THE POLITICS OF JEWISH COMMERCE

This study demonstrates the centrality of economic rationales to debates on Jews' status in Italy, Britain, France, and Germany during the course of two centuries. It delineates the common motifs that informed these discussions: the ideal republic and the ancient constitution, the conflict between virtue and commerce, and the notion of useful and productive labor. It thus provides the first overview of the political-economic dimensions of the Jewish emancipation literature of this period, viewed against the backdrop of broader controversies within European society over the effects of commerce on inherited political values and institutions.

By focusing on economic attitudes toward Jews, this book illuminates European intellectual approaches toward economic modernity, measured against traditional political and constitutional ideals. By elucidating these general debates, it renders contemporary Jewish economic self-conceptions, and the enormous impetus that Jewish reformist movements placed on the Jews' economic and occupational trans-formation, fully explicable for the first time.

Jonathan Karp is Associate Professor in the Judaic Studies and History Depart-ments at Binghamton University, SUNY. He is coeditor of *The Art of Being Jewish in Modern Times* (with Barbara Kirshenblatt-Gimblett, 2007). His current book projects are *The Rise and Demise of the Black-Jewish Alliance: A Class-Cultural Analysis* and *Philosemitism in History* (with Adam Sutcliffe; Cambridge Univer-sity Press, 2009).

The Politics of Jewish Commerce

Economic Thought and Emancipation in Europe,
1638–1848

JONATHAN KARP

Binghamton University, SUNY

CAMBRIDGE UNIVERSITY PRESS
Cambridge, New York, Melbourne, Madrid, Cape Town, Singapore, São Paulo, Delhi

Cambridge University Press
32 Avenue of the Americas, New York, NY 10013-2473, USA

www.cambridge.org
Information on this title: www.cambridge.org/9780521873932

First published 2008

Printed in the United States of America

A catalog record for this publication is available from the British Library.

Library of Congress Cataloging in Publication Data
Karp, Jonathan, 1960–
The politics of Jewish commerce : economic thought and emancipation in Europe, 1638–1848 /
Jonathan Karp.
p. cm.
Includes bibliographical references and index.
ISBN 978-0-521-87393-2 (hardcover)
1. Europe – Commerce – History. 2. Jews – Commerce. 3. Jews – Europe – Economic
conditions. 4. Jews – Economic conditions. 5. Europe – Economic conditions. I. Title
HF3495.K37 2008
381.089′92404–dc22 2007045443

ISBN 978-0-521-87393-2 hardback

*To my mother and father, Naomi and Martin Karp, with love,
gratitude, and admiration.*

Contents

Acknowledgments

This book has been many years in the making, during which time I have accumulated numerous debts of gratitude. The first is to my teachers at Columbia University. Professor Yosef Hayim Yerushalmi first pointed out to me the curious contrast between seventeenth- and eighteenth-century attitudes toward Jewish commerce. In approving my pursuit of this topic he provided abundant support of every kind – moral, material, and intellectual. Professor Michael Stanislawski, the finest teacher I have known, suggested the book's main title and helped me understand how pervasive the theme of Jewish occupational "productivization" has been in modern Jewish history.

My fellow Columbia graduate student and great comrade, Arthur Kiron, helped me at crucial junctures to think through some of the book's main arguments. My lifelong friend, Maurice Glasman, inspired me through his own work on related topics and raised my spirits over the course of many lengthy conversations. Charles Dellheim, Derek Penslar, David Ruderman, and Adam Sutcliffe read the entire manuscript and offered valuable criticisms. I would also like to thank Annette Aronowicz, Nicolas Berg, Lisa Makman, Ben McRee, Ezra Mendelsohn, Maria Mitchell, Jean Quataert, Gideon Reuveni, Abby Schrader, and Yumna Siddiqi for their many kindnesses. Andy Beck, my editor at Cambridge University Press, shepherded the book's progress with the right balance of patience and concern. Allan Arkush, the chair of Judaic Studies at Binghamton University, has been a friend and guide who gently prodded me toward completion of the manuscript. My History Department chairs, Don Quataert, Brendan McConville, Bonnie Effros, and Howard Brown, have supported my work in every possible way.

My parents, Naomi and Martin Karp, exhibited unconditional love throughout the incomprehensible processes of Ph.D. dissertating and manuscript preparation. As a token of my love and gratitude, I dedicate this book to them. My *machatonim*, Rivie Glasman and the late Collie Glasman, afforded me true spiritual sustenance. My children, Jacqueline and Isaac, kept me from despair and filled me with gladness. Finally, my wife, Gina Glasman, heard more, read more, and endured more of this book than any other person. For her countless suggestions and corrections, labor, humor in hard times and love always, I thank her with all my heart.

Introduction

This book analyzes the literature on Jewish commerce that emerged in Europe between the mid-seventeenth and mid-nineteenth centuries. It argues that much of this literature is only fully intelligible when viewed against the backdrop of broader controversies within contemporary European society over the effects of commerce on inherited political values and institutions. The works examined here are seen to operate on two levels: on the one hand, they are about Jewish economic life (including some written by Jews) and often aim to influence state policy on the local status of the Jews; on the other, they are concerned with the broader impact of economy, especially those aspects commonly identified with Jews (commerce, exchange, brokerage, and financial activities, particularly moneylending) on the political realm.

The period this book covers, roughly from the Peace of Westphalia to the Revolutions of 1848, was decisive for the Jews' acquisition of citizenship in the West and for the intellectual and spiritual modernization of Jewish life. The expulsions of the late Middle Ages had propelled Jews into North Africa, the eastern Mediterranean, as well as Poland and the New World. Despite the hardships they entailed, these shifts had the effect of expanding the Jews' commercial networks, the general benefits of which Jews were eager to advertise. By the late sixteenth century and throughout the seventeenth, as a result of the growth of their reputation as skilled merchants, brokers, and financiers, small Jewish settlements were reestablished in Western Europe. This sparked fresh debate about the religious, economic, and political merit of the Jews' incorporation into Christian society. The persistence of this debate for the next two centuries, its essential coherence as an ongoing discussion, as well as its given relationship to immediate and local historical circumstances, is what here constitutes "the politics of Jewish commerce."

This study asks how economic thought and ideology informed the discourse on Jewish status, including Jewish emancipation. Jewish historians

1

customarily apply the term "emancipation" to the acquisition by Jews of full citizenship rights, something that only occurred starting with the French Revolution. The term "emancipation" was a relatively late coinage, even postdating the Revolution, yet it should be remembered that it was never a formal legal term but always a rhetorical and even a metaphorical one.[1] For instance, in his "On the Jewish Question" Karl Marx used emancipation in its (by then) conventional sense to refer to modern citizenship generally and Jewish citizenship in particular. But he also used it to connote a broader form of liberation, the liberation of all mankind from oppressive market economy, from private property relations, and from commerce. At the same time, Marx employed the German word designating both Jews and Judaism (*Judentum*) as a synonym for commerce. Jewish emancipation, emancipation from Judaism, and emancipation from commerce were all interwoven in his exposition. Although not all of the commentators explored in this book were as rhetorically and philosophically dexterous, Marx's usage helpfully illustrates a general tendency. Jewish commerce provided a convenient and highly resonant means for analyzing the nature of commercial economy and assessing its social and political significance.[2]

A central argument of this book is the notion that a specifically *Jewish* commerce served a vital function in Western thought. It served to abstract various types of activities from the generality of economic life and, through their association with stigmatized Jews, make them vehicles for expressing widely felt anxieties about commerce in a manner that was politically safe and psychically tolerable. This is why the discourse on Jewish commerce can shed light on attitudes toward political economy that are often less apparent from other sources but might nevertheless be regarded as possessing a broad significance. It is legitimate to ask, however, to what degree were these anxieties genuinely reflective of Jews' economic practices and to what extent were they merely the product of fantasy and prejudice? The answer is that *Jewish* commerce had both real and nominal aspects. There were certainly specific commercial activities that Jews tended to concentrate in, first and foremost money and credit services such as lending, pawn brokerage, minting, tax farming, etc. Jews could also be merchants or traders, of course. But as traders they often functioned outside of existing corporate and guild structures, something that made their activities distinctive and controversial. Jews were conspicuous not only for trading in money and credit but also in information, as brokers, stockjobbers, and middlemen. These were by no means the only Jewish occupations, nor were Jews the only ones to perform them. Still, by virtue of their disproportional and conspicuous participation, these were often the activities associated with a recognizably "Jewish" commerce.[3]

Jewish commerce, however, was also a nominal concept. Distinctions between different kinds of exchange have a descriptive utility but not necessarily a functional one. Insofar as moneylending is commerce in money, it is not fundamentally different from commerce in other commodities whose price is determined by the law of supply and demand. Yet in premodern Europe (as in most premodern cultures) the abstract monism of market economy was unthinkable. Rather, the market was punctured by a dualism, a splitting in which activities that involved the buying and selling of money, credit, and information were regarded not as merely a special branch of commerce but as an opposing and negative principle within it. This duality was by no means confined to the contrast between virtuous Christian commerce and dangerous Jewish usury (as in the antagonism of Antonio and Shylock in Shakespeare's "The Merchant of Venice"). In looking at debates over Jewish commerce, it is a mistake to focus exclusively on usury. There were other dualities that at times were equally relevant to the understanding of Jewish commerce: retail versus wholesale trade, or retail versus peddling, guild versus freelance, speculative versus nonspeculative investment, manufacture versus distribution, as well as "useful" versus "nonproductive" labor.

These dualities reflect a powerful ambivalence. But it is not an ambivalence born simply of mental constructions and projections onto despised "others." Rather, it goes to the heart of what commerce is and does. Markets and exchange have always been important in European life, even during the early Middle Ages, bringing incalculable benefits and improvements.[4] At the same time, markets and exchange have always been threatening, creating instability and potential ruin to settled existence. At once conveying the "lifeblood" to and "sucking the blood" from European society (both metaphors were frequently used), commerce was the object of a sometimes valid and necessary criticism that itself could also pose a threat to a valid and necessary activity.[5]

This precarious circumstance made Jewish commerce a particularly useful construction. Jews were both religiously stigmatized *and* (not coincidentally) concentrated in precisely the types of commerce that attracted the greatest suspicion. For this reason, the protest against commerce could be directed at practitioners who were relatively safe to attack but who also plausibly epitomized its danger. This danger was both to persons (e.g., debtors, competitors, those vulnerable to deception and exploitation) and, on a loftier scale, to regimes. Was there a conflict between the virtuous citizenry a state required and the commerce on which it also depended? Because the cradles of modern political thought were mercantile city-states such as Florence and Venice, these questions were genuine and vexing. The Renaissance pursuit of the ideal polity through such channels as civic humanism (the late medieval and Renaissance revival of the classical political theory of Aristotle and Cicero) had to contend with the reality that a commercial revolution was simultaneously occurring in the Mediterranean world. Political theorists had to assess the implications of a globalizing trade for this potential conflict of virtue and commerce.[6] When Jews became prominent practitioners of this commercial expansion, the same problematic took on added intensity.

It must be emphasized, however, that Jewish commerce did not always have negative connotations. The debate was almost always over what Jews' economic activity implied for the real, imagined, or desired political structure of a given society. In this sense, economic *philosemitism* (admiration and appreciation of Jewish commerce) could be as pronounced as its antithesis. Clearly, the very fact that Jewish readmission and residential expansion did occur, although often under tight restrictions, attests to a widespread perception among political leaders, at least, that Jewish commerce was good for the state. For philosophers if not for practical politicians, the Jews' economic services could also be lauded as helping to resolve the conflict between virtue and commerce, since in the early modern period Jews engaged in trade while renouncing all claims to the political rewards their wealth might buy. It was an effective self-advertisement. In an age when land ownership was central to claims of political participation, Jews could own no land. Although they were considered to be aliens and infidels, they could therefore reasonably claim to pose no political threat. In fact by doing the necessary commercial "dirty work," some Jews argued, they were helping to underwrite the political stability of the regime and society as a whole.

Yet it was not difficult to stand this argument on its head. Jews possessed their own constitution, their ancient Mosaic law with its fiercely segregationist orientation. Political philosophers frequently lauded the Mosaic constitution (it was, after all, the Christians' "Old Testament"). A polity designed by God, legislated by a divinely anointed prophet, imbued with perfect laws that regulated agriculture and trade, established rigorous criteria of virtue for rulers, and provided inspiring models of national solidarity, the Mosaic political blueprint appeared to many political thinkers as the ultimate and ideal "ancient constitution."[7] But this sacred blueprint was one thing in the hands of virtuous Christians, another in the hands of vile Jews. The original Mosaic laws, such as those found in the middle and later chapters of Deuteronomy, had appeared to shun commerce and embrace agriculture, in part to protect the autonomy of an exclusive religious polity. Yet contemporary Jews were unmistakably mobile and mercantile! To some Christians, postbiblical Jewry had adopted commerce as a weapon to perpetuate the old Mosaic constitutional exclusivity (or misanthropy) through new and more insidious means.

In their eyes a diaspora population composed of merchants and middleman and animated by Mosaic precepts posed a danger to independent polities. "To receive the Jews ... into a commonwealth," insisted the English political writer James Harrington, "were to maim it."[8]

Although concepts such as the Mosaic Republic showed impressive resiliency, the terms of the debates over Jewish commerce shifted as attitudes toward politics and economics evolved. The debates of the seventeenth and eighteenth centuries had hinged on whether the inclusion of Jewish merchants and financiers posed a threat to idealized constitutional values of independence, frugality, and landownership, or alternatively, helped to expand liberty by weakening networks of entrenched economic power and privilege. In contrast, the eighteenth-century Enlightenment came increasingly to emphasize individual productive utility as the chief criterion of social and political legitimacy. In Enlightenment ideology, commerce was usually seen as a positive force so long as it was granted the freedom to enhance industry and productivity rather than strangle them. Jewish commerce appeared to violate this principle precisely because it was not free but rather imposed on Jews through centuries of prejudicial restrictions. To some *philosophes*, the Jews' *exclusive* specialization in exchange (that is, their lack of a more diversified occupational portfolio) appeared harmful and outmoded, a monopolistic vestige of the despised medieval order.

Intensifying this trend, the French revolutionary period gave rise to analogies between Jews and European nobilities. These analogies, although they appear counterintuitive today, were grounded in the two groups' shared association with the corporate structures of the *ancien régime*, as well as their assumed mutual evasion of "productive" labor and physical work. Such parallels, in turn, helped to promote historical investigations into the constitutional sources of the Jews' commercial orientation. Just as historical inquiry would expose the sources of noble power in the political and economic structures of the feudal order, an examination of Jewish history would reveal the constitutional factors that originally shaped the Jews' mercantile character. Was there something intrinsic to the Mosaic Constitution, or some later Jewish political incarnation, that led inevitably if paradoxically to commerce? Jews' evident failure to shift into agriculture and crafts, despite repeated calls and sincere efforts at their occupational reform beginning in the late eighteenth century, suggested that the hold of commerce over them might be deep and inveterate.

The Jews' seeming resistance to change fed curiosity about the historical reasons for their unshakable commercial orientation (a form of discourse that I term "historical economy"). Jews themselves engaged in such analysis (although gingerly), including the mid-nineteenth-century pioneers of *Wissenschaft des Judentums*, the academic study of Jewish history (often wrongly accused of ignoring economics altogether). In part because Jewish commerce was a live issue in contemporary debates of emancipation, these Jewish historians wished at one and the same time to diagnose the source of the Jewish "commercial caste," assert that its impact had been essentially benign, and persuade the public that only the Jews' full emancipation would make it dissolve. Less sympathetic minds were prone to different conclusions. In the period when this book concludes, the Jews' possible role in the formation of European capitalism, a concept just then crystallizing in European thought, was becoming the subject of intense scrutiny. Would capitalism destroy the material basis of Jewish existence by generalizing the Jews' historically specific economic functions? Or were the Jews really the high priests of this new commercial order? Such questions would underlie a great deal of both antisemitic and internal Jewish politics for decades to come.

This study is primarily an intellectual rather than an economic history. Its concern is not only to gauge attitudes but also to analyze arguments, to understand how they cohere and where and why they break down. The discussion relies on published materials, mostly pamphlets and books produced by contemporary philosophers, preachers, lawyers, theologians, as well as historians and political economists. Although the early modern period was precisely the era when a self-conscious body of economic literature first emerged, eventually developing its own terminologies, dogmas, and authorities, economic discourse remained highly porous. It was still an amateur's field. Adam Smith was a professor but of moral philosophy not political economy. Lengthy and detailed economic discussion might just as likely be found in a novel such as *Robinson Crusoe*, a travelogue such as Voltaire's *Letters Concerning the English Nation*, or a Jewish apologetic such as Simone Luzzatto's *Discourse on the Condition of the Jews* as in a mercantile treatise such as Thomas Mun's *England's Treasure by Forraign Trade*. Here, too, a focus on Jewish commerce helps to expand our understanding of what constituted economic discourse, who produced it, and why it became so pervasive and important during this period. This study demonstrates just how profoundly entwined economic concerns were with the broad social and political issues of the day.

Given the quantity of such sources produced over the period of two centuries, my own criteria of selection have been both stringent and subjective. I have concentrated on works that offer extended argumentation and reward close readings, works that are in conversation with one another, either because they directly respond to one another or because they focus on similar questions. Yet scholars of the history of economic thought may find the experience of this book somewhat disorienting; such of their mainstays as David

Hume, François Quesnay, Thomas Malthus, and David Ricardo, make at most only brief cameo appearances, whereas undoubted lesser lights such as Josiah Tucker and Adam Müller hog the stage. The script is not arbitrary, however. There are many ways to tell a story, and the first obligation in detailing the politics of Jewish commerce is to highlight authors who actually feature Jews centrally or significantly. Doing so makes it possible to ask if those who dealt with Jews evolved economic concepts differently from those who did not, such as Adam Smith. It will then be possible to ask if a politics of Jewish commerce sheds light on and helps to modify the standard narration of the history of economic theory in this period. Even so, though usually relegated to the chorus, throughout this study some familiar "stars" can still be heard.

Although I have strived to examine texts whose influence on emancipation debates is widely recognized (but whose economic dimensions are not), I have inevitably selected ones in languages I can read, French, Hebrew, German, and Yiddish, or in English translation. Because important literature on Jewish commerce also was produced in other languages, particularly Spanish and Portuguese as well as Polish and Russian, this limitation has serious implications for my narrative. Eastern Europe and the Ottoman lands, locales where the great majority of contemporary Jews resided, receive only cursory treatment here. This underscores the complaint recently voiced by Gerson David Hundert, the eminent historian of Polish Jewry, that historians have given too much emphasis to Western Jews.[9] However, such a complaint forgets that the experiences of Jews in the West and the discourses about them strongly influenced Jewish fate in other lands. It is my hope that this book will help others to trace the specific influences and divergences.

The evaporation in recent decades of the economic ideologies that had formerly animated Jewish politics (such as Zionism and socialism) has left no obvious *Weltanschauungen* to shape an overarching approach to Jewish economic life that contemporary historians might adopt or challenge. This is not entirely a bad thing; although it detracts from the appearance of concentrated effort by a body of scholars pursuing a focused set of critical questions, it allows for a healthy eclecticism too. Jonathan Israel, for instance, has labored heroically to set the study of Jewish economy in early modern times on a solid new foundation grounded in rigorous archival research combined with a comprehensive knowledge of contemporary political and intellectual developments. Readers will find many traces of his influence throughout the account that follows.[10] In contrast, Derek Penslar has pioneered a new field related to but distinct from that undertaken here, the study of Jewish economic "identity." His *Shylock's Children* partly intersects with this study in chronology and subject matter. Yet Penslar's account complements far more than it overlaps with mine. Although he in no way neglects the intellectual history of economic discourse on Jews, his is fundamentally a study of Jewish economic self-perceptions rather than of the economic debates over emancipation. In addition, Penslar's focus on philanthropy and "associational Judaism," particularly prevalent during the late nineteenth century, are fascinating and important topics related to Jewish economy that find no counterpart here.[11]

Finally, J. G. A. Pocock has exerted a major influence on my understanding of this history. His foci on the problematic of commerce in civic humanistic discourse and on the critical importance of historical narrative to the argumentation of political theory have proven apposite to the study of Jews in European political economy. In recent years, Pocock's paradigms have come under repeated assault, hardly a surprising development for a scholar whose work has proven so influential in so many areas. The brunt of the assault (aside from the effort to restore John Locke to preeminence in Anglo-American political thought, a figure whose wide influence Pocock challenged) is to claim that the simple binary of virtue versus commerce seriously underplays the degree to which commerce became broadly embraced in civic humanistic discourse and later related traditions, even well prior to the eighteenth century.[12] Pocock has responded by insisting that the key conflict was not always with commerce per se but with credit, including all the modern instruments of finance that appeared to undermine the fixity of property, especially land, on which man as a political actor was thought to depend.[13] Suffice it to say that when the issue becomes not just commerce per se but *Jewish* commerce and credit (topics that Pocock himself has not addressed), his approach finds strong confirmation here, as many of the chapters that follow attest.

Chapter 1 of this study introduces the theme of Jewish commerce and its relationship to the constitutional theories of seventeenth-century Jewish and English literature. Its central figure is the Venetian Rabbi Simone Luzzatto, author of the most influential Jewish economic apologetic of the age, the 1638 *Discourse on the Jews of Venice*. Luzzatto's main contribution to the politics of Jewish commerce was to demonstrate the unique utility of Jews as merchants, precisely because their statelessness and marginalized status ensured they would never be tempted to translate their commercial wealth into land ownership and political power. Chapter 2 centers on John Toland's 1714 *Reasons for Naturalizing the Jews in Great Britain and Ireland* and examines its connection with shifting conceptions of the ancient constitution in the party-political milieu of Augustan England. Toland's pamphlet was an unambiguously philosemitic work, strongly influenced in its understanding of Judaism by Luzzatto's earlier treatment. But contrary to the views of most historians, it was not, I argue, animated by simple conviction over the Jews' essential assimilability but rather by a secular millenarian faith in their constitutional uniqueness. Although gainsaying divine revelation, Toland still believed that the Jews' ancient endowment, including Jewish civil and religious principles, constituted an especial blessing to the Britain of his day.

Chapter 3 presents an analysis of the political economy of Rev. Josiah Tucker, particularly in reference to Tucker's advocacy of the Jewish Naturalization Bill of 1753 and his concomitant debunking of the ancient constitutional claims of the Bill's opponents. Tucker's philosemitism reflected his view that Jewish commerce could help under cut the monopolistic order that he believed still plagued British society, despite the watershed achievement of the Glorious Revolution, which in his view had ushered in a new commercial age. Chapter 4 shifts the scene to late eighteenth-century Germany and Christian Wilhelm von Dohm's influential 1781 *On the Civic Improvement of the Jews*. Dohm applied many of the same economic criteria utilized by Tucker to his analysis of the Jews, but with dramatically different results. He had absorbed the strong emphasis that economists such as Tucker had given to labor and industry, but Dohm rejected the ethnic division of labor that Luzzatto celebrated and Tucker sanctioned. Although Dohm was among the first European authors to demand the full civic emancipation of the Jews, it was central to his plea that Jews fully dissociate themselves from the commercial roles they had played under an antiquated constitutional regime.

Chapters 5 and 6 focus on the debates surrounding the French Revolution – not in connection with the Jews alone, but in regard to the European nobility as well. Here I explore the analogy between Jews and nobility that was sometimes drawn in the revolutionary period (depicting both as separatist estates whose status had derived from an outmoded feudal constitution and whose future depended on their successful economic regeneration). Yet what began as a set of parallels ended up as a study in contrast; for by the end of the Napoleonic period, nationalist writers were deploying the Jew-noble comparison in defense of noble inclusion and in opposition to Jewish emancipation. They did so by depicting nobles, in contrast to the Jews, as organically linked to the nation. By virtue of their status as a commercial caste acting in accordance with their misanthropic political constitution, Jews remained antipathetic to the *Volk*.

Chapter 7 demonstrates how the new movement of *Wissenschaft des Judentums* ("academic Jewish Studies" emerging in the 1820s) sought to counter these very claims. Jewish historians proposed alternative genealogies to the emergence of a Jewish "commercial caste" by offering a positive portrayal of the Jewish ancient constitution that had recently been attacked by the nationalist historians. They depicted Jewish society as an economically modernizing force in European society, albeit one whose capacity to induce positive change had been stymied by the backwardness of the feudal Christian constitution, an order that unfortunately still held sway.

In light of these claims, Chapter 8 considers the early emergence of a notion of "capitalism" in the writings of the young Karl Marx – a notion that Marx appeared to link to Jews and Judaism. Marx's 1844 "On the Jewish Question" exhibited a version of the basic socialist dichotomy inherited from Enlightenment and French economic discourse between productive and nonproductive activity. By associating Jews with the latter, socialists sometimes suggested that wasteful, exploitative, and unproductive capitalism was essentially "Jewish" in nature and origin. Marx's own treatment of the "Jewish Question" was an ambiguous one, however. On the one hand, his essay punctuated two centuries of discussion on the relation of Jewish commerce to the political constitution. On the other, the essay was unique precisely in its effort to subordinate the concept of politics to that of economics. "On the Jewish Question" likewise yielded two divergent conclusions on Jews: it suggested, in the first place, that Jews had been responsible for the emergence of the new economic order; yet at the same time, it implied that this selfsame new order had now rendered them obsolete. If commerce were to become the general order of things, then there could be no designated place for a group that presumably defined itself through its unique capacity to perform financial and commercial functions. Similarly, if commerce were to be overcome through the revolutionary eradication of the market system, Jews would finally achieve their liberation from "Judaism," and Jewish commerce would be no more.

The book concludes with an Afterward in which I demonstrate why the Industrial Revolution, starting its "take off" period in continental Europe by the mid-nineteenth century, provides a fitting terminus for this study. Industrialization appeared to many contemporary observers to demonstrate that production rather than exchange would be the true foundation of future economic life. In this sense it played into the earlier dichotomies that relegated the economic activities of Jews to a secondary or even negative status. It similarly reinforced an image of Jews – who in general terms were not at the forefront of industrial development – as backward and deserving of modernizing and reform. Jews ultimately benefited from industrialization, but ironically in ways that tended to reconstitute and reinforce their middleman orientation.

Most of the debates discussed in this book will seem strange and antiquated to readers today. I have tried to help make sense of them, not in order to justify their points of view but rather to convey why they might have resonated powerfully in their own time. In the final analysis, *The Politics of Jewish Commerce* seeks to contribute to the debates over commerce and economy both in the past and present. Although the end of the Cold War has softened the fevered tone of much economic debate, complacency over the role of economic forces in national and world politics seems a poor substitute for ideological zeal. Commerce and capitalism have been powerful, indeed revolutionary, forces in world history. Their capacity to transform our world beyond recognition proceeds without respite. To whatever degree we may acclaim or blame their advance we would be wise to do so equipped with knowledge of the insights and follies of those who have traversed this ground before.

1

ℭ

This Newfangled Age

The image of Shylock has dominated popular conceptions of the Jews' economic identity in early modern Europe.[1] Shakespeare's creation, a usurer, is the key economic stereotype associated with the Jew. Yet although moneylending was a core motif of anti-Jewish literature in the sixteenth and seventeenth centuries (and beyond), the Jew was famous not just as a moneyman but as a merchant as well.[2] In fact, from a historical standpoint, Shakespeare's antithesis between Shylock and Antonio (the actual "merchant of Venice") is misleading.[3] An actual Shylock, particularly if he had been a Sephardic Jew (i.e., a Jew of Iberian descent) residing in sixteenth-century Venice, could just as easily have been a merchant as a usurer. Indeed, he might even have been described in the same terms that Shakespeare used to describe Antonio, as possessing "an argosy bound to Tripolis, another to the Indies, . . . a third at Mexico, a fourth for England, and other ventures . . . squandered abroad."[4] Nor would Shylock the merchant have been unknown to Shakespeare's contemporaries. The Jew's reputation as a talented merchant preceded him – literally. Statesmen drew on it to design policies that afforded Jews residential privileges in return for their hoped-for commercial contributions. The Jews themselves, in the propaganda they produced to induce such invitations to settle, highlighted the mercantile and downplayed the usurious features of their national profile.[5] In part, this was simply because moneylending was no longer the attraction it had once been. With the expansion of credit institutions in the West and the increasingly open practice of banking and moneylending by Christians, the need for Jewish credit services declined – in Italy in the sixteenth century and in Germany and Central Europe in the seventeenth.[6] Instead, commerce became a selling point for Jewish settlement in the early modern world. And although denunciations of Jewish usury had been overwhelmingly theological in character (indeed, most of them had emanated from the Church) and were grounded in biblical, Aristotelian, and patristic rationales, the criticisms of

Jewish commerce were essentially political. That is to say, they assessed the potential impact of an international trade that was dominated by a foreign group of alien merchants on the inherited social, class, and constitutional arrangements in a given society. Some of these assessments were produced by economic organizations like guilds and competing merchant groups. But a number of them were produced by theorists of the state and the constitution.

By the late Renaissance period there were any number of writers who held modern-sounding economic views – views that, for instance, defined money as a commodity like any other.[7] Even earlier, underscoring the typical precedence of economic practice over theory, a battery of legal devices had been formulated by Catholic, Protestant, and Jewish scholars that rationalized various financial arrangements that were formerly held to be usurious.[8] Yet in a sense this progressive academic justification of interest hardly mattered. The understanding that usury (or rather, "excessive" interest) derived from scarcity of credit rather than from sinful intent did not in itself resolve the problem of how to conceptualize the role of economy in the ordering of political relations. On the contrary, the controversy stirred by novel forms of credit in the second half of the seventeenth century derived from sources that went well beyond traditional religious scruples.[9] As opposed to the usurious subsistence loans earlier associated with Jews, which tainted them as bastions of an exploitative feudal status quo, new credit institutions such as stock trading and the floating of state debts appeared frightening not just because they threatened the poor but because they seemed to challenge the established political order. Unlike the stereotypical usury of the Middle Ages, these novel credit and commercial institutions were part of the commercial revolution then sweeping the Atlantic and Mediterranean worlds. Jews found themselves implicated in the discourse of contemporary political philosophy because as stereotypical traders and creditors they symbolized activities which seemed to be transforming every facet of contemporary life.[10]

Why did Jews take on this symbolic importance? The answer requires a brief summary of the changes affecting Jewish economy in the late Middle Ages. By the thirteenth century, Western European Jews had long ceased to be the commercial avatars they had sometimes been in the ninth and tenth centuries. Christian merchants had long since come to monopolize most of the long-distance and regional trade in which Jews had formerly specialized. This was one of the reasons why in the eleventh and twelfth centuries – during a period of monumental expansion in the medieval economy – Jews became increasingly displaced from commerce and crowded into moneylending occupations.[11] Hence their surprising reemergence as important merchants in the sixteenth century requires explanation. It appears the more striking in light of the fact that, between the thirteenth and sixteenth centuries Jews had been physically excluded from much of Western and Central Europe. England expelled its Jews in 1290, France initially in 1306 and conclusively in 1394 (Provence, the home of a venerable Jewish population, had been incorporated into France in 1481 with Jewish expulsions ensuing), Spain and Sicily in 1492, Naples in 1541, and politically divided Central Europe through a series of local expulsions in the fifteenth and sixteenth centuries. This expulsion process climaxed in the mid-sixteenth century, although it continued at a local level in Italy and Germany. Yet even when expulsion reached its high point (or low, from the Jewish standpoint), factors were already in place that would lead to the eventual reversal of European Jewry's dislocation and ultimately give Jews a claim to being the international merchants par excellence.

This development was rooted in religious and economic transformations of the Iberian Jewish community (Sephardic Jews) that had begun in the fourteenth century. By the late fourteenth century, Spain was by far the largest Jewish community in Europe. Because Iberia was still both economically peripheral and engaged in a protracted war of conquest, the process that had led to the Jews' gradual economic marginalization in Italy and Northwest Europe was there not yet complete. On the contrary, the Hispano-Jewish population (as a consequence both of its size and the needs of the host community) was more occupationally differentiated than in most other locales.[12] This also meant that a Jewish merchant class persisted in late medieval Spain long after it had been reduced or eliminated in Italy and France.[13] In 1391, anti-Jewish riots engulfed the Jewish communities of Spain, dividing the survivors between Christian converts ("New Christians" or *conversos*) and Jews. These converts, many of whom continued secretly to practice Judaism (derisively labeled "*marranos*"), benefited from the removal of economic restrictions imposed on Jews.[14] This ensured that, among other opportunities, they had a greater chance to pursue their fortunes in large-scale or foreign trade. Such incentives no doubt contributed to the growth of the *converso* community in the fifteenth century, but a fraction of those *conversos* with the means to do so fled to Muslim territories in North Africa and the Ottoman lands, where there was nothing to prevent them from reverting to Judaism. Through the Spanish expulsion of 1492, these communities were supplemented by fresh Jewish refugees, who fled to parts of Italy as well. In 1497 the most numerous group, those who had migrated into neighboring Portugal, were forcibly converted en masse. King Manuel I had far more interest in retaining this population as nominal Christians than in expelling them as sincere Jews. As New Christians, they could remain within the Portuguese empire, including colonies in the New World, and still maintain commercial, familial, and even religious relations with other (mostly Sephardic) Jewish populations elsewhere.

Hence, as a result of Iberia's late economic maturation and ironically of its forcible large-scale conversion of Jews, the Sephardim retained a higher percentage of large scale merchants and international traders than other contemporary Jewish groups. Although the covert nature of their identity, especially once the Inquisition was in full throttle (c. 1540), renders accurate calculations of the quantity of their trade difficult to establish, there can be no doubt the Sephardic New Christians and Jews of the mid-fifteenth through the early seventeenth centuries became one of history's great trading diasporas. As Jonathan Israel has argued, no other trading group spanned the Ottoman and North African world (including the lucrative overland trade routes between "Romania" – present-day Croatia – and Italian port cities such as Venice and Ancona) as well as the evolving Atlantic trade linking South and Central America with Iberia and eventually with the Netherlands and Britain, too.[15] Although other Jewish groups continued to suffer local expulsions throughout the sixteenth and seventeenth centuries, particularly the Ashkenazic (northern European) and Italian Jews, a series of efforts, both overt and disguised, was made in the same period to restore small numbers of Sephardim to southwestern France, the Netherlands, and various of the northern German and Italian city-states, as well as to England in 1655.

In many cases, these groups were admitted as New Christians and then later (sometimes much later) allowed to revert to Judaism. For example, the New Christians invited to settle in Bordeaux by Henry II of France as early as 1550, did not publicly revert to Judaism until the mid-seventeenth century (and it was not until 1723 that they were formally given permission to do so).[16] In other cases, Jews who fled from Iberia to Ottoman lands and who became important either in maritime or overland trade with the Balkans and Italy were eventually offered trading privileges as well as temporary residence in various Northern Italian cities. At the same time, New Christians were fleeing to these same locales, usually with the tacit understanding that their Judaizing tendencies would be sheltered from the papal Inquisition by the authorities (sometimes including the Pope!). Ancona, part of the papal territories, granted privileges to Jews in 1514 and 1534, and to New Christians in 1541; the Duchy of Ferrara in 1538 for both Jews and, euphemistically, "Spaniards and Portuguese"; Tuscany for Jews in 1551; Savoy for Jews in 1572, although under Spanish Habsburg pressure the invitation was revoked a year later; and Venice for Jews (already present in the ghetto since 1516) in 1524 and in the 1580s for both "Levantine," that is, Ottoman, Jews and "Ponentine" ones, that is, those who had been or still nominally remained New Christians.[17] In 1593, the Dukes of Tuscany issued their famous "Livornina" welcoming Levantine Jews and New Christians (*Marrini*) into their newly constructed Ligurian port-city of Livorno, under exceptionally generous terms.[18] Meanwhile, New Christians living on the Atlantic seaboard – including Lisbon, Bordeaux, Rouen, and Antwerp – provided the base for the eventual expansion of a Jewish population, also initially comprised of New Christians, into Protestant Amsterdam and Hamburg at the end of the sixteenth century. Although a similar expansion of the Ashkenazic Jewish population from Poland westward into parts of Germany and eastern France took place during the seventeenth century, it was not accompanied by the same sweeping economic and religious privileges.[19] The Ashkenazim, who will be discussed later, did not possess the same economic profile as the Sephardim, though wealthy and enterprising Ashkenazic financiers were selectively invited to settle with their families and a small retinue as state bankers and suppliers (Court Jews). Sometimes, as with the case of the Jews in Alsace, larger and mostly poor groups of Ashkenazim were given limited settlement rights. Finally, with the seventeenth-century establishment of Dutch, French, and British colonial empires in the New World, Sephardic Jews and former New Christians acquired unprecedented economic freedom and civic protections as colonists and traders in such places as Dutch Brazil (1633–1654), Western Guiana (1657), and Suriname (1667); British Barbados and Jamaica (1655); and French Martinique and Guadeloupe (1671). Although Jewish status proved no more secure in the New World than it had in the Old, the privileges granted there were significant both because their terms sometimes exceeded those afforded in the metropole and because these privileges were almost invariably rooted in exclusively economic (if not always commercial) rationales.[20]

This remarkable process of readmission, whose "golden age" extended from 1550 to 1655, focused the attention of moralists, polemicists, and political philosophers on the Jews, their virtues and defects and their potential impact if permitted to resettle. Since Jews were generally invited to resettle *because* of the commercial roles they played, their place within their host societies came to be redefined in light of existing and ongoing debates over the political relevance of new economic phenomena.[21] The resulting literature is of a highly heterogeneous nature, in terms both of genre and authorship. No a priori distinction can be made, for instance, between the apologetic works produced by Jews to advance the cause of resettlement and the polemical tracts written by Christians to refute them. Each borrowed generously from the other. More to the point, both sides in the debate drew on a large body of economic and political outlooks inherited from the past – sometimes the remote past. Although a thorough cataloguing of this legacy is not possible here, some of its relevant features will be outlined before turning to discuss the literature on Jewish political economy itself.

COMMERCE IN HISTORY AND IDEOLOGY

As in all other areas, in matters economic early modern Europeans engaged with the legacy of classical antiquity. Yet in reviewing the history of economic attitudes, especially of intellectual and political elites, one should remember that that they provide no firm basis for assessing the actual extent of trade or the prevalence of markets in any given period. All too often, historians take the ideological and rhetorical hostility toward merchants found in eminent philosophical, theological, or literary works as evidence of the relative paucity of market exchange in a given time and place. Certainly this is the case with classical antiquity. When it came to trade, however, Greek and Latin writers did not always practice what they preached. There can no longer be any doubt that trade, particularly sea trade, as well as accompanying instruments of credit and insurance, were highly developed in the Mediterranean antiquity.[22] At the same time, the widespread involvement in commerce of the political elite often had to be disguised through legal fronts and fictions. In *The Laws* (4: 705), Plato insisted that the polity or republic be geographically distinct from the emporium, as Athens was from Piraeus and later Rome from Ostia. Contra Plato's intention, however, port and polis operated symbiotically.[23] The point is clear: although ancient societies could be commercially advanced, the prevailing ethic of their spokesmen was usually distinctly antimercantile. Indeed, those individuals who were overtly and more-or-less permanently involved in trade were distinct from those who practiced it on the side, or who employed agents to trade on their behalf, or who succeeded in freeing themselves of the taint of an earlier association with commerce by acquiring land, clients, and municipal offices.[24]

Merchants per se were generally excluded from full citizenship in the Hellenistic poleis. The metics who controlled much of the commerce of ancient Athens were outsiders lacking rights of political participation or landownership. M. I. Finley, who understated the *actual* quantity of trade in Greco-Roman antiquity nevertheless rightly remarked on the "universal rule that the ownership of land was an exclusive prerogative of citizens . . . ," which made it technically difficult to move from commercial wealth to landownership.[25] Landownership provided the condition of self-sufficiency requisite to the self-rule of free men. In contrast, commerce was usually perceived as a threat. Sallust and Juvenal described it as the source of corruption undermining the Roman republic.[26] Aristotle viewed commerce as conducive neither to stability nor independence, honor nor liberality. In his *Politics* Aristotle drew an influential distinction between production for use (necessary and virtuous) and production for exchange (parasitic and harmful).[27] This distinction paralleled another, viz., that between *praxis* (activity as an end in itself) and *poiesis* (activity as merely a means). The first category included politics and soldiery; the second, manual labor and trade.[28] Trade was thus regarded, at least by the elite, as parasitical and unproductive, as well as dishonorable, insofar as it entailed or related to menial activity. In fact, of authors in the classical canon Hesiod was one of the few with good things to say about physical labor.[29] The most influential ancient authority on such matters, Cicero, was far more typical in listing among the "mean" professions moneylenders, wage laborers, and merchants who buy in order to sell. Although Cicero (realistically) conceded that commerce "on a large and expansive scale, importing many things from all over . . . , is not entirely to be criticized," he insisted that those who have been enriched by it must be sure to "abandon the harbour for a country estate," that is, to employ their money in the purchase of land to retire on and bequeath to descendants.[30]

These attitudes were later reinforced through the cultural outlook of the European nobilities and Church.[31] The nobility had originally drawn its status from the fulfillment of a martial function. Its capacity to hold land had been a reward – at least in theory – for its performance of military tasks. This notion that landholders were society's noble warriors endured in the European mind long after the circumstances which had originally produced it began to fade. Although it is true that by the twelfth century wealthy merchants were frequently ennobled, this fact merely underscores the point that commercial values remained publicly subordinate to landed ones. Even in Italian city-states, where anticommercial prejudices among nobles were relatively weak, noble families generally sought to lay hold of burgher wealth by marrying their daughters to merchants, thereby retaining noble status, which was passed down through the son.[32] In contrast, during the high Middle Ages the nobility of France had vigorously opposed the practice of merchant ennoblement. It was this same northern French nobility that had developed the most stringent chivalric biases against mercantile life and which in the twelfth century had managed to extend its cultural influence throughout Europe.[33] Thus, although merchant ennoblement proceeded apace, noble families of recent vintage were understandably loathe to acknowledge their own commercial origins (and impoverished older noble families all too eager to remind them of it!).

Church doctrine, too, fortified many of these attitudes. The Church condemned not just the usurer but also (if somewhat less vehemently) the *mercatore*, the trader; indeed, it assigned a lowly place to the majority of mankind that was condemned to manual labor. Commerce, like labor, was a necessity but should be practiced as a means (to the distribution of goods) rather than an end in itself (personal enrichment). True, such views were tempered in the wake of the "commercial revolution" of the twelfth and early thirteenth centuries, and with the recovery of Roman law.[34] Moreover, the rise of Italian city-states, especially during the period of domination by the *popolo* – which included but was by no means confined to guilds – gradually forced a revision of the traditional Christian understanding of labor as penitence. Guilds were religious institutions as well as social and economic ones, and their members were understandably proud of the work they performed. Yet although artisan guilds produced pageants to celebrate their craft traditions and charitable activities to exhibit their pious beneficence, they did not produce many philosophers, theologians, and lawyers who could publicize their attitudes in writings that were likely to attain wide readership.[35] Until the sixteenth century, with the writings of figures such as Johannes Althusius, they lacked articulate spokesmen to propagate their value system within the clerical elite.[36] Moreover, when the Church did get around to altering its attitude on labor, it still retained much of its hostility to exchange. "Labor is holy," insisted the Dutch theologian Gerhard Groote, "but business is dangerous."[37] Thus, the historian Jacques Le Goff's characterization of early medieval religious attitudes can largely be applied to the late medieval and early modern periods as well. "Christianity," observes Le Goff, "tended to condemn all forms of *negotium*, all secular activity; on the other hand, it encouraged a certain *otium*, an idleness which displayed confidence in Providence."[38] In sum, it took the elite *interpreters* of Western culture quite a long time to acknowledge publicly the long-standing reality of the central role that commerce had played in the societies in which they lived and even in their own daily lives. In this sense, the Jews' commercial identities served as a barometer of shifting general attitudes toward commerce, money, and credit as a whole.

Although the Christian distinction between *otium* and *negotium* appears to mirror the classical one between *praxis* and *poiesis*, there was in fact a crucial difference. *Praxis*, in contrast to *otium*, encompassed politics, that is to say, the *vita activa* of public life. And it was precisely this notion of *praxis* that the political theorists of the Italian Renaissance sought to restore. Ever since the work of the historian Hans Baron, it has become commonplace to define a category of "civic humanism" as one of the central modes of Renaissance thought.[39] Although the prominence that Baron attributed to the political (not to mention the republican) in the overall agenda of humanism has been called into question, there is no doubt that the fifteenth and sixteenth centuries marked a revival of political theory, and that the "Machiavellian Moment," as J. G. A. Pocock labeled this phenomenon, was characterized by a renewed

interest in defining the qualities of political virtue.[40] In picking up the legacy of
pagan political philosophy, from Aristotle to Polybius and Cicero, Renaissance
authors could hardly ignore the fact that the leisured, agrarian, and antimercantile emphases favored by the classical tradition could not be easily fitted
into the social milieu of the Italian city-states, in which commerce and guild
life were so pronounced.[41] At the same time, as a wealth of recent scholarship
has shown, although the republican regimes of the Quattrocento employed a
rhetoric of *libertas* and depended heavily on the contribution of "bourgeois"
commerce, they were both oligarchical in structure and aristocratic in ethos.
These tensions or contradictions proved conducive to the creation of a rich
body of political writing. Works of Italian Renaissance politics engaged directly
with such dilemmas, among other things by presenting debates over the comparative merits of asceticism and acquisitiveness, by assessing the role of the
wealthy (and the poor) as both potential benefactors and possible threats to
the polity, and by evaluating how the division of labor functions to maintain
social solidarity.[42] Such works tended to divide society into social categories
based on wealth, power, function, status, and prestige with the aim of describing the conditions through which the interests of all such groups might be
balanced so as to perpetuate the stability of the whole. Although this, too, had
been an aim of classical authors such as Aristotle and Polybius, Renaissance
works were set apart by two important characteristics. First, the philosophical works of antiquity were often tied in with metaphysical schemas that the
Renaissance rejected and sought to replace. Second, the economic conditions
of the ancient polis had appeared relatively static in comparison with those
of the Italian city-states, and this contrast had somehow to be accounted for.
Thus, the recovery of ancient and pristine political virtues rooted in stable
landed wealth would have to take place under circumstances – such as the
dynamic ebb and flow of trade – which rendered their restoration extremely
problematic.

The well-constructed state envisioned by the Renaissance humanists sought
to establish a constitutional equilibrium between different social components
in which interests, abilities, and functions would be balanced through the
dispositional medium of civic virtue – the pursuit of the general good at the
expense of private interest. For the earlier generations of "civic humanists,"
this was to be achieved primarily via the inculcation of virtue, defined in terms
of classical education, self-discipline, rhetorical cultivation, and refinement.[43]
The innovation of Machiavelli, and the nature of his influence on subsequent
authors, was to recognize that the classical Aristotelian polity was inherently unstable, subject to inevitable degeneration, its ideal of virtue too static
and timeless to account for historical and class dynamics. Although Polybius

(c. 200 B.C.E.) had already called attention to this process of inevitable degeneration, Machiavelli's solutions to the problem were novel. Against the unpredictable but inevitable quality of *fortuna*, he offered a new image of civic action, one which wedded the ideal of freedom (of the individual but more pointedly of the collective) to political *virtù*, that is to say, virtuosity of skill, capacity for improvisation, tactical adroitness, and military determination – all of which, even without *fortuna*'s cooperation, might afford the republic a chance to endure.[44]

Individual qualities of *virtù*, moreover, would be supplemented by institutional processes. If by nature men were prone to corruption (confusing private and factional interests with the general good), the wisest policy would be to harness rather than suppress their aggressive energies. For Machiavelli, the Roman Republic had shown the way by evolving political institutions through which social and economic groupings, patricians and plebeians, could pursue their particular aims without ever fully realizing them.[45] If artfully constructed, the ensuing tension would help transform destructive impulses into productive ends. It is important to remember that *virtù* and institutionalized conflict were not intended to substitute for the classical ideal of harmony, but rather to supplement it. They pointed the way toward a realization of the ideal of self-rule within the framework of a new, more complex and pluralistic society. Although Machiavelli's own works were oriented to the more traditional view that associated most commerce with corruption,[46] his praise of institutionalized conflict could be and was employed by later writers to legitimate the pursuit of mercantile self-interests in buttressing political stability.[47] Machiavelli's works thus hinted at a possible reconciliation between the desire for social cohesiveness and the pursuit of economic self-interest, values that in classical and medieval discourse were generally viewed as incompatible.[48]

SIMONE LUZZATTO'S DEFENSE OF JEWISH COMMERCE

Simone Luzzatto's 1638 apologia for the Venetian Jews, *Discorso circa il stato de gl'hebrei et in particular dimoranti nell'inclita città di Ventia* (Discourse on the Condition of the Jews and Particularly those Residing in the City of Venice) marks the beginning of a theoretical literature on Jewish political economy. Luzzatto (1583–1663), a Venetian rabbi and the author of a Latin philosophical dialogue, wrote in full awareness of his work's continuity with the Renaissance discourse of civic humanism.[49] Indeed, even for an educated Italian Jew, Luzzatto possessed an uncommon familiarity with a wide range of contemporary non-Jewish philosophic, scientific, and economic doctrines. In spite of this, the *Discorso*, although long valued by students of Jewish history, has yet to receive the attention it deserves from historians of economic and political thought.[50] Luzzatto's achievement was not merely to weave a defense of Jewish merchant activities into late Renaissance political thought, but also to knit together two motifs that had earlier remained distinct: first, the problem of how a republic can preserve itself amid the tempests of time, and, second, the recipe for winning the state's fortune by foreign trade. Luzzatto believed that the problem of political stability must be solved by the expansion of trade. He shrewdly insisted that Venice could harmoniously achieve these dual aims if Jews were given permission to act as its principal agents of overseas trade.

The *Discorso* was occasioned by a threatened expulsion of Venetian Jewry as a consequence of a recent criminal scandal involving Jews.[51] But at a deeper level it was a response to the economic decline of the city (only recently apparent) and accompanying accusations that the republic was being dragged down by foreign merchants, including Jews, through their alleged displacement of the native Venetian merchant class.[52] Luzzatto did not spare the other foreigners – the Dutch, Genoese, Florentines among them – but he did sharply distinguish these from the Jews. His argument was not designed to show that the latter were more assimilable than the others, but, on the contrary, to emphasize the Jews' otherness. It is because the Jews are neither Venetians nor foreigners that that they can accomplish what the former will not and the latter ought not do. Jews are the ideal merchant class, he claimed, because they are stateless and devoid of permissible alternative occupations. This is fortunate; for the old Christian merchant class of Venice seems no longer to be interested in the arduous and risky business of foreign trade.[53] They now typically invest their profits in real estate and retire to lives of *rentier* gentility. Not so the Jews, who are permitted to own no land. The restrictions excluding them from agriculture and the crafts ensure that they will fulfill tasks indispensable to the common weal that others, granted the opportunity, would soon abandon. "If they left, no one else would come to dwell in the city in their place with the same restrictions and prohibitions."[54] As opposed to foreign merchants, moreover, Jews can neither export wealth to their home country – because they have none – nor exploit it to win political power in Venice itself – because for them politics is unthinkable.

Luzzatto built this ingenious argument on the notion that economic prosperity results from a division of labor between different segments of the population that are united through intricate networks of trade. In the Italy of 1638, such ideas were already commonplace. Fifteenth-century Florentines such as Leonardo Bruni (1369–1444) and Poggio Bracciolini (1380–1459) had praised merchants as stalwarts of the republic,[55] an attitude that persisted in much subsequent Italian political thought. The Florentine statesman, Bernardo

Davanzati, in his 1588 *Treatise on Money*, identified the polis as the proper locus of trade. The vaunted rusticity and self-sufficiency of country life might satisfy a barbarian, but urban life alone could supply the material bases for a truly civilized existence. Giovanni Botero (1544–1617), an important influence on Luzzatto, had written in elegiac tones about "the greatness of cities" and contrasted the healthy consequences of the Italian nobility's preference for town with its French counterpart's prejudice in favor of the backward country life.[56] Approaching the argument from a different angle, Girolamo Garimberto's *De regimenti publici de la città* (Venice, 1544) praised Venetian sagacity in devising an aristocratic republic reliant on foreign commercial classes that were naturally excluded from the city's political life.[57] Finally, the Neapolitan economist, Antonio Serra, emphasized the industrial potential of urban centers and the capacity of strong-willed men to arrest commercial decline or even transform, through innovation and application, backward societies into prosperous ones.[58]

Unlike their classical predecessors, Davanzati, Botero, and Serra did not view the polity as simply a necessary framework for public activity, a *res publica*. Rather, they understood cities to be microcosms and building blocks of what we might today call global interdependency, a world divided by labor so that it can be united by trade:

> So one city helps another, and one country parts with its superfluities to another, in lieu thereof it is from thence again supplied with what it wants. And thus all the good things of nature and art are communicated and enjoyed by the means of human commerce or traffick, which at first was but simple barter, or changing of once commodity for another, as it still continues in the uncivilized parts of the world. [59]

In his *Treatise*, Davanzati makes use of an organic metaphor that Luzzatto too would later employ, observing that if trade is the nutrient that nourishes the bodily organs, money is the blood that enables it to circulate. In adopting this image, Luzzatto provided a Jewish linguistic twist. By remarking that the Hebrew words for blood and money were near homonyms, *dam* and *damim* respectively, he underscored the idea that the Holy Tongue itself attests to a divine approbation of commerce and its tools.[60] Continuing with such biological images, Luzzatto then cited a different classical source, Socrates, to show that society is, like the human body, a composite of individual organs ("a multiplicity of men within a single man") that operate via commerce and the division of labor in perfect if unconscious harmony.[61]

Its classicism aside, all of this sounds enlightened and "modern" from the standpoint of later free market ideologies. Yet it would be a mistake to view Luzzatto as a prophet of "possessive individualism." In fact, his division of labor was corporatist to its core. The city is comprised of varied social and religious groups that perform specific economic functions and pursue distinct *group* interests.[62] Luzzatto seemed to be linking two distinct ideas: the first emphasizing the virtue of rational self-interest; the second portraying society as composed of different social groupings, each seeking to benefit itself by pursuing its narrow ends yet inadvertently (or rather providentially) benefiting the whole. He did not emphasize individual wealth-maximization but, rather, corporate egotism. Far from being an unalloyed vice, such self-interestedness greases the wheels of commerce, checks excess, and sustains equilibrium:

> What the moralists call excesses [*superfluità*], luxuries and vain objects of our acquisitiveness, the politicians who consider humanity as a whole define as the foundations of business, the elements of commerce, the checks on avarice, the equalizers of human conditions [*agguagliatori del stato humano*], the tenacious knot and glue connecting the ends of the earth.[63]

This argument, with its Machiavellian disdain for "moralists" and its contrasting high praise of the "politicians" [*il Politici*], enabled Luzzatto to acclaim the moral utility of Jewish enterprise by locating its specific function within the larger mechanism of Venetian social life.[64] Prevented from subsisting on their own lands, the Jews serve as customers for and transporters of the surplus agricultural produce of the Venetian peasantry: "Therefore, many persons here support themselves by selling them food . . . "[65] Similarly, Venetian artisans and tradesmen who manufacture goods benefit from the presence of Jews who supply them with raw materials, purchase their finished products, and distribute them in foreign markets. Like the disparate thoughts and impulses of the mind, the polity is comprised of a "combination of various fragments of common and precious little stones connected and combined together," a mosaic in which each component only appears meaningful in relation to the whole.[66]

Although the components act selfishly, they are not precisely free – and certainly not in the case of the Jews. On the contrary, Luzzatto implies that had the Jews not been legally excluded from farming and handicrafts, they would certainly have flocked to these other professions. It is only external force that keeps Jews in their middleman roles. Without the heavy hand of the state, in the form of restrictive laws, the entire mechanism would break down. This fit in with Luzzatto's insistence that the talent for commerce is not innate to Jews. The ethnic division of labor, he suggests, is not a result of wise statesmen aligning economic functions with inherent group abilities. Rather, it is an artificial order that consequently takes on a logic of its own. In a key passage of the *Discorso*, Luzzatto explains that it is the "school of hardship" and harsh necessity, not inclination, that accounts for the Jews' economic uniqueness:

> The Hebrews more than any other people have been educated and reared in the school of necessity under the rigorous discipline of want [*nella Scola del disàggio sotto la rigorosa discipli na di esso bisogno*]. They possess no stable properties, exercise no mechanical arts, are far from being able to profit from positions in the courts and other municipal offices, and are burdened with large families because their religious rites do not permit them celibacy. They must therefore earn their livings through diligent industry and make their way by painstaking determination and assiduity. Consequently, it is evident wherever the Hebrews reside there traffic and commerce flourish, as is attested by Livorno . . .[67]

Luzzatto's "rigorous discipline of want" possessed an ironic ring. The great sixteenth-century Venetian statesman, Paolo Paruta (1540–1598), whose philosophical skepticism and admiration of trade bears a strong resemblance to Luzzatto's, had likewise identified necessity as the true impetus to industry and innovation. But in Paruta's case it was the physical environment rather than man-made policy which dictated the terms of survival.[68] For Luzzatto, in contrast, the Jews' economic orientation is purely a function of Christians' prejudice. True, in imposing on them an economic otherness to match the religious one, gentiles have created a remarkable symbiotic order. Although Jews may suffer and perhaps chafe under such a regime, it has the distinct benefit of allowing them to survive. Yet Luzzatto deploys this fact to make an important apologetic point. It is the imperative of survival, he suggests, rather than any perversity or predisposition that has forced the Jews to become the commercial middlemen par excellence. The sacrifice of the Jews, their constriction to the field of trade and the consequent reduction of their full human personality to an unhealthily narrow sphere, although exacting a painful toll on their psyches, pays dividends for the Christian polity in achieving a richer, more diverse and eclectic environment. "Along with the transport of long-distance goods, are conveyed customs, arts, ideas, and civilization [*humanità*] itself."[69] If the Jews are prevented from becoming Renaissance men (a premise that Luzzatto's own achievements at least belied), they do nevertheless sustain and expand *civitas* for others. The symbiosis ordained by the Jews' restriction to the mercantile sphere occasions material prosperity, social solidarity, and cultural enrichment – ample reasons for the surrounding population to welcome them graciously, if not to free them from their special tasks.

Luzzatto's naturalistic rationale for Jewish toleration was highly innovative, but it had a conservative side, too. It was predicated on the Jews' acquiescence to their permanent confinement within a single economic sector and exclusion from any wider participation in Venetian society.[70] According to Luzzatto, the Jews have no interest in politics or ambition to exert authority over gentiles through the acquisition of land, titles, or offices.[71] Anticipating the charge later leveled against the Jews of diaspora-generated dual loyalty (i.e., the Jews of one country allied with those of another above the interests of their own rulers), Luzzatto insists that they regard it, "*as if* it were an unbreakable religious law, never to mix into affairs of state that involve the interests of rulers under whose protection other Jews are living."[72] Or, as Rabbi Menasseh ben Israel, who in 1654 would make extensive use of the *Discorso* to win Jewish readmission to England, later asserted, "[T]hey aspire at nothing but to preferre themselves in their way of Marchandize."[73] Jewish commerce makes the political liberty of the host society possible, because Jews themselves have no aspiration to the enjoyment of such liberty.

Libertas had been an overriding value in much of the political thought of the Italian humanists. In its Ciceronian sense, it connoted not so much individual freedom from governmental constraint as membership and participation in the free, i.e., self-governing, polity.[74] In foregoing any claim to *libertas*, Luzzatto was making a necessary though costly concession, for in the civic humanist terms that he himself employed, it meant depriving Jews of a key ingredient of their humanity (in the Aristotelian sense of man as properly a political being). Luzzatto acknowledged this point when he assessed the psychological toll that had been exacted on Jews by the narrowing of the scope of their activities to the monetary and commercial. "This nation possesses a weak and deeply enervated spirit, is incapable in its present condition of any political self-government [*d'ogni governo Politico*], and preoccupied with its particular narrow interests."[75] Pathetic as the concession may sound, it was eminently realistic.[76] No Jewish author of Luzzatto's day would have dared demand more than mere tolerance from the Christian authorities. Although Sephardic merchants in other corners of Christendom, such as Livorno or Amsterdam – or in some of the Dutch Atlantic colonies – might enjoy more privileges than those granted by Venice, with the exception of a relative handful of individual Jews who possessed extraordinary wealth and political value, they nowhere held the status of citizens. Citizenship itself was a relative term in the seventeenth century, one that generally connoted membership in an urban corporation rather than a national polity. Yet Jews, who as a rule enjoyed substantial degrees of autonomy and municipal self-government, were not citizens even in this sense.[77] Rather, they constituted a group whose protections were highly circumscribed in extent and duration, with privileges subject to periodic renewal, as was the case in Venice itself. Any claim, even a theoretical one, to their inclusion in the category of individuals enjoying real political rights in a Christian community would have been regarded as presumptuous if not downright preposterous.

COMMERCE AND AGRICULTURE IN SEVENTEENTH-CENTURY ENGLAND

Luzzatto's conservatism, like the Jews' captivity to commerce, was born of harsh necessity. It remains curious, however, that this insistent forfeiture in both Luzzatto's *Discorso* and the next text to be considered, Menasseh ben Israel's "Humble Addresses to Oliver Cromwell," of any claim by Jews to *libertas* occurred within works that were part of or related to the genre of contemporary political theory. This was particularly the case with Luzzatto's *Discorso*, a text replete with quotations from the kinds of classical sources, such as Tacitus and Aristotle, that were favored by late Renaissance political theorists, and one that also abounded in allusions to moderns such as Machiavelli, Justus Lipsius, Thomas More, and Botero. Luzzatto, it should be noted, was the author of a Latin philosophical work, *Socrate*, which, although containing smatterings of economic and political discussion, possessed no overt Jewish content.[78] This suggests a sensibility that felt entirely comfortable in two intellectual cultures or, more accurately, a mind convinced that the relationship between Renaissance humanism and Jewish learning was unproblematically harmonious. The short but fascinating succession of Sephardic and Italian Jewish writers who engaged with republican and civic humanist discourse, including Isaac Abravanel, Yohanon Alemanno, David De Pomis, and Menasseh ben Israel, were likewise men of two worlds. It would seem entirely natural that they should engage with questions that were of general intellectual or topical concern, such as the sources of political stability, or the relative virtues of monarchies and republics, in addition to ones that related directly to the current situation of their own coreligionists. Political theory and political economy provided a seemingly disinterested framework for dissecting society and diagnosing its ills; it also allowed for a treatment of the character and status of Jews that was relatively unfettered by religious and theological vocabulary. Religion could be discussed both abstractly and historically by asking presumably neutral questions about its political character. This was, of course, as true of Christian as of Jewish writers. Machiavelli could offer up devastating criticisms of Christianity's passive political orientation while leaving the reader uncertain about his own exact theological stance. In a similar way, Luzzatto found little difficulty in making use of the Hebrew Bible as a sort of political primer rather than as pure sacred writ, since the genre allowed sacred writings to function as more or less neutral political texts. In fact, reading the "Old Testament" as a work of political theory had become a well-worn tradition in civic humanist discourse by the time the *Discorso* was published, a subject to which we will return in Chapter 2.

This is not to say, however, that political theory was necessarily friendly to Jews. Despite the genre's defusing of dogmatic theology, biblical and classical sources supplied political philosophers with plenty of "secular" ammunition with which to attack the Jews. Tacitus and Seneca had written unfavorably about Jews, maligning them as misanthropic and seditious.[79] Although Moses was universally admired as a wise lawgiver and state founder (not least of all by Machiavelli), the rabbis – to put it mildly – were not.[80] Leaving aside such ancient prejudices, political theory also proved conducive to anti-Jewish sentiment because of the unease it expressed toward the place of merchants, especially foreign ones. In this light, Luzzatto's suggestion that commerce could successfully underwrite civic stability and independence was not necessarily the standard view. We have already noted that despite his advocacy of institutionalized class conflict, Machiavelli, for instance, displayed a mistrust of commerce for the same reasons Luzzatto had praised it: the prosperity, sophistication, and refinement that it brought to the populace. These qualities, Machiavelli believed, encouraged political corruption, patronage, dependency, factionalism, and reliance on mercenaries, as well as a kind of public effeminacy.[81] Although not all commerce was to be despised, excessive wealth and luxury, Machiavelli believed, would seduce the population into relinquishing its freedom.[82]

In seventeenth-century England – to which the remainder of this chapter is devoted – Machiavelli's opinions on these matters encountered a receptive audience. England had only recently become a commercial power; its principally agrarian orientation and relatively weak urban infrastructure made the growing power of merchants controversial within the dominant aristocratic culture. Whereas Florence, and still more Venice, had been cradles of European commercial and financial development, seventeenth-century England had but one major city. The northern Italian nobilities were scions of old mercantile families and had never lost contact with urban life. But the dominant classes in England were overwhelmingly landed, even if some of their members were business-minded "improving landlords." The fact that England's system of primogeniture often made it necessary for younger sons of gentry families to enter business did not always mean a softening of antimercantile attitudes, because status was still strongly associated with leisure and independency. In the minds of most aristocrats, the category of "merchant" overlapped with that of artisan and tradesman.[83] This suggested that merchants were to be classed among those who worked with their hands, something repellent to noble sensibilities. Although it is true that in the seventeenth century these attitudes came under increasing attack from political commentators and social critics, even praise of the merchant was usually qualified and reflected deep ambivalence.[84] It might be conceded that merchants had their place, but most agreed that it should be a restricted one. Town and country should be allied, so long as port remained subordinate to estate.

For political writers of a republican bent (in England, the term "commonwealth" was preferred), land was seen as a true source of civic virtue. This was so, among other reasons, because land provided the stable ground of self-sufficiency and independence that any true commonwealth required. The tradition of virtuous Sparta rather than the more cosmopolitan Athens prevailed. According to James Harrington, the leading interpreter of Machiavelli to seventeenth-century England, "Agriculture is the bread of the nation ... , a mighty nursery of strength, the best army and the most assured knapsack ... " He further expressed the view, citing Aristotle, "that [a] commonwealth of husbandmen (and such is ours) must be the best of all others." Harrington disdained the "culture of 'selling,' even likening it to a "Jewish humour."[85] He wove this position into a historical schema that identified the Tudor redistribution of Church lands with the growth of a broad-based class of gentry and yeomanry. This structural change made baronial feudalism obsolete and a restoration of Greco-Roman style republicanism both feasible and desirable, but significantly it did not restore the city-state to its former exalted position. On the contrary, one of Harrington's important innovations was to revise republican theory to fit the large territorial (and hence overwhelmingly agricultural) polity.[86] Harrington's antimerchant views were echoed by other republican stalwarts, such as Milton. But even the much larger category of authors who were not devotees of republican ideology tended to accord landownership a place of honor. In the English common-law tradition, government existed primarily to protect rights to property, which typically meant "real" or landed property.[87] Real as opposed to movable personal property often signaled full membership in the political community, which was one of the reasons why the question of whether aliens and eventually Jews could own land proved so controversial.

Naturally, real property accorded economic as well as political benefits. In a period when capital markets were still scarce and long-term investment in trade risky, land offered the safest outlet for surplus wealth (this was precisely why Luzzatto's Venetian merchant had sunk their profits into it). For the economists, as opposed to the politicians and lawyers, land also figured centrally in discussions of trade. Contemporary economic discussions often were geared toward defining the optimal uses of commerce for the maximization of state revenue to be achieved through productive agriculture, including the exportation of agricultural commodities. Thomas Mun's *England's Treasure by Forraign Trade* challenged the arguments of metalists by asserting that only through the free circulation of specie would foreign consumers possess the means to increase their purchases of English agricultural exports, thereby increasing demand, prices, rents, and revenue.[88] Josiah Child's attack on usury and high interest rates had less to do with traditional religious qualms than with the desire of gentleman farmers to secure low-interest loans in order to innovate and raise output.[89] Through low interest, agricultural investment would increase surpluses for export, advancing the cycle of rising production and demand, for "the produce of Land is the principle foundation of Trade."[90] William Petty's extensive surveys of agricultural conditions in England and Ireland provided innovative statistical models in addition to intensive discussions of comparative agronomy and effective estate management – all geared to the burgeoning revolution in agricultural productivity.[91]

Although important economic tracts were produced by merchants, these tended to be viewed, at least by the more academic-minded "political arithmeticians," as self-interested and suspect. In contrast, an "agricultural bias" runs like a golden thread through the arithmeticians' writings, culminating in *The Wealth of Nations* of Adam Smith.[92] This bias reflects, in part, a rational appreciation of a vital component of England's commercial advancement – innovation in the techniques of husbandry and crop production for the purposes of market sale.[93] But alongside the idealization of the improving farmer there was also a qualified diminishment of, and even a marked hostility toward, the figure of the merchant. In economic terms, the merchant was necessary yet unproductive. True, everyone understood that agricultural production for the market depended on the middleman, especially the overseas trader, yet his role was regarded as exclusively functional. He did not create wealth, he merely circulated it. For Petty, merchants exist only to "distribute back and forth the blood and nutritive juyces of the Body Politick, namely the Product of Husbandry and Manufacture." Their numbers and influence should be rigorously contained, lest they become "parasitical" off the wealth-producing classes of society.[94] The middleman does not sink his profit into the soil; hence, he is as economically unproductive as he is politically uncommitted. "The merchant . . . is not necessarily the citizen of any country," Adam Smith would later warn, for his primary loyalty is to reaping profit rather than creating wealth.[95]

There were countervailing opinions, to be sure. Reacting against J. G. A. Pocock's emphasis on anticommercial attitudes in seventeenth-century English political culture, historians such as Steve Pincus and Paul Rahe have pointed to the more sympathetic and pro-merchant sentiments of men such as Henry Parker, Slingsby Bethel, Sir William Temple, and Thomas Sprat.[96] To Parker, Bethel, Sprat, and others like them, England should look to Holland as a laudable example of a "commercial republic" whose prosperity and growing empire commands admiration and whose merchant-friendly policies merits emulation.[97] But although such examples suggest that Pocock's thesis requires amendment, they seem less important for the seventeenth than the eighteenth century, when a clear ideology of a commercially based and individualistic polity emerged. It has to be remembered that not every statement praising merchants reflected a proto-capitalist or proto-liberal outlook. The very term merchant could designate different things at different times. In one sense, merchants who were members of chartered corporations or possessors of the freedom of the city occupied a venerable and respectable position. They possessed arms as a privilege of their estate (and hence a capacity for the martial virtues), owned their own tools and workshops (and hence enjoyed freedom from dependence on others), and sold only within the narrow parameters permitted by the self-policed guild order. But these were less merchants in the modern sense than merchant-manufacturers, artisans, and craftsmen who employed laborers and exchanged the products produced in their workshops.[98] In contrast, the newer type of merchant – who was mobile, ever in search of novel sources of profit, and often geared toward finance and credit as much as toward manufacture and trade – was seen as less amenable to civic virtue and less devoted to the polity. By the end of the century, as we will see, this latter group became associated with such reputably sinister institutions as stockjobbing and currency speculation, which seemed seriously to threaten the landed order.[99]

These attitudes figured prominently in the debates that surrounded Jewish status in England. Jews there found themselves the objects of contention within a diverse body of discourse and concepts with which they themselves enjoyed only limited familiarity. As we have seen, these included classical and renaissance civic humanism, the ideal of the virtuous citizen and the correct balance of forces comprising the polity; political economy, its agrarian bias and qualified endorsement of trade; and the English common-law tradition with its conception of a landowning, or rather a freehold-possessing, elite enjoying hereditary rights enshrined in an ancient constitution. Nor were these traditions entirely separable from religion. The status of commerce and credit in Christianity was controversial; when Jews were added to the mix, it could become explosive. For instance, Jewish financiers and international merchants in late seventeenth-century Germany, the greatest of whom were Court Jews, sometimes became victims of an incendiary blend of populist economic attitudes and popular antisemitism. Yet while similar stirrings occasionally shook Anglo-Jewry (although rarely manifesting themselves in physical violence), the debates over the readmission of Jews that took place in the years 1654–1656 were notable for a different combination of features. Spiritual and messianic, rather than economic, impulses remained uppermost in the minds of English Protestant advocates of Jewish readmission. If anything these debates exhibited a combination of religious philosemitism, on the one hand, and economic antisemitism, on the other. As the historian David Katz has shown in his study of Jewish readmission to England, when economic rationales were employed in debates over Jewish readmission, they were adduced most often in opposition to rather than in favor of Jewish toleration.[100] Native merchants, fearing Jewish competition, tended vigorously to oppose proposals to readmit the Jews. The corporation of the City of London and the Levant Company produced tracts purporting to demonstrate that Jewish readmission would result in a disastrous diversion of foreign trade, since (these tracts argued) Jewish merchants, when not acting solely on their own behalf, served foreign commercial interests.[101] Nevertheless, as is evident from both Luzzatto's *Discourse* and from Menasseh ben Israel's *Humble Addresses*, such opposition, whether in Italy or England, indicated a widespread perception that Jews remained powerful economic actors whose presence would inevitably exert a significant impact not just on the nation's material condition but on its political affairs too. At the same time, pamphlets depicting this impact in a negative light required that pro-Jewish responses be formulated on the level of both economic and political reasoning. It is for this reason that Menasseh, in making his appeal for Jewish readmission to Lord Cromwell, shrewdly placed the mercantile, the religious, and the political rationales for Jewish readmission side by side.

MENASSEH BEN ISRAEL AND THE READMISSION OF THE JEWS

Menasseh was a Dutch Sephardic rabbi who enjoyed extensive contacts among Christian Hebraists, humanists, and millenarians. It was from the latter circle in England, including men close to Cromwell, that Menasseh received an invitation to visit London and confer with Cromwell about matters of common messianic interest. From the point of view of Menasseh and his Dutch coreligionists, obtaining permission from Cromwell to admit Jews, both to England proper and to its colonial possessions, was paramount for economic as well as for redemptive purposes. Jonathan Israel argues plausibly that Menasseh's embassy to Cromwell did not mark the apex of Jewish resettlement but, rather, a desperate effort to revive the fortunes of the Sephardic community in the aftermath of several powerful blows. First and foremost, the promising Dutch colony in Brazil had only a year earlier been lost to Portuguese reconquest after a protracted struggle in which Sephardim had participated fully. Not only was Brazil's sugar production key to Sephardic overseas commerce, but the colony also had offered a haven for increasing numbers of impoverished Jews. The Jewish poor were a mounting burden on the charitable resources of the Amsterdam Sephardic leadership, the *Mahamad*. Consequently, the *Mahamad* sought new territories where they could send the poor as colonists. The Amsterdam Sephardim had enjoyed positive economic relations with Portugal so long as the country was seeking its independence from Spain (which had acquired Portugal in 1580), but these declined once the goal was achieved in 1640. Relations were further aggravated by Dutch Jewish financing of the Dutch struggle to retain Brazil, including the subsidizing of pirate raids on Portuguese shipping.

The mid-seventeenth century marked the beginning of a decline in Portuguese New Christian fortunes both in Portugal itself as well as in Spain, where the fall of their protector, the Count-Duke of Olivares, in 1643, set the stage for a renewed persecution by the Inquisition. Outside of Iberia, the Venetian war with Crete, begun in 1645, would take a heavy toll on Venetian trade, including Venetian Jewish merchants. Although the impeccably well-informed Menasseh could not have been fully aware of the consequences of that war (which at any rate lasted until 1669), he was certainly conscious of the effects of the British Navigation Act on Dutch and Dutch Sephardic trade. Barring all transportation of the goods to and from Britain of one country in the ships of another, the Act effectively precluded Dutch trade with England and its colonies, a trade which had enjoyed extensive Jewish participation. Ratified by the 1654 Treaty of Westminster which concluded the First Anglo-Dutch War, the Act made it imperative for Sephardim to secure residence in England in order for the wealthy to trade and the poor to colonize other parts of the Americas now that Brazil had been lost. Indeed, Menasseh's appeal to Cromwell, to which we now turn, made sure to place heavy emphasis on the value to Christians of a Jewish presence in the New World. It seems that only by making Jews resident traders in England could the Sephardim's economic woes be stemmed.[102]

Menasseh understood that Cromwell required a religious rationale for promoting the Jews' economic goals.[103] We recall that Luzzatto had employed a sociological argument, explaining the Jews' concentration in commerce in naturalistic terms and justifying it in accordance with society's growing tendency toward occupational differentiation. Menasseh, in contrast, emphasized that the Jews were not merely driven into commerce by external circumstance but also drawn to it through a supernal influence. "Merchandizing," he wrote, is the "proper profession of the Nation of the Jews." This is to be accounted for, he insisted, by the "particular Providence and mercy of God towards his people." Banished from their own country but not from divine protection, "he hath given them, as it were, a naturall instinct" for commercial life. This "naturall instinct," implanted by God in his exiled flock, ensures that "they might not onely gain what was necessary for their need, but that they should also thrive in Riches and possessions; whereby they should not onely become gracious to their Princes and Lords, but that they should be invited by others to come and dwell in their Lands."[104]

It may appear strange, at first sight, that Menasseh should employ the object of his appeal, Jewish readmission, as an argument to achieve it. But what he is in fact asserting is that the Jews' return to Western Europe, although ostensibly motivated by their economic attractions, reflects a providential design to draw Jews into "all places & Countreyes of the World." Manasseh's biblical prooftext was *Daniel* 12:7: "And when the dispersion of the Holy people shall be compleated in all places, then shall all these things be completed." He indicated that "the opinion of many Christians and mine doe concurre" about how this prophesy should be understood. The Jews' universal dispersion, Menasseh explained, was a precondition for their restoration "into their Native Contreye." Restoration accompanied by messianic deliverance was now imminent.[105] In an earlier work, *The Hope of Israel* (1650), Menasseh reported the recent "discovery" that the Indians of South America were actually the Ten Lost Tribes of ancient lore.[106] In fact, he had been aware of such reports since the visit to Amsterdam of Antonio de Montezinos, a New Christian who claimed to have found a Jewish tribe on his travels through the Andes. In pressing this point, Menasseh was coloring his message for his Puritan readers.[107] Elsewhere, when writing for a Jewish audience, Menasseh had suggested that the presence in the Americas of Sephardic communities would be sufficient to fulfill Daniel's geographical requirements.[108] In *Humble Addresses*, however, he wished to play up the role of the Ten Tribes, doubtless in part for English consumption. Menasseh was no less messianic than Cromwell, but his notion of redemption centered on the idea that through Jewish dispersion the principles of the Torah would gradually become adopted by the Gentiles. "The Lord let the people of Israel be captive and scattered them amongst other peoples so that they might, as pilgrims, unite them in faith, for God does not wish for the death of the ungodly," he wrote in his *Piedra gloriosa o de la estatua de Nebuchadnesar*. In his *Humble Addresses*, however, he knew better than to mention these quasi-missionary aims.[109] Here instead he told his readers that the tribes of Judah and Benjamin were already "scattered through the whole World" (a point later underscored through his descriptions of the Jewish communities of India, Persia, Egypt, Turkey, Italy, Germany and Poland).[110] Only the Jews' restoration to England remained to fulfill the prophecy (*Angle-Terre* being the equivalent of Daniel's *ketsah ha-'arets*, the "ends of the earth"). This required English statesmen to recognize that Jews "do abundantly enrich the Lands and Countrys of strangers, where they live."[111] In the *Humble Addresses*, Menasseh frequently referred to the privileges that had been granted Jews in such places as Livorno, Venice, and Savoy. The effect was to demonstrate a providential pattern in recent history of expulsion followed by resettlement. In God's plan, the recent catastrophe in Brazil was a necessary prelude to the Jews' restoration to England. The economic self-interest of all the relevant parties would provide the motive power for the fulfillment of prophecy. In this way, Menasseh made the divinely implanted Jewish mercantile propensity instrumental to the messianic expectations of Jews and Puritans alike.

According to Menasseh, the commerce of the Jews is no calamity but has been ordained by God, among other reasons, for the material and spiritual welfare of Christian society. Yet although commerce is essential to the Jews' survival and ultimate salvation, Menasseh nevertheless regarded the Jews' practice of it as a taint on their character and a consequence of their sins. The Jews' instinct for commerce only became implanted, Menasseh tells us, when God banished them from their land. Before this fall from grace, they practiced commerce little or not at all. Hence, when the cycle is completed, and as the dialectic of exile and redemption renders the Jews' dispersion entirely fulfilled, they will return to their land and abandon its practice. ". . . [T]hey are forced to use marchandizing untill that time, when they shall returne to their own Country, that then as God hath promised by the Prophet Zachary, *Their shall be found no more any merchant amongst them in the House of the Lord*."[112]

Why did Menasseh offer this caveat? Luzzatto, a principal though unacknowledged source for the *Humble Addresses*, had also bemoaned the scars inflicted by commerce on the Jews' moral traits: a parsimony that approaches avarice as well as an ignorance of and indifference to the surrounding cultural environment, because they are "engrossed in their private interests."[113] But whereas Luzzatto described merchandizing as the most useful of trades, Menasseh depicted it as merely an instrument of divine expediency.[114] Perhaps he had the sensibilities of the English gentry and not just London merchants in mind. By insisting that the Jews' exilic confinement to commerce was divinely ordained to enable them to endure their punishment, Menasseh could concur with the antimercantile sentiments of his readers and, at the same time, reassure them that Jewish commerce presented no actual danger to the free-born natives since Jews also were obliged to obey the divine command to eschew exilic politics.[115]

It seems paradoxical that Menasseh, in his dedicatory preface to Cromwell, granted his rabbinical imprimatur, so to speak, to the 1649 regicide of Charles I and the founding of the commonwealth under the Lord Protector:

> It is a thing most certaine, that the great God of *Israel*, Creator of Heaven and Earth, doth give and take away Dominions and Empires, according to his owne pleasure; exalting some, and overthrowing others; who, seeing he hath the hearts of Kings in his hand, he easily moves them whithersoever himselfe pleaseth, to put in execution his Divine Commands.[116]

Medieval Jewish thought strongly favored monarchy. With the exception of the great Hispano-Jewish courtier, Don Isaac Abravanel, who with his fellow Jews was exiled by Ferdinand and Isabella in 1492, no major Jewish philosopher before Spinoza had advocated republican government. Luzzatto himself seemed at best ambiguous on the subject because his view appeared to shift depending on the specific agenda of a given work. In the *Discorso*, he depicted republican government as ideally suited to the commercial character of Venice, its political division between "the one, the few, and the many" ("the one" being the Doge) paralleling the division of labor in which Jews played an essential part.[117] But Luzzatto's *Socrate* was a distinctly monarchical work.[118] Like Luzzatto and Spinoza, Menasseh spent most of his life in a republic, or commonwealth, defined by mixed government and a federalist structure. In the *Humble Addresses*, he in fact offers no praise for the structural advantages of a republic but only for its utility within God's redemptive scheme favoring the settlement of Jews. Only under a commonwealth, he implies, with its fostering of political and commercial freedom, would the recognition of the "politique" value of Jewish merchants succeed in overcoming traditional Christian hostility: "that the Kingly Government being now changed into that of a Common-wealth, the antient hatred towards [the Jews], would also be changed into good-will."[119]

Menasseh arrived in London in September 1655 and remained there for two years, during which time no official decision was rendered on his petition for readmission. In fact, the end result of his efforts was disappointing. True, Jews did receive de facto permission to reside in England, but under conditions that required private worship and limited opportunities – far from the open invitation they had received in places such as Livorno or Dutch Brazil. The ambiguity of Jewish readmission lay in the negative formula in which their reentry was framed. In investigating the legality of Jewish readmission, the lawyers and antiquarians who gathered in the Whitehall Palace in December 1655 wished to determine whether existing statutes precluded it. The conference concluded in the negative but issued no declaration officially readmitting Jews. It was as if their restoration was instigated by a wink rather than a nod. Under these ambiguous circumstances, the debate quickly passed beyond narrow governmental circles to encompass merchants, clergy, and common-lawyers who weighed in on various sides. A steady stream of pamphlets emerged to promote or denounce the Jews, many of which directly took up or took on Menasseh's arguments. Although most emphasized the religious or commercial consequences of readmission, some also brought the argument around to politics.[120] One in particular, William Prynne's *A Short Demurrer to the Jews* (1656), linked Jewish readmission directly to the central issues of governmental rights, royal prerogative, parliamentary redress, and ancient constitutional standing. It was a work that, with its detailed excursus on the history of medieval Anglo-Jewry, would come to exert a substantial influence on legal debates over the status of English Jews in the following century. Its immediate effect, as we will now see, was to bring the apologetic discourse of Menasseh (and indirectly Luzzatto) into the arena of English political debate.

WILLIAM PRYNNE'S *SHORT DEMURRER*

Prynne (1602–1669) began his political career as a radical Puritan lawyer who achieved near-martyr status when his ear was severed in retribution for an act of *lèse majesté* against Charles I; it ended with his appointment by Charles II as the official keeper of the records at the Tower of London. What remained constant throughout these shifting allegiances was Prynne's overriding belief in the sanctity of the common-law tradition as a bulwark against the ungodly innovations of "this new-fangled age."[121] His *Short Demurrer* relied on and yet frequently criticized the historical researches of Sir Edward Coke (1552–1634). Coke was a Chief Justice and legal antiquarian who had dedicated himself to "recovering," in vast detail, the entire body of English common law in an effort to assert the ancient rights of the Commons that in Coke's view had been recently subverted by Stuart royal prerogative.[122] Prynne largely shared this aim. And like Coke before him, but unlike the later supporters of the Commonwealth, he proved his dedication to it by proclaiming the Crown and the House of Lords, alongside the Commons, as equally integral components of the ancient constitution. In fact, Prynne regarded the claims of hegemony asserted by the House of Commons after 1648 as violations of that very tradition.[123] Prynne could thus be described as a radical Puritan opponent of Oliver

Cromwell. In *A Short Demurrer*, he made the case against Jewish readmission by demonstrating its illegality in English common law.

The first point Prynne sought to make was an historical one, directly related to the Whitehall investigation, namely, that the record as he has unearthed it indicates there was no Jewish presence in England until the time of William the Conqueror.[124] Seventeenth-century interpreters of common law were divided over the issue of whether the Norman Conquest had represented any kind of fundamental break with ancient legal traditions. Most scholars of the time assumed that William had at least made innovations in the rules of land tenure, possibly including the introduction of *feuds* that defined the so-called feudal system. At the same time, many of these scholars were keen to show that that the law had evolved organically and without sudden breaks or sharp discontinuities. The question of the Jews' presence and historical status was an exception to this, at least in Prynne's mind. By insisting that Jews came into the constitutional picture in 1066, Prynne was demonstrating that they themselves enjoyed no part whatsoever in the original constitution, and that the Jews' initial presence in medieval England had been of doubtful legitimacy.[125] Similarly, the use to which the Jews were put by their royal patrons indicates that they had always played a subversive role with regard to the rights and privileges of the gentry freeholders' polity:

> None ever gain'd by the Jews introduction or continuance in any Christian State, but the King and some of his bribed Officers, and that by oppressing, squeezing, fleecing, taxing, excoriating, eviscerating, crucifying, pillaging, plundering the poor Jews in such an unchristian, inhuman, illegal, unrighteous manner, against the express commands of God, as made both Christians and Christianity most detestable to them . . . and [as] encouraged [the kings] to oppresse, fleece and pillage their Native Subjects, by illegal Taxes and Projects, and to use them rather like Jews than Christians, enforcing them thereby to take up arms against them for their Laws, Liberties and Properties just defense . . . [126]

Prynne himself had not originated the core argument here. Well before any concrete effort had been made to readmit them to England, Jews had functioned in common law discourse as symbols of the extreme measure of royal prerogative. It was a legal commonplace that the king's power was most absolute in relation to the Jews, their lives, and their property. This meant that for purposes of legal analysis, Jews were utterly alien and lay outside of the protections of the ancient constitution. But in practical terms, this categorical definition of the Jews as aliens par excellence (living under the mark of "perpetual enmity," as Coke put it) was only applied in legal cases involving non-Jewish groups, such as *native* commercial corporations. The legacy of medieval Jewry served as an abstraction or legal fiction to determine the precise application of alien law and royal prerogative to various actors in English society.[127]

Prynne exploited this abstract legal conception of Jewry as fodder for his rhetorical denunciation of Jewish readmission. He made use of their imputed status as rightless agents of the Crown to demonstrate the insidious constitutional effects that would ensue from their restoration. The original presence of Jews in medieval England had allowed the Crown to subvert the gentry's rights – indeed, "to use them rather like Jews." All the more reason, he insists, to block their readmission now, when, through an ironic twist, a parliamentary junta under Cromwell was seeking to deploy Jews with the same nefarious design. Although Prynne emphasized his religious opposition to Jewish readmission above all else, it is interesting to see how his Puritan fanaticism, legal antiquarianism, and civic classicism all converged to make exactly the same point. "For Reasons against their re-admission into England, they are divers, Theological, Political, and mixt of both."[128]

According to Prynne, the Jews were always a mortal threat to the Christian freeholding polity of England, an instrument of the royal usurpation of traditional liberties and a dagger at the heart of the commonwealth. Their expulsion in 1290 was one of the major steps, along with the Magna Carta and the creation of the Commons (1265), toward the eventual restoration of England's ancient rights.[129] Although Prynne was no civic humanist or republican (for men like Coke and Prynne, the ancient constitution was inconceivable without a monarchy, although a limited one), the Puritan legal tradition to which he belonged did share with humanist writings a similar devotion to classicism.[130] And there were other, related parallels between Puritanism and civic humanism, not least of all a common inclination to xenophobia.[131] Both viewed foreigners as a subversive and corrupting force, and foreign mercenaries in particular as mortal dangers to the land. Mercenaries were analogous to merchants in the sense that both sold to the highest bidder. Similarly, foreign merchants introduced an element into the polity whose loyalties were extraneous to it. As purveyors of foreign goods, especially luxury items involved in overseas trade, they threatened to erode the Spartan virtues of the citizenry. In delineating the reasons why contemporary German city-states had been long able to resist corruption, Machiavelli had emphasized their isolation from external contamination:

> ... [F]or their neighbors rarely visit them, and they rarely visit their neighbors. They have been content with the products of the local economy, eating

food grown and raised nearby, and dressing in wool from their own sheep. This removes the primary reason for contact with foreigners, and with it, the primary source of all corruption.[132]

Prynne echoes this same sentiment when he finds in classical sources ballast for his anti-Jewish arguments:

> ...hence Lycurgus the famous Legislator of the Spartans by his Law and advice, expelled all foraigners out of their city and country, lest by insinuating themselves amongst them, they should teach their Citizens some ill, introduce foraign manners, & an ill disordered kind of life upon which ground they also prohibited their Citizens to travel into foraign countries.[133]

Foreigners, according to Prynne, are like snakes taken into the bosom, "for as they being refreshed with heat do bite and sting: So these being enfranchised destroy the Republike ... "[134]

The deployment of a republican-*sounding* rhetoric by so unlikely a source as Prynne demonstrates just how pervasive and plastic civic humanist vocabulary had become in seventeenth-century England and how much it had in common with the theory of ancient and immemorial constitutional rights.[135] Prynne's pamphlets against stage plays and other iniquitous forms of entertainment, his diatribes against immigrants and Quakers,[136] whom he suspected of Jesuitical fifth-column activities, his fierce attachment to "those good old English Liberties which our noble Ancestors claimed, purchased, and transmitted to us as our richest Birthrights,"[137] even his admiration for the moral purity of the heathen "republike," far from being disparate elements in an incoherent mix, all attest to a deeply entrenched conservatism. "[E]very Nation hath its proper ceremonies which they bring along with them, and do not change with the climate when they come into another Countrey; wherefore there is great danger, lest by receiving strangers the ancient manners and Laws should be changed into new and foraign [ones]."[138]

Prynne informed his readers that his purpose in the *Short Demurrer* was to controvert the "worldly, carnal, sensuous" argument of Menasseh ben Israel that the Jews should be readmitted because they are profitable.[139] But far from helping the nation, the Jews only helped fleece its pockets. "The Trade of this Nation flourished more after their banishment hence, then ever it did before ... "[140] Prynne followed with several prescriptions for economic improvement which he believed would be far more efficacious than the benefits Menasseh promised through the readmission of the Jews. These included the removal of all new and (therefore) illegal taxes, the importation of bullion, and the redistribution of the spoils of English piracy to native English merchants rather than "to the use of that some stile, the Admiralty and State."[141] Prynne was a vigorous opponent of the New Model Army, not finding anything in the ancient constitution to legitimate its rule. In standing armies he saw only an instrument of centralization, tyranny, and corruption. Instead, he favored a restoration of what he called the "old unmercinary Trained Bands and Legal Militia."[142] In his *Short Demurrer*, we can thus see how the Jews – or the image of the Jews – fit into all the negative scenarios conjured up through the synthesis of conservative, Puritan, and civic humanist outlooks. The Jews were viewed as instruments not of legitimate commerce, but of fiscal centralization associated with illegal taxes, standing armies, and the subversion of native English merchants' inherited corporate privileges. Their economic activities could not be divorced from their political misuses.[143]

By the end of the 1650s, Prynne was campaigning for a restoration of the Stuarts. Although he had once been an important figure in the resistance to Charles I, he had grown disenchanted with the Independent regime. Yet if Prynne was disappointed by what the revolution had made, he must have been doubly frustrated by the restoration of monarchy that he hoped would provide its antidote. His disgust at such manifestations of impiety and social corruption as stage plays, the consumption of alcohol, and sexual permissiveness would not have been appeased by the moral laxity of the late Jacobean age. Nor would he have approved of its increasingly open acceptance of electoral patronage, the purchase of placemen, public complacency, and cynicism in the face of widespread political corruption. These were hard times for any moralist, and Prynne was not just any moralist but a fanatic. The late Stuarts' institutionalization of a standing army, not to mention their relative tolerance for the Jews who now trickled into Albion from Holland, Italy, and North Africa, would no doubt have outraged him deeply. Rewarded for his timely conversion to the Stuart cause with the position of keeper of the Tower records, it is fitting that Prynne's last years should have been taken up with a relentless search for documents pertaining to the original ancient constitution, a Puritan lawyer's last defense against the depredations of "this new-fangled age."

The political literature produced at the time of the Jews' restoration to Western Europe possessed two important motifs. The first was represented by Simone Luzzatto, drawing on the merchant-friendly doctrines of Italian predecessors such as Leonardo Bruni and Bernardo Davanzati. This genre saw commerce as a social glue, checking avarice and the excessive accumulation of power through its capacity for ceaseless redistribution, just as the circulatory system in a healthy body dissolves clots through constant movement. Rather than undermining the proper political order, a well-established commerce underpins it by reinforcing the division of powers with a division of labor – all the more so in the case of the Jews who are locked permanently into the mercantile role with neither hope nor desire for political influence.

The second strain, here illustrated through the *Short Demurrer* of William Prynne, identified the ideal not with any metaphysical conception of commercial integration but with the historical notion of ancient laws, customs, and traditions under perpetual threat from the forces of corruption and instability. In seventeenth-century England, the latter ideal was sometimes combined with "modernizing" trends in mercantile political economy designed to sustain the independent freeholders' polity through the limited endorsement of trade as an instrument of agricultural betterment. Such a typology rarely instanced pure forms, but the picture drawn thus far clearly suggests that, operating within this broad vocabulary of political concepts, debates on the place of a mercantile Jewish population in the coming century would have to contend with existing controversies over the relationship of commerce to the notion of inherited constitutional rights and of the ideal polity. Luzzatto had attempted to finesse this dilemma by insisting that the new and necessary institutions of trade could be made into a bulwark of the old order, because Jews were content to provide the commercial lubricant without desiring innovations, such as political benefits to themselves. Such an ingenious formula, however, would not survive the eighteenth century. It became increasingly obvious that Jews' economic integration could not be forever separated from the question of their political participation. Among the first to adumbrate this was the Deist philosopher John Toland. His 1714 work "Reasons for Naturalizing the Jews of Great Britain and Ireland" represented a remarkable convergence of the antiquarian and the avant-garde, projecting the restoration of ancient political constitutions into a world of commercial modernism and free trade. As we shall now see, Toland portrayed the Jews as a group that uniquely symbolized both.

2

From Ancient Constitution to Mosaic Republic

John Toland was born a Catholic in Londonderry in 1670, converted to Protestantism at the age of sixteen, produced a classic of deist literature (*Christianity not Mysterious*) at twenty-six, and until his death in 1722 pursued a career that precariously balanced abstruse philosophical investigation with paid political propagandizing.[1] In 1714, Toland published an extraordinary pamphlet entitled *Reasons for Naturalizing the Jews in Great Britain and Ireland on the Same Foot with All Other Nations*, which included the following propositions: (1) Jews should be naturalized as British subjects rather than merely tolerated; they should be granted many of the constitutional privileges of native-born Englishmen, including the right to purchase estates and to be eligible for some – although not all – state offices; (2) Jews should become more fully integrated into the general division of labor and need not be confined eternally to performing commercial tasks; (3) the faults attributed to Jews collectively are either exaggerated (in the sense that the vices of the few are attributed to the many) or where accurate merely reflect the scars of persecution; consequently, they will disappear once Jews are accorded better treatment.

Although historians generally agree that *Reasons for Naturalizing the Jews* impressively adumbrates the liberal outlook of the later eighteenth century, they have not viewed the pamphlet as part of an existing genre of Jewish political economy or sought to reconcile it with its author's own immersion in the party politics of contemporary Britain. The result has been a kind of critical schizophrenia, with some historians emphasizing the work's pathbreaking character as a plea for Jewish incorporation and others expressing wonder at a work that appears so "puzzling in the context of its times."[2] In fact, *Reasons* was both the product an immediate political context and of a long-term intellectual project.[3] Toland wrote the pamphlet when political warfare between Whigs and Tories had climaxed following England's controversial peace treaty with France to end the War of the Spanish Succession. The 1713

43

Treaty of Utrecht negotiated by the Tory leaders appeared to threaten Toland's hopes for a revived republic in Great Britain. Toland had played a key role in adapting the previous century's republican ideals to a nation that was both more commercially prosperous and more ideologically moderate than the one familiar to James Harrington or William Prynne. His *Reasons* was an expression of these circumstances and aspirations.

The Jews fit into Toland's republicanism for several reasons. First, he believed that a large-scale naturalization would enable Jews to strengthen Great Britain through their commercial skills. This was the most conventional aspect of his philosemitism. Second, Toland assumed that a liberal naturalization of Jews would immeasurably expand religious toleration in the country.[4] Related to this, however, were more peculiar goals. Toland was convinced that the Jews bore within them the latent political and military capacities of ancient Israelites. He was fascinated by the idea of the Mosaic Republic, the Hebrew state's "ancient constitution."[5] Toland thought that the Bible preserved only a semblance of the true Mosaic constitution. Living Jews could help to revive its spirit in Britain. Finally, Toland wanted Jews to colonize Ireland, where their presence would help to contain the political threat of fanatical Catholics.

These various aims, at once tolerant, militant, and messianic, were tied into an elaborately planned strategy to realize his vision within mainstream politics. Toland was a propagandist for Robert Harley, leader of the country faction, a hybrid grouping that combined aspects of both Whig and Tory agendas. On Harley's behalf, Toland produced pamphlets denouncing standing armies and infrequent Parliamentary elections as violations of the ancient constitution. Yet Toland's association with Harley and his defense of the ancient constitution eventually came into conflict with his own idiosyncratic political aims. Toland's embrace of both the Mosaic constitution and Jewish naturalization must be seen as part of his effort to thwart his conservative opponents and create an alternative future for Britain.

COUNTRY POLITICS

Sorting out these complex and contradictory aims is no easy task. For one thing, Toland made strenuous efforts to cover his tracks.[6] The fact that he lived by his pen required his subordination to the impulses and intrigues of powerful patrons. His career coincided with an age in which propaganda first became refined as a tool for manipulating public opinion while simultaneously revealing coded messages to party insiders.[7] Yet like Defoe, Swift, and other such paid literary performers, Toland viewed himself as an actor engaged in the political struggles of the time, not just as an instrument of wealthy and powerful patrons. This meant at one and the same time pleasing his superiors through the skillful execution of his literary assignments while seeing to it that his own ideological aims were in some way concretely advanced. As recent Toland biographers have shown, surprisingly often he succeeded in accomplishing this delicate task.[8]

Two elements in particular connecting Toland's ideology with his *modus operandi* complicate our efforts to assess his politics. The first reflects Toland's attraction to secrecy and deception: his possible membership in the Calves-Head Club, a reputed secret society of republican agitators devoted to debunking the royalist cult of Charles I,[9] and his own *Pantheisticon*, a clandestine symposium of pantheists for which he drew up plans in 1720.[10] Toland divided all philosophical knowledge into esoteric and exoteric categories, presumably including his own, and used coded language to signal insiders of his true meaning and intention. The second, closely related element has to do with Toland's penchant for literary deception. The historian, David Wootton, for instance, believes that Toland, who published an influential edition of James Harrington's works in 1699, invented one of the pieces he included under Harrington's authorship (*The Mechanics of Nature*) and significantly doctored another (John Halls's 1651 *Grounds and Reasons of Monarchy Considered*) – all in an effort to create a respectable genealogy for his own doctrines.[11] This should give us fair warning not to rely on the surface meaning of his actions and writings.

This much, at least, is certain: in the 1690s Toland became associated with a group known as commonwealthmen, young intellectuals who were dedicated to a revivifying of the civic humanist ideals of the Roman Republic.[12] This group, whose intellectual leader was Robert Molesworth, and that included such notables as Walter Moyle and John Trenchard, partly overlapped with the circle of politicians that regularly gathered at the Grecian Coffee House, among them the leader of the so-called country faction, Robert Harley. Harley, who would become the effective prime minister of several governments between 1701 and 1713, was one of the most innovative of British politicians of his day. He is credited with helping to pioneer modern organized political propaganda. His patronage of Toland, Charles Davenant, Daniel Defoe, Jonathan Swift, and various lesser talents, and his establishment of a system of nationwide distribution of "information", kept him and his country faction close to the reigns of power for nearly fifteen years.[13] Yet if Harley was a master of manipulation, he met his match in Toland. Their relationship was symbiotic and tactical. Toland saw Harley as an avenue to political influence. His own participation in both elite administrative circles and subversive secret societies suggests a conscious plan to use Harley and others to alter mainstream politics in fundamentally radical ways. Remarkably, Toland succeeded in achieving some of his aims. The same Toland who authored recondite tomes on the rites and religious practices of the ancient Celts and Jews, or who scandalized his readers with his mockery of the Anglican Church's "Protestant popery,"[14] was responsible at various intervals in the early eighteenth century for articulating the government's programmatic agenda.[15]

Toland was acutely aware of the schizophrenic character of his endeavors and strove to reconcile them. He formulated a rationale that comprehended, justified, and sustained his own juggling of roles as radical theorist and establishment political operative, effectively epitomized in the title page of his work, Tetradymus, the subtitle of which reads, "Clidophorus; or of the Exoteric and Esoteric Philosophy, that is, of the External and Internal Doctrine of the Ancients: the one open and public, accommodated to popular prejudices and the establish'd Religions; the other private and secret, wherein, to the few capable and discrete, was taught the real Truth stript of all disguises."[16] Toland correlated the "esoteric" with the internal and eternal verities of philosophy and the "exoteric" with external and provisional political circumstances. This distinction, one that Toland believed had been exploited by sages from Socrates and Christ to the present day, allowed him to create a hierarchy of ends and means in which some values could be legitimately subordinated to others, or compromised on their behalf, so long as progress toward the ideal was tangibly advanced.

The overt/covert dualism had its parallel in the confusing alliances Toland forged in his effort, at one and the same time, to earn his living by his pen, advance his ideological agenda, and be a player in the rough and tumble game of politics. As noted, Harley was Toland's conduit. Harley's country faction was a hybrid alliance comprised of Tory backbenchers and a small coterie of radical Whigs and commonwealthmen.[17] The "court" party that it opposed was built around a "modern" Whig establishment that had administered most of William III's governments, including the so-called Junto. These Whigs, descendents of those who had helped engineer the Glorious Revolution which in 1689 had ousted the Catholic James II, redefined their party as no longer an oppositional but, rather, a governing one. To advance the cause of the Protestant king, they employed the mechanisms of government centralization that their predecessors had formerly denounced, including the maintenance of a standing army, the resort to extensive systems of government patronage to protect parliamentary majorities, as well as the establishment and expansion of innovative mechanisms of government finance, such as the floating of state debt and the establishment of a national bank. All of this the country faction labeled "corruption," an identification that made it programmatically attractive to many who held "old whig" or "true whig," or even commonwealthman and civic humanist values. The country faction strenuously opposed these supposedly novel and extraconstitutional apparatuses of contemporary state power seen to undermine the political independence and economic potency of landed freeholders.[18] In this sense, the country faction's political program also was linked to the ubiquitous myth of the "ancient constitution," that is, the original and unalterable laws and institutions that from time immemorial had stood the breach against the sundry depredations of Crown and court.[19]

From the late 1690s until 1711, Toland balanced his commonwealthman and country faction allegiances, although he kept sight of his long-term aims, or "unalterable principles," throughout. These he defined as "civil liberty, religious toleration, and the Protestant succession,"[20] and can be briefly explicated as follows: civil liberty meant freedom of expression and dissent, the impartial rule of law, and respect for private property; religious toleration meant expanding the protections of the 1689 Toleration Act to include full political rights for dissenting Protestants; while the Hanoverian succession entailed the fulfillment, against the claim of the Catholic Stuart heirs of the deposed James II, of the 1701 Act of Settlement which directed that should Queen Anne (the Protestant daughter of the Catholic James II) possess no male heirs at the time of her death (as was expected), the crown would descend to the Electress Sophia of Hanover (the Protestant granddaughter of James I) and to her line, excluding any non-Protestant. For Toland – who associated Catholicism with political and religious tyranny – the Protestant succession mandated by the Act was a prerequisite for the achievement of liberty and toleration. Yet indicative of his ambiguous position, the same Act of Settlement, negotiated by his patron Harley, contained a stipulation that prevented naturalized or endenizened foreigners from holding office, "either civil or military," or obtaining grants of land from the Crown.[21] This provision, along with many other features of the Act, was designed to allay the country gentry's bugbears of foreign influence and ministerial corruption.[22] One of its effects, in combination with the various Test and Corporation Acts of the Restoration Period, was to preclude Jews from holding offices and, potentially, owning land. It was these disabilities, put into place by Toland's own country faction associates, which he came to challenge in his *Reasons for Naturalizing the Jews*.

I. POOR PALATINES AND INDUSTRIOUS ISRAELITES

In his *History of the Jews of England*, Cecil Roth drew attention to the fact that John Toland's 1714 pamphlet formed part of a larger contemporary debate over naturalizing foreign Protestants.[23] Toland's *Reasons* itself stresses this connection, its author recalling that he had "more than once or twice (as opportunity offer'd) enforced the necessity of a GENERAL NATURALIZATION."[24] The point in question was the passage in 1709 by a Whig-dominated Parliament of an Act of General Naturalization aimed at attracting foreign Protestants, as Toland put it, "like to add much strength and wealth to this country."[25] It is estimated that as a result of its passage over ten thousand mostly destitute immigrants from the Palatinate entered England in 1709 alone. This flood of "poor Palatines," whom Whigs claimed to be religious and Tories political refugees, created a political as well as a social welfare crisis.[26] In Toland's account, the 1712 repeal of the act underscored the moral blindness and "inhuman disposition" of the Tories – in power from 1710 to 1714.[27] By the autumn of 1714, with the Protestant Hanoverian succession assured and with the Whigs exultant over their coming election prospects, Toland clearly felt the time was ripe to revisit the topic of naturalization, only this time in relation to the Jews rather than the Palatines.[28]

It is interesting to see how closely some of Toland's arguments in 1714 follow those earlier advanced by other Whig writers on behalf of the Palatines.[29] The assertion that the wealth of a country is a direct function of the growth of its population, with the corollary that the immigration of skilled foreigners was inevitably an economic boon that state policy must promote, was already standard in Whig literature by 1714.[30] Daniel Defoe, writing in 1709, averred "that the opening of the nation's doors to foreigners has been the most direct and immediate reason of our wealth and increase, and has brought us from a nation of slaves and mere soldiers, to a rich, opulent, free, and a mighty people, as it is this day."[31] This Toland echoed in his *Reasons*, quoting his one-time patron John Locke to the effect that "numbers are to be preferred to largeness of dominions," and formulating as a general law of statecraft the proposition that the influx of foreigners are "the true cause of the land's felicity."[32] The argument was invariably weighted toward the goal of maximizing foreign trade. Competition at home will decrease wages, enhance productivity and allow for the sale of lower-cost goods abroad. As Toland put it, "This one Rule of More, and Better, and Cheaper, will ever carry the day against all expedients and devises."[33]

More significant than this echoing of the preceding century's "populationist" doctrines is Toland's specific *political* rationale for advocating immigration and naturalization. In this regard, his views on Jews and Judaism were heavily indebted to the *Discorso* of Simone Luzzatto, a work he had read well before 1714.[34] Toland drew on Luzzatto's depictions of Judaism to combat antisemitic and xenophobic elements in the civic humanist tradition, particularly those expressed by James Harrington, who was also a key figure in Toland's pantheon. Because Luzzatto was a Jew and an economist entirely conversant with (if not always sympathetic to) the civic humanist tradition, he was the ideal source to facilitate Toland's reworking of that tradition in a philosemitic manner. But although Luzzatto's *Discorso* has long been recognized as a major influence on *Reasons*, it would be more accurate to describe it as a springboard.[35] From each significant premise that Toland shared with the Venetian, he derived a set of radically divergent conclusions. In particular, Toland resolutely rejected Luzzatto's political quietism.

Like Luzzatto, Toland began his discussion in *Reasons* by asserting that the Jews' characters conform to those of the environment. Thus "... they have no common or peculiar inclination distinguishing 'em from others; but visibly partake of the Nature of those nations among which they live, and where they were bred." Yet from this same starting point he drew a critical inference that Luzzatto had taken pains to avoid. According to Toland, it is political rather than economic mechanisms that account for why the Jews "do now almost entirely betake themselves to the business of Exchange, Insurances and improving of money upon Security." Toland's point was that unlike economic verities, political institutions can be altered.[36] Luzzatto had insisted that Jews aspired neither to landownership nor the political rights that accompanied it. Toland contended otherwise: Jews should be allowed to own land in Great Britain and reap the rewards in honor and authority that such property afforded. Yet although Toland disagreed with Luzzatto on this specific point, his real opponent here was Harrington, who in his 1656 *Oceana* had emphasized that the creation of a free polity or republic required the proper distribution of land. Harrington had claimed that England's still feudal political institutions were out of sync with the great expansion of freeholds that had taken place since the sixteenth century. Toland admired Harrington greatly as a "commonwealthman" but sharply disagreed with the master's rejection of Jewish readmission to England itself. That point will be discussed in detail later, but what is directly pertinent here is that Toland came to view the Jews' exclusion from landownership as the key to their historically marginal status in European society:

> for it may be easily demonstrated, that the want of immovable property is the true Reason, and not any pretended Curse or other ridiculous fancy,

why none of the vast Estates they so frequently acquire seldom or ever descends to the third generation; but are always floating and unfixed, which hinders their families from growing considerable, and consequently deprives them of the credit and authority, whereof all men of worth may be laudably ambitious.[37]

Whereas for Luzzatto and Harrington (if for different reasons) the Jews' historical disabilities were precisely what recommended them as commercially beneficial and politically tolerable, for Toland their restored access to land would have the effect of supplementing their economic utility with the "authority" that demands and reflects true membership in the polity.[38]

Why was Toland prepared to go further than almost any philosemitic predecessor by insisting that Jews should be enabled to own land throughout Great Britain? It is tempting to see Toland here as an exemplar of Lockean principles, viewing Jews as fully corrigible and the possessors of natural rights like all other men. Locke, however, is unlikely to be the key source for Toland's unusual sympathy for Jews. Not only had Locke written very little about Jews, but Locke's penchant for abstract reasoning and arguments rooted in natural law harmonized poorly with Toland's antiquarian mind-set. Toland, for instance, laid great emphasis on Jewish history.[39] In seeking to free the Jews from the bonds that had traditionally enchained Jews to commerce, Toland did not aim to detach them from their ancient inheritance. On the contrary, in demonstrating their capacities for landownership, Toland stressed the need to reconnect Jews with their own ancient heritage. For they had once been "Shepherds in MESOPOTAMIA, Builders in Egypt, and Husbandmen in their own Country."[40] Toland insisted that these same ancient skills could now be reactivated – in the interests of both Jews and Britain – if through naturalization their capacity to acquire land were at last restored. In making this argument, moreover, Toland was not simply supporting his earlier contention that, as demonstrated by the variety of their historical experience, "they have no common or peculiar inclination distinguishing 'em from others." Rather, he believed that Jews' historical legacy as republicans was what rendered them especially valuable to Britain.

If his *Reasons* had been written much later in the eighteenth century (and perhaps in French or German), we might have expected Toland to extol the benefits that would accrue to the Jews through the reawakening of their dormant rustic capacities. Their free exercise of agrarian skills would endear them to the virtues of labor required to achieve their integration. It would facilitate their exodus from a debilitating habituation to commerce as well as their regeneration through physical labor. In looking closely here at Toland's *Reasons*, we see just how far he remains from such an outlook. Toland was not an exponent of religious equality or of a fully liberal and neutral state, at least not in the short run. Rather, his rationale for naturalizing the Jews had as much to do with aiding the cause of British Protestants against Catholics as it did with assisting the Jews' in their rehabilitation or their acquisition of abstract equality. This is especially evident from Toland's remarkable proposal to revive and expand Harrington's 1656 recommendation (examined below) to employ Jews in the colonization of Ireland.

Whigs had supported the granting of estates and titles in Ireland to worthy foreigners from the early days of William III. Following the latter's conquest of Ireland in 1688–1689 from the Catholic supporters of James II, William had sold large tracts of arable land to his Dutch and Huguenot lieutenants and granted peerages to several, practices bitterly denounced by the Whigs' opponents. Xenophobia as well as accusations of corruption resulting from the centralization of court power through land grants fed this opposition. Harley's country faction had inspired the prohibition written into the Act of Settlement of "any grant of lands, tenements, or hereditaments from the Crown" to foreign-born subjects. A year before the Act of Settlement the country faction had also engineered an Act of Resumption, which forced some of William's grantees to forfeit their Irish lands. In part this reflected a degree of Tory sympathy for the displaced Irish Catholic landholders, in part it epitomized the Tory hostility to foreign, for example, Dutch, Huguenot, and German Protestants. The two were dynamically related. Between 1641 and 1665 the percentage of Irish land in Catholic hands had fallen from three-fifths to one-fifth.[41] Subsequently, Ireland had been the scene of repeated Jacobite uprisings, usually with French backing, in 1689, 1697, and 1708. Whigs reacted in 1697 and 1703 with legislation aimed at prohibiting the sale of "Protestant" land to Catholics. And, in 1709, Lord Wharton, the Whig lord lieutenant of Ireland, proposed that the "Poor Palatines" be settled there to dilute or displace rebellious Catholics, a proposal subsequently put into effect.[42] In his *Reasons*, Toland added the Jews to these same colonization schemes.

As Toland insisted in *Reasons*, Protestant colonization of Ireland still remained woefully incomplete. Ireland must not only be repressed as a seat of Jacobite rebellion but exploited economically as well. The Catholic population lacked industry; its priests ("half the population," in Toland's characterization) were incapable of "exercising honest callings, to the great detriment of Trade, as well as the manifest depopulation of the Country," whereas the rest of the Catholic inhabitants remained enervated through the inactivity induced by countless holidays and pilgrimages, "idly neglect[ing] the business of the publick and of their families . . ."[43] Instead of colonizing Ireland with Protestants alone, Toland wondered, why not do so with Jews as well? The Jews "encrease the number of hands for labor and defence, of bellies

and backs for consumption of food and raiment, and of brains for invention and contrivance."[44] They might therefore become effective participants
in the colonization of the "Heaths, Moors, Bogs, Fens, and Commons" of
which "there is still but too great a quantity in Scotland and Ireland (and
even in England itself) . . ."[45] Moreover, their former military prowess suggests a capacity for the kinds of martial qualities essential to such a colonizing mission. Jews had been valiant soldiers in the service of the Assyr-
ian, Egyptian, Greek and Roman powers. "Now I ask man, why they may
not as well do the same (if lawfully made capable) in GREAT BRITAIN and
IRELAND?"[46]

Toland penned his *Reasons* shortly after he had severed all ties with his
longtime patron Harley (since 1711 the Earl of Oxford). Toland's devotion to
Harley and the country faction agenda had always been merely provisional,
subordinate both to his immediate financial needs and to his enduring constitution ideal, the aforementioned "unalterable principles" of civil liberty,
religious toleration, and the Protestant succession.[47] In the years 1710–1714,
those principles appeared in mortal danger. Harley had gone over decisively to
the Tories, becoming the leader of a ministry that in Toland's eyes had signed a
traitorous peace treaty with Louis XIV. In relinquishing Spain to the House of
Bourbon, Toland believed, the 1713 Treaty of Utrecht had squandered twelve
years of British military sacrifice in return for only the territorial concessions
of Gibralter and Minorca in Europe, along with the morally dubious *asiento*,
or slave-trade monopoly. Although in truth the treaty required Louis XIV to
recognize the Hanoverian succession, Harley and his governmental colleague
and rival, Henry St. John (Viscount Bolingbroke), who negotiated the treaty,
had corresponded directly with the Pretender, whose restoration St. John at
least definitely favored.[48] This, combined with Harley and St. John's sponsor-
ship of the 1714 Schism Act, which threatened to outlaw Dissenters' schools
and academies, convinced Toland that Harley had placed Toland's "unalterable
principles" in mortal danger. In *The Art of Restoring*, which Toland composed
shortly before *Reasons for Naturalizing the Jews*, he chose to portray his former
mentor as George Monk, the Cromwellian general who in 1659–1660 had engineered the restoration of Charles II, then ensconced at Versailles. In likening
Harley to Monk, Toland was insinuating that through "secret provisions" in
the Treaty, Harley had similarly plotted with France to restore the Pretender to
the British throne.[49] This potent analogy underscores Toland's deep commitment to the commonwealthmen tradition that, in his view, Harley had now
betrayed. The "art of restoring" was tantamount to the wickedness of destroying the old commonwealthmen dream of a future genuine republic, a true
republic without a king, although one for which the Protestant succession

in the person of George I would be paradoxically a precondition. Toland's republican ideal, the proverbial "good old cause" of Parliamentary rule following the execution of Charles I, remained very much in his mind when he wrote his *Reasons* in the late summer or early autumn of 1714. Indeed, the role he assigned to Jews in *Reasons* was precisely to resurrect their republican capacities – their ancient agrarian and military skills – at a moment when Britain appeared to be reactivating its own.

II. JAMES HARRINGTON'S *OCEANA* AND JOHN TOLAND'S *RESPUBLICA JUDAICA*

Toland's proposal to grant Jews land as colonizers of Ireland recalls an earlier project, his editing of James Harrington's *Oceana and Other Works* (1700), to which he had appended a long biographical introduction; for in 1656 Harrington himself had proposed colonizing Ireland with Jews.[50] That Harrington did so in a work, *Oceana*, which possessed an explicitly republican orientation, suggests that at least in an indirect way Harrington had himself linked Jewish readmission to *Britain* with the ideal of a revivified *English* republic. As noted, Toland's own decision to revisit Harrington's Jewish colonization proposal in the autumn of 1714 attests to his continued commitment to the republican ideal. Yet Toland's republicanism was no slavish recapitulation of Harrington's. On the contrary, his disagreement with Harrington over the place of the Jews demonstrates his distance from the master's teachings. To explicate the contrast, it will first be necessary to examine Harrington's original proposal and show how it fit into the broader aims of *Oceana*.

Harrington's scheme entailed colonizing Ireland with Jewish merchants as well as farmers. His opening of an avenue for Jews to pursue agriculture was significant given the privileged position he accorded to farming. For Harrington, the merit of an agrarian over an urban population was that it afforded citizens independency and the state stability. "A people not educated or led by the soul of government, is a living thing in pain and misery," wrote Harrington in *Oceana*.[51] The republican ideal is that of self-rule, and among the many obstacles to it none is more crippling than dependence upon another more powerful. Machiavelli saw the antidote to dependency as arising only from the capacity for ruthlessness expressed by an armed *popolo*. For Harrington, however, the armed urban *popolo* would necessarily prove unstable because it lacked a grounding in an enduring material foundation. "Otherwise, a commonwealth consisting but of one city would doubtless be stormy, in regard that ambition would be every man's trade: but where it consisteth of a country, the plough in the hands of the owner findeth him a better calling, and produceth the most innocent and steady genius of a commonwealth, such as is that of Oceana."[52] To ancients like Aristotle and Cicero, landed estates worked by slaves provided their proprietors with the leisure conducive to participation in the forum. To republicans of all ages, land provided the freedom from dependency on others, which was a prerequisite for virtuous self-rule. But Harrington's point – although not excluding these others – is that landownership inculcates psychological virtues of honesty, simplicity, and rootedness in "tillage," which would prove most resistant to the dandified corruption of king and court. "Ambition, loving to be gay and to fawn, hath been a gallantry looked upon as having something of the livery, and husbandry or the country way of life, though of a grosser spinning, as the best stuff of a commonwealth . . ."[53] It is in the context of subordinating the city and its mercantile interests to the political virtues of the countryside that Harrington's discussion of Jews should therefore be understood.

Harrington did not wish to banish merchants from his utopia or deprive them of citizenship – far from it. But he did believe that the size and economic diversity of a large territorial state would help dilute the internally destabilizing struggle between political forces and factions that had brought earlier republics such as Athens and Rome to ruin. Merchants would occupy a limited position, one far outweighed by the middling landowners. Moreover, overseas colonization would function to further dilute economic faction. It helped that *Oceana* was an island fortress commanding the seas around it and that it had "anciently subjected" the neighboring lands of Marpesia, "being the northern part of the same island" (Scotland), and Panopea, a nearby island (Ireland). In gratitude for liberating it from the feudal yoke, Panopea now serves Oceana "as an inexhaustible magazine of auxiliaries." Panopea, "the soft mother of a slothful and pusillanimous people," nearly depopulated for rebelling against its powerful neighbor, was "at length replanted with a new race." Alas, however, the new race degenerated like the old, depriving Oceana of an industrious subject people to till the rich soil and man the "commodious ports of trade" for Oceana's enrichment.[54] It was at this juncture that Harrington broached his proposal for Jewish resettlement. Writing in 1665–1666 (shortly after the Menasseh ben Israel had proposed Jewish readmission to Britain as a whole), Harrington suggested that the exploitation of Panopea's natural wealth might have been better accomplished:

> if it had been thought upon in time, by planting it with Jews, allowing them their own rites and laws, for that would have brought them suddenly from all parts of the world, and in sufficient numbers; and though the Jews

be now altogether for merchandise, yet in the land of Canaan (since their exile from whence they have not been landlords) they were altogether for agriculture; and there is no cause why a man should doubt but, having a fruitful country and good ports too, they would be good at both. Panopea well peopled would be worth a matter of four millions dry rents, that is besides the advantage of the agriculture and trade, which with a nation of that industry comes at least unto as much more. Wherefore Panopea, being farmed out unto the Jews and their heirs forever, for the pay of a provincial army to protect them during the term of seven years, and for two millions annual revenue from that time forward – besides the customs, which would pay the provincial army – would have been a bargain of such advantage, both unto them and this commonwealth, as is not to be found otherwise by either.[55]

Like Toland in 1714, Harrington presumed that the Jews' ancient preoccupation with agriculture meant that, while they were presently "altogether for merchandise," they could "be good at both." Nevertheless, the fact remains that Harrington wished to circumscribe the commercial in general and the Jewish element in particular by confining the Jews to Ireland alone. Polis (or commonwealth) and port (or colony) would be kept as distinct from one another as Christian and Jew. Harrington therefore denied Jews true membership in the polity. On the contrary, he insisted that granting it would be to sabotage the republic itself:

> To receive the Jews after any other manner into a commonwealth were to maim it; for they of all nations never incorporate but, taking up the room of a limb, are of no use or office unto the body, while they suck the nourishment which would sustain a natural and useful member.[56]

This attitude, reminiscent of the xenophobic harangues of Puritan opponents of Jewish readmission such as William Prynne, expressed Harrington's view of both Jews and trade as necessary evils. The same view permeated the country faction ideology of the late seventeenth century. By contrast, Toland's *Reasons* fully supported Jewish colonization not just of Ireland but of Scotland and England as well, including Jews' eligibility to *own* land in England proper. And although Harrington had suggested that the Jews would require the armed protection of *Oceana's* provincial army, Toland exhibited confidence in their capacity for self-defense once they were granted arms. The institution of landownership and arms-bearing were core to the republican ideal of citizenship; Toland's readiness to accord both to Jews exemplifies his inclusive approach to a revivified English – or better yet, British – polity.[57]

The question remains: why did Toland believe the Jews could be virtuous and useful members of a British commonwealth and why did he apparently discount the warning issued by his commonwealthman master, Harrington?[58] The answer lies partly in the two men's different assessments of the original political character of the Jews. Both viewed Jews as inheritors of an ancient political legacy. Indeed, Harrington's views on the political character of biblical Hebrews were no less decisive for his attitude toward contemporary Jews than Toland's own antiquarianism was to *his* rationales for Jewish naturalization, as we will see.

Large portions of *Oceana* as well as Harrington's 1659 *The Art of Lawgiving* are taken up with the politics of biblical Israel.[59] By the time that Harrington wrote his works the use of the Old Testament as a political primer was a fairly commonplace practice; before Harrington, the Italian writer Carlo Sigonio (1524?–1584), the Swiss Protestant, Cornelius Bertram (1531–1594) and the Dutch, Petrus Cunaeus (1586–1638) had all produced lengthy, and in the latter case, widely read analyses of the political character of *De republica Hebraeorum*.[60] Machiavelli himself had frequently cited Moses's actions as an exemplary lawgiver, politician, and military leader.[61] The popularity of the Bible as a political proof-text was a result of its inimitable combination of unimpeachable authority and doctrinal malleability, because the scriptural narrative could be as readily employed to support divine-right monarchy as theocracy or popular sovereignty. Harrington's own agenda in describing the "Mosaical commonwealth" was complex. As with the preceding authors, he sought the authority of scripture to support his political prescriptions for his own nation, particularly apposite in the context of the Puritan-dominated English commonwealth of Harrington's day. But Harrington also wished to demote biblical Israel from its sui generus status as divinely instituted polity. He was at pains to demonstrate that many of its institutions, for example, its Sanhedrin or "senate," were borrowed from republican neighbors, such as the Midianite nation.[62] The point was intended less to demonstrate the derivative character of the mosaic commonwealth than to illustrate its foundation in *human* reason and action. Men not God made the Israelite constitution, just as men today, employing their "prudence" or reason, could make a commonwealth in Britain. In fact, Harrington suggested, today we have the advantage of being able to learn from Israel's mistakes and improve on the biblical model. In particular its admirable agrarian law, exemplified by the Jubilee, which sought to protect the "balance" of landownership from the engrossment of a small minority, failed to achieve perfection, according to Harrington, because the Hebrews had neglected to carry out the divine command to root out the Canaanite population. As a consequence, insufficient land existed to allow for a wide distribution to citizens, a fatal flaw in the execution of the constitution, resulting in its inevitable if protracted demise.[63]

This indictment of the Hebrews' excess toleration, leading to their fraternization with the Canaanites, loss of rustic militancy, and consequent "effeminizing" by luxury, appears ironic in light of the criticism we have seen Harrington make of contemporary Jews, viz., that they are too xenophobic to "incorporate" into England and must be confined to the Irish periphery. In nevertheless recommending them as Irish colonizers, Harrington must have concluded that Jews – if given a second chance – would not make the same mistake twice, especially if backed by Protestant arms in their expropriation of Canaanite – or, rather, Catholic – land. But there is another reason why Harrington distinguished biblical from modern Jews. In Book II of *The Art of Lawgiving*, Harrington actually described two different polities, the Mosaic and the Jewish, the former based on Scripture, the latter on rabbinic oral law, or "cabala." This second polity, Harrington observes, crystallized around the time of Hadrian's expulsions (second century); it thus possessed a diasporic character that rendered its law appropriate for a landless people. Devoid of an institutional basis in landholding, the rabbinic Jewish polity, in contrast to the Mosaic, was nondemocratic and oligarchic; its system of granting authority, namely, ordaining judges through the laying on of hands, failed to accord lawmaking powers to the people at large. Instead, it replaced the popular component of the Mosaic "mixed constitution," the twenty-four thousand large assembly or "congregation of the Lord," with a "junta of fifty presbyters," Pharisees who were "not elected by the people," and who contemptuously regarded the masses as the "*populus terrae*, the rascal rabble."[64] This underlying motif of a Jewish fall resembles traditional Christian denigration of postbiblical Judaism. No doubt this (perhaps unconscious) Christian prejudice partly accounts for why Harrington believed that modern "cabalistic" Jews would be unfit as citizens of Oceana proper. About this rationale, too, Toland disagreed.

Toland had once described Harrington as "the greatest Commonwealthman in the world."[65] But in his *Nazarenus* of 1718, he accused Harrington of having misunderstood the nature of the ancient Mosaic commonwealth. In that same text, Toland promised he would soon issue a work to set the record straight.[66] This was to be his *Respublica Mosaica or The Commonwealth of the Jews*, a work that Toland apparently never completed and for which no drafts have yet been found.[67] Although his *Respublica Mosaica* eludes us, we may still be able to piece together some of its elements from scattered remarks found in Toland's other writings. Indeed, although scholars have generally sought out adumbrations of the Mosaic Republic in other works, some of the best evidence of its character comes from Toland's *Reasons for Naturalizing the Jews*. Scholars have tended to separate Toland's views on contemporary Judaism (assuming these views to be tolerant but hardly complimentary) from his celebration of the ancient Mosaic legislation (which in any case was enacted for only a brief time and grossly distorted in the Pentateuchal record). Yet Toland did not always rigorously distinguish them. For instance, in his *Reasons* Toland insists that the Mosaic legislation was essentially political, not religious. It was a law designed for a theocratic polity wherein ritual observance became reducible to the aim of instilling obedience to the established governmental order. Turning to Judaism as it is presently practiced and citing Simone Luzzatto as his source, Toland dichotomizes Judaism into first, a legal system designed to imbue devotion to the republic and, second, a value system corresponding to doctrines of natural religion:

> Luzzatto expressly maintains, that as their religion, consider'd as it is JEWISH, or distinct from the LAW OF NATURE, was solely calculated for their own NATION and Republic; so they were never commanded to instruct others in the peculiar rites and ceremonies, tho they are every where enjoin'd to magnify to all the world the divine goodness, wisdom, and power, with those duties of man, and other attributes of God, which constitute NATURAL RELIGION.[68]

Here Toland, taking Luzzatto at his word, read back into the Bible a complementarity of universalistic and particularistic elements that actually reflected a more recent Sephardic tradition, one rooted in the Iberian Jewish elite's exposure to Greek philosophy and European "feudal" jurisprudence. The tradition can be traced to the fifteenth-century Hispano-Jewish philosopher and courtier, Don Isaac Abravanel, who formulated a Jewish version of the medieval Christian distinction between temporal and spiritual, or human and divine, realms of government. For Abravanel, a part of the Mosaic code was civil in function, if also perfect and divine in nature. In his presentation of the Bible's "mixed constitution," Abravanel (like many Christian Hebraists after him) projected back into the Mosaic era the existence of a Sanhedrin or secular judicial court. As scholars have noted, Abravanel's depiction of a Mosaic hierarchy of elected and appointed secular and ecclesiastic courts reflected his keen knowledge of contemporary governmental structures, such as those prevailing in Venice, where he lived out his later years, as much as the biblical text itself.[69] Following Abravanel, it was the Venetian Rabbi, Simone Luzzatto, who elaborated on this image of Moses both as the founder of an exclusivist Jewish polity and the legislator of a code of universal law, comprised of or at least compatible with natural law. In his apologetics, Luzzatto gave considerable emphasis to so-called Noahide commandments, a set of precepts akin to but not identical with the Ten Commandments, that had been exegetically derived from Hebrew scripture by the rabbis of late Antiquity.[70] According to rabbinic tradition, these laws represent the minimal legal obligations imposed on mankind as a whole – although it remained unclear whether their fulfillment was considered valid if rooted in reason alone rather than derived from Hebrew Scripture, at least indirectly.[71] For Luzzatto (whose apologetic purposes encouraged him to downplay this qualification), the fact of these dual codes – one for Jews, the other for gentiles – demonstrated that Moses was a superior legislator to Solon, Lycurgus, Romulus, and the others. Whereas they had devised codes possessing a dual system of morality for citizens and foreigners, "the law of God, promulgated by Moses, provided and cared for the good of the entire species."[72] Aligning Judaism with Ciceronian principles of cosmopolitanism to fend off Tacitian accusations of misanthropy, Luzzatto insisted the Mosaic credo prescribes that "every man must consider himself as a citizen of a single republic."[73] Jewish "particularism" is not at odds with but, rather, fully complementary to an ethic of universal brotherhood. Jews are commanded to desist from proselytizing, obey gentile authority, and behave with pure benevolence toward non-Jews.[74]

Toland's eclectic use of sources has led to some confusion about the key influences informing his views on the Mosaic republic, with many scholars identifying the philosopher Baruch Spinoza or the legal scholar John Selden as paramount. Yet Luzzatto was clearly his most significant informant. Although Selden, too, had generously praised the Mosaic constitution, and – like Toland, had highly esteemed the Noahide commandments – it was the Bible's integration of sacred and profane rather than its inherent toleration that Selden admired most.[75] As for Spinoza, whose philosophical radicalism and pantheism make him seem an obvious precursor, he held a far less laudatory view of Moses than had Toland. Spinoza, for instance, would have laughed at the notion that Moses could have been a source of his own (Spinoza's) pantheism. In contrast, in his *Origines Judaicae* from 1709, Toland had approvingly cited the hellenistic geographer Strabo of Amaseia to the effect that Moses, whom Strabo claimed had originated as an Egyptian priest, regarded God as synonymous with nature.[76] Strabo has Moses declare that "[G]od is the one thing alone that encompasses us all and encompasses land and sea – the thing which we call heaven, or universe, or the nature of all that exists."[77] In his work *Adeisidaemon*, which accompanied *Origines Judicae*, Toland had identified ancient Egypt with the origins of superstition and idolatry.[78] "Such were only the most degraded expressions of a widespread deficient conception of divinity as a force existing outside of nature and possessing will and intelligence," he observed. Although Toland did not label Moses an "atheist" (but identified him instead as a "Spinozist"!), he did portray him as a pantheist who rejected all conceptions of God as existing above and beyond nature.[79] Toland similarly depicted Mosaic ceremony as the essence of simplicity, combining devotion to the Sabbath with respect for natural law, at least until corruption and degeneration had led to its unnecessary elaboration, albeit (in contrast to Harrington) not to the point of invalidating later Judaism.[80]

Although Toland's account traced the broad trajectory of Spinoza's narrative of Israel's decline, there is thus little resemblance between the two. To the extent that Spinoza spoke favorably of any biblical polity, it was the short-lived "theocracy" of the period between the Hebrews' initial Sinaitic acceptance of divine lordship and their subsequent agreement to move from the direct rule of God (i.e., of themselves democratically) to that of an intermediary, interpreter, and cleric – namely, Moses.[81] Of course, it was Spinoza – on this point following Machiavelli – who had presented the most powerful portrait of the Mosaic religion as a brilliantly effective fig leaf for political domination. As a number of scholars have noted, Toland's own emphasis on the political benefit which classical legislators like Moses and Numa derived from instituting a state religion not only had ancient sources in Critias and Cicero but also contemporary parallels in such works as the anonymous *Traité des trois imposteurs* (1719), a scandalous portrayal of Moses, Christ, and Mohammed as mere political manipulators.[82] Yet while Toland fully shared the religious skepticism of the *Traité*, he offered a far more positive interpretation of the Mosaic legislation, not just in its original "pantheistic" incarnation but even in its later theistic and rabbinic expression.[83] According to Toland, the Bible's "peculiar rites and ceremonies" – its particularist rather than the universal element – correspond to the internal laws of the Jewish republic. Although provincial, these laws are nevertheless republican in the sense that they are self-imposed. For that reason, they mark the Jews as political beings capable of self-rule in the Aristotelian sense. Not only does Toland disagree with Spinoza in regarding Mosaic Israel as genuinely republican and democratic, he differs from both Spinoza and Harrington in insisting that *rabbinic Judaism* possesses sufficient continuity with the biblical past to render it an adequate vehicle for contemporary Jewry's recovery of its republican capacities.[84] Again, Luzzatto's apologetic likely exerted a decisive influence on Toland in this regard. In contrast to Harrington (but consistent with Luzzatto), Toland makes no absolute distinction between the original Mosaic republic and the rabbinic "cabala." And although Spinoza viewed the Jews' retention of their ancient constitution under diasporic conditions as pathetically anachronistic, Toland insisted that such longevity attested to the matchless potency of their doctrine and ceremonies. Their creed is republican without being xenophobic. It exercises the capacity for self-government precisely by requiring that it never be imposed on others. The Mosaic law is compatible with the English ancient constitution and the common law because it is legislation for Jews alone and not, it must be emphasized, a system of arbitrary powers to be foisted on other nations in rank violation of their own capacities for self-government. In other words – and here Toland demonstrates his distance as well from other deists like Anthony Collins – Judaism is neither the source nor the equivalent of papism.

JACOBITES AND JEWS

Toland's championing of the Jews, so often presented as the epitome of liberal precepts, was in fact premised not only on antiquarian concepts like the Mosaic republic, but equally on a rampant hatred of Catholicism. "We Britons," says Toland, "further perceive that the governing Principle of Rome is worldly, earthly, tyrannical; and that the Papal Hierarchy is a mere Political Faction, erecting a splendid, pompous, and universal Empire over Mankind..."[85] It is the alternative of empire versus republic that Toland's "Britons" must now choose, and Protestantism, although in its present form a deeply imperfect substitute for Mosaic toleration, has at least the advantage of being in close enough genetic proximity to it to serve as a provisional bulwark against imperial papal tyranny. It must be remembered that one of the legacies of Stuart rule had been to so grossly magnify the popular association between Catholicism and royal absolutism as to render the two practically synonymous. Andrew Marvell's *Account of the Growth of Popery and Arbitrary Government* (1678), along with countless other tracts, underscored this same psychologically potent connection between Catholicism and absolutist tyranny, which political events both at home and abroad appeared vividly to confirm.[86] The revocation of the Edict of Nantes in 1685 weighed heavily on the minds of those descendants of Whig politicians who had tried since 1679 – in the face of new and startling revelations of a "popish plot" – to exclude the Catholic James II from the succession. In his too-late effort at resistance to William, James's stirring of Irish Catholics to rebellion seemed to confirm the danger he had represented all along.[87] In facing periodic rebellion at home, seemingly abetted by an implacable enemy abroad, England continued to view itself as an embattled Protestant island, a bastion and holdout against Catholicism on the march. It had good reason to feel defensive. As Diarmaid McCulloch points out, by 1690 Protestant territory in Europe had contracted to about one-fifth of what it had been a century earlier. The massacre of Huguenot refugees in Savoy, the rooting out of Calvinism from Counter-Reformation Poland, the destruction of numerous German Protestant cities, the isolation

of Protestant Geneva, France's near defeat of Holland in the 1670s, all contributed to a sense of Whig foreboding.[88] In 1689, at the start of William
III's Nine Years' War, England, too, appeared poised for a near total military
defeat at French hands, the implications of which seemed too devastating to
contemplate.[89] These were formative years politically and psychologically for
Toland, and it is tempting to read into his own Irish-Catholic origins, as well
as his conversion to Protestantism at age sixteen, a personal dimension to his
construction of the papist leviathan. "I was born in the bosom of a church
that has surfeited me with 'em, and made me hate 'em ever since," he once
wrote of intolerant Catholic priests.[90]

The truth is that Toland saw religion almost entirely in political terms;
Protestantism was desirable because it at least left room for reason, autonomy
and liberty to breathe. To this degree, Toland felt it imperative that Protestant
Europe be protected and if possible expanded. This entailed, among other
things, the incorporation of Jews into a Protestant polity whose fundamental
principles derived, in Toland's mind, from the Mosaic republic.[91] The connection, in fact, reached back to Christian Britain's earliest beginnings, for
Toland's genealogical researches had suggested that both Jews and Judaism
had been organic to the original British Protestant polity. The ironical dedication of *Reasons* "to the most Reverend the Arch-Bishops, and the Right
Reverend the Bishops, of both Provinces" was intended as a jab not just at the
High Church's virtual papism but also at the Laudian assertion that Anglicanism was the pristine form of English Christianity.[92] If, as Laud had claimed,
original Anglo-Christianity had been conveyed directly from Palestine to the
British Isles (bypassing Rome), then its first apostles, Toland concluded, also
must have been Jews: "as by your Learning you further know how considerable
a part of the British inhabitants are the undoubted offspring of the Jews (to
which the [papist] Irish can lay no claim)."[93]

It was precisely this conflation of religious and political spheres that allowed
Toland to trace a continuity between ancient and modern. In *Nazarenus*, published in 1718 though partly based on manuscripts written nine years before,
Toland set out to prove that the original Christianity of the first-century
apostles was essentially Jewish (a point, as noted, mischievously hinted at
in *Reasons'* dedication) as well as republican before it became intolerant
and tyrannical through the infusion of pagan mystery rites and priestcraft.[94]
Toland's thesis was that first-century Palestinian Christians (Nazarenes and
Ebionites) felt obliged to continue observing the ceremonial law while at the
same time fully exempting from it pagan converts to the Gospel.[95] According to Toland, these Jewish-Christians fully maintained Luzzatto's dichotomy
between a national ceremonial legislation and the universal religion of reason

that Toland assumed to be the hallmark of authentic Judaism. But original Christianity, which modern Protestantism imperfectly sought to replicate, was in turn merely a semblance of the Mosaic Republic that had never itself been erected in full conformity with its own pristine design; "for everything diminishes the further it proceeds from its original."[96] Had the authentic Respublica Mosaica been even once accomplished, it could never have been destroyed, even though a republic is "to be reckon'd one of the things in nature the most subject to revolutions." A perfect republic, Toland remarks, citing Cicero – must by definition be "a government immortal."[97] And a people once connected with even the blueprint of the perfect commonwealth must still carry with them a trace of its immortality: "... for notwithstanding the Mosaic plan was never wholly executed, and that the imperfect imitation of it, under various denominations, is long since destroy'd; yet the Jews continue still a distinct people from all others, both as to their race and religion."[98]

This "distinct people," inheritors and protectors of the Mosaic constitution, could prove indispensable to the new Great Britain. But why limit Britain to Oceana, Marpesia, and Panopea? In picking up on the Jews where Harrington had left them off, Toland evoked the dream of commonwealthmen such as Marchamont Nedham to establish a great North European Protestant alliance, including a British republic allied or even unified with the Dutch.[99] In 1709, the Whigs saw the naturalization of dissenting foreign Protestants as helping to increase their political base at home as well as fulfill a 'national mission' abroad to defend the interests of persecuted Protestants everywhere. Toland turned his attention to the Jews in 1714 because it was precisely in that year that Whig fortunes had seemed to come full circle and that prospects for the expansive Protestant commonwealth had risen phoenixlike from the ashes. The initial descent into despair had added high drama to the eventual Whig triumph. In the face of Queen Anne's decrepitude, St. John's ascendancy, Harley's dickering with the Pretender, and the Act of Schism, that spring had brought perhaps the most intense period of Whig panic since the 1680s.[100] Yet by autumn, exuberance filled the air. With Hanover dynastically aligned to (and Scotland since 1707 united with) England, the goal of a Whig-dominated Protestant Europe seemed closer to consummation than ever before.[101] Surely, the papist onslaught could be checked and perhaps even reversed. Reality now seemed in the process of conforming to Toland's ideal: a Whiggism that would be British, even European and "Jewish," rather than merely English.[102] The ideal future republic would be outward-looking rather than insular, cosmopolitan rather than nationalistic, embracing tolerance instead of xenophobia (in part, through the vanquishing of Catholic power). In short, it would be a revivification of that Respublica Mosaica which Toland claimed to admire "infinitely, above all the forms of Government that ever yet existed," both actual and imagined.[103]

By now it should be clear that Toland accorded the Jews, or rather the image he had concocted of them, a key role within his grand scheme. The restoration of the ancient though esoteric Mosaic commonwealth entailed a descent into sometimes ruthless party-political struggle as well as the abandonment of principles once regarded as sacred to the civic republican and country faction traditions. Defending the innovative Whig program in 1717, which embodied such formerly heretical institutions as the standing army and septennial elections, Toland claimed to know no reason "... why the Legislature ... might not, as well as six or seven ages ago, make new laws, limitations and precedents; which will be the Ancient Constitution (if there be any charm in this expression) to our posterity, six or seven ages hence."[104] Of course, this flexible and seemingly modern outlook masked an impulse toward restoration, which was of a far more radical character than anything conceived of in the antiquarian minds of an Edward Coke or a William Prynne. But it did suggest that the path of return could only be pursued by advancing, and in 1714–1722 this meant defending all the new political and financial arrangements that were seen to be upholding the Whig regime, even if these may have violated the privileges of freeborn country English squires. The naturalization of the Jews, a nation of traders, would, Toland believed, lend additional economic weight to this regime. But the dialectic of a future past also entailed the restoration of the Jews' own civic republican capacities, first as landed freeholders and soldiers in Britain, and eventually in a reconstituted commonwealth of their own. "Now if you'll suppose with me (till my proofs appear) this pre-eminence and immortality of the Mosaic Republic in its original purity," pleaded Toland in the conclusion of his "Appendix" to Nazarenus:

> it will follow; that as the Jews known at this day, and who are dispers'd over Europe, Asia, and Africa, with some in America, are found by good calculation to be more numerous than either the Spaniards (for example) or the French: so if they ever happen to be resettled in Palestine upon their original foundation, which is not at all impossible; they will then, by reason of their excellent constitution, be much more populous, rich, and powerful than any other nation now in the world. I would have you consider whether it might be not both the interest and duty of Christians to assist them in regaining their Country.[105]

It would be interesting to know what "good calculation" Toland had at his disposal, because it might help account more generally for the gross overvaluation in his writings of the Jews' political relevance. This passage certainly evokes the medieval legends of Prester John, described by fabulists such as Sir John Mandeville, including the hoary tail of the captive Ten Tribes poised to battle Antichrist in the coming Armageddon, though Toland had reworked this old motif into a modern parable that combined tolerant religious ireni-cism with a call for Holy War.[106] In terms of the latter, Toland's comparison between the Jewish masses and the populations of Spain and France was hardly insignificant, these being the two most powerful Catholic nations (at war with England when Toland wrote the 1709 draft of *Nazarenus*), which would become dynastically aligned through the Tory-negotiated Treaty of Utrecht in 1713.

It is precisely this quality of realpolitik combined with political messianism that marks Toland's peculiar "moment." Toland's importance to republican political and economic theory on Jews lies precisely in the fact that he looks both forward *and* backward; that is, he enunciates concepts in a secular form that curiously evoke the millenarian philosemitism of seventeenth-century England.[107] By emphasizing the Jews' civic and political capacities, inherited directly from their own ancient constitution, Toland had directly challenged the indigenous model of English political antiquarianism as well as the quietist premises of earlier apologists for Jews. Without dismissing the issue of the Jews' economic utility entirely, he had shifted the emphasis to those spheres which his predecessors most emphatically renounced: Jews' military and civic benefit to the independent commonwealth. In so doing, he also had employed the Jews and their constitution as a means to invigorate the timeless spirit of republican traditions by freeing it from the hoary letter of ancient English law. Yet if Toland had challenged some of the presuppositions of his civic republican inheritance, he had not entirely transcended them. Historians must therefore be careful not to confuse a Whig with a whiggish interpretation of Toland and the Jews. As we have seen, Toland still operated within the framework of the millenarian and antiquarian, however idiosyncratically. It is this that separates him decisively from the Jewish emancipation debates to come. Those debates would focus on the question of the Jew's *individual* corrigibility, theoretically freed from all historic and corporate associations.[108] Despite distinct echoes of some of Toland's arguments within the later emancipation pleas, the new emphasis would be on the Jews' claims to citizenship *in spite* rather than because of their allegiance to a Mosaic constitution.

Within Anglo-Jewish history, the significance of Toland's pamphlet lay in its effort to shift the historical focus away from the mythical constitution of the Goths, Anglo-Saxons, Celts, and other ancient Britons so esteemed in Whig mythology. In this light it is interesting to note that concurrently with Toland's career, historical scholarship was beginning to challenge the historicity of the ancient constitution and to ridicule its feudal "Gothic" underpinnings. The purposes behind such criticisms had little direct connection with Toland's own arcane researches, yet they nevertheless tended to support his goal of promoting foreign immigration and naturalization. This is apparent from the writings of the political economist and proponent of the 1753 Jewish Naturalization Bill, the Rev. Josiah Tucker, to which we turn next.

3

∾

A New System of Civil and Commercial Government

When in 1753 Parliament passed a law making possible the naturalization of foreign Jews, it was in a form far narrower than the one Toland had envisioned in 1714. It also sparked a national debate whose anti-Jewish vehemence might have surprised him, and whose result – the bill's repeal in late 1753 – would certainly have disappointed him. The Jewish Naturalization Bill sought to eliminate the Alien duties (excise taxes) imposed on that small number of foreign-born Jewish merchants who possessed sufficient wealth to practice large-scale international trade. That it would do so by circumventing the Protestant oath normally required for naturalization frightened many Englishmen into believing the claims of propagandists that the bill constituted a mortal threat to the country's Christian character. This fear was greatly exacerbated by rumors that the bill aimed to naturalize all foreign Jews presently residing in England (about one-half the Jewish population there) as well as to invite much larger numbers of Jewish immigrants into the country. In truth, the bill stipulated that individuals seeking naturalization would be required to obtain a special act of parliament in their behalf, a procedure whose expense would have been prohibitive to all but a few. Moreover, eligibility was confined to those who had established residency in the country for a minimum of three years and demonstrated a proven utility.[1] These naturalized Jews would be "admitted as Subjects of the Realm, but not properly as members of the Constitution," that is, like Protestant dissenters and Catholics, they could still enjoy no government offices or membership in most corporations.[2]

But such details, although repeated ad nauseam by the bill's supporters, did little to quell the anxiety unloosed by the Tory opposition press. In fact, the success of the hostile campaign led some Whig proponents to acknowledge that they had been tactically outfoxed;[3] hence the characteristically acid tone of the Rev. Josiah Tucker's assessment, published a year after the events:

> . . .[S]uch is the Force of a proper Title [Tucker concluded], that if the late Jew Bill itself had been called, A Bill to prevent the Jews from profaining the Christian Sacraments (which was the real Tendency of the Bill) instead of, – A Bill to enable Parliament to naturalize Foreign Jews, all would have been well; and the Zeal for Old England! and Christianity forever! would have still been asleep.[4]

Tucker's sarcasm went hand-in-hand with an outspoken directness that would have found the subterfuges of a John Toland entirely foreign. An occasional writer and a noted political economist of his day, Tucker was little deterred by controversy or the ridicule his opinions provoked. His figure was burned in effigy in 1747 by a London mob celebrating the defeat of a Protestant naturalization bill he then supported. Six years later, the Tory press christened him "Josiah ben Tucker ben Judas Iscariot" for his efforts on behalf of the Jew Bill.[5] Tucker fought back with equal if less crude invective. His favorite target, as suggested earlier, was the cult of nostalgia surrounding "Old England" – especially the cherished image of the ancient constitution that Tory writers regularly depicted as under siege from a new order of financiers, foreign creditors, and assorted parvenus.

In the Jew Bill the Tories had stumbled onto an issue that seemed to encapsulate many of their long-standing criticisms of the existing order. The Jew Bill appeared to conjure up, out of a past that one might have assumed forgotten, the old controversies of Queen Anne's day. Both the bill's friends and foes commented that the clamour it generated recalled the 1709 trial of Dr. Sacheverell, which had led to frenzied cries of "Church in Danger!" and contributed in no small way to the Tory election triumph of the following year. The Treaty of Utrecht was likewise dredged up in the Parliamentary debates, suggesting that old partisan wounds remained fresh despite the passage of almost half a century.[6] Of course, these were the same episodes that had mapped John Toland's odyssey from despair to triumphalism, culminating in his own plea for Jewish naturalization in 1714. What was odd about the Jew Bill, however, was that unlike Toland's pamphlet, which made little immediate impression, the Jews now took on a key symbolic role in contemporary politics. As Thomas Perry notes in his study of the Bill, ". . . in the political vocabulary of 1753–54 the words 'Jew' and 'Whig' became practically synonymous."[7] Why this should be so requires a brief discussion of the ideology of the Tory Party as it developed before 1753.

The Tories' long exclusion from ministerial responsibility (since 1714) had given it the freedom to develop a radical critique of the world the Whigs had made. Much of this critique will be familiar to us from earlier renderings. What had changed since the days of Robert Harley's ministry, however, was the much-refined capacity of one party to maintain a monopoly over governmental institutions through the liberal dispersion of preferments, favors, and funds. The British electoral system, after 1734, witnessed the striking irony of one political party whose public support was steadily in decline attaining ever greater Parliamentary mastery over another that was increasingly more popular.[8] In the eyes of the excluded Tories, the source of this unjust condition was the institution of government borrowing backed up by high land taxes on rural freeholders and exorbitant excises on merchants.[9] Because the Whigs controlled the votes of a majority in Parliament, no reforms could be expected from within the system itself – and this despite the perennial attempts by the opposition to push legislation for annual parliamentary elections and the elimination of paid placeholders.[10]

As the historian Isaac Kramnick details, the "Patriot" and Country party critique of Whig Prime Minister Robert Walpole's political machine, the so-called "Robinocracy," was part of a broad Tory indictment of contemporary society. Writers of the caliber of Swift, Pope, Gay, Fielding, and Goldsmith – the whole circle assembled around Bolingbroke's *The Craftsman* – depicted in satire and tragedy the decline of a way of life, a social ethos, and traditional order associated with rural England, the country village, and the mixed constitution. All this, "That noble fabric, the pride of Britain," in the words of Bolingbroke, was being sacrificed, it was now claimed, to the gluttony of "a race of pygmies," rentiers and idle creditors lacking any natural ties to the land or its traditions and subsisting parasitically off the interest paid by the depleted gentry on the National Debt. Tory journalists and pamphleteers bemoaned the disease now eviscerating "that middle class of men, higher than the peasant, lower than the gentlemen," the yeomen who had "withstood the fury of popular insurrection and the arrogant encroachments of greatness," but who were now "hastening to annihilation."[11]

The persistence of civic humanism well into the middle of the eighteenth century, and particularly Pocock's model of an ongoing opposition between "virtue" and "commerce," has been sharply criticized in recent years, not least of all by Kramnick himself. He and other critics of Pocock rightly if too narrowly emphasize that by this time, at the latest, political discourse in both England and America was marked by a "bourgeois radicalism" or "commercial republicanism," which redefined virtue in a way that was fully compatible with the new commercial values, not to mention the evident prosperity occasioned by it.[12] Virtue now meant the work ethic, industriousness, as well as (if not entirely consistently) manners, politesse, sociability, and refinement. The Machiavellian political model of independence and participation, if not exactly extinct, was no longer inextricably allied with rusticity or irreconcilably divorced from "corruption."[13] Commerce exerted beneficial political effects by channeling aggression away from violent feuds and insurrections and into getting and spending instead. Commerce also helped to create precisely the kinds of durable institutional mechanisms which Machiavelli and Harrington had rightly desired but mistakenly sought in political activism or the restoration of inappropriate, grossly outdated classical political models. As David Hume insisted, "Laws, order, police, discipline . . . can never be carried to any degree of perfection, before human reason has refined itself by exercise, and by an application to the more vulgar arts, at least, of commerce and manufacture." Such application to the vulgar arts as Hume spoke of epitomized the unabashed materialism of the day, in which a well-made constitution reflected specialized skill and craftsmanship. As Hume went on to ask rhetorically, "Can we expect, that a government will be well modeled by a people, who know not how to make a spinning-wheel, or to employ a loom to advantage?"[14]

In this sense, Hume's Whiggish disposition and Tory allegiances seem entirely consistent. Indeed, criticism of the virtue/commerce opposition received surprising support from a far less temperate figure, that is, Bolingbroke himself, who was in fact no real foe of commerce per se. Although he had condemned the overweening "power of money,"[15] it was not so much money in its traditional forms, even including most types of credit, to which he objected, as its misuse and manipulation through speculation made possible by paid political influence.[16] Bolingbroke valued the role of merchants as agents of foreign export. "No Commodity is truly an Increase of the National Stock, but that which is exported, and all Trades receive their Life and Vigour from the Merchant." In the period in which he edited *The Craftsmen* (1726–1736), he spoke out repeatedly against incorporated trading companies (which were at any rate often the backers of Walpole), denounced monopolies, and defended "freedom of Trade" (the "Spring of Riches").[17] Yet, as Geoffrey Holmes has noted, he:

> always made a clear distinction between his attitude towards 'the merchant who brought home riches by the returns of foreign trade,' which was enthusiastic, and his distaste for what he considered to be the parasitic element among the men of capital – the stockjobbers, the financial manipulators, the big government creditors, the war contractors.[18]

It was "Stockjobbing" that for Bolingbroke represented "the bane of Trade, and the fatal Rock, on which our happy Constitution had like to have been lost . . ."[19] Stockjobbers "delude and ruin many Thousands of innocent and unwary Persons." The broader charges against the "financial interest" were indistinguishably ethical and economic. Riches in the hands of a few parvenus deprives land of its real value and diverts capital from the merchants who need it most.[20] At the same time, "this easy way of getting Money engross'd the Time and Attention of many wealthy Persons and others, who might be usefully employ'd in the Service of their Country as well as Themselves . . . "[21]

This limited critique of "stockjobbers" rather than merchants demonstrates just how respectable commerce had become in mid-eighteenth-century England. But it would be a mistake to assume that because the tide had shifted: politics was now free of storms over the proper place of money and trade within the constitution. On the contrary, the Jew Bill episode shows that, so long as commerce could be identified with a politically suspect group, the old fears of corruption and the old resort to ancient constitutionalism could reemerge with surprising vigor. Antisemitism and xenophobia, potent forces in their own right, also functioned as smokescreens for social criticisms that were difficult to express directly. These criticisms reflected a concern to protect the monopolistic character of English commerce as well to preserve the status of the landed gentry whose holdings were vulnerable in an increasingly monetized economy. John Bernard, representing the Corporation of the City of London, neatly combined these two anxieties in his attack on the Jew Bill. Displacing native English with Jewish merchants, claimed Bernard, also would prevent straitened gentry families from sending their youngest sons into commerce, thus bringing ruination on both town and country alike.[22] The parliamentarian George Lyttelton, a participant in the debates of 1753, assumed religious objections served as merely a pretext to protect landed privilege from the encroachments of the money men and insisted that "this [bill] had no more to do with religion than any turnpike act we passed in [this] session . . . "[23] Recognizing, if too late, that the religious arguments would have to be neutralized if the Act were to survive, Whigs such as Sir Robert Nugent suggested that widespread Jewish landownership would lead to the Jews' rapid assimilation, even religious conversion, as evidenced by the case of Ireland, where Catholic estate holders, complying with a natural hatred of "being out of fashion," had already led the way in turning Protestant. As if this wasn't sufficient provocation for Tories, Nugent proceeded to argue that Jewish naturalization would have the beneficial effect of driving up the price of land, increasing its value and facilitating its agricultural improvement.[24]

These rationales, with their dim echoes of Toland, played directly into the hands of the other party. Opponents responded by insisting that the right to acquire and bequeath freeholds had never been granted Jews, even those born in England or its dominions, and had in fact been expressly outlawed by medieval law, or even from time immemorial. The Jew Bill aimed to do far more, therefore, than naturalize a handful of Jews; it would retroactively reverse the provisions of the English constitution to allow all Jews native and foreign, through the wealth obtained by their commercial devices, to engross English estates and thereby achieve political domination in Britain. The methods Jews would use to achieve this, according to opponents, ranged from "uncontrolled bribery and corruption, upon the freedom of elections" to the buying of a (papist?) mercenary army to seize control by force, forcing us to "abjure our present royal family, that we all might be harmoniously naturaliz'd under a king of the Jews."[25] By freeing Jews of the restraints "laid on them by the antient and fundamental laws of the Kingdom," the bill thus threatened to turn over governance to a religiously and politically alien power.[26] At the same time, the Jews' own constitution was utterly incompatible with English common law. The egalitarian institutions mandated by Mosaic law – the requirement that estates be divided equally among sons, the insistence on the remission of debts every seven years and on the reversion of landed property to its former owners every jubilee – are both antithetical to legitimate notions of private property but conducive to the Jews' own aims to monopolize the soil.[27] The Jews, one pamphleteer was prepared to concede, "may be good servants in *a commercial state*; but they are very improper masters for a *free people*."[28]

JOSIAH TUCKER AND THE COMMERCIAL DEFECTS OF THE ANCIENT CONSTITUTION

Opponents proved effective in framing the debate in antiquarian legalistic terms – the importance of protecting the ancient constitution's wise denial of full subject status to Jews – while larding their arguments with religious vitriol and crude caricature. It was a difficult, perhaps impossible combination to beat. Nevertheless, of all the combatants in the Jew Bill controversy, pro and con, it was Josiah Tucker who best combined economic abstraction, historical irony, and denunciatory élan.[29]

In his two major pamphlets of 1753 Tucker met the constitutional arguments head on, but without confining himself to legal history alone. Indeed, his counter-reading of the development of medieval law was merely one parry within an all-out assault on the "Gothic Government" (Tucker's derisive label for the Tory ancient constitution). In the sequel to his government-sponsored *Letter to a Friend Concerning Naturalizations*, Tucker set forth a history of the Jews in England from the conquest to the expulsion that he promised would illustrate the many changes that had since taken place in "our ancient Constitution."[30] This constitution, as he described it, was not peculiar to medieval England but, rather, "only a Part of that Gothic Government" that had been set up throughout Europe by the barbarian Germanic tribes.[31] This meant that in its structural and constitutional origins England lacked that quality of historical singularity that in the minds of seventeenth-century Whigs and eighteenth-century Tories was presumably its celebrated mark. Just as important, the ancient constitution actually possessed no semblance of the liberal constitutional freedoms they had made so much of. Instead, it mandated a rigid division of the population into hereditary orders of military and servile classes in which "... all Persons whatever were, in some Sense, either fighting Men or Slaves."[32] Tucker proceeds to deflate nostalgia for these halcyon days:

> Doubtless these were happy Times! And what a Pity is it, That these Persons who are so lavish in their Praises of Old England, and dissatisfied with our present modern Constitution, had not lived in these golden Days, when they might have enjoyed Old England in Perfection.[33]

Tucker's savagely wrought sarcasm aside, there was really little new in his deflation of the cult of Old England. His true innovation – and a remarkable one at that – was to adapt a well-worn critique of Tory historiography to encompass regulations dealing with medieval and modern Jews, indeed, deploying Jews as the very symbol of constitutional progress. To understand exactly how he pulled this off, it will be necessary to rehearse the broader narrative framework of English constitutional history available to Tucker.

As early as the 1670s, writers who sought to adapt Harrington's civic humanist approach to the uncomfortable realities of Stuart restoration – Pocock's so-called neo-Harringtonians – had attempted (in a thoroughly un-Harringtonian manner) to align the idea of an ancient constitution with England's own feudal past.[34] For Harrington himself, feudalism had represented both a cause of the decline of ancient republicanism and an obstacle to its restoration.[35] But starting with Shaftesbury's *A Letter from a Person of Quality to a Friend in the Country* (1675) a view began to emerge that saw feudalism as the true embodiment of agrarian virtues as well as the social foundation of all constitutional protections (i.e., mixed and counterbalanced institutions) against Court authority. As Pocock points out, "this was less an idealization of feudalism than a defeudalization of medieval reality." But it did help make possible, however violently, a harmonizing of the Machiavellian picture of republican Rome with the social structure of a gentry-dominated England.[36]

By viewing English republicanism through the lens of a feudal commonwealth, the inherited political structure could be endorsed without, at the same time, relinquishing ground to the prerogative claims of crown and court. The ancient and Gothic constitutions were one. Not surprisingly, this interpretation left an opening for a counterattack by historians with royalist leanings who, in contrast to the neo-Harringtonians, set out to depict the Gothic period as a veritable Dark Age of cultural barbarism and baronial tyranny. For royalist sympathizers such as Robert Brady, the key strategy was to sever the imputed link between ancient Anglo-Saxon freeholding rights and postconquest institutions such as the Magna Carta and the House of Commons. A royal physician as well as one of Prynne's successors as Keeper of the Records of the Tower, Brady insisted that there had been no such freeholding rights in the Anglo-Saxon period, because in that period too the social order had been merely feudal and tyrannical. At the same time, institutions such as Magna Carta and the House of Commons had arisen within the framework of the royal and baronial prerogatives confirmed by William the Conqueror. Such freeholding "rights" as subsequently came into existence had therefore evolved historically as part of a relaxation rather than a relinquishing of the royal authority.[37]

The debate continued with some modifications into the eighteenth century. After 1714 most Tories had become fully accommodated to the settlement of 1688 (if not to the Hanoverian Succession), and indeed fit the Revolution comfortably into their preferred account of recent history.[38] Within that larger text, Tories presented English history as an age-old struggle between freeholders on the one side and barons and kings on the other. The ancient liberties had flourished within the Saxon commonwealth and its proto-Parliamentary Witenagemot. The Norman Conquest proved only a momentary setback. The constitutional liberties it assaulted were soon restored through the Magna Carta and strengthened immeasurably by the Tudor land-redistribution. This same static dialectic was applied to seventeenth-century history, when the Glorious Revolution succeeded in squelching the revanchist Stuart power play.[39] Of course, there was also a sequel to this story: the eternal struggle between Crown and Commons continued down to the present day; only now, the threat to the constitution came from a corruption-wielding Whig ministry employing debt and patronage rather than overweening royal prerogative.

If this roughly was the eighteenth-century Tory analysis of English constitutional development, it found its match in contemporary Whig literature. As Kramnick notes, the Whig response initially came via its party-controlled journals. To the foundation constructed in the previous century by Robert Brady and Henry Spelman, the Whig press added an interpretive superstructure that attributed the erosion of medieval feudal institutions to the gradual rise of trade and industry, centered initially in the boroughs but eventually infiltrating the whole agrarian economy. A version of this interpretation would later appear in the economic writings of the Scottish Enlightenment, in works

such as Adam Smith's *Wealth of Nations* (Book III), which depicted the feudal nobility as having self-destructed through its spendthrift addiction to the
baubles proffered by local merchants.[40] As we will see in a subsequent chapter,
a version of this narrative would also recur in the radically different setting
of Revolutionary France, particularly in the writings of the pamphleteer, the
Abbé Sieyes.

The basic story detailed in the eighteenth-century Whig press juxtaposed
mercantile commoners to wastrel aristocrats locked in a struggle that would
lead first to the enrichment of towns and freeholders through the exportation
of wool, then with the increased circulation of money to the commutation
of feudal dues, and finally to the acquisition of chartered rights and parliamentary representation.[41] The Revolution of 1688 provided the narrative's
denouement by permanently securing the mixed constitution through its
vesting of sovereignty in King-in-Parliament. The postscript, in the face of
a now-supreme Parliament, was to show how constitutional balance needed
to be maintained by artificially strengthening the authority of the weakened
Court, if necessary through the very institutions of patronage and placehold-
ing that the opposition in its short sightedness denounced as corrupt.[42] From
the viewpoint of inherited civic humanist doctrines, this argument entailed
the peculiar twist that a society that was excessively virtuous would eventually
destroy itself by draining the lifeblood from its own economic and political
institutions; hence the moral defense of not just enlightened self-interest but
even of occasionally outright selfishness that can be found in the works produced by some of Robert Walpole's paid literati, such as Bernard Mandeville.

What Tucker added in his *Second Letter* to Whig historiography was the
sketch of a feudal society so primitive in its institutional capacities that it
could not fit Jews – and by implication all other useful outsiders – into any
appropriate place within its legal or social structure.[43] They could not be
absorbed into any of the recognized castes: not the fighting lords, because Jews
were not authorized by the Gothic military code to carry arms; not into the
burgher class, because their commercial contributions were not tolerated by
the egoistic spirit of "Monopoly and Self-Interest"[44]; and not into the servile
class of woodcutters and ploughmen ("as far as Knowledge of the Plough and
Agriculture obtained in those barbarous Times"), because, as Tucker notes
without elaboration, "the Jews were bred up to other Employments."[45] In this
way the ancient constitution was exposed as fundamentally defective, subvert-
ing the very ends it was supposedly created to serve. Its crude construction
created a situation in which the Jews were forced to seek the protection of
the Crown; their usurious activities, amply taxed by the king, enlarged the
resources he could exploit for his own fiscal independence and hence for the

exercising of his royal prerogative against the nobility and the corporations.[46] This part sounded like William Prynne's account of the Crown's use of the Jews to oppress the commons. But in truth it was a pointed rejoinder from Tucker to those representatives of the "Patriot" and "Country" parties who would deny the right of Jews to acquire landed estates in 1753, on the basis of the precedent of medieval royal prerogative.[47]

Perhaps because the Jews were expelled early on in the process, Tucker did not elaborate further on their possible role within the historical sequence of feudal decline. He may have felt he had said enough to expose the Gothic Constitution for what it really was, and hence proceeded to describe why what had replaced it was infinitely better. "... [T]he Glorious Revolution put an entire Period to the very Remains of those shocking Tyrannies and Oppressions; and begun a New System of Civil and Commercial Government."[48] Tucker depicts this new system of government, which he viewed as having been crystallized and reaffirmed by the Whig policies of Robert Walpole, as the moment of disjuncture with the feudal past. The Glorious Revolution institutionalized Protestant monarchy, Parliamentary supremacy, and commercial liberty. Yet Tucker could not hide the fact that although 1688 was a watershed date in English history, aspects of the old order persisted beyond the Glorious Revolution. Indeed, it was essential to his arguments over the Jew Bill to show that an element of historical continuity existed between the old "Gothic" and the new "Commercial" phases. As we will see, the Jews themselves symbolized this continuity.

AN UNFINISHED REVOLUTION

In order to understand the central role that Tucker accorded the Jews in completing the unfinished Glorious Revolution, it will be necessary to examine the crux of the legal debate over Jewish naturalization: landownership. We have already seen that the Jews' ineligibility for landownership was central to the analyses of their proper status by Luzzatto, Toland, and others. In the England of 1753, Jews could and did own land; the question that resurfaced in the Jew Bill debates was whether they were in fact legally entitled to do so.

The nebulous legal circumstances through which Jews had been readmitted to England – assuming that they had been legally readmitted at all – underscored the possible relevance to the Jew Bill's validity of medieval statutes relating to their privileges and status. Certainly, this was the position of many of the Bill's opponents, who exploited the ambiguity surrounding both the thirteenth-century expulsion and the seventeenth-century readmission of the Jews to discredit the Act. The opposition suggested that an Act "to naturalize certain foreign Jews" could hardly be valid if even native-born Jews lacked real status as British subjects. It is worth noting that despite this implicit threat, virtually no subsequent effort was made following the successful repeal of the Jewish Naturalization Act to deny Anglo-Jews rights they had previously enjoyed, including the ownership of immovable property. This suggests that the episode was in part merely a reprise of the constitutional controversies of a previous era, for which the Jews happened to provide a convenient occasion. At the same time, and more seriously, the Jew Bill debate provoked a clamorous public inquiry into whether the nation still retained its collective Protestant identity and existed in essential continuity with its past despite the recent dynastic and constitutional changes. This is why it focused so strongly on the past, and particularly the remote past relating to the nation's constitutional origins. In this light, the fact that Jews offered the opportunity for this backward glance is significant. Jews represented a group that was linked to England's remote past as well as to its immediate present. Yet the connection between medieval and modern Anglo-Jewry remained as blurry as the circumstances of their seventeenth-century readmission. They therefore represented an ideal test case for measuring England's own constitutional continuity after 1688 and 1714.

Despite the tone of so much of the propaganda, the debate over Jewish status underscored the reality that much had changed since medieval times. Even the erudite and incisive opponent of the Jew Bill, Joseph Grove, was prepared to acknowledge that medieval law was no longer fully operative when it came to determining Jews' property rights. According to Grove, medieval statute held "that no Jew may have a Freehold in any Manors, Lands, Tenements, Fees, Rents, or in any Tenures whatever, either by Deed, Gift, Feoffment, Confirmation, or any other Obligation, or any other manner whatever."[49] But the importance of such a precedent was not, suggested Grove, to prevent future rulers from expanding Jews' access to property, but rather to preserve their ultimate status as aliens. Even today they remain *Ferae Bestiae*, wild beasts; "such as Birds of Passage, Fishes in the open, unclaimed Sea, and Bees flying in the Air at a Distance from their Hives, for in all such Animals, as no one can claim a distinct Right they consequently belong to, and are esteemed the Property of, the Person occupying."[50] In other words, the constitutional principle of Jewish servitude that had rendered medieval Jews *servi camerae* (serfs of the royal chamber) still holds. Jews today live in Britain only at the pleasure of the king. They hold property only because the king authorizes them to do so, and this authorization can only be accorded to individuals for the duration of their lives. Jews cannot pass property to their offspring, said Grove, except through the king's act of renewal.[51] This certainly sounds like a reversion to feudal law. Yet it is interesting that Grove justifies this claim not on the basis of medieval precedent but rather of the eternal Law of Nations. Because Jews are stateless aliens, their lack of sovereignty prevents them from according reciprocal protections to subjects of other states. They can therefore be entitled to none themselves.[52]

Tucker did not directly respond to Grove's learned arguments. Instead, he depicted the opposition as deluded victims of foolish nostalgia who refused to recognize that times had irrevocably changed – and for the good! Unlike some apologists for the Jews, such as Philip Carteret Webb, Tucker was not interested in the minutia of Latin legal records on medieval Jewry's property qualifications. In fact, relying on such documents would have undermined his central point: that the Gothic constitution was not merely defunct but had long been bankrupt. The new constitutional order, however, is perfectly clear in its *silence* regarding any such Jewish disabilities, since it contains none. "... I leave it to your own Judgment to determine whether there is any thing in the Nature of our present Constitution that forbids Jews to class with the Rest of the Subjects, as far as relates to Matters of mere civil Concern in a private Station."[53] Having established this point to his satisfaction, Tucker was still left with explaining why Jews remained excluded from certain institutions, such as guilds and trading companies, which did not legally require an Anglican or even a Protestant or Christian allegiance. The reason, he concluded, was that although the constitution had changed, the old "monopolizing Spirit" of medieval trading corporations had not. Indeed, this spirit, Tucker lamented, was still "exerting its baleful Influence" on our politics.[54] The City of London, the Levant and other chartered trading companies, had spearheaded opposition to the Jew Bill. As a genuine proponent of free market principles, Tucker wished to see their exclusive privileges eliminated.[55]

In his historical sensibility Tucker appears as a modern in a much more straightforward sense than, for instance, John Toland. Instead of projecting into a hoped-for future the image of an idealized antiquity, he insisted on judging the past critically in relation to the present. If, as opponents of the Jew Bill claimed, medieval Anglo-Jewry had been guilty of "excessive Usury and monstrous Extortion," this had not been the fault of the Jews but rather of "foolish absurd Laws" against lending at interest that in the Reverend Tucker's estimation also grossly misinterpreted Scripture.[56] The consequence of these laws "was, that the Jews had the Monopoly of Money in their own Hands, and could make a Prey of the Kingdom at their Pleasure + *Just as our exclusive Companies do now*."[57] It follows that if the Jews' anomalous position under the Gothic constitution had led to their eventual expulsion from the country, the chartered monopolies' anomalous position under "new System of Civil and Commercial Government" ought now to result in their own elimination. "Did the Jews ever receive a greater Profit than the Hudson's Bay Company have done?"[58] Ergo: the Jews are now the antimonopolists, whereas the chartered companies are today's Jews.

In a further point of contrast with Toland, Tucker anticipated that the Jews' contribution to Britain would be almost purely mercantile. This was in line with his intention of according Jews civic rights only, and not, as with Toland, a broader form of membership in the commonwealth.[59] And although Tucker certainly favored granting wealthy individuals permission to acquire estates, there is no mention in his writings of Jews colonizing territories or manning militias. To Toland, the immigration of Jews was part of a larger reclamation project designed to strengthen and unite the non-Catholic populations in a future north European commonwealth dedicated to religious toleration, civic and political liberty, and the cultivation of reason. To Tucker Jews are useful traders and moneymen who, as part of a larger absorption of industrious foreigners, enhance the commercial strength of the country while helping to erode the vestiges of feudal corporatism. Although Toland emphasized the Jews' capacity for all sorts of work, and denied that God or nature predisposed any nationality to one particular line, Tucker suggests that Jews do have a kind of commercial instinct and, indeed, that all men are ordained by Providence to play a particular role, based in "Instinct," within the general division of labor.[60] These assertions, aligned with his expertise in political economy, place Tucker closer to the tradition of Simone Luzzatto and Menasseh ben Israel than of Toland.

Discussions of the Jew Bill tend to focus on its politics and prejudicial mentalities, whereas the relevant economic issues get lost. Tucker's participation in the debate offers a glimpse into the relationship between emerging economic ideologies and contemporary representations of Jews. His reflections on trade, finance, industry, and governmental policy, to which we now turn, thus shed considerable light on his stance in the controversies of 1753.

THE ELEMENTS OF COMMERCE

When we look at Tucker's economic writings, we see how far European political economy had come in the century since Simone Luzzatto's *Discorso*. It is true that the basic elements found in Luzzatto are still present: physical necessity driving the production of goods, the urge for greater convenience leading to their exchange and the drive for greater efficiency bringing about a ramified division of labor wherein each through his specified role becomes interconnected with the larger whole. What has changed is that Tucker has taken all of these basic elements, dissolved them into their component parts, and then reconstructed them into an intricate theory of moral, psychological, and social behavior.

Tucker published his principal work on political economy, *The Elements of Commerce*, in 1754, two years after David Hume's *Political Discourses*, containing most of the latter's essays on economics, appeared.[61] Although posterity justly celebrates Hume for his influence on and anticipation of Adam Smith, Tucker remains a rather neglected pioneer of economic thought.[62] Both Hume and Tucker were incisive critics of what Smith would label "the mercantile system," and both embraced the principles of *laissez-faire* while rejecting the agrarian orientation of contemporary Physiocratic writings. Although no match for Hume as a philosopher, Tucker did – as we shall see – work out a complex psychological theory of labor and commerce that in some ways resembled the Scotsman's doctrines of moral philosophy. On more technical economic topics, Tucker and Hume held similar views of the nominal character of money and made similar distinctions between productive and nonproductive occupations. In one famous instance, Tucker influenced Hume to modify his own theories when Tucker attacked the static implications of Hume's so-called rich country-poor country hypothesis.[63] This is enough to suggest that Tucker was an important and influential figure in the development of classical political economy. And because neither Hume nor (even less so) Smith focused on Jewish commerce, Tucker may serve as a useful "stand in" indicating what those authors might have said had they addressed that topic.

Tucker begins his *Elements of Commerce* with the individual as the most basic unit of social analysis. Each of us, he contends, comes into the world with both less and more than other animals. Humans possess fewer of the natural and instinctual protections and must consequently compensate by combining with others. But they are also endowed with unique and individual talents that far exceed those of the brutes.[64] This means that although men form societies for purposes of protection, they do so through establishing a division of labor built on intrinsic distinctions of talent. Although this division leads to an initial exchange of goods, this stage, insists Tucker, comprises only the "First Draught, or Rudiments of Commerce." What makes a more fully-fledged commercial life possible is the generation – once society has achieved a modicum of material security – of a secondary level of "needs," which Tucker designates "Artificial Wants."[65]

But why should a society capable of self-sufficiency seek to acquire more? The answer that Tucker gives directly concerns his own relationship to the civic humanist ethic, and shows why and how he departs so fundamentally from it. That ethic had tended to view man's political life as the preeminent fulfillment of his uniquely human personality. In Aristotelian fashion, it viewed man as a political animal who could only realize his truest nature by participating actively in the public sphere, the *respublica*. This, in turn, necessitated the virtues of public-spiritedness and devotion to the common good, which, formulated negatively, could be described as the constitutional wherewithal to withstand individual and collective corruption. Such a supremely difficult task would stand the best chance of succeeding if certain external conditions remained operative, principally the material and military self-sufficiency associated with land-holding and an armed citizenry. Although some strands of civic humanism did assign an important role to commerce, its conception of virtue naturally favored frugality and simplicity while condemning the acquisitiveness associated with social complexity and the mobility of wealth. In a like manner, the ideal of a mixed constitution conformed to a classical aesthetic of simplicity, balance, and harmony.

This is precisely the point that Tucker – here reflecting a broader eighteenth-century trend promoting the benefits of both luxury and "*doux-commerce*" – wished most strenuously to controvert.[66] Fleshing out the heresies of Mandeville (while tempering his provocations), Tucker insisted that not just self-interest but self-love and not just necessities but superfluities, are what make the world go round. A society existing at the level of rustic frugality would be more than harsh, it would be positively barbaric. Such a society, Tucker suggested, would not have curbed human selfishness but magnified it instead. Rather, it is self-love and acquisitiveness, leading at a certain stage of material development to the pursuit of "Artificial Wants" and hence to a fully-fledged commerce, that possess the power to tame the more vicious passions. "If Self-Love is restrained from doing Good to Society, it will do mischief." In other words, the self-love of one is inevitably ranged against self-love another; the only question is whether the confrontation will occur through violence or trade. As Keynes would later put it, "It is better that a man should tyrannise over his bank balance than over his fellow-citizens." For Tucker, self-love must be harnessed through the rational, disciplined, and civilizing framework of material exchange.[67]

By Tucker's day, this emphasis on the utility of self-love was already fairly commonplace, yet he complicated this view of human nature in an important way. For him – as for contemporaries such as Samuel Clarke, Francis Hutcheson, and David Hume – man's self-regarding instincts are supplemented by a slight but equally in-built capacity for benevolence.[68] In itself, the benevolent instinct is exceedingly weak and can do little. That is why it must operate in alliance rather than in opposition to self-love, helping to direct the latter to ends that are socially beneficial rather than destructive. Insofar as self-love, "the great Mover of Created Beings," is directed to the acquisition of material benefits ("Artificial Wants"), it also greatly expands the power of human benevolence to exert its influence. This happens, says Tucker, because from their different starting points self-love and benevolence combine to impel the individual to engage in commerce with others (commerce here implying all forms of sociability as well as trade).[69] Similarly, in a society in which the division of labor has ripened, both self-love and benevolence draw men to value the ranks and distinctions reflecting different talents, abilities, and merits. Ambition, desire, need, and want will no longer be limited to accomplishing their ends through brute aggrandizement, but will instead discover that emulation provides a surer route to success, one that also accords better with the innate social sentiments.[70] In summary: necessity draws men to combine into societies organized through a division of labor; self-love feeds the desire for artificial wants, thus compelling the further refinement of that division, which in turn gives rise to commerce; market exchange then conditions men to recognize that the gratification of long-term interests necessitates the emulation of and respect for the skills and offices of others; finally, this recognition, although it operates imperfectly, hones the capacity of reason to fit means to ends, or to coordinate these various elements into a policy of enlightened self-interest.

It is not hard to see how from these premises a doctrine justifying at least a limited amount of state intervention might arise. What human nature and providence legislate can be assisted and accelerated through wise policy. Formulated negatively, misguided government or poorly conceived constitutions can easily frustrate nature's scheme.[71] The ancient constitution was just such a failure, in Tucker's view, because by institutionalizing rank and privilege, it encouraged men's self-regarding instincts to be unleashed toward selfish ends. Corporations and monopolies were the result of a public policy and a constitutional arrangement that bottled up trade and imposed artificial hierarchies in the place of natural ones.

> Hence it is, that Monopolies are formed, and Charters granted, under the absurd Pretence of the Public Good, when, in Fact, private Advantage is the only Point aimed at. Hence it is, that unjust Combinations are sanctified by positive Laws, and those very Exclusions are stiled Rights and Liberties, by which other Men have the Rights taken away from them, and are denied the Liberty of being Useful to themselves, and serviceable to their Country.[72]

The Gothic baron and the exclusive trading company were equally the expressions of a monopolizing spirit, however sanctified they might appear in the eyes of custom and law. The result was the blocking of the very commercial expansion and wealth production that would have helped to curb the passions of aggrandizement.[73] Tucker expresses it as a law that a society that does not advance through commerce into a prosperous social order grounded in merit will necessarily stagnate into an impoverished feudal system rooted in force.[74] Still, law and constitution are instruments of policy, and although Tucker might have agreed that no laws are better than bad laws, he greatly preferred the use of positive laws, even authoritarian ones, to bring about socially beneficial results. Most expedient of all, however, was to so formulate policy that men were induced to "choose" the socially desired course:

> ... a lasting and extensive National Commerce is no otherwise to be obtained, than by a prudent Direction of the Passion of Self-Love to its proper Objects, – by confining it to those Objects, – and there giving it all possible Assistance and Incouragement. The Passion of Self-Love therefore must be taken hold of by some Method or other; and so trained and guided in its Operations, that its Activity may never be mischievous, but always productive of the public Welfare. When Things are brought to that pass, the Consequence will be, that every Individual (whether he intends it or not) will be promoting the Good of his Country, and of Mankind in general, while he is pursuing his own private Interest.[75]

This theme of the unintended but inevitable benefits of self-interest was of course one that Mandeville had broached in *The Fable of the Bees* and Adam Smith would elucidate in *The Wealth of Nations*.[76] Where Tucker differed from Smith was in his insistence on a set of positive policies to abet and guide this process. State policy, for instance, must intervene to channel self-love into socially beneficial ends. The immigration of foreigners (such as Jewish settlers) provides a case in point. Tucker's earliest economic writings, right up through the *Elements of Commerce*, put population increase (especially through immigration) at the center of all good policy.[77] Although this theme was hackneyed by the year of the Jew Bill, in Tucker's case it fit integrally into a broader moral and social outlook. As noted, the populationist doctrine that "the most decisive mark of the prosperity of any country is the number of its inhabitants," constituted a veritable dogma of seventeenth- and eighteenth-century political economy, both in England and on the Continent.[78] But what is here expressed in terms of a result was more often than not conceived of as a cause. Joseph Schumpeter, in his *History of Economic Analysis*, describes as "manifestly correct" the proposition underlying all populationist doctrine that "under prevailing conditions, increase in heads would increase real income per head."[79] One such condition was the stagnation in population during the sixteen hundreds after more than two centuries of unprecedented expansion, a phenomenon that when recognized fed a widespread perception that Britain's demographic health was in crisis. Because cities such as London and Paris had grown phenomenally during much of this period, contemporary observers assumed that internal migration to the cities had come at the expense of depopulation of the countryside.[80] Such concerns were aggravated by the presumption, which Tucker shared, that the overseas colonies were draining off huge numbers from the mother country. For this reason, Tucker opposed the acquisition of empire, especially through the agency of chartered monopolies, while at the same time strongly favoring foreign immigration to Britain.[81] For him, the alignment of forces was unmistakable: monopolies pursued empire by draining human resources from the metropole while at the same time protecting their exclusive privileges by opposing the naturalizing of foreigners, including Jews. So long as empire and charter persisted, so long as Jews and other industrious immigrants remained excluded from England's key commercial enterprises, the new system of civil and commercial government would remain incomplete.

"MONEY WITHOUT INDUSTRY, IS AN HURT, NOT A BLESSING"

Both proponents and opponents of the Jew Bill drove their economic arguments around depictions of the commercial character of Jewish immigrants. The question usually involved defining the specific moral and political consequences of Jewish commerce. These arguments almost always cut both ways. The proponents' emphasis on the "Utility of introducing rich Persons into a State" was exploited by opponents to frighten the population into believing that foreign Jews would use their fantastic wealth to purchase all the estates in the land.[82] Undeterred, the Bill's propagandists such as Philo-Patriae argued along typically mercantilist lines that because domestic trade, in and of itself, produces no new wealth, only the settlement of wealthy foreign groups such as Jews would increase the nation's riches, since they are "particularly industrious, in importing Specie."[83] Opponents parried by insisting that Jews would seek to monopolize overseas trade to the detriment of native merchants and the general good. Some insisted that Jews merely replicate skills the country already possesses in abundance. For all their reputed talents and international connections, Jewish merchants offer nothing that is not currently available from native ones; indeed, the latter are superior because their very Englishness allows them to exert "influence over, almost, all parts of the world, in favour of English manufactures..."[84] The City of London's John Bernard presented a more striking argument. He denied the essential likeness of Jewish and English merchants. The Jews could not act as substitutes for English merchants since they were really merchants of a special, and incompatible, kind. What Bernard meant was that Jews deal exclusively in exchange and not at all in manufacturing, which is "the origin of trade in all countries." "[T]herefore they can never be the beginners of trade in any country." "No instance can be given, Sir, of the Jews having been the beginners of trade in any country, but many to the contrary. In Poland, there have been multitudes of Jews of many ages, yet no man will say that Poland is a trading country..." Only at one stage in a nation's commercial history can the Jews be of any real benefit, Bernard conceded, and that is when a surplus of commodities has already been developed yet the capital and overseas connections to distribute them do not yet exist. Clearly this was not the case with Britain, where Jews would find no niche and consequently must drain employments and resources from the domestic economy.[85] Bernard's point was that Jews were good only for financing and organizing distribution to international markets (something other countries might require but that England at present did not need). This argument was readily compatible with the distinction between the manufacture of and trade in commodities (what Lord Egmont labeled "real commerce"), on the one hand, and trade in money and information, on the other. Jews' specialty, Bernard suggested, was "usury, brokerage, and jobbing, in a higher or a lower degree."[86] Bernard was not directly laying out a religious argument against usury here, but was, rather, expressing a contemporary economic prejudice (one perhaps unconsciously grounded in religious assumptions). Finance was secondary to industry and distribution.[87]

Although Tucker did not share Bernard's belief that Jewish brokers would stifle virtuous English merchants, he did articulate a more sophisticated version of Bernard's assertion that finance has less priority than industry. This would become a central point in almost all future discussions of Jewish economy. In understanding how Tucker arrived at this position we must return to the topic of population and immigration. Although state economic policy in sixteenth-century Venice and Tuscany, seventeenth-century Colbertist France, or eighteenth-century Electoral Brandenburg was interested chiefly in attracting foreigners with specific skills, there had been a strong impetus in contemporary Britain toward raising the numbers of even unskilled laboring poor. "The surest Wealth consists in a Multitude of laborious Poor," wrote Mandeville. In this he echoed sentiments voiced frequently by authorities such as Child, Petty, and Charles Davenant (although notably not Hume or Smith).[88] A large population of poor folk, it was held, would depress the price of labor and engender cheaper production costs and lower prices. A growing awareness among economic writers of the elasticity of demand also helped to break down the old prejudice that sale for the internal market merely shifted wealth without increasing it.[89] To Tucker, immigrants were useful in part because they exerted a salutary effect on the native population, both rich and poor. Tucker subscribed at one and the same time to the doctrines of the "utility-of-poverty" and the elasticity of demand. Assuming, as Tucker did, that most newcomers were men of means, bankers, merchants, and craftsmen, their presence in large numbers would be ideally suited to challenging the sanctioned privileges of chartered monopolies. Analogously, foreigners of more modest means would compete with native English artisans and through this intensified competition help stamp out the complacency of English workers. The general charge by Tory opponents of the Jew Bill and other naturalization legislation was that rapacious immigrants would undercut the earnings of common laborers and invade the established markets of native merchandizers and manufacturers. Tucker readily agreed:

> ... it will be objected, That foreigners will live more frugally, and consequently will work cheaper, than our own People; and that the reducing [of] the Price of Labour will take the Bread out of the Mouths of our own Poor. But surely the lazy and idle Manufacturer, who, by the present high Price of Labour, riots in Idleness Two or more Days out of Six, and is therefore the Cause of our being underworked, and consequently undersold, by Foreigners in Branches of our Exports, deserves no other Regard or Attention from the Legislature, than the endeavoring to bring him back to a reasonable Frugality, and temperate way of Living...[90]

Competition breeds respect for merit. Climbing the social or economic ladder demands industry, frugality, and other virtues arising from the acquisitive spirit tempered by commercial government. This is why social hierarchy born of the division of labor is so important. It creates natural ranks that instill a desire for emulation through diligent application and hard work. "[L]et superior industry and skill, integrity and virtue receive all your Incouragement," exhorted Tucker, "because they deserve it ... "[91] Immigrants have already passed this test; their enterprising and adventurous spirit attests to their talents, industry, and frugality.[92] Although other defenses of the Jew Bill emphasized mercantilist rationales – viz., as the "Utility of introducing rich Persons into a State"[93] – for Tucker, it is labor alone that is "the true Riches, and money [merely] the Sign or Tally."

Tucker was able to fit the Jews into a new social ethic in which commerce and virtue were seen to complement rather than contradict one another.

Tucker's approach to related issues was similarly integrative. The Jews' conspicuous absence from agriculture cast no blemish on their characters. On the contrary, the evident hostility of landed gentlemen to merchants and the supposed opposition between real and mobile wealth reflected shortsighted, dangerous prejudices.[94] Although for purposes of analysis commerce might be broken down into its constituent elements, in the last event it was all of one piece. In an economy such as Britain's, where subsistence farming was dying out, where enclosure had been proceeding for centuries, and where "improvement" had now become a watchword (even if usually only lip service was paid to it), Tucker could look on agriculture as a purely commercial endeavor. Like Hume, almost going out of his way to controvert Physiocrat doctrines, Tucker asserted that agriculture possessed no special claim to moral or economic preeminence.[95] In fact, in his taxonomy of occupations he pointedly subsumed it under the rubric of manufacturing, of which farming constituted merely a special branch. "[T]he Ground or Soil is properly the raw Material, and the Land-Owner or Farmer is the head Manufacturer."[96] Likewise, merchants should be viewed as components of the agricultural and manufacturing processes, as transporters and distributors of raw materials and finished goods. "This being the Case, it must necessarily follow, that every general Principle of Commerce, which tends to establish and promote other Manufacturers, must likewise be productive of good effects in Husbandry."[97] Foreign merchants not only provide a direct service to farmers, but by adding to the total number of consumers they help expand the size of the domestic markets. In exemplary fashion, Tucker concludes by juxtaposing bad with good policy, attacking the subsidizing of exports for the benefit of the landed interests while praising instead schemes to import industrious foreign merchants and mechanics.[98]

There is a final point to be made in this context, the explication of which sheds light on the transformation of eighteenth-century attitudes to Jewish economic life. It is true that for Tucker the elements of commerce constitute a unity – with self-love and benevolence, virtue and trade, agriculture and manufacture, production and distribution, all functioning together in harmony. But it is also the case that he subordinated each of these dualities to a further and yet less easily reconcilable one. Despite Tucker's friendliness to a wide range of occupations, we should not lose sight of the fact that at the foundation of his outlook lay that ethic of work and that distinction between productive and unproductive labor that in future would help shape the terms of the Jewish emancipation contract.

Industry, frugality, sobriety, policy, emulation, and merit are the cardinal virtues extolled by Tucker the economist and clergyman. Commerce and "good morals" are "inseparably connected"; likewise, "universal commerce,

good Government, and true Religion, are nearly, are inseparably connected."
The implanting of self-love in the hearts of men discloses a providential plan, a
preestablished harmony wherein "private coincide[s] with public, present with
future Happiness."[99] The moral economy comprises a perfect "Machine," a
Newtonian timepiece defined by its "constant and regular Motion."[100] Monopolies and corporations are reprehensible because they interrupt the regularity
of this machine by privileging idleness over industry and instituting false hierarchies of useless over useful people. Conversely, immigration is invaluable
because it awakens the whole population to the virtues of diligence while
engendering a natural order of merit and skill:

> [A]nd the better any Person discharges the Duties of that Sphere of Life he
> belongs to, the more he will be enabled to contribute to the present Happiness
> of Society, by promoting a regular and permanent circulation of Industry
> and Labour, through the several Ranks he is connected with.[101]

Thus a literal and conceptual vocabulary borrowed in part from theology was
now being enlisted to preach a gospel of labor. It is tempting to speculate here
over whether the messianic connections between commerce and redemption
drawn by Menasseh ben Israel had found their latest apostle in Josiah Tucker;
except that for Menasseh commerce was merely an instrument, one to be
relinquished on Israel's restoration and not, as would seem the case for Tucker,
the very substance of redemption itself.

Yet theology aside, hard-nosed economic rationales sustained Tucker's elevation of labor. The school associated with "mercantilism" (a crude but
inescapable term), with its focus on achieving favorable balances-of-payment,
seemed to imply that precious metals did not just measure wealth but were
actually its true source. Against this, a number of economists – Thomas Mun,
Josiah Child, Dudley North, and John Locke among them – set out to prove
that specie was, as Aristotle had written long ago, merely a social convenience, a token or sign, and not that actual repository of value signified by
it.[102] This debate over money precipitated further investigation into the true
sources, meanings, and measures of value. The question was of more than mere
academic concern, because its resolution had the potential to alter existing
political arrangements. The schemes of a John Law, for instance, or a government's momentary adoption of Physiocratic doctrines on the free trade in
grain could and did provoke upheaval.[103] With the Physiocrats, we are entering a period when, to paraphrase Keynes, the arcane speculations of "some
defunct economist" could have devastating effects on entire populations.[104]

Tucker's own intermediate position between older and newer forms of political economy is nowhere more apparent than in his "labor theory of value."

The imprecision involved in assigning a labor theory to Adam Smith applies equally to the case of Tucker. For Tucker, this was largely because his position on value was so completely intertwined with his populationist doctrines that it was difficult to determine whether for him labor or demography should be given first priority. What is certain, however, is that he viewed both labor and population size as factors that far outweighed land or money. The priority of labor and population becomes clear, says Tucker, when we consider that land prices in densely populated regions are proportionately higher than those in scarcely populated ones.[105] As for money, it is equally apparent, he notes, that it will always follow the flow of population, so long as population growth gets effectively translated into industry. "For if Great Britain hath Industry, and another Country Money, the Industry of the one will soon extract the Money of the other, in Spite of every Law, Penalty, and Prohibition that can be framed."[106]

It would thus appear that Tucker saw population growth as the key to the rise of industry, and "industry" (in both senses of the term) as what in turn produced wealth.[107] To indicate this Tucker proposed that a "Ballance of Industry" be substituted for the more traditional "balance-of-trade" as the correct formula in assessing wealth production. Not money, but labor was what really mattered: "...for Money without Industry, is an Hurt, not a Blessing."[108] Money without equivalent industry is potentially inflationary; or could give rise to the fantastic schemes of financial "projectors."[109] Hume held a similar position, noting that "The greater number of people and their greater industry are serviceable in all cases; at home and abroad, in private, and in public. But the greater plenty of money, is very limited in its use, and may even sometimes be a loss to a nation in its commerce with foreigners."[110] Thus, in prioritizing the factors of production (or the "elements of commerce," as Tucker called them) money must not be seen as an absolute value, but rather as a convenience, in itself almost arbitrary, facilitating the circulation of actual wealth. It should be noted that as a sign of things to come, this very doctrine was deployed during the debates of 1753 to attack the Jew Bill. Indeed, the *Westminster Journal* published an article that summer proclaiming that the influx of Jewish financiers must not be confused with the addition to the country of actual wealth, because money will be found to be beneficial only to the extent that it is productive, that is, to the extent that it enhances manufacturing and employment. "[M]oney, or credit, circulating through a nation, from hand to hand, without producing labour and industry in the inhabitants, is direct gaming; and what else can be expected from the *Jews*, upon their naturalization."[111] Such arguments would reverberate later in the eighteenth century in denunciations of Jewish commerce. But Tucker, even disregarding of his pro-Jewish stance, would have found the reasoning specious. Jews are people and not a personification of money. As such their labor – whether commercial, financial, or otherwise – comes first, and wealth flows organically from it. In contrast to slave societies, where labor is coerced through artificial and counterproductive means, a free and prosperous society will allow the natural forces of population growth to spur activity. Nevertheless – and this point bears emphasis – the coercive power of government can and must be brought to bear in maximizing the laboring potential of the population through all legitimate means. That is to say, the state can act, first and foremost, to enhance population growth, and second, to ensure that growth does not lead to a proliferation of the wrong kinds of professions.

We have noted earlier how Tucker urged government to use all means at its disposal to encourage foreign immigration. This was to be supplemented, however, by policies geared toward influencing the birth rates of the native-born population. Tucker proposed that severe penalties be imposed on bachelors and other such "unproductive" people. Those who do not reproduce labor in the form of offspring were conflated in his mind with those whose labor contributed nothing to "industry."[112] This is important as well, because it connects two modes of eighteenth-century economic analysis that might otherwise be thought of as distinct. Policies intended to increase population were by this time a standard device of state management. But if utility was conceptualized in terms of both productive and reproductive capacities, then additional avenues would be opened up for state supervision. For reasons that should now be apparent, Tucker assumed that expansion of the numbers of laborers and expansion of "industry" effectively amounted to the same thing. His analysis of the benefits of population increase, one of Tucker's economic rationales for Jewish naturalization, went hand in hand with his differentiation of productive and nonproductive forms of work, a distinction that would take on enormous significance in later discussions of Jewish economy.

Tucker's notion of unproductive work can be broken down into two subsets. The first, which includes actors, publicans, prostitutes, distillers of alcohol, and so on, represented all those engaged in marginal or sometimes criminal activities which tended to weaken work discipline and redirect sexual appetites into unfruitful (and unwholesome) channels.[113] The second category, comprising most of the previous category but now supplemented by intellectuals and literati, though in some cases not exactly useless from a cultural standpoint, was regarded by Tucker as economically unproductive and hence subject to restriction by law: "... as these Scholars and literary Gentlemen live by the Labour of others, the Increase of their Numbers would be so far from adding to the Public Stock of Wealth, that it would greatly diminish it in every view."[114] Although these categories were comparatively limited ones, they still suggest that distinctions between productive and unproductive professions were implicit in all theories of value that placed labor at their center. Labor is productive insofar as it creates exchangeable commodities or insofar as it provides the conditions of material production through finance, investment, transport, and sale. This, it should be noted, is the maximal definition of productive labor in the time period we are now concerned with. For Adam Smith, the category of those designated useful but unproductive was much larger than for Josiah Tucker, including, among other groupings, both household servants and soldiers. A growth in the numbers of such professions would be harmful, possibly even destructive to the nation.[115]

What differentiates Tucker and Smith is not so much their definitions as the extent to which each was willing to countenance positive state policies to ensure that organic developments did not miscarry. Despite an intense hostility to all traditional forms of combination – guilds, corporations, chartered companies, and so on – Tucker's readiness to accord "policy" a central role in his theory indicates that he still remained at least partly rooted in Aristotelian definitions of economy as estate management. This is notable in light of Tucker's utter detestation of the civic humanist tradition with its own ideal of the gentleman farmer rooted in the Aristotelian ideal of the *oikos*. Yet we have seen that Tucker's critique of that tradition still managed to salvage from it a not wholly unrelated conception of virtue as industry, independence, and frugality. What was different, of course, was that the adherents of Patriot and Country principles approved of commerce insofar as it served the political ends of their own agrarian and gentry-based political ideology, whereas for Tucker politics or policy comprised merely the "visible hand" offering a small dose of paternal guidance to a more or less self-generating moral economy.

MERCANTILE PHILOSEMITISM

Josiah Tucker represents the high-water mark of so-called mercantile philosemitism, an appreciation of the Jews' presumed commercial and financial capacities translated into practical programs and policies to ensure their settlement and at least limited toleration. As we have seen, such arguments were strongly influenced by seventeenth-century Jewish apologists such as Simone Luzzatto and Menasseh ben Israel. But it was not until the end of the seventeenth century that non-Jewish authors began independently to employ them (as opposed to state policies and privileges). As the eighteenth century wore on, and as pro-merchant "mercantilist" doctrines began to merge with (until they were later overtaken by) laissez-faire principles that challenged privileged monopolies and championed new commercial groups, economic thought became increasingly sympathetic to a Jewish commercial function.

This somewhat inchoate period of "late mercantilism" also possessed a frequent if muted and universalized religious dimension, with the image of globalizing commerce indicating the divinity's benevolent intentions for mankind.[116] "Trade makes the People of the whole Earth as one great Family supplying each other's wants" was a typical expression of this outlook.[117] Differences in the resource (or factor) endowments of different nations make it necessary for commerce to deliver these diverse benefits to all. Thus, God or "Nature has given various Products to various Countries, and thereby knit Mankind in an Intercourse to supply each other's Wants."[118] Jews, as both the Chosen People and a trading nation, readily fit into this universal pattern. Writing in the earlier part of the eighteenth century, Joseph Addison called them ". . . the Instruments by which the most distant Nations converse with one another, and by which Mankind are knit together in a general Correspondence: They are like the Pegs and Nails in a great Building, which, although they are but little valued in themselves, are absolutely necessary to keep the whole Frame together."[119] John Toland, whether sincerely or ironically, echoed Genesis 12:3 ("I will bless those that bless thee and curse those that curse thee") in his observation that Jews bring bounty where they are welcomed but leave desolation where they are forced to depart. "What a paltry fisher town was Livorno before the admission of the Jews?" Toland observed, "What a loser is Lisbon since they have been lost to it?"[120] Seeming to adhere to such advice, the author of an anonymous pamphlet published during the Jew Bill debate informed his fellow Christians that they must express toward Jews "more friendship and greater cordiality than any other strangers or foreigners upon the face of the earth, as those people are known all over the world to be all merchants and traders, from the highest to the lowest . . . "[121]

Similarly pro-Jewish sentiments were aired fairly frequently during the decade surrounding the Jew Bill. This appears to have been the case not just in Britain but in France and Germany as well. In his historical narration of the rise of *doux-commerce*, Montesquieu credited the Jews with rescuing trade from scholastic obscurantism through their invention of a financial device, letters of credit, that fortunately rendered the policing of credit virtually impossible: ". . . in this way commerce was able to avoid violence and maintain itself everywhere, for the richest trader had only invisible goods, which could be sent everywhere and leave no trace anywhere."[122] Montesquieu's insistence on religious toleration, his praise of commerce, and his ascription to the Jews of a heroic role in the restoration of commerce in modern Europe all suggest a favorable attitude on his part toward their renewed presence in France. On this point, his younger contemporary Ange Goudar was far more explicit. Employing familiar populationist arguments to advocate for the expansion of Jewish settlement, Goudar insisted that Jews, though potentially injurious to small and poor countries, would be highly beneficial to France. Goudar adduced a host of familiar arguments culled from Luzzatto and Menasseh ben Israel stressing Jews' apolitical orientation, single-minded devotion to commerce, general moral rectitude and propensity to multiply – all features, he argued, that a resource rich but commercially underdeveloped state like France required.[123]

A still more generous assessment emerged from an anonymous document published in Berlin (in the year of the Jew Bill), containing a dialogue attributed to the probably fictitious Levi Isaac, who is also a character in the presented dialogue. Although recent scholarship has tended to posit a Jewish authorship, there is good reason for supporting earlier contentions that it was the work of the philosopher and champion of Jewish toleration, Gotthold Ephraim Lessing. Indeed, whether or not he was the actual author, Lessing strongly supported the pamphlet's contention that (a) merchants are society's true benefactors in the circulation of goods both regionally and between different classes and orders; (b) an influx of Jews will stimulate productivity, intensify competition, consequently lower prices for consumers while increasing revenue to the crown; and (c) Jews should be granted wide freedom and occupational latitude.[124]

These works, as well as those of Josiah Tucker, were all published within the space of a decade. What is most impressive, beyond their combination of temporal proximity and geographical diversity, is the fact that the "mercantile philosemitism" they expressed would so quickly wane. The reason why – the topic of the next chapter – is already implicit in some of the very philosemitic doctrines Tucker expressed. Already in Tucker's day, Jews were starting to be assailed for exemplifying an outmoded economic order: "[M]oney, or credit, circulating through a nation, from hand to hand, without producing labour and industry in the inhabitants..." Although this theme would echo in the subsequent history of Anglo-Jews, its strongest intonations were heard in continental Europe. For this reason, the exploration of Tucker's political economy both illuminates the economic arguments surrounding the Jew Bill and anticipates a future politics of Jewish commerce.

4

∾

The Natural Relation of Things

Of all the Enlightenment-era treatments of the Jewish political economy, it was the work of a young official in the Prussian foreign affairs ministry, Christian Wilhelm Dohm (1751–1820) that came to exert the most far-reaching influence. Dohm's 1781 *On the Civic Improvement of the Jews* (*Ueber die bürgerliche Verbesserung der Juden*) dominated discussions of Jewish civic status for decades. Any commentator – apologetic or denunciatory – who hoped to shift public opinion on the Jewish question was obligated to reckon with Dohm's analysis. By portraying Jewish economic life as profoundly distorted, while laying the blame on oppressive conditions imposed on Jews rather than their own natures or religion, Dohm formulated a new paradigm. At once sympathetic and critical, embracing economic freedom along with paternalistic state remediation, Dohm's approach suited an era of profound social reform. *On the Civic Improvement of the Jews* remained the touchstone of Jewish political economy through the early 1820s and retained its influence if not its vibrancy even well beyond that date.

What made the work so effective was its unusual mixture of sobriety and advocacy, its qualities of informed and incisive analysis, of perceptive criticism and humane sympathy. More empirical in approach than even a philosemitic treatment like *Reasons for Naturalizing the Jews*, Dohm's book eschewed the messianic utopianism of Toland's pamphlet, even though its conclusions were essentially optimistic. Dohm possessed a richer store of historical knowledge about the Jews than did Toland, especially regarding their medieval circumstances, and at the same time shared little of the latter's antiquarian fascination with the esoteric components of the Jews' ancient constitutional lore. Like Josiah Tucker, Dohm took political economy seriously, and his economic conceptions, however retrograde they may appear today, were progressive in the context of their times.

That seems surprising in light of the traditional scholarly disparagement or neglect of German economic thought before Marx. It is eighteenth-century English political economy that usually appears state-of-the-art, built on a unique set of empiricist traditions that originated in Bacon's critiques of Aristotelian science, in Hobbes' view of human nature, and in Locke's theories of property and civil contract.[1] In this triumphalist narrative of the rise of British political economy, the French Physiocrats, having demolished the protectionist rationales of mercantilism, were in turn vanquished by Adam Smith, who finally cleared the way for economics to emerge as a true science of market exchange. Meanwhile, the German tradition of political economy, to the extent that it has merited any attention in standard histories, has usually been dismissed as backward and irrelevant.[2]

Treatments of the Jewish question in contemporary economic literature might appear to reinforce such a judgment. It would be an easy matter (indeed, it has been done many times) to survey the history of German commentary on Jewish commerce from the period of Dohm up through the mid-nineteenth century and characterize much of it as the expression of a sickly anxiety and phantasmagoric Judeophobia. Germany's inflation of the Jewish commercial bogeyman seemed to exemplify its backwardness and abnormality in comparison with Britain, where a Josiah Tucker could champion Jews or – more remarkable still – where an Adam Smith could ignore them altogether in a work devoted to wealth and trade.

Yet traditional Jewish historiography has not focused on Britain but on the German lands as the setting for the onset of Jewish modernity.[3] It has been argued that German Jews were modern first because Germany's imperfect liberalism had prompted them to devise uniquely creative strategies in their efforts to forge a distinctive sense of membership within an environment that lurched between efforts to incorporate *and* ostracize them.[4] In comparison, Britain's attitude to Jews appears relatively relaxed. Whereas Jews were readmitted to the British Isles without special permission and gradually emancipated in them without much in the way of momentous legislation, Germany's "thorny path" to emancipation stands out for the ostentatious manner in which it seemed to belabor and begrudge every friendly gesture or positive move.[5] If this was a function of Germany's retarded or distorted adoption of political liberalism, why not also see it as a reflection of the primitiveness (or rather, quaintness) of its economic conceptions, its economists' emphases on the maximizing of state revenues, their focus on the satisfaction of needs rather than on the operation of market forces, and their insistence on deriving economic formulae from historical narratives rather than timeless analytical abstractions?

Such a contrast, however, both caricatures German economic approaches and misrepresents British ones. A focus on revenue, demand, and historical narrative characterized seventeenth- and eighteenth-century English and Scottish economic literature no less than its German counterpart.[6] The Scottish Enlightenment first formulated the kinds of stadial theories of economic development that would later become associated with the German style of economic thought. Resembling each other in their approaches to economic life, British and German discussions of Jewish commerce also had much in common. Toland's pamphlet exerted an impact toward the end of the eighteenth century, and Jew Bill debates resulted in an early plea for civic and economic emancipation.[7] These broad similarities only underscore the revolutionary character of Dohm's treatise. A Josiah Tucker, whose views often presaged Smith's, is at the same time found to have important connections to the work of a Prussian professor of finance, Dohm, including a shared faith in the absolute value of population, a joint emphasis on governmental intervention (*Polizei*) as the nexus between state and economy, and a common skepticism toward Physiocratic doctrines. Yet such resemblances prepare us poorly for Dohm's novel take on Jewish economy.

Although Dohm (or at least his book) has long featured centrally in discussions of Jewish emancipation, too little attention has been paid to how his economic conceptions shaped his approach to the Jewish question. Ilsegret Dambacher focused crucially on Dohm as an economic thinker, yet aside from treating his relationship to such broad categories as "physiocracy" and "mercantilism," she did not situate *On the Civic Improvement of the Jews* within its own generic framework: the Italian, English, and French literature on Jewish economy that preceded it.[8] When Dohm is viewed in relation not just to a Tucker or Toland but to a Simone Luzzatto, his radical break with the earlier discourse becomes apparent. Although Dohm's political economy loosely fits into that broad and nebulous category of "late mercantilism" (a category displaying significant thematic overlap with classical economics), his book's innovative character is due less to a new conception of the economic universe than to a self-conscious rethinking of the Jews' place within it. Dohm was no enemy of trade (as some interpreters have claimed); on the contrary, he was typically an enthusiastic proponent of economic freedom. As with most other contemporary proponents, however, he did offer occasional qualifications, ones that appear paradoxical but are nevertheless often cogent when viewed in their historical context. For instance, with regard to the Jews, Dohm believed that creating the conditions for laissez-faire necessitated a compulsory diminution of Jewish involvement in trade.

CAMERALISM TRANSCENDED

Dohm's proximity to English economic thought was not fortuitous. Like many of his generation of civil servants emerging from the University of Göttingen, he had imbibed that institution's Anglophile spirit at its peak. In his *History of the English and French in the East Indies* (1776), Dohm adopted an English and Western European model for Prussian international trade. Like Tucker, he roundly condemned the colonialist greed of merchant corporations and monopolistic trading companies.[9] The emulation of the economic prosperity of the West, while avoiding its moral pitfalls, describes Dohm's general approach to topical affairs. As founder and editor of a periodical, *Deutsches Museum*, the type of reformist journal that abounded in the second half of the eighteenth-century Enlightenment or *Aufklärung*, Dohm hoped to enlist educated public opinion to influence the development of state policy. The strategy was to offer statesmen and the public at large the fruits of social-scientific research (*Statistik*). Policy should be informed by objective knowledge. The British press and Parliament offered a model of how the presentation to the reading public of such empirical data could inform intelligent debate and deliberation, or so Dohm and his fellow Anglophiles (for example, his friends the publicists and reformers Christian Garve and August Ludwig von Schlözer) believed.[10]

On the Civic Improvement of the Jews was written at the behest of another of Dohm's friends, the German-Jewish philosopher Moses Mendelssohn (1729–1786). Mendelssohn had hoped to find a way of galvanizing public sympathy in the aftermath of anti-Jewish riots that took place in Alsace during the summer of 1780.[11] Those riots and the anti-Jewish pamphleteering (and his forgery of Jewish debt receipts on behalf of Alsatian peasant borrowers) of their ringleader, François Hell, not only occasioned Dohm's book but would also given rise to the 1785 essay contest sponsored by the Metz Royal Academy of Arts and Sciences on ways of making the Jews "happier and more useful (*plus heureux and plus utiles*) in France," which formed part of the background to the 1790–91 debates over Jewish emancipation in the French National Assembly.[12] In a sense, then, Dohm's book was the first salvo fired in a decade of argument over the Jews' capacity for "improvement" (*Verbesserung, régénération*).[13] Mendelssohn believed that Dohm, the young and scholarly civil servant whom he had met only months earlier, would prove a more credible and effective advocate than he himself of the Jewish cause. Dohm exceeded Mendelssohn's expectations – and certainly the brief he had given him. Not confining himself to events in Alsace, Dohm broadly surveyed Jews' present circumstances throughout Europe, especially in the German lands.

The underlying question he raised was whether and under what conditions Jews could acquire the virtues deemed necessary for their fuller participation in the civic life of the surrounding communities.

That such a question could be asked suggests that Dohm shared many of the prejudices of most educated Europeans regarding the nature and moral character of Jewish society. Jews, it was widely assumed, held a moral double standard when it came to dealings (especially business dealings) with outsiders; they lacked, moreover, a sense of civic duty and devotion to the common good as well as the will and capacity to perform physical labor.[14] In examining these criticisms of Jews, especially in contrast with Toland's and Tucker's praise, it is important to remember that Dohm confronted a different set of circumstances from those encountered by his earlier British counterparts. As late as 1753, it was still possible for sympathizers such as Tucker to assume that the bulk of Jewish immigrants would be affluent merchants who, as advocates of Jewish readmission had argued for centuries, would fertilize the local economies through their commercial activities. Writing thirty years after Tucker and in a different social and political setting, Dohm was far more aware of the reality of widespread Jewish poverty, a subject we will return to later. What is important to note here is that while Dohm offered occasional praise of wealthy Jews and Sephardic merchants, the emphasis of his book lay on reforming rather than lauding Jewish economic life. And although his book contained many apologetic and some philosemitic elements, it essentially lay outside of those traditions.

A further difference generating this contrast was the legal situation of Jews in most of continental Europe (excluding the Netherlands) in comparison with that of Britain. Constitutional issues surrounding the Jewish debates in Britain had been directed chiefly at foreign-born Jews. As Tucker had noted with only slight irony, "the Genius of the English Constitution" already ensured that *native-born* Jews would be British subjects and suffer only minor forms of civic or political discrimination.[15] In Germany and France, however, the Jewish populations were proportionally larger, with significant segments (the so-called *Landjudenschaften*) located in rural areas, that is to say, in direct contact with the kind of traditional peasantry that no longer existed in England.[16] This meant that Jews concentrated in both peddling and moneylending provided a source of friction with the local community to a degree not applicable to early modern Britain.[17] Moreover, in Germany and France (and throughout the Continent generally), Jews were subject to an array of severe restrictions on such essential matters as their places of residences, marriages, numbers of offspring, and – crucially in this context – occupations. These limitations imposed tremendous hardships on Jewish populations, reflecting a degree of municipal and guild regulation as well as a state bureaucratic apparatus that had no real equivalent in contemporary Britain.[18] Finally, in Germany, because of its more than three hundred jurisdictional sovereignties (and countless other quasi-sovereignties) prior to the Napoleonic period, the legal position of the native-born Jews was not only harsh, but also intensely convoluted, because it depended on minute details of locality, and even within a given locality might vary significantly between individuals.[19]

In light of Dohm's new take – as well as his keen awareness of the volatility of antisemitism in the countryside – it seems surprising that he should begin his innovative work with the stock theme of populationism drawn from the older vocabulary of pro-Jewish economic literature. The book opens by defining a continuously expanding population as the single most important factor in maximizing the economic well-being of the nation, and then proceeds faithfully to recite many of the same populationist rationales made familiar by writers such as Botero, Child, Petty, Toland, and Tucker. A large population enhances military security, enlarges internal markets, increases domestic production, and, hence, expands international trade. " ... [M]ost important, the industry and general prosperity of the citizens cannot be more effectively enlivened than through the constant enlargement of the population."[20] Although Dohm concedes that some small countries may achieve an optimal level of population, he denies that this point has currently been reached by any of the large or medium-sized states.[21] This is plain from the fact that no state has yet approached anything like a maximal exploitation of its agricultural or industrial capacities.

> None has achieved an improvement [*Verbesserung*] of the soil to the utmost degree possible; none raised all the natural products of the soil that it might – and those that it has, not yet to the highest level of quality and quantity; none has yet processed all of the native and foreign materials it can; none has been able to exploit all its advantages of condition and relation to the extent that it perhaps could.[22]

Dohm, like Tucker, sees population growth as the critical condition for the fullest possible utilization of a nation's material resources; similarly, he defines industry, in the form of productive enterprise, as the function of a perpetually expanding and hence ever more diligent labor force.[23]

Yet what is missing from the passage is also significant. Whereas Tucker had subsumed agriculture and manufacturing under the general category of commerce and implied that productivity was not at all confined to the growing and making of things, here and throughout *On the Civic Improvement of the Jews*, Dohm downplayed the role of exchange as a branch of "industry."

Exploiting a standard feature of contemporary social analysis – distinguished through "the nature of the civil constitution" – Dohm divided contemporary society into three functional and status categories: producers, salaried officials, and nobility. In this schema, merchants fall between the first and the second. Their potential contribution to productive labor is conditioned on the relative degree of independence they are able to attain from monopolistic associations. Dohm did not seek a narrow definition of productive labor. In opposition to the Physiocrats, for instance, he insisted that artisans, and not just agriculturists, are economically productive.[24] Merchants too perform an indispensable function, circulating material commodities as well as specie. Nevertheless, this function is logically dependent upon and consequent to the industry embodied in material production.

It may be true, as his biographer has emphasized, that Dohm gave more emphasis to the circulation of money as an independent stimulant to productive enterprise than either David Hume or Adam Smith, both of whom Dohm professed to admire. But this in itself did not produce as fundamental a difference as she suggests.[25] First, despite their attacks on (and often caricatures of) mercantilist doctrine on money, both Smith and Hume acknowledged that while money is not itself wealth, under certain circumstances its influx and increased circulation could serve as a stimulus to productive activity.[26] Dohm's stated rationale in promoting tolls was to free up specie that he believed would otherwise stagnate in the coffers of chartered merchants, so that it might filter down to industrious small freeholders and independent artisans. "Every hand through which it passes employs it to new production and multiplies its worth."[27] Tolls and duties were justified only to the extent that they function as redistributive mechanisms to pry loose capital and redirect it toward enterprising entrepreneurs instead of state treasuries or privileged monopolies.

Viewed in the context of his populationism, Dohm's position on commerce was thus analogous to the view of Tucker that "Money without Industry, is an Hurt, not a Blessing." Without the productive energy of material combined with manpower money had nowhere to go but into the pockets of feudal oligarchs and monopolistic corporations.[28] As we shall see, Dohm's relative depreciation of merchants stemmed from a number of considerations, not least of all his specific diagnosis of the crisis afflicting the Jews. But like Tucker, Dohm's image of merchants was shaped in part by the way in which guilds and trading companies had historically operated to secure exclusive privileges and maintain rackets. Merchants in traditional European society were monopolizers not liberators, which is why even Adam Smith tended to mistrust them.[29] Without stretching the comparison, Smith's point was that by nature all men are merchants and so should they be in society, but designating merchants as a privileged caste inhibited this goal.

Of course, Dohm's hierarchy has antecedents in German political economy too. The label Cameralism that is often applied to German economic literature of the late seventeenth through the late eighteenth century derives from *Kammer* (*camera*), the state treasury, or more broadly the court, chamber, or ministry. Cameralists were ministerial experts advising the prince on the management of his territories, which they regarded as an extended estate or royal household (*oikos*). Cameralists endeavored to explain how best to conduct public administration so as to maximize and extract state revenues. This was an especially pressing need in the wake of the Thirty Years' War, when Cameralism first emerged. With its vast cost in human life (up to 20 percent of the German population as a whole with a far worse toll in specific regions), the war made repopulation perhaps *the* major economic priority for many of the German states after 1648.[30] This would account for much of the emphasis in Cameralist literature on populationist doctrines. Although most of the losses were of peasant populations, the war also contributed to the stagnation, if not outright decline, of precisely those components of the older medieval economy responsible for artisanal production and trade, the guilds and the free cities, on which a considerable part of the ruler's tax base depended.[31] These centers of earlier urban industry also were damaged by mounting competition from rural industry and the broader shift in European economy favoring the Atlantic coast.[32]

The deterioration of guild power and productivity presented the princes with both an opportunity and a challenge. The decline of the urban estates – along with the simultaneous waning of imperial authority in Germany proper – provided space for the consolidation of princely power. Yet the erosion of competing centers of political and economic authority also ensured they would be on their own when it came to raising the cash necessary for building armies and financing court life. Rulers faced psychological as well as political obstacles to realizing these aims. For instance, although centralization is usually assumed to have been an overwhelming priority during this period, Cameralist authors continued to think in terms of the existing system of estate privilege and to accept the spirit of pervasive localism.[33] The difficulty Cameralists faced was thus to champion the role of the state as the supreme organizing principle binding together the panoply of regional and municipal jurisdictions. With their princes' legitimacy dependent upon maintaining the trappings of the feudal order, Cameralists had to perform a tightrope act by identifying new and as yet untapped sources of wealth without, at the same time, unduly upsetting established economic relationships and privileges.[34]

One means to accomplish this was through the use of state-sanctioned merchants and mercantile enterprises (*Verlage*), designed to develop new markets which, or so it was argued, would not impinge on existing ones.[35] The novel moral aspect of Cameralist literature, in this light, was its legitimation of new kinds of merchants and commercial activity in the face of the ingrained hostility of traditional German society, the estates and the clergy (both Catholic and Protestant), to mercantile innovation. In the social ethic of the guilds and merchant corporations, the unaffiliated merchant was an intruder, a "jackrabbit." Such accusations, with the added incendiary of religious hostility, would be regularly leveled against Jews. They were said to undermine legitimate trade, to deal indiscriminately in a variety goods normally distinguished and separately regulated by guild custom. As one petition condemning their presence put it, they "wander in the villages and in the cities, peddle and force their way on the people,... sell their goods, which are for the most part old and dilapidated, at a cheaper price, and thereby attract and allure the buyer, a man from the countryside, in effect, however, cheating him."[36]

Because they were free of established institutional ties, Jews' pursuit of profits was viewed as unencumbered by traditional codes of restraint, honor and propriety. And although few Cameralist writers championed Jews outright, they often identified at least the *Verlag* merchant as a useful and convenient agent of the common weal. He was likened to an alchemist, one who seeks to generate riches not through artificial or occult means but rather through the *acceleration* of natural and organic processes.[37] Yet just as the alchemist, because of his involvement with highly combustible agents, requires outside supervision, so the merchant needs the guidance of the prince and the state, acting as prophylactics in defense of traditional and established commercial jurisdictions. It was thus the achievement of seventeenth-century Cameralist writers to carve out a limited space of legitimate mercantile innovation, one that at least implicitly included Jews, within such a highly territorialist and deeply conservative corporate polity. The enterprising merchant was linked with the prerogatives of the prince, who in turn was depicted as the chief guardian both of the public welfare encompassing traditional structures (*Wohl*), and the general prosperity extending beyond them (*Wohlstand*) – two terms that appear again and again in Dohm's text.[38]

Dohm's *On the Civic Improvement of the Jews* marked both a continuation of and a departure from these central Cameralist themes. The emphasis he gave to population growth and to state supervision were certainly in the Cameralist tradition.[39] But his relative depreciation of the role of commerce – even in the qualified form of his Cameralist predecessors – indicated a shift in priorities. Most striking, Dohm severed the traditional Cameralist link between populationism and the promotion of Jewish commerce.[40] In his *On the Civic Improvement of the Jews*, after delineating the many virtues of population growth, Dohm proceeded to inquire why Jews had hitherto failed to benefit from them. If governments today universally agree that population is key to economic improvement, he asks, then why have they so rarely included Jewish immigration in their prescriptions?[41] This, too, is unexpected. Elementary familiarity with European Jewish policies for the preceding century or more would indicate that Jews had been invited into to many regions on the basis of their imputed capacity to generate wealth through commerce.[42] Dohm, who had made a special study of medieval and postmedieval state policies on Jews, was as aware as anyone of this. In fact, his devoted service to Frederick the Great, whose treatment of the Jews exclusively as fiscal instruments appeared to belie his enlightened reputation, proved consistently frustrating on this score.[43] The best explanation for his failure to mention it is that in making his case on behalf of the Jews, Dohm deliberately eschewed all arguments acclaiming the special role played by merchant groups.[44] He did so not because he was opposed to commerce per se but because, like the contemporary Cameralist Johann von Justi, albeit for different reasons, he believed that commerce was too important to be left to Jews.

That Dohm adopted a position that was effectively both pro-Jewish but opposed to Jewish commerce reveals just how radically he veered from earlier apologetics. In the writings of a Davanzati or Botero, commerce was what bridged the productive and consumptive activities of the community; it was the axis on which the division of labor turned. Simone Luzzatto had brilliantly insinuated a Jewish component into this formula by locating the Jews' specific economic function at the point of the exchange of commodities produced by other groups, such as manufacturers, artisans, estate-owners, and peasants. Luzzatto accepted these groupings as both given and inevitable. Jewish commerce was a stabilizing and conservative force upholding both Venetian republican traditions and its existing corporatist order. What Luzzatto had sought to do was to weave the Jews back into a prefabricated social tapestry. Although aware that identifying them wholly with trade might give ammunition to the Jews' opponents, he attributed this identification to necessity rather than propensity. Instead of attacking the Jews, Gentile society should recognize that they had made a virtue of necessity, to the collective benefit of all.[45]

But this was exactly the point that Dohm wished to overturn. Yes, the Jews had been compelled by external forces to concentrate in trade, but this had not led to virtue – either for the Jews or the society that hosted them. Writing in the wake of widespread peasant attacks on Jewish merchandizing and moneylending (in the conditions of rural Alsace the two were functionally inseparable), Dohm recognized that strategies such as those employed by Luzzatto, Menasseh ben Israel, and even Toland or Tucker, had failed.[46] As both a historian and Prussian civil servant, he was acutely aware of the long legacy of governmental privileges that had been accorded to Jews on the basis of their commercial and financial identities. Such policies, and the accompanying promotion of the Jews' mercantile contributions, did not diminish popular hostility to them. On the contrary, these had only succeeded in intensifying popular anti-Jewish hostility by reinforcing rather than weakening the basis on which it depended.

This basis of this hostility to the Jews, Dohm suggests, is precisely the economic utility imputed to the Jews, most recently by their apologists but long before by kingdoms and states that for at least a millennium had evaluated them on the basis of economic considerations alone. It did not particularly matter whether such evaluations had been justified on grounds of the Jews' inherent or acquired mercantile characteristics. In the final analysis, any rationale for tolerating them that was rooted in their purported commercial value would be bound to confine and reduce their value as persons and citizens. How, Dohm asked, can we insist that Jews give their obedience and love to a state that assesses them solely on the basis of their financial contributions? And what must be the effect on their persons and reputations of evaluating them in terms of, and thus confining them solely to, the function of trade? Evaluations and policies of this kind, he concluded, had led both to widespread public prejudice against Jews as well as to their own internal degradation, indeed to the wholesale distortion of their personalities, characters, and values.[47]

Whatever one thinks of this claim it is certainly not utilitarian, as some commentators have labeled Dohm's position on the Jews. And however much Dohm may in the process of defending the Jews have appeared to indict them, he also clearly rejected the calculative model on which Cameralist toleration of Jews had formerly depended. Moreover, although Dohm was guided by a paternalist conception of the role of the state, his statism led him to approach the topic of Jewish economy from an educative rather than an exploitative perspective. It is true that the key role he would assign to the state in "ameliorating" the Jews' condition suggests that Dohm's break with Cameralism was less than complete. Yet at the same time his determination to wean them from commerce indicates a fundamental rejection of a tradition that viewed the population – and particularly the Jews – as little more than figures in a ledger.

Yet Dohm's transcendence of Cameralism only partly explains his disparagement of Jewish commerce. What else accounts for his thoroughly negative assessment, particularly from an observer who was ostensibly arguing *on the Jews' behalf.* Even Mendelssohn, as we shall later see, balked at some of the unflattering characterizations his friend had made.[48] Dohm himself insisted emphatically that the blame for the Jews' degradation did not lie with themselves but with the European states that had so cruelly misused them.[49] But that the Jews at present were essentially corrupt and degraded was a fact that Dohm did not question.

Dohm's indictment of Jewish commerce was rooted in several factors. Like Tucker, he viewed economic productivity as a function of population growth that would intensify competition and fuel the spirit of industriousness. As a government official, Dohm had to moderate his criticisms of the corporate order; as an economist trained in the Cameralist tradition, he could not entirely exclude guilds and merchant associations from his *Weltanschauung.* Still, Dohm anticipated their steady if gradual decline. What was anathema was an ethnic division of labor along the lines praised by Luzzatto and instituted in European Jewish policy for centuries. Dohm's conception of human nature also contributed to his critical views on Jewish commerce. He was strongly influenced by the ideas of John Locke, particularly as mediated through such contemporary psychologists as Charles Bonnet, which suggested that men's characters were shaped by their environments and experiences rather than some ingrained and intrinsic character.[50] Dohm explored the psychological and behavioral effects of Jews' persistent exposure to commerce. *On the Civic Improvement of the Jews* presented a lengthy historical portrait of how the political isolation to which Jews had been subjected, their exclusion from civic participation, and their consequent confinement to a stigmatized commerce had shaped their present personalities. His diagnosis led him to offer a set of prescriptions to remedy this crisis of Jewish life.

All of these dimensions will be explored in detail below, but first it is important to recognize that the crisis Dohm diagnosed was one afflicting German and not just Jewish society. Dohm, like so many of the figures discussed in this book, believed that the Jews symbolized the defects (as well as, in some cases, the hopes) of society as a whole. This was a core theme when it came to Enlightenment philosophic and theological conceptions of Judaism, as Adam Sutcliffe's recent study shows.[51] But it was also a central dynamic in the perceived dynamic between Jews and economic life. In his *On the Civic Improvement of the Jews,* Dohm was nothing if not ambitious. Not only did he critique Jewish economy in its totality, but he depicted the Jews' situation as symptomatic of the ills he believed currently afflicted Europe. Jewish economy signaled a condition of profound unfreedom for the entire population. Their *Verbesserung* would thus mark the emergence of a healthier economic life for the entire community, one fully in tune with nature's laws. Dohm sought a basis for resituating the Jews within the larger social and political order, which would have the effect of transforming that order beyond recognition. As we will see, Dohm's vision related to but also transcended the civic republicanism of a Harrington and a Toland, or even the "new system of civil and commercial government" embraced by Tucker. But first, we must consider what had changed in the landscape of Jewish life, apparently undetected for the most part by Toland and Tucker, that prompted Dohm to offer dramatic new vision of Jewish "betterment."

SHYLOCK ECLIPSED – THE EIGHTEENTH-CENTURY DECLINE OF JEWISH ECONOMY

One of the differences between Dohm and advocates of Jewish commerce such as Luzzatto, Menasseh ben Israel, Toland, and Tucker was that the latter had focused their attention primarily on Sephardic rather than Ashkenazic Jews. As noted, Sephardic Jews commonly enjoyed the reputation (indeed, themselves promoted it) of being "all of them merchants" (rather than moneylenders), of possessing, in contrast with their Ashkenazic coreligionists, "purer morals" as well as a greater capacity to absorb the manners and mores of the civilized peoples among whom they lived. In his famous exchange with Voltaire, Isaac de Pinto, the Dutch-Sephardic *Philosophe*, insisted that "A Portuguese Jew of Bordeaux and a German Jew of Metz appear two beings of a different nature!"[52] Yet when not addressing such Gentile eminences as Voltaire but writing instead for internal Jewish consumption, de Pinto wrote despairingly of the mounting poverty within the Sephardic communities themselves, recommending that indigent Sephardim be sent as colonists to Guyana.[53] Although Dohm remained unaware of this mounting poverty in the Sephardic community and, indeed, subscribed to what has been called the "myth of the Sephardi economic superman," he did not believe that western Sephardim provided a realistic or even a desirable occupational model for German Jews to emulate.[54]

The persistence of a "myth" of Sephardi prosperity amidst the reality of a mounting burden of poor relief epitomizes the plight of contemporary Jewish economy as a whole. The historian Jonathan Israel has argued persuasively that the overall economic profile of European Jewry deteriorated substantially in the years following Toland's pamphlet, a contention that is supported by a raft of recent scholarship.[55] According to Israel, the various interlocking Jewish economies of Europe – Portuguese, German, and Polish alike – experienced a sequence of blows that began in the mid-1700s, although their effects would not become fully apparent until the following century.[56] First, the crucial links between New Christian bankers and merchants in Iberia and their Sephardic Jewish cousins in the Atlantic world (principally Amsterdam, London, Hamburg, and the American colonies) were rocked by a series of seventeenth-century disasters, such as the Planters' Rebellion in Brazil (1645–1654), which destroyed both a promising center of Sephardic colonial trade and the source of the contraband sugar trade from Brazil to Amsterdam, the 1647 ousting of the clique of Portuguese *converso* bankers who had formerly dominated royal finances in Madrid, and finally the catastrophic conclusion of the War of the Spanish Succession, which sapped what remained of the vitality of New Christian economy in Spain and fueled a last intense wave of Inquisitorial persecution.[57]

A second development was the contraction of the substantial Sephardic participation in Atlantic colonial trade when, in the wake of three successive naval wars and England's increasingly effective enforcement of the Navigation Act, the Netherlands lost its commercial dominance to Britain, a realm where Jews could play only a relatively minor commercial role.[58] Supplementing this was the late-seventeenth-century decline of trading networks between Italy and the Ottoman Empire, culminating in the loss by 1716 of most Venetian territories in Greece, marking the definite eclipse of a major sixteenth-century engine of Jewish settlement and prosperity in the eastern Mediterranean and Balkans.[59] There occurred, moreover, a decline in industries where Jews had formerly enjoyed strength (usually also tied to the colonial trade), most notably the 1720 demise of the tobacco processing industry in Amsterdam, much of it owned by wealthy Sephardim who often employed German and Polish Jews. Outside of Poland, where the manufacture of alcohol remained a virtual Jewish monopoly, the only important industries in eighteenth-century Europe where Jews maintained a stronghold were book printing, and diamond cutting and coral polishing in centers such as Livorno, Antwerp, Amsterdam, and Hamburg.[60]

Finally, Jewish demography in this period appears thoroughly out of sync with the deterioration of economic opportunity. Although population growth in western and central Europe leveled off by the mid-1700s, this appears more than compensated for by the continued – indeed, intensified – migration of Jews from Poland, where population was only starting a remarkable ascent that would continue unabated until 1900. Such growth generated a vast increase in the number of Jewish poor by the end of the century. That is, although the total population of European Jewry more than doubled (from around 850,000 to just under two million), the relative proportion of the poor and destitute probably increased by well over 100 percent.[61] It has been estimated that, for Germany, 66–75 percent of the Jewish population resided in the lower classes by the end of the century, a rise of about 10 percent from 1750, whereas in Amsterdam, with the largest population of Jews in Western Europe, perhaps 50 percent of Sephardic Jews and 80 percent of Ashkenazim qualified as poor.[62] Amsterdam Jewry's efforts at poor relief crippled the community's institutions by the end of the century, with expenses tripling between 1650 and 1793.[63]

It is also possible to assume that while economic decline was not uniform in all regions of Jewish settlement, each region was in some degree affected by it. Similarly, although not every stratum of the Jewish population suffered in the same manner, all classes and strata of the Jewish community felt the ill effects. In part, this was because the structure of both the Jewish communities and the Jewish economies was highly integrated, so that the deterioration of a single industry – such as tobacco processing in Amsterdam after 1720 – would exert a ripple effect extending far beyond those immediately displaced. Court Jews employed the services of a network of lesser financiers, brokers, and even rural peddlers to help with their provisioning; the decline of the court Jew enervated the entire system.[64] Similarly, any increase in the number of poor within a given community, either because of migration or internal economic crisis, would have an impact on almost the entire community. This was because the requirement that almost all Jews be affiliated with the local Jewish communal institutions – mandated both by the external authorities and internal religious, social, and cultural obligations – meant that the entire community was responsible for taxes and fines on individuals as well as for the maintenance of social services, including poor relief.[65] Isaac de Pinto denounced the "tyrannical" tax burden imposed on Amsterdam's upper stratum by the demands of poor relief. This fed into a vicious cycle, with the well-off seeking to opt out of communal responsibilities, whereas the poor but able-bodied young men were forced to seek opportunity outside of established communities. Amsterdam may have lost much of its future productive citizenry through emigration of this kind.[66]

Shifts in European economy and state economic policy were behind much of this dislocation. As noted, the deterioration of locales where Jews had been prominent – the Balkans and Venice after 1650, Northern Italy (with the exception of Livorno) following the wars and floods of the late seventeenth century, Ottoman Turkey after 1683, Iberia after 1711, and Amsterdam as a manufacturing and export if not as a financial center after 1720 – and the concomitant rise of new centers, principally London and Paris, where Jews failed to establish a stronghold, was certainly a key factor.[67] Jews were increasingly ill-placed to benefit from the economic changing of the guard. Additionally, Jews suffered from the shift in emphasis in Western European economy toward the processing of raw materials and the production of manufactured goods principally for the domestic rather than the overseas markets. This complex development meant greater competition for domestic manufacturing jobs in which the guilds, reacting against governmental efforts to pry open the artisanal economy, pressured for the further exclusion of Jews and other outsiders from craft production (a policy pursued in Prussia, for instance, by Frederick William I).[68] This in turn entailed a still greater concentration of Jews in petty trading occupations at a time when their numbers in this area were already excessive. There is also evidence of expanding restrictions on foreign imports, curtailing the Jews' activity in international trade and, in the case of Holland, further exacerbating the plight of domestic export trades.[69]

Finally, political and state institutional transformations played a role in diminishing the importance of Jewish finance. Israel has argued, for instance, that the relative peace reigning among the major European powers between the Treaty of Utrecht in 1713 and the wars of the French Revolution precipitated the decline of the European court Jew, whose very raison d'être had been to finance and supply princely armies.[70] Although Berlin's Jewish financial elite reaped great benefits from their services to Frederick the Great during the Seven Years' War, the generalization still holds.[71] But it is also worth stressing that state finances as a whole underwent a transformation in the eighteenth century, particularly in Britain and Prussia but also (with remarkable experimentation if less success) in France. French administrators hired by Frederick the Great introduced the "Régie" system into his lands, which replaced contractors and tax farmers with state officials, effectively revolutionizing Prussia's state finances.[72] These processes rendered court Jews increasingly obsolete by mid-century. And this in turn suggests a kind of decapitation of the Jewish economy, with the groups best placed economically and politically to attain privileges for the rest either losing their power or seeking external outlets for investment. This latter point, involving a reallocation of resources away from the Jewish populations, may in turn have contributed to the court Jews' gradual cultural disengagement from the traditional community.[73]

It is true that almost every one of these points can be challenged. Records on population and poor relief are less than reliable prior to the early nineteenth century; hence we are often forced to rely on exaggerated figures and impressionistic reports.[74] There is also evidence of countervailing trends, including Jewish economic expansion at this time: in the flourishing port towns of Livorno and Trieste, in German textile manufacturing, or in the importation of novelty items such as coffee and chocolate, as well as in a wide range Polish handicrafts, trade, and transport.[75] Poland, in fact, may be a case in which overall economic decline served the immediate if not long-term interests of

Jews who were now often able to take over sectors of the local economy formerly protected by Christian guilds.[76]

It is, indeed, possible that the degree and extent of overall decline has been exaggerated, not so much through an overestimation of the crisis afflicting many Jewish communities at this time, as by an excessively favorable assessment of earlier conditions. Those contemporaries who reported so enthusiastically on the contributions of sixteenth- and seventeenth-century Jews were not overly zealous in calling attention to the plight of the poor in their own day. Simone Luzzatto spoke almost exclusively of Sephardic Jewish merchants, although petty moneylenders, pawnbrokers, and impoverished peddlers were more typical of Italian Jewry as a whole.[77] John Toland believed that the amassed wealth of the Jews was as great or greater than that of Britain; Josiah Tucker assumed that most Jewish immigrants to England would be either well off or else highly industrious members of the middling classes. It was in the nature of the apologetics and state mercantile policies of the time to paint as favorable a picture as possible of Jewish economic vitality.[78] The image of a "Golden Age" in early modern Europe of Jewish commercial ascendancy cannot disguise the reality of pervasive Jewish poverty throughout this entire period.[79]

Throughout the period in which Jews were restored to parts of western and central Europe (roughly 1550–1710), principally on the basis of their assumed economic benefits, demands were voiced for Jews to abandon their trafficking and usurious ways and take up "useful and honest," that is, manual, trades. The earliest demands (although never enforced) for Jewish occupational restructuring go back the medieval reigns of Edward I and Louis IX.[80] Centuries later, in his 1543 "On the Jews and their Lies," Martin Luther proposed "putting a flail, an ax, a hoe, a spade, a distaff, or a spindle into the hands of young, strong Jews and Jewesses and letting them earn their bread in the sweat of the brow...," a demand subsequently echoed on countless occasions by guilds fearful of Jewish commercial competition.[81] In the mid-seventeenth century, a time when the French minister Colbert, the Prussian Great Elector, Frederick William, and Simone Luzzatto and Menasseh ben Israel were proclaiming the unparalleled commercial utility of the Jews, other voices proposed removing them from commerce and making them artisans and farmers.[82] We have already seen that Harrington and Toland wanted to employ Jews as agricultural colonists in Ireland. For different reasons, German guilds in this same period demanded as the price of their tolerance that "these idle people take up agriculture like Christians and with plow in hand sweat out the slothfulness from their limbs."[83] Similar sentiments, although obviously with a more benevolent intent, were in fact voiced within the Jewish community itself. In 1642, at the very apex of its economic fortunes in Amsterdam, the Sephardic community there established the charitable Avodat Hesed Society to habituate refugees from Eastern Europe to manual trades.[84] As an alternate strategy – although in this case directed at the Sephardi poor – the Amsterdam *Mahamad* evolved numerous schemes to remove able-bodied poor to agricultural colonies in Guyana and Suriname.[85]

Still, if the picture of the earlier period was not as bright as it has sometimes appeared, there can be little doubt that it became progressively bleaker in the eighteenth century. Even the negative attitudes toward Jews underwent a demotion, so to speak.[86] As in the related case of Jewish impoverishment, Jewish criminality was a serious problem well before it achieved a high level of public saliency in the mid-eighteenth century. Toland's *Reasons for Naturalizing the Jews* provides hints of a rising perception of growing criminality within the immigrant Jewish community. Toland, while admitting that there were, "to be sure, sordid wretches, sharpers, extortioners, villains of all sorts," among the Jews, defused the accusation with what would soon become a classic liberal retort "not to impute the faults of a few to the whole number."[87] In fact, Toland lifted the latter statement almost verbatim from Simone Luzzatto's *Discorso*, a work occasioned by a threatened expulsion of Venetian Jews purportedly because of a recent scandal involving Jewish smugglers, fences, and violent criminals in the Ghetto.[88] The phenomenon of *Betteljuden* (begger Jews and Jewish vagrants) can be traced back as early as the fifteenth century, a period of widespread expulsions from German cities and towns whose consequent dislocations appear to have created continuous waves of uprooted Jews.[89] Most *Betteljuden* were not participants in criminal gangs, of course; in fact, although frequently the subject of hostile, even draconian legislation, in a number of cases in early modern Germany they were treated by the authorities with a surprising degree of tolerance.[90] But historians believe that it is from their ranks that the first significant criminal associations were formed in central Europe, sometime in the late sixteenth century. In retrospect, it seems that Jewish prominence in criminal activity was overdetermined: Jews' mobility and poverty, their institutionalized concentration in commercial spheres that lay outside the regulated economy of Christian guilds, their involvement with moneylending, minting, pawnbrokerage, and peddling, their activity as military suppliers who had to place a premium on the ready acquisition of all manner of goods, as well as their contacts with segments of the population that were also often drawn into criminality, such as soldiers, and not least of all, their extreme insecurity, all surely contributed to the phenomenon. At the same time, established Jewish communities were highly vulnerable to the charges made against them by Jewish and non-Jewish informers (often the purchasers of stolen goods), as well as by Christian guilds seeking their expulsion or restriction and so had a cardinal interest in attempting to police their coreligionists.[91]

The image of Jews as burglars and thieves took time to penetrate the consciousnesses of Christians. In England during the Jew Bill campaign of 1753, the *Gentlemen's Magazine* and other Tory journals were already reporting on the activities of Jewish criminal groups. By the 1770s, this was becoming a stock representation of Jewish immigrant society in Britain.[92] In Germany and Holland, news reports began to surface earlier, in the wake of the mid-seventeenth-century upheavals, of bands of destitute Jews, among them beggars, thieves, con men, fences, and other sordid types loosely associated with the *Betteljuden*.[93] The Sephardic community of Amsterdam apparently shared some of the same presumptions about the criminal predilections of immigrants from Germany and Poland as the police superintendents of Berlin.[94] Yet for non-Jews, the picture they presented was very different from that of earlier, medieval images of Jewish criminality. The latter had usually revolved around wealthy Jewish usurers, coin-clippers, and exploiters of Christians and of the poor, often possessing occult, even demonic attributes.[95] Although this image would persist into the modern period, it would now be supplemented by another that was in certain respects more relevant – that of a Jewish criminal underworld, of thieves disguised as ragmen, gangs of burglars, urchins, pickpockets, prostitutes, and the like. The German reading public developed a fascination with the figure of the Jewish *Gauner* (crook) and robber band mastermind. In this light, Gotthold Ephraim Lessing's 1749 play, "The Jews," provided a fitting eighteenth-century counterpoint to Shakespeare's "The Merchant of Venice." For the play to achieve its ironic effect the audience must assume that "as many as there are of [the Jews], without exception, are swindlers, thieves, and highwaymen . . ." Thus, the eighteenth-century reader would be apparently shocked to discover that the virtuous traveler who rescues a German aristocrat from a gang of murderous thieves is in fact himself a Jew.[96]

Unlike Lessing, Dohm was not interested in deflating the stereotype. This is because he largely accepted it. Yet his collective portrait of the Jews as disfigured by commerce, however prejudicial, was not born of mere fantasy. Rather, it was the result of an effort to confront the underlying causes of a major social problem. As far as Dohm was concerned, the source of Jewish degradation did not lie in poverty per se, not in some recent deterioration of the Jewish economy, such as we have described earlier. Rather, their confinement to mercantile livelihoods of all kinds, large and small, had long ago laid a foundation that, unless removed, would ensure their permanent unhappiness. Whatever the impact recent developments may have had on Dohm's perception of Jews, he himself remained convinced that the sources of the problem were far older and deeper.

THE ALTERATION OF THEIR ORIGINAL SPIRIT

This problem Dohm summarized as "the [Jewish] nation's overwhelming attraction to every kind of profit, its love of usury, and of deceitful gain."[97] This "attraction" [*Neigung*] was the product of the Jews' persistent and exclusive association with a set of activities that over the course of many centuries had impressed their nature fully on their personalities. Dohm's approach to psychology owed its basic outline to Locke's educational theories in which experience shapes consciousness. The Swiss pathologist Charles Bonnet, one of the founders of "sensationalism," had adapted Locke through his insistence that the body itself would become internally altered as a consequence of physical repetition. Similar ideas were applied to pedagogy by the educational reformer Johann Bernhard Basedow, founder in 1774 of the experimental Philanthropin school in Dessau. In Basedow's pedagogical theory, the roles of subject and object were reversed, with the child not merely the passive recipient of external impressions but an actor in the shaping of his own character, principally by means of imitation. Thus, exposure was decisive not just in providing proper models but in inspiring his desire to emulate them. The greatest attentiveness must be paid to the pupil's environment since it would inevitably become the material of his soul.[98] Dohm, who came to admire the work of both Bonnet and Basedow as a student in Göttingen, was interested in applying their insights to the world of work.[99] In his *On the Civic Improvement of the Jews*, the Jews offered Dohm ideal material for sounding out these theories.

Work was the subject of moral and psychological analysis among some eighteenth-century economists. Adam Smith famously worried about the mental debilitation induced by the repetition of minute tasks, rendering the laborer "as stupid and ignorant as it is possible for a human creature to become." Smith assumed this to be an inevitable consequence of the subdivision of labor but one whose dire effects on civic life must be counteracted by a least a modicum of publicly funded education.[100] At a more abstract level, Josiah Tucker depicted work as the principal mode of striving rationally over the long term to gratify an in-born drive of self-love. Because it necessitated a sublimation as well as a fulfillment of that drive, it had unintended but beneficial effects for society as a whole. Work was a form of the disciplined pursuit of wants that inculcated patience as well as an appreciation for the achievements of one's betters.[101] Dohm's view was not unrelated; yet it was far more concretely tied to grasping the specific effects, not of work as such but of particular kinds of work, whose qualities and characteristics as modes of activity imparted something of their natures to those regularly engaged by them.[102] Tucker did not directly face the possibility that if work was a means toward an end that also affected its psychological results through process, it might be the case that a particular type of employment could involve a process that in itself counteracted the desirable aims of "industry." Dohm, in contrast, was directly concerned with the moral and psychological implications of various forms of labor. He did not therefore accuse Jews of laziness, idleness, drunkenness, or any of the other vices of the poor regularly denounced by British political economists.[103] On the contrary, the effects of the Jews' enforced preoccupation with commerce and moneylending had been to render them constantly alert and zealous, even diligent in the pursuit of their "overwhelming attraction."

In *On the Civic Improvement of the Jews* Dohm presented a typology of the different professions and their psychological effects. "Every type of occupation and trade has its characteristic effects on the mode of thinking and moral character."[104] Although these effects may vary in individual cases, subject to modification on the basis of temperament, education, and environment, generalizations will be found to hold for occupational categories as a whole. These Dohm divides into two principal sets: first, occupations characterized by a regularity of activity and reward, and, second, those that are erratic in both practice and result, where fortune plays a key role and where earnings vary from day to day. In the first category, Dohm singled out the crafts [*Handwerk*] as the kind of activity most conducive to calm, consistent endeavor, possessing a rhythm attuned to the shifting phases of the day, consequently inducing a healthy, placid, unreflective enjoyment of life.[105] In the second, Dohm classed both manufacturers [*Fabrikanten*] and merchants [*Kaufleuten*]. Both must depend on the vagaries of the market, hence on good fortune [*Glück*], yet neither can afford to. They must possess intelligence to limit as much as possible the effects of chance, as well as courage to take the kinds of risks that make chance remunerative. This in turn requires calculation and foresight. Hence these men are always living for the future, never – like the craftsman – in the present. Their spiritual mood tends naturally toward anxiety, but this, too, must be disguised, since competition amongst themselves requires dissimulation. In fact, there is a tendency to look at others instrumentally, as objects, obstacles, or opportunities.[106]

This objectification of others, inseparably attached to the activity of profit-seeking, entails yet another set of consequences: the merchant and the manufacturer (both, in effect, salesmen) also must face a powerful temptation to overstep the strict bounds of the law. Their survival, one might say, depends on the adoption of a mercenary outlook that cannot afford to forego any and all possible advantages. Because the craftsman depends on buying and selling the goods that he himself creates, his reputation for honesty must inhere in the products of his labor.[107] The manufacturer and merchant, however, sell goods produced by others, and this implies that trickery toward both employees and customers is possible and even necessary.[108]

These tendencies vary, however, in relation to the size of the business and the amount of profit it can rake in. The small merchant, lacking the means or hope of attaining real security, will train his senses to detect any marginal opportunity for gain. He quickly acquires the habits of stinginess and petty-mindedness [*einem Kleinigkeiten-Geist*], a grasping manner and a narrow perspective.[109] The large or substantial merchant, by contrast, develops almost the opposite qualities. In perpetual pursuit of the windfall, the big deal, he must spend lavishly to impress his customers. He will employ vulgar display as a device for elevating his social standing and gaining access to old money. He will therefore assume the cloak of the aristocrat, although he lacks the education, taste, and refinement of the truly noble. Indeed, he will be readily seduced by his own extravagance, seeing it as an end rather than a means and acquiring a wastrel addiction to base pleasures and luxury consumption. (He is thus hardly an exemplar of Max Weber's Protestant ethic.)[110]

However badly the practice of commerce has disfigured these men, its effects on their Jewish counterparts have been far worse, claims Dohm. This is because, although the Christian has rarely been exclusively a merchant, the Jew has rarely been anything else. The Christian merchant descends from a family in which a diversity of professions has likely been practiced, with one sibling going into the ministry, another into the military or civil service, and so forth. The Jewish youth, on the other hand, sees nothing around him but haggling and negotiation, because this is all that Jews have been permitted; he quickly comes to realize that trade will provide him with his only means of livelihood. His entire worldly education is therefore oriented to absorbing and mastering its methods. If he possesses less general knowledge than the non-Jew, he also enjoys less exposure to other sensations, including the "feeling of honor" [*Gefuhl von Ehre*]. Although Gentile society only recently and halfheartedly began to follow the ways of commerce, the Jews have been traversing its paths for well over a millennium. Therefore, "the petty arts of gaining advantage must be better known to them" than to others.[111]

Dohm insists again and again that this defective existence did not stem from some original depravity of the Jewish soul. His occupational typology was designed to show precisely how experience, especially the experience of work, molds personality. It is important to grasp just how deeply the experiential aspect of his diagnosis went. Men, asserts Dohm, are influenced not just by their present circumstances and occupations but also by their histories. The concentrated experience of a thousand years of merchandising, according to Dohm, compounded immeasurably the occupational hazards of the Jew's commercial existence. Like work, history constitutes a mass of accumulated experiences that helps to shape character, outlook, institutions, and mores. To substantiate this claim, Dohm embarked on an extended discussion in *On the Civic Improvement of the Jews* of the legal, and especially the economic, aspects of Jewish history. The purpose of this excursion was not just to elucidate the baneful effects of the Jews' long-term occupational confinement but to highlight its causes as well.

As we have seen on several occasions the discourse on Jewish commerce is replete with historical excursuses. Pocock's studies amply demonstrate that historical narrative was integral to contemporary debates over the proper place of commerce; because the advent of commercial society was commonly viewed as a recent one, its progress and effects had to be assessed genealogically. What then might be termed Jewish "historical economy" was equally central to discussions over the Jews' proper place. Because Jews were indubitably a commercial people, the nature of their economic life was an essential factor in their relationship to the rest of European society. It helped, of course, that the Bible amply attested to the Hebrews' agricultural and pastoral orientation, or that a well-known ancient historian such as Josephus had insisted in his *Contra Apionem* that "we [Jews] neither inhabit a maritime country, nor do we delight in merchandise." If this was the case, then how had Jews so utterly altered the character of their material life? In the eyes of Christians, did their descent from natural to artificial economy mirror their spiritual fall through their rejection of Christ? If so, might their future material regeneration or *Verbesserung* prepare the ground for a civic and spiritual redemption as well?

If such historiosophic questions in any way inspired Dohm's historical account of Jewish decline, they were amply disguised by both his religious latitudinarianism and his hard-nosed scholarship. As in so many other areas, Dohm's use of Jewish history set him apart from his predecessors. He was, for one thing, far better informed about it than most of those we have discussed. For instance, whereas Toland had relied on Luzzatto as well as various English antiquarian studies (e.g., Coke's *Institutes* and Prynne's *Demurrer*), and whereas Tucker had depended primarily on D'Blossiers Tovey's *Anglia Judaica*, Dohm proved himself familiar with a far wider range of both primary and secondary source materials. A glance at his citations indicates that he had scanned Basnage's *Histoire des Juifs,* Ulrich's *Sammlung jüdischer Geschichten,* Büsching's *Geschichte der jüdischen Religion;* and Shudt's *Jüdische Merckwürdigkeiten,* among numerous others. He had examined medieval Jewish privileges and charters in German, Latin, French, and English; and he had combed through voluminous legal compendia such as the *Schwabenspiegel* for materials relating to the Jews.[112] By the standards of his day, Dohm had undertaken a thorough program of research into the relevant legal and economic material. That he had hoped to do even more is evident from the preface he wrote to *On the Civic Improvement of the Jews:*

> The author of this work made a plan many years ago to study the history of the Jewish nation since the destruction of its own state [encompassing]: the moral and political relations in which the Jews of different times and places found themselves; the mutual influences of the nations amongst whom they lived, the consequences of the different persecutions, the direction of [the nation's] character as a result of its previous occupations; and the influence which it has exerted in matters of industry, trade, and morals.[113]

From this passage, it is apparent that Dohm's particular interest lay in dissecting the relationship between "matters of industry, trade, and morals"; that he also would seek to understand the role that persecutions had played in conditioning that relationship; and that he would attempt to explain, by reference to a series of developments occurring in the interval between the destruction of Jewish state and his own times, how the diaspora history of the Jewish nation had effected an "alteration of its original spirit" [*die Abänderung ihres ursprünglichen Geistes*].

We have seen that Dohm was not the first to insist that the Jews "had once been farmers in their own land."[114] Menasseh ben Israel and especially John Toland also had emphasized this fact. Toland wished to show that the Jews' occupational profile was not fixed in stone, that a precedent existed for their future restoration to agriculture and soldiery. Dohm shared with Toland a naturalistic belief that government and education "are the true Springs and Causes" of men's different group characteristics.[115] For Toland – borrowing directly from Simone Luzzatto – the Jews had long ago lost their common traits and: " . . . since their dispersion, they have no common or peculiar Inclinations distinguishing 'em from others; but visibly partake of the Nature of those Nations among which they live, and where they were bred."[116] For Dohm, however, this was too easy a solution, and the relatively higher degree of complexity he exhibited toward his subject matter derived from his awareness that history was not just a record of precedents but also a burden of experience.

The main burden of Dohm's historical account was to show that medieval religion and law had conspired in the degradation of the Jewish spirit. What is fascinating about this narrative is that while underscoring the shift from being agriculturalists in their land to merchants in their exile, Dohm was insistent that Diaspora was not itself the cause of this transformation. On the contrary, they had continued to practice agriculture and even to serve honorably in civic offices under the Empire for several centuries after the destruction of their state. Nor, Dohm insisted, was Diaspora incompatible with the acquisition of urban citizenship on the ancient model.[117] For a period of over four hundred years, then, until the Emperor Honorius in 418 initiated the process of their debarment from civic and military offices, the Jews had proven themselves good and worthy members of civil society.[118] Would that the influence of fanatical churchmen had never been permitted to disturb these "wise principles of the Roman government." The Jews would certainly be more enlightened and less corrupt had the old Roman laws been allowed to stand.[119]

The impact of church fanaticism on civic administration had an additional implication for the condition of the Jews. Not only were they now excluded from most forms of public service, but the purview of self-government formerly permitted them was, according to Dohm, radically diminished. This combination of factors seemed to Dohm a foreshadowing of the process of severe occupational contraction that Jews would later experience in the Middle Ages. Although they were not yet confined to one or two professions, they were on the way to being deprived of any real participation in recognizable civic and political functions. What initially seems like a contradictory set of tendencies – the Jews' removal from Roman offices and their loss of internal civic jurisdiction, on the one hand, leading to a more total subjugation to Roman institutions, on the other – actually represented for Dohm part of a single, unified process of depriving the Jewish personality of its civic and political dimensions.[120] In light of the old Aristotelian concept of human nature, this was a devastating blow.

Yet if the earlier centuries of enlightened Roman government constituted Dohm's model for what a future Prussian state might become, as Jonathan Hess has insightfully argued, religious fanaticism was hardly the sole threat. The immediate cause of the Jews' *economic* degradation was not church fanaticism, or even the later implementation of its policies on usury. For all the virtues of Hess's analysis, he is committed to a reading of Dohm as an advocate of Prussian autarchy, a claim that is irreconcilable with Dohm's broad economic and philosophic outlook. Indeed, in the historical section of *On the Civic Improvement of the Jews*, Dohm aimed his sharpest rhetorical at the myth of

Germany's tribal "natural economy." What had sealed the fate of the Jews was not Christianity's erosion of Roman religious toleration but the barbarians' replacement of its cosmopolitan and mercantile culture with feudalism.[121]

In German historical discourse, discussion of the *Volkswanderung* played a roughly parallel role to that of the "Gothic" constitution in Britain or the Frankish conquest in France. Since the late Renaissance, legal historians in Europe had been preoccupied with unraveling the impact that German tribal institutions had exerted on earlier Roman law.[122] Tacitus' *Germania* proved a central text for such scholarship.[123] For Tacitus and his later admirers the Germans embodied the primitive martial, political, and domestic virtues that had fallen away from contemporary Roman usage or become lost to modern, civilized Europeans. Such arguments, already in vogue in his day, Dohm altogether rejected. He viewed the tribes as barbarians addicted to cruelty and xenophobia, in whose hands both the wise old Roman laws and the conquering new Christian faith could only become instruments of savagery. In the barbarians' eyes, what so compromised the standing of the Jews, aside from the religious difference, was the fact that they were no longer warriors; for, according to Dohm, the Germans "knew no other virtue than the martial."[124] That the Jews were no longer warriors represented a further legacy of their civic disfranchisement under the late Empire, but its impact only became fully apparent once the Empire had been overrun. The effect of the *Volkswanderung* was to exclude the Jews culturally as well as institutionally from the life of the majority. They could enjoy no standing within a Gothic society that valued only martial virtues.[125]

So far this account seems not dissimilar to Josiah Tucker's depiction of the primitive Gothic polity. As we recall, Tucker had divided Gothic society into warrior and servile orders, classing the armed burgesses with the former, whereas the Jews remained outside the constitutional arrangement altogether. With nowhere else to go, they were forced to seek the direct protection of the Crown. Dohm would offer a roughly similar scenario but with one important addition. In Tucker's Gothic polity, the monopolistic protections of the urban burgesses had had the effect of keeping trade underdeveloped, yet vestiges of commerce persisted. This seems to have been a consequence of the self-interested ethos of the English medieval corporations that sought to monopolize trade but not to destroy it.[126] To Dohm, however, the Germanic nobility was far too primitive to organize any system of trade whatsoever, even a monopolistic one. Its utter fascination with the warrior ethic, whereby land was valued exclusively as the reward for military service, precluded even the rudimentary beginnings of a commercial system of agriculture, such as Tucker had allowed for medieval Britain. This circumstance both reflected and reinforced the ingrained cultural hostility of a caste that "knew no virtue other than the martial" against all forms commerce and against the kinds of landless, unarmed men who engaged in it. For this reason, says Dohm, the burgher classes remained undeveloped in early medieval Europe, and there was no one to fill the void but the Jews.[127]

Dohm has been accused of lacking originality when compared with earlier historians of the Jews such as Basnage, but nothing could be further from the truth. Dohm's historical excursus contained the seeds of an approach that would later animate both German and Jewish treatments of Jewish economic history.[128] According to Dohm, the Germanic invasions (*Volkswanderung*), having destroyed the old Roman trading networks, created for a period of several centuries a commercial vacuum that only the Jews could fill. It had been a widespread assumption in the earlier apologetic literature that the Jews were pushed into trade because they had been pushed out of all other livelihoods. This was an argument that Dohm too partly adopted, as we have seen. Yet although placing responsibility for the Jews' plight firmly on the backs of the gentile authorities, Dohm also pointed to a number of additional factors that stemmed directly from the cultural character of the Jews themselves. Luzzatto, Menasseh ben Israel, and Toland had already identified the Jews' geographic dispersion and linguistic uniformity as qualities that made them particularly well suited to undertaking commercial roles.[129] What made Dohm's account appreciably more complex, however, was his belief that these characteristics would not in themselves have led inevitably to a Jewish mercantile concentration. Rather, it was the Jews' presence at a specific juncture in European development that rendered these intrinsic "Jewish" qualities into causal factors leading to the Jews' full-scale adoption of trade. This historical juncture, according to Dohm, was the moment in time when the Jews enjoyed a higher cultural standing than that of the warlike German conquerors.

Jews alone could fill the vacuum created by the underdevelopment of the native Germanic *Mittelstände* because, in addition to their demographic and linguistic advantages, among the former inhabitants of Greco-Roman civilization only they retained the technical skills required for organizing a vast international network of trade. This is not a point on which Dohm much elaborates, but it is critical to his historical and rhetorical arguments. The disjunction between a primitive Germanic population and a civilized, technically proficient Jewish element created a tension and resultant force that propelled the Jews into a specified position within the social totality, a position that once locked into they could never escape from. In short, the Jews became drawn into commerce because "very probably, there was once a time when the greatest amount of European Enlightenment [*die gröste europäische Aufklärung*] was to be found amongst the circumcised":

> The Jews brought with them from the Roman Empire more knowledge and culture than the ruling nations of the first period of the new states possessed. They were not deranged by primitive moral codes and feuds, nor stultified by scholastic monkish philosophy and superstitions.[130]

Here Dohm was not suggesting that the Jews carried with them into the early Middle Ages commercial skills honed earlier in the period of Antiquity (an argument that others would later develop). On the contrary, he was asserting that although the Jews had not always been a mercantile people, they had once constituted a highly enlightened one, far superior to the ancestors of today's "ruling nations." The Jews' future improvement would be conditioned, therefore, on the restoration of capacities whose former existence and vitality were apparent from a common history. But history was itself relative. By positing a cultural discrepancy between Germans and Jews at an earlier period in time, Dohm was both exposing the latter's corruption as a product of an earlier historical disjunction and at the same time revealing how their future redemption might progress now that the tables had been turned and the "ruling nations" were in ascendance.[131]

Dohm's account was rhetorically oriented toward exposing the historical ironies of European transformation rather than constructively toward the elucidation of developmental laws. For Dohm history was ironic because it revealed the medieval Jewish experience to be an enormous mistake, one that resulted initially from the paradoxical fact of the Jews' own enlightenment. Obviously, such a mistake could only occur – and persist – in a host society whose prevalent ideals and dominant institutions remained backward, even if its technical capacities had in subsequent centuries advanced considerably. Once the mistake had been made and the Jews were ensconced entirely in mercantile life, a downward spiral ensued – and this despite the technical development of European society in the following period. Their increasingly one-sided involvement with commerce now began to exert its limiting effects on the Jews' own moral and cultural outlook, thus reinforcing their isolation and estrangement from the larger society. Degeneration from within was continuously reinforced by self-seeking and shortsighted policies from without. The most diverse elements – if from conflicting and contradictory motives – seemed now to conspire in tightening the yoke. Kings and princes, grasping that their need for capital could be satisfied by maintaining a mercantile group in abject dependency, worked to further degrade the civic status of the Jews to the point where their very toleration became exclusively a function of their imputed financial utility at any given moment. The corporate orders (*Stände*), fearing the Jews' competition and suspicious of their usefulness to the Crown, lobbied conjointly to exclude them further from a broadening range of occupations and confine them to usury instead. Finally, the Church, in keeping with its misguided outlook on a range of social and economic issues, vilified and proscribed moneylending activities to the point that their pursuit became the monopoly of a single pariah group.[132]

This last point, viz., that traditional medieval attitudes to usury were misguided, suggests that contrary to the tendency of much of our earlier discussion, Dohm did not negate the general value of commercial or banking occupations but rather only the wisdom of confining the Jews to them. In turning now from Dohm's historical account to his policy prescriptions on contemporary Jewry, we should keep this distinction in mind. From Dohm's occupational typology, we know that prolonged habituation to the ways of commerce – as amply demonstrated in the historical experience of the Jews – was bound to lead to moral corruption. Yet, at the same time, Dohm echoed Tucker in demanding a liberalization of state commercial and financial policies, suggesting that commerce must be expanded while the role of the state in managing it be made to contract.[133] We recall that Tucker, too, had denounced medieval theology for its failure to grasp the authentic nature of credit and interest (even accusing the Church of grossly misinterpreting Scripture). Dohm was prepared to go still further: the modern state itself had yet to institute policies that afforded sufficient freedom to the movement of capital or adequate security to the acquisition of property. With reference specifically to the nature of credit, Dohm concluded that "[n]o European state has yet comprehended the true and natural concepts involved in this business" – not even the advanced commercial governments of England or Holland.[134]

ANCIENTS AND MODERNS: MENDELSSOHN VERSUS DOHM

What in retrospect appears as Dohm's economic modernism emerges particularly in his insistence that the greatest possible freedom be granted to contracting parties who alone possess the requisite information to determine which interest or profit rates are necessitated by given sets of circumstances.[135] Whereas for Tucker, freedom was valued chiefly for the impetus it gave to individual industry, Dohm (like Adam Smith) valued it principally as an epistemological precondition for society's economic advancement. As Smith put it, "What is the species of domestic industry which his capital can employ, and of which the produce is likely to be of the greatest value, every individual, it is evident, can, in his local situation, judge much better than any statesman or lawgiver can do for him."[136] No government, corporation, or similar institution legislating from above – not even "a monopoly of angels with perfect knowledge," in the words of the French economist Turgot – could possibly collect and assess all of the vital information that individual contracting parties hold as a matter of course at their fingertips.[137] This in itself was a startling concession from the pen of a Professor of *Statistik*. It amounted to a repudiation of the whole premise of Cameralist government, namely, that the prince or state alone possessed the requisite knowledge and vantage point to keep its own economic house in order. Democracy, while potentially dangerous in the political arena, is absolutely essential in the realm of commercial decision making; for markets depend on free choice, and choice is at bottom a function of knowledge.

This same knowledge-based argument, it is worth mentioning, went hand in hand with a legal and ethical claim: enlightened policy, as Dohm put it, must never make laws that would inevitably have to be broken. To say this was implicitly to recognize an authority that stood above human government – not natural law in the medieval Scholastic sense, but, rather, what Dohm referred to as "the natural relations of things" [*die natürlichen Verhältnisse der Dinge*]. The natural relation of things is the timeless manner in which business gets conducted. It is the foundation of human government and law in the commercial or economic sphere.[138] An enlightened government will therefore structure its laws so as to enhance the conditions for the realization of the "greatest possible freedom" [*die großmöglichste Freiheit*] in matters of individual commercial decision making. For this reason, Dohm (here taking a somewhat more liberal position than Smith) suggested that if governments insist on establishing maximum interest rates, they should at least set them well above the natural price of money – that is to say, the going market rate.[139]

Where, however, government can prove more valuable still is in the institution of positive laws to protect contracting parties against those "harmful abuses" [*schädlichen Misbräuchen*] – principally, cheating and fraud – that threaten to undermine the natural order itself.[140] This point returns us directly to Dohm's analysis of contemporary Jewry and even serves to unite many of the disparate elements in his discussion. The harmful abuses that inhibit the natural order and necessitate government intervention are exactly the kinds of economic crimes often associated with the mercantile practices of the Jews. Dohm's warnings against the promulgation of laws that cannot be enforced underscore the paradox of the Jews' status within contemporary European life. The effect of hypocritical legislation that confines Jews to usury while condemning the activity itself has been to implicate both Jewish and gentile society in the web of restrictions that inhibits progress for the community at

large. In this way, the question of usury encapsulates in microcosm the entire
medieval legacy of Jewish corruption. The corruption of the Jews, we remember, was first made possible by the condition of general backwardness that
characterized European society after the Germanic invasions. Dohm's thesis
was that the backward spirit of the Middle Ages lives on today wherever Jews
continue to be relied on as a means of circumventing the illegality of various
forms of monetary exchange that are in reality legitimately ordained by the
"natural relation of things."[141] Thus, the Jews have paid the heaviest of prices
for bad governmental policies – not only in assuming the guise of illegality but
more importantly in absorbing its actual spirit. This is the cumulative effect
of having been forced for centuries to pursue a mode of livelihood that, under
the conditions it was permitted them, had necessarily entailed the regular
resort to criminal methods.

Two further and even contrary inferences might be drawn from this conclusion. The first was developed by Dohm's friend and ally Moses Mendelssohn,
the second by Dohm himself. For Mendelssohn, there was nothing inherently
degrading in the nature of the Jews' traditional occupations. On the contrary,
such activities as the Jews performed were genuinely useful to society at large.
Criminality and immorality, to the extent that they existed among the Jews,
were the consequence of society's marginalizing of the Jews' professions and
the moral taint it unjustly placed upon them. A general freeing up of the
avenues of exchange, a recognition of the authentic principles guiding commerce and trade, would therefore help to legitimize the Jews' traditional roles
and allow their full utility to be at last acknowledged.[142] Dohm, as we have
seen, could not accept such a view. Although he agreed with Mendelssohn that
age-old restrictions on the Jews' occupational life were to blame, he remained
convinced that the damage to their characters had already been done. Although
commerce needed to be liberalized, the Jews ought to be discouraged from
continuing to pursue it, at least for the time being.

Dohm's position will become clearer if we examine further the bases of
Mendelssohn's criticisms. Mendelssohn had presented his objections in the
preface to a German translation of the *Vindiciae Judaeorum* of Menasseh
ben Israel. Needless to say, there was considerable irony in the fact that he
chose to use Menasseh's text – a classic exemplar of the older style of Jewish
apologetic – to challenge some of the premises underlying the new style of
Enlightenment economic critique now being leveled at the Jews. On the one
hand, Mendelssohn's criticisms of Dohm reflected his concern that the latter had failed to present the liberal case in its full strength, and had indeed
retreated dangerously on key positions. Specifically, Mendelssohn did not
at all approve of Dohm's sensationalist psychology or of his imputation of

ingrained character flaws to the mass of Jews.[143] Nor did he believe that the Jews required further restrictions on their economic activities in order to prepare them for greater freedom. Here Mendelssohn sounds refreshingly modern – an unabashed defender of commerce and free trade – and, indeed, many commentators have depicted these views as such. However, it is important to note that Mendelssohn's position remained in certain respects rather closer to the older style of Jewish apologetic associated with a Menasseh or a Simone Luzzatto than to the classical economy of Tucker and Smith.

Mendelssohn showed that he was acutely aware of the changes in attitude that had occurred since Menasseh's day. A masterful ironist, he used his preface to deflate the image of progress he saw papering over the prejudice inherent in the new "enlightened" approach to the Jews. It was true, he began, that in the superstitious times preceding our own prejudice had taken a fantastic and violent form. This was because of the religious fanaticism of the age, its assumption that because the Jews were so perverse as to reject the revealed truth they would be capable of any and every crime against the true faith: the desecration of churches, the poisoning of wells, even the murder of children. Fortunately, now that times had changed, accusations such as these would no longer find as receptive an audience as in the past.[144] But from the point of view of the current Enlightened age, Mendelssohn noted sadly, this change coincided with a curious reversal of roles. Now it was the gentiles who were seen as enlightened and the Jews as backward, fanatical and superstitious. Now it was the Jews who "lacked ethical feeling, taste, and refined morality," who showed "an incapacity for art, science, and useful professions (chiefly those of a military and civic character)." The charge leveled against Jews, of possessing "an unconquerable addiction [Neigung] to fraud, usury, and lawlessness, has replaced those coarser accusations [of former times]." Adding injury to insult, it has also "removed us from the category of useful citizens and expelled us from the maternal protection of the state." Whereas formerly every effort had been expended to make Jews Christians, now the Jews were simply neglected, regarded as useless, and all but discarded. "Our lack of culture has been made the basis for our further oppression. They tie our hands and then reproach us for not using them."[145]

It is clear that although Mendelssohn did not have Dohm exclusively or even principally in mind in this passage, he had indeed zeroed in on the latter's key supposition that the Jews had fallen from a position of former cultural superiority to one of marked inferiority. Mendelssohn did not necessarily object to the assumption that Jews were in need of enlightenment, merely to the implication that they were appreciably less enlightened than the mass of their non-Jewish counterparts. Moreover, he was highly sensitive to the possible misuses of the enlightenment concept. In the religious sphere, he remained suspicious of deism as a new and subtle tool for securing the Jews' eventual conversion.[146] Here he showed himself to be equally cautious regarding a mode of economic thought that posed as enlightenment liberalism but was actually constructed on unenlightened premises.

Both of these specific concerns had been recently crystallized for Mendelssohn through the issuance in January 1782 of the *Toleranzpatent*.[147] This was one in a series of decrees issued by Joseph II of Austria aimed at attracting immigrants to the imperial domains and rationalizing legal and economic policy toward all alien groups, including Jews. To the latter it promised, among other reforms, to "remove obstacles in any honest ways of gaining . . . a livelihood and increasing general industriousness." This meant that Jews would in theory be permitted to join Christian artisan guilds (although not as yet to become guild masters) and that other restrictions on the Jews' access to livelihoods would be relaxed. Although most of his Jewish admirers hailed the *Toleranzpatent* as marking the start of a new era, Mendelssohn viewed it suspiciously. True, the *Toleranzpatent* did not in any way attempt to limit Jewish participation in trade (as Dohm might have recommended). But it did insist that the Jews' commercial records be kept in German, and no longer in Hebrew or Yiddish, in order to maintain "common confidence." It also expressed a general intention "to make the Jewish nation useful and serviceable to the State . . . by directing them to the sciences, the arts and the crafts."[148] Evidently, Mendelssohn detected a prejudicial and coercive intimation in the document, the faint suggestion that the Jews at present were in fact neither honest nor useful to society and that state institutions would find additional justifications to forcibly render them so. He seems to have feared that the *Toleranzpatent* was a manifestation of precisely that impostor Enlightenment he had so often warned against; that it signified a new strategy for breaching traditional Jewish defenses so as to undermine the already fragile Jewish economy and secure through "toleration" the same missionary aim that more forcible methods had earlier failed to achieve.[149]

Mendelssohn had the *Toleranzpatent* in mind when criticizing Dohm's book. He was deeply concerned that the categories of the emancipation debate not be misconceived. He rejected entirely what he viewed as an emerging quid pro quo arrangement, whereby Jews would have to prove their value in order to merit their civic membership in society. Such an arrangement would violate the premise of natural rights that he felt ought to underlie the state's contract with its citizens. Moreover, he wished to controvert the assumption he detected in both *On the Civic Improvement of the Jews* and the *Toleranzpatent* that the Jews were presently not beneficial subjects; for all subjects, he averred, were inherently useful. He did not object to the notion that citizens had obligations to fulfill, rather only that groups, such as Jews, should be singled out for special treatment. In fact, Mendelssohn strongly implied that if special conditions were to be established for the Jews' emancipation, they might choose voluntarily to forego it.[150]

Thus, there was something new and something old in Mendelssohn's position. What was new (in contrast to the Jewish apologists of the past) was the premise of natural rights and of reciprocal obligations objectively imposed. What was old, or what harkened back at least to earlier approaches, was the apparent willingness to countenance a return to an earlier condition wherein the Jews' mercantile value and utility were fully acknowledged. In economic terms, Mendelssohn defended the old categories drawn by Simone Luzzatto. The superstitious and backward societies of earlier times had at least recognized how invaluable the Jews' occupations were. They had never, thought Mendelssohn, questioned the utility of a population that could serve as a source of ready credit and commercial transport. Menasseh ben Israel, like Luzzatto, had grasped the point that a division of labor in which some tend the fields, others manufacture, and others carry and exchange the resulting products is the most efficient and sensible of arrangements. Therefore, it was absurd to draw a distinction between productive and nonproductive labor:

> Not only making but also doing [something] is called producing [*hervor-bringen*]. Not only he who works with his hands, but, generally, whoever does, stimulates, occasions or facilitates anything that can afford use or pleasure to his fellow men, deserves the name of producer; and he sometimes deserves it all the more the less you detect a movement of his hands and feet.[151]

This argument was consistent with Mendelssohn's broader natural rights view that everyone who obeyed the law ought to be valued as a subject or citizen.[152] It bridged the gap between the political and economic spheres, just as it established a link between the old mercantile apologetics and the new political economy. The genuine abuses of middlemen, such as price-fixing, resulted from the unjust and misguided regulations imposed on them, and not from the activities in themselves. Mendelssohn sounded very much like Josiah Tucker (or David Hume or Adam Smith) when he called on government:

> ... to curtail as much as possible all restrictions; to abolish monopolies, exclusive and privileged rights; to accord equal right and freedom to the smallest jobber and the largest commercial firm; in a word, to promote competition of every kind between middlemen; to encourage rivalry between them so that the price of things finds its equilibrium, ingenuity encouraged, on the one hand, and on the other, every consumer allowed to benefit, without excessive effort, from the industry of others.[153]

It is through competition not prohibition that "the ragman, the jobber, the wandering Jew" can be rendered "of very considerable utility." Such competition and rivalry rest upon a legal foundation of "unlimited liberty and equality of right [*uneingeschränkte Freyheit und Gleichheit der Rechte*] between buyers and sellers regardless of station, reputation, or creed..." The egalitarianism evidenced here was imported by Mendelssohn directly into the occupational sphere, where, he claimed, even "the pettiest trafficking Jew is...a useful inhabitant (I ought not say citizen) of the state, a true producer."[154]

Certainly, this sounds like state-of-the-art political economy. Its ring of theoretical sophistication can probably be accounted for by Mendelssohn's wide reading in the literature of the English and Scottish Enlightenments.[155] Yet how carefully had Mendelssohn actually read? There were very few political economists of the time who altogether rejected the distinction between productive and unproductive labor. We have seen it employed, for instance, by Josiah Tucker. Physiocratic doctrine rested in significant part on its identification of productive and sterile classes. Although hardly a Physiocrat, David Hume adhered in similar fashion to a hierarchy of use in matters of commerce. For Hume, it was, above all, merchants who "beget industry," whereas lawyers and physicians acquire riches merely "at the expence of others..."[156] Adam Smith, far less prone than Hume to encomia on merchants, devoted an entire chapter of *The Wealth of Nations* to refining the productive/nonproductive distinction (a point discussed later). These differences suggest that the impulse toward categorization, however formulated, transcended theoretical abstractions. On the one hand, economists were busily seeking out an Archimedean point – the location of the source of value (usually in one or more of what would later be designated "the factors of production," labor, land, or money) – on which to ground their theoretical enterprise. On the other hand, the language of political economy could not be easily separated from the broader Enlightenment preoccupation with "utility," which was not a technical concept but a moral one.

In this light, Mendelssohn seems to have conflated the technical term of productive (*hervorbringend*) with the moral one of useful (*nützlich*). To a Physiocrat like Quesnay, the "sterile classes" were deemed *useful* insofar as their reworking and circulation of goods, as well as their expenditures, found their way back into the hands of farmers. But the latter alone (or rather both farmers and miners) were *productive* in that since they alone extracted value from nature, only they produced a surplus (*produit net*) over and above their own consumption.[157] Adam Smith rejected the physiocratic doctrine mostly on the grounds of its denial of a productive status to artisans and merchants; yet he still held rigorously to the basic distinction. For Smith soldiers, for instance, might possibly be useful, but they were never productive. This was because the soldier's labor did not get embodied in a tangible commodity enduring in time past the moment of creation to generate further labor and productivity.

> Their service, how honorable, how useful, or how necessary soever, produces nothing for which an equal service can afterwards be procured. The protection, security, and defence of the commonwealth, the effect of their labour this year, will not purchase its protection, security, and defense for the year to come.[158]

As noted, this was a technical distinction but still one of considerable import to Smith. Soldiers were consumers who needed to be paid; their soldiering would not in itself generate or reproduce the wealth they consumed (except perhaps through conquest and booty). Farmers, by contrast, although likewise consumers, would in most circumstances create and procure the means of their own subsistence season after season. A society that was comprised entirely or predominantly of soldiers, actors, lawyers, professors, or merchants would never survive; but one composed exclusively or preeminently of farmers might.[159] (It should be noted, however, that although Smith was deeply concerned with defining an optimal ratio of productive and nonproductive labor, he marveled at the capacity of a commercial society to live well *despite* sustaining an unprecedented number of the latter.[160]) Mendelssohn, steeped as he was in the German rationalist tradition, insisted that man does not live by bread alone. He therefore concluded that "[t]he soldier produces [*bringt hervor*], for he creates peace and security for the state; the scholar produces – admittedly rarely something that is tangible but nevertheless goods which at the very least are equally as valuable: good advice, instruction, diversions, and entertainment."[161] Superficially, such a view appears to anticipate the criticisms later made of Smith by the great French economist Jean-Baptiste Say (1767–1832). Regarding value as a *subjective attribution of utility* rather than a tangible essence, Say claimed that anything bought or sold on the market was a commodity and therefore genuinely the end result of productive activity. "There is no doubt that the performance of a stage play gives as much pleasure as a pound of chocolate or a piece of fireworks." Nevertheless, Say proceeded to note, "a nation having a crowd of musicians, priests, and government employees might be a nation well entertained, well indoctrinated, and well governed. But that would be all. Its capital would receive no direct growth from the labor of these industrious men."[162]

So it seemed to most contemporary economists that some formal distinction was required in order to demonstrate how a growing population with increasing numbers of men removed from the soil would be fed and clothed, as well as entertained and amused. So far as Smith was concerned, there was indeed an important distinction between "making something and doing something." There was a hierarchy of labor in which the production, first of the biological means of subsistence, and second of objects like tools and machines that enhanced future productivity, enjoyed a necessary priority over the procurement of other services and the facilitation of commodity exchange.[163] The key point was not that Smith viewed such activities as mutually exclusive, but, rather, that he felt it legitimate to try to quantify the best possible ratio between the various categories. "A man grows rich by employing a multitude of manufacturers, he grows poor by maintaining a multitude of servants."[164] The same could be said for a society or nation as a whole. It is true that Smith regarded the proliferation of nonproductive persons to be a necessary consequence of the very division of labor that had made countries such as England and Holland prosperous. But it was also plausible to him that a land could generate, through bad laws and practices, an unnecessary superabundance of unproductive laborers whose consumption of the annual produce would choke off the supply of subsistence goods available to the productive classes and thereby progressively kill off industry. This, in his view, was exactly what was now taking place in France, Poland, and other European countries.[165]

This was precisely the charge currently leveled against the Jews, if not directly by Dohm then certainly by other German economic writers.[166] Johann von Justi, the leading Cameralist writer of the mid-century, for instance, devoted a short chapter of his 1760 *Foundations of State Power* to the question of Jews' economic utility. After considering and then rejecting a number of economic accusations against Jews, von Justi claimed he could nevertheless "regard it as by no means permissible to allow them to [continue to] practice commerce (*Commercien*)." How peculiar, von Justi noted, given that the entire well-being (*Wohlfarth*) of the state depends on commerce – "*so sie sind eine sehr zärtliche Sache*" – that governments would place the critically important task of merchandising in the hands of Jews and other foreigners, while denying them access to other, less vulnerable fields. Justi was enough of a mercantilist to fear that the use of Jews and other foreigners in trade ran the risk of allowing them to withdraw capital from the country. He favored increasing Jews' numbers (in accord with his populationism) while transforming them into industrial artisans (*Fabrikanten*). Not only would this remove them from the strategically delicate mercantile sphere, but it also would allow the state to scrutinize their activities more directly.[167]

A similar proposal was proffered in 1776 by Johann August Schlettwein (1731–1802), the leading apostle of Physiocracy in Germany.[168] It is worth noting that despite his Physiocratic orientation Schlettwein at no point advocated directing Jews into agriculture (although such was a common tendency among non-Jewish, as opposed to *Jewish*, advocates of productivization). Rather, like Justi, he wished to see them channeled into *"Handwerk, Kunst, und Manu-facturarbeiten."* Nevertheless, Schlettwein's rationale differed from Justi's. It was not the fact that Jews were foreigners that rendered them dangerous, but, rather, that they were *superfluous* middlemen (*Zwischen–händler*). The profits they accumulated from transporting goods between country and town raised prices for consumers and lowered earnings for producers. Because it is likely that Schlettwein was among those Mendelssohn had in mind in his response to Dohm, it is worth pausing to consider his actual standpoint. Schlettwein did not ignore the fact that middlemen are necessary. Rather, he assumed that it was governmental restrictions and not market forces that had driven the Jews into trade. The state was operating under the mistaken assumption that by forcing the Jews into commerce and then imposing special taxes on them it would acquire additional revenue for itself. The state's fallacy lay in the fact that the Jews merely passed along these added costs to others. Indeed, Schlettwein's charge recalled traditional accusations that the Jews provided the authorities with a means to extract additional and illegitimate taxes from the laboring population. Jews were forced to underpay peasants; consequently, peasants were compelled to borrow money (from Jews!) to meet their added costs. For Schlettwein the way out of this vicious cycle was to open up *Handwerk* to Jews (he said nothing, unfortunately, about eliminating their unjust taxes). Doing so, he believed, would allow them to render a true economic service: as refiners if not producers of raw materials they would lower labor costs and as consumers they would spur overall productivity.[169]

In returning now to Dohm, we can see that the breadth of his approach set him apart from predecessors like Justi and Schlettwein. Neither, for instance, had considered the moral and civic benefits of Jews' occupational produc-tivization, and neither had tied this productivization into the question of civic incorporation. Moreover, there is no evidence that Dohm agreed with Schlet-twein that the perpetuation of the small Jewish minority's current occupa-tional profile would be ruinous to the German economies as a whole. Instead, he feared that the lack of proportionality between what the Jews and the rest of society did represented a most serious obstacle to their civic incorporation. The impact of this imbalance on the non-Jewish community was less real than symbolic. The Jews' now internalized confinement to commerce epit-omized European society's failure to consummate its own full adoption of liberal principles. Yes, the disproportionate involvement of Jews in usury and petty retail trade (*Detailhandel*) confined their moral outlook and constrained their civic virtue; yet the effect also has been to implicate gentile society in the web of restrictions that inhibits progress for the community as a whole.

Even if Jewish-gentile relations constitute a relatively minor sphere of social interaction, the treatment of the Jews is still indicative of a much larger crisis afflicting contemporary life. In short, it is the crisis of a society that legislates criminality.[170]

If a market economy conformed to the "natural order of things," its realization would nevertheless require state intervention to remove the stubborn detritus of bad medieval policy. The common association between commerce, moneylending, and criminality, for which the Jews have tragically paid the price, can only be eliminated by pressuring them to change their occupations. Dohm's approach commanded that a freer and more liberal economy, one in which commerce and banking could enjoy their rightful place, would have to be predicated on freeing up these very occupations by dissociating them from their traditional practitioners. The approach was not unique to Dohm. Although Adam Smith evidently hesitated to countenance the employment of coercive measures by the state even for liberal ends, such sympathetic contemporaries as Turgot and Cordorcet assumed the necessity of "planning for competition," as Friedrich von Hayek would later put it.[171] In Dohm's presentation, too, there is no moral contradiction (or paradox) between what may rightfully be prescribed for the ailments of society as a whole and the treatment he proposes for the suffering of the Jews. "Only first will the unnatural condition in which the [Jewish] nation now finds itself need to be reversed through the imposition of various not entirely natural means..." Whoever protests against such artificial means fails to consider that at present our own general circumstances are hardly the natural ones either.[172] Therefore, both society in general and the Jews in particular will symbiotically benefit from the latter's occupational restructuring. The Jews constitute a clot in the circulatory system of market economy that can only be removed through an effort of the state to force them out of their traditional professions.

The contradiction, if there is one, lies in the fact that on the road to greater civic freedom the Jews must first traverse the path of further restrictions.[173] Commerce needs to be freed of Jews and the Jews of commerce. Both ends can be achieved through reeducation; their systematic training in more directly productive and less morally vulnerable occupations (Dohm was keen on artisanry for Jews, regarding its effects as emotionally stabilizing, less so on agriculture, which was prone to bad weather and anxiety).[174] This is the first hint that we have seen of an emerging quid pro quo arrangement, whereby in return for their acquisition of civic equality Jews would be expected to demonstrate a capacity for moral, cultural, and occupational reform. The quid pro quo could operate – as recommended by Dohm in 1781 and as legislated a decade later by the French Revolution's National Assembly – on the basis of future expectations, or on the basis of compulsion, as decreed by the Emperor Napoleon in 1808. The route of compulsion (withholding emancipation until Jews made themselves occupationally productive) was the one taken by most of the German states following Napoleon's defeat in 1815. This quid pro quo was thus the working out of the same paradox implicit in Dohm's original recommendation: that of applying special treatment to a group in order to accord its members individual equality.[175]

For Dohm, the paradox was a necessary and resolvable one. His optimism was based on the singular premise that "everything of which the Jews are accused is the result of the political constitution under which they presently live..."[176] This brings us back from the realm of economy to that of politics and from the question of occupations to that of constitutions. Dohm insisted that men are above all shaped by political institutions; even the occupational distortion of the Jews was in the final analysis the result of Europe's own flawed political arrangements, its constitution. If the constitution were to be reformed to incorporate Jews into the broader polity (notwithstanding the few special and temporary measures noted earlier), then their cultural and occupational uniqueness would gradually wither away. Here we see how the quid pro quo operated in reality to transform society as a whole, and how the question of the Jews was ultimately subsumed under the question of the constitution (a point not lost on several of Dohm's readers).[177] Under a proper constitution the state would no longer, as Dohm's Cameralist predecessors had recommended, seek to maintain a rough and sustaining equilibrium between religious and corporate orders. Rather, it would endeavor to soften the fabric of internal allegiances, so as "to weaken the exclusivist foundation of [all] these different societies." This, according to Dohm, was the "great and noble business of government." It was a business that would only be completed "when the noble, the peasant, the scholar, the artisan, the Christian and the Jew are, above all of these things, citizens."[178] Although *On the Civic Improvement of the Jews* was directed at just one of these groups, Dohm intended that all of them would undergo systematic "improvement."[179]

Historians have long recognized Dohm's importance to the story of Jewish emancipation. The eminent scholar Jacob Katz even dated the inception of the Jewish emancipation process to the publication of Dohm's *On the Civic Improvement of the Jews*.[180] Dohm's critique of Jewish commerce is part of his historical importance, because the reform of Jewish economic life was inseparable from his call for Jewish rights. That the two goals are interdependent is apparent from the title of his book, in which *Verbesserung* refers both to the improvement of the Jews' civic status and of their civic behavior.[181] Yet Dohm transformed the discussion of Jewish life not by his indictment, because others before him had attacked Jewish commerce with far more virulence. Nor was Dohm the first to call for the Jews' occupational transformation. Rather, his innovation was to conceive of a future society in which Jews could be fully incorporated by abandoning their occupations rather than their religion. He could see no good reason why commerce should remain a defining feature of Jewish identity. If this were to happen it could only mean one thing: that the Jews remained victims of discrimination, that they had not been accepted, or, something he could not imagine, that they did not wish to be accepted.

Finally, it should be recognized that Dohm's conception of productivization was not retrograde. In the late eighteenth century, agriculture and crafts *were* (or could be) modern activities. Indeed, the productivization of agriculture was key to modernization. Only be creating surpluses of food, fuel, and textiles could the division of labor sufficiently progress to fuel economic growth. This was the English model, although one greatly admired on the continent.[182] Unfortunately, an agricultural revolution along the lines of English enclosure and improvement would prove extraordinarily problematic for a country such as Prussia with its traditional peasantry, nobility, and guilds. Hence, by emphasizing Jewish agriculture and especially artisanry, Dohm was not – in the context of his times – exhibiting a romantic nostalgia for the past. He was once again revealing himself as a keen modernizer. Dohm would modernize Jews by making their occupational structure more proportionate to that of the population at large. In turn, this would help render the old estate structure more flexible, leading to its gradual dissolution. In its place, a "natural order" would emerge, one built on the mobility of merit and on the mandates of markets. The obstacle to this, Dohm recognized, was not at all the Jews but rather the nobility. In his eyes, they were the recalcitrant and all too powerful impediment. Thus the challenge Dohm faced was essentially the same as that confronted by moderate leaders of the French Revolution who also would recognize a certain parallel between the reform of Jewish society and that of the noble estate. But in their effort to overturn a backward and unjust order, these revolutionaries would sweep Jews up into a social ferment that would change their condition forever.

5

〇〜

A State within a State

"In 1789 nobles were the kingdom's Jews." So quipped Guy Chaussinand-Nogaret in his classic study of the French nobility of the Eighteenth Century.[1] At first glance, the comparison seems merely fanciful. The nobility, in theory at least, existed at the very apex of society, whereas Jews were widely seen as at the bottom. The nobility was defined by its preeminent claim to honor, a quality of which the Jews were thought bereft. The nobility's prestige was based on its presumed martial expertise. Jews in early modern Europe had largely been excluded from the military duties which gentile commentators (John Toland notwithstanding) thought them incapable of performing. The nobility's power was built on its predominant and in principle exclusively rightful ownership of land. Jews, in contrast, were excluded almost entirely from land ownership. By law, the nobility could not engage directly in commerce. Jews, as we have seen, were often legally confined to the practice of trade. All of these distinctions would seem to render the two groups polar opposites. And yet in a sense they resembled each other profoundly: both were despised minorities which, in the eyes of many, constituted a self-enclosed international network, a foreign element that lived parasitically off the labor of the vast majority and that contributed nothing to society at large.

In the period 1789–1816, the noble-Jew analogy produced a fascinating set of associations. As a French revolutionary discourse started to crystallize in early 1789 a new definition of the nation began to emerge, one formulated in deliberate contrast to a society of Estates (*état* or *Stand*). Insofar as the nation was now synonymous with the Third Estate (commoners), the nobility (the combined First and Second Estates) became classified as an estate within the state as well as a nation within the nation. The application of this same derisive term to the Jews during the 1789–1791 debates over their emancipation in the French National Assembly reflected a comprehensive assault on the corporatism of the ancien régime. Not only were nobles and Jews rhetorically confronted with the same set of alternatives (amalgamation into versus exclusion from the nation), but the same means of regeneration was prescribed for both (the habituation to productive labor). Later, as reaction against the Revolution crystallized in central Europe, charges originally leveled against the nobility's social parasitism became gradually displaced onto the Jewish population. In part this was because an attack on the Jews, as opposed to an attack on the nobility, could present itself as a form of opposition to the ancien régime without, at the same time, acceding to the radicalism of the Revolution. Just as the Revolution's original attack on the nobility entailed investigations into the historical sources of its privileges (the nobility's "ancient constitution"), so, too, the controversies surrounding the Jews' emancipation surfacing in Germany in the Napoleonic period would impel new researches into their original historical and constitutional character. This new interest in the Jews' historical-economy was intended to show that, contra Dohm, intrinsic constitutional rather than extrinsic political factors had produced and maintained the Jews' orientation to commerce.

Historians have for some time been aware of this similarity in revolutionary discourse on Jews and nobles. In *The Origins of Totalitarianism*, Hannah Arendt explored the links between antiaristocratic politics and antisemitism in the early nineteenth century, concluding that the two groups privileged disutility provided the common denominator.[2] Dealing with an earlier period Arthur Hertzberg suggested that Enlightenment era critiques of Jewish economy were sometimes thinly disguised attacks on the nobility.[3] More recently, Derek Penslar has observed that the late Enlightenment indictment of Jewish "backwardness" (economic and otherwise) was part and parcel of a broad assault on corporate privileges and states within the state, including the nobility, monastic orders, and the poor. Reformers, as Penslar demonstrates, deemed all of these groups ripe for regeneration and integration.[4] Finally, Deborah Hertz, in discussing the intimate relations between groups of nobles and Jews in late-eighteenth-century Berlin, notes various social and economic similarities between the two, population size, early marriage patterns, and control over liquid capital.[5] In what follows, these insights will be developed in detail, with specific attention given to illustrating how and why the parallel arguments on Jewish and noble regeneration momentarily merged before once again diverging at the end of the Revolutionary era. Political economy provides a touchstone throughout this excursion, because its conceptual language of productivity and utility were central to treatments of both Jews and nobles. This chapter focuses on the great revolutionary pamphleteer, Emmanuel-Joseph Sieyes (1748–1836), who utilized economic and occupational categories to frame his indictments of noble privileges, and the German philosopher Johann

Gottlieb Fichte (1762–1812). Fichte is not normally thought of as an economist, yet in his early writings he interpreted the French Revolution as a clarion call for economic reform, starting with the destruction of noble monopolies. Although Sieyes did not discuss Jews, his critique of nobility almost certainly set the terms of debate over Jewish emancipation in the National Assembly. Fichte, however, did draw an overt and extremely critical link between Jewish commerce and the noble ancien régime.

THE ABBÉ SIEYES

Qu'est ce que le Tiers état? (What is the Third Estate?), published in 1789 by the Abbé Emmanuel-Joseph Sieyes, the religiously indifferent vicar-general of the bishopric of Chartres and avid political-economist, was one of the most significant tracts in modern European history.[6] It possesses a status in the history of the French Revolution akin to that of Thomas Paine's *Common Sense* in the American, albeit with Sieyes enjoying a major advantage over the Englishman. As a delegate to the Estates General (and later the National Assembly), he was able to transform the rhetoric of his pamphlet into a programmatic blueprint for the actual policies the National Assembly pursued during the initial phase of the Revolution.

The system of estates was moribund in France when Sieyes wrote *Qu'est ce que le Tiers état?*, which is to say that the traditional division of European society into three groupings, the clergy or first estate ("those who pray"), the nobility or second estate ("those who fight") and the commoners or third estate ("those who work") had long ago ceased to correspond to practical reality. Most higher clergy were nobles; many nobles were former commoners who had been elevated by virtue of the riches they had won in commerce. The majority of nobles were no longer warriors (including the theoretically abolished *noblesse militaire* and *noblesse par fiefs*) but, rather, *noblesse de robe*, *noblesse par charges* and *noblesse par lettres*. French nobilities differed, moreover, not only by category but also by region.[7] In most parts of the country, feudalism, properly speaking, as a system of hierarchy, reciprocity, and a set of rules governing the status of land, also was a thing of the remote past. Absolutism, absentee landlordism, and rentier capitalism had rendered the term virtually meaningless.

Long before Sieyes penned his famous pamphlet, the nobility had been recognized as a serious problem. Ironically, through much of the eighteenth century this problem was not construed as one of overweening power and privilege but rather of overpopulation, degradation, and poverty. The rural nobility, in particular, often existed in a state of crisis, clinging to a privileged status while lacking even sufficient means. As the commentator La Bruyère declared, the rural nobility was "inutile à sa patrie, à sa famille et à lui-même."[8]

This decline was brought into sharp relief by the growing utilitarianism of the absolutist regime and of French culture more generally. Colbert's policies, sometimes described as an effort to organize the French economy into a single machine, aimed at freeing portions of the nobility from rules and customs of "derogation" (*dérogeance*) – the loss of noble status for engaging in commerce or physical labor. The aim was to elevate the status of commerce, in the wake of the revocation of the Edict of Nantes, as much as provide an outlet for hard-pressed nobles. A series of edicts from the late seventeenth and early eighteenth century opened large-scale commerce to nobles, although these changes would yield little practical result. With the rise of the philosophes the question of *la noblesse commerçante* became a topic of public debate, however. Voltaire, in keeping with his general Anglophilia, professed to admire the readiness of the English nobility to engage in business, a further indication of that culture's healthy attitude toward commerce. Montesquieu, fearing that the combined weight of inherited privilege and commercial wealth would prove damaging to both the nobility *and* the economy, decried the notion, insisting that "commerce is the profession of equal people."[9] The debate culminated with the furor surrounding the publication of *La noblesse commerçante* by the Abbé Coyer in 1756. Coyer demanded the complete abrogation of "*cette loi singulière et gothique de dérogeance*," and the revitalization of the nobility – or a segment of it – through commercial endeavor.[10] In doing so, he reiterated a crucial if not always clear distinction that had been present from the start: that between petty or "detail" commerce from which all nobles should desist, and large-scale trade, which alone should be permitted to them.[11] Still, with the genie out of the bottle, fresh voices now emerged to propose other more radical means of noble rehabilitation, such as the creation of a *noblesse cultivatrice*, if not actually performing physical labor in the fields then at least adopting the manner of the English yeoman or "improving farmer."[12]

Although the debate waned in the second half of the eighteenth century, it will be important to keep it in mind in what follows. First, it reinforces the analogy we will gradually draw between noble and Jewish occupational regeneration, with the significant proviso that for nobles regeneration could mean engagement with commerce while more often than not for Jews it entailed the opposite. Second, we should keep in mind the debate over *La Noblesse commerçante et cultivatrice* while considering both Sieyes's arguments and his rhetoric – because, rather oddly, he himself barely addresses it. Not only did his pamphlet make little reference to the large numbers of impoverished nobles, treating them all as more or less equal members of a monstrously powerful and unjust caste, but Sieyes hardly mentioned this once lively discussion to which nobles themselves had contributed on both sides. True, there was a sense in which this background hardly mattered. Noble privilege remained embedded in laws and many institutions, including the tax system as well as access to material goods and cultural status, a situation that made it possible for Sieyes to strike a chord of deep resentment in French public opinion.[13] Indeed, Sieyes was keenly aware of the disjuncture between the de facto and de jure status of the estates, and his pamphlet exploited it mercilessly. He knew that the way French society actually worked was so remote from the theoretical categories of estate function as to render their continued use absurd and intolerable.

Qu'est ce que le Tiers état? drew liberally if imprecisely on the vocabulary of contemporary political economy to make the case that the nobility did nothing whatsoever productive or useful. Sieyes merged the Physiocratic and Smithian category of "productive" with the Mendelssohnian category of "useful" by contrasting both to a third category, one that Smith hesitated to employ and which Mendelssohn refused to acknowledge: the useless. That Sieyes was aware of the difference between productive and useful is apparent from the pamphlet's opening chapters in which he devotes considerable attention to categorizing contemporary occupations as private or public, as relating to: (1) primary production (agriculture and mining); (2) secondary production (artisanry and refining): (3) transport and exchange; or (4) administrative, as well as intellectual and scientific endeavors.[14] Sieyes initially grounds his distinctions hierarchically in terms of their proximity to production before proceeding to lump all of the above classes together – *without distinction* – as all equally either "useful and industrious" (*laborieux et utiles*) or "useful and pleasant" (*utiles ou agréables*). Virtually all of the occupations in society receive the author's approval – that is to say, all of the forms of labor included in the vast territory between "useful" and "pleasant" receive equal approbation. This is because Sieyes's categories, unlike Smith's, are not grounded in function alone but in caste. The key distinction is less between the nature of the activity being performed than between the legal, social, and political position of the persons who perform them. It turns out that virtually all the industrious, useful, and pleasant functions in society are performed by the same people. On the one hand, "the activities which support society," that is, productive endeavors, are performed entirely by the Third Estate. And even with regard to the public services of army, law, church, and bureaucracy, in which the First and Second Estates naturally play a role, the Third Estate performs, according to Sieyes, "nineteen-twentieths" of the labor and indeed "all the really arduous work." This taxonomic strategy enables Sieyes to have it both ways: he can associate the Third Estate with the most economically essential activities, farming, crafts, and manufacturers, and by subtly blending the category of productive with the "useful," the "pleasant," the "distinguished," the "menial," and so on, he can incorporate virtually all of those who perform any kind of labor whatsoever into the category of commoners. As a result, he redescribes society from a tripartite into a bipolar formation, from a system of functional status gradations, on the one side, into a black and white dichotomy of just producers and parasites, on the other. In *Qu'est ce que le Tiers état?* Sieyes combines the imagery of class warfare based on economic activity with depictions of national struggle based on estate division:

> The most ill-organized state of all would be the one where not just isolated individuals but a complete class of citizens would glory in inactivity amidst the general movement and contrive to consume the best part of the product without having in any way helped to produce it. Such a class, surely, is foreign to the nation because of its *idleness*.[15]

The Third Estate performs all the real labor in society, whereas the First and Second Estates – both synonymous with the nobility[16] – "glory in idleness amidst the general activity." Hence, as the title of his first chapter has it, "The Third Estate is a complete nation," whereas the others are merely "foreign."

This brings us to the question of Sieyes's use of the term "nation." When on June 16, 1789, the delegates of the Third Estate designated themselves the "National Assembly" they effectively defined the nation as the supreme political category in the land. A month later, the concept reemerged in the "Declaration of the Rights of Man and Citizen," which declared that "the source of all sovereignty resides essentially in the nation" and that "no body and no individual may exercise authority which does not emanate expressly from the nation."[17] In the century before the Revolution a nation could likewise signify the total population of subjects encompassed within a sovereign territory. But a nation also could designate a corporate body that existed within that territory or even both within and beyond it. Isaac de Pinto, for example, had referred in his letter to Voltaire both to the "nation" of the Jews who lived scattered about the world *and* to the (Sephardic-Jewish) "Portuguese nation of Bordeaux."[18] This same duality was mirrored in the self-definition of the nobility. In the eighteenth century, the French nobility insisted on its exclusive status as the political nation; it depicted itself as the nation existing before and standing in opposition against the usurpation of legitimate authority by the absolutist regime.[19] Yet although the nobility claimed to be *the* nation within a given territory, it also was manifestly *a* nation transcending territorial

boundaries. Throughout the century the French nobility, for instance, continued to absorb foreign members into its ranks.[20]

Sieyes's understanding of "nation" must be viewed within this framework
of prior noble assertions. By insisting that the Third Estate is the nation unto
itself, he defined "nation" in deliberate contradistinction to noble claims. And
by defining the nation as the Third Estate and the Third Estate alone as those
who perform all that is useful in society, he located national membership in
the concept of economic utility (a conception later echoed in Article 1 of the
"Declaration of the Rights of Man and Citizen," which declared that "social
utility cannot be founded but on common utility").[21] Sieyes rendered the
nation sovereign by grounding its definition in law while at the same time
making law the expression of its own will. "What is a nation? A body of associates living under a common law and represented by the same legislature."[22]
Because only a society of the Third Estate can be said to live under a common
law (i.e., the law of commoners), a national legislature (in contrast to the
Estates General) must be composed only of the Third Estate.[23]

This construction of the term "nation" helps explain how such expressions
as "a nation within a nation" and "a state within a state" became applied both
to the nobility and the Jews, among others, in the period surrounding the
French Revolution. Jacob Katz has noted that the formulation "a state within
a state" was first directed against Huguenots in the early seventeenth century.
Later on, it was used to insinuate conspiratorial designs on the part of groups
such as Jesuits and Freemasons, before eventually being employed as a weapon
in the struggle against Jewish emancipation. Katz's thesis is that although Jews
had indeed resembled a separate corporation in premodern Europe, until
the prospect of their political emancipation became real they were not yet
considered a part of the body politic and therefore not regarded as a political
threat to it.[24] In light of previous chapters, we see that this argument requires
qualification: even in relatively tolerant Britain men like Prynne, Harrington,
and the later opponents of the Jew Bill regarded Jews as both alien and a
potential political threat. But there is another sense in which Katz's thesis
should be modified. It was not just changes in the potential status of Jews,
but, rather, the emergence of a conception of social distinctions grounded
in utility alone that rendered both Jews and nobility susceptible to the state
within a state label in 1789.

The contrast between nation and estate (as well as between state and estate)
emerged when it did for a reason. In the period immediately before the Revolution authors such as Sieyes had still to contend with the fact that the Third
Estate's own claim to be the "*nation complette*" remained frustrated by the
nobility's monopoly on actual sovereignty[25] Thus, Sieyes likened the Third

Estate to a "strong and robust man with one arm still enchained."²⁶ Those chains are the foreign element, the nobility, which exists as a burden (*une charge*) on the body politic, in it but not of it. Remove the privileged orders and the nation would be "not something less but something more." Until that is accomplished, the nobility remains a deadly threat to the nation. It is not itself a sick man, on the verge of collapse, but, rather, a parasite, "a horrific disease consuming the living flesh off the body of an unfortunate man."²⁷ In the final paragraph of the first edition of *Qu'est ce que le Tiers état?*, Sieyes similarly compares the privileged orders to a "malignant tumor" on the body of a sick man which must be "neutralized" to keep it from destroying his life.²⁸ It is curious that at one and the same time he likens the Third Estate to a robust man and a diseased figure. The nobility must be subtracted from the nation in order to make it whole.

Sieyes's historical remarks in *Qu'est ce que le Tiers état?* convey his sense of how this paradoxical condition arose. Here he plays on the nobility's own historical claims to governance (its so-called racial myth) constructed on the basis of the ancient Frankish conquest of Gaul and the eternal rights of possession thereby acquired.²⁹ For Sieyes, this foreign conquest was precisely an argument for excluding the nobility from membership in nation, because, "[t]hey are foreign to the nation . . . because of their origin . . ."³⁰ The law of conquest from which the nobility derived its original privileges is no longer valid today since the system which generated it has dissolved. That law was part of the matrix of feudalism, a system in which the noble was defined in contrast with "commoners, peasants and villeins." These designations, according to Sieyes, corresponded to a legal status that had once been legitimate, at least within the framework of the feudal system. It was based on two categories, serfs and nobles. Because no status other than these was possible, the nobility possessed all rights and privileges exclusively. "In former times the Third Estate was serf, and the noble order was everything."³¹ Although the feudal system was indeed "barbaric," it was legitimate to the extent that it provided security and livelihood under the primitive conditions of the time. However, with the alteration of circumstances, the system not only lost its former raison d'être but in a sense its actual existence, too. This was because feudalism, in Sieyes's definition, depended on the presence of only two classes, serfs and nobles. As soon as significant numbers of persons emerged who no longer fit these categories, the system became outmoded.

What might strike us initially is how Sieyes's historical treatment of feudalism contrasts with Dohm's. Dohm depicted the Jews as the group designated to fill the commercial vacuum created by the barbaric feudal ethos, subsequently disfiguring both the Jewish population and the society at large. Here

Sieyes offers a rather different narrative, one later borrowed by Marx, in which commerce emerged within the interstices of feudal society to gradually render that society obsolete, despite the feudal nobility's stubborn insistence on perpetuating its privileges.[32] Finally, as the result of a lengthy process of commercial and urban development there emerged a gross disproportion between the number of privileged persons and of commoners – according to Sieyes's estimate, there are today less than two hundred thousand nobles in a total population of twenty-five to twenty-six million. Commoners, who had once been synonymous with serfs, now constituted a vast population of freemen, whereas a tiny race of nobles, who had once been lords, continued to live off them like parasites. The nobility, having lost any semblance of its former military and administrative *functionality*, is now noble in word alone. "... [B]ut under the cover of this word, and solely through influence of a false opinion, *a new and intolerable aristocracy* has illegally insinuated itself."[33] The privileged estates are impostors, usurpers, and intruders into the body politic. They comprise an "aristocracy," which bears no resemblance to the ancient class of Frankish conquerors. Yet precisely *because* of their impostor status they represent a more deadly threat than any previous ruling estate. The nobility is a "phantom" [*ombre*], but a phantom "seeking ... to terrorize an entire nation."[34]

Sieyes thus effectively interwove two insinuations – viz., that of the nobility as an impostor class and that of the nobility as an alien body – into a portrait of fifth column usurpation that has been accomplished through public brainwashing. It is through the force of its own carefully constructed mystique that this spectral class of aristocrats has managed to induce the members of the nation to submit when in truth they ought to command. The noble estate is a foreign occupying power impersonating a once-legitimate ruling class to which the nation has acquiesced out of its own misplaced sense of inherited obligation. And because the First Estate actually means to do the nation harm, its monopoly of power goes beyond mere nepotism to take on the character of a sinister foreign conspiracy. Through its control of the *capitus* – the royal court – it holds captive the nation and the king:

> And what is the court if not the head of that immense aristocracy that rules over every part of France and through its members seizes upon everything while controlling in all places what is essential to every aspect of public affairs [*de la chose publique*]?[35]

The noble estate is an aristocracy both foreign in its interests and castelike in its control over key functions. Boring from within and pursuing a set of egoistic interests fatal to the general good, it is a "state within a state," an *imperium in imperio*.[36]

To better appreciate the novelty of Sieyes's formulation, we should note that his illustrious predecessor, Montesquieu (among a host of earlier authors) had celebrated the nobility's capacity to provide the constitutional counterweight against tyranny in both its monarchical and democratic forms.[37] Yet as we have seen, by formulating a critique of political arrangements drawn primarily from economic categories, Sieyes had little need of a doctrine of countervailing powers based on the perpetuation of a blood aristocracy. For Sieyes, the division of labor rather than inherited estate distinctions ought to define the character and parameters of government. Why should a group that does nothing useful be permitted to rule? Political economy offered the capacity both to diagnose social illness and prescribe the cure. The efficiency model provided by the division of labor undermined the claims of corporate utility that had hitherto justified a system of separate estates. Yet, at the same time, it was the division of labor divorced from the corporate order that provided the means of regeneration. The division of labor decoupled from religion, ethnicity, and caste would make possible the reintegration of the individual members of corporate groups such as Jews and nobles into the general polity.

It should be stressed that those who advocated such integration were not necessarily naïve or utopian. Dohm, for example, assumed that the effect of a group's long immersion in a specific type of labor would be to imbue its practitioners with the qualities and characteristics of their occupations, making their adjustment to meritocracy a long and arduous one. In *Qu'est ce que le Tiers état?* and Sieyes's other writings he presented a similar hypothesis regarding not the nobility but the laboring classes. Accoring to Sieyes, men's habituation to manual labor rendered their perspectives myopic, their horizons narrow, their senses dull. Astonishingly, he proceeded to argue that the nobility's familiarity with leisure has enabled some of its members to acquire a broad humanistic outlook and farsighted perspective that most other members of society lack.[38]

As William Sewell has argued, this undercurrent in *Qu'est ce que le Tiers état?* – hinting at the possible superiority of leisure over labor – appears to counteract the express ideology of the pamphlet. In *Qu'est ce que le Tiers état?* Sieyes presents a brief discussion of the relationship between categories of work and qualifications for political office. Those to be excluded from political (although not necessarily civic) rights include women ("rightly or wrongly"), individuals performing menial tasks, and all who labor "under the domination of a master." Similarly, in his other political writings, Sieyes drew a sharp distinction between citizens, on the one hand, and those who perform the nation's drudgery ("working companions" – *compagnons du travail*), on the other. This recalls Sieyes's occupational typology at the beginning of *Qu'est ce que le Tiers état?*, in which he first worked out a detailed hierarchy of activities, from those closest to those furthest removed from primary production, only to dissolve these distinctions later on. We have seen that one effect of this move was to establish that the Third Estate held a virtual monopoly on all activity that was productive, useful, or pleasant. Yet a second effect was precisely to limit the political application of this claim: contrary to the earlier implication, if transport, exchange and administration occupy the same general category of beneficial endeavors, then no social priority need inhere in agriculture or artisanry from which special rights might be derived. On the contrary, the occupations of farming and crafts, while possessing no extraordinary economic status, tend to disqualify their practitioners politically. This is because "the capacity to grasp the grand relations of society" validating political participation manifests itself only in men who possess leisure and means. And because political participation is itself a legitimate form of useful enterprise, such participation may be justifiably restricted to individuals capable of devoting time and energy to public service, rather than to the larger body of *compagnons du travail*.

> To be a citizen, it is necessary to know the relations of human associations, and in particular those of the society of which one is a member. Men who cannot improve themselves, or whom one cannot raise to this knowledge, are only working companions.[39]

Thus, the most influential French revolutionary theorist appears to have maintained a position oddly reminiscent of Plato. Not the simple and virtuous citizen-farmer of ancient Athenian democracy, but the leisured and educated gentleman alone possesses the qualifications – knowledge and vision – to hold and elect public offices.[40] Politics is a profession requiring a mastery of skills acquired through preparation and training. Its effective practice is therefore premised on a mental outlook rooted in technical competence as well as in freedom, i.e., the leisure and independence afforded by property.

In his study of Sieyes, William Sewell astutely identifies many of these tensions but neglects to mention Sieyes's efforts to resolve them. In fact, Sieyes did not gloss over the contradictions in his account but confronted them directly. He was aware, for instance, that polity and economy were distinct if interrelated spheres. He could not entirely divorce the question of political rights from the notion, to which he was entirely committed, of the Third

Estate as the nation. He struggled over the proposed exclusion from political rights of "the vast majority of those who do the useful work of society..."[41] and of "nine-tenths of the nation."[42] In truth, Sieyes could see only one way out: "We must invite governments to metamorphose human beasts into citizens, to make them participate actively in the benefits of society."[43] As with Tucker, Dohm, and Smith, the internal tensions and contradictions between the various elements of political economic argumentation were to be resolved through the *deus ex machina* of state intervention.[44]

For Sieyes, regeneration directed by the state represented the key medium for establishing a meritocracy that, if genuine, would operate on principles of fairness and equality. Such principles could be established only within a polity prepared through state intervention both to terminate inherited privilege and to institute methods of education into citizenship. As noted, not only vagabonds and mendicants but also "anyone under the dominance of a master" could not be allowed "to figure among the representatives of the nation..." Nevertheless, such "human beasts," as he notes, would certainly confront fewer obstacles in their acquisition of citizenship than those currently faced by a recalcitrant nobility: "...for a mendicant, a foreigner, has perhaps no interest in opposing the interests of the Third Estate, whereas the noble and ecclesiastic are, by their status [*par état*] allies of the privileges which profit them."[45] The Third Estate only potentially and inadvertently constitutes a danger to itself. But the noble estate is a mortal threat to the nation.

By contrast, because of its freedom from toil the nobility potentially possesses the broad perspective to see beyond its own egoism, to engage society from the vantage point of "justice and humanity." Whereas Third Estate must acquire vision to accomplish its transformation from "human beast to citizen," the nobility must use its capacity for broadmindedness to effect its own reform:

> Why may not reason and justice, as mighty some day as vanity, compel the privileged, through a new but truer, more social interest, to demand of themselves their own rehabilitation [*réhabilitation*] within the order of the Third Estate?[46]

Rehabilitation means dissolving the noble order and merging its individual members into the Third Estate (if only to lead it!); it means ceasing to be a nation unto itself and integrating into the nation at large. Doing so is not merely a gesture of will, it is also a material concession. Sieyes makes it clear that the members of the noble estates must not only relinquish their privileges but also habituate themselves to the habit of labor, if not to debilitating manual work then at least to commerce and trade. Renouncing privilege and acquiring industry are inseparable acts, since, under the threat of losing noble status *par dérogeance*, the nobility's privileges have up to now served legally to bar them from entering "degrading" spheres of labor and trade. "What kind of society is it," asks Sieyes, "where one who works must *forfeit* [*fait déroger*]?"[47] In the odd paradox established in *Qu'est ce que le Tiers état?*, one estate must transcend the effects of its labor, the other acquire its habit.

Paralleling these distinctions between laboring and idle castes is a further one between compulsion and choice. Sieyes implies that "human beasts" are incapable of being humanized on their own and therefore require the agency of the state. The nobility, by contrast, is not a conglomeration of human beasts but a caste of willful aliens who might, through a voluntary act, come to "demand of themselves their own rehabilitation." Yet alongside this olive branch, Sieyes also brandished a sword. The noble estates can choose rehabilitation or, alternatively, they can bring about their own exclusion. Sieyes was prepared to call the bluff of the noble Estates, when in the Winter–Spring of 1788–1789 its representatives threatened to "secede" from the Estates General should the Third Estate achieve its own aim of "doubling" its representation:[48]

> They have dared to pronounce the word *secession* [*scission*]. In this they have threatened both King and People. Well! Good Lord! How happy for the nation if so desirable a secession could be rendered permanent! How easy it would be to do without the privileged! How difficult it would be to induce [*amener*] them to become citizens![49]

If the nobility insisted on remaining a state within a state, then the nation must be prepared to exclude them permanently. The choice, Sieyes suggested, would be theirs alone.

THE EMANCIPATION OF THE JEWS OF FRANCE

Less than six months after the publication of *Qu'est ce que le Tiers état?*, the National Assembly declared "Financial, personal, or real privileges to be abolished forever," decreed that all remnants of personal service – likewise judicial fees, tithes, and exclusive hunting rights – be eliminated without compensation, and announced it had "abolishe[d] the feudal system entirely."[50] Relatively few nobles actively opposed these August Fourth Decrees, most had passively acquiesced to them and a small number even supported them enthusiastically. Reaction was only slightly more intense the following summer when titles too were outlawed. In the first year of the Revolution, fewer than 10 percent of nobles emigrated and outside of a few regions rebellion or sabotage were infrequent or halfhearted. It was only with the later radicalization of the Revolution that the picture changed dramatically. Nobles were severely persecuted under the Terror and in 1797 they were deprived en masse of citizenship.[51] Although by the time of the Restoration, if not well before, members of the former nobility had begun to find their places in a new French society, the intervening period exhibited all of the alternative possibilities posed by Sieyes, acquiescence, incorporation, resistance, rejection, and exclusion.

The experience of French Jewry during the Revolutionary and Napoleonic periods was not entirely dissimilar although certainly far less violent and destructive. The Sephardic Jews of Western France were granted citizenship in late 1790, whereas the Ashkenazim, whose relations with the peasantry of Alsace had long been troubled, were made citizens in late 1791, after considerable debate. With the renewal of conflict over "Jewish usury" in 1806, Napoleon convened an Assembly of Notables to reform Judaism in conformity with the duties of citizenship. Their formulae ratified by a "Sanhedrin" the following year, the state imposed a set of occupational and residential disabilities on the Ashkenazic population for a probationary period of ten years, compromising the Jews' status as full citizens until and unless they curbed their usurious behavior and instituted necessary reforms. Thus the Franco-Jewish experience in this period exhibited the two versions of quid pro quo implicit in Dohm's and Sieyes's formula: equal status in anticipation of regeneration, or partial exclusion in order to compel it.

What made the Jews analogous to nobles in the initial stages of the Revolution – and what made them unlike other candidates for citizenship such as French Protestants or persons with unsavory professions such as actors and executioners – was their identification as both foreign and unproductive. Like nobles Jews were labeled a parasitic *imperium in imperio* and *une nation dans une nation*. In opposing Jewish emancipation in 1789, the Abbé Maury insisted that the Jews were not simply members of another French denomination but citizens of their own nation whose ostensible religious law was in truth a national constitution. "The word 'Jew' is not the name of a religious sect but of a nation," he intoned. To grant them citizenship would be absurd: like "saying that, without letters of naturalization and without ceasing to be English or Danes, the English or Danes could become French." Yet unlike Englishmen or Danes, there was an intrinsic connection between the Jews' national law and their exploitative commercial professions: for their Sabbath precludes military service, their dietary laws rule out fellowship with gentiles, and their numerous national holidays ensure that they cannot devote themselves to agriculture. Hence, "they have never done anything but trade in money [*commerce de l'argent*]. They have been the scourge of agricultural provinces. None of them has tried to ennoble his hands by handling a plow-share or cart." Nevertheless, although granting Jews equality would be ruinous to the peasantry, they should be tolerated, Maury proclaimed. "They are men, and they are our brothers [*ils sont hommes et ils sont nos frères*].[52]

Although Maury was by no means the only opponent of Jewish emanci-pation, he as much as anyone came to the heart of the matter. The charge of loyalty to a foreign constitution that sanctioned the economic exploitation of nonmembers and precluded their own engagement in productive labor resonated with many delegates. Even many on the other side (and even some Jews such as the acculturated Zalkind Hourwitz) acknowledged that the Jews were guilty of many abuses.[53] Particularly effective was Maury's insistence that it had not been Christian compulsion but Jewish law that had led them into usury, for this directly assaulted the Dohm's key premise that "everything for which the Jews have been accused is the effect of the political regime under which they have been forced to live, and any other group of men, subjected to the same circumstances, would surely become guilty of the same crimes." Because Dohm and other advocates of Jewish emancipation had already con-ceded the Jews' "crimes," this assertion of premeditation sapped the defense of its vitality.

Despite this weakness, the Jewish case was finally won because of the sheer momentum of revolutionary optimism. In the final analysis, historical argu-ments such as those adduced by Dohm or Maury were irrelevant. At this moment of transformation, history must be construed as an instrument rather than an end. The delegates to the National Assembly were conscious that they had achieved a triumph of freedom over necessity. They were not just inherit-ing history but making it. This same freedom offered ample hope that under an entirely new set of circumstances the Jews could transcend the burdens of the past. The supporters of emancipation even recognized that forging a new world took time. The future was to be the workshop of the Jews' transforma-tion. "*[R]égénération des juifs... ne peut pas s'opérer en un instant, ni même dans le cours de plusieurs années.*"[54]

As has often been observed, Jewish emancipation flowed from the logic of the French Revolution, which was determined to recognize as participants in its polity not members of corporations and estates but individuals alone. Just as Sieyes confronted nobles with the alternative of dissolving into the Third Estate or seceding, the Jews were offered the choice of full incorporation as individuals or full exclusion as a group (amounting, in a sense, to the same thing).[55] As Count Clermont-Tonnere famously intoned to the Assembly, "It is intolerable that the Jews should be come a separate political formation or class in the country. Every one of them must individually become a citizen;

if they do not want this, they must inform us and we shall then be compelled to expel them. The existence of a nation within a nation is unacceptable
to our country."[56] If a sort of fiction was to be maintained that the Jews
must be emancipated not as a collectivity but rather en masse as a totality of
individuals, then it also was presumed that the Jews must cease to act collectively in the social, political, and especially their economic life. Because the
centuries-long development of ideas of toleration in Europe had focused narrowly on religion, religious difference could be countenanced as compatible
with national cohesiveness where group cultural or economic distinctiveness
could not. Jewishness must therefore be constituted by religion alone, whatever
national characteristics it may once have possessed. At the same time, amid this
leveling ethos Jews' economic difference stood out perhaps more than any of
their other distinctions. Aside from their autonomous governmental institutions, Jews' commercial character was largely what made them resemble a
corporation. Corporations of the ancien régime were, among other things,
economic and occupational orders. Their divestment of commerce would
be their gesture of self-sacrifice to the enterprise of nation building. Their
abandonment of usury would be the sign that they no longer constituted a
special interest, for as Sieyes phrased it, if corporate interest is egotism, then
virtue must be the national interest. Occupational amalgamation into the
nation meant that in future the Jews must no longer exhibit an occupational
character markedly distinct from that of the population in general. Given the
social structure of France at the time this could only mean that a majority of
Jews must dissolve into the peasantry or find their way into industrial workshops.

When in the following decade and a half this unlikely scenario failed to materialize, the Revolution appeared to lose patience. Still, although Napoleon's
decrees of 1808 seemed to call into question the very terms of the emancipation
contract, it would be a mistake to view them as decisive to the fate of Jewish
emancipation in France.[57] It was not merely that the regulations were badly
enforced or that they admitted of countless exceptions. What mattered was
that their real intention was forcibly if clumsily to advance the amalgamation
of Jews into French society, not permanently to exclude them from it. And
despite the fact that the hoped-for restructuring of the Jews' occupations had
still not occurred by 1818 (the conclusion of the ten-year trial period), the
decrees were not renewed. Hence, although they created a humiliating hardship for the Jews of eastern France, their ultimate effect, at least in terms of
the Jews' future legal status, proved minimal.[58]

It turns out that the decrees would have far greater impact on the citizen
status of German than of French Jews. In France, the decrees were abandoned

after 1818. But in the German states they were utilized as a precedent and rationale for slowing and even reversing progress toward full emancipation. This
curious fate of the decrees reflects a more fundamental distinction. The Jews
of France were originally granted citizenship through a Revolution, one that
profoundly altered the legal structure of French society.[59] The Revolution abolished chartered corporations, guilds, and seigniorial privileges. It destroyed
the nobility as a legal category. This meant that in France, as opposed to
Germany, the problem of entrenched noble privileges – as opposed to inherited material advantages – was effectively resolved in August of 1789, so much
so that in 1801 both Napoleon and Sieyes felt the time was ripe to reconstitute a ceremonial nobility of merit to substitute for the nobility of blood
that had been purged. Thus, despite the fanfare surrounding the Napoleonic
"Sanhedrin" of 1806, the problem of French Jews' recalcitrance in regenerating
themselves was never linked to the threat of a reconstitution of legal "feudalism," even despite its essentially cosmetic resurgence following Napoleon's
fall.

In Germany, however, aristocratic legal privilege was weakened but not
destroyed by the reforms instituted during the Napoleonic period. On the
contrary, the question of distinct legal privileges for the nobility, as well as
a possible restoration of privileged estates, would resurface powerfully after
Napoleon's defeat, particularly in Prussia. This was not only because of the
relatively stronger position of the German nobility and Germany's comparatively weak and conservative Third Estate, but also of the fact that in Germany
the French Revolution had served as both an impetus for internal regeneration
and a warning against radical efforts at social and political reform. These two
factors would at times join together in support of arguments against Jewish
emancipation. On the one hand, the weakness of the Third Estate made it far
more possible in Germany than in France to view Jews as a part of the "old
order" against which revolutionary sympathizers must struggle. On the other
hand, because after 1791 Jewish emancipation in Germany also was linked
to the French model of Revolution, it was difficult to dissociate the Jews'
cause from the Revolution's radical and during the Napoleonic period foreign
imperial aims.

Thus, from various and sometimes antithetical political standpoints the
parallels between Jews and nobility, merely inferred by us in the case of Sieyes,
became explicit in the writings of several prominent German intellectuals.
Jews could be depicted as an estate of the ancien régime and therefore as
partners of the nobility in the upholding of an outmoded and unjust system;
they could be depicted as prototypes and models of European aristocratic
degeneration whose own ancient constitution had likewise fallen far from the

grace of its original, pristine purity; or, finally, they could be portrayed as the embodiment of a negative inversion of the noble aristocratic ethos, an egoistic and exclusivist society bent on domination, the kind of fifth column and pretender caste reminiscent of Sieyes's own characterizations of the First and Second Estates. In what follows in this chapter and the next all of these associations, and the political-economic conceptions that lay behind them, will be examined.

JOHANN GOTTLIEB FICHTE

In contrast to Sieyes, Johann Gottlieb Fichte did address the question of Jewish emancipation, briefly and in a notoriously hostile manner. Fichte's remarks in his 1793 *Beitrag zur Berichtigung der Urtheile des Publikums über die französische Revolution* (Contribution to the Correction of the Public's Judgment on the French Revolution) appeared so incendiary that his Jewish contemporary, Saul Ascher, published a lengthy rejoinder entitled *Eisenmenger the Second*, likening Fichte to the infamous seventeenth-century traducer of Judaism.[60] Modern Jewish historians have not been much kinder, with some even identifying Fichte as the creator of a new and virulent strain of modern antisemitism.[61] What is too often overlooked, however, is the actual book in which Fichte's remarks appear. There his comments on Jews take up three pages in a work of over three hundred. More relevant than the issue of proportion is that of context. Fichte's attack on Jews is a small though potent element in a full-scale assault on the nobility and the ancien régime. Although his remarks on Jews exhibit all the traces of traditional Christian antisemitism, their significance cannot be understood without recognizing this noble-Jew connection.[62] Fichte, who in the years 1794–1796 supervised a German edition of Sieyes's writings, extended Sieyes's attack on the unproductive noble estate into an elaborate critique of the nobility's dominant system of property relations, one in which Jews performed the commercial function.[63] Having indicted the noble regime for its despotic gluttony, Fichte then made a surprising move. In a subsequent work, *Der geschlossene Handelsstaat* (The Closed Commercial State), he extended his attack on the noble order by identifying it not with Jewish commerce but with capitalism in general, or at least with the system of private property and free markets that was now becoming dominant in Germany. In a similarly counterintuitive manner, Fichte proposed establishing a rigorously planned economy in order to transcend this medieval anachronism. As becomes clear in the following chapter, this had an unanticipated effect on the German discourse concerning Jewish emancipation. Fichte's linkage of free markets with noble rule helped set the stage for Romantic political

economists and historians to detach these negative critiques of feudal aristocracy from the nobility itself and apply them exclusively to Jews.

Fichte like Sieyes stemmed from humble origins. The son of a ribbon maker,
he was born in Rammenau, in Upper Lusatia in 1762. And as with Sieyes,
Fichte's advancement depended on noble patronage. His education at the
Shuls-Pforta had been subsidized by a local nobleman; likewise his later university education at Jena, Wittenberg, and Leipzig. When his benefactor died,
Fichte was thrown back upon his own resources. This moment coincided
with and perhaps even prompted his turn toward philosophy. Fichte would
later credit his break with the determinism of his Protestant upbringing to his
encounter at this time with the works of Kant.[64] In grateful appreciation he
made a pilgrimage to Königsberg in the summer of 1792. His first work, published anonymously, was taken by reviewers as one of Kant's own. The success
of his literary debut was sealed when Kant publicly revealed the author's true
identity and acclaimed his work. By early 1794, Fichte's growing reputation as
an original interpreter of the critical philosophy won him a professorship at
Jena, an achievement all the more remarkable given his outspoken support for
the French Revolution. Prussia had been officially at war with France for nearly
two years, and although Jena lay outside of Prussian territory, prominent liberals throughout Germany were by this time denouncing the Revolution in
droves.[65]

Yet Fichte was not one to pull his punches. His 1793 Beitrag presents a defense
of the Revolution from the perspective of German philosophical idealism. The
fact that it makes little mention of specific events in France was due less to
caution on the part of the author than to Fichte's intention to unhinge the
Revolution from its geographical and historical moorings, and by means of
philosophical abstraction demonstrate its relevance to European society as a
whole.

The work's starting point is a reinterpretation of Sieyes's notion of secession. Whereas Sieyes presented secession as a violation of national sovereignty,
Fichte depicts it as an expression of freedom and the will to self-determination.
Secession from a given political union is fully legitimate because contracts are
by their nature susceptible to cancellation. This does not mean that contracts
can go unilaterally unfulfilled, but rather that no contract can persist indefinitely without the assurance of continuous mutual consent. In the Beitrag,
Fichte views every state as the product of just such an original contract. Consequently, and without even the pretext, per Locke, that a ruling party has
already violated and hence invalidated its contract, Fichte insists on the right
of the ruled to opt out, so long as it provides compensation. It is the exercising
of this right of secession that Fichte here calls a revolution.[66]

For Fichte secession is not, as for Sieyes, a threat or bluff directed by the noble estates against the Third. Rather, it is the revolution itself. Any group of subjects or citizens enjoys the right to secede from the state and form a new one. Fichte's model here is so abstract and rationalistic that he conceives of neither secession nor statehood in spatially exclusive terms. Should an individual or group wish to terminate its contract and constitute itself anew as a polity, it can do so even while remaining *within* the territorial boundaries of the existing state. Fichte's point is that a state is less a territorial than a legal category, and in situations where the two conflict the latter definition must take precedence. He does not, it is true, ignore all of the practical difficulties that might arise from an act of internal secession, for "both my neighbors right and left remain in the old [state]; and so the whole immeasurable expanse is all mixed up; what confusion and disorder would not follow?"[67] But he insists that as discomforting as it may be, such an outcome cannot be rightfully opposed.[68]

In justification of this right of secession, that is, the right of revolution, Fichte defends precisely what Sieyes had unambiguously condemned: *imperia in imperio*. He does so, however, by contrasting legitimate "states within a state" (such as in the case of the "secession" described above) with illegitimate ones:

> You who so much fear the threat of these relationships [created by secession or revolution], have you never thought to consider your own situation; have you still failed to discover that these dangers, magnified a hundredfold, already surround you continuously?[69]

In these lines, Fichte was addressing himself to conservative writers such as August Rehberg who had deployed, *inter alia*, the "state within a state" argument against the legitimacy of revolutions. Even before 1789 (and to the publication at the end of that year of Edmund Burke's *Reflections on the Revolution in France*), Hanoverian conservatives such as Rehberg, Ernst Brandes, and Justus Möser, with their strong Anglophile tendencies, had championed the organic and evolutionary model of the English constitution over the natural law ideal of Rousseau, Sieyes, and Kant. For these authors, England had managed to preserve intact "the old German constitution" from the period of late antiquity, whereas Germany, following the Peace of Westphalia, had lost its own "ancient constitution" through the baneful influence of French absolutism.[70] The many virtues they attributed to the English constitution included its capacity to maintain political stability and equilibrium through the vehicle of functionally and legally separate estates. Rehberg viewed the estates as prophylactics against despotic power, whereas Fichte saw them instead as the props of absolutism.[71] Although Rehberg and Brandes recommended a reform of existing German estate structures, including the abolition of numerous feudal privileges, their ultimate goal was to strengthen the *Stände* over the long haul rather than to weaken or gradually phase them out, as Dohm had recommended.[72]

Fichte's natural law defense of states within states was designed to attack his opponents' organic theory at its heart. In contrast to "states" created through legitimate acts of secession, Fichte insisted, it was the *Stände* and corporate bodies of the existing regime that constituted a true threat to the public good. This point is amply demonstrated, he maintains, by looking at some of the actually existing "states within states" (*Staaten im Staat*), such as the churches, the guilds, and the military. Members of the military, for instance, are subject to their own constitution, jurisdiction, rules of conduct, and codes of morality. This membership in a privileged society affords them a carte blanche to demean with impunity the occupants of all other civil stations and terrorize mercilessly the persons and property of burghers and peasants. Yet Fichte also notes that the cruelty exhibited by soldiers toward civilians is only the flipside of the demeaning condition of subordination to which their own state-within-a-state constitution subjects them:[73]

> If a *Stand* is removed from the general and led to the particular court of justice; if the laws of this court are far removed from the general laws of all morality; if their petty infractions are punished with strict harshness while their real crimes are overlooked . . . , so would such a *Stand* constitute a separate interest and a distinct morality and reach the level of a dangerous state within a state. Whoever [by demonstrating honorable behavior] escapes the seductions of such a constitution would be ever so noble a man; but he would not contradict the rule, merely prove the exception.[74]

It is at this point that Fichte calls attention to another such state-within-a-state: the Jews. Jews share the characteristics of other dangerous *Stände*, including internal moral codes harmful to the general good, laws that undermine rational norms, a license to act with impunity against outsiders, an egoistic guild spirit, enforced endogamous marriages, and castelike mores. At the same time, Fichte directs several accusations at the Jews, which appear to render them distinct from the other corporations. They are a "powerful, hostilely disposed state" dispersed throughout Europe, which stands in "perpetual war with, and presses down hard upon, the citizenry." Their oppression is not just, as with the military's, a by-product of an inhumane self-disciplinary code. Rather, according to Fichte, it is a manifestation of a religiously induced misanthropy; ". . . [they] are so dangerous, not just because they constitute a separatist and strongly-linked state . . . , but because their state is constructed upon a hatred of the entire human race."[75]

Although, as noted, Fichte has been accused of founding a new school of antisemitism, many of these charges sound familiar. He identifies, for instance, the Jews' misanthropy as a symptom of their Old Testament allegiances, of subordination to "*einen menschenfeindlichen Gott.*" Like John Chrysostom, or the later Martin Luther, Fichte implied the Jews were irredeemable. Their egoistic mentality is so engrained that to change their minds (and make them citizens) would necessitate chopping off all their heads in a single night and replacing them with others "containing not a single Jewish thought."[76] Nevertheless, there was indeed something new here, the first hints of what might be called a "left-wing" indictment of Jews' social functions.[77] Fichte molded inherited Christian denunciations of Jewish perversity into a set of radical political criticisms that made the Jews willing instruments of an oppressive order. Thus, for Fichte, the Jews' misanthropy has definite uses for the unjust corporate order. Jews enjoy special dispensations from the ruling authorities, including economic ones not accorded to even the governing *Stände*.

The first such dispensation is that – as a group designated by the feudal constitution to perform commercial and fiscal functions denied to all others – Jews are enabled, even encouraged, to violate otherwise sacred property laws:

> . . . [T]hat in a state where the absolutist king may not deprive me of my paternal hut and where I maintain my right against the all-powerful minister, the first Jew whom it pleases can plunder me with impunity.[78]

The Jews are the exception that enforces the rule of corporatist despotism. It is their anomalous religion that allows them to live by a different set of rules, both in the sense of mandating a distinctive way of life and of permitting exemption from constitutional norms. It is thus fitting that their second dispensation is a radical theological dissent denied to others. Their non-Christian or anti-Christian religious beliefs – manifestly antithetical to reason – are tolerated by a political order that in turn refuses to permit genuinely rational forms of dissent.[79] As with the Jews' protected system of economic exploitation, their tolerated religious outlook indirectly helps to prop up the repressive regime. Fichte lampoons the apologists of absolutism who embrace religious toleration. They do so, he avers, as a sop with which to clamp down on political criticism:

> O, [the Jews] have different beliefs and that is sufficient for me. Believe in Zoroaster or Confucius, in Moses or Mohammed, in the Pope, Luther or Calvin, it's all the same to me. If only you don't believe in an alien reason [*eine fremde Vernunft*]. But you want to have reason itself and that I will never tolerate. Remain in your condition of immaturity,[80] for otherwise you would become too much for me![81]

It does not follow from this, Fichte insists, that he actually opposes the toleration of Jews and Judaism. "I do not wish to say that one should persecute the Jews for their beliefs, but rather that absolutely no one ought be persecuted for such."[82] In words reminiscent of the Abbé Maury, although reflecting an opposite political conception, Fichte avers that the Jews should be accorded human rights but not citizenship, at least not so long as they subscribe to "different moral laws" [*verschiedene Sittengesetze*][83]: "... for the Jews, who are citizens of a state excluding you, which is tighter and stronger than all of your own, would absolutely trample under foot your other citizens... if you also gave them the rights of citizens..."[84]

This is what advocates of Jewish emancipation, in Fichte's view, have failed to grasp. "It seems to me that the *method* of many of the more recent authors in regard to the Jews appears very confused..."[85] Although he does not identify the specific proponents of these views or explain precisely how their "method" is flawed, it is apparent from the context of his remarks that to Fichte popular hostility toward Jews represents an historically explicable if morally illegitimate response to a genuine rather than illusory threat. Employing the argument that Maury had leveled against apologists such as Dohm, Fichte insists it would be illogical to assume that the Jews' flaws derive exclusively from their external oppression. Rather, it is their own internal religious constitution that has generated their egoistic behavior. At the same time, the Jews' constitution is part of the larger feudal corporate constitution. Jewishness is an integral component of an intolerable and outmoded regime, a noble regime. With the exception of the Jews and the guilds, the other "states within states" attacked in the *Beitrag* – the military and clergy – can be characterized as noble in their personnel and privileges. Because Fichte dismisses the guilds as weak and insignificant, it is fair to conclude that his principal target remained the nobility, to whose mode of domination he also linked the Jews.

Abstracted from the familiar vestiges of Lutheran antisemitism, what was new in Fichte's understanding of Jewish commerce was its clear identification with the old order of feudalism. In the early twentieth century, the economist Werner Sombart would argue the position against Max Weber that Jews rather than Calvinists and Quakers were the originators of modern capitalism. Whatever the merits of Sombart's argument, the association between Jews and economic modernity has been commonplace ever since. Fichte offered the germ of an alternative narrative, one that had roots in Dohm and Luzzatto and that would be restated in the mature Marx's historical remarks on capitalist development. Jews provided the commercial mechanism that helped to sustain seigniorial authority. Their economic activity was part and parcel of the system of lordship that dominated Europe from the Middle Ages to the French Revolution and beyond. Fichte's identification of Jews with the system of noble estate privilege possessed a degree of historical plausibility as well. In late medieval and early modern Germany Jews had been employed by princes and territorial nobility as a source of revenue, taxes that from the subjects' point of view violated customary law, precisely as Fichte charged. Extending from their medieval condition as "imperial serfs," whole communities of Jews were not infrequently pawned by emperors to their vassals: for example, electoral princes, territorial nobles, urban noble patriciates, and clerical nobility as well. Jews had served as pledges for loans to be recouped through their own commercial and credit activities. In addition to providing a special source of revenue, nobles also had found Jews useful as fiscal and commercial wedges for breaking the power of municipalities and guilds.[86] In more recent times, as the historian Deborah Hertz has observed, Prussian mercantilist policy employed a small sector of Jewish financiers to streamline the state fiscal apparatus. "In this fashion the monarchy attempted to promote Prussia's economic development without allowing any competition within the gentile social structure that would threaten the domination of the nobility." Yet Hertz also notes that these wealthy Jews' utility to the crown and nobility depended on their pariah status, something Fichte neglected to mention.[87] Fichte's linkage of Jews and nobility, although possessing a degree of historical veracity, fails to register the high price that Jews were forced to pay for their service as a "privileged" state within a state.

Although Fichte said nothing more about Jews in the *Beitrag* (and relatively little for the rest of his career), the remainder of the book also possesses a direct relevance to the politics of Jewish commerce. Fichte's analysis of feudal relations and his prescription for transcending them offer a remarkable blueprint for the theory of regeneration that would so often be applied to the Jews. The regeneration that Fichte demanded of the nobility, a regeneration of nobles' capacity to perform constructive and creative labor, bore a marked similarity to the idea of Jewish occupational productivization that would be explored by *Haskalah* or Jewish Enlightenment. To understand how Fichte moved from an indictment of the corporate regime to the establishment of a new and free constitutional order built on the principal of the common participation of all citizens in creative labor, we must first return to Fichte's discussion of contracts.

OVERCOMING FEUDAL ANARCHY

Fichte's attack on both Jews and nobility was tied to an abstract theory of property rights through which he hoped concretely to benefit the principal victims of this noble regime – the peasantry. As Fichte described it, the system of *Stände* forms a giant "*Hierarchie-Maschine*" of oppression, starting from the absolutist princes at the top and descending down "to the slaves who cultivate the fields."[88] Fichte explains in the *Beitrag* that the initial contract that established the current system of privileges – of nobles over peasants or, more broadly speaking, of feudalism – is invalid on two counts. It is illegitimate, first, insofar as it presumes a category of property over persons rather than things, and, second, insofar as it assumes that such a contract – even over things – could extend indefinitely through the course of innumerable generations. As noted earlier, there exists a valid right to secession, so long as it is based on the free will of the seceding party and so long as it in turn establishes a polity founded on natural rights. But, short of secession, that is to say, revolution, contracts can be renegotiated in such a way that the division of one polity into two can be avoided. In the case here described, this assumes that the initial contract, in addition to its multiple illicit grounds, also contains grounds that are licit and thereby continue to impose obligations. Insofar as there exists a valid contract over things, however wrongly interpreted during the course of centuries, that contract remains operative with respect to the legitimate forms of property, which serve as its true foundation.

This is where Fichte's natural rights theory combines with a view of political-economy already familiar to us from Dohm, namely, the latter's account of the disastrous consequences of the triumph of feudalism in Germany. According to Fichte, the original "state within the state," the one that in a sense constitutes all the others, is the nobility, for it is the nobility that has usurped the state itself.[89] Just as Sieyes insisted on an earlier stage of legitimate feudalism, Fichte posits that the nobility's original contract with the commoners was based on the concept of a fair exchange of two forms of property, land and labor. Insofar as the contract gave rise to a later fiction that these two modes of property should be removed from the realm of free exchange, it became invalid. But, in dispelling this fiction, the party that originally contracted to provide its labor in return for the use of the other's land can only cancel or alter the contract by agreeing to provide compensation. In other words, the owners of labor in withdrawing from the contract nevertheless enjoy no right to expropriate their masters' lands.

The "revolution" that Fichte seeks is to be accomplished not through expropriation but through the simple replacement of privileges (over persons) by property (over things), that is, through a return to the original contract. This will accomplish a restoration of labor in the one case and a validation of land in the other as the rightful properties of their respective owners. However, for Fichte this can be only the first condition of any solution. His natural rights theory premises two other necessary conditions: first, that all who labor enjoy an inalienable right to property, and, second, that all who are propertied maintain the reciprocal obligation to work. Fortunately, both of these conditions can be realized through a single process, one that will ensue of itself from the restoration of property and elimination of privilege. For, as a consequence of the former, the owners of labor will be placed in a position to sell their property to the highest bidder. Forced to pay a high price for the labor they had traditionally received through privilege, the owners of land will likewise be forced to sell a portion of their property on the open market. Land will become available at a cheap price to those whose property formerly consisted of labor alone. Ultimately, this will lead to an effective subdivision of landed estates and redistribution of immovable property through natural market processes and without resort to either state intervention or popular insurrection. The sellers of labor (the peasants) will now become owners of land, and the labor they exert on their own property will ensure their material well-being as the rightful reward for their productive toil.[90]

But what of the formerly privileged? How will they be able to achieve a similar harmony of these two fundamental human activities, producing and consuming? The privileged, that is, the nobility, have become habituated physically and mentally to engaging only in consumption and never in productive work. Clearly, their partners to the previous contract can no longer continue to supply them indefinitely "with the requirements of an unlimited luxury." And yet "everyone must have what is indispensable . . . ; [for] that is an inalienable human right."[91] Because those previously advantaged by the contract have lost the use of their own labor due to "our good-natured promises to supply them continuously"; because the nobility became debilitated by an arrangement which for so long precluded its own acquisition of skills; in short, "insofar as justice *permits* it from the one side and *demands* it from the other,"[92] the nobility will be entitled to a temporary period of acclimation to the life of labor during which it will gradually take on more and more the complete responsibility for its own upkeep. In the interim, nobles should receive the support of the peasants on whom they once depended. However arduous this transitional stage, Fichte insists on its necessity:

> The suffering that this exertion of labor may cause him does not in the least enter into consideration, for it is a suffering that nature has laid upon us for benevolent ends and which certainly we have no right to relieve him of. *No man on earth has the right to allow his powers [Kräfte] to go unused and to live through the powers of others . . .* [93]

Those supplying temporary subsidies during this transitional period (the peasants, drawing from the produce of former noble estates) maintain "the right of supervision," says Fichte, to ensure that sufficient progress is achieved over a reasonable although here unspecified period of time. Such progress must involve not just the acquisition of the skills and habits of work but also the gradual weaning of the advantaged from their accustomed "luxury," their "imaginary needs governed by display and fashion":[94]

> He must from the moment of the cancellation of our contract learn to deny himself gradually the satisfaction of ever more requirements. We will give him at the start ... what remains over from his previous income; then less, then gradually ever less, until his needs come into balance approximately with our own. And thus he will have reason to complain neither of injustice nor of excessive harshness. If through these efforts he should become even good and wise he will yet thank us that *out of a wasteful idler we have made him into a frugal laborer and from a useless sack of clay into a productive member of human society.*[95]

More than recalling Sieyes on the First Estate, this passage brings to mind a number of Dohm's prescriptions for the economic reform of the Jews. In both Fichte and Dohm, it is recognized that the defects in question currently exist because society no longer requires either group to perform the specific castelike functions that once justified a special social status (military functions in the case of the nobility and commercial ones in the case of the Jews). Because these moral defects have been historically conditioned through the complicity of others, they cannot be viewed as the products of mere choice. In addition, because these defects have been inculcated over the course of many generations, they have now become ingrained and self-sustaining. Finally, as a consequence of this habituation, any moral regeneration to be accomplished through labor will only succeed on the basis of a gradualist approach.

In both Dohm's rendering of the predicament of the Jews and Fichte's of the nobility, what was formerly functional and to this extent justified has long since lost its legitimacy. Given the fact that the commoners' own collective martial power now far surpasses that of the nobility, society neither needs the latter's protection nor does the nobility actually continue to provide it. For Dohm, too, we recall, the general society has now completely surpassed the Jews in the sphere of commercial attributes. This further analogy exposes a distinction, however, between Dohm and Fichte. Fichte (like Sieyes) does not appear to regard the current military activities of the nobility as a form of useful labor. For him, the nobility is entirely idle. But this was not the case with Dohm's depiction of the Jews. As we recall, Dohm viewed industry as a virtue already present in the character of the Jews. It is simply that from today's perspective their industry has become socially and morally misplaced and thus requires redirecting – whereas for Sieyes and Fichte, the industry of the nobility must be created from scratch. Although neither martial characteristics nor commercial orientations should be eradicated from society as a whole (on the contrary, they must be broadly disseminated on a roughly equal basis), these characteristics do need to be restricted or eliminated within those groups that formerly bore them as their own exclusive marks of identity.

This leads to another point: Fichte and Dohm both saw merchant activities as necessary and useful, yet for different reasons both expressed serious reservations about the nature of commerce in modern life. Their contrasting criticisms of commerce reflect differences in the broad mentalities in the respective periods in which they wrote. Dohm had faith that once state policy had brought about an erosion of the corporate order the free market would operate to produce and distribute goods. Fichte, in his *Beitrag* period, was impatient with Dohm's gradualism but shared his goals. Yet Fichte's views on commerce and free markets evolved. He came to see Dohm's "natural order of things" as anarchic. True freedom, he concluded, lay in applying human reason to blind market forces. This transformation in Fichte's thinking occurred against a backdrop of growing national self-awareness in Germany. Despite the fact that revolutionary France was increasingly recognized as a threat to German autonomy, its experiments in state control of the economy provided a nationalist countermodel to the free market ideology increasingly associated with England.

English political economy was still ascendant in Germany when Fichte launched his assault. By 1800 the ideas of Adam Smith had found a ready reception.[96] As noted, German was the first foreign language into which *The Wealth of Nations* had been translated, only a year after its publication in English. Reviews, synopses, additional translations, studies, and critiques would quickly follow. Fichte's one-time ally, the philosopher Friedrich Jacobi, had been one of Smith's early admirers.[97] At Göttingen, the jurist J. S. Pütter became an influential proponent of the new economics, and a number of his students – among them future officials in the reform regimes of Stein and Hardenberg – carried the gospel forth.[98] Not only Smith, but the whole array of British and French political-economists, Mirabeau "the Elder," Sir James Steuart, Adam Ferguson, Arthur Young, among others, were widely known in precisely those circles that would help to reform German economic life after 1806. Königsberg, where the young Fichte had sought an audience with his hero Kant, was, like Göttingen, a center of Smith studies. There the economist Christian Jakob Kraus proved himself the most dogged and systematic advocate in Germany of Adam Smith's doctrines in Germany.[99] There is no reason to assume that Fichte remained isolated from such currents. Although he rarely referred in his writings to specific influences, he remained up to date not only on contemporary theory from abroad but also on the political events and social trends of his time. He followed closely the economic turmoil then occurring in revolutionary France as well as the contrasting commercial progress of Great Britain. Like other admirers of the Revolution, Fichte did not attempt to disguise his contempt for Britain's commercial and imperial expansionism, which in his view was constructed at the behest of a mercantile aristocracy on the backs of a displaced peasantry.[100]

Fichte's break with the liberalism of his *Beitrag* days appears to have begun in the late 1790s, paralleling other personal and intellectual ruptures of those years, his forced departure from Jena under the charge of promoting "atheism" and his controversy with the philosopher Friedrich Jacobi. Fichte's attempt in 1796–1797 to develop a theory of social contracts and natural rights independent of the influence of Rousseau and Kant was also undoubtedly critical to this development.[101] Equally important was Fichte's emerging conception of labor as one of the chief means of individuation, that is, of the individual's recognition of his essential self (what Fichte called the *ich*) through his confrontation with the external environment (the *nicht-ich*). This was a confrontation that physically and cognitively *purposeful* (*zweckmässig*) labor, among other things, effected.[102] Crucial to its realization, Fichte concluded, was the self's acknowledgement that the existential limitations of its will require the complementarity of other selves, other people.[103] Labor, which in modern societies in conducted through the rational division of functions, serves as a principal means by which the individual acknowledges the limitations on his self. Paradoxically, it is through "interaction" (*Wechselwirkung*) that the individual is rendered more complete and society more whole.[104] In the *Beitrag*, Fichte had already insisted that "no man on earth has the right to allow his powers [Kräfte] to go unused and to live through the powers of others…"[105] Now he was less concerned with rights and obligations than with linking the pursuit of self-consciousness and self-realization with social solidarity. These shifts toward a more collectivist, less market-oriented view of the ideal society were subsequently consummated in his 1800 *Der Geschloßne Handelsstaat* (The Closed Commercial State).

The *Handelsstaat* represented Fichte's attempt to formulate the social and economic foundations for a *Vernunftstaat* – a fully rational state. Its value to our analysis lies in its identification of commerce preeminently, albeit counterintuitively, with the feudal nobility. This would prove to be a crucial link in a chain of associations in German literature between the fate of Jewish and noble castes. As we have seen, Fichte himself initiated this link when in the *Beitrag* he depicted the Jews as props of the noble regime. But (as we will see in the next chapter) it was his critics, rather than Fichte himself – figures such as Adam Müller and Friedrich Rühs – who extended and then eventually dissolved the association when they attempted to free the nobility from the aspersions that Fichte, in his *Beitrag* and *Handelsstaat*, had cast on it.

Although Fichte's starting point had barely changed since the days of the *Beitrag*, his conclusions were startlingly new. In the earlier writings, Fichte had focused on the individual's participation in a community of individuals activated by the pursuit of freedom through the social application of the categorical imperative. The obligation to labor, derived from the obligation to both self-sufficiency and the service of others, must be predicated on the possession of sufficient property to make equal economic interaction possible. In the *Handelsstaat*, the obligation to labor was defined far less in terms of the autonomy of the individual, the microcosm, and far more in terms of the autonomy of the community, the macrocosm. The effect of this change was to strengthen and formalize the institutional bases that Fichte now believed must secure individual rights and obligations to the greater whole. In the *Beitrag*, he had assumed that the full restoration of alienable property in labor and land would, by means of natural market processes, gradually produce a set of equitable economic arrangements. In the *Handelsstaat*, however, it was to be the managerial and redistributive capacities of the state, acting on the basis of its sovereign coercive authority, that ensured the right of each *laboring* individual to a life of equal well-being. This did not signify a complete contradiction of his earlier conception of the nature of the state. The state was still not viewed as an end in itself. Rather, whereas in 1794 Fichte viewed the state as merely a legal framework for free and autonomous activity, by 1801 it had become a means – and in fact the chief means – through which the citizens achieve economic equality.[106]

The intention of the closed commercial state was not – as in mercantilism – to harmonize and control traditional social groupings by bringing them under the umbrella of the state, but rather to construct new sets of social institutions based on a continuous, centrally managed refinement of the division of labor.[107] Fichte assigned to the administrative stratum (standing outside of the tripartite estate mechanism) the role of regulating the proportions of men allotted to each *Stand*, a withdrawal from his earlier principle of absolute individual autonomy in the determination of vocation.[108] Conditions of equal comfort can only be assured if collective productivity is made the criterion of divisions in labor. This could not be left for the market to decide. Only the state possessed the power and authority to back up what common knowledge understood to be the shared needs of society as a whole:

> A state in which agriculture is backward and more hands are needed for its improvement, in which a normal mechanical artisanry is absent, can have no luxury. It is unacceptable that one should say, "I, however, can afford to pay for it." It is even unjust that one can pay for the inessential while some other of his fellow citizens lack the necessities... [109]

State administration must determine which occupations require more hands and which do not. The priority of productive over nonproductive, useful or merely pleasant labor found in Josiah Tucker, the Physiocrats, Adam Smith, and Dohm (but not in Mendelssohn or Sieyes) was retained and even expanded by Fichte in his socialist tract. "[T]here must not be more non-producers employed in a state than can be sustained through the products of the same." [110]

If the emphasis on the *Stände* sounds like an idealized vision of the medieval Christian order, Fichte nonetheless rejected all parallels between his closed commercial state and economic systems of the past. Indeed, far from seeking a return to medieval economy, Fichte believed that his closed commercial state would constitute the first genuine effort to free man from the clutches of his inherited economic past. Fichte conceived of that past as medievalism in the economic sphere. In his historical account (inverting the assumptions of nearly all contemporary political economists), he represents the modern free market system as a continuation of rather than a departure from medieval theory and praxis. We recall that for Sieyes the growth of commerce had long ago rendered authentic feudalism and its attendant noble privileges obsolete. Fichte had more or less echoed this view in his *Beitrag* of 1794, there depicting the allodium (alienable land) as the once-dominant mode of medieval property (authorized by the original constitution) whose place had later been usurped by the feodum (inalienable estates). Consequently, Fichte concluded in the *Beitrag*, the feodum must now be destroyed and a free market in land and labor installed in its place. [111] In the *Handelsstaat*, however, Fichte's historical account shifted. In contrast both to his own earlier views and to those of Sieyes, he now presented private property, alienable land, and unregulated trade as part of the modern triumph of the medieval feudal regime.

In this new conception, medieval Europe had once comprised a single broad entity – a body unified through common Christian religious and Germanic tribal ties, rather than national and political ones. In the face of weak states and primitive, half-forgotten constitutional traditions, the peoples of

Europe had come to consider themselves members of a single Christian commonwealth, one devoid of strict internal borders or significant cultural and political (i.e., national and constitutional) distinctions. "Each individual traversed the ground of the other, always finding himself everywhere at home."[112] Commerce and trade were likewise organized on the basis of this same borderless universality. "There was a common means of exchange, gold and silver, that had essentially the same worth in all parts of the great commercial state and circulated unhindered from one part to the other." Merchants traversed this vast territory unhindered in their solicitation of wares. "Trade was, in this circumstance, thoroughly free, without regulation and likewise without restriction."[113]

Fichte did not intend to discount the prevalence of social hierarchies and estates in the Middle Ages, but rather to demonstrate that these hierarchies had originated under conditions in which centralized states were still weak. The process of state-building, initiated and impelled by the late-medieval recovery of Roman law, had led gradually to the establishment of separate nation-states and distinct legal sovereignties. But, he emphasized, state-building was a process that had been left tragically incomplete. Religious unity had been broken by the Reformation; cultural and political unity by the reassertion of old tribal cultural ties. Thus, Christendom had gradually given way to Europe, but there was one exception. The third source of medieval unity, the free market, although antithetical in its very nature to the rationalizing prerogatives of the modern state, had been left undisturbed. Although Fichte did not explain the reasons underlying this failure, he left no doubt as to its consequences. The first was that the most powerful of the old medieval hierarchies was left intact. That is to say, instead of exerting its capacities to redistribute property in the most equitable possible way, the modern state had legitimated and formalized the same unequal property relations it had inherited from the preceding period. The second consequence was similar in its effect yet more fundamental in its cause, namely, the incomplete state left intact the pan-European character of medieval commerce which had produced these economic injustices in the first place. Political anarchy had been tamed, but only to give economic anarchy freer reign.[114] Fichte posed the resulting dilemma as follows:

> ... if the whole of Christian Europe, with the acquired colonies and ports in other parts of the world, is [to remain] forever a unity, then obviously the trade of all parts with all must [also] remain as free as it originally was. [But] if, to the contrary, [Europe] has become divided into various integral states existing under different governments, then it must likewise be divided into various thoroughly closed commercial states.[115]

A Europe comprised of numerous political sovereignties, yet at the same time constituting a vast economic republic, would be a monstrosity. To permit unrestricted commerce is to concede failure in the whole project of constitutional reform. This is because "[a]ll institutions which permit or assume unregulated commerce between citizens of one and another state consider both as fundamentally citizens of the same state."[116] The error is not merely one of logic nor the resulting deficiency simply in the realm of state power. Rather, the effect of free commercial relations is to deprive the concept of citizenship of its core meaning. For Fichte, citizenship is an enabling condition whose value lies in its guarantee for all of the means of life and livelihood. Yet the free market leads not to freedom in the Aristotelian or Machiavellian sense, but to its opposite: the liberty of men "to mutually destroy one another." Retention of the medieval economic order within the novel and complex circumstances of modern life means placing men's fates in the hands of a constitution, which "has long ago been dissolved."[117] Hence, the retention of even the economic clauses of this outmoded constitution would naturally lead to a:

> ceaseless war of all against all,...which becomes the more dangerous the more the world becomes populated, the more the commercial state expands through [colonial] acquisitions, the more production and skill rise and the number of wares in circulation along with the accompanying general wants multiplies and diversifies. What had occurred without great injustice and oppression in the simple life of the nation is now through expanded acquisitiveness being transformed into the most crying injustice and the greatest source of poverty.[118]

Consequently, the closed juridical state, defined by political citizenship and legal equality, can only be realized and made meaningful through a closed commercial state constituted by economic equality and guaranteed livelihood. The state is to be "closed" in the sense that virtually no foreign trade is to be permitted; and it is to be "commercial" insofar as a merchant estate will exist to internally redistribute goods.

Here Fichte must be measured against the long line of political philosophers who had identified land ownership as the authentic basis of political citizenship. One might see the closed commercial state as Machiavelli and Harrington translated, *mutatis mutandis*, into Kantian terms. From Fichte's standpoint, Harrington and others of the same tradition had fallen into the trap of defining property "medievally" in terms of land. In the *Handelsstaat*, Fichte pointed out that landownership (as "real estate," the archetypal mode of private property) is the expression of the medieval class par excellence, the nobility. If land is the only *real* property, then land-owners are the only real citizens. "What a marvel it is that . . . we see here a theory according to which the *Stand* of the great landowners, or the nobility, is the only true property owner who alone is the politically-constituted citizen . . ."[119] Autonomy and self-rule, as celebrated by the republican tradition, were thus inevitably defeated by the republican emphasis on land. By defining independent landownership as the fulcrum of political freedom, power was handed over to – or retained in the hands of – the landed nobility. Thus, the nobility is the commercial class par excellence.

Fichte went one step further. He attacked not just the ideal of private property in land, but the idea of private property in general, identifying the former as merely the chief characteristic instance of the latter and both as equally the expressions of noble interests (the feodum as inalienable landed property). In this way, Fichte had closed the circle first traced by Sieyes. The latter, in his *Qu'est ce-que le Tiers état*, had explicitly renounced "noble" constitutional models, such as the English, which had hitherto provided reformers in France and Germany alike with their ideal of organic constitutional development, of mixed estates that highlighted the successful integration of landed and commercial interests. Sieyes rejected this reformist tradition as well as all other celebrated constitutional models from ages past. Noble constitutions, even "balanced" ones like the English, held no attraction for him. As we have seen in the case of Jewish emancipation, the radicalized atmosphere preceding the Revolution encouraged not just antinoble sentiment, but a preference for free creation and fresh starts.[120]

In the *Handelsstaat*, Fichte echoed Sieyes's insistence on breaking the mold of history, severing the ties that bound men to past arrangements. He, too, singled out Britain, with its mixed constitution, as the model of economic injustice, aristocratic property relations, and the commercial expansionism of the landed interests. Yet Fichte also went beyond Sieyes's conception. For, as we have seen, in the *Handelsstaat* he rejected Sieyes's supposition that noble and third estates were truly opposing principles. Whereas Sieyes saw the productive capacity of the bourgeois commercial order as the death knell of the Middle Ages, Fichte incorporated private property and free markets into a nightmarish vision of medieval property relations gone awry. This leads back to the question, left dangling earlier, as to why in the *Handelsstaat* Fichte had neglected to state the reasons for the modern state's failure to complete its rationalizing mission. The answer appears to lie in Fichte's inability to reconcile the antiaristocratic emphases of the French Revolution with its own espousal of market-driven economy. For how could a Revolution that defined itself by the intention of destroying medieval privilege, nevertheless retain intact, and indeed fortify, the Middle Ages' most characteristic economic feature? Unable adequately to answer this question, Fichte passed it over with a gloss.

This element of confusion in Fichte's historical-economy will prove invaluable to the next phase of our analysis, an examination of German Romantic political-economy and the Jews. By attacking the nobility for the creation of free markets, Fichte had opened a breach in the polemical arsenal of the Revolution, which could then be turned against the Third Estate itself. This is precisely what the Romantic political-economist Adam Müller did. As we will see, Müller would seek to deflect Fichte's accusations against the feudal aristocracy. But to do so, he would first have to recover some constitutional principle that he could describe as thoroughly uncontaminated by all taints of property and commerce. It was just such a constitution that Müller claimed to find in the Mosaic Republic of the Jews.

6

&

The Israelites and the Aristocracy

In 1799, as Fichte was composing his *Closed Commercial State*, the poet Novalis (Friedrich von Hardenberg) produced a classic German romantic depiction of feudalism and the Middle Ages. In language both vivid and analytic, Novalis's "Christianity or Europe" glorified the old corporate order of estates, guilds, and churches, while excoriating the Reformation and Enlightenment for fragmenting Europe and shattering its spiritual foundations.[1] Approximately a decade later, as popular resistance the French Revolution climaxed, Adam Müller (1779–1829) inaugurated his project of extending Novalis's critique of Enlightenment to the field of political economy. In a sequence of works produced throughout the Napoleonic era, Müller drafted his own original historical model of Western and European socioeconomic development. As part of his effort to glorify the social relations of the Middle Ages, Müller identified the conceptual foundations of feudalism with the ancient Mosaic Constitution. He asserted that the Old Testament provides the original model of a true aristocratic polity. Its rejection of absolute private property and its conception of landownership as temporary usufruct; its restrictions against commerce and its outlawing of usury; its ideal of the nation as a spiritual entity and of society as a corporate family; its heroic and bellicose spirit exemplified by the people and its leaders – all amply demonstrate that the Mosaic constitution was the true originator of the medieval. At the same time the present degraded condition of both the Jews and the nobility reveals just how far both have fallen from their former state of grace. In fact, Müller claimed that the nobility's degeneration had been prefigured ages ago by the similar fall of the Jews. The nobles, he asserted, can only reclaim their honor and restore their right to govern by reviving the ancient constitutional principals first perfected by the Jews. The question, however, is whether Jews today can do the same.

Müller is a neglected figure in the history of European political economy, from the perspective of subsequent neoclassical doctrine perhaps deservedly so. Yet there have been other traditions, for instance, the German Historical School of Wilhelm Roscher and Gustav Schmoller that in turn strongly influenced the political economy of Max Weber; the "natural economy" of Karl Bücher, that was later revived by Karl Polanyi and Moses Finley, not to mention in the antisemitic economic theories of National Socialism, as well as the modern American school of institutional economics founded by Thorstein Veblen, in relation to all of which Müller might be justifiably assigned a grandfatherly role. Equally important in the present context is Müller's position as the principal figure in the German transmission and restoration of the Mosaic Constitution that featured prominently in the early chapters of this book. As a force in modern political thought, the Mosaic Constitution had appeared to play itself out by the late seventeenth century, to be replaced by the social contract doctrines of Locke and later Rousseau. In a recent essay celebratory of the role of the Mosaic Constitution in Western political thought, the intellectual historian Fania Oz-Salzburger reaches precisely this conclusion. Oz-Salzburger argues persuasively that interpretations of the Mosaic Constitution in early modern political discourse helped shape emerging concepts of sovereignty, of federalist structures, and of "moral economy," that is, institutions safeguarding the poor. Yet she confines her discussion to early modern British and Dutch political literature and stops in the late 1600s, after which point she believes the influence of the Old Testament on European political thought waned. Although accurate for England and Holland, this thesis does not take the German and French situations into account.[2] German Romantics in particular drew sustenance in their assault on the Aufklärung from the Hebrew Bible, with its apparent endorsement of "mixed government," its strong tribal and nationalist flavor, and its emphasis on economic solidarity.

As in the British case, German political philosophers saw the Mosaic republic as potentially relevant to the working out of their own pressing constitutional dilemmas. And as with early modern Britain, albeit far more acutely in early nineteenth-century Germany, the status of contemporary Jews was one of those dilemmas. Despite these similarities Romanticist configurations of political Hebraism possessed a different intonation, not to mention a contrary ideological tendency, from seventeenth-century models such as those of James Harrington and John Toland. Often bombastic in his language and nebulous in his terms, Müller, for example, clearly viewed himself not as the spokesman of civic humanist ideals but as the savior of the *Adelsstand*, the noble estate. Yet in light of the stereotyped image of German Romantic and *Volkisch* ideology, in which *Judentum und Deutschtum* usually appear as antitheses, Müller closely associated his sacred nobility with the commercial *Handelsvolk* of Jews. His formulation of a pro-noble ideology exerted a strong influence on German conservatism following Napoleon's defeat. What did not survive, as explained later, was his linkage of the nobility and the Jews. On the contrary, amid the drive to construct a postwar constitutional framework for German society, many conservatives who were influenced by Müller, much like liberal adepts of Fichte, aimed to restore the civic dignity of the nobility while impugning that of the Jews.

THE ROMANTIC CRITIQUE OF POLITICAL ECONOMY

Müller himself was neither a noble nor a Jew. The son of a minor Prussian official, he earned his living as a tutor, a publicist and a paid political propagandist. He had trained in the fields of *Staatswissenschaft* and Cameralism at the University of Göttingen in the years 1799–1801, years when the doctrines of Adam Smith attained their peak influence there. With his dandyish appearance, attractive if overblown conversation and wide-ranging knowledge of contemporary politics, Müller soon became a presence in Berlin salon society. His first major work, *Die Lehre von Gegensatz* (The Doctrine of Oppositions), written in 1802, sought to resituate aesthetic theory on the basis of dialectical principles, and presented a conception of the beautiful as a composite of antitheses (Müller would offer a similar formula for attaining the ideal condition of economic equilibrium).[3] The publication four years later of his *Vorlesungen über die deutsche Literatur* (Lectures on German Literature) affirmed his position as a major presence within the younger generation of German Romantics.[4] In 1805, Müller had converted to Catholicism, establishing a precedent soon followed by other notable Romantics such as Ludwig Tieck and Friedrich Schlegel. The combination of his new Catholic creed and increasingly reactionary politics would later bear fruit when, after the defeat of Napoleon, Müller was employed by Metternich to perform diplomatic and literary services on behalf of Austria, the leading Catholic power of the Restoration period.[5] But it was in the preceding years of revolution and reform that Müller made his lasting mark intellectually. In 1808, he completed the lectures that formed the basis of his *Die Elemente der Staatskunst* (Elements of Statecraft).[6] This was a monumental attempt to apply his aesthetic notions to political science and economy. Along with his 1811 *Versuche einer neuen Theorie des Geldes* (Attempt at a New Theory of Money),[7] it established Müller's reputation as the leading German Romantic author in the field of political theory and economy.[8]

Although Müller's wide reading in contemporary political economy was rivaled by few Germans of the time, his own economic conceptions, including his depiction of feudalism, found little support within the leading political circles of the day. This was certainly true among liberals, especially in the years before 1815 when the reformist campaign was in full swing. Characteristic was Müller's defeated bid in 1810 to win the chair in *Kameralwissenschaft* at the University of Berlin, and its award instead to the Smithian, Johann Gottfried Hoffmann.[9] What is more surprising, given Müller's reactionary outlook, is that his reception among the conservative elite was only slightly less unfriendly. This was not a consequence of Müller's own humble origins. Esteemed conservative thinkers such as Justus Möser, August Rehberg, and Ernst Brandes (and later the Jewish convert Friedrich Julius Stahl) were not of aristocratic birth either. Rather, most conservatives regarded Müller's views as simply too radical. They tended to view his theories as the nostalgic schemes of a beautiful dreamer, or, worse, the apocalyptic thunderings of a disguised revolutionary.[10] As in the case of Robert Harley's relationship with John Toland, conservative statesmen such as Metternich employed Müller as a propagandist but distanced themselves from his more far-ranging ideas.[11]

Müller's conservative critics, it turns out, were not far wrong.[12] Never one for half measures, at least not in the rhetorical sphere, Müller claimed to reject not just the latest trends in political-economy but, indeed, the whole tradition of modern economic thought dating back to the Renaissance – encompassing mercantilism, physiocracy, cameralism, and the various other "modern" schools. To Müller, the similarities between these systems far outweighed the differences. First, he attacked the methodology of economics itself. In his view, economics had defined itself as a calculative science, when in fact it should be considered as the art of balancing, of achieving geometric harmony.[13] Second, Müller called into question the very ends of political economy, namely, society's wealth-maximization. To Müller, wealth was at best merely a means to serve rather than replace human spiritual wants and, thus, should never be defined as a *telos* or *summum bonum*.[14] Similarly, Müller chastised the political economists for their preoccupation with categories of productivity and growth; he dismissed the various competing schools as differing merely in approach. The goal, whether realized through free trade or governmental regulation, remained invariably the same: the ceaseless accumulation of riches and power.

the number of residents, the stock of heads to be brought under weapons, and the sum of money-revenue; and, as if international law were nothing other than a facet of political arithmetic, the entire emphasis of administration is geared toward arithmetic expansion, expansion of square miles, of residents, troops, and revenues...[15]

In this sense, laissez-faire represents just a more extreme form of mercantilism. Both systems wish to break society down into atomistic components so as to advance a common goal of optimizing state power.[16]

This last point requires emphasis when seeking to uncover Müller's intellectual influences. Müller certainly acknowledged his spiritual kinship with the British statesman Edmund Burke, who had similarly praised the feudal spirit and the genius of the unwritten constitution. Yet it would be a mistake to view him as an acolyte. Despite Burke's impact on Müller's historical and aesthetic conceptions (elaborated on later), and despite Müller's close friendship with Friedrich Gentz, Burke's admiring German translator, Müller's political economy remained quite distinct. Emma Rothschild has rightly noted that "there was no German Burke to claim freedom of commerce as the fulfillment of feudal wisdom."[17] Burke was essentially a free trader, who regarded the aristocracy as the proper practitioners of commerce as much as of chivalry. Müller's views, as we shall see, were altogether different, defining a division of labor through which each estate represented a contrasting and exclusive social principle.

If Müller's connection to Burke was hardly straightforward, then his relationship to Fichte was unambiguous and entirely antagonistic. Müller's initial encounter with Fichte (his very first publication was a review of Fichte's *Handelsstaat*) proved to be his most fateful.[18] In reading Müller's economic works, one is struck by his consistent and systematic determination to invert Fichte's ideas. A number of examples can be cited. Whereas Fichte employed the imagery of the machine to define the instrumentalist function of the state, Müller condemned the analogy, insisting instead that the state was a living organism, the brain and heart of society.[19] Although Fichte emphasized that property could be legitimate only in relation to things and not persons, Müller drew a mystical equation between objects and people. Objects possess personality. They take on the character of the human lives which employ them, while at the same time the personality of human beings is inevitably rooted in the character of the objects among which they live.

Thus, although Fichte, with his Kantian perspective, warned repeatedly of the dangers of treating rational persons as material things, Müller warned against the dangers of depriving objects of their human individuality. In his 1794 *Vorlesungen*, Fichte had emphasized that men inherit a preexisting material culture, the legacy of labors past, which affords the present generation advantages and places it in the debt of preceding ones. From this, Fichte derived the principle that man has a moral obligation to engage in productive labor, for this is the only means at his disposal to repay the debt he owes to his ancestors.[20] Yet, at the same time, Fichte insisted that men should assert their independence from the intellectual and institutional legacy of the past. Fichte wished to set men free to create the future in the image of reason rather than of tradition. Müller, in contrast, viewed the debt of the present generation in cultural rather than simply material terms. Man is not only born into a world of existing material culture but into a realm of preexisting ideas and institutions as well as laws and social arrangements. "These are nothing other than the fortunate hands of his great forefathers extending themselves to him, supporting him and upholding his brief, ephemeral existence; in short, laws and institutions are true persons."[21] Thus, at any given moment, the state is comprised not just of *Zeitgenossen* [contemporaries], all of whom inhabit the same space at the same time, but also of *Raumgenossen*, those present, past, and future generations that have occupied or will occupy the same space at different times. Drawing here on the views of Burke, whose *Reflections on the Revolution in France* exerted tremendous influence on German conservatism, Müller held that past and future generations are to be regarded as equally citizens of the state.[22] The interests of both the ancestors and posterity require protection against the vagaries of present momentary expedience. Custom and tradition should provide countervailing balance against fashion and whim.[23]

Adapting such Burkean themes, Müller set out to constrain the impulse of the ephemeral present always to reshape the world in its own passing image. To do so necessitated investigation of the authentic values of the medieval past. Müller's forays into medieval history bear resemblance not just to Burke but also to the Scottish historical sociologists William Robertson and Adam Ferguson. The Scottish authors were at pains to show that the Middle Ages had not been entirely the era of "religion and barbarism" that Enlightenment philosophes such as Voltaire and Gibbon had claimed. On the contrary, chivalry had softened the warrior ethos of the feudal aristocracy, leading to the rise of "manners" moderns so loved to celebrate. Robertson, Burke, and Ferguson believed that, mediated through the sociability introduced by chivalry, the noble classes had managed to achieve a healthy equilibrium between martial and commercial virtues.[24] Although Müller acknowledged that this was true of England, he insisted that, for reasons elaborated on later, it did not occur in Germany. There, because commerce had been forced to wage a vicious struggle to gain a foothold, it was more determined to achieve domination. Instead of the "balance" characteristic of English life, Germany has succumbed to a one-sided materialism. Müller illustrated this by drawing an analogy between the closed Gothic constitution of medieval Germany and the closed Mosaic constitution of the Israelites. In both cases, a virtuous aristocratic culture had been felled by the overweening commerce it tried so hard to exclude. As a consequence, the personalities of both nobles and Jews had now become distorted by a materialistic one-sidedness alien to their authentic and proud aristocratic spirit.

In his historical conceptions, Müller made a strenuous effort to redescribe Fichte's earlier narrative by reversing its array of heroes and villains. This can be seen in his effort to rehabilitate the feudal and the medieval economy as paradigms of the natural order. It also applies to the more specific case of defining the original sources of European medievalism and tracing the specific causes of medieval decline. Müller agreed with Fichte that medievalism had been progressively undermined through its gradual absorption of an alien and inimical Roman element. But Müller scored points by exposing a contradiction in Fichte's narrative. Müller identified Roman law not just as a rationalizing administrative force but also as a juristic system that affirmed private property rights in the strictest sense. How then could Fichte claim that private property and markets were an illegitimate carry-over from the Middle Ages and Roman law a foundation for modern economic autarky? On the contrary, insisted Müller, the little that the feudal age knew of private property was in direct proportion to the small extent to which Roman law had penetrated its life.[25] Thus, Müller understood *modern* political economy as the fully worked-out expression of Roman property concepts.

When it came to the question of estates, Müller similarly inverted Fichte's formulations. We recall that in his *Handelsstaat* Fichte had made provision for a rational order of *Stände* (agricultural, artisanal, and distributive) in which individual membership would be determined by the administrative judgment of the state. But for Müller, the *Stände* were not to be evaluated on the basis of productive criteria, but rather in accordance with spiritual considerations. Müller assigned distinct national, religious, and gender symbolism to each of the *Stände*. In this, he rejected the modern substitution of functional estate categories for organic ones. According to Müller, the moderns treat state and society "as a machine with component functional parts; whereas the state should conform to nature in nature's natural division."[26]

Thus, for Müller, the true mixed constitution could not be founded on the rationalist theories of philosophers such as Fichte and Montesquieu. It corresponds instead to the ideal of the social order as an extended family, one in which function follows from intrinsic nature and internal tensions create an insoluble corporate whole.[27] It is an order in which the institution of private property and the activity of commerce, as represented by the burgher estate, are both held in check by the spiritualizing and collectivizing authority of aristocracy and clergy. In accordance with "Nature's natural division," each *Stand* possesses its defining principles. The burgher estate or *Nährstand* is Roman, pagan, and masculine in nature. It is the *Stand* of the *Zeitgenossen*, representing individualism, man's domination over objects, and the interests of the immediate present. In contrast, the noble estate, the *Wehrstand*, is Mosaic in origin and feminine in gender. It represents the *Raumgenossen* – the defense of ancestors, tradition and land, the nation's enduring symbol. Finally, whereas the *Wehrstand* represents the past and the *Nährstand* the present, it is the *Lehrstand* (the clergy) that stands for the future. The *Lehrstand* is Christian and celibate (remember Müller's Catholicism); it mediates between the Judaic and pagan elements of the other estates and administers the sacraments to them, as to husband and wife.[28] Within this social trinity, it is the *Lehrstand* that stands for salvation and eternity.[29]

If this was the balanced order that had once characterized Europe, then what had occurred historically to upset it? How did one of these *Stände*, the Third Estate, manage to grow sufficiently powerful to usurp the others and establish its rule? To answer these questions, we need to look back at Müller's depiction of the original feudal constitution – the Mosaic law – and its practitioners – the Israelites.

Israelites and Jews (corresponding respectively to biblical and postbiblical adherents of Mosaic law) occupy distinct roles in Müller's analysis. Israelites are the originators of the feudal constitution, whereas Jews provide the archetype of aristocratic decline. The transformation of Israelites (landed adherents of the Mosaic constitution) into Jews (a despised and stateless caste) mirrors the fall of the nobility from feudal grace to bourgeois damnation; hence the causes of the Israelites' decline help to explain the reasons for the nobility's descent.

One of the core motifs within the Mosaic Constitution was the suggestion that Moses had stood in the first rank of ancient lawgivers, along with Solon, Lycurgus and Romulus. In one sense, this could take the form of damning through faint praise, at least insofar as the intention was to expose the divine law of Moses as a merely human invention, a kind of political pious fraud that employed the cover of the sacred to advance a set of secular political aims. This was the view of Machiavelli and later of Jean-Jacques Rousseau, although both authors admired Moses no less for his political acumen.[30] Alternatively, Moses was described by a number of sixteenth- and seventeenth-century authors as the founder of the ultimate republic whose legislation truly expressed divine wisdom in the political sphere.[31]

If one might say that John Toland fell somewhere eccentrically toward the middle of this spectrum, then it was Adam Müller who appeared finally to establish a direct link between the various indigenous, national, and feudal

"ancient constitution" ideals and the "Jewish" Mosaic Republic itself. Modern
historical analysis has barely considered the prominence of ancient constitutional motifs in the German lands during the early modern period. Yet the
territories of the future Germany were replete with constitutional traditions
that were genetically related or else phenomenologically analogous to many
of the ancient constitution ideas of seventeenth-century Britain: indeed, the
former took a bewildering variety of forms. One was the notion of the ancient
Reich, the Holy Roman Empire, whose original though now defunct constitution conjured up the image of a pan-European Christian imperium, or even
a vast European republic of mixed constitutional forms.[32] In addition to the
imperial, there also were localized "old constitution" traditions, emphasizing
customary law and regional self-government, in opposition to the centralizing encroachments of a remote, mechanized, and alien state. Such traditions
could be found celebrated in Justus Möser's Osnabrück, Hegel's Württemberg,
as well as in many other small and embattled polities.[33] A third source, a more
or less domesticated import from Britain, was to be found in the writings
of Edmund Burke, particularly, as noted, his *Reflections on the Revolution in
France*, which had effectively squared the circle of Whig political theory by
rendering the constitutional settlement of 1688–1689 (Tucker's "new system
of civil and commercial government") into a timeless expression of ancient
political prudence. Burke had breathed new life into the mixed constitution at
a time when British models had come under fire from enthusiasts of the Revolution. Burke's unabashed medievalism, moreover, proved uniquely appealing
to Romantic sensibilities like Müller's.[34]

Müller, one might say, took the constitutional approaches of Montesquieu
and Burke and gave them a romanticized aesthetic gloss. An endless body
of contrasts (*Gegensätze*) and infinite array of particularisms mark the ideal
constitution. The constitution is a work of art that reflects the genius of God,
as variegated, "anarchic," and yet orderly as divine creation itself. It is these
same qualities that inhere in the Mosaic constitution, with its devotion to
transcendence, eternity, and divine rule. For some of its seventeenth-century
admirers, the Mosaic state had been supremely republican precisely because
of its replacement of monarchical with monotheistic kingship. For Müller,
in turn, the Israelite polity was "feudal" by virtue of its substitution of Lord
for king: "Jehovah [was] the owner of the land . . . ," his subjects mere "stew-
ards of the fields" and "temporary recipients of its usufruct . . ." Even when
a monarchy did come into existence, Jehovah remained "lord suzerain" to
whom all mortal kings owed fealty. In a political order such as this, land could
not be subjected to merely human dominion, for "the earth is the Lord's." And
because Hebrews could not treat objects as mere property, they also could not

treat persons as mere objects. "Whoever knows how to treat material property as a person can be permitted to treat persons as material property." Ancient Hebrew slavery was thus the true prototype of medieval serfdom, according to Müller, with its network of reciprocal obligations and secure protections. The Hebrew notion of servitude, he added, stands in stark contrast to chattel slavery, a characteristic expression of an ignoble, Roman and bourgeois conception of "things."[35]

Indeed, chattel slavery was a commercial institution of Greco-Roman derivation, according to Müller. But the ancient Israelites, especially in their formative period, knew little of commerce – a remarkable fact given the location of Palestine at the crossroads of Near Eastern trade. It might be noted that here Müller veered from the argument of Josephus, as interpreted by authors such as Cunaeus, that Jews lived far from the crossroads of trade "and so they long kept their manners uncorrupted, and none of those exotic things pertaining to luxury and riot was imported, whereby most potent nations are undone."[36] He evidently wanted to underscore the point that it was not an accident of geography but the intent and effect of the Mosaic legislation that prohibited active trade with outsiders.[37] Because the soil is the mirror of the heavens, Moses did all in his power to root the nation in the life of the land:

> ... the agriculturist, whose entire activity is continuously interwoven into the shifting of the seasons, becomes ever more enamored of the soil on which he stands and holds constant to the strict and simple life dependent on invisible forces – and even to the idea of a single, highest god, if such a notion has even once seized hold of him.[38]

In a Romantic gloss on the kind of typology encountered earlier in Dohm, Müller notes that the activity of merchants and manufacturers thrives independently of nature and thus of the temporal sources of tradition, faith, and solidarity. Thus, the merchant "puts his faith more readily in his own cleverness and skill..." than in God, nation, or state.[39] Moses recognized that if the severest restrictions on commerce and usury were not imposed, a burgher class would eventually arise "to bring about an erosion of all nationality" and "divert the eye [of the nation] from its ancestors and descendants."

> ... in commerce every individual acquires for himself; Moses desired, in order that national existence or the freedom of all be collectively possessed, that all life possessions be held far more by the nation through the long course of centuries than by individuals through the moment.[40]

It is tempting to see here Romantic glosses not just on Dohm but on Machiavelli and Harrington as well. But in terms of the political traditions that we have discussed earlier, the Romantic conception of the ancient constitution diverged significantly. It is not just that Machiavelli despised noblemen and Harrington feudalism. It is, rather, that the Romantic longing for restoration had itself been forged in self-conscious awareness of a fatal and irreparable breach with the past.[41] Müller expressed this in his insistence that what really separated all original feudal models from the future hoped-for one was that the latter would not be imposed through blind faith but through self-conscious choice, not through haphazard fortune but through deliberate planning, and not through prophetic decree but through the *wissenschaftlich* activities of a scholarly class. This is precisely why the future constitution would prove superior to the ancient one and why it alone would manage to avoid the pitfalls that had destroyed past incarnations, the Mosaic included.[42]

Müller was attracted to ancient Mosaicism because he saw it as both a sacred guide and a cautionary tale. According to Müller, the stability of any order depends on its capacity to absorb and balance antithetical principles. This capacity reflects the recognition that a dominant principle, whether monotheistic, like the Israelite, aesthetic, like the Greek, or legal, like the Roman, can only be meaningful if it coexists in perpetual tension with the variety of principles that oppose it. "One-sidedness" is the fatal flaw of past constitutions. As Müller, with his fondness for paradox, put it, the idea of one God need not contradict that of many gods, the idea of one Law need not contradict that of many laws (i.e., state and corporation law), or the idea of one state that of many states (i.e., "states within states," or estates).[43] Echoing an older strain in German idealist thought, Müller insisted that true unity must be a function of harmonic multiplicity. "Nothing can unite so much as true division itself."[44] The masculine exists only for and through the feminine, the bourgeois only for and through the aristocratic. Contrariwise, the effect of attempting to suppress social oppositions is to create precisely the sort of one-sidedness that ultimately enables the triumph of violent antagonisms, as occurred in the French Revolution. The mentality of the modern era – particularly of Revolutionary France, with its emphasis on legal uniformity – has thus made intolerance a watchword. Its republican self-identification is a counterfeit one, because mutuality is the true mark of a republic and one-sidedness the symbol of tyranny. Yet one-sidedness is also the real source of constitutional degeneration. Hence, like all despotic systems, the modern revolutionary one, according to Müller, must sow the seeds of its own destruction.[45]

According to Müller, this dialectic of one-sidedness and degeneration was already prefigured in the case of the ancient Israelites. Degeneration was a paradoxical consequence of the Mosaic constitution's own determined republicanism, which was forced to succumb not only to kingship but, more importantly, to commerce. It was precisely because the Mosaic legislation insisted on commercially isolating the Israelite nation that it became vulnerable to foreign imperial conquest. There can be no "closed commercial state," for its fortress walls actually weaken the internal life of the *Stände*. The irony is that ancient Israel, because of its well-intentioned but excessive efforts at autonomy, wound up succumbing to foreign domination. This led, ironically, to a thriving domestic and foreign trade and, precisely the result the lawgiver most feared, to the growth of an overweening mercantile class. Thence, a whole set of opposing tendencies came into play. The monotheistic principle, originally geared to the maintenance of agricultural exclusivity and the protection of national solidarity, legislated a complete proscription of neighboring polytheistic systems as well as of the nations that harbored them. What had begun as a set of salutary institutions, including the notion of national submission to a cosmic divinity, ended up as an ethic of chauvinistic intolerance manifested in devotion to a national god. What had started as a struggle for freedom and independence won through arduous struggle, suffering, and heroism became transformed into a debilitating addiction to *ressentiment*. "And so from the originally just and noble pride there henceforth emerged a disagreeable, intolerable arrogance." The subversion of the original principles of a people, nation, or culture not only brings with it an ironic adoption of its own opposing principles but also a retention of the original but now insupportable self-image. "They now conceived of the national nobility in a bourgeois [*bürgerlich*] and Roman manner." "[T]he ancient nobility became henceforth a curse, as all profaned nobilities necessarily must come to the most extreme depravity."[46] As with Fichte and so many others, the Christian myth of Jewish blindness and fall from grace here finds creative reformulation in Müller's secularized historical narrative. In this case, however, the tale of the Jews' descent into commerce was not meant to prefigure their own eventual conversion but to point the way to the resurrection of noble authority after it had been crucified by Rome – that is to say, Napoleonic France.

In contemporary Europe, the feudal class – like the Israelite nation before – has become "profaned." The source of its downfall lies in its own "excesses" and one-sidedness, here likewise exacerbated by the intrusion of alien forces. Although vague about the nature of these original excesses, Müller suggests that they centered on the areas of "canon and feudal law."[47] This implies that a sufficient balance between agriculture and commerce had been lacking in the original feudal polity; which is to say that, as in the Mosaic case, legal and religious norms were so weighted as virtually to exclude a functioning Third Estate. Müller may have adapted this interpretation from Edmund Burke, who in his *Reflections* identified as one of the causes of the baneful Revolution the noble estate's excessive efforts to suppress commerce and keep the moneyed and landed interests rigorously separate, a misguided policy that Burke believed led the resentful Third Estate to an equal overreaction.[48] But Müller's account also reminds us of Dohm's portrait of the barbaric period of European development, when a dangerous vacuum existed within the tribal social structure.[49] In Müller's case, that vacuum was not filled by Jews (who now existed merely on the sidelines, as symbols of noble degeneration) but by the Roman element in its progressive diffusion through the medieval legal system. Further evidence for this contention comes from Müller's discussion of the English constitution. Its "national genius" had made provision for commercial development within its own system of common law (as Burke too boasted) and was thus never forced to turn to Roman property concepts to simulate a constitutional balance, as occurred on the Continent. Thus, for Müller, the English constitution is now the only surviving legacy of the Mosaic (a notion John Toland might have enjoyed). Even Britain's fabulous enrichment through international trade has not dimmed its original spirit, for "[w]orld commerce and the vast expansion of industry have penetrated England, yet the spirit of narrow property rights never attained dominance over that of feudal right." The same English constitution that Fichte had cited to support his theory of the aristocratic character of private property gave added proof to Müller that the only secure polity is the one in which noble and burgher estates act to rein each other in.[50]

We will return to Müller's depiction of the Mosaic constitution, but first we must see how the feudal conflict with Roman law played itself out. For continental Europe and Germany were not destined to enjoy England's happy fate. Although the English had done it right, the Germanic nobility had sought to impose its ideals monolithically. Consequently, society was forced to admit the alien influence of imperial Rome in order to fulfill its material needs. Initially, this recovery of Roman learning had served a beneficial purpose, helping to curb the "excesses" of the feudal and canon codes. But having once gained a foothold, in the medieval as in the Mosaic worlds, Roman law and culture sought an ever-wider sway. Müller's account so telescopes events that they appear in an almost unnavigable blur. But it does seem correct to say that the twelfth-century Renaissance during which Europe reabsorbed Roman law coincided with what historians would later designate the "commercial revolution of the Middle Ages." This coincidence of the Renaissance (i.e., the recovery of Roman sources) and commercial expansion would then repeat itself in early modern Europe. The Renaissance of the fifteenth and sixteenth centuries was responsible for infusing into Europe that mercantilist spirit that would drive state policy toward inexorable disaster. Mercantilism proper, as

Müller understood it, was the economic policy of the new absolutist state made feasible through the rationalizing and centralizing impetus of Roman law.[51]

But the rise of this absolutist state marked the first serious blow to the nobility. This occurred for two reasons. First, mercantilist policies threw the full weight of governmental authority behind the new commerce and its practitioners. This meant that the real power of the Third Estate grew to unprecedented proportions, although for the time being the bourgeoisie remained in a constitutionally subordinate position. Second, absolutism sought to appease and co-opt the still-dominant nobility by transforming it from a "natural" estate into a privileged corporation. This meant securing for the nobility as exclusive property the landed estates that it had formerly held as mere usufruct, subject to the full range of feudal limitations and obligations. The nobility – caught, as it were, unawares – now became both the beneficiary and the victim of Roman concepts, while losing sight of its own. "The sublime idea of personal service, suzerainty, and feodum . . . [were made to] yield . . . to the concepts of money dues, worldly sovereignty and strict possession."[52] Consequently, absolutism, which knew no "higher bond than the worldly, material bond of state and property," was able progressively to render the nobility into a kind of mutant bourgeoisie endowed with special legal and constitutional privileges – into what Müller labeled, as had Fichte before him, a *Geburtsadel*. Denuded of their authentic nature and purpose, noble privileges were now perceived by the rest of society – particularly the Third Estate – as unjust, and their bearers as unworthy. "And so the bourgeoisie found the nobility unbearable because they could find no honor in them and yet still had to abide their privileges."[53] In this way, the ground for French Revolution had been prepared centuries in advance.

We have now observed three separate accounts of noble degeneration. For Sieyes the new nobility was both foreign and phantom, a potent illusion holding the nation captive through historical amnesia. For Fichte, the nobility had undergone successive incarnations, which led from a status derived from military prowess and reciprocal obligation to one rooted in the arbitrary privileges of birth. For Müller, too, the modern nobility had forfeited its mission by succumbing to and absorbing into itself the ethos of Roman property law. Like the ancient Israelites, it, too, had become "profaned."

In relation to Sieyes, Müller's thesis allowed for a fundamentally novel interpretation of the French Revolution. Müller insisted that, contrary to the theories of "state historians," the Revolution had not been a conflict between antithetical principles of bourgeois and aristocrat. Rather, both of these groupings had long since succumbed to the force of private property and had thus equally sought life "in dead possessions."

> ... those who defended feudalism or inequality based themselves on a right which in their hands became a dead right. Those who attacked feudalism and yearned for equality wanted dead right and lifeless possession, nothing more. Consequently, it is thoroughly false when it is assumed that two [opposing] political systems confronted each other in the French Revolution. Rather, they were only two different property estates [*Besitzstände*]: one effectively established in the days of yore, and another conjured up by the present generation ... [54]

Here was truly a game of one-upmanship on Sieyes. For, by definition, an authentic Third Estate would wish not to be "everything," as Sieyes had demanded, but merely something "in equal weight alongside the other two estates."[55] Therefore, a Third Estate that claimed to be the nation would truly be neither, or rather, it would be precisely the sort of impostor class that Sieyes had previously accused the nobility of being.[56] Inverting, in like manner, Sieyes's own attacks on the "foreignness" of the nobility, Müller now labeled the Third Estate an alien force, a Roman *civitas* that had usurped the place of the old bourgeoisie. But Müller could only make this point at the expense of conceding Sieyes's: that is, by acknowledging that the present-day nobility was also essentially illegitimate. No wonder conservatives found many of his views unpalatable. Müller had forged a double-edged indictment of the European social system as a counterfeit (or inorganic) polity that had abandoned its original constitutional heritage. The question that remained was how to get it back.

Did the example of contemporary Jews offer any guidance? As noted, in his *Elements*, Müller implicated commerce in the undermining of the old European constitutional balance. But it was a commerce born of Roman property law rather than some usurious "Jewish spirit" that had damned Europe to commercial slavery. At a time when Jews and commerce, or Jews and usury, often were depicted as synonymous, this distinction enabled Müller to represent the Jews as still the bearers of a positive constitutional model rather than as an economic threat. By transforming itself into an egoistic monopoly, the nobility had fallen into the same trap as, and had indeed now come to resemble, the Jews in their fallen state. Yet Müller did not intend this comparison to flatter the former. As he noted, unlike the European aristocracy, the Jews – even in their "profaned" condition – had not fallen entirely from grace. Although they had come to conceive of their own noble character in a *bürgerlich* manner, they nevertheless retained important vestiges of their ancient heritage. Having replicated the fate of the Jews of old, it was time perhaps for the nobility to look to contemporary Jews as a model of regeneration. It is true, Müller conceded, that "[n]o one will envy the present political circumstances of the Jews; nevertheless, I maintain it as my solemn duty to consider the serious matter [of our fate] from the standpoint of this nation."[57] In addition to their state, what the Jews had clearly lost was their virtuous professions, particularly their agriculture: "of the patrimonial customs and manner of living little more remains."[58] Yet, despite this shortcoming, the genius of the Mosaic constitution still shines through.

What is it that nobles have lost but the Jews still possess? In defining the reasons for the decline of the European nobility, Müller remarked that feudal law can only survive if its idea is animated by religious feeling, by which he meant a sense of subordination to a principle higher than that of private property. One effect of the penetration of feudal by Roman property concepts was to deprive the former of their religious content, that "spirit of freedom, mutuality and worthy obedience which were inseparable from them from the start."[59] Analogously, what still inoculates the Jews from the all-too-common charge of base avarice is the fact that, even today, they have never abandoned their original faith. On the contrary, it is what defines them and maintains them in their unity. Thus, "[m]uch that in our misery is most lacking to us we could learn from them: the secret of political endurance and unshakable faith."[60] For Müller, the two secrets are one and the same. By making faith the foundation of his constitution, Moses ensured that neither commerce nor statism would penetrate to the core of Jewish nationality. Although debilitated by the acquisition of commerce and the loss of its state, the political unity of the Jewish nation remains strong. Whereas the ancient Greeks had pioneered in the creation of the constitutional state, they lacked a religious idea to animate their sense of nationality. Thus, the Greeks today remain on their own soil, still practicing their age-old customs, although without any residue of their ancient political forms. By contrast, "that there can be found so little in the Mosaic legislation of positive state law is the reason why the essence of the Jews' political unity can endure alongside all later Christian and Mohammedan constitutions."[61] In Judaism, property never replaced God.

So, too, the European nobility must now rediscover its faith – or forge it anew – if a perfected feudal society were in future to emerge. As noted, this would require the reconstitution of a scholarly-clerical class capable of "scientifically" recomposing all of the elements of statecraft, the Mosaic, the

Roman, and the Greek, into an ideal balance. In this, the Mosaic would be the most important single element, because it would supply the aristocratic principle and ground statecraft in the soil of religious devotion.

Müller's historical economy had aimed to expose the dangers inherent in the ideas of Adam Smith, Sieyes, and Fichte: gross materialism, one-sidedness, and bourgeois egoism. It was a well-timed exposition. French revolutionary expansionism had now aroused Germany from its slumber. As Germans prepared to throw off the Napoleonic yoke, they had a rare opportunity to define their own future. From Müller's standpoint, this should be a project undertaken not just by the *Zeitgenossen*; full respect must be paid to the *Raumgenossen*, the past and future generations, as well. A reconstituted *modern* feudalism, in Müller's view, one that reflected the English and Mosaic constitutions, would be the ideal model for Germany from both a historical and religious point of view. Naturally, this would be a far cry from what Dohm had envisioned. Although Müller professed to admire both ancient Israelites and modern Jews, the restoration of the noble order could afford the latter only a highly circumscribed status. The noble-Jew analogy had proved fruitful in revealing the historical character of the aristocracy, its fall from grace and its future resurrection. Its mission fulfilled, it could now be laid to rest.

CHRISTENTUM UND DEUTSCHHEIT

Thus far, we have discussed the Jews only as a historical symbol – albeit one of contemporary significance, as we have just seen. But what of the immediate practical problem of Jewish emancipation in Germany? In the last section of this chapter, we will see how the progression of images – from Sieyes's depiction of the nobility as corrupt although corrigible idlers, to Fichte's definition of both Jews and nobility as execrable "states within states," and, finally, to Müller's characterization of both groups as "profaned" aristocracies – helped to inform the literature on German-Jewish emancipation in the first years of the Restoration regime.

In the years 1811–1812, Müller helped to found Berlin's *Christliche-Deutsche Tischgesellschaft* (later the *Christliche-Germanische Tischgesellschaft*), a patriotic society composed of Romantic and conservative writers who opposed most of the recent social reforms in Prussia and who urged the government to adopt a stronger stance against Napoleon.[62] "Women, philistines, and Jews" were excluded by the by-laws. This was intended as a stab at the earlier Berlin salons, which were often hosted by Jewish women and which, in the eyes of the patriots, had exhibited altogether "philistine," bourgeois and Francophile tendencies.[63] A number of the members of this *Tischgesellschaft* – for example,

Achim von Arnim, Clemens Brentano, Friedrich Karl von Savigny – openly opposed proposals for Jewish emancipation on the grounds that through it Jewish "merchants, money-changers, and brokers" would buy up noble estates (noble lands had been made alienable in 1809) and drag the peasantry into further ruin.[64] Müller's own opposition, however, rested on somewhat different grounds. As we have seen, he favored not just a Christian state but a corporate one as well. Hence, he not only rejected Jewish emancipation, but emancipation in general. For him, the old Fichtean accusation that the Jews constituted a "state-within-a-state" was no mark against them, because in his view society *should* be composed of states-within-states, so long as they remain commonly subordinated to the mixed constitution. Thus, Müller argued in favor of a return of Jews to their medieval status as a self-governing but restricted religious corporation, although free from persecution. Jews should be accorded their own legitimate place within the constitution, not as individuals adhering to a private sect, because Müller had no truck with individual rights on the French model, but as a corporation among other corporations.[65] Fanciful or frightening as such a notion appears, it would subsequently enter into the repertoire of conservative policies regarding the Jews. As we will see, it later became a pet project of the Prussian King Frederick William IV, who in the early 1840s sought to implement a restoration of the *Standestaat*, highlighted by a full return of the Jews to their medieval status.[66]

But this was still in the future. Despite the opposition of many conservatives, Prussian Jewry was emancipated on March 11, 1812, one of a series of reforms instituted by the Stein and Hardenberg governments after 1806. As in the case of the French Revolution, so, too, with Prussian reform, Jewish emancipation went hand-in-hand with the legal demolition of the "feudal" regime – the elimination of guild privileges and town monopolies, the termination of serfdom, the conversion of labor service into monetary compensation, the admission of commoners to military offices, and the alienability of noble estates.[67] Yet in the wake of Napoleon's defeat, Jewish emancipation came to be challenged with a renewed vigor. The Napoleonic decrees of 1808 supplied a convenient precedent and rationale; indeed, after 1818 when the decrees in France were allowed to lapse, a number of German states renewed them independently. Amid negotiations to create a German Confederation to replace the now defunct *Reich*, the question of Jewish emancipation became a sticking point. The matter emerged as a topic of heated public discussion infected with the spirit of what the Jewish reformer, Saul Ascher, labeled "Germanomania." Yet Jewish status was only one among many difficult questions surrounding the effort at this time to forge a new postrevolutionary German polity and identity. Many Germans hoped that a new constitution would now point the way to national unification.

Following the "war of liberation," pressure arose from within veteran and student groups hoping to accelerate the pace of constitutional reform. At the same time, the lower nobility, guilds, and municipalities – reeling from the blows suffered at the hands of reformers – were pressing for a constitution with guaranteed representation for the estates. Constitutionalism, opposed by the Austrian minister Metternich as a ploy to bring revolution and by Prussian bureaucrats as an obstacle to efficiency, nevertheless provided common ground for liberals and conservatives alike to advance their distinct visions of the German future. At the same time, negotiations over the constitution could sometimes lead them to compromise. For instance, the fear of being of being tarred with the label of "leveller," associated with the hated French, provided an incentive for liberals to moderate their rhetoric against the old *Stände*, whereas the fait accompli of the earlier reforms supplied a rationale for conservatives to scale back demands for a full restoration of feudal institutions, along lines proposed by Müller.[68] Moreover, although doctrinaire conservatives opposed both market and constitutional reforms, practical Restoration policy in Prussia and elsewhere tended to split the difference by pursuing economic at the expense of political innovation.[69] Because Jewish emancipation had both economic and political dimensions, conservative notables were divided on the question. Metternich, for instance, favored retaining the emancipation that other conservatives associated with Napoleonic rule, whereas the arch-conservative Friedrich August Ludwig von der Marwitz (who like Metternich employed Müller as a secretary) and the political philosopher Karl Ludwig von Haller, wanted the retraction of Jewish citizenship. Liberals were likewise split. For instance, Friedrich Buchholz, a determined enemy of the "feudal monarchy" and an enthusiastic proponent of Adam Smith, was also the author of virulently antisemitic works.[70] Nationalism tended to be a liberal cause yet it could prove as hostile to Jewish emancipation as any social or religious conservatism.[71]

Amid this ideological web, one source of consistency in the anti-Jewish rhetoric of this period was the demise of the noble/Jew analogy. Whether formulated as a critique of the corporate bases of the ancien régime, as a demand for the two groups' regeneration through productive labor, or an apologia for their lost aristocratic ethos, the recent social upheavals in Germany had brought an end to this fruitful motif. One reason is that by 1815 the alliance between the two groups had itself effectively concluded. The Jewish elite had formerly functioned, in the manner characterized by Simone Luzzatto, to provide fiscal and commercial services for the state in a manner that protected the nobility's precious monopolies and prerogatives. Jews did not just serve the noble interests indirectly, however. They also supplied credit to nobles in financial straights, and through the salons established in Berlin by wealthy Jewish women, provided them with cultural and literary forums they had otherwise lacked. The reforms of the early nineteenth century rendered many of these functions redundant or obsolete. Whereas the nobility's prospects for survival looked grim in the mid-eighteenth century, by 1815 they had rebounded remarkably. The formal elimination of feudalism turned out to be rather a boon for many, at least the wealthiest. The conversion of peasants into agricultural day or seasonal workers proved economical for noble estates, whereas the conversion of labor services into monetary fees infused badly needed capital into noble hands. Complementing this, the liberalization of the social order, as Deborah Hertz observes, allowed noble families to channel younger sons into new professions, thereby freeing themselves of the heavy burden of supporting them at home. In fact, as a consequence of the reforms, the Prussian nobility now succeeded in doing what many nobles elsewhere in Europe had done before: purge their ranks of the poor "sandaled" or "cabbage" nobles and then buy up their former lands. Although noble fates varied by region in Germany, on the whole the reforms had allowed them to modernize without actually dissolving, something that Jews, too, would attempt in the nineteenth century. Yet this final similarity did not salvage the relationship. Nobles were now free (or freer) of their humiliating dependency on Jewish money. They could at last publicly exhibit disdain for Jewish philistinism and vulgarity without biting the hand that fed them or appearing to be hypocrites. Müller's *Tischgesellschaft* was a perfect expression of this liberation.[72]

The nationalism of the *Tischgesellschaft* underscores the fact that on ideological grounds as well the noble/Jew linkage had lost its utility. To its conservative organizers, religious and national identity should go hand-in-hand. Even if all of the participants in the club did not adhere to its *standisch* ideals, in light of the experience of French tyranny and exploitation, all could concur that *national* solidarity should trump class conflict. For the conservatives, short of their conversion, the Jews' only place in the new Germany would be as a tolerated cast; for the liberal nationalists, hostility to the rule of money and corporate egoism could now be displaced almost entirely onto the Jews, who would no longer be required to share this onus with their former noble allies.[73] Liberal nationalists had begun this process as early as 1803 when a series of pamphlets were published denouncing the Jews as an egoistic caste of usurers and exploiters whose emancipation would give them free reign to conquer Germany. Works of a similar nature, produced by the aforementioned

Buchholz, as well as by C. W. F. Grattenauer, Christian Ludwig Paalzow, and E. T. von Kortum, attracted a wide readership. They denounced Jewish commerce as a plot to bring the nation to ruin, but at the same time linked the Jews to other states-within-the-state, reflecting the paranoid temperament of these years of continued revolutionary upheaval and Napoleonic conquest.[74] In contrast, the antisemitism that materialized in the following decade isolated Jews from a broader critique of society; or, rather, concentrated onto the Jews the criticisms formerly leveled against a range of foes. Jews were poised to play the role of the new nobles, now a nobility of finance and usury. In a bourgeois order, money rather than pedigree would control land. This theme had already been adumbrated by the French conservative de Bonald, who in 1806 had decried "cette nouvelle féodalité des juifs, véritables *hauts et puissans seigneurs* de l'Alsace."[75] In the immediate Restoration period, fantasies of a Jewish takeover reminiscent of the Tory anti-Jew Bill propaganda erupted in Germany. As the powerful nobleman and Müller's patron, von der Marwitz, exclaimed, "so soon as landed property will have sunk to such a level that they can acquire it advantageously, ... *they* will become, as landowners, the chief representatives of the state, and so our old honorable Brandenburg Prussia will become a new-style Jewish state (*ein neumodischer Judenstaat*)."[76] Two prominent instances of the same theme, one from a liberal Fichtean, the other from a conservative Müllerian perspective, will suffice to illustrate the point.

BETWEEN *GEBURTSADEL* AND *GELDADEL*

A Kantian professor at the University of Heidelberg, Jacob Friedrich Fries is best known to posterity, however, through his political activities, particularly his participation in the nationalist Wartburg Festival in 1817 and in the student groups (the *Studentenbünde* and *Burschenschaften*) that had organized it.[77] Although the student movement included disparate political strains, its essential outlook was both nationalistic and liberal-constitutional. It favored the establishment of a federated German republic or constitutional monarchy, a *Rechtstaat*, with expanded rights for the citizenry (such as press freedoms, rights of habeas corpus, and of public assembly).[78] Fries's own political position was not all that different from that of Fichte in his later years. His nationalism tended to be *volkisch* in the liberal sense, identifying the common people as the progressive element in the nation and the educated classes as the mediators of national values. Yet, at the same time, Fries rejected social leveling of a radical nature, fearing that it might lead to social fragmentation along French Revolution lines. He was thus willing to concede a degree of legal inequality among citizens (including some political privileges for the nobility) if necessary to advancing the national interest.[79]

In this light, what is striking about Fries's "On the Danger of the Jews to the Well-Being and Character of the Germans" is not so much its evocation of Fichtean state-within-a-state imagery, by now already a commonplace in anti-Jewish literature, but, rather, its attempt to build on Fichte's original association between Jews and nobility without, as was the case with Fichte, directly attacking the nobility itself. This is not to suggest that Fries was dissembling in "On the Dangers" or that he was consciously employing the Jews as decoys. Rather, his formulation – according to which contemporary Jews constitute "the last vestige of the caste system in our times" – flowed directly from the effort to forge a liberal-nationalist basis for political reform while eschewing any hint of revolutionary radicalism.[80] As Fries remarked in an 1816 pamphlet on the German constitution, in contrast to France, where the poor were driven to behave like "cannibals," Germans have "gradually softened or abolished unjust noble privileges and harmful feudal servitude of almost every kind." Thanks to the foresightedness of its government reformers, they have continuously advanced the welfare of the people through their "ennobled national education" and "benevolent institutions."[81]

Fries's criteria for civic incorporation were based less on the idea of a mixed constitution à la Montesquieu than an organic nationalism, wherein all "authentic" elements were to be accorded their proper place in the polity and at the same time subordinated to its larger ends.[82] Fries supported gradualism in the pursuit of legal equality as a bar to the excessively rationalizing effects of French radicalism. His Rousseauian or Fichtian denigration of "factions" and "private interests" was conceived of as much in spiritual and nationalist as in material and social terms. The nation should be more than a collection of public-spirited individuals; it should reflect a harmony of its distinctive but integral elements. Fries expressed faith that the nobility, over the course of time, could be subordinated to and assimilated through the agency of the state precisely because, as an indigenous and Christian component of the nation that functioned integrally within it, the nobility had never truly sealed itself off from outside influences and effects. Not so the Jews, whose occupational structure remains overwhelmingly commercial. Jews have failed to amalgamate economically into the *Volk*. Indeed, they comprise one of the last remaining "closed societies" [*geschlossene Gesellschaft*] in Germany, one whose own internal constitution – combining the elements of "nation," "political alliance," "religious party," and "commercial caste" [*Handelskaste*] – precludes its submission to a higher cause. Each of these components, according to Fries, would serve as an argument against Jewish emancipation; but in combination they are devastating.[83]

Of the four constitutional elements mentioned earlier, it was the *"Handelskaste"* that Fries labeled "most dangerous of all."[84] Unlike Fichte in his *Handelsstaat*, Fries refrained from endorsing direct state supervision of the economy, insisting only that the state aim to coordinate commerce with other positive institutions, such as law, science, the military, and religion, that embody the national will. Yet Fries did indicate that commerce comprises a highly volatile activity, one that could help bind society together or else rend it apart. Which effect it would exert was a matter of the degree to which its practitioners comprised a distinct political grouping whose ends conflicted with those of the nation as a whole.[85] The nobility, according to this definition, does not constitute a commercial caste, or, in the true meaning of the term, a caste of any kind. This is clear, according to Fries, from the fact that members of the nobility are today found in a wide variety of fields, including "science, art, industry or commerce," without monopolizing any one of them.[86] That is to say, while remaining in various ways distinct, they are also in the process of integrating themselves into civil society.

Fries insists that aristocratic egoism is now the defining characteristic of the Jews and no longer of the nobility itself. The present contrast between the former erstwhile allies could not be more plain. The Jewish caste resembles not the aristocracy properly speaking but, rather, a "portion of the landed nobility," one that "hundreds of years ago" had cut itself off from the larger body of the *Wehrstand* and organized itself into a separate and distinct criminal class, namely, the *Raubadel* or noble "robber barons" of the late Middle Ages. Their depredations in the countryside, according to a thesis popular among nineteenth-century German historians, had led to the rise of fortified cities, which then became commercial centers.[87] In Fries's account, the criminality and "lawless brutality" of the *Raubadel* left the princes no choice but to take up the sword and violently smash this sect.

> What now, if these *Raubadel* had taken the notion to proclaim their own religion, to announce that conscience did not permit them to eat and drink with other folk and to take up some occupation other than highway robbery – would the princes have restrained themselves from putting an end to the abomination? Or more likely would they not have employed the sharpest measures against it? It is an entirely similar matter with regard to the Jewish case and its caste isolation.[88]

In this manner was the link between Jews and nobility, as between two states-within-states of the ancien régime, reduced to an historical analogy between a "secret society" of present-day Jews and an outlaw sect of nobility destroyed long ago.

Fries insisted that not external historical forces but rather internal constitutional ones best explain why Jews have amalgamated into a *Handelskaste*. By this means he sought to preempt the charge of circular reasoning, that is, blaming Jews for a condition that had been imposed on them against their will. At the same time, and despite the frequent violence of his imagery, Fries claimed to bear only sympathy for the Jews as men. It was not against Jews as persons, Fries insisted, but against Judaism as a religious-political doctrine, that he had felt compelled to write. Here, too, Fries protested his liberalism and sought to reconcile it with his nationalism. His opposition to rabbinic Judaism, he averred, involved not questions of religious freedom – which at any rate enjoyed his full support – but, rather, "the most sacred matters of right and moral national development [*sittlichen Volksausbildung*]."[89] This meant, apparently, that Judaism was not merely a religion but an alien political doctrine and code as well. Similar views had been expressed during the French Revolution by the Abbé Maury and by Fichte, among others. The difference was that then opposition to the Jews' internal political code was part of a far broader effort to purge society of all legal distinctions and traditional social privileges. In the case of Fries, in contrast, it appears to substitute for many of those broader aims.

Fries stopped short of demanding Jews' conversion to Christianity, maintaining instead that "breaking the chains of Talmudism," along with "harsh measures" directed against Jewish commerce, would be sufficient to turn Jews toward "respectable professions." The wealthy among the Jews could be made to subsidize the vocational education of the poor, while at the same time "every productive trade should be rendered as accessible as possible to the first generations."[90] If Fries seemed unclear as to what a Judaism minus its ceremonial law might entail, he nevertheless left no doubt as to the nature of the "harsh measures" to be applied should the Jews refuse to be reformed.

> If our Jews do not wish to abjure entirely the abomination of the ceremonial law and rabbinism and to adopt reason and right in doctrine and life to an extent that allows them to amalgamate with Christians into a civic union [*zu einem bürgerlichen Verein verschmelzen können*], then they may be declared by us as debarred from all civic right and, as in Spain, deprived of the privilege of residing in this land.[91]

Such a statement recalls the choice that Sieyes had offered to the nobility in 1789 as well as the stricture against the Jews leveled by Fichte in 1794. Yet, in

"On the Dangers," Fries eschewed the radical assault on the nobility employed by these predecessors.

In a pamphlet published the previous year, the historian Friedrich Rühs employed a similar approach, but in his case the chief influence was not Fichte the liberal revolutionary but, rather, Adam Müller the Romantic reactionary. Rühs was a professor at the University of Berlin, a specialist on the history of Scandinavia and the author of a major textbook on the Middle Ages. His two polemics, "On the Claim of Jews to Civic Rights" (1815), and "The Rights of Christianity and the German Nation" (1816) proved influential when the Congress of Vienna's deliberations prompted renewed debates on Jewish emancipation.[92] Although some scholars have asserted that Rühs's pamphlets merely reprised traditional Christian antisemitic motifs, this in fact is a gross underestimation.[93] Like most secular antisemites of the time, Rühs did repackage the old Christian charges of Jewish blindness and misanthropy in a modern ideological garb. But Rühs's attacks on Jewish emancipation also exhibited newer elements. He wrote not only as a professional historian cognizant of recent innovations in research methods and approaches but also as a nationalist who at the very moment of challenging Jewish emancipation had also produced a bitterly denunciatory portrait of France's policies toward Germany.[94] He had absorbed the jingoism and the currently fashionable "Germanomania" that had barely existed even a dozen years earlier, let alone during the Christian Middle Ages he so admired.[95] Finally, Rühs wrote as a Romantic, that is, as someone who attempted to apply Müller's critique of the Enlightenment, and of its political economy in particular, to the question of Jewish citizenship and emancipation. All of this, combined with the fact that Rühs produced his pamphlets *after* rather than before Jews had attained emancipation, lent a certain immediacy to his approach. Amid an atmosphere of reaction against the previous decade of French-inspired reform, his pamphlets appeared as timely reassessments, formulated on the basis of new and urgent criteria, of the disastrous policies of an earlier age.

Rühs set out to show that, contra Dohm, intrinsic rather than external factors had decisively shaped the Jewish economy. This claim entailed a two-part approach: first, the demolition of Dohm's lachrymose conception of Jewish history; and second, the forging of a link between Judaism as a national religious constitution and Jews' historical predilection for commerce.

Although acknowledging an element of persecution in the Jewish past, Rühs insisted that the author of the *Verbesserung* had exaggerated both its extent and influence.[96] He pointed, for instance, to a wealth of privileges and protections from which numerous Jewish communities had benefited during the

Middle Ages.[97] He noted that Jews had been granted a high degree of autonomy, the right to worship freely and to live by their own law. He cited the
protections enjoined for "priests, clerics and widows, and all orphans, traders
and Jews" in the *Schwaben-* and *Sachsenspiegel*.[98] He called attention to the
state's enforcement of debts owed to Jews, the permission granted them to
charge high interest rates, and the exemptions from prosecution accorded
them for receiving stolen goods in pawn.[99] He pointed to the near universal
prohibitions in this period on the forced conversion of Jews. He further indicated that in the High Middle Ages German Jews had lived under the direct
protection of the emperor, and that in this their standing was superior to that
of many other groups. He pointed to the fact that the *Wergeld* exacted for the
murder or injury of a Jew was often higher than for many classes of Christians
(and indeed, in some cases akin to that of a noble), and that less severe penalties might be imposed on Jews than on Christians for numerous categories
of crimes.[100] Of critical importance, he adduced concrete instances in which
Jews had not been entirely restricted to the credit and commercial spheres: in
Spain and England, in which they had been permitted to own land; in Italy
and in Poland, in which they had been free to engage in a variety of crafts.
According to Rühs, the fact that in these major cases Jews had still by and large
clung to their stereotyped roles afforded further proof that their occupational
focus had been a matter of choice rather than compulsion.[101]

There can be no doubt that Rühs's presentation contained numerous errors
of fact and interpretation (most significantly, his failure to distinguish early
from late medieval policy on Jews).[102] Nevertheless, it also must be remembered that Dohm's unremittingly bleak portrait of Jewish life in the Middle
Ages had provided no less a distorted picture than Rühs's rosy portrait of
comfort and privilege. Rühs had thus provided an equally partial, but also an
equally accurate, set of characterizations and generalizations of Jewish status
in premodern Europe. This in itself was sufficient to damage if not displace a
central pillar of Dohm's edifice, viz., that distortions in both the occupational
structure of the Jews and in their personal characters were not the consequence
of their own intrinsic natures (or religious constitution) but of external forces
alone.[103]

If this in itself was not an entirely new argument, the facility that Rühs
brought to the medieval sources and the welter of detail he plucked from
them supplied it with a fresh vitality. And although Rühs's efforts to prove
the existence of a Jewish *Handelskaste* in the period of antiquity fell flat, he
had more success linking aspects of the Jews' commercial orientation with
their ancient and immutable constitution. Here it is worthwhile noting that
we are still not at a stage in which coherent formulations have been devised

to demonstrate a dynamic and intrinsic connection between the spirit of commerce and the *theology* of Judaism. Such formulations only begin to appear in later decades through the influence of Hegelian thought, as the following chapter shows. Yet, in retrospect, it is indeed possible to discern in figures such as Fries and Rühs an initial groping toward defining such a link.

This tendency is apparent in Rühs's attempt to apply the theories of Adam Müller to an understanding of Jewish mercantile life (recall that Müller himself identified the spirit of commerce with Rome not Jerusalem). Rühs links Müller's criticisms of Enlightenment political economy to the dominant style of Jewish apologetics familiar from Dohm. That is to say, he attacks Dohm for an approach to both statecraft and Jewish toleration grounded in a mechanistic notion of state and society, as "a machine or clockwork." Dohm's "natural order of things" is one in which "heads are counted, souls exchanged, balances drawn, bartered, liquidated and made the subject of all manner of experiments."[104] This crass conception, suggests Rühs, derives from the same superficial culture of French Enlightenment that has historically inflicted so much suffering on the German nation.[105] Rühs thus insinuates a connection between French imperialism and emancipation of the Jews, both of which are born of mechanical and materialist notions of statecraft and economy. These constitutional notions contrast profoundly with and operate inimically to the more organic conception of nation and state that have traditionally anchored German life. For "neither numbers, nor feverish activity, nor industriousness make a healthy state, but rather only the spirit which enlivens a nation, unites it and links its individuals into an indissoluble whole..."[106]

In Rühs's vulgarized version of Müller, the original German Volk, anciently immortalized by Tacitus, underwent countless historical alterations in the face of changed circumstances while still remaining eternally true to itself. But after 1648 a tragic rupture occurred, although not because of any internal dissolution stemming from inherent constitutional weaknesses (as Müller had proposed), but, rather, purely by dint of the insidious alien force of French absolutism. Following the Thirty Years' War, France succeeded in inflicting its alien character on Germany's indigenous institutions. Germany's petty absolutist courts aped Versailles, while German intellectuals mimicked Gallic cosmopolitanism along with the French tongue. Napoleonic imperialism was merely the culmination of a conquest that had begun centuries earlier.[107] Borrowing another motif from Müller, Rühs claimed that laissez-faire political economy was a powerful weapon employed by France to secure its domination. It is the very spirit of utilitarian calculation found in the works of Dohm and other Germans whose minds were corrupted by French ideals.[108] The French and the Jews – distinct principles in their own rights, but like-minded in their will to rule – have thus united in the effort, first to foist the Jews as tolerated aliens on a trusting and virtuous people, and then to accord them full citizenship in German lands. Jewish emancipation in Germany could only have occurred, Rühs suggests, because the German spirit had already become enervated by the absorption of French doctrines such as free trade. The free exchange of goods across borders and sovereignties thus prepared the way for the entry of a Jewish population that is loyal to its own foreign constitution, one that is fundamentally inimical to the German. Unregulated commerce, usury, and exploitation have only followed in its wake.[109]

Frenchmen and Jews each seek domination in their distinctive "national" ways, according to Rühs. Materialism, rooted in Gallic and Roman law, is what defines France at its core, as aristocracy defines the Jews. Rühs in no way intends "aristocratic" as a compliment along the lines of Müller. This is not a result of any hostility he that may have felt toward the noble estates but, rather, to the distinction he now drew between authentic and counterfeit nobilities. According to Rühs, the aristocratic principle of the Jews is of a distinct kind, an aristocracy of money [*Geldadel*] and knowledge rather than of warfare and land. It is through their claim of exclusive descent from the biblical patriarchs that the Jews conceive of themselves as uniquely noble. Thus, according to Rühs, the same Jews of medieval Spain who had voluntarily eschewed land ownership were also the first group in the country to affix the aristocratic title "Don" to their names.[110] Yet at the same time Rühs was careful to emphasize that not all Spanish Jews had been permitted to bear such noble titles. His core point here was that the Jews are themselves constitutionally divided between a rabbinic aristocracy and the nonrabbinic masses. Judaism is outwardly "aristocratic" precisely as a consequence of the internal composition that it legislates for Jewish society. That society is composed of two elements, rabbis and masses, which correspond, respectively, we might add, to the noble and Third Estates:

> Their rabbis are at the same time their masters, to whom the people are obliged to give the greatest devotion and the blindest obedience. They constitute, like the Brahman among the Indians, the nobility, the exclusively authorized power.[111]

There were precedents for this sort of analogy in earlier German and even German-Jewish literature. In an appendix to his 1791 *Autobiography*, the Jewish philosopher Solomon Maimon, an associate of Mendelssohn and friend of Saul Ascher, had characterized Diaspora Judaism as a religious polity grounded in an aristocratic constitution, one in which a rabbinic elite subsisted parasitically on the labor of the Jewish masses. "The Jewish constitution is therefore in its form aristocratic, and is accordingly exposed to all the abuses of an aristocracy." Sounding very much like Sieyes, Maimon depicted the "unlearned classes of the people" as "burdened with the support not only of themselves but also of the indispensable learned class," a fact that accounts for why they are too enervated to effect their own liberation.[112]

A second "precedent" was of far older vintage. In his 1543 "On the Jews and their Lies," Martin Luther had referred repeatedly to the Jews as a self-styled nobility which would "not give up [its] pride and boasting about ... nobility and lineage."

> Therefore they boast of being the noblest, yes, the only noble people on earth. In comparison with them and in their eyes we Gentiles (Goyim) are not human; in fact we hardly deserve to be considered poor worms by them. For we are not of that high and noble blood, lineage, birth and descent.[113]

Not only do Jews "boast ... of the noble blood inherited from their fathers," but they have also hoodwinked the German nobility into letting them extract "additional taxes" from the hard-pressed peasantry. "Thus the lords are taking from their subjects what they receive from the Jews."[114] In this manner the Jews ("lazy squires") "hold us Christians in captivity in our own country."[115] Luther made a distinction between the ancient Hebrews living in the land under Mosaic Law and contemporary Jews who had renounced the Bible and pledged fealty to the emperor. Although the former are "blood relatives, cousins, and brothers of our Lord,"[116] the latter are those "of whom Moses knows nothing, nor they of him."[117] Their claim to noble lineage is all the more arrogant in that it is entirely counterfeit.

Hence, although Rühs's picture of a Christian state held captive by an alien *Geldadel* had its immediate sources in postrevolutionary German nationalism, it also evoked antisemitic images from an older Protestant tradition. It was Rühs's capacity to synthesize these many sources that made his pamphlet effective. He did not simply echo Luther, Sieyes, and Maimon. Rather, he provided an original contribution of his own by linking the Jews' internal constitutional structure to their imputed outward mode of conduct. According to Rühs, Judaism's rigid division into rulers and ruled, rabbis and masses, must invariably seek its own externalization. The absolute obedience commanded by the rabbis could only be maintained by foisting the illusion on all Jews, even the impoverished masses, that they exist in relation to the world as the rabbis exist in relation to them – as a nobility divinely commanded to dominate and control.[118] The Jews' compulsion to lord it over Christians is merely a projection of the degradation they are made to suffer at the hands of their own lords. Domination is a form of compensation through which the Jewish masses are promised a life free of honest toil, which their rabbis have taught them to despise. Commerce is therefore intrinsic to the "aristocratic" Jewish constitution because it affords the opportunity to rule others and because it provides a livelihood without labor, both requisite conditions for an aristocratic life.[119]

Like Fries, Rühs grounded his attack on Jewish emancipation in the distinction between Jews and Judaism and between masses and rabbis. That at present this distinction was merely a theoretical one only served to reinforce the conclusion that currently no Jews whomsoever should be entitled to citizenship. And, like Müller, Rühs insisted that German Jews be restored to the condition they had enjoyed in the Middle Ages, with all the necessary restrictions that accompanied that status (perhaps betraying a crack in his own historical argument against Dohm). But in contrast to Müller, this recommendation was not part of a broader reactionary program of general medieval restoration. Rather, Rühs singled out the Jews for special treatment. He did so on the grounds that the German constitution must not be defined by excessive distinctions of class or estate; rather, it must unify the nation socially and politically through the medium of common religion. Thus it would be "a marvelous contradiction that a citizen of the Jewish state, or empire, could be a citizen of a Christian state." Like Fries, Rühs left open a window for eventual Jewish emancipation, but in his case only a mass conversion to Christianity, rather than a mere purging of rabbinic elements, would do the trick. Presumably, a Judaism without rabbis was as inconceivable to Rühs as an aristocratic constitution without nobles.[120]

It is hardly surprising to learn that the French Revolution profoundly transformed Jewish life in Europe. What has not been as well understood is how the revolutionary turmoil, particularly the effort to overthrow "feudalism," altered the discourse on Jewish status and economy. Jews in this period were more often viewed as bastions of the old order rather than harbingers of the new. Although Jews' economic profile in central and western Europe had not fundamentally altered since the middle of the eighteenth century – a mass of poor traders, petty moneylenders, and impoverished clergy, alongside a wealthy stratum of manufacturers and financiers – the Jews' core relationship with the nobility was undergoing profound change. This connection, which had its roots in late medieval times and was reconstituted during the sixteenth and seventeenth centuries, began to crumble during the Revolutionary period. This was certainly true in most of Germany, but it also characterized, albeit much more gradually, the situation in Poland, where Jews and nobles had comprised an alliance of enormous significance to that country's economy and politics. The growing political chaos in eighteenth-century Poland, culminating in three successive partitions (in 1772, 1793, and 1795) eventually led during the Four Year Sejm (1788–1792) to efforts to reevaluate the position of Jews there, reinforced by translations of Dohm's treatise and the National Assembly debates. Unlike western or central Europe, Jews constituted perhaps a majority of the "bourgeoisie" in eastern Poland, a fact that ensured the greater longevity of their subordination to the noble economy.[121] Yet the underlying crisis of the Polish nobility in the early nineteenth century dealt a severe blow to their fateful collaboration. It was only in Hungary that the Jewish-noble relationship retained or intensified its vitality during the second half of the nineteenth century.[122]

In Germany itself, the decades of Revolutionary and war had cast both Jews and nobles into sharp relief. However much contemporaries viewed their relationship through a glass darkly, or through ideological or antisemitic blinders, it was inevitable that their multifarious links would be reflected in the social and political criticism of the Age. The story initiated in the previous chapter ends in this one with the degeneration of this social criticism into nationalist chauvinism and unalloyed antisemitism. Nevertheless, the relationship between antisemitic discourse and "the stories Jews tell about themselves," to borrow Ronald Schechter's phrase, is never a simple one.[123] Not only do Jews sometimes devise criticisms of their own institutions that seem to echo antisemitic ones (without necessarily constituting "self-hate"), but antisemitism has been known on occasion to stimulate highly creative Jewish responses. The arguments of Fries and Rühs were taken seriously by many of their contemporaries, Jewish and gentile.[124] In the next chapter, we find that the outlook that had crystallized in Rühs's pamphlets, specifically the focus of the internal class and constitutional mechanisms of the Jewish *Handelskaste*, supplied rich material for future discussions of the politics of Jewish commerce. But it would now be Jews who pursued their own investigation of Jewish historical economy. If criticisms like those of Rühs had shattered Dohm's historical paradigm, then the time had come to search deeper into the authentic records of the Jewish past to construct a better one. Likewise, if a historical link between Jewish religion and Jewish economy had ever truly existed, then only an objective investigation of the internal sources of the Jews' constitution could bring it to light.

7

ॐ

Jews, Commerce, and History

Jewish Studies scholars have long assumed that the movement *Wissenschaft des Judentums* ("the academic study of Judaism") was exclusively preoccupied with intellectual history and had little if any interest in economics or sociology.[1] *Wissenschaft* has typically been viewed as a *Geistes- und Leidensgeschichte*, a history of scholarly accomplishment and physical suffering. In keeping with the apologetic orientation of its early practitioners, so this view goes, they avoided discussion of the controversial aspects of Jewish material life, such as usury or Jews' fiscal alliances with the nobility and the crown, except occasionally to note that these unfortunate practices had been forced on the Jews by a backward, hate-filled society. In his outstanding recent study of economics and Jewish identity in modern times, Derek Penslar restates this view with little modification. *Wissenschaft* pioneers such as Isaac Marcus Jost "placed economics in the service of apologics," whereas "economic themes were muted" in the work of the great nineteenth-century Jewish historian Heinrich Graetz. High culture and lachrymosity marked the perimeters of German-Jewish historiography, whereas Jewish economic life remained peripheral at best. Only when a *Wissenschaft* movement emerged in Eastern Europe in the late nineteenth century, or following the 1911 publication of Werner Sombart's *The Jews and Modern Capitalism*, did the field of Jewish economic history really take off.[2]

This characterization of *Wissenschaft* has had significant repercussions, given the movement's important contribution to the development of modern Jewish consciousness. For one thing, it suggests that the bourgeois central European Jews who created *Wissenschaft des Judenthums* were preoccupied only with religious, literary, and cultural matters and lacked a strong sense of the crisis affecting contemporary Jewry's material circumstances. Only with the emergence of Jewish socialism and Zionism, the argument continues, were Jewish historians willing to reckon with (and help to rectify) the pressing problem of Jewish occupational backwardness. Yet although it is certainly true that economics was never central to early Wissenschaft, it was not at all neglected. From its inception, the movement was closely connected with the Jewish Enlightenment (*Haskalah*), which had made Jewish economic restructuring a key feature of its reform agenda. As detailed here, many of the founding institutions and individuals of *Wissenschaft des Judenthums* participated in programs designed to provide Jews with vocational training and occupational restructuring. Beyond this, *Wissenschaft*'s intellectual modus operandi, its effort to scientifically historicize Judaism and the Jews, to replace Judaism's traditional faith in God as the architect of collective Jewish fate with a naturalistic understanding of human social and intellectual development, had ample room for economic conceptions. The founders and early practitioners of *Wissenschaft*, men such as Leopold Zunz, Isaac Marcus Jost, and Eduard Gans, developed far-reaching historical schemas to account for the epochal emergence of Jews as a *Handelsstand* (a merchant caste) and demonstrate how the Jews' mercantile character could and would become transformed through emancipation. Despite their frequently abstract formulations the historical approaches they adopted had practical reformist ends, further underscoring the movement's genetic links with the *Haskalah*. Indeed, this tension between *Wissenschaft*'s academic and reformist tendencies proved to be highly productive. It resulted in a literature of historical economy that is both fascinating in its own right and valuable to any understanding later economic thought on Jews. As we will see, *Wissenschaft* proves to be an important link between Enlightenment and eventual Marxist and socialist approaches to the economic Jewish Question.

POLITICAL ECONOMY AND THE HASKALAH

In his *Autobiography*, the Polish Jewish philosopher Solomon Maimon noted that "from time to time men have arisen out of the legislative body itself [i.e, the rabbinic class], who have not only denounced its abuses, but have even called into question its authority." This remark recalls the observation of the French revolutionary, the Abbé Sieyes that, before the Revolution, challenges to the system of aristocratic privilege arose largely from within the aristocracy itself.[3] So, too, according to Maimon, with the Jewish scholarly class, which alone has possessed the knowledge, leisure, and perspective to grasp the disastrous consequences of its own system of control.

In referring to these rabbinic and scholarly dissidents, Maimon could have had in mind, in addition to older traditions of rabbinic dissent, the contemporaneous movement of "Jewish Enlightenment" (*Haskalah*), which had emerged in Germany during the second half of the eighteenth century. The *Haskalah*, in its initial German-Jewish incarnation, can be broken down loosely into "conservative," "moderate," and "radical" tendencies.[4] Maimon, although an idiosyncratic figure, is to be associated with the radical wing.[5] It was this faction that laid primary responsibility for the ills afflicting Jewish life at the feet of the rabbinic class. Maimon, who had trained as a rabbi in Poland, believed that because he had once stood within rabbinic culture, he could now stand outside it and view it clinically. He could claim neutral status for himself because he had chosen to exchange rabbinic privilege and livelihood (meager though it actually often was) for a life of still greater poverty and uncertainty as a European philosopher and intellectual. From Maimon's point of view, *Haskalah* was thus a kind of self-critique, his autobiography a record of his own education to liberation and dissent.[6]

In the *Haskalah* as a whole, including its radical and conservative wings, the Jewish occupational structure constituted but one target in a far broader critique. The *Haskalah* was premised on a belief that the non-Jewish cultural environment had become transformed through the development of religious toleration and through the application of rational criteria to contemporary social and cultural concerns. Hence, a Jewish ethos that had historically arisen in response to gentile persecution could no longer be a desirable or a tenable one. Whether or not these changes required a fundamental reform of the Jewish religion remained open to debate.[7] But all adherents of *Haskalah* agreed, at the very least, that Jews must become better integrated into the general environment; forge ties of solidarity with their non-Jewish fellow subjects; and recognize the validity of the secular dimension of life alongside the sacred.[8]

In practical terms, this meant the acquisition of European languages and other "useful" forms of secular and technical knowledge. It also required habituation to established codes of civility and adaptation to the economic and social categories pertaining in the wider world. Whereas Jewish adaptation in the economic sphere had formerly entailed filling an occupational niche, it now necessitated that Jews incorporate themselves on a roughly proportional basis into the division of labor characteristic of European society as a whole. Jews' occupational "productivization" was part and parcel of the larger aim of achieving integration, not merely by conforming the Jewish occupational structure to the general pattern but also by reforming the Jews' personality. Through labor, man joins the nature that is within himself with that which exists outside, an act that transforms and improves God's bounty. The unifying activity of work creates a condition of harmony between man, his environment and his social world, a harmony whose offspring are material well-being, social wealth, and individual creative gratification. At least, that was the Enlightenment theory as absorbed and adapted to Judaism by the *Haskalah*. From a practical standpoint, this meant recognizing the primacy of agriculture and crafts for most Jews and acknowledging the merely tertiary role of exchange. Fellow Jews must be encouraged to eschew petty trade and moneylending and to recognize the harm caused by these pursuits both in moral and practical terms.[9]

Proponents of *Haskalah* viewed rabbinic culture in its present state as a chief obstacle to achieving these aims. Moderates such as Naphtali Herz Wessely perceived the narrowness of the rabbinic outlook as an understandable if outmoded response to what had formerly been a genuine need. In the face of external hostility, in order merely to survive, Jews had been forced by the gentile environment to acquire a degree of cultural insularity. As Wessely intoned in his groundbreaking 1782 *Words of Peace and Truth*, "[i]t is the gentiles who are to blame for our misfortune." Having "for more than a thousand years" excluded Jews, "the hearts of our community subsequently... [grew] dark." Mistreated by the world, Jews came to "despise worldly things." They abjured politics, astronomy, agriculture, navigation, and construction. For they said: "Let us abandon these studies and occupy ourselves with trade and commerce to enable ourselves to live and feed our children, for only this have they left us." According to Wessely, the scholars, who had been entrusted with the leadership of the nation, abandoned the teaching of secular sciences, including creative manual labor, because they saw that such knowledge could be of no practical avail.

> They cannot work in field or vineyard, or in the construction of towers, fortresses and cities. These nations have not permitted them to work in any practical crafts.[10]

Worldly knowledge was relinquished, ironically, because in the conditions of the time it was *useless* to Jews. Unfortunately, now that times have changed, recapturing this forgotten knowledge and skill would require strenuous effort and sacrifice.

A major obstacle to Jews' readjustment, Wessely suggested, lay in their present cultural overemphasis on knowledge of the sacred (*Torat ha-'Elohim*) at the expense of the secular (*Torat ha-'Adam*).[11] From this same notion, Wesseley and other advocates of *Haskalah* drew the inference that Jewish society suffered from an overproduction of clergy and a deficit of practical men. Thus, a curious sort of connection became established between the petty mercantile and the rabbinic, with Jews afflicted by an overabundance of both. The Jewish *Aufklärer* David Caro insisted that rabbinic positions be severely regulated so that only those morally and intellectually equipped would be able to attain them.[12] Wessely likewise suggested that too many young Jewish men were being indiscriminately trained in advanced rabbinic learning to the detriment of themselves and Jewish economy generally.[13] According to this argument, the overproduction of rabbis was draining Jewish society of its productive capacities, including its capital. Caro advised, among other practical remedies, that the traditional religious obligation to give charity for the support of scholars be replaced by an obligation to contribute funds to the erection of vocational schools.[14] David Friedländer, a disciple of Mendelssohn, albeit a far fiercer critic of rabbinic culture than his teacher, went further still. Only through a complete elimination of rabbinic academies would the mass of Jews be able to liberate themselves from a life of idleness. For Friedländer, this is the case not only because the majority of rabbis contributes nothing that is economically useful, but also because the cultural and political power they wield serves as a barrier against practical, vocational education.[15] Although Friedländer was himself a wealthy merchant, and although he defended commerce as a civilizing force that helped to bind mankind, he drew a sharp distinction between affluent merchants and petty traders. Echoing Dohm's behaviorist model, Friedländer insisted that a life of petty trade almost inevitably instills moral vices its practitioners. Although economic freedom is a sine qua non for improvement, poorer Jews must use it to obtain vocational training and enter agriculture and crafts.[16]

Of course, not all proponents of *Haskalah* expressed the same degree of hostility to rabbis as had Maimon and Friedländer. Nevertheless, if most stopped short of seeking the rabbis' elimination, they did attempt to reshape inherited rabbinic attitudes, including attitudes toward labor, by turning the rabbis' own words, so to speak, against them. For instance, in his *Wine of Lebanon*, Wessely extended his earlier distinction between sacred and secular knowledge by articulating a distinction between the Hebrew terms *'avodah* and *mela'khah*. In traditional Judaism, the former term denoted both physical labor and divine service (worship or prayer). *Mela'khah*, in contrast, was usually employed in connection with those categories of labor prohibited to Jews on the Sabbath. Wessely inverted the mundane and sacred connotations of both terms, first by defining *'avodah* as rote mechanical labor, or submissive ritual devotion, and, second, by defining *mela'khah* as the mode of creative work that alters nature to fashion a unique and beneficial product. Through this interpretation, Wessely attempted to restore to Judaism what he viewed as its own original notion of productive labor, that is, of labor as a semblance of the act of divine creation. For according to rabbinic tradition, the labor (*mela'khah*) prohibited on the Sabbath is a likeness of the activity from which

God had desisted on the seventh day. Wessely extolled such creative work as a sacred act of *imitatio dei*, while at the same time devaluing both rote labor and mechanical ritual emptied of their creative impetus.[17]

Those who promoted *Haskalah* wrote in the language of traditional Judaism because that was the language that their intended audience understood.[18] But, as demonstrated in the case of Wessely, they also sought to reinterpret inherited Jewish concepts in light of their own values and aims. For the most part, this reflected the conviction that their own interpretations best conformed with those of original, biblical Judaism and even with rabbinic culture in its pristine form. Not only were Jews once "farmers in their own lands," as the Bible amply demonstrates, but the rabbis of the talmudic age, in pointed contrast to their modern counterparts, had diligently tilled their own fields and produced handicrafts. Their aim at all times, according to Wessely and others, was to strike the correct balance between spiritual and material domains.[19]

Proponents of *Haskalah* were fond of repeating the rabbinic instruction to "combine torah study with a worldly occupation" (*talmud torah im derekh 'erets*). For the *Haskalah*, the term *derekh 'erets* signified more than the rabbinic "worldly occupation." Rather, the phrase served as a recipe for integrating not only sacred and secular but traditional learning with productive *physical* labor as well. In a similar manner, *Haskalah* literature adduced a host of traditional rabbinic terms to demonstrate that original Judaism had placed a premium on independent labor and self-sufficiency, even if, during the darkest of days, such emphases had been obscured. As Mordecai Levin has shown, terms such as *bitaḥon* ("trust" or "faith"), *tsedakah* ("charity"), and *ma'aseh bereshit* ("divine creation") were divested by the *Haskalah* of their inherited meanings and imbued with new and more timely ones. *Bitaḥon*, for instance, no longer referred to fatalism, or to absolute dependence on God's inscrutable will, but, rather, to self-reliance; for God had made man responsible for his own destiny, good or bad, as well as for his own livelihood. Similarly, *tsedakah* did not mean the maintenance of the poor and idle, as misguided Jews persist in believing, but rather the active promotion of their own regeneration through labor. The concept of *ma'aseh bereshit* [God's creation of the world], which among traditional Jews often connoted Kabbalistic mysteries, was now interpreted, as with Wessely's notion of *mela'khah*, as the divine model for and sanctioning of creative human labor.[20]

Going beyond individual terms to reinterpret an entire literary genre, Mendel Lefin of Satanov (1749–1826) produced a work of *musar*, Jewish literature of moral reproof, designed to instill in its readers worldly habits of frugality (*kimuts*) and industry (*haritsut*). Much traditional *musar*, especially works produced late medieval Ashkenaz, possessed a fire and brimstone quality. These works sought to bring readers into a condition of penitential piety, urging them not only to asceticism but also to the minimizing of worldly pursuits in favor of time devoted to Torah study.[21] Lefin adopted the *musar* form to convey a much different message, one directly borrowed from the moralistic works of Benjamin Franklin. Lefin's *Ḥeshbon Ha-Nefesh* (Moral Stocktaking) employed Franklin's method of repetition so that the reader, once fully habituated to virtue, would become an exemplar of the work ethic, endowing worldly labor with sacred value.[22]

These were some of the basic responses of Jewish Enlightenment to the challenge of occupational productivization. In turning now to *Wissenschaft des Judentums*, we will examine how these and other core *Haskalah* motifs, including occupational productivization, were absorbed into the *Wissenschaft* movement during its initial phase, only to be purged from it later on. Indeed, the various tensions and dualities that existed within *Wissenschaft* helped to generate its own unique approach to Jewish historical-economy. In particular, *Wissenschaft* conceptualized the question of Jewish occupations in terms of (as one of its founders described it) the duality of "inner" and "outer" Jewish history. This duality corresponded to an array of further distinctions: between Jews and Judaism, between external persecution and internal development, and between political-economic and religious-cultural existence. Initially, the founders of the *Wissenschaft* movement hoped to integrate these oppositions into a single grand theory of Jewish material and spiritual development. Their failure was not merely a result of the project's grandiose nature but also of the self-identity of the movement as it gradually crystallized in the first two decades of its existence. It was in this period that *Wissenschaft* came increasingly to identity its own prerogatives with the internal component of Judaism and to associate its predecessor movement, the *Haskalah*, with the external. Hence, in asserting its independence from *Haskalah*, *Wissenschaft* eventually came to relegate the material and economic dimension of the Jewish past to a separate and subordinate status. It will be one of the burdens of this chapter to show, however, that this was not the case at the start.

FROM HASKALAH TO WISSENSCHAFT

The *Haskalah* is best understood as a cultural and educational movement. Its chief aims were the promotion of emancipation from without and regeneration from within. In this sense, *Wissenschaft des Judentums* represented both a continuation of and departure from the Jewish Enlightenment. Like the *Haskalah*, it, too, sought to advance the cause of emancipation, which in Germany through the period of its emergence remained incomplete and

often unfulfilled. But instead of simply lamenting the Jews' current backwardness, conditioned by its history of persecution, *Wissenschaft des Judentums*
affirmed a different proposition: viz., that the Jews had advanced historically
and evolved progressively in tandem with the rest of Europe, both alongside
and within it.[23]

Emerging at a moment of European national awakening, the *Wissenschaft*
movement applied organicist models of national development to the Jews' own
historical experience. Its affirmation of Jewish national identity was intended
to show that Jews bore an essential likeness to other advanced nations of
Europe and hence possessed an equal claim to civic and cultural incorporation.
In this light, the "nationalism" of the *Wissenschaft* movement was of a highly
attenuated kind. It was applied primarily to the Jewish past rather than the
present, and was geared toward supporting individual citizenship rather than
collective self-determination. Although it did proclaim a Jewish collective
identity of sorts – as a phenomenon of demonstrated historical dynamism –
it was an identity that no longer needed to be constituted as separate polity
or even a distinct linguistic and cultural entity.[24]

The self-emancipatory component of *Wissenschaft* lay in its treatment of
Judaism (in the broadest sense of the term) as an object worthy of scientific inquiry. "Science," in its early nineteenth-century German connotation,
involved a process of both discernment and transmutation. To study something scientifically was to elevate it ontologically.[25] The reader will recall a
similar conception in the writings of Adam Müller (discussed in Chapter 6).
Müller hoped to revive feudalism as the social system of the future by subject-
ing its core components to "scientific" analysis. For Müller, original feudalism
was inferior precisely because it lacked this element of self-knowledge.[26] Similarly, to the founders of *Wissenschaft*, Judaism had as yet failed to examine itself
in this same scientific spirit, to become conscious of itself, and to integrate
itself into the totality of vital human knowledge. Wissenschaft, its proponents
believed, would help to consummate Jewish acculturation. For one thing, to
insist that Judaism could be the worthy object of scientific and historicist dis-
section was to imply that the Jews' own nationality had now ripened to full
maturity and that integration would follow organically from disintegration.
By contrast, it also suggested that the creative well-springs of "Judaism" (again,
broadly conceived) had perhaps not entirely exhausted themselves and might
yet prove capable of evolving new and dynamic forms.[27]

Wissenschaft des Judentums thus tended to differ from *Haskalah* not only
in many of its theoretical assumptions but also in its practical evaluations of
the different eras of Jewish history. The *Haskalah* sought its "usable past" in
the biblical and, to a more limited extent, in the early rabbinic period. In this,

as Shmuel Feiner has shown, it proved itself in accord with the periodiza-
tion schemes then common to Enlightenment Europe. It identified antiquity,
in its near-Eastern and Greco-Roman variations, with the first flowering of
civilization, subsequently stultified in the pall cast by the Christian Middle
Ages, only to be revived and advanced once again, steadily if not smoothly, in
the centuries beginning with the Renaissance. Some viewed the Jewish "Dark
Ages" as of even longer duration. "Since the destruction of the Temple in
70 AD," Lazarus Bendavid remarked, "Jewish history has sunk for over
1,700 years into an oppressive, impenetrable darkness."[28] Yet the effort to
apply this sort of schema to a specifically Jewish past created difficulties. For
if antiquity was a Hebraic golden age, the *Haskalah* on the whole rejected the
applicability of Judaism's national-political origins to its own contemporary
praxis. In contrast, *Wissenschaft des Judentums* proved capable of devising a
more nuanced conception of progress, one that could explain the fanatical
excesses of the Middle Ages as a necessary if unfortunate by-product of man's
collective spiritual growth, rather than merely as a tragic error or inexplicable
aberration. Thus, whereas the *Haskalah* generally depicted the Middle Ages as
a period of darkness and degeneration, *Wissenschaft des Judentums* was capable of casting medieval Judaism – or at least aspects of it – in a more positive
light. This was certainly true of *Wissenschaft's* celebration of the well-rounded
Jewish culture of medieval Spain.[29] But *Wissenschaft* also was able to find a
measure of beauty and heroism in aspects of medieval Ashkenazic culture
as well.[30] Indeed, one of the central preoccupations of the movement was to
demonstrate that the Jewish contribution to civilization had not ended with
the rise of Hellenism, or with the career of Jesus of Nazareth, but had instead
endured into the Middle Ages and right up through present times.[31] In contrast
to *Haskalah, Wissenschaft des Judentums* therefore offered a relatively more
coherent vision linking past and present. It was no longer forced to think in
terms of restoring ancient Jewish virtue while at the same time detaching that
virtue from its original national-political framework. Instead, *Wissenschaft*
could outline a theory of developmental progress which, by affirming the historical legitimacy of postbiblical Judaism, helped to prepare the ground for
Jews' full entry in European national civilization.

One of the factors underlying its distinctive outlook lay in *Wissenschaft's*
emergence during a period when emancipation had been already partially
achieved, or fully achieved and partially withdrawn. By 1820, German states
had retreated, sometimes substantially, from the promise of full equality, a situation that persisted until the 1850s and 1860s.[32] This paradox of fulfillment and
incompleteness left its psychological imprint on the generation that founded
the movement. The founders recognized that at least in the German lands

much of the *Haskalah's* program of regeneration had already been fulfilled. By the 1820s, German-speaking Jews abounded. There was even a small yet articulate and visible minority of university-trained Jews.[33] Reflecting – indeed, exaggerating – these changes, the octogenarian David Friedländer, whose life span and organizational affiliations bridged the gap between *Haskalah* and *Wissenschaft*, boasted that in the Germany of 1819 all German Jews knew how to speak the native tongue, worship in a rational manner, and abide by the general codes of civility. According to Friedländer, German Jewry had now successfully banished all vestiges of rabbinic medievalism from its midst. But for Friedländer, this remarkable success had raised a number of difficult questions. If Jews had fulfilled their end of the bargain, why had the state reneged on its own? Why, moreover, had respected figures such as Rühs and Fries lashed out so virulently against the Jews? And why, finally, had the temper of German public opinion, especially its youth, appeared to turn violently against emancipation?[34]

David Friedländer, Leopold Zunz, Eduard Gans, and others of the early *Wissenschaft* movement expressed a combination of perplexity, anger and defiance at these developments. They pointed to the contributions and sacrifices of Jewish soldiers to the Wars of Liberation, which they believed had once and for all given the lie to the accusation that Jews would not die for the nation that made them its citizens. They even questioned whether the vaunted cultural superiority of Germany did not disguise a still-potent barbarism festering just beneath the surface.[35] Yet all of this righteous indignation could not obscure a single stubborn reality, one that Friedländer and Zunz, among others, felt obliged to concede. In one area, at least, German Jews had as yet failed to pass the test of regeneration. In their occupational profile, they had changed relatively little since the late eighteenth century.[36]

In the emancipatory quid pro quo that had been woven into the legal fabric of all German states at this time, the occupational factor stood out. It was the common thread in German policy toward Jewish subjects. It was the area in which reform had proved most difficult. Hence, it was the component of the emancipation contract that conservative statesmen could most easily fall back on to support their stand. German law discriminated not just between Jews and gentiles but also between various categories of Jews, as had also been the case in premodern times. One approach was to exclude from the category of full citizens all those engaged in "petty trade," which typically meant the vast majority of Jews resident in a given state. As the Württemberg Diet pronounced in passing its discriminatory legislation in 1833, a prerequisite for the granting or restoration of full rights would be demonstrated success in transforming "the consuming Jew into the productive citizen."[37] In

Prussia, with by far the largest German-Jewish population, legal distinctions were drawn between native-born Jews and those resident in recently acquired territories. The latter were generally poorer, less acculturated, and more narrowly concentrated at the bottom of the commercial hierarchy. Although Jews in the old territories of Prussia suffered relatively minor disabilities, such as exclusion from public offices and from university posts, those in the newer were subjected to a legal status reminiscent of the eighteenth century, including restrictions on occupations, residency, and marriage.[38] Thus, the quid pro quo generated its own subsidiary paradoxes. There were Jews who were prevented by law from entering the very trades that would ostensibly prepare them for citizenship.

Yet even those disabilities pertaining to Jews in Prussia proper, insofar as Jewish intellectuals felt them most acutely, remained linked to the productivization issue. An examination of the antiemancipation literature of the decade 1810–1820 suggests that the real object of attack was often not impoverished Jews and petty traders but, rather, Jews higher up on the occupational ladder.[39] Numerous pamphlets opposing emancipation emphasized the dangers of recent laws permitting the alienation of noble estates, either in whole and in part.[40] It had been a standard claim of earlier debates on emancipation that, given both land reform and Jewish legal equality, Jewish capital would be able to take over the market in land. Jews, it was claimed, would employ their newfound power in real property to exert undue political and economic control. By the late 1810s, a number of German authors professed shock at learning that a stratum of wealthy Jewish landowners had now actually emerged.[41] Moreover, anti-Jewish opinion became further scandalized by another recent phenomenon: the movement of Jews into German university life. Given the disabilities that Jews had traditionally endured, it was indeed a striking fact that by 1815 the proportion of Jewish university students had already risen above the Jews' percentage of the general population, a phenomenon that would only intensify in decades to come.[42] This new visibility of Jews among landholding and academic elites was thus a source of distress for German nationalists and conservatives alike. It appeared to confirm their fears that, granted equality, Jews would not seek out humble positions as peasants and craftsmen, but, rather, attempt to infiltrate the commanding heights of German society.

This last factor (the disproportionate number of Jews at German universities) was relevant in at least two ways to the establishment of *Wissenschaft des Judentums*. First, as controversy increased surrounding their presence at academic institutions, Jews began to form their own separate student organizations. One of these was a scholarly society formed in 1816 at the University of

Berlin – the predecessor organization to the 1819 "Society for Culture and Science among Jews," which would inaugurate the *Wissenschaft* movement. What is interesting to note is that although this society was composed exclusively of Jews, it initially displayed little interest in Jewish scholarly matters. On the contrary, its purpose was apparently simply to provide social and intellectual fellowship to Jewish students who felt otherwise excluded and embattled.[43] It was only in the wake of the 1819 anti-Jewish "Hep Hep" demonstrations that this same grouping (although with slightly changed personnel) crystallized as the *Verein für Cultur und Wissenschaft der Juden.*

This suggests that the movement toward a "science of Judaism" was a gradual one, entailing a sequence of factors: the entrance of Jews into the university system in the 1810s; the post-Napoleonic reevaluation of and partial withdrawal from emancipation; and finally the intensification of anti-Jewish sentiment in Germany (and in German academia specifically) toward the end of the decade. Although the formal prohibition on Jews holding positions at state universities would not go into effect until 1822 (Eduard Gans, the then President of the "Society," was the test case), by 1819 there was already reason for Jewish students who aspired to professional academic careers to fear that their religious origins would hinder their advancement.[44] This, in turn, suggests that at least a part of the impetus behind a "science of Judaism" derived from the emancipatory quid pro quo that now appeared increasingly likely to threaten the careers of would-be Jewish academics.[45] In this light, a science of Judaism would be useful, since that which legitimated Jewish culture would of necessity legitimate the scientific credentials of its practitioners.

Second, when pointing to the disproportionate number of Jewish university students, it is necessary to remember that the Jewish occupational structure in Germany was an anomalous one. The sociologically relevant factor conditioning Jewish university affiliation was the relatively greater extent of urbanization and commercial activity among Jews than among other Germans.[46] On the one hand, it is fair to assume that the ideological pressure on Jews to become secularized, as well as to extricate themselves from "traditional" occupations, was greater than that placed, for instance, on the German peasantry or German artisans at this time.[47] On the other hand, the traditional Jewish occupations also were arguably more conducive to the production of a professional class and intelligentsia than were the occupations still engaged in by the majority of non-Jewish Germans. For these reasons, the impressive growth of a Jewish intelligentsia, a factor directly conditioning the rise of the *Wissenschaft* movement, was structurally linked with the already existing phenomenon of Jewish occupational disproportionality. Whether or not this connection was consciously recognized or intuited by the founders of *Wissenschaft des Judentums* remains an open question. But that the movement was itself hostile to petty commerce and moneylending, and that *Wissenschaft* viewed itself as an alternative to these professions, there can be no doubt.[48]

In light of these two factors, it is possible to see why, to its founders, the movement's initial dual aims of productivization and science, appeared to be complementary ones. Indeed, the movement's original twin tendencies were implicit in its own organizational title, which referred both to Jewish culture and Jewish science. A *Verein für Cultur und Wissenschaft der Juden* would thus be directed, first, at elevating Jewish culture in Germany, a goal to be achieved in part through occupational productivization, and, second, at altering the environment for Jews in German academic life, an aim to be accomplished by rendering Judaism the subject of scientific inquiry. The first goal represented a continuation of earlier *Haskalah* themes, whereas the second constituted a new departure. On one level, these goals overlapped: removing Jews from tainted and degrading occupations would help make their religious conceptions and practices more scientific; likewise, opening German academia to Jewish Studies would advance and expand Jewish occupational opportunities. But on another level they existed in tension because pragmatic and utilitarian aims could come into conflict with scientific and disinterested ones.

The intermixture of *Haskalah* and *Wissenschaft* orientations was noticeable from the start. Thus, the "Society for Culture and Science Among Jews" was engaged not only in grandiose plans for the comprehensive investigation of Jewish history and culture but also in more mundane and pragmatic vocational schemes involving agricultural and artisanal education for the children of the Jewish poor. Initially, the Society originated plans for four institutional components: (1) an "Institute for Research" to investigate the sociological conditions and historical experience of the Jews; (2) an "Archive for Correspondence" to link the Society with sister organizations throughout the Jewish world; (3) a journal, the *Zeitschrift für die Wissenschaft des Judenthums*, to publish theoretical discourses and empirical research; and (4) a school to train young Jews in modern secular studies.[49] To these, Eduard Gans, the Society's president from 1821 to 1825, proposed adding a fifth – a component that would be geared directly to the goal of productivization. Although in principle Gans regarded the training of impoverished Jews in agriculture and crafts as the responsibility of the state, he also insisted that the Society could not afford to avert its eyes from a problem of such pressing magnitude.

[W]e lack entirely an institute for agriculture, crafts, and the lower professions. Indeed, until now we have limited ourselves entirely to the scientific
[sphere], but should this limitation persist forever? If even its full realization
must be left to the future, ought we not begin a comprehensive effort to
establish such sections?[50]

Members of the Society introduced a variety of such practical schemes,
although few ever came to fruition. Although individual members affiliated
themselves with vocational schools that had been established by Jewish phi-
lanthropists, the Society itself lacked sufficient resources to create its own.[51]
Indeed, the proposals that came before the Society regarding vocational training, agricultural colonization, and the like were almost invariably framed in
terms of research and scientific inquiry. Thus, Moses Moser, a founding member of the *Culturverein*, proposed sending a young researcher to Poland and
Hungary to study the source of the "wandering beggar Jews" currently plagu-
ing Germany and to discover how "a spark of culture might be ignited" in their
breasts.[52] Plans for establishing the aforementioned institute for agronomy
were to be preceded, according to Gans, by research into the precise numbers of Jewish farmers and landowners presently existing in Germany. In his
address of May 1823, Gans reported that the "Agricultural Commission . . . had
begun its first comprehensive work, viz., the production of a list of all Jewish
farmers [*Ökonomen*] by means of official correspondence." He expressed the
hope that experiments undertaken by "foreign members," in America and
elsewhere, would provide a comparative record of achievement and help prepare the ground for concrete successes at home.[53] It appears, therefore, that
despite its conviction that productivization was a pressing need, the Society
lacked not only the material resources, but equally important, the particular
mind-set required to attack the problem directly. Although it did not shun the
issue, it trained its own sites on science – *Wissenschaft* – as the proper means
of preparation for practical Jewish regeneration.

In the early literature of *Wissenschaft*, a number of efforts were made to
acquire this preparation by investigating the historical origins of the contemporary Jewish economic problem. Here, too, this duality between pragmatic,
Enlightenment-style approaches, on the one hand, and historical, theoretical ones, on the other, was evident. The *Wissenschaft* writings that fell into
the former category tended to attribute primary responsibility for the Jews'
occupational distortions to Christian persecution, while at the same time conceding an historical pattern of Jewish habituation to and internalization of the
Handelsgeist. These writings tended to draw moral and cultural distinctions
between Jews engaged in large-scale trade or finance and "common Jews"
immersed in *Kleinhandel*. The solutions they proposed also tended to echo

Dohm's: vocational education on the positive side, and special legal restrictions, on the negative.

Yet even in writings displaying these older tendencies the lines between *Haskalah* and distinctively *Wissenschaft* approaches were often blurred. In light of the fact that generations had now passed without the expected transformation of Jewish economy, the *Wissenschaft* literature of the 1820s came to temper its Enlightenment and *Haskalah* optimism with historical realism. Frustration engendered lowered expectations and even a measure of defensiveness. What had taken centuries to produce could not be expected to come undone overnight. Emancipation advocates such as Dohm and Grégoire had likewise urged patience in regard to the timeframe of regeneration.[54] But in the 1810s and 1820s, these warnings would take on the sobering weight of experience. This increased awareness among *Wissenschaft* authors of just how stubborn the occupational problem might be began to encourage a greater willingness to examine internal factors in the shaping of Jewish economy, extending well beyond the *Haskalah* emphasis on external persecution. This was in keeping with the nature of the challenges to emancipation produced by Rühs, Fries, and others. It also was consistent with the conviction on the part of *Wissenschaft* authors that modern Jewish life had developed along its own internally conditioned course and that tracing the inner, spiritual history of the Jews must precede any diagnosis.

An early example of this approach was the 1819 collaboration between the young *Wissenschaft* scholar Leopold Zunz and the Jewish educator Levi Lazarus Hellwitz. Their "Organization of Israelites in Germany" combined an account of the historical causes underlying the Jews' degeneration with a set of proposals aimed at accomplishing Jewish *Verbesserung*.[55] Although the historical sections of the pamphlet displayed a strong *Haskalah* intonation – emphasizing external persecution, above all – a more novel theme also was broached – viz., the possible conceptual link between Jewish religion and Jews' commercial economy. In "The Organization of Israelites" this link took the form of a parallelism: both Judaism and commerce had for centuries functioned as twin historical surrogates for the fuller range of political and occupational activities that Jews had been compelled to forego.

Cut off from participation in government, excluded from offices, guilds and honors, removed from any sense of community with Christians, despised by his fellow men, homeless yet still regarding the dispersed Israelites as his brothers, insecure in his possessions, and in constant terror of the outbreak of popular rage, – he was forced to turn [inward] towards the lost fatherland. And all the many flames which burned in the free citizen – love of fatherland, and of king, of the laws, of fellow men, of heroism, of science, freedom and domestic happiness, mental development, faith and virtue – were all united within the Israelite in the one fire of religion.[56]

Just as the purview of the Jewish religion had been forced to expand to fill the vacuum created by intellectual and political deprivation, so, too, commerce had been forced to expand to fill the void produced by Jews' exclusion from a varied physical and occupational existence. Commerce – and its derivative, moneylending – thus eventually became the sole fields of endeavor on which the full variety of Jewish talents and aspirations were left to play themselves out. "Since offices and titles could bring no consideration, money would have to; since activity and craft pursuit could produce no inner satisfaction . . . , the stock of money would have to suffice." Money became the source not just of livelihood but also of life itself. "The Israelite, whose wealth consisted of dead currency alone, was forced to find life therein." Because commerce had to encompass so many other functions and fill such a variety of psychological and material needs, the Jew came to practice it with a misplaced intensity. Finally, because the Jew had become entirely habituated to commercial life, he also had become incapable of seizing upon alternatives once they were eventually presented to him. In the Jew's own mind, commerce was both his birthright and "hereditary occupation." He could not grasp that his condition had resulted from a set of past circumstances that were no longer applicable. Viewing his traditional life as both natural and inevitable, he became incapable of conceiving of any other. "He no longer knows why he trades," and yet he trades. The end result has been, Hellwitz and Zunz concluded, a tragic postponement of the Jew's desired reconciliation with gentile society.[57]

The implication of Hellwitz and Zunz's analysis was clear: the Jews themselves are chiefly responsible for their failure to wean themselves from commerce. Both past persecution and the present-day refusal on the part of European states to grant Jews full emancipation are not in themselves sufficient to explain why the Jews cling stubbornly to traditional occupations (on this point, conceding the challenge of Rühs). Yet, for precisely this reason, Jewish history might reveal further *internal* factors that were still functioning to maintain this attachment.

For the early practitioners of *Wissenschaft*, these considerations yielded a variety of practical conclusions as well: the aforementioned insistence that more time would be needed to effect the necessary change; the accession to the legitimacy of special laws directed against Jews; or, conversely, the demand that emancipation be granted as a basic human right and therefore decoupled from unrealistic expectations that occupational reform will rapidly follow. Thus, the anonymous reviewer of Alexander Lips's 1821 *The Civil Rights of Jews*, writing in the *Zeitschrift für die Wissenschaft des Judentums*, readily conceded that weaning Jews from commerce would be exceedingly difficult, because it would violate their own ingrained values:

> ...the reviewer has himself, through ample experience, witnessed how parents, and especially mothers, are so reluctant to remove their sons from the trader class. The reviewer knows families which have little more than their wretched piece of bread, but which nevertheless will not allow their sons to subject themselves to the labor of the *Handwerker*.[58]

Jewish reformers repeatedly warned that regeneration would not succeed unless Jewish women, the bearers of domestic culture, received a proper religious education. Precisely because the home was seen as the feminine sphere, critics viewed women's religious conceptions as profoundly significant to their husbands' and sons' own occupational choices.[59] As the reviewer put it, as a result of their ignorance of authentic Jewish tradition, Jewish mothers regard manual labor as a taint on their men's (and by extension their own) reputations. But such a "horrendous belief," although controverted thoroughly by the Talmud, should not be combated through force. For only "time, and with it, the enjoyment of freedom, will alter [it], and make parents prefer...an honorable *Handwerker*...to an itinerant merchant who trusts less in his own labor than in the pity of others."[60]

For the authors of "The Organization of Israelites," in contrast, the occupational problem required a two-tiered solution. Because the source of commercial addiction was primarily cultural, secular scholarship or "*Wissenschaft*" would offer the most radical and far-reaching cure. "Only where the atmosphere and conditions for science exist has the *Schachergeist* been destroyed, necessity and conditioning overcome, [and] hate and neglect obliterated." Nevertheless, as the authors maintained, *Wissenschaft* could be an appropriate cure for only a small minority of merchants, those wealthy, leisured Jews whose fortunes depended on large-scale trade and finance. It was inappropriate for the "common Israelite" immersed in his "*Kleinhandel*." In the latter case, only the carrot and stick of vocational training and legal restriction would produce the desired result.[61]

This formula of culture and science for an elite and vocational training for the masses was subsequently echoed and problematized by another member of the "Society," Isaac Marcus Jost. As noted, the proponents of eighteenth-century *Haskalah* had insisted that only a small minority of Jews should receive rabbinic training because most lacked the necessary intellectual and spiritual aptitude. The practitioners of *Wissenschaft des Judentums* likewise viewed it as neither feasible nor desirable that large numbers of Jews should follow in their wake. The internal impulse driving young Jews to academic pursuits, combined with the legal restrictions deterring them from teaching at state universities, were seen as generating precisely the sort of crisis that *Wissenschaft des Judentums* was designed to prevent. In an 1820 letter to his former teacher, Samuel Meyer Ehrenberg, Jost complained that under present conditions "university students simply cannot find employment." If sufficient productive work were not soon generated, Jewish intellectuals would be forced to convert in order to obtain university positions. "If we don't push the crafts, our entire next generation will turn Christian."[62]

The notion that divisions in Jewish society, not just between rabbis and laymen but also between rich and poor, might have been a causative factor in the development of the Jewish economy was one that would reappear in the *Wissenschaft* literature of subsequent decades. As we will see later, Jost would explore the topic at length in his *History of the Israelites*, published during the late 1820s. Yet class analysis, to the degree that it became a component of *Wissenschaft*, was itself a reflection of the attempt to work out the relationship between intrinsic and extrinsic, organic and artificial in the shaping of Jewish economy.[63] In the "Organization of the Israelites" we observed Hellwitz and Zunz depicting Judaism and commerce as functionally analogous phenomena: that is, as dual historical substitutes for the fuller civic and material activity that in the past was denied to Jews. It was this same link between "Judaism" and "commerce," variously formulated, that made its mark on the early programmatic literature of the *Wissenschaft* movement, to which we now turn.

THE *STATISTIK* OF THE JEWS

Zunz's own programmatic essays of the early 1820s expanded on the linkage he had previously drawn in his collaboration with Hellwitz – but now in a more abstract and less utilitarian form. This shift reflected a new emphasis on contemporary philosophical and Romanticist approaches. Consequently, it is possible to discern in Zunz's early programmatic statements, as well as in those of Eduard Gans, the beginnings of an anti-*Haskalah* tendency in *Wissenschaft*, opposed to both Enlightenment materialism and to the Enlightenment's use of history as a means for advancing its utilitarian aims. As Gans suggested in an "Address to the Society," pragmatic concerns threatening to overwhelm scientific ones, impeding objectivity, and reducing life and history to a set of spiritless mechanical operations, needed to be shunted aside.[64] The movement's twin influences of Romanticism and Hegelianism, otherwise frequently at loggerheads, were at one in their mutual condemnation of the Enlightenment's historical approach. The Society's pragmatic

concern with productivization was thus at odds with its own spiritual orientation. Its focus on internal, organic development was at odds with the
Haskalah's "lachrymose conception" of Jewish history. Organicism and the
theory of immanent national-historical development appeared at odds with
depictions of economic experience drawn almost exclusively from images of
gentile persecution. The *Wissenschaft* emphasis on internal development, on
spiritual and intellectual *Geistesgeschichte*, appeared irreconcilable, in light of
Diaspora conditions of statelessness, with discussions of political and economic conditions imposed on Jews from the outside.

Yet those modern historians who claim that *Wissenschaft des Judentums*
lacked a political and economic dimension tend to ignore the fact that politics
and economics could be defined as the products of *internal* constitutional
identity rather than of external experience alone.[65] Moreover, idealist conceptions of history did not in themselves preclude a form of economic analysis.
This was true both of the general German historical writing of the time and
of *Wissenschaft des Judentums* in its early phase. We have seen that political
and economic life need not be conceived of as reflecting conditions imposed
from outside, even under Diaspora circumstances. The challenge presented
by Friedrich Rühs, among others, was precisely to home in on the internal,
constitutional, and religious components of Jewish life as the fulcrum of the
nation's political and economic character. In the early decades of its existence, *Wissenschaft des Judentums* sought to take this challenge up, albeit in a
piecemeal and occasional fashion. As Zunz protested, the field of economic
history is one that "remains somewhat foreign to us."[66] However foreign,
the *Wissenschaft* response took forms that mirrored contemporary German
approaches to historical-economy, as demonstrated in the case of Zunz's own
proposed "Statistics" of the Jews.

It is a curious fact that although German historicism, like *Wissenschaft
des Judentums*, has been scolded by later scholars for its neglect of economic life,[67] both the terms "economic history" (*Wirtschaftsgeschichte*) and
"statistics" (*Statistik*) were first coined by German authors.[68] What is so striking about the latter coinage is that in German literature the term *Statistik*
refers to a genre and body of literature that was often entirely devoid of
numbers.[69] The term was first employed by Gottfried Achenwall in 1749.
Its derivation from the Latin "status" – meaning both "state" in the political sense (*Staat*) and in the sense of condition (*Zustand*)[70] – underscores its
initial functional relationship to the literature of German Cameralism and
Staatswissenschaft. Eighteenth-century *Statistik*, pioneered by figures such as
Achenwall and August Ludwig von Schlözer, initially was a by-product of
both Cameralism and English "Political Arithmetic." It was "statistical" in the

sense that it aimed to condense into digestible form the mass of data relevant to its given subject matter. It was "Cameralist," at the same time, in virtue of its orientation to the prerogatives of state management. In its original function, *Statistik* sought to provide the prince with a survey of national-territorial conditions, incorporating descriptions of farmland, climate, geology, population, customs, as well as natural and human history – in short, all of the information deemed essential to wise government.[71]

As noted, in contrast to "Political Arithmetic," German *Statistik* (at least, up through the middle of the nineteenth century) granted no special priority to numbers, tables, or calculations. Historical and descriptive components were accorded greater weight than analytical ones. And although the *Statistiker* did not always refrain from appending his own opinion, it was characteristic of the genre that the "facts" be left alone to speak for themselves. This quality of bureaucratic reticence suited the princely readership for which *Statistik* had been originally designed. But by the late eighteenth century, practitioners of *Statistik* such as Christian Wilhelm von Dohm and August Lüdwig von Schlözer increasingly viewed their work as a tool to stimulate public opinion and enhance its critical judgment on questions of general concern. Dohm and Schlözer initiated the practice of publishing their statistical findings in periodical journals accessible to a general reading public.[72] This increasingly democratic tone also manifested itself in a shift in the presumed mediating nucleus of society from the personal figure of the prince to the abstract apparatus of the state. Here, too, it was Schlözer who, from his perch at the University of Göttingen, helped to stimulate an appetite for *Statistik* within a generation of reform-minded German civil servants.

But *Statistik* underwent a further transformation, one that would make it particularly relevant to the early phase of *Wissenschaft des Judentums*. In the aftermath of the Wars of Liberation, increasing stress was laid on the cultural totality of the nation rather than on the formal borders of a territory as the focal point of analysis.[73] This emphasis, which dovetailed nicely with contemporary idealist and Romanticist conceptions of national development, was to leave a lasting imprint on the future character of German political-economy.[74] By the second or third decade of the nineteenth century, *Nationalökonomie* had become the standard German term to designate the science of economy as a whole. The substitution of "national" for "political" suited the circumstances of a disunited Germany. The nation could be made central because, under conditions of political fragmentation, it alone provided the abstract unifying framework that could transcend the territorial limitations of existing states. This, in turn, lent German economics a certain distinctiveness in comparison with its French and English counterparts. For, given their emphases on publics, states, governments, and nations, both *Nationalökonomie* and *Statistik* were able to avoid the kind of rigid distinctions between political and cultural topics, or between sociological description and historical analysis, that would become increasingly common elsewhere.[75]

In this light, German *Statistik* appeared tailor-made for a *Wissenschaft* diagnosis of Jewish economy. Zunz's 1823 "Outline of a Future Statistics of the Jews" combined an eclectic conception of the relevant statistical data with a set of insistent instructions on how such materials should be correctly organized and interpreted. Its ambitious program called for the collection, country by country, of all literary, geographical, epigraphic, demographic, and archeological data pertaining to Jews. This comprehensive mass of detail would then be distilled to its representative essence. The result, according to Zunz, would be a snapshot portrait of national development at a given moment of time (*Geschichts-Differenziale*), a freeze-frame picture of historical movement in perpetual flux, and a code through which the full course of past and future national evolution might be correctly inferred. A *Statistik* of the Jews would thus capture what Zunz called the "upshot of history halted in its present course."[76]

Given the stakes – the capturing of the very essence of a people – Zunz warned that:

> A non- or a false statistic will ... arise out of one-sided, inappropriate and incorrect observations, out of unfamiliarity with history, with the present, the sensibility and needs of the people, out of false or falsified history, out of foreign, incidental intermixtures, out of preconceived opinions lacking in substantiation, out of the neglect of existing needs, and out of the lack of scientific method in general.[77]

A true *Statistik*, in contrast, would be consequent not just of evidentiary completeness and interpretive fair-mindedness (*Vorurtheillosigkeit*) but also of the successful organization of historical materials on the basis of applied organic priorities. In this light, Zunz insisted that a *Statistik* must reflect the correctly proportionate degree of interplay between internally and externally derived national attributes. To accomplish this, a threefold structure must be imposed, consisting of the categories of "elements," "principles," and "results." *Die Elemente*, as Zunz defined them, comprise the formative and shaping forces of national identity, such as language, religion, and state. The more derivative class of *die Principe*, in contrast, refers to the internal yet secondary manifestations of national life, including constitution, morality, folkways, and occupations, all of which depend "on the more or less immanent character of the elements." Finally, *die Resultate*, reflect the "relationship [of the nation] to the foreign environment, derived from the external history of the *Volk*, whether it be of a subservient, dominant, or neutral character."[78]

That which is genuinely authentic in a nation's development, according to Zunz, results from the interplay between original, constitutive factors and temporal, conditioning circumstances:

> So it follows once again that out of both components, namely, on the one hand, the advancement of the people through time and, on the other, the consideration of still-existing ideal elements, the essential and inner character of [the nation's] *Statistik* is formed.[79]

This, it should be noted, does not mean that original characteristics are alone statistically valid. Rather, change and adaptation are legitimate to the extent that they function to undergird the elemental features. However, should foreign elements overwhelm indigenous ones, "the totality as such will cease, and along with it its *Statistik*."[80]

The question now arises as to how these general rules might apply in the case of the Jews. But here, as Zunz cautions, a severe modification must be imposed. For lacking such elemental features as national language, territory and state, only two primary components remain: religion and tribal descent. "... [S]o in the absence of a state, [and] consequently of a historical unity, an ideal element, namely Judaism, is to be placed at the head..." On the one hand, because of this lack, the Jews' nationality must necessarily be a limited one. On the other hand, "Judaism" itself can no longer to be construed in strictly religious terms. For (and here in a manner reminiscent of his "Organization of the Israelites") Judaism qua religion has been forced to absorb into itself all of the other primary elements of nationality, such as language, territory, and state. As an "ideal element," Judaism both incorporated and supplanted the more concrete, worldly, and mundane categories that would otherwise typify national norms.[81]

What then of the relationship between Judaism as the supreme "ideal element" and that most mundane of human activities, the pursuit of livelihoods? In the absence of territorial unity, Zunz suggests, the conditions of occupational development would have been entirely different for Jews than for other peoples. The collection of statistical data relating to Jewish economic life must therefore focus equally on "the occupations and trades which [Jews] did *not* practice, [either] from voluntary reasons or out of [external] coercion."[82] In his earlier programmatic work "Something regarding Rabbinic Literature," to which his *Statistik der Juden* supplied the companion piece, Zunz called for scholarly investigation of the technical contributions that Jews had made to European economic civilization, its credit devices, promissory notes, bills of exchange, and paper money.[83] In this, he appeared to embrace that from which much of the *Haskalah* had fled – identifying aspects of *Jewish* finance with the advancement of European culture.[84] In his *Statistik*, Zunz went further by placing Jewish occupations not in the tertiary category of *die Resultate* but in the secondary category of *die Principe*. He thus implied that Jews' occupational structure was somehow authentic rather than foreign. For it had developed out of the peculiarity of the Jews' own *Statistik*, in which the ideal element of Judaism had come to substitute for the material categories of state and territoriality.

Zunz still left unresolved the question of whether Jews' economic life reflected "the active" or "the passive properties of living Jews" (*des passiven... Zustandes der lebenden Juden*) – whether their means of livelihood was a consequence of national "necessity, freedom, or compulsion." His condemnation of the "one-sidedness" and distortion of a "false *Statistik*" indicates how little prepared he was to accept the constitutionalist theories of a Fries or Rühs, in which a rabbinic aristocracy, built into the original structure of Judaism, had predetermined the nation's future occupational character. In this light, Zunz did in fact leave open the possibility that the Jewish commercial orientation had expressed an aspect of Jews' external relations in the Diaspora, determined through gentile hostility, Jewish economic functionality or both. Yet, at the same time, he expressed little inclination to fall back on this type of *Haskalah* analysis. On the contrary, the peculiarity of the Jews' religion-state remained a primary factor underlying their economic distinctiveness.[85]

Eduard Gans also was interested in the production of a Jewish historical *Statistik*, beginning with "the collection of all laws and regulations imposed upon the Jews..." This comprehensive collection would form, according to Gans, a significant part of the "preparation" [*Vorbereitung*] for a "sound, thorough and from all sides complete history of the Jews."[86] Like Zunz, Gans wished to define the correct relationship between the "inner" and "outer" realms of Jewish history. Gans too presumed a normative statistical model, one that classified the inner history of a nation as "its preceding existence,... its constitution and its law, its customs and beliefs, its language and its commerce, its science and its art." Finally, like Zunz, Gans also considered the relationship between external and internal history to have been entirely unique in the case of the Jews.[87]

According to Gans, a nation's "outer history" is normally the "bearer" [*Trägerin*] of its inner development, corresponding to its "shell." "Of no history is this more true than of the history of the Jews, and of none is it less." What this means, apparently, is that, "in earlier times,... outer history frequently had almost no influence whatsoever on the inner development of the Jews."

But, according to Gans, this in itself is an inaccurate statement, because European Jewry's very isolation *was* in fact the prime factor conditioning its inner development. In other words, isolation and estrangement [*Entfremdung*] were themselves the external conditioning factors relevant to Jews' internal development. This was important in light of Gans' contention – to be explored later in some detail – that external *Entfremdung* had produced a condition of extreme spiritual stasis within medieval Diaspora life.[88]

For Gans, medieval Jewry was entirely lacking in the kind of rich external life enjoyed by other nations, one replete with political and military conflicts, affairs of kings and dynasties, and heroic struggles to achieve and maintain national independence. This was equally true of the Jews' economic as of their political life; both remained unchanged amid the long centuries of European travail. Thus, according to Gans, by the period of late Antiquity, the Jews' medieval economic identity had already been determined in all its essentials. Their mercantile orientation had ensued simply and logically from their prior Diaspora condition.[89] In this sense, the "outer history" defined by European state policy produced no real shift; Europe's Christian states avidly maintained the Jews' dispersion (as well as, consequently, their commercial orientation), but never actually caused it. And if, according to Gans, the Jews' geographical dispersion determined once and for all their commercial functionality, then it was precisely this mercantile utility that consistently regulated their legal status. The whole process played itself out according to script – or, rather, to scrip: "[w]here they were accorded privileges and rights, it was in exchange for pounds, as tokens for the barter of silver..." This merely functional relationship, reduced to its lowest common monetary denominator, could in turn effect no further transformation of the Jews' internal existence: for "there must the inner life go its unchanging, independent way, without consideration of the arbitrary gain or loss in the acquisition of rights or of the outer field of profit."[90]

During the period of Gans's participation in the Society, he produced two studies of the "external relations" of Diaspora Jews, one on "The Legislation on Jews in Rome," the other on "The History of Jews in Northern Europe and in the Slavic Lands." As with so many of the activities of the short-lived Society, Gans intended these studies as initial down payments on a far more grandiose project. What Gans apparently had in mind was a full-scale analysis of the total body of legislation pertaining to Jews, not merely in all European states but also in Europe's individual towns, because "in no sphere of public legislation was the particular and divergent more beloved than in this one."[91] But if, as Gans asserted, the Jews' external Diaspora relations exerted no real effect on their internal development, then the question must arise as to why he deemed it imperative to assemble, classify, and analyze the totality of legislation imposed on them.

One of the defining features of a *Statistik* was its capacity to utilize history to render an objective portrait of the present. Gans, no less than Zunz, was interested in the contemporary implications of his legislative data-gathering enterprise. For both of these authors, part of what defined the spirit of the present age was its historical self-consciousness. Thus, to say that medieval Jewry lacked an outer history was not sufficient. The point, rather, was that medieval Jewry lacked an outer history in part because it lacked the consciousness of possessing one. This is what Gans meant when he claimed that the historical interaction of internal and external elements was at one and the same time both most and least applicable to the case of the Jews. To say that nothing external could penetrate the shell's surface was to say that the shell itself was impervious, because of its construction, to external influences. Medieval Judaism's inability to problematize its own insularity was thus a contributing cause of its isolation.[92] In seeking to restore contemporary Jewry's own "outer history," that is, its proper relationship with and involvement in the life of contemporary Europe, *Wissenschaft* had also to restore contemporary Jewry's consciousness of its own past "outer history." What this meant, strange as it may sound, was that *Wissenshaft* had to make contemporary Jews conscious of their own self-imposed past insularity.

This, in turn, could be accomplished only through the scientific affirmation of the actual rather than the mythological conditions in which Jews existed under gentile rule.[93] Thus, Gans was at pains to establish that, although persecution of Jews had been a constant in Diaspora history, the causes, motivations, and rationales behind it had shifted constantly. Not only this, but the legal-historical status of Jews, according to Gans, had to be measured in relation to that of other marginalized groups, such as Moslems, pagans, and heretics, in comparison with which Jews had often received favored treatment.[94] Indeed, such qualifying factors could be multiplied exponentially through the assemblage of the "particular" and "divergent" legislation of European town law, a rich and multifaceted body of material relating to Jews' "outer history." If, as Gans insisted, "outer history is merely the bearer of inner history," it is only through a scientifically precise rendering of this vast range of external conditions that a true "inner history" of historical Judaism would emerge. A comprehensive picture of the Jews' outer life would thus be preparatory to a description of their spiritual development. And this was the case even though – or rather, precisely because – that outer life (despite its own actual variegation) had made no impression on the Jews' self-conception. According to Gans, such a picture would therefore be necessary, "... so that the spiritual life, operating for the most part independent of external relations, might follow."[95]

How then might a thoroughgoing portrait of external conditions be preparatory to an account of the Jews' occupational development? As noted, Gans attributed the Jews' *Handelsstand* origins to their condition of Diaspora statelessness – an external factor.[96] Yet, as we have seen, he also categorized the Jews' characteristic occupations with their inner, spiritual life – that is to say, their religion. In sorting out this difficulty, it is important to keep in mind Gans's overall indebtedness here to Hegelian concepts. By the late 1820s (and by then as a convert to Christianity and a professor of Law at the University of Berlin), Gans would become one of Hegel's closest disciples.[97] Yet back in his *Wissenschaft* days, when Gans had already come under Hegel's spell, he had still to face the challenge of reconciling Hegelianism and Judaism. The problem, in particular, was how to account for and justify Judaism's persistence past the moment when, according to Hegel, its historical mission had already been fulfilled. In his 1822 "Address to the Society," Gans sought to provide an answer, one that, as we shall see, linked the theme of Jewish monotheism with the emergence of a Diaspora Jewish *Handelsstand*.

Gans insisted that ancient Judaism had constituted a rational advance on paganism precisely through its abstraction of divinity from nature. But although Judaism deserved historical credit for first uncovering the essential unity of thought and being (i.e., monotheism), its achievement had been partly negated by the forms that this religious expression took, by literalism, legalism, and localism. Emerging out of this negation, Christianity was originally constituted as a synthesis of paganism and Judaism. Through the figure of Christ, it was able to restore the divine to the realm of everyday life. Moreover, Christianity was able to demolish the notion of mere national divinities that in their distinctive ways had characterized both paganism and Judaism alike. Yet, at the same time, Gans insisted that Christianity had itself suffered a negation, and this at the very moment of its inception. For in its original synthesis of pagan and Judaic elements, Christianity had been forced to strike so fine a balance between opposing principles that it could not help but take on an excessively doctrinal orientation as the mark of its essential character. This dogmatic tendency, according to Gans, was bound inevitably to give rise to controversy and sectarianism and thence to the violent suppression of dissent. Thus, Christianity was rendered a fundamentally intolerant and repressive faith. And in light of this defect, Judaism retained its relevance, for Judaism's own unique conception of unity represents an enduring alternative to Christianity's at best equally flawed approach. Christianity thus bears the relation to Judaism not of a successor, as both Hegel and ancient Christian tradition claimed, but of a worthy competitor.[98]

But, according to Gans, Judaic unity was not made manifest in mere concepts alone but also in the very structure of civil society. In the sociological as in the theological realm, historical Judaism represented the unity principle operating within human history. This claim emerges from Gans's depiction of Judaism's self-adaptation, on the basis of its ancient constitution, to the Jews' condition of Diaspora statelessness. For Hegel, the imperfection of the ancient state lay in its one-sidedness, that is, its total subordination of private existence to public aims. According to Hegel, the ancient state failed "to come to terms with the principle of self-sufficient particularity," that is, with individual and corporate plurality, which is the ideal expression of *Geist* in civil society.[99] This one-sidedness, or "substantiality," as Hegel calls it, was, as Gans agrees, entirely characteristic of the ancient Jewish state as well. For Gans, ancient Judaism's theological unity concept was paralleled by – or embedded within – a constitutional one: thus "[i]n the earliest period, appointed as guardians of the idea of the unity of God, it was necessary that even the state, morality, laws, and religion would appear as an undifferentiated sameness." Again, the originality of Judaism lay in its theology, not in its ancient constitution, which was "indistinct from [that of] any other oriental people."[100] With the advent of Christianity, the Jews' theological innovation was bequeathed to the wider world; hence, its theological self-justification could no longer reside in its monopoly over monotheism itself.

Yet, precisely here, according to Gans, Judaism evolved a further innovation, one that it accomplished, paradoxically, by remaining exactly the same as it was before. Whereas before the rise of Christianity, Judaism had been theologically novel but constitutionally generic, in the wake of the Christianity's emergence, Judaism lost its theological uniqueness while acquiring a constitutional one instead. Judaism sought to retain its old constitutional form as an undifferentiated polity, but now in the absence of a state. Indeed, in the absence of its state, and under conditions of dispersion, Judaism could retain its constitutional unity through one method alone: by transforming itself into a commercial estate, *ein Handelsstand*. "When their state was destroyed, they held onto the concept of this unity, latching themselves onto a class, *a trading class*."[101]

The transformation of Jews into a *Handelsstand* was consistent with (although not identical to) Judaism's original theological and political structures. But Gans suggests that it was also anachronistic in two respects. First, it represented a form of adaptation that sought to maintain political unity long after the constitutional structure requiring such unity had been destroyed.

Second, it was anachronistic in the sense of being premature. As Gans tells us, the Jews' singular estate form represented a kind of embryonic incarnation of the very civil society that would characterize Europe as a whole during modern times. "Besides the unity which it nevertheless afforded there existed in this [form of *Handelsstand*] the possibility, as in no other, of development into all the general classes [*Ständen*] of society."[102] For Gans, as for Hegel, civil society is properly divided into three estates: the substantive [*substantielle*], the reflective [*reflectierte*], and the general [*allgemeine*]. We recall that Sieyes had divided all occupations into four general classes: agriculturists, artisans, merchants, and service workers and professions. Fichte, in his *Closed Commercial State*, had defined three estate categories, agricultural, artisanal, and mercantile. Indeed, despite the top-heavy administrative apparatus that his *Handelsstaat* required, Fichte made no special estate provision for a civil service and bureaucracy. Hegel differed on precisely this key point. Hegel's estates correspond, first to the agricultural, second to the artisinal, industrial, and mercantile, and third to the bureaucratic categories.[103] Thus, when Gans states, without further elaboration, that the medieval Jewish *Handelsstand* contained within it the potentiality of all the other classes of society, he could mean one of two things. He could mean either that the unity of the *Handelsstand* did not in itself preclude Jews' historical integration into the other major estates of medieval society, or he could mean that the *Handelsstand* instanced by medieval Jews was a kind of anticipation of modern bourgeois society, as we shall now explain.

In the first case, it is difficult to see how the structural unity afforded by the *Handelsstand* could have been compatible under Diaspora conditions with the dispersion of medieval Jews into other occupations.[104] Yet, in the second instance, it is also not entirely clear why Gans would have considered a commercial estate as somehow prototypical of modern developments. After all, in Hegel's political theory, it is the bureaucratic class (his third estate) that serves as the mediating force in society, for it alone "has *the universal interests* of society as its business."[105] Yet there is evidence from Gans's later writings that he himself attributed greater universal relevance to the commercial element of the "reflective estate" than did Hegel. First, Gans viewed the expansion of the commercial segment of the "reflective class" as one of the hallmarks of modern *Nationalökonomie*. Second, Gans classified large-scale landowners (to whom Hegel had accorded special political privileges), as well as factory owners, as within the "general" rather than the commercial estate. He defined estate owners and rentiers as idle elements to be included in the "universal" *Stand* simply because they performed no *particular* activity. He thus indicated that, in contrast with Hegel, his own classification scheme followed from the specific nature of the activity performed rather than from the social-psychological standpoint it supposedly afforded. Third, Gans asserted that among the three estates, only members of the "reflective" had need of subdividing themselves into distinct corporations. This was significant in the sense that, as we shall see momentarily, Gans believed that corporative existence, organized on a free and voluntary basis, was essential to modern civic life.[106] Hence, if we take Gans's later conceptions as applicable to his 1822 "Address" (admittedly, a risky assumption), then it is indeed possible to interpret him as identifying the medieval Jewish *Handelsstand* with the prototype or embryo of a modern commercial society.

We stand on more solid ground in addressing the question of why this Jewish *Handelsstand* never realized its potential – that is, why the Jews continued up to Gans's day to constitute a largely undifferentiated commercial nation. If the ancient state had been "one-sided," then in accordance with Hegelian dialectics it had engendered its own negation. This negation was accomplished through the agency of political or constitutional ideals that in Antiquity were still basically religious in form. Thus, for Hegel, Christianity spelled the end of the ancient state through its own affirmation of individuality and personality.[107] Yet at the same time Hegel regarded the principal shortcoming of Christianity as its other-worldliness. This ensured that the individuality it had introduced could only express itself in the sphere of private thought, hope, and activity.[108] For Gans, this emphasis on the private went hand-in-hand with the fragmentation of Christian society into the kind of egoistic corporate existence that had epitomized the Middle Ages. What characterized medieval estates and corporations was precisely the fact that they were "unfree . . . , in which the freedom of the individual was negated":[109]

> The medieval estates represented not the state, rather [only] their own business. They advanced through their own right, not the right of the state.[110]

Like Hegel, Gans argued that modern civil society should retain a likeness of these "corporate" institutions, but in a highly modified form. As voluntary associations such corporations would serve a number of beneficial purposes: they would help prevent society's fragmentation into atomized individuals; they would help redirect individual self-seeking into socially useful ends; and (of particular importance for the *Wissenschafter* Gans) they would help protect group diversity in an age of homogenizing pressures. According to Gans, genuine unity can only be achieved by insuring "a wealth of particularities."[111] But, needless to say, such socially useful and socially mediating modern corporations would be far removed from their medieval prototypes. Thus, in a circumstance in which society was composed exclusively of private, self-seeking, and closed corporations, the medieval Jewish *Handelsstand* could neither dissolve itself into the full range of occupations, nor effect the kind of unity-through-particularity that for Gans reflects the Hegelian *Geist* in its mature incarnation:

> That this was nevertheless delayed for millennia is primarily due to the fact that society itself had still not reached a full development, that where there existed so many masses not yet brought into alignment, the one particularism appeared scarcely as such. Cut off and excluded, [the Jews] thence followed a singular history paralleling that of world-history, through the elaborate interaction of their family, political and religious life, as much as through their isolation from all general classes of society.[112]

The tragedy of Jewish Diaspora history was thus epitomized by the failure of a corporate society to incorporate the Jews.

According to Gans, this means that in the present age two forms of emancipation must now occur. First, Europe must be emancipated from the lingering vestiges of its corporative medievalism. For, even in its present condition, Europe has still failed to grasp that its own unity can only be made possible through a corporative multiplicity, one that guarantees both individual freedom and voluntary group affiliation. Second, Jews must now be emancipated from their own inwardness, characterized by the persistence of their "parallel" history and manifested in their own lingering corporate insularity.[113] In fact, both emancipations would be interdependent; for the Jews' diffusion through "all the general classes of society" would be dependent on the emergence of an open corporative society, while at the same time such a society, through its acceptance of a distinct Jewish (cultural) corporation, would help to realize its own liberal Hegelian perfection. Needless to say, by making Jews aware of their inherited indifference to external change, as well as by demonstrating to Europe how its corporatism has thus far fallen short, *Wissenschaft* could play a major role in helping to effect both emancipations.

Gans had formulated an impressive response to the challenge of Rühs. Like Rühs, he had connected the emergence of the Jewish *Handelsstand* with the inner theological and sociological character of "Judaism." But, at the same time, he had done so in a manner that allowed him to connect that which was unique in Jewish monotheism with that which was particular to premodern Europe's social and economic character. Moreover, like Rühs, Gans, too, had shunned much of the lachrymose conception, but in his case he had done so without attempting to exonerate Christianity's theological intolerance or civic parochialism. His was thus a relatively more sophisticated – and, needless to say, a far more sympathetic – portrayal of Jews and Judaism. For instead of rendering Judaism an alien element, he depicted the Jewish *Handelsstand* as a model – albeit an imperfect one – for indigenous European development.

Yet for Gans personally, the price of his own exclusion from Christian Europe proved too great. In 1825, both he and his fellow Society member Heinrich Heine accepted baptism. As Heine famously put it, baptism was to be an entry-ticket to the opportunities of a wider European culture, by which he meant, a professional academic career.[114] It is impossible to say what Gans might have contributed had he remained part of *Wissenschaft des Judentums*. But given his great interest in the history of inheritance law – a legal-economic topic if there ever was one – his departure could only mean a loss to future *Wissenschaft* historical-economy.[115] As we now turn back to examine some of the figures who remained in the movement, we will see that the kinds of synthetic approaches outlined here would no longer be pursued. Indeed, it appears that Gans's effort increasingly to wean *Wissenschaft* from its *Haskalah* influences constituted one of his last enduring legacies to the movement. By severing that tie, the possibility of further developments along the lines of Zunz's and Gans's *Statistik* was momentarily closed off.

THE *DOPPELBILD*

When, during the 1820s, Isaac Marcus Jost began to issue successive volumes of his *History of the Israelites*, he was criticized by Zunz, Gans, and others of the *Wissenschaft* circle for undertaking a full-scale, comprehensive history of the Jews from biblical to modern times before the necessary "statistical" preparation had been completed.[116] In his defense, we might now say that Jost had been the first Jewish historian to attempt seriously to supply the *empirical* background for a future economic history of the Jews.

Almost alone among the early practitioners of *Wissenschaft*, Jost examined the mundane mechanisms of actual economic experience. He was the first to investigate the practice of Jewish money-lending in a detailed way, categorizing different types of loans and delineating the factors generating variations in rates of interest. Moreover, his *History* was the first to discuss the internal composition of the medieval Jewish community on the basis of its integrated occupational functions. Jost sought to relate the shifting status of Jews regionally and chronologically to changes in the value of their economic services to the state. At the same time, he tried to discern how various economic groupings within the Jewish community had operated conjointly to satisfy external demands.[117] All of this might seem praiseworthy from the standpoint of the *Statistiker* Zunz. But in actuality what Zunz appears to have found most disturbing about Jost's synthesis was not its premature character. Rather, it was the fact that by the time of its publication, Jost's *History* had already been rendered obsolete. That is to say, Jost's history was too polemical, too preoccupied with external causes, and, at the same time, too superficial in its negative portrayal of rabbinic Judaism to satisfy contemporary *Wissenschaft* tastes.[118] It read, in short, too much like a *Haskalah* history of the Jews.

Jost's depiction of the Jews' occupational development was a case in point. In radical *Haskalah* fashion, he attributed the Jews' occupational deformity to a combination of rabbinic obscurantism and gentile persecution. On the one hand, the progressive expansion of Jewish law had allowed for the incursion of rituals and restrictions into every aspect of daily life, thus choking off the time available for "productive" vocations.[119] On the other hand, external factors such as the Jews' exclusion from public offices and military service, the prohibition on their employment of Christian slaves in agriculture, and the rise of exclusionary Christian guilds, had had the effect of confining their livelihoods to the various rungs of the exchange economy.[120] Thus, although Jost provided a more detailed account of all these matters than had his *Wissenschaft* contemporaries or *Haskalah* predecessors, his explanatory apparatus and theoretical presumptions appeared to be out of step with the contemporary intellectual *Zeitgeist*.

Even in the one area in which Jost appeared most original – in his "class analysis" – his deployment of Jewish history as a tool of contemporary social criticism tended to rankle. Jost identified sharp social divisions within medieval Jewry, not just between rabbis and laymen, but between wealthy merchants and bankers, on the one side, and the ignorant and impoverished Jewish masses, on the other. He attacked the wealthiest elements in medieval Jewish society as self-serving agents of the gentile aristocracy who repeatedly failed to recognize that the status and power afforded them through wealth rendered the entire community vulnerable to attack. "And the Jews would stand higher had they never been placed in such positions, or had they declined to accept them."[121] Because as high-level financial agents they required the subordinate services of petty traders and moneylenders, they helped bring about the creation of an entire class of petty traders and itinerant "beggar Jews" [*Betteljuden*]. These "Jewish-Gypsies, charlatans and criminals," as Jost refers to them, were loathed by non-Jews and feared by their coreligionists as well:

> If we knew of their condition merely from historical testimony we might regard their portrayal as distorted and subject to serious doubt . . . , but unfortunately it is still the case today in our civilized (*gebildeten*) states and humane age, that we observe such mischief in many places.[122]

This aside was typical of Jost's use of history as a tool of contemporary social criticism; for his account of the present plague of *Betteljuden* was placed within a discussion of Jewish life during the fifteenth century!

But, despite the tendentious anachronisms that marred his *History*, it is now possible to see that Jost's contribution to Jewish historical-economy was a genuine one. First, he helped begin the effort on the part of Jewish scholars to attend to the social character of historical Judaism. This could be approached either through criticism, as was often the case with Jost himself, or through praise. Thus, Ludwig Philippson, the Jewish Reform leader and editor of the influential *Allgeimeine Zeitung des Judentums*, was able to draw selectively on Jost's *History* to produce a portrait of medieval Judaism's social ethic as a model of enlightened liberalism, social justice, and economic equality.[123] A more substantive effort was the theological-historical writings of Abraham Geiger, one of the leaders of nineteenth-century Reform. Geiger adapted Jost's class analysis to construct a grand schema of Jewish theological development. He interpreted Jewish religious development, especially during the Hellenistic period, in terms of the competing party-political agendas of different social strata. His 1857 *Urschrift und Übersetzungen der Bibel in ihrer Abhängigkeit von der inner Entwickelung des Judenthums* [Original Text and Translations of the Bible based upon the Inner Development of Judaism] utilized the categories of Jewish aristocracy, clergy, and bourgeoisie to depict the triumphant emergence of a populist Pharisaic Judaism at the time of the Maccabees.[124] Nevertheless, neither Geiger, Philippson, nor other contemporaries were able to make significant advances on Jost's analysis of the core problem of Jewish occupational development.

A second legacy of Jost – one alluded to earlier – lay in the relatively greater empirical detail he provided on Jewish economic life. But here, Jost's influence on future *Wissenschaft* historians was of an indirect kind. When we examine the successor effort within classical *Wissenschaft* to produce a full-scale, multivolume history of the Jews – Heinrich Graetz's monumental *Geschichte der Juden* (first edition: 1859–1877) – we find that, notwithstanding accusations to the contrary, the author did manage to weave into his narrative an extensive array of economic-related materials.[125] This was because by the time he completed the second edition of his *Geschichte* a significant amount of the preparatory spadework had already been done. Specifically, non-Jewish researchers such as the German historians Georges-Bernard Depping and Otto Stobbe carried on what Jost had inaugurated.[126] And it was to these authors, rather than to Jost himself, that Graetz acknowledged his debt.[127]

Yet, despite the fact that Graetz did make ample use of these researches, his integration of the "inner" and "outer" dimensions of Jewish history was accomplished only through a feat of great narrative skill. In this light, Ismar Schorsch's verdict that Graetz was "... the first *Wissenschaft* historian to integrate the external and internal history of ancient and medieval Jewry into a single work of scholarship" needs to be qualified.[128] Graetz did not so much integrate these dimensions as place them side by side. What this means is that he offered little insight into how the one side might have influenced or even reflected the other. On the contrary, what Graetz presented was by his own admission a *Doppelbild*, a "double-image." It was the image not of one but of two Jewish histories: the first of "ceaseless martyrdom, degradation and humiliation," the second of "relentless mental effort, of indefatigable scholarship."[129]

Graetz's *Doppelbild* symbolized the compromise that classical *Wissenschaft des Judentums* had at last settled on in its effort to answer Friedrich Rühs's challenge of 1815. With Gans departed, Jost superseded, and Zunz's "Future *Statistik* of the Jews" abandoned, it would be many decades before a novel conception Jewish historical-economy again emerged from within the tradition of *Wissenschaft des Judentums*.[130] Perhaps the reason for this, as Zunz once put it, was simply that economic matters still remained "somewhat foreign to us." But the deepening emphasis on spiritual history appears also to have been connected with the movement's internal dynamics, and particularly its increasing effort to distance itself from its materialist and pragmatic *Haskalah* links.

Striving to establish its independence from Enlightenment apologetics, *Wissenschaft* had hoped to use history to reconcile Jews with the modern age. In the movement's various attempts to account for the development of a Jewish *Handelsstand*, fragmentary though they were, it had sought to embrace the spirit of organicism in order to fend off the attacks of a hostile Romanticism. If this turned out to be a difficult or even an impossible task, it suggested, as we shall see in the next chapter on Karl Marx, that a new approach – one that would employ the tools of historicism to refashion and revitalize older materialist conceptions – would first have to emerge if the *Doppelbild* were to be effectively transcended.

8

⌀

Capitalism and the Jews

Eduard Gans never completed his plan to collect and analyze all the legislation pertaining to Jewish Diaspora status. Yet he appears to have known in advance what its final result would be. In his "Legislation on the Jews in Rome," Gans employed the term "*Halbheit*" ("half-measure") to explain the overall character of Jewish status as it had evolved in Christendom. According to Gans, over the course of many centuries Christian Europe had exhibited a profound ambivalence toward Jews and Judaism. It had sought neither fully to extirpate the Jews nor to incorporate them; it had accorded Jews a special status as sole tolerated dissenters while at the same time rendering them the peculiar objects of its wrath.

For Gans, it was Christianity's own intimate ties to Judaism that best explained this paradox. A part of Christianity's legitimacy depended on its own claims to Jewish descent. Christian doctrine, moreover, looked forward to the ultimate conversion of the Jews as the culmination of its spiritual mission. For these reasons, Judaism, in contrast with both paganism and heresy, could not be destroyed. "The destruction of Judaism would have involved the dual sin: against the legacy of the past, and against the promise of the future." Yet for Gans, this same condition of dependency also best explained Christianity's animosity to Jews. That is to say, at its core, as well as in numerous of its particulars, Christianity viewed Judaism as being too close for comfort. This resemblence, in both the genetic and typological senses, produced a concomitant animosity, an "anxiety of influence," one might say, that drove Christianity periodically to vent its rage against its proximate other.[1]

Like Gans, the young Karl Marx in his 1844 "On the Jewish Question" (*Zur Judenfrage*) undertook to account for the phenomenon of Jewish survival. Gans and Marx were both disciples of Hegel. For both of these figures, the question of Jewish survival remained an equally vexing dilemma. If history constitutes a zigzag march of progress, then the persistence of Judaism was either a historical irrelevance or a sign of significant defects within the Hegelian synthesis itself. Hegel himself wrestled with this paradox, alternatively labeling Jewish endurance as the reflection of a "fanaticism of stubbornness" or of an "admirable firmness."[2] Unlike the master, Gans and Marx connected the question of Jewish survival not merely with a consistency of Jewish will but with the evolution of a Jewish *Handelsstand*. Both sensed a link between the Jews' theological conceptions and their material, economic existence, and both were at pains to define the connection between Jewish and Christian economic theology.

As examined in the preceding chapter, during his *Wissenschaft* years Gans had attempted to use Hegelian concepts to explain Jewish survival and advance Jewish emancipation. He viewed the successful linkage of Jews' "inner" and "outer" histories as essential to realizing these ends. The Jews' "outer" history was epitomized by their *Halbheit* legal status; their "inner" history by stasis and insularity. Hence the theoretical determinants underlying their "halfway" status would be of direct practical relevance to the Jews' external emancipation and internal self-development. For if Christian ambivalence was responsible for confining the Jews to an isolated *Handelsstand*, then the Jews' own inner productivization – as demanded by the emancipatory quid pro quo – could only occur within a pluralistic society defined by open corporations and free *Stände*. The realization of such a society would, in turn, depend on the elimination of a subordinate legal status that ultimately derived from Christian theology.[3]

In this sense, too, the same interdependence of inner and outer, and of theory and practice, applied to the relationship between past and present. Although the Jews' marginalization in Christendom had at one time been historically explicable, and in that sense perhaps justified, it seemed to Gans incomprehensible and intolerable that it should persist in modern Europe. The expansion of the "reflective" estate had productivized Europe to the point where society now comprised a unity of distinct yet integrated economic elements. As Gans had shown in his writings for the *Culturverein*, uniformity in the sociological as in the theological realm was inimical to genuine unity. The old Christian rationale for tolerating Jews in a subordinate status no longer applied. Judaism must either be recognized as a legitimate and alternative form of monotheism or else eliminated. What could not be permitted, however, was the perpetuation of the *Halbheit*. As Gans wrote with evident exasperation:

> How long must [it] ... persist! Has not history sufficiently taught us that there are only two paths to choose from: either to proceed from the principle of an exclusively saving Church and from strict – and in this regard, at least,

praiseworthy – logic and wipe the Jews from the face of the earth and fill the resulting space with their buried limbs; or to forget that there is such a thing as a Jew from a legislative standpoint, and so fill that space with their resurrected spirits? Only what lies in-between is the evil.[4]

Gans wrote these words in 1823, but they could easily have reflected the sentiments of many German Jews in the early 1840s. In fact, it was likely the case that the "Jewish Question" provided a more salient topic of general debate in the latter than in the former period. This was because by the early 1840s general liberal opinion in Prussia had adopted Jewish emancipation as one of its causes.[5] The pressure to resolve the Jewish Question had been recently intensified by the actions of King Frederick William IV of Prussia. Soon after his 1840 accession to the throne, the king issued a secret directive to his ministers instructing them to find ways of restoring Jews' medieval corporate status.[6] The king's proposal was an attempt to resituate the Jews within an idealized medieval polity. Soon leaked to the press, it served as a trial balloon for a broader program of reconstituting Prussia as a *ständisch* Christian state, an idea that hearkened back to the teachings of Adam Müller and Karl Ludwig von Haller. No wonder that, when word of the proposal came out, it scandalized both Jewish and general liberal opinion.[7]

In the face of organized opposition, and of intense disagreement among government ministers, parliamentary debates on the proposal were postponed for several years. The Prussian United Diet declined to pass the law in the form proposed, agreeing only to ascribe separate status to Jews in the religious sphere. Still, for all intents and purposes crown policy toward the Jews assumed the Christian character of the state and aimed to treat Jews administratively as members of corporate *Judenschaften*.[8] The controversy, particularly during the early part of the decade, generated dozens of pamphlets, of which Marx's was among the least noticed at the time, although it is the only one still read today.[9] In this light, it is well to remember that Marx's "On the Jewish Question" was not merely an abstract exercise in philosophical criticism but also an analysis of a topical question of immediate public concern. It was Frederick William's medievalist proposal on the Jews that drew Marx into a debate with his former collaborator Bruno Bauer over the significance of Jewish status to such matters as individual citizenship versus medieval corporate identity, the liberal versus "Christian" states, and bourgeois versus socialist emancipation.[10] These were the problems that Marx wished to take on in "On the Jewish Question."

Although "On the Jewish Question" addressed a topical issue, Marx's treatment of it attracted little immediate attention.[11] Marx published the essay in the Spring of 1844 in the pages of the *Deutsch-Französische Jahrbücher*, a journal issued in France with articles written exclusively in German. Its language tended to reduce sales in France, whereas the Prussian censor, which immediately confiscated all copies it could locate, virtually precluded them in Germany.[12] Further obscuring the breakthrough character of "On the Jewish Question" was the fact that Marx's essay was couched as a review of two polemics published a year earlier by his former collaborator Bruno Bauer. It was Bauer's essays rather than Marx's critiques of them which drew fire. Bauer was the author of famously controversial works on the New Testament and had become a cause célèbre when dismissed by the government from his position as Professor of Theology at the University of Bonn in March 1842. In his own "The Jewish Question" (Die Judenfrage), Bauer had rejected Jewish emancipation on the grounds that in a politically backward "Christian" state such as Prussia the claims of Jews qua Jews to citizenship amounted to special pleading. For Bauer, Jewish emancipation was itself a Halbheit, since it would merely mark a Jewish exception to the general rule of a corporate society.[13] Jews always insist on being the exception to the rule, said Bauer, and they always accept the rule! He demanded that Jews abandon their religion and make common cause with atheistic German liberals before they could reasonably expect their own emancipation, a demand that drew impassioned responses by liberal Jewish spokesmen such as Abraham Geiger and Samuel Hirsch.[14]

In contrast, the fame (or infamy) of Marx's early Jewish essay came only later,[15] when Marxism had become a driving force in the European workers' movement and, ironically, when Marx himself had long since abandoned the type of analysis he formulated in 1844. The essay came to be regarded by many later Marxists as a seminal work in the history of Marx's development as a theoretician.[16] By making it appear as a necessary step on the road to historical materialism, "On the Jewish Question" escaped orthodox censure for both its theoretical sloppiness and its anti-Jewish prejudices.[17] Some Marxists, Karl Kautsky, for instance, apparently did find the essay embarrassing. Kautsky feared it might be exploited to taint the Social Democratic Party, not to mention the reputation of its author.[18] Kautsky's worries aside, interest in the essay did not dim. In fact, the analytical literature on "On the Jewish Question" is vast and continues to grow.[19] But for reasons that should now be apparent, critical discussion has tended to focus either on its place in the history of Marx's intellectual evolution, or somewhat incongruously, on the question of whether or not (or to what degree) it demonstrates Marx's antisemitism.[20] Here the aim is different: to show how Marx's ideas creatively recapitulated and transcended treatments of Jewish commerce encompassing figures such as Luzzatto, Toland, Fichte, and Dohm.

With regard, for instance, to *Wissenschaft des Judentums*, what is of concern here is Marx's attempt to resolve the puzzle of the *Doppelbild*, the separation of external and internal, material and theological, commercial and spiritual in depictions of the Jewish past. As noted, "On the Jewish Question" was composed at a time when Marx was attempting to work out the nature of such dynamics as they operated within society as a whole.[21] Indeed, part of the essay's fascination resides in its evident uncertainty as to where the source of ultimate causal priority for the development of capitalist modernity should lie. In this sense too, the essay represents a *Halbheit*. What sets the work apart from previous Hegelian writings is the author's shifting deployment of both "idealist" and "materialist" conceptions. This approach, applied to a topic that seems to demand such eclecticism (Judaism and commerce), is what lends the piece much of its power and weight. "On the Jewish Question" was written during a phase when Marx was neither fully Hegelian nor fully Marxist, thus, at the one moment when he was able to make use of both approaches simultaneously.[22]

THE EVERYDAY JEW

Early on in "On the Jewish Question" Marx announces his intention to tackle the issue from a new angle: "Let us consider the real Jew," he says, "not the *sabbath Jew* ..., but the *everyday Jew*." "Let us not seek the secret of the Jew in his religion, but rather let us seek the secret of the religion in the real Jew [*im wirklichen Juden*]."[23] What is the secret of religion and what is the real Jew? At first glance, and with Marx's later writings in mind, these statements evoke the "materialist" conception of history, a conception in which Hegelian "being" (*Dasein*) is separated from and made generative of Hegelian "spirit" (*Geist*). According to this approach, the secret of ephemeral religion must lie in something far more substantial than mere theological formulae.[24] Dissolve Judaism's mystifying force and you will discover the workaday life of the Jew, that is, the moneylender, merchant, financier, petty trader, and huckster. The implication is that the social relations inherent in these kinds of commercial activities have produced a specific brand of religion. Judaism is not an arbitrary belief system but a belief system mirroring a given way of life. If it is also a false or dangerous belief system, then it can only be changed or eliminated by altering or abolishing the way of life which produces it. If the "secret of the religion [is] in the real Jew," then Judaism cannot be reformed or done away with without reforming or doing away with the real Jew – the huckster.

Yet two problems emerge from this reading of Marx. First, assuming that the above interpretation is correct and that Judaism is a false or dangerous belief system, then the question arises: whom does it endanger? Marx asserts that "Jewish emancipation, in its final significance, is the emancipation of mankind from Judaism."[25] Clearly, Marx here suggests that Judaism endangers *both* Jews in particular and mankind in general. Is Marx then saying, in the fashion of a William Prynne or Jacob Friedrich Fries, that Judaism is a form of exclusivist and domineering religious constitution that threatens to enslave all foreign nations that come into contact with it? Or are Marx's antecedents even older than these, recalling instead Christianity's age-old abhorrence of the "Judaizing heresy" perpetually threatening to infect adherents of the new covenant with the outworn beliefs of the old?[26]

There is a second difficulty involved in this "materialist" reading of Marx's essay. If the "real Jew" is more real and substantive than his religious smoke screen, then, according to this "materialist" reading of his essay, Marx should presumably call for the destruction or the elimination of the real Jew. Such an approach would be analogous to his insistence in later writings that only the active elimination of the bourgeoisie would destroy the ideological constructs generated by its mode of class domination.[27] Yet in Marx's proposed solution to "the Jewish Question" he does not call on society to rid itself of, to emancipate itself from, Jews. Rather, he concludes that the mankind's enemy is not the Jews but Judaism, that is, not their physical beings or intrinsic natures but their beliefs. Society frees itself not by ridding itself of Jews but of Judaism. Here Marx appears to be saying that the Jews are a part of society, that they are men who have been distorted and denatured by their particular faith. They are harmful insofar as they are instruments and agents of that faith, but they are also harmed because of it. Hence, in "On the Jewish Question," Marx insists that the Jews will be emancipated only when the condition of their existence, namely, Judaism, is eliminated. In this light, he appears to be seeking the secret of the real Jew in his religion rather than the secret of his religion in the real Jew.

We might find a way out of this conundrum by making use of the interpretation favored by one of Marx's biographers, David McLellan. McLellan notes that in the German of Marx's day the word *Judentum*, which meant both Jews and Judaism, also had the tertiary meaning of "commerce" (Marx's term, *Schacher*, implies a combination of commerce, usury, and hucksterism).[28] Thus, when Marx says Judaism, he means not the religious system designated by that term but, rather, the activity of commercial exchange. In this way, according to McClellan, much of "On the Jewish Question" should be read as "an extended pun."[29] But this solution also creates difficulties. For if Marx intended Judaism to mean simply "commerce," then his equation would not form a pun but a tautology. He would be saying, in effect, that we should

"seek the secret of commerce in commerce." This hardly seems a satisfying conclusion. Moreover, if as McLellan claims, Marx's "Judaism" had "very
little religious . . . content," then we must ask why in "On the Jewish Question"
Marx proceeded to treat the reader to an analysis of Judaism as a *theological*
system, one that possessed a very definite historical and conceptual relation
to Christianity? If Marx theologizes in "On the Jewish Question," it suggests
that his conception of Judaism/commerce was at least partly an "idealist" one
that renders the huckster a product of Jewish religion as much as it makes
Jewish religion a product of huckstering. Thus, to address the questions we
raised above – viz., who are the Jews?, what is their relation to mankind?, and
which enjoys causal priority, the "real Jew" or Judaism? – we must now do
what Marx himself did and make a brief excursion into theology.

As noted, Marx was interested in the same question that engaged the
practitioners of *Wissenschaft des Judentums*: why Jews and Judaism have survived long after Christians and Christianity had supposedly superseded them.
According to Marx, Judaism can be said to have survived because "it constituted the religious criticism of Christianity, and embodied the doubt concerning the religious origins of Christianity . . ."[30] Bauer had employed very
similar phraseology in his *Die Judenfrage*. But as was often the case with Marx's
relation to Bauer, similarities in language did not necessarily mean identical
conceptions.[31] Here, Marx's interpretation was closer to that of Gans than of
Bauer, whereas both the explanations of Gans and Marx echoed a common
source in patristic doctrine. According to St. Augustine, for instance, Jews must
be tolerated in the Christian polity (among other reasons) because they dispel
rather than embody a doubt: that is, they serve as uncomprehending witnesses
to the prophesied Christ, in opposition to pagan critics who would challenge
Christ's historicity and divinity. Marx alludes to such traditional interpretations, but he refuses to accept them as sufficient, even in the secularized
formulations of writers such as Gans. Judaism has equally survived alongside
Christianity, says Marx, because "the practical Jewish spirit" has perpetuated
itself in Christian society, "and has even attained its highest place there."[32]
This argument of a "Judaization" (*Verjudung*) of Christianity – preparatory of
a Judaization of modern society as a whole – also evoked Christian theology.[33]
Paul and Luther had associated what Marx calls the "practical Jewish spirit"
with the effort to seek salvation through works. For Luther, Judaism had persisted because the Roman Church had failed to purge itself of its own Judaic
ritual, erroneously believing it capable of justifying man in the eyes of God.[34]

Here then is where Marx's "materialist" conception, problematic though
it may be in "On the Jewish Question," comes into play. To Marx (at least
at the time when he wrote the essay), historical Judaism, like all religious

conceptions, represented an attempt to solve the fundamental problem of "human need" [*Bedürfniss*].[35] Human need is the biological demand for the extraction of life-sustenance from nature. In "On the Jewish Question," Judaism reflects the effort to solve the problem of human need by resolving it, first, into "practical need," and second, into monotheistic divinity. What Marx means by "practical" is "subjective" or "egoistic" (*Das praktische Bedürfniss, der Eigennutz*), as opposed to "theoretical" and "objective."[36] That is to say, Judaism deified (or reified) material need into the Jewish national God. Because Marx does not provide us here with a religious anthropology of antiquity, his conception of the specific relation of Judaism to ancient heathenism cannot be determined with certainty. But one suspicion deriving from earlier Hegelian formulations and later developed by the philosopher Ludwig Feuerbach is that Judaism sought to deify human need in a manner that would distinguish its own exclusive group conceptions from those of its heathen surroundings.[37] This involved two elements: exclusivity, or the Jewish doctrine of chosenness (what Marx means by the adjectives "practical" and "egoistic"); and transcendence of, or alienation from, nature, as we shall now explain.[38]

In a direct effort to counteract heathen nature-worship, Judaism deified human need by abstracting it from the natural realm and elevating it into the transcendent. The Jewish God embodied human need as something removed and remote from its actual sources in the soul, in human labor and in the world of flora and fauna. The invisible Jewish God, and not the rain, crops, soil, and sun, agriculture and crafts, or their corresponding divinities, was to be the provisioner of mankind. The flip side of this lofty conception was that Judaism's desacralization of nature rendered its notion of material properties characteristically perverse. It became, claims Marx, a "... real contempt for, a practical degradation of nature, which in the Jewish religion exists only in the imagination."[39] Of course, such assertions of a Jewish alienation from nature were by now commonplace. They were implicit in Enlightenment critiques of Jewish economic life divorced from physical labor and uprooted from the soil, and they were explicit in Hegelian doctrine on Judaism, a major source for Marx here.[40] Bauer himself had applied it to the Jewish "fetishizing" of laws and rituals abstracted from their original social, political, and historical contexts.[41]

But this is not Marx's meaning at all. Rather, Marx takes the familiar Hegelian theme of the Jews "stepping out of nature" and applies it to their material origins. For it is here that Judaism's distinctive relation to commerce first emerged. To transform human need into divinity while separating it from nature entirely is, according to Marx, to transform practical need into money and commerce. Why? Because as an abstraction money can be a provisioner of practical need without itself being in any way a part of nature. Indeed, what lends money its unique qualities is that it is artificial and unnatural. Writing like a faithful antimercantilist political economist, Marx recognized that money is an arbitrary representation of value and not value itself. It is, one might say, always by definition a substitute. Just as the classical economists protested against the mercantilist conflation of money and value, Marx viewed money as an imposter that seeks to usurp the role of value. Thus, money bears a relation – admittedly, not necessarily as equivalence but at the very least as parallel – to the monotheistic, transcendent God. Both are supernatural and universal media that seek to monopolize the claim to represent value and that, because they seek to impose their domination over all, will brook no counterfeit currency. Money is not only "the jealous god of Israel, before which no other god may exist," but it also "subjugates all the gods of mankind and transforms them into commodities." Jewish money and Jewish monotheism equally reduce human and natural products to a common denominator, which itself is neither human nor natural. The God/gods of Israel (Jehovah and Mammon) therefore represent "the alienated essence of man's work and existence; [the] essence [that] dominates him and that he worships..."[42]

THE JUDEO-CHRISTIAN ORIGINS OF MODERN ECONOMY

If the preceding associations sound far-fetched, some of them were nonetheless already familiar in the literature of Young Hegelianism and early left-wing German socialism. As Julius Carlebach points out, in his "Philosophy of the Deed," the socialist writer Moses Hess had devised a bizarre set of anthropological linkages in order to demonstrate an intrinsic connection between money and the Jewish God. F. W. Ghillany's 1842 *The Human Sacrifice of the Ancient Hebrews* provided Hess with his springboard through its sensational account of the Moloch cult, which Ghillany regarded as Israelite in origin. Hess posited a sublimation on the part of the ancient Hebrews of human sacrifice into a cult involving the payment of ransom to Yahweh in return for the life of the first-born (*pidyon ha-ben*). For Hess, the Christian practice of communion provided a later "incarnation" of the same theme, albeit one characteristically denuded of its base monetary connections.[43] With regard to the latter, Hess appeared to be building inadvertently on the older association of blood and money (the Hebrew *dam* and *damim* respectively) that had appeared *inter alia* in Luzzatto's *Discorso* and that reflected the persistent image in early modern political economy of money as the lifeblood of the healthy polity.[44]

The professor of Law, Heinrich Leo (a representative of the "Historical School" of jurisprudence that Marx had earlier singled out for criticism), drew a further linkage between the God of Judaism and money.[45] For Leo, it was Judaism's antithetical relationship to nature as defined by its transcendent divinity that had generated a characteristic tendency toward abstraction within the Jewish mind. This, in turn, led Jews to adopt a kind of suprarationalism through which every natural object, including man himself, was to be dissociated from its intrinsic qualities and evaluated instead exclusively from the standpoint of abstract (monetary) value:

> In the same way that there exist some fountains that would transmute every object thrown into them into stone, thus the Jews, from the very beginning until this very day, have transmuted everything that fell into the orbit of their spiritual activity into an abstract generality [*ein abstract-Allgemeines*].[46]

We can assume that for Marx (as for Leo), commerce and money were not the immediate expressions of Judaism in its Mosaic form. But these phenomena did evolve immanently out of Judaism's original character. This means that although commerce and money are two of the forms that historical Judaism took, they are not Judaism in itself. Here, once again, Marx is found to employ associations rooted in traditional Christian polemics against Judaism. Christian tradition equated Judaism's character not just with money but with legalism and carnality. Put otherwise, it was not money that Christianity sought to negate in Judaism, but, rather, Judaism's ritualistic emphasis and its legal formalism. Marx appears to concur with this characterization in "On the Jewish Question." "The monotheism of the Jews," he says, "is . . . in reality, a polytheism of the numerous needs [of man], a polytheism which makes even the latrine an object of divine regulation."[47] Whatever its offensive resonances, this formulation suggests that for Marx Judaism's effort to produce monotheism by abstracting practical need from nature failed precisely on its own terms. The effort to constrict human materiality into an abstract divinity produced a God who was preoccupied with regulating human needs in every detail. One might say that this God was not so much in the details, he *was* the details. Hence, although Judaism did produce a concept of unitary divinity, it was a divinity that manifested itself in formalized categories, rigid divisions, minute distinctions, and strict orders of purity, a veritable "polytheism of the numerous needs of man." Obviously, neither Marx nor traditional Christianity were willing to concede that Judaism's approach to law and ritual might have expressed an effort to transcend the mundane or even to sanctify it. Instead, Christianity claimed for itself the exclusive means of transcendence, while viewing paganism as merely a misguided attempt to sanctify what was in fact hopelessly profane.[48] Against Judaism, however, Christianity maintained a somewhat different charge, one that also was echoed by Marx: the charge of materialism, of mistaking the letter for the spirit.[49]

According to Marx, Christianity arose as a negation of this Judaic materialism. But precisely for this reason, it, too, failed in its mission. In its rejection of Jewish legalism, Christianity demonstrated its own inability to resolve the problem of human need. Christianity could reject Judaism's baroque focus on "the numerous needs of man" only through its own fantastical denial of those same needs. Hence, the Jesus of the Gospels rejected the notion that humans could or should rely on themselves to perpetuate their earthly survival. "Therefore I tell you, do not worry about your life, what you will eat or what you will drink, or about your body, what you will wear."[50] But this initial negation of human need, as Marx explains, proved impossible to sustain. When immediate redemption did not materialize, Christianity faced the necessity of coming to terms with human need. It was forced to make its peace with human necessity and thus with its own Judaic origins. The nature of that peace, suggests Marx, was synthetic. That is to say, Christianity affirmed private property (Moses), but it sought to do so without, at the same time, abandoning its own communalism (Christ). In a parallel manner, Christianity reabsorbed Judaism's materialist, and thus immanently commercial, spirit, while at the same time holding a part of itself aloof from that spirit.[51] As we shall now see, it was this very synthesis of, or compromise between, Christianity and Judaism that proved fateful for the future development of Western economy.

It is in the interstices between Christianity and Judaism that Marx locates the origins of modern economy. Marx suggests that the essential contrast between the two religions is that Judaism is "practical" while Christianity is "theoretical." What this means is that Christianity sought to carve out a pure sacred space, "the ethereal realm" [*die blaue Luft*], from which it would entirely exclude carnality or "practical need."[52] Through this act of integration with and reseparation from Judaism, Christianity was able to apply Judaism's religious formalism, its "polytheism of numerous needs," to the management of society's mundane existence (its sphere of social relations, particularly the economy) while still retaining its own lofty position above (because Christ's kingdom is "not of this world").

In here discussing Christianity's dependence on Judaism, Marx was echoing not just Augustine but sources closer to home. The German-Jewish writers Ludwig Börne and Heinrich Heine, both converts of convenience from Judaism, had identified the roots of antisemitism in Christian Europe's use of Jews as commercial surrogates. Jews were Christianity's designated usurers. They dealt exclusively in money and trade so that Christians could avoid the taint. Now that commercial capitalism had actually conquered Europe, Heine and Börne noted, Christians could no longer disguise the fact of their own immersion in it. But this did not necessarily result in an abatement of anti-Jewish hostility. On the contrary, they still hated the Jews, but now no longer just for fulfilling a despised function, but for exposing Christians' own duplicity and fall from grace.[53]

Despite his abstract terminology, Marx was suggesting something similar, although he did not at all share the interest of Heine and Börne in deflating antisemitism. Marx's point went far beyond merely exposing Christian hypocrisy. "On the Jewish Question" had the ambitious aim of outlining the entire history of the development of civil society, or even of capitalism (a term Marx did not yet employ). As Marx suggested, Christianity's reabsorption of Judaism and its subsequent employment of a division of labor, with Judaism handling business below and Christianity organizing salvation above, had enormous ramifications. By separating the ethereal and worldly spheres, while at the same time making them interdependent, Christianity eventually achieved a rationalization of both domains. This rationalization was a gradual as well as a recurring process in European history. Just as Christianity had early on sought to protect its aloofness from Jewish materialism, at the end of the Middle Ages it strove to achieve what Marx calls the "perfection" of civil society. Civil society would be perfected by its creation of a new institution to occupy the supernal realm. That institution was the state, now elevated above society to the "ethereal" position.[54] Where civil society was private and egoistic, the state would be public and neutral.

It was through the creation of the state as an ethereal realm – that is, through the state's formal separation from civil society – that both realms thus became complete. The state became the sphere formally divorced from commerce and from private property relations. Conversely, civil society became the realm of pure commerce and property rights. The state became the domain of communalism, and civil society that of commerce. In this sense the original synthesis effected by Christianity now replicated itself. For just as Christianity had once been forced to reincorporate a Judaic element, so, too, its modern apotheosis (the perfected state) was now forced to accomplish a restoration of the Jews. Christian tradition regarded the final conversion of the Jews as the crowning event in Christ's return. So, too, according to Marx, the Jews' political incorporation into Europe would seal the perfection of the secular state. For it was through the implementation of the perfected state [der vollendete politische Staat] that the institution of modern citizenship had first emerged in the period of the French Revolution. And insofar as citizenship was to be applied equally, regardless of private religious affiliations, it would have to encompass the Jews as well, even in Prussia. In this manner, the issue that had occasioned Marx's essay, the question of Jewish citizenship, was revealed as the endpoint of the entire historical-theological process just described.

Like Eduard Gans, Marx had redescribed the evolution of Jewish historical economy to account for the development of a Jewish *Handelskaste*, a caste whose purpose was to perform economic functions directly prohibited to the rest of society. What Marx also showed was that this *Handelskaste* must inevitably be dissolved through the logic of Christian theology. The state could only express its perfection through the ideal of citizenship and civic equality, which included Jewish emancipation. At the same time the state's perfection coincides with and reflects the perfection of civil society, that is, its thoroughgoing commercialization, a development that eliminates the need for Jewish mercantile specialization. After all, what need of a *Handelskaste* if private property and commerce are now the province of all? Marx insisted that his was to be an investigation of the "everyday" workaday Jew. The conclusion of his investigation was that the workaday Jew (as a Jew) would soon be out of a job.

EMANCIPATION FROM EMANCIPATION

The question of Jews' legal equality was not itself the endpoint of Marx's essay. His real concern was not whether the adherents of Judaism could be granted legal equality, since in a "perfected" state (i.e., one with a pure separation of church and state) it was obvious that they could. Rather, Marx both agreed that Jews *ought* to be politically emancipated and at the same time insisted that their political emancipation would not be sufficient. Instead, he anticipated a second Jewish emancipation, one that he believed would help prepare the way for a far broader liberation for mankind as a whole. It is worth recalling that Marx's predecessor, Bruno Bauer, also had demanded that the Jewish not be decoupled from the general emancipation. But although Bauer had argued that Jews had no business pursuing legal equality for themselves before seeking it for society as a whole (as men not Jews), Marx insisted that mankind's liberation actually *depended* on the prior liberation of the Jews.[55] The question is why.

To understand what Marx intended by defining a Jewish emancipation as prepatory to a general one, it will be useful to compare his essay with various older strains within European thought, some of which have appeared in previous chapters.

A thematic link exists between "On the Jewish Question" and the deist writings of the early eighteenth century, for example. Deists were adherents of "natural religion," the belief that man did not require revelation to achieve salvation, but could discern the essential divine truths through the reasoned contemplation of nature. Many deists viewed a Christianity purified of its superstitious and intolerant "Jewish" roots as essentially compatible with natural religion, and, like Marx, argued that Christianity's revolution against Judaism remained incomplete. Christianity's manifest intolerance was a carryover from its roots in Jewish chosenness, they insisted. Consequently, the critique of Judaism must be preparatory to the restoration of Christianity's pristine message, one that had thoroughly rejected Jewish exclusivity and that combined natural religion with the simple moral virtue exemplified by Christ. In this manner, the deists reasoned, a de-Judaized Christianity could help pave the way for the emergence of a broad and tolerant secular society.[56]

This deist formula possessed political ramifications that would be drawn out in later Enlightenment thought. The creation of this secular sphere, for instance, conditioned partly on the purging of Christianity's "intolerant" Jewish inheritance, would necessarily require the institution of a neutral state. Religion would be relegated to the private sphere, as a matter of individual conscience. At the same time, civil society also would be reorganized. Corporations, guilds, and estates, all of which were founded on group privilege, would be proscribed, and the corporative constitution that made them possible revised on the basis of individual equality.[57]

A structural transformation of this sort also entailed a Jewish critique, in this case not of Judaism per se but of the traditional corporate life of the Jewish community. As in "On the Jewish Question," the Enlightenment's theological critique of Judaism paralleled the social one of the "real Jew." Dohm, for instance, had argued that the Jews were not corrupt through any flaw of their own but as a consequence of their enforced occupational confinement. At the same time, Dohm insisted that commerce was not itself to blame. Rather, Christian Europe had been at fault for the Jews' degraded condition. For it was partly as a consequence of Christianity's proscription of usury that Europe had failed to acknowledge commerce as its true lifeblood.[58] With the dispelling of such outmoded notions, said Dohm, it would be possible to see that commerce was too important a function to be relegated to an outcast group. As part of that process, the Jews must be freed of commerce and commerce of the Jews. Dohm thus brought together many of the various Enlightenment arguments on Judaism and Jews. He believed that the creation of a religiously neutral sphere (Marx's "perfected state") would be a precondition for channeling Jews into the full range of occupations and livelihoods. This, in turn, would help bring about the salutary commercialization of society as a whole.[59]

Although Marx agreed with the deists that Christianity had perpetuated Judaism by other means, he did not at all concur with the notion that Christian society could survive a full purgation of its Judaic elements. Without its Jewish component, Christianity had proved "too ethereal" to survive on its own. Moreover, Marx was not convinced that the relegation of religion to the private sphere would ultimately weaken its influence, as Bauer, for example, assumed. Responding to Bauer, Marx claimed that the separation of church and state, as, for instance, in the United States, actually intensified religious feeling. By creating a fully fledged private realm, the perfected state made religion into a private activity, one entirely compatible with the pursuit of individual self-interest. Religion and bourgeois economy fueled one another. Although Bauer assumed that a formal church-state separation would eventually lead to widespread atheism, Marx insisted that the perfecting of the state would enable religion to flourish as never before.[60]

Moreover, just as the perfected state had not solved the problem of religious delusion but rather aggravated it, so too the perfection of civil society had not solved the problem of human need.[61] For Marx, Jewish emancipation along the lines that Dohm and other liberals envisioned it was the logical conclusion of the entire misdirected Judeo-Christian course. From both theological and material perspectives, the Judeo-Christian experiment had failed.

The obstucted effort to transform medieval corporate society into a modern liberal order, a failure epitomized by the *Halbheit* in contemporary Prussia, provided Marx with a sociological laboratory in which to dissect and diagnose the nature of this failed experiment. In 1843 feudalism still blocked the path of the emerging commercial regime. In Germany, as opposed to France and the United States, it was the corporative quality of the "old society" [*die alte Gesellschaft*] that prevented the state from becoming fully transformed into an "ethereal realm." The restrictions of the "old society" had blocked the Jewish *Handelsstand* from becoming universalized. This peculiarity led Marx to investigate the relationship between Jews as a feudal *corporation* and the new perfected civil society still seeking its own consummation.

In the old society, according to Marx, the state had stood within rather than above civic relationships. It could not monopolize the communal, ethereal realm because guilds, corporations, and estates still retained a political character of their own:

> The old civil society had a *directly political* character; that is, the elements of civil life such as property or family or the manner and means of livelihood were raised, in the form of lordship, estate and corporation, to elements of political life. They determined, in this form, the relation of the individual to *the state as a whole* – that is, his *political* relation; that is, his separation and exclusion from the other elements of society.[62]

Under feudalism what would eventually become the private sphere within a perfected system was still the public one. For this reason, the individual in the "old society" enjoyed no direct relationship with the state. Rather, his own connection to the state was expressed in and confined to his position within his corporation and his corporation's position within the state. Conversely, although the elements of civil society – guild, caste, corporation – were politically constituted under feudalism, they lacked a fully social or economic identity of their own:

> For this organization of national life did not raise property and labor to the level of social elements, but rather it far more completed their *separation* from the state as a whole, and constituted them as *distinct* [political] societies within society.[63]

Economic activities in feudal society were organized on a distinctively group or corporative basis, in the form of states-within-the state, or, rather, of states-within-society. And although some corporations may have fulfilled exclusively economically functions, they still operated as essentially political entities.

The establishment of perfected, or modern, civil society reversed all of these relationships. Freeing property and labor from the bonds of corporate life enabled them to become purely economic elements. The political revolution par excellence, the French Revolution, thus paralleled what we characterized earlier as Christianity's elevation of the state into the "ethereal realm." Political life, the life of the state, now became the exclusive corporate sphere, the only one that henceforth would be allowed to exist, where individuals joined together in a common endeavor. Meanwhile, social and economic life became entirely individualistic, a war of all against all. Defined in religious terms, political life became, as we have already seen, purely Christian (the communal quality that Marx understood to be distinctive in Christianity), whereas civic life became Jewish (a set of formal, contractual property relationships).[64] Judaism's "polytheism of the numerous needs" of man came to pervade the realm existing outside of the state.

Once again, from the standpoint of Christian theology, Marx's exposition was highly ironic. Just as Heine and Börne had remarked, Christianity, expecting its own fulfillment to bring about the final conversion of the Jews, instead produced a universal Judaizing of society. Or as Marx put it, "It is from its own entrails [*Eingeweiden*] that civil society ceaselessly engenders the Jew"[65] Civil society *engenders* not only the "real" Jew but now the Christian Jew as well.[66] It is only poetic justice that the "real Jew" should benefit from this apotheosis and accord himself the political emancipation whose very properties derive from the transfigured principles of his own religious faith.

It is also in the transformation of the "old" into the new society that the living, material identity of the Jew first comes into question. Here it is not so much a question of what the real Jew is as whether or not he still actually exists. In the old society, there could be no doubt about the Jew's tangible reality. He existed as part of a specific corporation, defined, as with all corporations, by its political character. As a politically constituted unit, the Jews comprised a "nation," one of the many nations-within-the-nation of the ancien régime. The Jews' corporative life was constructed in national-political terms so that they could perform commercial and credit functions within a society incapable of separating its social and economic from its political domains. Hence, Jews comprised what Marx called a "trading nation," in which the Jew possessed "... the nationality of the trader, and above all of the money-man."[67]

Marx's invariably nasty and antisemitic tone should not obscure the degree to which his analysis fit into and expanded on the preceding discourse on Jewish commerce. It is interesting to note, for instance, that Marx refers to the Jews' nationality as "chimerical," a term that also was employed by Bauer. For Bauer, the Jews are a "chimerical" people [*das Volk der Chimäre*] because they have stubbornly refused either to contribute to or benefit from mankind's general progress, but, rather, only seek selfish advantage within it.[68] For Marx, in contrast, they are a chimerical nation because of the *Halbheit* status that they retain in a state that stands on the brink of of its own perfection. The Jewish nation is not characterized by language, territory, or any other of the characteristics by which nations were generally defined in the nineteenth century. Rather, up to now (or at least since the loss of their ancient state), the Jews have been a nation merely by virtue of their corporative status and functions, as traders, moneylenders, and financiers. And yet with corporations on their way out, and with the corporate functions of finance and trade now being taken over by civil society as a whole, in what sense might the Jews still be described as a nation? They may be traders, moneylenders, and financiers, yet they are by no means the only traders, moneylenders, and financiers. In this sense, too, the Jews' nationality is "chimerical." It exists only insofar as civil society exists, but it is not to be mistaken for civil society itself. "The Jew, who occupies a distinctive place in civil society, only manifests in a distinctive way the Judaism of civil society."[69] No other nation is as dependent on civil society for its existence, and none more threatened by it. For if civil society succeeds in becoming "perfected," then the Jews should no longer remain distinctive in a national, that is, corporative way.

Yet in the circumstance of the *Halbheit* this has not yet occurred. Indeed, because Judaism has become the order of the world without the world recognizing it, the Jews have not been able to disappear. "It is because the essence of the Jew was universally realized and secularized in civil society, that civil society could not convince the Jew of the *unreality* of his *religious* essence . . ."⁷⁰ For somewhat different reasons, this describes a thoroughly bourgeois society, on the one hand, as well as a Germany on the cusp of the new society but still grasping at the delusions of the old, on the other.⁷¹ It is the circumstance of a Prussia under Frederick William IV, yearning to return to a medieval *Standestaat*, beginning, significantly, with the restitution of the Jewish estate. As editor of the *Rheinische Zeitung* Marx had recently become aware not just of the extent of poverty during the "Hungry Forties," but of the degree to which state institutions, the legal system, the *Landtag*, and the estates, were rigged against the poor. To the young Marx, these hardly seemed the universal mediating institutions that had been so celebrated by Hegel. Marx's *Critique of Hegel's Philosophy of Right*, written in the summer of 1843, was intended to expose these deficiencies.⁷² His "On the Jewish Question," composed shortly afterward, extended inquiry into the stubborn persistence of the *Halbheit* by highlighting the absurdity of continuing to stigmatize Jews when society had itself undergone *Verjudung* (Judaization). For it is not so much that the Jew still performs indispensable economic functions that accounts for society's determination to keep him apart, as that his creed is now the adopted, although *unacknowledged*, standpoint of society as a whole. Why should the Jew abandon his religion or his professions, asks Marx, when he sees Judaism's "tenets" (commerce and huckstering) all around him?

From Marx's standpoint, we can say that it was Frederick William's temptation to go backward – to a time and condition in which the Jewish nation was not yet chimerical, but, rather, still constituted as the commercial corporation par excellence. Bauer's inclination, in contrast, was to take a half-step forward and then stop – with the Jews emancipated from only their chimerical national ties, although still enslaved to their religion (the collective commercial creed of civil society as a whole). What then might be said of the Jews' own choice? Marx suggests that if society were to eliminate the occupations of trader, moneylender, and financier, the real Jew would also have to disappear. Is it then possible for the Jews to emancipate themselves by changing their occupations? According to Marx, ". . . when the Jew recognizes his *practical* [i.e., "egoistic"] nature as invalid and works [*arbeitet*] towards its abolition, then he works his way out of [*herausarbeitet aus*] his previous development; he works for general *human emancipation* and against the *supreme practical* expression of human self-estrangement."⁷³ It is implied here that the Jew can be an actor in his own emancipation if only he will *work* to abolish his "practical" nature. What is the Jew's practical nature? As we have seen, the "profane basis of Judaism" is practical or egoistical need. Hence, the path to the Jew's own emancipation, as well as his honest endeavor for general, human emancipation, begins when the Jew abandons hucksterism and moneylending as the distinctions of his chimerical nationality.

But abandoning commerce is not enough. The material basis of Jews' existence cannot be eliminated simply by their abandonment of financial and mercantile professions. For there is no reason to conclude that these professions will not continue to be performed without Jews. And if that is the case, then with or without the "real Jew," society will continue to be made up of "Jews." Ultimately, then, it is up to society to eliminate the empirical basis for Jewish existence by doing away with commerce and finance as a whole. In so doing, society liberates the Jew as well as itself.

Here Marx at last returns to the essentially pagan starting point from which he initially launched his analysis. The wrong turn taken by Judeo-Christianity was the effort to transcend nature, to transcend material reality through the act of abstraction. Not the gods of nature but the processes of nature – labor and production – are the correct answers to the problem of human need because only labor and production genuinely reflect human nature, at its core. The consciousness that practical need should create is the consciousness of labor as the collective, creative enterprise of all mankind. It is the consciousness of man's "species being" [Gattungswesen] i.e., his recognition that his nature is determined by collective endeavor and common engagement in human work.[74] When the Jews become productivized, become producers rather than exchangers in a society of other laborers and producers, they, too, will become conscious of their own species being. Then "[t]he subjective basis of Judaism – practical need – is humanized [vermenschlicht], because the conflict between the individual, sensuous existence of man and his species-being, is negated."[75]

The political emancipation of the Jews, the question that had preoccupied so many of the figures we have examined in this study, stands exposed as merely a penultimate emancipation. The emancipation of the Jews is symbolic of an unbridling of "Judaism" that allows liberal, commercial society free reign. It serves as a barometer of commercial society's maturation, its loss of its former sense of shame and inhibition. It is definite progress but also at the same time the realization of a Hobbesian nightmare of egoism run amok. The Jews and mankind must therefore be emancipated from emancipation. They must be socially rather than just politically emancipated, something which can only occur when the bonds of the perfected state have been thoroughly transcended. The communal life that can possess only a narrow political reality under the perfected state must be extended to encompass man's full existence, his full material life. This occurs when civil society becomes truly communal, when private property is socialized, and individual egoism thereby defused. It is not simply the elimination of the Jewish huckster and financier, not simply the "productivization" of the Jews that will transform them, but rather the elimination of all huckstering and all finance, as well as the productivization of society as a whole, which transforms it.

CAPITALISM, SOCIALISM, AND THE JEWS

To gauge the full impact of "On the Jewish Question" we must now situate the essay within the broader corpus of Marx's philosophy and political economy, as well as measure the analysis he presents in 1844 against other contemporary and subsequent socialist views of Jewish commerce. Finally, we must address the question of how "On the Jewish Question" broadly influenced Jews' own ideological conceptions of economic and social emancipation.

Returning first to the matter of emancipation, it seems that we are now back at our starting point. For the question still remains: does the "real Jew's" social emancipation enjoy causal priority in Marx's account, or is it society itself that must first eliminate Judaism in order to liberate the Jew? Presumably, if mankind is liberated from Judaism/commerce and the Jews are a part of mankind, then they, too, will be liberated. Yet this is not how Marx concludes "On the Jewish Question." Instead, Marx concludes his essay by affirming that "[t]he social emancipation of the *Jews* is the emancipation of mankind from Judaism."[76] Perhaps Marx intended merely to say that since Judaism is the ultimate source of commerce, then the "real Jew" must be its most primitive and basic expression. If there are no more "real Jews," it will be a sure sign that there can be no more commerce. This again conjures up the old Christian image of the Jews' final conversion. But if that is the theological paradigm underlying Marx's schema, it begs the question of why Judaism, or for that matter any religion, should be identified as the source and *locus classicus* of an entire social and economic system.

To solve this riddle, we must delve deeper into the sources of Marx's analysis. Marx says that Judaism emerged out of the conflict between "the individual, sensuous being of man and his species consciousness [*Gattungsexistenz*]."[77] This is the conflict between Hegelian *Dasein* (being) and *Geist* (mind) that Marx, following in the footsteps of the philosopher Ludwig Feuerbach, believed Hegel himself had never properly resolved. According to Feuerbach, the conflict between *Dasein* and *Geist* is in reality man's own conflict within himself. For Feuerbach, it is a conflict that emerges through error – the error of separating body and spirit, heart and mind, being and consciousness.[78] The error derives from man's dishonest humility, his unwillingness to face facts, his stubborn refusal to recognize himself as all too human. Man projects God as an objectified force existing outside of himself. He takes his own noblest aspirations, his highest self, loftiest thoughts, and foists them on a creature of his own imagining. He thereby reduces himself to something lowly, profane, creaturely, and in consequence, begs forgiveness from the very God he has invented.[79]

In "On the Jewish Question," Marx took this basic conception of Feuerbach and applied it to political economy. His own interest in economy dated from 1842 when, as noted, he covered the Rhenish Landtag's investigations into peasant conditions in the Moselle for the *Rheinische Zeitung*. It was then, as Marx later recalled, that he "experienced for the first time the embarrassment of having to take part in discussions on so-called material interests." After his resignation from the newspaper, in March of 1843, Marx engaged in further contemplation of these "material interests."[80] Specifically, he began to develop Feuerbach's critique of Hegel in a manner that would emphasize labor as the central condition and activity of man. There was precedent, even within the German idealist tradition, for such an emphasis. Both Fichte and Hegel had incorporated labor as the very model of human intersubjectivity.[81] But it was the application of labor to Feuerbach's critique of theology that for the moment chiefly interested Marx.

In "On the Jewish Question," man's original sin is defined as his negation of that which is most truly human, creative labor (the unity of body and mind). It is because man degrades labor that he reifies God into commerce and money as the objectified representations of his own sensuous nature. Commerce and money, as noted, are equivalent to God in that they are equally the expressions of man's self-alienation.[82] Money and commerce are both based on the fiction that the products of labor can be equivalents and therefore subject to market exchange. Marx's own political economic conception assumed that two different products can have nothing in common but their mutual sources in human production. Thus, the social links that money defines, links between man and man, are ghostly substitutes for the social links that only labor-in-common can truly provide. "Money is the estranged essence of man's labor [*Arbeit*] and his being [*Dasein*] . . ."[83] Genuine human community, in this light, can only emerge when labor replaces money as the universal source of value and when mankind replaces God as the subject of need.

Man's failure to recognize this elementary truth could only have arisen as a failure of consciousness. This is why in "On the Jewish Question" an "ideal" construct, religion, can be viewed as the source of a system of social relations, commerce. In this sense, Marx's pun on "Judaism" was no tautology. At the same time, it was no materialist conception either. If this last fact has been little recognized by scholars, it may be because Marx did not recognize it himself. By the time he wrote "On the Jewish Question," he had already arrived at the conclusion that civil relations generate political ones. This was essentially the analysis he presented in his 1843 "Contribution to the Critique of Hegel's *Philosophy of Right*," published before "On the Jewish Question."[84] As mentioned, Marx wished to tackle the Jewish Question precisely because it presented itself as an immediate practical problem concerning the relation of society to politics. But in working within the constraints of an *actual* Jewish Question, Marx was forced to admit certain ambiguities into his analysis. For whatever else it might have been, the Jewish Question also was a question about Jews. And who were Jews if not the adherents of Judaism? Marx tried to resolve this difficulty by identifying Judaism with civil society and Christianity with the political state. This implied that the chronological (and therefore the causative) priority lay with commerce. But in the theological realm, it was Christianity that had made Judaism "universal." In itself, as Marx insisted, "*Judaism could not create a new world*"; Judaism could only be realized "under the sway of Christianity."[85] In this manner, social relations were made dependent on political ones, commerce on religion, and the material on the ideal. If it had been Marx's intention to expose the Jewish Question as one of material relations, the Jewish Question itself had undermined his intentions.[86]

One might say that from the perspective of later Marxism, Marx's analysis "ought" to have been viewed as the product of mental error. For how could Jews, who do not themselves comprise a social class, have produced capitalism? As we noted earlier, Marx did not employ the term capitalism in his essay. When Marx did later refer to capital if not to capitalism, he used it to refer to a specific "mode of production," that is, an economic system characterized by a given set of class relations. But the concept of class relations was also nowhere apparent in "On the Jewish Question."[87] Instead, Marx was concerned there with commerce and money, not with capitalism and class. In "On the Jewish Question," he viewed the predominance of exchange as the hallmark of the "new" society. In his later works, however, although Marx would retain this emphasis on exchange, he also would identify capitalism with the growth of the bourgeoisie, not with Judaism, or with Christianity, or with the perfected state. What made capitalism possible for the later Marx was not merely the rise of a commercial burgher class, as had already occurred in the Middle Ages, but, rather, the emergence of a fully fledged bourgeoisie capable of instituting a mass production of commodities through the commodification of labor, that is, through industrialization. Yet the bourgeoisie of Marx's 1848 *Communist Manifesto* was the opposite of the stereotypically unproductive Jews. It was a stunningly productive class, one that had utterly revolutionized the forces of production. In no sense, then, could it be conflated with the pitiful Jewish *Krämer* or *Schacherer*, or even with the isolated Jewish financiers [*Geldmenschen*] who traverse the pages of "On the Jewish Question." Thus, when Marx abandoned his Feuerbachian approach to economy, he abandoned the Jews as well. They would play no part in a "Marxist" conception of capitalism.

Even so, a degree of continuity existed between Marx's analysis in "On the Jewish Question" and his later conceptions. As Jerry Z. Muller observes, with reference to Marx's relationship to Jewishness, there is a link in Marx's writings between "the traditional stigmatization of usury and the new anathemization of industrial capitalism . . ."[88] As noted, Marx celebrated industry for its revolutionizing of the means of production required for the eventual emergence of a socialist society. Industrialization marks the start of the transition from the realm of necessity into freedom, from prehistory into history, from scarcity to "postscarcity."[89] To the extent that the bourgeoisie organizes industry, it performs an essential task. But once past that stage, it has outlived its utility and becomes *merely* parasitic and exploitative.

In his analysis of capital Marx referred to the ancient Aristotelian distinction between the "use" and "exchange" values of commodities, between, for example, a sandal to be worn and a sandal to be sold. The former is the intrinsic value of an object which, according to Marx's interpretation, reflects the amount of concrete labor embodied in it. Exchange value, by contrast, is the price that the object fetches on the open market. Marx believed that exchange value is in itself illegitimate because, as earlier explained, it reifies a human value (labor) into an abstract value (money). In *Capital*, Marx extended this distinction when he sought to unravel the mystery of the source of profit. Because Marx believed that labor is the sole repository of value, he concluded that profit can only exist if it is extracted from it. Only by employing the worker for longer hours than are actually required to produce a commodity can the capitalist skim profit from what Marx called his "surplus labor." Surplus labor is thus what yields "surplus value" or profit.[90] In this sense, capital bears comparison with interest and the capitalist with the usurer, who gets back more than he invested without performing any labor for it. Just as in "On the Jewish Question" the Jew is the equivalent of money, so in Marx's *Capital* "the capitalist is merely capital personified and functions in the process of production solely as the agent of capital."[91]

Marx provides an analogous formulation in *Capital* when he distinguishes between different forms of commodity exchange to determine which is distinctly capitalist. The first formula, $C - M - C$, describes the sale of a commodity (C) for the money (M) needed to purchase a second commodity. This is sale for consumption, a process corresponding to use value since the point of the entire exchange is use. Marx's second formula is M – C – M, which designates buying simply in order to sell rather than to consume. As Marx dryly notes, because "one sum of money is distinguishable from another only by its amount": the only conceivable purpose of buying in order to sell is to increase the amount. This is indicated by Marx's final formula: M – C – M' where M' is the enhanced or "surplus value" resulting from the exchange. Because money lacks the power to increase in its own right (it in fact has no value of its own) it can only be enhanced from one source, C, a commodity that embodies the labor required to produce it. When M – C – M' becomes an entire modus operandi, a continuous process, it deserves the name capital. In such a process, "money ends the movement only to begin it again," its circulation for the sake of accruing surplus value is "an end in itself" that itself can never end.[92] Yet it does end. Marx suggests that the process fueled by the drive for M' leads to the massive expansion of C to such an extent that both industrialization and the mass conversion of men into proletarians ensue. C is now capable of providing adequately for the material needs of all humanity and no longer requires M. Consequently, C and M wage a struggle to the death with C ultimately emerging victorious. In the end, the bourgeoisie (equivalent to M' or capital) will be "swept out of the way and made impossible."[93] In "On the Jewish Question," something similar, although without the threat of violence, happens to the Jews when their "emancipation" is made equivalent to their disappearance.

Despite Marx's (and later Engels's) claim to have replaced "utopian" with "scientific" socialism, this duality between M and C pervades socialist thought as a whole and not just mature Marxism.[94] As Muller and others have observed, it is rooted in ancient economic and scholastic economic morality which socialism had in part adopted. But it is also present in the Enlightenment's distinction between productive and unproductive labor or in Josiah Tucker's proclamation that "Money without Industry, is an Hurt, not a Blessing." For the Enlightenment, industry and utility are the sources of value; money can be harmful if it is not subordinated to these. This means that there are essentially two types of capital, the productive and the parasitic kind, corresponding to the two types of persons who represent them, what Marx called "those who work" and those "who do not work."[95] As we have observed, although Adam Smith regarded merchants as productive, he relegated them (retail merchants even more than wholesale ones) to the lowest productive category, since in comparison with the farmer, artisan, and manufacturer they set into motion the least amount of capital.[96] As for financiers, both Smith and Hume dismissed them as "idle people, who live on their revenue; our funds, in that view, give great encouragement to an useless and unactive life."[97] Socialism, in part, grew out of the classification schemes of classical economics. French socialists of the early and middle nineteenth century lent the distinction between productive and nonproductive labor even greater emphasis than had the Physiocrats or Smith. Charles Fourier, to cite a prime example, differentiated between "*le classes esssentielles, le propiétaire, le cultivateur, le manufacturier,*" "*et une classe accessoire..., une classe d'agents parasites et improductifs, qui sont les Négoçiants.*"[98]

These same schemes could and often did take on an antisemitic flavor. Within Fourier's "accessory class," he included "soldiers, bureaucrats, merchants, lawyers, prisoners, philosophers, Jews, and the unemployed."[99] Pierre-Joseph Proudhon distinguished between fertile capital, on the one hand, "attributable only to the creations of human industry," and a bogusly profitable capital, on the other, which he identified with *tokos*, the Greek term for usury. Useful capital invigorates industry; harmful capital seeks profits without production.[100] In this light, Proudhon's image of Jews resembled Hume's view of rentiers and stockjobbers: "The Jew is by temperament an antiproducer, neither a farmer nor an industrialist nor even a true merchant.... He knows but the rise and fall of prices, the risks of transportation, the incertitudes of crops, the hazards of demand and supply..."[101] Fourier, Proudhon and many contemporary socialist sects identified harmful capital and unproductive labor with Jews.[102] In France before 1848 the relatively greater prominence of high finance than large-scale industry reinforced the image of the banker, in particular Jewish bankers such as the Rothschilds, as "the kings of the age."[103] The old analogy of Jews and nobility was revived, with terms like "nobility" and "feudalism" now employed to identify rentier capitalists as parasites lording it over the productive classes. The Fourierist Alphonse Toussenel's 1845 book, *Les Juifs, rois de l'epoque: histoire de la féodalité financière*, took "Jews" as a synonym for all members of the Fourier's unproductive "accessory" class who, or so Toussenel claimed, today ruled France and lived the idle life of kings.[104]

What for Marx and Engels made these socialist doctrines unscientific was their failure to define classes rigorously and recognize the primacy only of the bourgeoisie and proletariat. Henri de Saint Simon for instance defined two essential classes, but he did so along seemingly arbitrary lines, distinguishing *actifs* (farmers, artisans, manufacturers, merchants, scientists, artists, "good lawyers," and "a few good priests") from *oisifs* (nobles, rentiers, soldiers, most lawyers, and most priests).[105] For Saint Simon, moreover, artisans were "all those who work with material products, to wit: the farmers, the manufacturers, the traders, the bankers, and all the agents whom they employ."[106] Marx and Engels could only throw up their hands at the notion of a banker who is both an artisan and a member of the *industriel* class. Yet the Marxian Social Democratic and Saint Simonian traditions had one thing in common: in comparison with other contemporary European socialist movements, both were relatively little infected by antisemitism. Although value judgments transposed from Christianity underlay the anti-Jewish attitudes of some socialist sects, they were by no means the only factor. Perhaps more important than religion was the fact that many of the socialist movements tended to glorify the petty artisan and proprietor.[107] They could thus readily view "Jewish capital" or usury as a sinister force that was destroying their industrious and virtuous way of life. In contrast, the Saint Simonians put great emphasis on managerialism and a large-scale planned industry. Hence (and despite their own messianic Christianity), they lacked this idealization of the little man common to many forms of economic antisemitism. Saint Simon and his acolytes afforded managers, scientists, and even bankers an important role in their utopia. The disproportionate number of Jews within the group, including the bankers Isaac and Emile Péreire, must be understood as partly a product of this rare socialist affirmation of such typically "Jewish" activities.[108] By contrast, precisely because it committed itself to a binary industrial class struggle of bourgeoisie and proletariat, Social Democracy, whatever its other shortcomings with regard to Jews, was ideologically antipathetic to Jew hatred.

Although later Marxists would no longer conflate the Jews *simply* with the bourgeoisie, "On the Jewish Question" did not thereby lose its relevance. On the contrary, it continued to provide creative sustenance both to those who would identify Jews with the new society and to those who would proclaim them as condemned with the passing of the old. In "On the Jewish Question," Marx had suggested that Judaism, if not Jews, had been instrumental to the rise of the "new society." At the same time, he had implied that the chimerical nation of the Jews constituted a component of the moribund corporative world. Here the tensions between religion and people that *Wissenschaft des Judentums* had also tried to confront remained intact. But after 1848 these tensions were no longer expressed in terms of the conflicts between men and their political or religious constitutions but rather between old and new economic systems. This was precisely because in the period following 1848 the notion of "capitalism" as a fundamentally new form of economy truly began to emerge.

Hitherto, as we have seen, novel economic phenomena tended to be understood in terms of political constitutions: conceived of variously as old and new societies, "new systems of civil and commercial government," corporative, perfected, and closed commercial states. It was even possible, as with the case of Fichte, to identify "modern" commerce with the prerogatives of a land owning nobility or with a medieval juridical anarchy gone awry. In the decades following 1848, this was far less the case in the Europe west of the Elbe. In central Europe, the post-1848 decade was the period of industrial "take off."[109] In Britain, the twenty-five years after 1848 marked "the high point of laissez-faire capitalism."[110] The revolutions of 1848 had been animated, in part, by artisan classes seeking to reconstitute their guild protections within the fabric of a new democratic regime.[111] Yet, after the revolutions' failures, the novelty of industrialization could no longer be dismissed as an alien and momentary accretion.

This shift in consciousness could be measured in various other ways. But its implications for the politics of Jewish commerce are what concern us here. For now, the old dualities of Jews and Judaism, inner and outer history, began noticeably to shift. Now the central debate was not so much over what had caused the Jews' commercial propensity in the first place, but, rather, what long-term effect this propensity had exerted on modern Europe. Were Jews and Judaism responsible for capitalism, were they a key modernizing force, or were they rather a chimerical corporation, one whose very existence was threatened by the new relationships? For Marx's later disciples, Marx's ambiguity on this point left a legacy of confusion as to the Jews' true relationship to economic modernity and its implications for Jewish survival.[112]

For those who viewed commerce, in and of itself, as the motor of capitalism, it was not difficult to identify the Jews with its origins. But for those who believed commerce had been a necessary but insufficient condition for capitalist industry, the Jewish role would now be relegated to the sidelines.[113] The Historical School of German economics tended to identify commerce rather than industry as the quintessence of capitalism. This premise could and on occasion did lead to a focus on the Jews' historical role in its development. Werner Sombart and Max Weber are today the best-remembered representatives of this school. Sombart and Weber disagreed over whether commerce or industry was the defining feature of capitalism, and consequently over whether Jews bore responsibility for its inception. Although the writings of both men, particularly Sombart, exerted a significant impact on Jewish political economy, it was the Historical School's founder, Wilhelm Roscher, who enjoyed the most far-reaching influence. Roscher's famous essay, "The Status of the Jews in the Middle Ages, considered from the Standpoint of General Political Economy," was not published until 1875, but the bare kernel of his theory of Jewish historical economy was already present in his *Outline of Lectures on State Economy, according to the Historical Method,* published in the same year as Marx's "On the Jewish Question."[114] Although Roscher did not use the term, his was essentially a "middleman minority" theory. In fact, his 1875 essay compared Jews with other *Handelsvolke* such as Indian "Banians," Quakers, Armenians, and Lombards. According to Roscher, there was nothing in the internal character of these groups that predisposed them to commerce, merely their advanced technical culture in relation to surrounding "younger" nations. Trading nations are older, more advanced peoples who serve less developed nations by performing their commercial functions. They are diasporic for various historical reasons, such as exile, religious persecution, or migration in search of livelihood. As the "natives" develop their own institutions and are forced to compete, they subject the *Handelsvolk* to persecution, something Roscher claimed happened to Jews when individual European nations began to produce indigenous bourgeoisies. Eventually, Roscher suggested, after much hardship on the part of the minority *Handelsvolk*, a developmental threshold will be achieved, at which point fully commercialized societies no longer feel threatened by mercantile minorities and can integrate them back into their national communities. Roscher assumed that western and central Europe had now reached the stage at which the Jews could be assimilated into their own national bourgeoisies.[115] In this sense, his analysis premised Jewish emancipation not on the productivization of the Jews but on the productivization of the populations among whom they live.

Not everyone influenced by Roscher was quite so optimistic. The Russian Jew Ber Borochov integrated Roscher's conception of "national economy" with Marxism to produce his own hybrid theory of Jewish emancipation. Borochov was less interested in the question of the Jews' role as capitalist pioneers than in assessing the effects of capitalist triumph on Jewish survival. What Roscher held to be true of the Middle Ages – that to develop the "younger nations" of Europe had to cast off Jewish commercial tutelage – Borochov took to be a permanent iron law, at least within capitalist society. Borochov picked up on Marx's implication that the onset of capitalism had rendered the Jews' old commercial estate – their "chimerical nationality" – obsolete. Because Borochov did not believe that assimilation, à la Roscher, was possible for the Jewish masses, he insisted that Jews would have to reconstitute their nationhood through economic and occupational restructuring. Only through their territorial isolation, in a land of their own, he argued, could the Jews restore the economic foundations of their nationality, this time as a proletariat committed to socialist development rather than a petty bourgeois or commercial caste.[116]

Later, Borochov's formulation would supply one of the theoretical pillars of labor Zionism, perhaps the dominant economic ideology in the early history of the State of Israel. The Left Po'ale Zion platform he inspired emphasized the need to develop a more or less exclusive Jewish economy in Palestine. Only separation would ensure that Jewish workers would not revert to a middle class orientation while reducing Arabs and other non-Jews to permanent proletarian status, thereby partly replicating the fatal class structure of Jews' European past.

On a distinct but related level, Borochov also would provide the inspiration for the school of Jewish materialist historiography in interwar Poland, the *Yunge Historiker*. One need only cite the 1911 programmatic statement of the founder of *Yunge Historiker*, Ignacy (Yitzhak) Schipper to recognize traces not only of Borochov's but of Marx's approach to Jewish commerce as well:

> "The [nineteenth-century] leaders of Jewish historiography accomplished many things . . . [Schipper acknowledged]. "Thanks to them we possess an impressive picture of the spiritual directors of Diaspora Jewry. But what is completely lacking is the history of the hundreds of thousands who have left a trace for the future, not of the spiritual riches but of their toil and drudgery as well as of their speculative abilities. In short, we know about the Sabbath Jew and his extra [Sabbath] soul. But it is time we got to know the history of the weekday Jew and his weekday thoughts, . . . the history of Jewish working life."[117]

Labor Zionism and the demand for a new Jewish economic history may seem like odd metamorphoses for Marx's "On the Jewish Question," but they are only some of the enduring paradoxes of the politics of Jewish commerce.

Afterword: Industrialization and Beyond

The economic ideologies surveyed in this book were all formulated before the advent of the European Industrial Revolution. Because this was the watershed event of economic modernity, it will be worthwhile considering the legacy of the doctrines explored earlier to the industrial and postindustrial world. With the exception of the kinds of Jewish nationalist formulations associated with Zionist economic ideology, the period from 1638 to 1848 produced a comprehensive vocabulary of economic concepts, images, and arguments that would be reiterated, adapted, and deployed by later generations (although few were aware of the original sources). In the literature of this period, Jews had acquired contradictory identities: as an economically outmoded group or a nation of relentless modernizers; as part of the old order or the vanguard of the new; as a people gifted with commercial talents to fructify local economies or parasites draining the inherited order of its natural vitality; as emblems of slavery, exploitation, or of emancipation; as poor *schnorrers* or "kings of the age."

In the middle and late nineteenth century, a Jewish population encumbered by these binary images confronted industrialization. It was a bizarre encounter. The Industrial Revolution appeared to profoundly transform everything but the Jews. How was it possible that "probably the most important event in world history" (Eric Hobsbawm) so little altered their core economic orientations?[1]

Historians have become sensitive to the gradual, piecemeal, and variegated character of European industrialization (no longer seen exclusively through the lens of eighteenth-century Britain).[2] But this current awareness does not diminish the Industrial Revolution's psychological impact on all who witnessed or considered its awesome capacity for transformation. As Samuel Johnson prophesied in the mid-eighteenth century, henceforth "all the business of the world is to be done in a new way."[3] If anything, Johnson's vision proved too modest. The capacity of industry to sustain populations far larger than hitherto believed possible (higher fertility, lower mortality, and the end of famine) suggested that nothing was truly impossible. It fed into the romantic dream of man exceeding, excelling, and transcending the world of nature through the realization of his own nature, of man reborn, liberated, unbound. This unbound Prometheus took on immense historical significance.[4] Marx described the rupture of industrialization as separating necessity from freedom and prehistory from history; for Weber, it was a triumph of instrumental rationality (*Zweckrationalität*) over mystery, the necessary but bittersweet denouement to the centuries-long process of man's disenchantment, his denaturing.[5]

Clearly the Jews, numerically a comparatively small people in Europe, concentrated far from the centers of the new factory production in England and Germany, enmeshed in their "unproductive," commercial and financial, nonagricultural, and at best small-scale manufacturing and outmoded artisanal occupations, were in no way central to this transformation. Yet, by contrast, given their long-standing identification with the economic life of Europe, it was hard for many contemporaries to imagine that they were not somehow deeply mixed up in it. As noted, to those who defined the new age primarily as a revolution in productivity, the Jews had no significant role to play but were instead part and parcel of the old outmoded nonproductive world.[6] Only those like Werner Sombart or later Milton Friedman, economists who understood capitalism to be a relatively old system, defined first and foremost by financial and commercial operations and only secondarily by industry, could regard the Jews as genuine capitalist "pioneers."[7] Sombart, committed to the socialism that idealized craft production yet at the same time powerfully attuned to the creative genius of financial capitalism, not only recognized (and exaggerated) the historical importance of Jews to capitalist development; he also was among the first historians to locate the crucible of capitalism in the medieval Italian banking houses and communes of Genoa and Florence.[8] Sombart's vision of capitalism as a product of the *la longue durée*, if not his specific formulations, would exert a powerful influence on subsequent European social and economic history, through the work of scholars such as Marc Bloch, Hans Baron, and Fernand Braudel. Here was a twentieth-century school of social and economic thought that had not become overawed by the specter of the nineteenth-century industrial Prometheus.[9]

Still, even for Sombart, the main contributions of the Jews lay in the past. Other than a few brilliant eccentrics such as Thorstein Veblen, or a rather large number of crude antisemites fixated on Jewish conspiracy theories, the Jews' remarkable success *amid* industrialization went unexplained.[10] Although seemingly little impacted directly by the growth of heavy industry, it was precisely European Jewry whose population experienced the demographic transformation linked with industrialization earlier and faster than did most other Europeans. Although often still residing in small towns and villages until the late nineteenth century, Jews were nevertheless urbanizing at far higher rates than the surrounding populations. Indeed, wherever Jews enjoyed freedom of movement and access to secular education, their *embourgeoisment* progressed at a rapid pace. It is difficult not to be stuck by the figures cited by historians and sociologists such as Raphael Mahler, Jacob Lestschinsky, Arthur Ruppin, Calvin Goldscheider, or Yuri Slezkine that display the gross disproportionality of Jewish urbanites, professionals (particularly in law and medicine), and, of course, businessmen, merchants, and entrepreneurs in most areas of Ashkenazic Jewish settlement during the mid-nineteenth to the mid-twentieth centuries.[11]

The Industrial Revolution affected Jews differently from the majority of the population: it seemed to make them more themselves. Sometimes richer, often far poorer, they symbolized an obsolete social and economic order, yet one – we can in retrospect see – that was well situated to reconstitute itself once modernization had more fully gotten under way. Of course, in asserting this, we gloss over the enormous sustained cost of Jewish impoverishment (often culminating in "pauperization") that Jews endured between the late nineteenth century and the early decades of the twentieth, if not beyond.[12] Yet those Jews who managed to survive, or who immigrated to the West or became absorbed into Soviet Russia, eventually did prosper in relation to the surrounding populations. Keynes's famous rejoinder to the panglossian optimism of much economic prognostication ("in the long run we're dead") is gallows humor in the context of twentieth-century European Jewish history. But those Jews whom fortune granted a "long run" authored a success story that went well beyond mere survival.

Even Jewish poverty seemed sufficiently prodigious to suggest the presence of a group compelled by its unique internal structure, historical background, inherited skills, and experience to skip or radically foreshorten the stage of proletarianization (the shift out of the peasantry and into the factory) so that it could eventually jump the ladder back to a commercial and later a professional rung. This smacks of determinism, but how else do we account for the rapidity with which Jewish artisans abandoned their traditional fields in twentieth-century immigrant New York, and the degree to which even many of the numerous professed socialists among them found their way into business?[13] More striking still is what Nathan Reich, in referring to the pre–World War II period, termed "the marked reluctance of American born young Jews to follow in the footsteps of their parental store-and shop-keepers"; instead of inheriting and perpetuating the business, more often than not the sons (and sometimes the daughters) abandoned it for clerical or professional work.[14] And although the American Jewish experience of mobility was more rapid and dramatic than Jewish experiences elsewhere, it was not qualitatively unique.

Indeed, the phenomenon of professionalization and *embourgeoisment* was not even confined to capitalist Europe or America but manifested itself equivalently in the Soviet Union. Yuri Slezkine's book detailing (*inter alia*) Jewish mobility in Soviet Russia is only the latest and most sensational presentation of this phenomenon. Wherever industrialization and modernization occurred, even in a nascent or mongrel fashion, large percentages of Jews seemed prepared to make the most of it, often despite the existence of other severe constraints on their movement. And what was the nature of this preparation? Undeniably, it was the Jews' legacy as a middleman minority dating back to medieval times; their essentially urban, mediating, and commercial skills.[15] It is remarkable that in the conditions of political backwardness, anti-Jewish discrimination, and slow uneven industrialization in Eastern Europe during the late nineteenth and early twentieth century, this very heritage should seem to put Jews at a gross disadvantage, so much so that the route to modernization appeared to proceed not along the familiar road of commerce but by adopting a radically different course: immersion in the proletariat or, more radically still, autotransformation into agriculturists. It seems perverse indeed that the more typical formula of modernization, pithily formulated by Eugen Weber as "Peasants into Frenchmen," should in the case of perhaps the most radical modernist movement in Jewish history, Zionism, be inverted into the intuitively countermodern project of making Jews into peasants. Suffice it to say that from the mostly negative and pessimistic assessments of the Jewish economic future rendered by social scientists at the end of the nineteenth century one would never have predicted the arrival of a new "Jewish Century" marked by so much tragedy but also by such a high degree of economic success and successful adaptation.

Why were the social scientists so wrong about the Jews?[16] For one thing, the formulae of progress and growth that they emphasized, entailing productivity, productive labor, primary and heavy industry, commercial agriculture, mass production and industrialization – in short, *industrial revolution* – only partly hit the mark. As I suggested earlier, in the post-classical period economists came to recognize that consumption and demand are also important, that demand is elastic and can be inflated through promotion, merchandising, and advertising, not to mention through state fiscal and monetary policy; that distribution does not always follow production but may rather impel it; that finance and accounting can themselves be "productive" and not merely deceptive, and that credit is an essential impetus to growth.[17] Because of their "traditional" occupations, these are all areas in which many Jews enjoyed experience, possessed knowledge, and – not least important – transmitted these skills to succeeding generations (through education, not genes). Even more than this, in a postindustrial age like our own, the long-term value of service industries is far more important than it appeared to be in the late nineteenth century. It is now increasingly clear that intellectual capital, adaptability, and flexibility are capacities that transcend the relatively short-lived modernizing spurt fed by industrialization. And here, too, Jews' "premodern" inheritance would hold them in good stead.[18] If it did not exactly make them modern before their time, it enabled them to rapidly become modern when the time had come.

Of all the intellectual tendencies reviewed in this book, it therefore appears that the economic philosemites and apologists of the early modern era were in the end the most prescient. Their notion of Jews as commercial specialists, as a middleman minority (before the term was coined), turned out to possess greater sociological longevity than anyone might have expected. Admittedly, these apologists were hawking their ideas in society that was still corporatist and pre-emancipatory. It was a society too hierarchical and, by our standards, too unjust to serve as exemplary for our own times. Moreover, this society was not compatible with the type of unitary citizenship that was ultimately championed by the Enlightenment. But the latter corrective to corporatism proved itself to be also deeply flawed, just as the French revolutionary ideal of abstract citizenship and unitary equality proved inadequate to the needs of a complex and diverse society. Instead, some degree of cultural and political pluralism has come to seem more in keeping with the realities of modern life. It is therefore worth asking to what degree *economic* pluralism, or an ethnic division of labor, one in which Jews or some other group could play a disproportionate role in the society's commercial life, is compatible with sound liberal ideals, including integration and individual freedom. The United States appears to point the way toward such a workable synthesis, however imperfectly.[19]

Another legacy of eighteenth-century Enlightenment proved fateful but not always salutary for the politics of Jewish commerce. The misreading of productivity as rooted in productive labor alone ultimately put the Jews at war with their own economic inheritance and alienated them psychically and politically from the commercial orientation that they could not at any rate avoid, or could avoid only at their peril. Although the foundation of productivist ideologies was laid in the period surveyed here, it was really in the following century, the industrial age from 1848 to 1948, that their full impact became clear. The ferociously anticommercial ideologies of communism and fascism (as well as various forms of Zionism) swept up masses of Jews in a futile and tragically destructive effort to transform them in the wrong direction, if not destroy them outright. In contrast to pluralistic liberalism, these movements marked a grotesque intensification of the politics of Jewish commerce. Their destructiveness, however, should not blind us to the rational and humane complaints against capitalism that these ideologies exploited and cannibalized. The dilemma of capitalism and its discontents, of commerce and its critics, trapped the Jews in its clutches. The earlier history that we have surveyed is essential to understanding these later developments, to making sense of them and of the entire era of hyperproductivity and hostility to commerce that has now at last faded away, if indeed it truly has.

Notes

INTRODUCTION

1. Jacob Katz, "The Term 'Jewish Emancipation': Its Origin and Historical Impact," *Studies in Nineteenth-Century Jewish Intellectual History*, edited by Alexander Altmann (Cambridge, MA, 1964), pp. 1–25.

2. Karl Marx, "Zur Judenfrage," in *Deutsche-Französische Jahrbücher*, edited by Arnold Ruge (Paris, 1844).

3. *Economic History of the Jews*, edited by Salo W. Baron and Arkadius Kahan (New York, 1975); Mark Wishnitzer, *A History of Jewish Crafts and Guilds* (New York, 1965).

4. Peter Spufford, *Money and its Use in Medieval Europe* (Cambridge, 1988).

5. Karl Polanyi, *The Livelihood of Man*, edited by H. W. Pearson (London, 1977); idem., *The Great Transformation: The Political and Economic Origins of Our Time* (Boston, 1957).

6. J. G. A. Pocock, *The Machiavellian Moment: Florentine Political Thought and the Atlantic Republican Tradition* (Princeton, NJ, 1975).

7. Kalman Neuman, "The Literature of the *Respublica Judaica*: Descriptions of the Ancient Israelite Polity in the Antiquarian Writing of the Sixteenth and Seventeenth Centuries" (Hebrew). Ph.D. dissertation: Hebrew University of Jerusalem, 2002; idem., "Political Hebraism and the Early Modern 'Respublica Hebraeorum': On Defining the Field," *Hebraic Political Studies*, vol. 1, no. 1 (Fall, 2005), pp. 57–70; Jonathan R. Ziskind, "Cornelius Bertram and Carlo Sigonio: Christian Hebraism's First Political Scientists," *Journal of Ecumenical Studies* (Summer–Fall 2000), pp. 321–32; Frank Manuel, *The Broken Staff: Judaism through Christian Eyes* (Cambridge, MA, 1992), pp. 121–27.

8. James Harrington, *The Political Works of James Harrington*, ed. J. G. A. Pocock (Cambridge, 1977), p. 114.

9. Gerson David Hundert, *Jews in Poland-Lithuania in the Eighteenth Century* (Berkeley, CA, 2004), pp. 1–20.

10. Jonathan Israel, *European Jewry in the Age of Mercantilism, 1550–1750* (Oxford, 1985); idem., *Diasporas within a Diaspora: Jews, Crypto-Jews and the World Maritime Empires* (1540–1740) (Leiden, 2002).

11. Derek Penslar, *Shylock's Children: Economics and Jewish Identity in Modern Europe* (Berkeley, CA, 2001).

12. E.g., David Wootton, "The Republic Tradition: From Common Wealth to Common Sense," pp. 1–41 in *Republicanism, Liberty, and Commercial Society, 1649–1776*, edited by David Wootton (Stanford, CA, 1994); Mark Jurdjevic, "Virtue, Commerce, and the Enduring Florentine Republican Moment: Reintegrating Italy into the Atlantic Republican Debate," *Journal of the History of Ideas*, vol. 62, no. 4 (Oct. 2001), pp. 721–43.

13. J. G. A. Pocock, "Gog and Magog, The Republican Thesis and the Ideologia Americana," *Journal of the History of Ideas*, vol. 48, no. 2 (April–June, 1987), pp. 325–346; idem., Introduction to Edmund Burke, *Reflections on the Revolution in France*, edited by J. G. A. Pocock (Indianapolis, 1987), pp. xx–xxi.

1. THIS NEWFANGLED AGE

1. John J. Gross, *Shylock: A Legend and Its Legacy* (New York, 1992); for a corrective, see Joseph Shatzmiller, *Shylock Reconsidered: Jews, Moneylending, and Medieval Society* (Berkeley, CA, 1990).

2. James Shapiro adopts a similar position but for rather different reasons in his *Shakespeare and the Jews* (New York, 1996), p. 3.

3. A pioneering study of the play's Anglo-centric economic context is John W. Draper, "Usury in 'The Merchant of Venice,'" *Modern Philology*, vol. 33, no. 1 (August, 1935), pp. 37–47.

4. William Shakespeare, *The Merchant of Venice*, Act I, scene iii. See Leon Poliakov, *Les Banchieri Juifs et le Saint-Siègle* (Paris, 1965), p. 280. Jewish prominence in shipping would only grow in the seventeenth and early eighteenth centuries. See Gino Luzzatto, *Sulla condizione economica degli Ebrei veneziani nel secolo XVIII*, in *Sritti in onore di Riccardo Bachi* (Perugia, 1950), pp. 161–72.

5. Abraham Melamed, *Ahotan ha-Ketomah shel he-Hakhmut ha-Mahshavah ha-Medinit shel ha-Hogim ha-Yehudim be-Renesans ha-Italki* [Wisdom's Little Sister: The Political Thought of Jewish Thinkers in the Italian Renaissance] (Hebrew). Ph.D. dissertation: Tel Aviv University, 1976, p. 385.

6. Robert Bonfil, *Jewish Life in Renaissance Italy* (Berkeley, CA, 1994), p. 97; David Sorkin, *The Transformation of German Jewry, 1780–1840* (New York, 1987), p. 43; Penslar, *Shylock's Children*, p. 19.

7. Among the many works, see Benjamin N. Nelson, *The Idea of Usury: From Tribal Brotherhood to Universal Otherhood* (Princeton, 1949); John T. Noonan, *The Scholastic Analysis of Usury* (Cambridge, MA, 1957) and Raymond de Roover, *La Pensée Économique des Scolastiques: Doctrines et Méthodes* (Montréal and Paris, 1971), pp. 76–90; Jacques Le Goff, *Your Money or Your Life: Economy and Religion in the Middle Ages* (Cambridge, MA, 1988); T. P. McLaughlin, "The Teaching of the Canonists on Usury," *Medieval Studies*, I (1939), pp. 81–147. See also the examples cited by Joyce Appleby, *Economic Thought and Ideology in Seventeenth Century England* (Princeton, NJ, 1978), pp. 39–40, 65–72. For rabbinic attitudes, see Siegfried Stein, "Interest Taken by Jews from Gentiles," *Journal of Semitic Studies*, vol. 1, no. 2 (April, 1956), pp. 141–64; Aaron Kirschenbaum, "Jewish and Christian Theories of Usury in the Middle Ages," *Jewish Quarterly Review*, new series, vol. 75, no. 3 (Jan. 1985), pp. 270–89. David B. Ruderman, "Champion of Jewish Economic Interests," in *Essential Papers*

on Judaism and Christianity in Conflict, edited by Jeremy Cohen (New York, 1991), pp. 514–35.

8. Kirschenbaum, "Jewish and Christian Theories of Usury," pp. 273–74. Nelson, *The Idea of Usury*, pp. 23–25, and 25, n. 58; R. H. Tawney, *Religion and the Rise of Capitalism: A Historical Study* (Gloucester, MA, 1962), pp. 47–53; Lester K. Little, *Religious Poverty and the Profit Economy on Medieval Europe* (Ithaca, NY, 1978), pp. 180–83.

9. P. G. M. Dickson, *The Financial Revolution in England: A Study in the Development of Public Credit, 1688–1756* (New York, 1967).

10. Jews were sometimes explicitly associated with more novel and complex variations of old usurious concepts, such as the "compound interest" described by the sixteenth-century French mathematician Jacques Chauvet as "abominable" "usury on usury" employed exclusively by the Jews. See Natalie Zeman Davis, "Sixteenth-Century French Arithmetics on the Business Life," *Journal of the History of Ideas*, vol. 21, no. 1 (Jan.–Mar. 1960), pp. 24–25. As a rule, during the Middle Ages, when overtly religious conceptions of usury prevailed, it was a frequently expressed sentiment that "Christian usurers are worse than Jews," because Jews at least possessed divine permission, however misconstrued, to lend at interest "unto a stranger," which Christians did not. With the Reformation's gradual acceptance of usury as an economic necessity and private matter, Jews were distinguished by their cruel and zealous desire to exploit economically beyond the exigencies of productive commercial arrangements. See Nelson, *The Idea of Usury*, pp. 10–12, 65–66, 71.

11. Wilhelm Roscher, "Die Stellung der Juden im Mittelalter, betrachtet vom Standpunkte der allgemeinen Handelspolitik," in *Zeitschrift für gesamte Staatswissenschaft*, XXXI (1875), pp. 503–26.

12. Yitzhak Baer, *A History of the Jews of Christian Spain*, 2 vols (Philadelphia, 1961), I, pp. 40–41; II, p. 247.

13. Ibid., I, pp. 84–85; Bonfil, *Jewish Life in Renaissance Italy*, pp. 62–63.

14. Jane S. Gerber, *The Jews of Spain: A History of the Sephardic Experience* (New York, 1994), p. 121.

15. This is the central thesis of Jonathan Israel's second major study of early modern Jewry, *Diasporas within a Diaspora*, pp. vii, 1–9.

16. Arthur Hertzberg, *The French Enlightenment and the Jews* (New York, 1968), pp. 50–51.

17. Israel, *Diasporas within a Diaspora*, pp. 61–70; Benjamin Ravid, "A Tale of three Cities and the Raison d'Etat: Ancona, Venice, Livorno, and the Competition for Jewish Merchants in the Sixteenth Century," in *Mediterranean Historical Review*, vol. 6, no. 2 (December, 1991), 138–62.

18. See, generally, Bernard Dov Cooperman, *Trade and Settlement: The Establishment of the Jewish Communities of Leghorn and Pisa*, Cambridge, MA: Ph.D. dissertation: Harvard University, 1976.

19. Moses A. Shulvass, *From East to West: The Westward Migration of Jews from Eastern Europe During the Seventeenth and Eighteenth Centuries* (Detroit, 1971).

20. See the articles collected in Paolo Bernardini, Norman Fiering, eds., *The Jews and their Expansion to the West, 1450–1800* (New York, 2001).

21. Jonathan Israel, *European Jewry in the Age of Mercantilism* (Oxford, 1991), puts this into the framework primarily of policies of "reason of state" and "mercantilism,"

rather than political-economy and political theory in the sense discussed here. See pp. 51–52, 116–17, 202–03.

22. This is an old debate dating back to the late nineteenth century. The original antagonists were the "primitivist" economist Karl Bücher and the "modernist" Eduard Meyer. The modernist view was subsequently championed by the Russian émigré historical economist, M. I. Rostovtzeff. The primitivist view was powerfully revived in the 1970s by Moses I. Finley, building on the economic theories of Karl Polanyi. Now the pendulum seems to have swung back to the other side. See Elio Lo Cascio and Dominic Rathbone, editors, *Production and Public Powers in Classical Antiquity* (Cambridge, 2000); Edward E. Cohen, *Athenian Economy and Society: A Banking Perspective* (Princeton, NJ, 1992). For comprehensive but highly polemical statements of the modernist position, see Morris Silver, *Economic Structures of the Ancient Near East* (Totowa, NJ, 1986); idem., *Economic Structures of Antiquity* (Westport, CT, 1995). A modified restatement of the Finley approach is found in Philip Jones, *The Italian City-State: From Commune to Signoria* (Oxford, 1997), pp. 5–10. The *origins* of the original "Bücher-Meyer" debate have not been considered in terms of the ideologies surrounding the depiction of Jews' and other middleman minorities' historic economic roles. Such an analysis, as the second half of this book suggests, would indicate that the core debate is really considerably older.

23. I owe this insight to Maurice Glasman, "Roman London, Imperial Emporium," (unpublished research paper).

24. Even so, the profits to be made by patricians through high interest loans were so great that Seneca reported boasted of his gains. See Jean Andreau, *Banking and Business in the Roman World* (New York, 1999), pp. 11–14; Keith Hopkins, "Taxes and Trade in the Roman Empire (200 B.C.–A.D. 400)," *The Journal of Roman Studies* LXX (1980), pp. 105–06.

25. M. I. Finley, *The Ancient Economy* (Berkeley, CA, 1985), p. 48.

26. Quentin Skinner, *The Foundations of Modern Political Thought*, vol. 1 (Cambridge, 1978), p. 43.

27. Aristole, *The Politics*, translated by T. A. Sinclair (London, 1981), pp. 344–46.

28. J. G. Melquior, *Liberalism Old and New* (Boston, 1991), p. 31.

29. Hesiod, *Works and Days*, ll. 11–24.

30. Cicero, *On Duties*, edited by M. T. Griffin (Cambridge, 1991), pp. 58–59. As noted, these remarks emerged from a society in which international commerce was important to the economy, perhaps especially to the political elite. Scholars have sometimes been tempted to cut the resulting Gordian knot by simply asserting that the ancient authors' pro-mercantile attitudes have not been properly acknowledged. This is the approach taken by even so profound a historian as Hans Baron in his "Franciscan Poverty and Civic Wealth as Factors in the Rise of Humanistic Thought," *Speculum*, vol. XIII, no. 1 (January, 1938), pp. 1–37, who remarks that humanist thought of the fifteenth century, in contrast to the sentiments of predecessors like Petrarch and Boccaccio, properly understood the outlook of Aristotle and Cicero praising wealth (and implicitly industry and commerce). Although it is true that these ancient authors validated wealth, it was landed wealth whose by-product was leisure. Those who engaged in menial labor and (especially petty) commerce were necessary but nevertheless contemptible. That is the real paradox.

31. See P. D. Anthony, *The Ideology of Work* (London, 1978), pp. 17–18.

32. David Nicholas, *The Later Medieval City, 1300–1500* (London, 1997), pp. 192–93.

33. Robert L. Reynolds, *Europe Emerges: Transition toward an Industrial World-Wide Society, 600–1750* (Madison, WI, 1961), pp. 262–63. Northern nobles tended to regard their Italian counterparts are too commercial and insufficiently martial, therefore inadequately honorable. See Jones, *The Italian City-State*, p. 301.

34. See John F. McGovern, "The Rise of New Economic Attitudes in Canon and Civil Law," *The Jurist*, 32 (1972), pp. 39–50.

35. Unlike merchants, who did generate a significant body of literature, such as handbooks offering advice on trade practices that implicitly dignified merchant activity. See John F. McGovern, "The Rise of New Economic Attitudes – Economic Humanism, Economic Nationalism – during the Later Middle Ages and Renaissance, A.D. 1200–1550," *Traditio*, XXVI (1970), p. 227.

36. Antony Black, *Guilds and Civil Society in European Political Thought from the Twelfth Century to the Present* (London, 1984), pp. 15–27, 89, 133–42. Hans Baron, "A Sociological Interpretation of the Early Renaissance in Florence," *The South Atlantic Quarterly, South Atlantic Quarterly*, XXXVIII (Oct. 1939), pp. 434–36 and, following him, McGovern, "The Rise of New Economic Attitudes," see a shift in attitude toward labor among humanists and canon lawyers already by the fifteenth century. Still, it remains to be said that the "work ethic" they endorsed constituted a form of social control over the "idle" poor, a form of "economic nationalism," as McGovern labels it, which largely affirmed antique aristocratic attitudes regarding the virtue of labor for the masses while protecting the leisure of the elite to engage in learning and conduct politics. Baron may be correct that a new attitude toward time, reflecting merchant sensibilities, had now emerged; yet the sensibility was still fundamentally classical. As Baron himself notes, *otium* did not signify a vegetative or hedonistic state but to Hellenistic philosophers a condition on intense intellectual focus and activity. In his *De Re Publica* (I, 17, 27), Cicero has Scipio Africanus Maior say himself, "He ... never did more than when he did nothing." Hans Baron, "Cicero and the Roman Civic Spirit in the Middle Ages and Early Renaissance," *Bulletin of the John Rylands Library*, vol. 22 (1938), p. 74.

37. Quoted in Anthony, *The Ideology of Work*, p. 37.

38. Jacques Le Goff, *Time, Work, and Culture in the Middle Ages*, translated by Arthur Goldhammer (Chicago, 1980), p. 61.

39. Hans Baron, *The Crisis of the Early Italian Renaissance: Civic Humanism and Republican Liberty in an Age of Classicism and Tyranny* (Princeton, NJ, 1955).

40. Perhaps it is more accurately a "Ciceronian Moment," because Cicero was initially the most important influence. Alister E. McGrath, *The Intellectual Origins of the European Reformation* (Malden, MA, 2004), p. 36; Baron, "Cicero and the Roman Civic Spirit"; Carrie Nederman, "Nature, Sin, and the Origins of Society: The Ciceronian Tradition in Medieval Political Thought," *Journal of the History of Ideas*, vol. 49, no. 1 (Jan.–Mar., 1988), pp. 3–26. The criticism that civic humanism was more a rhetorical stance than a consistently applied contemporary ideology does not invalidate its impact. To say otherwise, it seems to me, would be to engage in a genitive fallacy that confuses original intent with long-term significance. Other recent critics of Baron claim to find precursors in medieval Italian political thought or locate a more authentic civic republicanism in late-thirteenth-century Florentine guild ideology. See the evaluations summarized in James Hankins, "The 'Baron Thesis' after Forty

Years, and Some Recent Studies of Leonardo Bruni," *Journal of the History of Ideas* 56, no. 2 (1995), pp. 309–38 and idem., *Renaissance Civic Humanism: Reappraisals and Reflections*, edited by J. Hankins (Cambridge, 2000).

41. See Jones, *The Italian City-State*, p. 331. Florentine guilds may have supplied a "precursor" to the emergence of civic humanist thought, as is argued by John Najemy, "Civic humanism and Florentine politics," in Hankins, *Renaissance Civic Humanism*, 75–104, but the humanist movement as a whole also has been described as a "program of the ruling classes," which disdained the lower orders and manual labor. See Lauro Martines, *Power and Imagination: City-States in Renaissance Italy* (New York, 1979), p. 207.

42. See Mark Jurdjevic, "Virtue, Commerce, and the Enduring Florentine Republican Moment: Reintegrating Italy into the Atlantic Republican Debate," *Journal of the History of Ideas*, vol. 62, no. 4 (October 2001), pp. 721–43.

43. Hankins, "The 'Baron Thesis', pp. 229–330. Hankins regards rhetoric as far more important than constitutionalism in the civic humanist agenda. But as Carrie J. Nederman suggests, the two were closely intertwined. See Nederman, "Nature, Sin and the Origins of Society," p. 23.

44. On *virtù*, see Neal Wood, "Machiavelli's Concept of *Virtù* Reconsidered," *Political Studies*, (June 1967), pp. 159–72.

45. Machiavelli, *Selected Political Writings*, ed. David Wootton (Indianapolis, 1994), pp. 93–95 (*Discourses*, Book I, Chapter II); Compare also the idea formulated by Donato Giannotti (1492–1573), Florentine author of the *Libro de la Republica de Vinitiani* of establishing within a republic "*un modo de vivere* "between different social groupings; cited in Pocock, *The Machiavellian Moment: Florentine Political Thought and the Atlantic Republican Tradition* (Princeton, NJ, 1975), p. 299.

46. Ibid., pp. 156–82. Jurdjevic, "The Enduring Florentine Republican Moment," pp. 730, 742, is right to note statements in Machiavelli's *Discourses* and *The Prince* that express a more favorable view of commerce, but wrong to imply that these somehow cancel out his even more forthright statements denouncing wealth and the effeminizing cosmopolitanism that derives from international trade.

47. See, generally, Albert O. Hirschmann, *The Passions and the Interests: Political Arguments for Capitalism before its Triumph* (Princeton, NJ, 1977).

48. Claude Mosse, *Le travail en Grece et a Rome* (Paris, 1980), pp. 9–25; J. P. Vennant, *Mythe et Penseée chez les Crecs* (Paris, 1965), pp. 197–99; but Ellen Meiksins Wood, *Peasant-Citizen and Slave* (London, 1988), pp. 126–72 offers some useful qualifications.

49. *Socrate, overo dell'Humano Sapere exercitio soriogiocoso di Simone Luzzatto Hebreo Venetiano* (Venetia, 1651). On this work, see David B. Ruderman, *Jewish Thought and Scientific Discovery in Early Modern Europe* (New Haven, CT, 1995), pp. 171–78.

50. Several fragments of the *Discorso* translated into English by Felix Giovanelli appeared in *Commentary* magazine (April 1947, May 1947, and June 1952); a long-awaited complete English translation is in the works from Benjamin C. I. Ravid.

51. Benjamin C. I. Ravid, *Economics and Toleration in Seventeenth-Century Venice: The Background and Context of the "Discorso" of Simone Luzzatto* (Jerusalem, 1978), pp. 10–18; Leone Modena, *The Autobiography of a Seventeenth-Century Venetian Rabbi, Leon Modena's "Life of Judah,"* edited and translated by Mark R. Cohen (Princeton, NJ, 1988), pp. 143–46, 249–51.

52. Simone Luzzatto, *Discorso circa il stato de gl'Hebrei in particolar dimoranti nell' inclita Citta di Venetia, di Simone Luzzatto, Rabbino Hebreo* (Venice, 1638). The charges emerge from reports of the Venetian Board of Trade frequently leveled when bills faced the Venetian Senate for the renewal (and often expansion) of Jewish commercial privileges. Such charges focused on accusations that Jews were increasingly monopolizing trade with the Levant; that their existing privileges gave them unfair advantages over Christian merchants; and that Jews removed their wealth from Venice. See Ravid, *Economics and Toleration*, pp. 41–48.

53. Robert Lopez influentially argued that the Venetian and Florentine merchant classes abandoned commerce in favor of investment in land and art as early as the fourteenth century. See Robert Lopez, "Hard Times and Investment in Culture," reprinted in *Social and Economic Foundations of the Italian Renaissance*, edited by Anthony Molho (New York, 1969), pp. 95–116. A transition of the sort described by Luzzatto (although no doubt he greatly exaggerated it) did occur – part of a larger "Aristocratic revival" in sixteenth-century Europe – although it was a gradual movement by a minority of the Venetian elite, which had at any rate always been quasi-noble, and which pursued land and agriculture for rational economic reasons, among others. Indeed, Venice's acquisition of a sizeable inland empire, and the city's key role as node of overland trade from Germany and Central Europe, made landed estates an inviting prospect. See William J. Bouwsma, *Venice and the Defense of Republican Liberty: Renaissance Values in the Age of Counter-Reformation* (Berkeley, CA, 1968), pp. 104–06; Peter Musgrave, *The Early Modern European Economy* (New York, 1999), pp. 49–52. These shifts, however, could not permanently arrest Venetian decline. In Luzzatto's day, its immediate source was competition from England and the Netherlands, which having negotiated peace treaties with Spain in the early seventeenth century, could use their superior merchant fleets to trade directly with the Levant. This in turn resulted in stepped-up efforts within the Venetian Senate to encourage the immigration and naturalization of "foreign," that is, Western merchants. See Frederick C. Lane, *Venice: A Maritime Republic* (Baltimore and London, 1973), pp. 331, 400–02.

54. Simone Luzzatto, *Discorso circa il stato de gl'Hebrei et in particular dimoranti nell'inclita Citta' di Venetia. Facsimile dell'edizione veneziana del 1638 coredato di una notta di Riccardo Bachi su La dottrina sulla dinamica delle città secondo Giovanni Botero e secondo Simone Luzzatto (Bologna, 1976),* Considratione VIII, p. 28. Idem, *Ma'amar 'al Yehudei Yenetsiyah [Discourse on the Jews of Venice]* (Hebrew), translated by Dan Lattes (Jerusalem, 1954), p. 98.

55. See Skinner, *Foundations*, I, pp. 73–74; Jurdjevic, "The Enduring Florentine Republican Moment."

56. Giovanni Botero, *The Reason of State*, translated by P. J. Waley and D. P. Waley, and *The Greatness of Cities*, translated by Robert Peterson [1606], (New Haven, CT, 1956), pp. 259–61.

57. Martines, *Power and Imagination*, pp. 313–14.

58. Antonio Serra, *Breve trattato delle cause che possano far abbandonare li regni d'oro et d'argento dove non sono mintiere, con applicatione al Regno di Napoli* (Naples, 1613). On Serra, see Theodore A. Sumberg, "Antonio Serra: A Neglected Herald of the Acquisitive System," American Journal of Economics and Sociology, vol. 50, no. 3 (July 1991), pp. 365–73. I must express my gratitude to Professor Giuseppe Veltri for calling my attention to Serra's influence on Luzzatto. See also Giuseppe Veltri,

"Alcune considerazioni sugli Ebrei e Venezia nel pensiero politico di Simone Luzzatto," in *Percorsi di storia ebraica: Atti del XVIII convegno internazionale dell'AISG, Cividale del Friuli-Gorizia, 7/9 settembre 2004*, edited by Cesare Ioly Zorattini (Udine, 2005), pp. 247–66.

59. Bernardo Davanzati, *A Discourse on Trade*, translated by John Toland (London, 1695), p. 16; cf. Terence Hutchison, *Before Adam Smith: The Emergence of Political Economy, 1662–1776* (Oxford, 1988), p. 57.

60. "And indeed the word 'money' [*damim*] has two meanings in Hebrew: both 'blood' [*dam*] as well as 'currency' [*al Danaro*]," Luzzatto, *Discorso*, Consideratione VIII, p. 28; Idem. *Ma'amar*, p. 97.

61. On Luzzatto's use of imagery drawn from recent and contemporary scientific discourse, see Ruderman, *Jewish Thought and Scientific Discovery*, pp. 157–58.

62. Luzzatto, *Discorso*, Consideratione VI, pp. 22–25; Idem., pp. 93–95.

63. Ibid., p. 81.

64. Cf. the eighteenth-century Italian philosopher Vico: ". . . the passions of men who are entirely occupied by the pursuit of their private utility are transformed into a civil order which permits men to live in human society." Quoted in Hirschman, *The Passions and the Interests*, p. 17.

65. Luzzatto, *Discorso*, p. 28; idem. *Ma'amar*, p. 98.

66. Luzzatto, *Discorso*, p. 32; idem. *Ma'amar*, p. 105, cf. 97.

67. Luzzatto, *Discorso*, Consideratione IV, p. 19; idem. *Ma'amar*, pp. 89–90.

68. On Paruta, see Bouwsma, pp. 206–12, 240–79. Serra also emphasized the virtue of overcoming challenges. See Serra, *Breve trattato*, p. 232; Sumberg, "Antonio Serra," p. 367.

69. Luzzatto, *Discorso*, Consideratione I, p. 9; idem. *Ma'amar*, p. 81.

70. This has been noted by Ravid, *Economics and Toleration*, p. 98.

71. Luzzatto, *Discorso*, Consideratione III, pp. 15–16; idem. *Ma'amar*, pp. 86–87.

72. Quoted in Yitzhak F. Baer, *Galut* (New York, 1957), translated by Robert Warshow, p. 86 (my emphasis).

73. *Menasseh ben Israel 's Mission to Oliver Cromwell*, edited by Lucien Wolf (London, 1901), p. 89. The argument would resound throughout the eighteenth century. John Toland would employ it in a qualified way, as explored in chapter 2 of this study. In the middle of the century, the French economist Ange Goudar recommends Jews as the ideal commercial specialists because they are both industrious and apolitical. "Cette Secte, établie chez nous, ne sçauroit donner du mouvement à l'ambition d'un parti. L'intrigue & la cabale sont entiérement inconnuës. C'est dans la nature de la chose. Sa sureté le demande ainsi. Si les Juifs cessoient un moment d'être fidéles, ils se perdroient pour toûjours. Errans, sans Chefs, sans patrie, & par consequent, sans moyens pour résister à la plus petite Puissance qui voudroit les détruire, la premiére maxime politique pour eux, est celle de n'en avoir aucune." Ange Goudar, *Les interets de la France mal entendus dans les branches de l'agriculture, de la population, des finances, du commerce, de la marine, et de l'industrie* (Amsterdam, 1757), vol. I, p. 422.

74. Iseult Honohan, *Civic Republicanism* (London and New York, 2002), p. 36.

75. Luzzatto, *Discorso*, Consideratione XI, p. 18; idem. *Ma'amar*, pp. 105–06.

76. Luzzatto did offer a faint qualification by adding the words, "in its present condition."

77. For the late medieval period, see Kenneth Stow, "The Jewish Community of the Middle Ages was Not a Corporation," (Hebrew) in *Kehunah u-Melukhah: Yahase Dat u-Medinah be-Yisra'el uva-'Amim [Priesthood and Monarchy: Relations of Religion and State in Israel and Among the Nations] (Hebrew)*, edited by Isaiah Gafni and Gabriel Motzkin (Jerusalem, 1987), pp. 141–48.

78. *Socrate, overo dell'humano sapere exercitio seriogiocoso di Simone Luzzatto Hebreo Venetiano* (Venice, 1651).

79. John Gager, *The Origins of Anti-Semitism* (New York, 1985), pp. 55–66.

80. On Moses in Machiavelli, see Abraham Melamed, *The Philosopher King in Medieval and Renaissance Jewish Thought* (Albany, NY, 2003), pp. 151–54.

81. Machiavelli, *Selected Political Writings*, p. 151.

82. For a different conclusion, see Jurdjevic, "The Enduring Florentine Republican Moment," pp. 730, 742, who mentions but does not examine Machiavelli's antimercantile statements.

83. Richard Grassby, *The Business Community of Seventeenth-Century England* (Cambridge, 1995), p. 45.

84. See Steve Pincus, "Neither Machiavellian Moment nor Possessive Individualism: Commercial Society and the Defenders of the English Commonwealth," *American Historical Review*, vol. 103, no. 3 (June 1998), pp. 705–36.

85. Quoted in Pincus, "Neither Machiavellian Moment nor Possessive Individualism," p. 716.

86. Pocock emphasizes that Harrington himself exhibited no special prejudices against merchants per se but, rather, only against those whose occupation and form of labor rendered them dependent on others. See Pocock, *Machiavellian Moment*, pp. 391–92.

87. J. P. Sommerville, *Politics and Ideology in England, 1603–1640* (London and New York, 1986), pp. 88–89, 94–95, 106.

88. Appleby, *Economic Thought*, pp. 59–63.

89. David McNally, *Political Economy and the Rise of Capitalism: A Reinterpretation* (Berkeley, CA, 1988), pp. 56–57.

90. Ibid., pp. 54–55.

91. Ibid.

92. See Lawrence Dickey's "Appendix III on Book IV" to Adam Smith, *Wealth of Nations* (Indianapolis, 1993), pp. 226–42.

93. Even if a truly widespread agricultural "improvement" in England had to await the eighteenth century. See Peter S. Stearns, *European Society in Upheaval; Social History since 1750* (New York, 1967), p. 74.

94. McNally, *Political Economy*, p. 49; note, too, the use of the Davanzati's and Luzzatto's circulatory metaphor, only here with a negative connotation.

95. Smith, *The Wealth of Nations* (Chicago, 1976), i, p. 444; Smith's sentiments on merchants are frequently sour: they complain of high wages, but are "silent with regard to the pernicious effects of their own gains," p. 110; they make the best improvers when they retire to country estates, but are filled with "clamour and sophistry" in seeking to convince others "that the private interest of a part [of society] ... is the general interest of the whole," p. 143; nevertheless, the modern commercial system is so constructed that today "every man ... lives by exchanging, or becomes in some

measure a merchant..." On Smith's "ambivalence" to markets, see David McNally, *Against the Market: Political Economy, Market Socialism and the Marxist Critique* (London, 1993).

96. Pincus, "Neither Machiavellian Moment nor Possessive Individualism"; Paul A. Rahe, "Antiquity Surpassed: The Repudiation of Classical Republicanism," in *Republicanism, Liberty, and Commercial Society, 1649–1776*, edited by David Wootton (Stanford, CA, 1994), pp. 232–69.

97. Pincus, "Neither Machiavellian Moment nor Possessive Individualism," pp. 720–21; Istvan Hont, "Free Trade and the Economic Limits to National Politics: neo-Machiavellian Political Economy Revisited," in *The Economic Limits to Modern Politics*, edited by John Dunn (Cambridge, 1990), p. 55.

98. Andy Wood, *Riot, Rebellion and Popular Politics in Early Modern England* (New York, 2002), p. 122 refers to a redefinition of this group as a "middling sort," a new term when applied to a population group at this time, but suggesting that the traditional class of urban commoners was now being supplemented by other mercantile and artisanal elements.

99. The so-called neo-Harringtonians (discussed in Chapter 2) stressed that only independent freeholders were truly independent in the sense that affirmed their capacities for political virtue. Yet at the same time, they held themselves up as defenders of "trade" per se, and reserved their severest condemnations only for "finance" and "stockjobbing." *The Machiavellian Moment*, pp. 447–48.

100. David S. Katz, *Philo-Semitism and the Readmission of the Jews to England, 1603–1655* (Oxford, 1982), p. 7. But cf. Todd Endelman, *The Jews of Georgian England, 1714–1830* (Philadelphia, 1979), p. 17; Don Pantinkin, "Mercantilism and the Readmission of the Jews to England," *Jewish Social Studies* 8 (1946).

101. Endelman, *Jews of Georgian England*, p. 24.

102. Israel, *Diasporas within a Diaspora*, pp. 389–417; cf. David Katz, *Philosemitism*, p. 29.

103. Clearly he knew his audience, as the statement of Major-General Edward Whalley affirms: "It seems to me that there are both politique and divine reasons; which strongly make theyre admission into a cohabitation and civill commerce with us." Quoted in *Katz, Philosemitism* p. 7.

104. *Menasseh ben Israel's Mission*, p. 81.

105. Ibid., p. 79.

106. Ibid., p. 20.

107. His personal opinion was that the American Indians constituted only a branch of one of the far-flung Tribes. See Richard H. Popkin, "The Rise and Fall of the Jewish Indian Theory," in *Menasseh ben Israel and His World*, edited by Yosef Kaplan, Henry Méchoulan, and Richard H. Popkin (Leiden, New York, København, and Köln, 1989), pp. 68–70.

108. Israel, *Diasporas within a Diaspora*, p. 387.

109. Henry Méchoulan, "Menasseh and the World of the Non-Jew," in Kaplan et al., *Menasseh ben Israel and His World*, p. 86.

110. *Menasseh ben Israel's Mission*, pp. 79, 84–9.

111. Ibid., p. 83.

112. Ibid., p. 82 (Zachariah 14:21).

113. Luzzatto, pp. 104–06; Ravid believes Menasseh did not directly cite Luzzatto because the heavy restrictions Venice imposed on Jewish civic and economic activities provided a poor model for what he hoped to achieve in London; the greater likelihood, however, is that despite extensive Jewish involvement in Venetian trade, the city's economy was in serious decline. See Ravid, "How Profitable the Nation of the Jews Are': *The Humble Addresses* of Menasseh ben Israel and the *Discorso* of Simone Luzzatto," in *Mystics, Philosophers, and Politicians: Essays in Jewish Intellectual History in Honor of Alexander Altmann*, edited by Jehudah Reinhartz and Daniel Swetschinsky (Durham, NC, 1982), p. 170.

114. Melamed, *Ahotan ha-Ketomah*, p. 348.

115. *Menasseh ben Israel's Mission*, p. 89.

116. Ibid., p. 75; In a Hebrew letter written shortly before his journey to England and addressed "to all persons of the Hebrew nation living in Asia and in Europe, especially to the Holy Synagogues of Italy and Holstein, S. P. D.," Menasseh offered a religious-historical rather than political explanation of why a Jewish restoration to England was now possible. "Today this English nation is no longer our ancient enemy, but has changed the papistical religion and become excellently affected to our nation, as an oppressed people whereof it has good hope." In Cecil Roth, ed., *Anglo-Jewish Letters* (London, 1938), pp. 47–48.

117. Luzzatto, pp. 86–87.

118. Melamed, *Ahotan ha-Ketomah*, 328; idem., *The Philosopher King*, p. 136; idem., "Medieval and Renaissance Jewish Political Philosophy," in *History of Jewish Philosophy*, edited by Daniel H. Frank and Oliver Leaman (London, 1997), pp. 415–19.

119. Ibid., p. 77; Menasseh's rhetoric also appears to reflect what Blair Worden has labeled a mid-seventeenth-century "crisis of monarchy," with rebellions raging in France, Portugal, Holland, and the Ukraine. See Blair Worden, "Marchamont Nedham and English Republicanism," in Wootton, *Republicanism*, p. 72.

120. See S. B. Liljegren, *Harrington and the Jews* (Lund, 1932) and the sources cited therein.

121. W. M. Lamont, *Marginal Prynne* (London, 1963).

122. Lawrence Stone, *The Causes of the English Revolution 1529–1642* (New York, 1972), p. 105.

123. Avrom Saltman, *The Jewish Question in 1655: Studies in Prynne's Demurrer* (Ramat-Gan, 1995), p. 83.

124. William Prynne, *A Short Demurrer to the Jews Long Discontinued Rarred Remitter into England* (London, 1656), p. 4.

125. Glenn Burgess, *The Politics of the Ancient Constitution: An Introduction to Enlgish Political Thought, 1603–1642* (University Park, PA, 1992), pp. 92–93; Marjorie Chibnall, *The Debate on the Norman Conquest* (Manchester and New York, 1999), pp. 35–38.

126. Prynne, *A Short Demurrer*, p. 121.

127. Jonathan A. Bush, "'You're Gonna Miss Me When I'm Gone': Early Modern Common Law Discourse and the Case of the Jews, "*Wisconsin Law Review* (September/October 1993), pp. 1225–85.

128. Prynne, *A Short Demurrer*, p. 83.

129. Saltman, *The Jewish Question,* p. 100.
130. J. P. Sommerville, *Politics and Ideology in England, 1603–1640* (London and New York, 1986), p. 59.
131. For other similarities as well as crucial differences, see Worden, "Marchamont Nedham," p. 48.
132. Machiavelli, *Selected Political Writings,* p. 151.
133. Prynne, *A Short Demurrer,* p. 95.
134. Ibid., p. 96.
135. Pocock himself underscores this point by his characterization of royalist political tract, "His Majesty's Answer to the Nineteen Propositions of Parliament," produced in the name of Charles I on the eve of the civil war, as carrying "essentially republican language." See his Introduction to *Harrington,* p. 19.
136. Pocock, *The Machiavellian Moment,* p. 396.
137. Prynne, *A Short Demurrer,* p. 142.
138. Ibid., p. 96.
139. Ibid., p. 119–20.
140. Ibid., p. 122.
141. Ibid., p. 123.
142. Ibid., pp. 122–23.
143. Ibid., p. 136.

2. FROM ANCIENT CONSTITUTION TO MOSAIC REPUBLIC

1. John Toland, *Christianity Not Mysterious* (London, 1696).
2. Heinrich Graetz described the *Reasons* as "... the first word spoken in behalf of [Jews'] emancipation". See his *History of the Jews,* vol. v (Philadelphia, 1895), pp. 197–98; according to Salo W. Baron, its author "was the first to advocate full emancipation..." See his "The Modern Age," in Leo W. Schwarz, *Great Ages and Ideas of the Jewish People* (New York, 1956), p. 319; in Jacob Katz's estimation, Toland "anticipated a social trend that was to emerge at a later date." See Katz, *Out of the Getto: The Social Background of Jewish Emancipation, 1770–1870* (New York, 1978), pp. 39–40; in the opinion of Shmuel Ettinger, "there is hardly an argument that appeared afterwards in Jewish apologia in the eighteenth and nineteenth centuries which was not mentioned by Toland." See Ettinger, "The Beginnings of the Change in the Attitude of European Society towards the Jews," *Scripta Hierosolymitana,* VIII (1961), pp. 218–19; Idem., "Jews and Judaism in the Eyes of the English Deists of the Eighteenth Century" (Hebrew), *Zion,* xxix (1964), p. 257; At the same time, Isaac Barzilay sees it as "puzzling in the context of its times," "in many ways a curious work," whose author's motives are "in themselves unclear." See Barzilay, "John Toland's Borrowings from Simone Luzzatto," *Jewish Social Studies,* vol. xxxi, no. 2 (April, 1969), p. 75. In Herbert Mainusch's estimation, the pamphlet exists out of time, for it cannot be "connected with any definite [political] happenings." See Mainusch, "Einleitung" to John Toland, *Gründe für die Einbürgerung der Juden in Grossbritanien und Irland,* edited and translated by idem. (Stuttgart, 1965), p. 21. And Todd Endelman regards Toland's own ideological intentions as irrelevant because the author wrote merely as "a literary hack in the pay of various political figures." See Endelman *The Jews of Georgian England* (Oxford, 1978), pp. 26–27. Justin Champion similarly formulates

this interpretive divergence in his "Toleration and Citizenship in Enlightenment England: John Toland and the Naturalization of the Jews, 1714–1753," in *Toleration in Enlightenment Europe*, edited by Ole Peter Grell and Roy Porter (Cambridge, 2000), p. 133.

3. Recent scholarship has partially rectified this confusion by clarifying some of the work's philosophical bases. Justin Champion has advanced our understanding of Toland's convoluted literary stratagems, into which *Reasons* no doubt fits, whereas Silvia Berti has endeavored to situate *Reasons* in the framework of his various other writings about Jews. Yet despite these efforts, the task of connecting Toland's *Reasons* to the broader history of Jewish political economy and to specific party politics of early Augustan Britain remains incomplete. See Justin Champion, "Toleration and Citizenship," pp. 133–56; idem., *John Toland and the Crisis of Christian Culture, 1696–1722* (Manchester, UK, 2003); Silvia Berti, "At the Roots of Unbelief," *Journal of the History of Ideas*, vol. 56, no. 4 (October, 1995), pp. 555–75.

4. It is true that Toland allowed Jews to be excluded from holding high offices, yet even here one detects only a half-hearted concession current to political realities. On Toland's early life and career, see Stephen H. Daniel, *John Toland, His Methods, Manners, and Mind* (Kingston, ON, 1984), pp. 5–10.

5. Two partial exceptions are Ettinger, "The Beginnings of the Change," and Berti, "At the Roots of Unbelief," pp. 568–70. Both articles note the connection in suggestive but brief and passing remarks.

6. The best example – and one of the harshest modern accounts – is Paul Hazard, *The European Mind* (London, 1973), pp. 176–80.

7. See J. A. Downie, *Robert Harley and the Press: Propaganda and Public Opinion in the Age of Swift and Defoe* (Cambridge, 1979).

8. Robert Reese Evans, *Pantheisticon: The Career of John Toland* (New York, 1991).

9. Champion, among others, assumes the Calves-Head Club was the fantastical invention of a Tory pamphleteer, Ned Ward. See Champion, *John Toland*, p. 86. Robert E. Sullivan notes the dubiousness of the source for Toland's participation in this "Calves Head Club" ritual, "that Grub Street perennial 'Ned' Ward," without, however, dismissing the account altogether, see *John Toland and the Deist Controversy* (Cambridge, MA, 1982), pp. 14–15. For less skeptical views, see William Kolbrener, "'Commonwealth Fictions' and 'Inspiration Fraud': Milton and the *Eikon Basilike* after 1689," *Milton Studies*, 37 (1999), p. 168 and Michael Mendle's H-Albion review of Andrew Lacey, *The Cult of King Charles the Martyr*. Studies in Modern British Religious History Series. (Woodbridge and Suffolk, UK, 2003). Available at: http://www.h-net.org/reviews/showrev.cgi?path=255891083547450.

10. The structure and rites of the society are presented in Toland's *Pantheisticon. Sive Formula celebrandae sodalitatis Socraticae, in tres particulas divisa; quae pantheistarum, sive sodalium, continent I, Mores et axiomata: II, Numen et philosophiam: III, Libertatem, et non fallentem legem, neque fallendam. Praemittitur de antiquis et novis eruditorum sodalitatibus, ut et de universo infinito et aeterno, diatriba. Subjicitur de duplici pantheistarum philosophia sequendi, ac de viri optimi et ornatissimi idea, dissertatiuncula* (London, 1720). In 1751, an English translation was published in London by M. Cooper under the title *Pantheisticon: or, The form of celebrating the Socratic-society*. As with the Calves-Head Club, Toland's participation in many of these societies remains a matter of historical debate. The strongest proponent of Toland's

proto-Freemasonry, is Margaret C. Jacob, *Living the Enlightenment: Freemasongry and Politics in Eighteenth-Century Europe* (New York and Oxford, 1991), pp. 66–67, 91–95; for contrary views, see Chiara Giuntini, *Panteismo e ideologia republicana: John Toland (1670–1722)*, pp. 483–85 and Sullivan, *John Toland and the Deist Controversy*, pp. 201–04.

11. See Wootton's Introduction to his *Republicanism, Liberty, and Commercial Society*, pp. 29–31. For a further instance of a possible Toland's "semi-forgery," see Blair Worden, "Whig History and Puritan Politics: The *Memoirs* of Edmund Ludlow Revisited," in *Historical Research*, vol. 75, no. 188 (May 2000), pp. 209–37.

12. Margaret Jacobs, "John Toland and the Newtonian Ideology," *Journal of Warburg and Courtauld Institute*, XXXII (1969), pp. 307–31.

13. Speaker of the House of Commons 1701–1705; 1704–1708: Secretary of State 1710–1714 Chancellor of the Exchequer. Only in the period 1708–1709 was Harley out of governmental power. See Downie, *Robert Harley and the Press*, passim.

14. Champion, *John Toland and the Crisis of Christian Culture*, p. 134.

15. Evans, *Pantheisticon*, pp. 174–75; Downie, *Roberty Harley*, pp. 43–44.

16. John Toland, *Tetradymus* (London, n.d.), title page; on the influence of Giordano Bruno's hermeticism on Toland, see Stephen H. Daniel, *John Toland*, p. 10; Evans, *Pantheisticon*, p. 117; Sullivan, *John Toland and the Deist Controversy*, pp. 198–202. Champion, rather unaccountably, rejects the application of an esoteric/exoteric duality to Toland as an oversimplification of his work and one that reifies an "authentic" Toland behind the constructed exterior. Rather, one might say that recognizing this duality is necessary but insufficient to distinguishing, to the best degree possible, Toland's ends and means. The duality can be traced back as early as Toland's 1704 *Letters to Serena*. See Champion, *John Toland and the Crisis of Christian Culture*, p. 231.

17. J. R. Jones, *Country and Court England, 1658–1714* (Cambridge, MA, 1979), pp. 273–74.

18. See David Hayton, "The 'Country' Interest and the Party System, 1689–1720," in *Party and Management in Parliament, 1660–1784*, edited by Clyve Jones (New York, 1984), pp. 37–85.

19. On these themes, see also Pocock, *The Machiavellian Moment*, pp. 423–61.

20. Evans, *Pantheisticon*, p. 128; Pierre Des Maizeaux, ed., *A Collection of Several Pieces of Mr. John Toland*, vol. II (London, 1726), p. 223.

21. The Act states that "no person born out of the kingdoms of England, Scotland, or Ireland, or the dominions thereunto belonging (although he be naturalized or made a denizen), except such as are born of English parents, shall be capable to be of the Privy Council, or a member of either House of Parliament, or enjoy any office or place of trust, either civil or military, or to have any grant of lands, tenements, or hereditaments from the Crown to himself, or to any other or others in trust for him." See *English Historical Documents, 1660–1714*, edited by Andrew Browning (London, 1953). pp. 129–34

22. J. H. Plumb, *Sir Robert Walpole: The Making of a Statesman* (Cambridge, MA, 1956), pp. 95–96.

23. Cecil Roth, *A History of the Jews in England*, 3rd edition (Oxford, 1978), p. 213.

24. John Toland, "Reasons for Naturalizing the Jews in Great Britain and Ireland," in Paul Rudin, *Pamphlets Relating to Jews in England during the Seventeenth and Eighteenth Centuries* (San Francisco, 1939), p. 44.

25. John Toland, *State-Anatomy of Great Britain* (London, 1717), pp. 55–56.
26. H. T. Dickinson, "The Poor Palatines and the Parties," *English Historical Review*, vol. lxxxi (1967) pp. 464–85.
27. Toland, *State-Anatomy*, p. 56.
28. Giancarlo Carabelli dates the publication of *Reasons* between October 1 and December 1, 1714. See Carabelli, *Tolandiana: materiali bibliographici per lo studio dell'opera e della fortuna di John Toland* (Florence, 1975), pp. 188–89. The effort to sponsor the Palatines was only the latest in a series of bills proposing the naturalization of foreign Protestants..." Earlier efforts were made in 1667, 1672, 1680, and 1694. See Thomas W. Perry, *Public Opinion, Propaganda, and politics in Eighteenth-Century England; a Study of the Jew Bill of 1753* (Cambridge, 1962), p. 31, n. 22. The possibility exists that Toland wrote *Reasons* at least in part considerably earlier and only published it in 1714. Toland himself refers in his *Reasons* to Luzzatto's *Discorso* as a work "written above 60 years ago," which would suggest that he was writing sometime between 1698 and 1708. Barzilay suggests the Toland may not have had the text of the *Discorso* in front of him when he wrote and misremembered, a possibility that cannot be verified. See Barzilay, "Borrowings," p. 76, n. 9. More decisive are Toland's allusions in *Reasons* to his support for recent legislation supporting Protestant naturalization but defeated by the Tories, suggesting that the pamphlet was written sometime after 1712. The overarching point, however, is that he published the work at a moment of maximal optimism for a future Whig polity.
29. This is emphasized by Barzilay, "John Toland's Borrowings," p. 78, who calls attention to Toland's "mercantilist" thinking. In contrast, Endelman, *The Jews of Georgian England*, sees him as one of the earliest exponents of "liberal capitalist thought" on the Jewish Question. See p. 213.
30. On early "populationist" doctrines see Terence Hutchison, *Before Adam Smith: The Emergence of Political Economy, 1662–1776* (Oxford, 1988), pp. 38, 249–50; Joseph Schumpeter, *History of Economic Analysis*, edited by Elizabeth Boody Schumpeter (New York, 1954), notes that, from about the sixteenth to the middle of the eighteenth century, economists "were as nearly unanimous in this 'populationist' attitude as they have ever been in anything," p. 251.
31. Quoted in Dickinson, "The Poor Palatines," p. 474.
32. Toland, "Reasons," in Rudin, *Pamphlets*, p. 58.
33. Ibid., p. 58.
34. As Barzilay noted, Toland refers in his *Reasons* to Luzzatto's *Discorso* as a work "written above 60 years ago." Barzilay conjectures that Toland's error (the *Discorso* was published in 1638, that is, seventy-six years before the *Reasons*) was because "Toland, while writing this, did not have the *Discorso* in front of him, or that some years separate its actual writing and publication." Barzilay, "John Toland's Borrowings,' p. 76, n. 9. Evans states that an early and partial formulation of the Mosaic Republic appeared in Toland's 1701 *Limitations for the Next Foreign Successor*, thus published some sixty-three years after the *Discourse*. Evans, *Pantheisticon*, p. 169. In 1695, Toland had translated the Italian Bernardo Davanzati's *A Disourse on Trade* (on behalf of John Locke and in light of contemporary debates over the proposed recoinage). It is thus possible that Toland had come across Luzzatto's *Discorso* when he was researching Italian commercial treatises and that his dating of Luzzatto as it appears in the *Reasons* was culled from an initial set of notes he had taken on the *Discorso* sometime between 1699 and 1701.

35. Barzilay, "Borrowings,"
36. Toland, "Reasons," in Rudin, *Pamphlets*, p. 48.
37. Ibid., p. 60.
38. In citing the similarities between Luzzatto and Toland, Barzilay neglects to distinguish the intentions, see Barzilay, "Borrowings," p. 81.
39. See Melinda S. Zook, *Radical Whigs and Conspiratorial Politics in Late Stuart England* (University Park, PA, 1999), p. xvi. For an opposing view, one reasserting the influence of Locke if not on Toland than on some of his commonwealthmen contemporaries, see Michael Zuckert, *Natural Rights and the New Republicanism* (Princeton, NJ, 1994).
40. Toland, "Reasons," in Rudin, *Pamphlets*, p. 48.
41. McNally, *Political Economy*, p. 46. Between 1641 and 1703, the amount of Irish land in Catholic hands had fallen from 59 to 14 percent. J. G. Simms, *The Williamite Confiscation in Ireland, 1690–1703* (London, 1956), p. 195.
42. J. G. Simms, *The Williamite Confiscation in Ireland*, p. 195.
43. Toland, *State-Anatomy*, p. 19. The idea of a mercantile colonization of Ireland by Jews was first broached in 1607 by the adventurer Thomas Shirley in a proposal to James I. See Edgar R. Samuel, "Sir Thomas Shirley's Project for the Jews – The Earliest Known Proposal for the Resettlement," in *Transactions of the Jewish Historical Society of England*, vol. xxiv (Spring, 1975), pp. 195–97. Sir William Temple had recommended colonizing Catholic lands with productive and loyal Protestants as early as 1673. Istvan Hont, "Free Trade and the Economic Limits to National Politics: Neo-Machiavellian Political Economy Revisited," in *The Economic Limits to Modern Politics*, edited by John Dunn (Cambridge, 1990), pp. 52–55.
44. John Toland, *Reasons for Naturalizing the Jews in Great Britain and Ireland* (London, 1714), p. 6.
45. Ibid., pp. 6–7. ·
46. Toland, "Reasons," in Rudin, *Pamphlets*, p. 49.
47. Evans, *Pantheisticon*, p. 128; Pierre Des Maizeaux, ed., *A Collection of Several Pieces of Mr. John Toland*, vol. II (London, 1726), p. 223.
48. Toland believed the Treaty's "secret provisions" included the restoration of the "Old Pretender," James Francis Edward Stuart. J. G. Simms, "John Toland (1670–1722), a Donegal Heretic," in idem., *War and Politics in Ireland 1649–1730* (London, 1986), p. 42.
49. See previous note. In actuality, Bolingbroke wanted the Pretender to succeed Queen Anne but only if he converted to Anglicanism, something James refused to do. See Plumb, *Sir Robert Walpole*, pp. 188–89.
50. *The Oceana of James Harrington and his other Work* (London, 1700).
51. James Harrington, *The Political Works of James Harrington*, ed. J. G. A. Pocock (Cambridge, 1977), p. 14.
52. Ibid., pp. 158–59.
53. Ibid., p. 158.
54. Ibid., p. 159.
55. Ibid.
56. Harrington, *The Political Works*, p. 114.
57. Toland was even prepared to allow Jews to occupy fiscal offices, such as those of the Exchequer, Customs, Excise, City of London and East India Company directorships,

and cited the long tradition of Jewish courtiers as precedent; see Toland, "Reasons," in Rudin, *Pamphlets*, p. 60.

58. In this light, Pocock's thesis that Harrington contravened Machiavelli's fatalistic view of corruption by locating its source in sociological circumstances, that is, the opportunity for landownership, rather than exclusively in human nature, seems to fit Toland's approach to Jewish regeneration. See Pocock, *The Ancient Constitution and the Feudal Law: A Study of English Historical Thought in the Seventeenth Century* (New York, 1967), pp. 146–47. Toland may be said to have applied Harrington's precepts more consistently to the Jews than had Harrington himself.

59. For Harrington the Mosaic commonwealth was "a true classical republic," one governed by laws and one in which the people elected the clergy. A theocracy is in this sense a republic in which citizens are sovereign under God, see Pocock, *Machiavellian*, p. 398; Pocock, "Introduction," *The Political Works of James Harrington*, pp. 80–81.

60. Cornelius Bonaventure Bertram, *De Politia Judaeorum, tam Civilis quam Eccksiatica iam inde a suis primordiis, hoc est ab Orbe Condito* (Geneva, 1574); Carlo Sigonio, *De republica Hebraeorum* (Bologna, 1582); Petrus Cuneaus, *De republica Hebraeorum* (Leiden, 1617). See Kalman Neuman, *The Literature of the Respublica Judaica: Depictions of the Ancient Hebrew State in the Antiquarian Writings of the Sixteenth and Seventeenth Centuries* (Hebrew) (Ph.D. Dissertation, Hebrew University, 2002); idem., "Political Hebraism and the Early Modern 'Respublica Hebraeorum': On Defining the Field," *Hebraic Political Studies*, vol. 1, no. 1 (Fall, 2005), pp. 57–70; Jonathan R. Ziskind, "Cornelius Bertram and Carlo Sigonio: Christian Hebraism's First Political Scientists, *Journal of Ecumenical Studies* (Summer–Fall 2000), pp. 321–32; Frank Manuel, *The Broken Staff: Judaism through Christian Eyes* (Cambridge, MA, 1992), pp. 121–27. Lea Campos Boraleva, "Classical Foundational Myths of European Republicanism: The Jewish Commonwealth," in *Republicanism, a Shared European Heritage*, vol. 1, edited by Martin Van Gelderen and Quentin Skinner (Cambridge, 2002), pp. 247–62.

61. See Melamed, *The Philosopher-King*, pp. 141–66.

62. Harrington, *Political Works*, 616–17.

63. Ibid., p. 632.

64. Ibid., pp. 648–49.

65. Quoted in Simms, "John Toland," p. 39.

66. John Toland, "Appendix" to *Nazarenus or Jewish, Gentile, and Mohametan Christianity* (London, 1718), pp. 7–8; the "Appendix" took the form of a letter written by Toland in The Hague on October 16, 1709. See Ettinger, "Beginnings," p. 216. On the background to and theology of *Nazarenus*, see Gesine Palmer, *Ein Freispruch für Paulus: John Tolands Theorie des Judenchristentums* (Berlin, 1996).

67. Champion suggests Toland may not even have started it but here, as on other occasions, was "merely circulating the idea of a text." Yet clearly Toland had done much of the preparatory work for such an undertaking and was intellectually committed to it. See Champion, *John Toland and the Crisis of Christian Culture*, pp. 49–50.

68. Toland, "Reasons," in Rudin, *Pamphlets*, p. 62.

69. This seems to me to go well beyond Maimonides classic distinction between the "welfare of the [social] body" (*tikkun ha-guf*) and of the soul (*tikkun ha-nefesh*). See B. Netanyahu, *Don Isaac Abravanel* (Philadelphia, 1982), pp. 158–94.

70. A trace of this idea is already found in the prerabbinic *Jubilees* 7:20–21; the earliest appearance in a rabbinic work is Tosefta to Avodah Zarah 8.4; the laws are later elaborated in the Babylonian Talmud, Sanhedrin 56b. See David Novak, *The Image of the Non-Jew in Judaism: An Historical and Constructive Study of the Noahide Laws* (Toronto, 1983), pp. 6–35 and passim.

71. Medieval rabbis differed on various constructions of this position but all shared it in essence. Full Noahide status required revelation, not merely natural law or deduction by reason. See Jacob Katz, *Halakhah ve-Kabbalah* (Hebrew) (Jerusalem: Hebrew University Press, 1984), pp. 270–74; idem., *Exlusiveness and Tolerance: Studies in Jewish-Gentile Relations in Medieval and Modern Times* (West Orange, NJ, 1961), pp. 172–79; Novak, *The Image of the Non-Jew*, pp. 355–56. Cf. Steven S. Schwarzschild, "Do Noachites have to Believe in Revelation," *The Jewish Quarterly Review*, 52 (1961–1962), pp. 296–306 and 53 (1962–1963), pp. 30–65.

72. On similar ideas held by the Dutch Sephardic Rabbi Elijah Morteira, see Adam Sutcliffe, *Judaism and Enlightenment* (Cambridge, 2003), p. 109 and the references there.

73. Luzzatto, *Discourse*, section xiii, p. 113. This passage is also discussed in Bernard Septimus, "Biblical Religion and Political Rationality in Simone Luzzatto, Maimonides and Spinoza," in *Jewish Thought in the Seventeenth Century*, edited by Isadore Twersky and Bernard Septimus (Cambridge, 1987), p. 428.

74. Moses Mendelssohn's classic defense of Jewish "revealed legislation," like that of Toland, was clearly influenced as much by Luzzatto's positive interpretation as by the far more hostile one of Spinoza, despite almost exclusive scholarly emphasis on the latter. See Moses Mendelssohn, *Jerusalem, or, on Religious Power in Judaism*, edited by Alexander Altmann, translated by Allan Arkush (Hanover, NH and London, 1983), pp. 89–95, 127–33. Of course, Mendelssohn diverged from all his predecessors in insisting on the noncoercive nature of Judaism with regard to the policing of its members' praxis.

75. Reid Barbour, *John Selden: Measures of the Holy Commonwealth in Seventeenth-Century England* (Toronto, 2003), pp. 50–51; in his writings Toland cites Selden with great respect, but this is not necessarily determinative of influence. Cf. Jason P. Rosenblatt, *Renaissance England's Chief Rabbi: John Selden* (Oxford, 2006), 272–73.

76. John Toland, *Adeisidaemon, sive Titus Livius a superstitione vindicatus. Annexae sunt ejusdem Origines Judaicae.* (The Hague, 1709; reprint Amsterdam, 1970); Sutcliffe, *Judaism and Enlightenment*, pp. 199–200; Champion, *John Toland*, 174–77.

77. Menahem Stern, *Greek and Latin Authors on Jews and Judaism* (Jerusalem, 1974), pp. 299–300.

78. Michael Palmer, *Adeisidaemon, Vernunft zwischen Atheism und Aberglauben: Materialismus und Commonwealth bei John Toland.* Ph.D. dissertation (University of Berlin, 2002), p. 108.

79. Jan Assmann, *Moses the Egyptian: The Memory of Egypt in Western Monotheism* (Cambridge, MA, 1997), pp. 93–97.

80. Toland, *Adeisidaemon*, pp. 157–58.

81. Spinoza, *Theological-Political Treatise*, translated by Samuel Shirley (Indianapolis, 1998), pp. 189–90.

82. See Champion, *John Toland*, pp. 170–85; Palmer, *Adeisidaemon*.

83. On Toland's equation of theism and superstition, see his *Adeisidaemon* and its skillful exposition in Palmer, *Adeisidaemon*, pp. 94–105.

84. Spinoza attempted to explain the Jews' preservation entirely through naturalistic means. His ambiguous statement that "They are preserved largely through the hatred of other nations…," refers to both the enmity of non-Jews *and* Jewish misanthropy and self-isolation, the latter enforced through customs such as *kashrut* and circumcision. This contrasts sharply with Toland's praise of the Jews' timeless constitution. See Spinoza, *Theological-Political Treatise, p. 45*.

85. Toland, *State-Anatomy*, pp. 21–22.

86. Jones, *Country and Court*;, pp. 171–209.

87. Jim Smyth, *The Making of the United Kingdom, 1660–1800* (New York, 2001), p. 69.

88. Diarmaid MacCulloch, *The Reformation* (New York, 2003), pp. 646–47.

89. Jones, *Country and Court*, pp. 258–59.

90. Quoted in Evans, *Pantheisticon*, p. 91. None of this is to deny, of course, that Toland's anti-Catholic rhetoric was equally or perhaps primarily directed at High Church Tories of the Sacheverell variety. Toland supported membership in the Anglican Church because he recognized the utility of a prevailing civic religion, while at the same time striving to make Anglicanism as much a "big tent" as possible. See J. A. I. Champion, *The Pillars of Priestcraft Shaken* (Cambridge, 1992), pp. 194–95.

91. In the *State-Anatomy*, Toland defined as "Protestant" any group opposing Catholicism, including Jews; see Evans, *Pantheisticon*, pp. 183–84.

92. Champion, *The Pillars of Priestcraft*, pp. 53–98.

93. Toland, "Reasons," Sig. A4; On supposed Jewish connections to the history of Scotland of Scotland, see Arthur H. Williamson, "'A Pil for Pork-Eaters': Ethnic Identity, Apocalyptic Promises, and the Strange Creation of the Judeo-Scots," in *The Expulsion of the Jews: 1492 and After*, edited by Raymond B. Waddington and A. H. Williamson (New York, 1994), pp. 237–58.

94. Toland, *Nazarenus*, p. 77.

95. According to Toland, it is evident from canonical and noncanonical gospels, "… that all the Jews which became Christians were still zealous for the Levitical Law. This Law they looked upon to be no less national and political, than religious and sacred: that is to say, expressive of the history of their peculiar nation, essential to the being of their Theocracy or Republic, and aptly commemorating whatever befell their ancestors or their State; which, not regarding other people, they did not think then bound by the same, however indispensably subject to the Law of Nature." *Ibid.,* p. 38.

96. Ibid., p. 16.

97. Toland, *Appendix*, p. 2.

98. Ibid.

99. See Blair Worden, "James Harrington," in Wootton, ed., *Republicanism*, p. 102; J. P. Kenyon, *Stuart England*, 2nd edition (London, 1990), pp. 185–87.

100. In *The Grand Mystery Laid Open*, published only half a year before the "Reasons," Toland openly expressed his sense of panic and despair. See J. P. Kenyon, *Revolution Principles: The Politics of Party, 1689–1720* (Cambridge, 1977), pp. 156–68.

101. In 1711, at a low point in Whig political fortunes, Toland's old fellow commonwealthman Robert Molesworth demanded an extension of Whigism not just to

Scotland and Ireland, but "were it in our power," to France itself, see Kenyon, *Revolution Principles*, pp. 156–58.

102. The same association between "Whig" and "Jew" would resurface, on both sides of the Jew Bill debate, in 1753–1754. See Perry, *Public Opinion*, p. 74.

103. Toland, *Appendix*, p. 1.

104. John Toland, *State-Anatomomy*, p. 10.

105. Toland, "Appendix," p. 8.

106. On the seventeenth-century background, see Nabil Matar, "The Idea of the Restoration of the Jews in English Protestant Thought: Between the Reformation and 1660," *Durham*, pp. 25–26. Matar's depiction of Toland as rejecting the Jews' restoration to Palestine in favor of their integration into Europe is inaccurate, a further example of the tendency of scholars to fit Toland into a narrow conception of Enlightenment liberalism. See Matar, "The Controversy over the Restoration of the Jews in English Protestant Thought, 1701–1753," *Durham University Journal* 80 (1988), pp. 248–49. Nevertheless, in Toland's *Hodegus*, a work devoted to a secular but mostly favorable treatment of the Hebrew Bible, Toland dismissed the conventional millenarian legend of the Ten Tribes while affirming his philosemitism. "Finally, the Jews expect, that, upon the future return of the twelve Tribes, at the coming of their MESSIAH, from all the countries where they are dispers'd; this [miraculous] *Cloud* will again precede them to the holy land, which I wish them a good journey: tho, during the time of their waiting, I am farr from being weary of their company here; where they are most useful subjects, and many of 'em my very good friends." Contained in *Tetradymos* (London, 1720), p. 43.

107. Although he rejects the term "philosemitism," Matar provides a generally excellent analysis of English millenarian proto-Zionism. See N. I. Matar, "The Idea of the Restoration of the Jews in English Protestant Thought, from the Reformation to 1660," *Durham University Journal*, 78 (1985), pp. 23–36.

108. I do not mean to suggest that the views of Dohm, Grégoire, Clermont-Tonnerre, and others associated with the later drive for Jewish emancipation were entirely free of "millenarian" or biblicist political notions. After all, the demand for the Jews' *regénération* seems to suggest the kind of restoration Toland had in mind. But *regénération* was conceived of as a liberation of nature from history and was applied not just to the Jews but to French society as a whole. At any rate, the question of the Jews' capacity for allegiance and service to the state was what overwhelmingly concerned the participants in the emancipation debates. In this light, Judaism as a religious and political regime was viewed as a key obstacle. Although Jews were not asked to renounce their creed, which would have been a violation of article 10 of the "Declaration of the Rights of Man and of the Citizen," it was expected that the *political* component of their religion be negated.

3. A NEW SYSTEM OF CIVIL AND COMMERCIAL GOVERNMENT

1. See Thomas Perry, *Public Opinion, Propaganda, and Politics in Eighteenth-Century England; a Sudy of the Jew Bill of 1753* (Cambridge, MA, 1962), pp. 81–86.

2. Philo-Patriae, *Considerations of the Bill to Permit Persons Professing the Jewish Religion to be Naturalized by Parliament, in Several Letters from a Merchant in Town to his Friend in the Country, wherein the Motives of all Parties interested therein are*

examined; *The Principles of Christianity, with Regard to the Admission of Jews, are fully discussed; and their Utility in Trade clearly Proved* (London, 1753), pp. 3, 5.

3. Holmes and Szechi conclude that it was Whig leader Henry Pelham who in reality outfoxed the Tories: "The Jewish Naturalization Act of 1753 briefly threatened to raise a popular clamour which they could have exploited in the traditional role as the defenders of the Church, but Pelham defused the issue by calmly allowing the act to be repealed." See Geoffrey Holmes and Daniel Szechi, *The Age of Oligarchy: Pre-Industrial Britain, 1722–1784* (London, 1993), p. 268.

4. Josiah Tucker, *The Elements of Commerce* (1754), p. 38; compare Tucker's remarks with those uttered by the Earl Temple in the debate of the November 1753 repeal of the Act: "I believe the clamour was chiefly if not entirely owing to the act happening unluckily to get a wrong title; for if instead calling it an act for permitting the Jews to be naturalized, it had been entitled an act to prevent the profanation for the holy sacrament of the Lord's Supper, I believe, no objection would have been made to it, but on the contrary every man would have applauded our zeal for the honour of the religion we profess…" William Cobbett, *Parliamentary History of England from the Earliest Period to the Year 1803*, vol. XV (London, 1813), p. 110.

5. George Shelton, *Dean Tucker and Eighteenth-Century Economic and Political Thought* (London, 1981), pp. 70, 84.

6. For example, the speeches of Henry Pelham, Horace Walpole, and William Northey in Cobbett, *Parliamentary History*, vol. XV, pp. 143, 147, and 152. See also Perry, *Public Opinion*, pp. 28, 157–58.

7. Perry, *Public Opinion*, p. 74.

8. On the decline in Whig support after the "Excise Crisis," see Paul Langford, *A Polite and Commercial People: England 1727–1783* (Oxford, 1989), p. 33; on the decline in Tory electoral fortunes, see Holmes and Szechi, *The Age of Oligarchy*, p. 37.

9. See, for example, the Duke of Bedford's attack on the bill in Cobbett, *Parliamentary History*, vol. 15, p. 109.

10. Ibid., pp. 37–42, 267–69; Pocock, *The Machiavellian Moment*, pp. 477–86.

11. Isaac Kramnick, *Bolingbroke and his Circle: The Politics of Nostalgia in the Age of Walpole* (Ithaca, NY, and London, 1992), p. 6.

12. See, for example, Isaac Kramnick, *Republicanism and Bourgeois Radicalism: Political Ideology in Late Eighteenth-Century England and America* (Ithaca, NY, 1990); for one of the earliest such critiques, see Ralph Lerner, "Commerce and Character: The Anglo-American as New-Model Man," *The William and Mary Quarterly* 36 (January 1979). On the backdrop of undeniable commercial prosperity, see Neil McKendrick, John Brewer, and J. H. Plumb, *Birth of a Consumer Society: The Commercialization of Eighteenth-Century England* (Bloomington, IN, 1982), pp. 19–23.

13. Paul A. Rahe, "Antiquity Surpassed: The Repudiation of Classical Republicanism," in Wootton, ed., *Republicanism*, p. 242.

14. David Hume, *Writings on Economics*, edited by Eugene Rotwein (Madison, WI, 1955), p. 24. See also M. M. Goldsmith, "Liberty, Virtue, and the Rule of Law, 1689–1770," in Wootton, ed., *Republicanism*, pp. 197–232 and Fania Oz-Salzburger, "The Political Theory of the Scottish Enlightenment," in *The Cambridge Companion to the Scottish Enlightenment*, edited by Alexander Broadie (Cambridge, 2003), p. 166.

15. Quoted in Kramnick, *Bolingbroke*, p. 28.

16. McKendrick, Brewer, and Plumb, *Birth of a Consumer Society*, pp. 199, 229.

17. Lord Bolingbroke, *Contributions to the Craftsman*, edited by Simon Varey (Oxford, 1982), p. 33.
18. Geoffrey Holmes, *Politics in the Age of Queen Anne* (New York, 1967), p. 167.
19. Bolingbroke *Contributions*, p. 34.
20. John Brewer, *The Sinews of Power, War, Money and the English State, 1688–1783* (Cambridge, MA, 1988), pp. 206–07.
21. Bolingbroke *Contributions*, pp. 57–58.
22. Perry, *Public Opinion*, pp. 82–83.
23. See Cobbett, *Parliamentary History*, vol. XV, pp. 128–29.
24. Cobbett, *Parliamentary History*, vol. XIV, 1384–87.
25. Cobbett, Parliamentary History, vol. XV, p. 109; "Old England," in *A Collection of the Best Pieces in prose and verse against the naturalization of the Jews* (n.a., London, 1753), p. 11.
26. *A Collection of the Best Pieces*, preface.
27. Joseph Grove, *A reply to the famous Jew question: in which, from the public records and other undoubted authorities, is fully demonstrated ... that the Jews born here before the late act were never intitled to purchase and hold lands to them and their heirs ... In a letter to the gentleman of Lincoln's Inn*, p. 16; *Collection of the Best Pieces*, pp. 15–16.
28. Jonas Hanway, *A review of the proposed naturalization of the Jews being a dispassionate enquiry into the present state of the case: with some reflexions on general naturalization* (London, 1753), p. 75 (emphasis in original).
29. This is not to deny that there were other notable and effective combatants. As prime minister, Henry Pelham, though an able pamphleteer and expert in financial matters, had confined himself parliamentary speeches and behind-the-scenes maneuvering. Philo-Patriae, whose identity still eludes historians, proved an effective mouthpiece for the government. The learned Philip Carteret Webb produced two meticulous apologies for the Jewish cause (having been hired by the London Jewish community to do so) whose dry erudition was unequal to, or made irrelevant by, the strident polemics arrayed against him. On the other side of the debate, Jonas Hanway was an experienced merchant with a lively pen and puritanical views. But beyond the countless crude and witty scribblers for the London Evening Post or anonymous literary henchmen such as "Old England," only Joseph Grove (to be discussed below) combined impressive historical command with at least a semblance of Tucker's literary skill. Jonas Hanway, *Letters admonitory and argumentative, from J. H − −y, merchant, to J. S − − r, merchant in reply to particular passages, and the general argument, of a pamphlet, entitled, Further considerations on the bill, &c.* (London, 1753); idem., *A review of the proposed naturalization of the Jews*; Philip Carteret Webb, *The question, whether a Jew born within the British Dominions was, before the making the late act of Parliament, a person capable by law to purchase and hold lands to him and his heirs, fairly stated and considered* (London, 1753, reprint New York, 1978).
30. Josiah Tucker, *A Second Letter to a Friend Concerning Naturalizations* (London, 1753), p. 4.
31. Josiah Tucker, *A Second Letter*, p. 5.
32. Ibid., p. 10.
33. Ibid., p. 9.

34. Pocock, *The Machiavellian Moment*, pp. 415–16.
35. Ibid., p. 404.
36. J. G. A. Pocock, *Virtue, Commerce, and History* (Cambridge, 1985), p. 176; Worden, "James Harrington," in Wootton, ed., *Republicanism*, pp. 83, 141, 151–52. For a modification of "Neo-Harringtonianism," see Alan Houston, "Republicanism, the Politics of Necessity, and the Rule of Law," in Alan Houston and Steve Pincus, eds., *A Nation Transformed: England after the Restoration* (Cambridge, 2001), p. 257.
37. Pocock, *The Ancient Constitution*, pp. 207; Chibnall, *The Debate on the Norman Conquest*, pp. 42–43.
38. For Bolingbroke, armed uprisings and Jacobite threats were the overblown pretexts of Whig apologists employed to explain away the true constitutional threat represented by governmental corruption and usurpation. See David Armitage's "Introduction" to Bolingbroke, *Political Writings* (Cambridge, 1997), pp. xv–xvi.
39. Kramnick, *Bolingbroke*, pp. 178–79.
40. Smith, *The Wealth of Nations*, pp. 420–46; Pocock notes the much earlier case of Andrew Fletcher's 1698 *A Discourse of Governmnet with Relation to Militias*, where the Renaissance revival of arts led to a multiplication of cultural and material wants in the hearts of independent Gothic freeholders, with ultimately self-destructive consequences. Fletcher, however, was not discussing economic development per se, but, rather, the circumstances that led to the unfortunate replacement of the civic militias with a centralized standing army. See Pocock, *The Political Works of James Harrington*, p. 139.
41. Kramnick, *Bolingbroke*, pp. 133–34.
42. *Ibid.*, pp. 122–23.
43. Tucker devoted a large portion of his *Reflections* to detailing the historical record of English xenophobia. See pp. 56–69.
44. Tucker, *Second Letter*, pp. 10–11.
45. Tucker, *Second Letter*, p. 11.
46. Because Gothic law demanded the fealty of each to his superior, the Jews, according to Tucker, had to substitute their own persons for the military service they would otherwise have provided as armed vassals of the Crown. See ibid., p. 12.
47. Tucker, *Second Letter*, p. 26.
48. Ibid., p. 12.
49. Joseph Grove, *Reply*, p. 10.
50. Ibid., p. 70.
51. Gavin Langmuir, "'Judei nostri' and the Beginning of Capetian Legislation." *Traditio* 16 (1960), p. 203–40, esp. p. 206; idem., "The Jews and the Archives of Angevin England: Reflections on Medieval Anti-Semitism," *Traditio* 19 (1963), pp. 183–244. The concept has roots in canon law but in various forms appears in law codes throughout Europe. A good summary statement is from fifteenth-century Magdeburg: "As subjects of the princes Jews enjoy no rights except those bestowed upon them by princes." Quoted in Guido Kisch, *The Jews in Medieval Germany: A Study of Their Legal and Social Status* (Chicago, 1949), p. 168.
52. Joseph Grove, *Reply*, pp. 65–66.
53. Tucker, *Second Letter*, p. 14.
54. Ibid.

55. What Tucker did not acknowledge was that the corporations' influence owed much to the Whig-dominated legal system itself. As an admirer of Robert Walpole, Tucker elided the fact that the "Robinocracy" had enjoyed the support of the major chartered trading companies – a fact that had never escaped Bolingbroke himself. Thus the break with the ancient constitution established by the Glorious Revolution was not as clear-cut as Tucker made out.

56. Tucker, *Second Letter*, pp. 36–37.

57. Ibid.

58. Ibid.

59. "And then I leave it to your own judgment to determine whether there is any thing in the Nature of our present Constitution that forbids *Jews* to class with the Rest of the Subjects, as far as relates to Matters of mere *civil Concern* in a *private* station." Tucker, *Second Letter*, pp. 14–15 (his emphasis).

60. Tucker, *Elements*, p. 5, 18.

61. David Hume, *Essays Moral, Political, and Literary*, edited by Eugene F. Miller (Indianapolis, 1985). Of the important essays, only "Of the Jealousy of Trade" was published later, in 1758.

62. The economist Salim Rashid has written a number of works seeking to realign Tucker's reputation vis-à-vis that of Hume and Smith. See for instance, *The Myth of Adam Smith* (Cheltenham, UK, 1998); idem., "Josiah Tucker, Anglican Anti-Semitism, and the Jew Bill of 1753, *Historical Magazine of the Protestant Episcopal Church* (June 1982), pp. 191–201.

63. For Hume's revised views, see his "On the Jealousy of Trade in Hume, *Essays*, esp. p. 283 and Hume, *Economic Writings*, pp. 199–204. Most of Tucker's original correspondence on the matter has been lost, but he reiterated his arguments in *Four Tracts on Political and Commercial Subjects* (Gloucester, 1774). See Eugene Rotwein's lengthy introduction to *Hume's Economic Writings*, pp. lxxvi–vii and his footnote on p. 204. For a somewhat different view, one that credits Tucker's impact on Hume but views Hume as generally more progressive, see Istvan Hont, "The 'Rich Country – Poor Country' Debate in Scottish Classical Political Economy," in Istvan Hont and Michael Ignatieff, *Wealth and Virtue: The Shaping of Political Economy in the Scottish Enlightenment* (Cambridge, 1985), pp. 285–301.

64. Tucker, *Elements*, pp. 3–4.

65. Tucker, *Elements*, p. 6.

66. The concept is most often associated with Montesquieu but has a much broader eighteenth-century application. Charles de Secondat, baron de Montesquieu, *The Spirit of the Laws*, translated by Anne M. Cohler, Basia Carolyn Miller, and Harold Samuel Stone (Cambridge, 1995), Part I, Bk. 5, Ch. 6. See Lawrence Dickey, "*Doux-Commerce* and the 'Mediocrity of Money' in the Ideological Context of the Wealth and Virtue Problem," in Adam Smith, *An Inquiry into the Nature and Causes of the Wealth of Nations* (Indianapolis, 1993), pp. 243–59.

67. Ibid., p. 7.

68. See J. B. Schneewind's Introduction to David Hume, *An Enquiry Concerning the Principles of Morals* (Indianapolis, 1988), pp. 1–10.

69. Tucker, *Elements*, pp. 6–7.

70. Ibid., pp. 6–9; idem., *Reflections on the Expediency of a Law for the Naturalization of Foreign Protestants*, Pt. II (Holborn, 1751), p. 10.

71. Tucker, *Elements*, p. 7.
72. Ibid., p. 6.
73. Ibid., p. 12.
74. Ibid.
75. Ibid., p. 9.
76. Smith, *Wealth of Nations*, Book I, Ch. 2.
77. Shelton, *Dean Tucker*, p. 55.
78. Adam Smith quoted in Joseph Schumpeter, *History of Ecomomic Analysis*, ed. Elizabeth Boady Schumpeter (New York, 1954), pp. 257–58; see also, Hutchison, *Before Adam Smith*, pp. 38, 249–50.
79. Schumpeter, *History*, pp. 251–52.
80. Jan De Vries, *The Economy of Europe in an Age of Crisis* (Cambridge, 1988), pp. 4–12.
81. Tucker, *Elements*, p. 15. Although antipopulationist treatises were produced as early as the sixteenth century, they did not gain a foothold until the end of the eighteenth, with the publication of Malthus's *Essay on Population*. See Schumpeter, *History*, p. 257.
82. Philo-Patriae, *Further Considerations*, p. 8.
83. Idem., in Rudin, *Pamphlets*, p. 90.
84. Cobbett, *Parliamentary History*, vol. XIV, pp. 1367–68.
85. Ibid., 1390–91.
86. Ibid., p. 1424. Philo-Patriae, the pseudonymous author of two widely circulated pamphlets supporting the Jew Bill, insisted on the dogma that domestic trade in and of itself can acquire no new wealth. As foreign traders Jews would increase the nation's riches, because they are "particularly industrious, in importing Specie." In Rudin, *Pamphlets*, p. 90; see also Perry, *Public Opinion* p. 7, pp. 82–83.
87. As Bernard's reference to Poland suggests, attacks such as his took full advantage of the growing awareness that England's Jewish population was less and less characterized by Sephardic grandees and increasingly comprised of Ashkenazim. The latter were easier to caricature as usurers rather than merchants and plebian rather than patrician. Thus, the image of the Jew conjured by opponents of the Bill was impressively malleable and ranged from overweening wealthy monopolists to unassimilable impoverished "brokers, peddlers, or hawkers." This point is also made by Perry, *Public Opinion*, p. 7.
88. D. C. Coleman, "Labour in the English Economy of the Seventeenth Century," *Economic History Review*, series 2, vol. 8 (1955), p. 280, n. 3; Hume, *Economic Writings*, pp. xlii–xliv; Idem., *Essays*, pp. 271–74. Smith's words are worth quoting: "The liberal reward of labour, as it encourages the propagation, so it increases the industry of the common people.... A plentiful subsistence increases the bodily strength of the labourer, and the comfortable hope of bettering his condition, and of ending his days perhaps in ease and plenty, animates him to exert that strength to the utmost. Where wages are high, accordingly, we shall always find the workmen more active, diligent, and expeditious, than where they are low..." Smith, *Wealth of Nations*, p. 91 (Bk. I, Ch. viii).
89. De Vries, *Crisis*, p. 179.
90. Josiah Tucker, *The Expediency of a General Naturalization of Foreign Protestants and Others* (London, 1751), p. 12.
91. Josiah Tucker, *Elements*, p. 7.

92. "And indeed it is scarce possible, that any Foreigners should succeed, but those who are conscious to themselves of superior Talents, Industry, or Frugality in some respect or other . . . ," Tucker, *Elements*, p. 32.

93. Philo-Patriae, *Further Considerations*, p. 8.

94. *Reflections*, p. 50.

95. Antoin E. Murphy, "John Law and the Scottish Enlightenment," in *A History of Scottish Economic Thought*, edited by Alexander Dow and Sheila Dow (London and New York, 2006), p. 14.

96. Tucker, *Elements*, p. 42.

97. *Ibid.*, p. 43.

98. Tucker recommended channeling the funds used to subsidize corn exports into schemes for enhancing immigration instead, see ibid., p. 32; similarly, Tucker addressed the problem of debt in the hands of foreign creditors, "chiefly Dutch, Flemings, Swiss, and Jews . . . ," by proposing that they be encouraged to reside in Britain instead. See Tucker, *Expediency*, p. 15.

99. Tucker, *Elements*, p. 8. On these themes, more generally, see Salim Rashid, "Christianity and the Growth of Liberal Economics," *Journal of Religious History* (1982), pp. 221–32.

100. Tucker, *Reflections*, Part II, p. 11.

101. Ibid., p. 10.

102. Joyce Appleby, *Economic Thought*, p. 231.

103. Pierre Goubert, *Initiation à l'histoire de la France* (Paris, 1984), pp. 188–89; Istvan Hunt and Michael Ignatieff, "Needs and Justice in the *Wealth of Nations*: An Introductory Essay," in *Wealth and Virtue: The Shaping of Political Economy in the Scottish Enlightenment*, edited by idem. (Cambridge, 1985), pp. 17–19.

104. J. M. Keynes, *General Theory of Employment, Interest and Money* (New York, 1936), p. 312.

105. Tucker, *Reflections*, Pt. II, p. 22.

106. Tucker, *Elements*, p. 99. Hume makes this same point repeatedly in his essay, "Of the Balance of Trade," *Hume's Economic Writings*, pp. 60–77.

107. At times, Tucker appeared to reduce the entirety of political-economy to the science of population study, see *Reflections*, Pt. II, p. 22.

108. Tucker, *Elements*, p. 103.

109. Ironically, John Law, the most infamous projector, in the eyes of economists like Tucker, Smith, and Hume, appears to have held a similar view. See Jean Claude Perrot, *Une Histoire Intellectuelle de 'l'économie politique, xviie–xviiie* (Paris, 1992), p. 199.

110. Hume, *Essays*, p. 283. Hume did acknowledge some exceptions, particularly the interval between the initial influx of money and the moment when it begins to raise prices. In this interval, the importation of precious metals could serve as a beneficial economic stimulant. See p. 286.

111. *A Collection of the Best Pieces*, pp. 43–444 (emphasis in original).

112. Tucker, *Elements*, pp. 18–20.

113. Shelton, *Dean Tucker*, p. 59.

114. Tucker, *Elements*, p. 92.

115. Smith, *Wealth of Nations*, i, pp. 351–71.

116. There was a continental parallel to this phenomenon, particularly under Jansenist influence in France. For a fascinating discussion, see Perrot, *Une histoire intellectuelle*

de l'économie politique, pp. 345–53. On the roots of the doctrine in patristic literature, see Jerry Z. Muller, *The Mind and the Market: Capitalism in Modern European Thought* (New York, 2002), p. 7.

117. Arthur Dobbs quoted in Richard C. Wiles, "Mercantilism and the Idea of Progress," *Eighteenth-Century Studies*, vol. 18, no. 1 (Autumn, 1974), pp. 67–68.

118. Matthew Decker, quoted in Dobbs, "Mercantilism and the Idea of Progress," p. 68.

119. Joseph Addison and Richard Steele, *The Spectator*, vol. 3, edited by Henry Morley (London, 1891), number 495.

120. Toland, *Reasons for Naturalizing the Jews*, p. 34.

121. From an anonymous pamphlet appended to *A letter to the Right Honorable Sir Thomas Chitty, Knt. Lord Mayor of London* (London, 1759).

122. Montesquieu, *The Spirit of the Laws*, pp. 386–87 (Pt. 4, Bk. 20, Ch. 20).

123. See Goudar, *Les interets de la France*, vol. I, pp. 421–30. See also Arthur Herzberg, *The French Enlightenment and the Jews* (New York, 1968), pp. 66–67.

124. *Schreiben eines Juden an einen Philosophen nebst der Antwort*, (Berlin, 1753). See most recently, Gad Freudenthal, "Aaron Salomon Gumpertz, Gotthold Ephraim Lessing, and the First Call of an Improvement of the Civil Rights of Jews in Germany (1753)," *AJS Review*, 29:2 (2005), 299–353. On Lessing's economic views, see John Walter Van Cleve, *The Merchant in German Literature of the Enlightenment* (Chapel Hill, NC, 1986).

4. THE NATURAL RELATION OF THINGS

1. Admittedly, the German theorist of natural law, Samuel Pufendorf, as well as the Dutch statesman Hugo Grotius, have been incorporated into this narrative. See Istvan Hont and Michael Ignatieff, "Needs and Justice in the *Wealth of Nations*: An Introductory Essay," in idem., *Wealth and Virtue*, pp. 35–42.

2. For instance, Eric Roll, *A History of Economic Thought* (New York, 1992), pp. 218–27.

3. This has been recently challenged by David B. Ruderman, *Jewish Enlightenment in an English Key* (Princeton, NJ, 2000). For other critiques of the Germanocentric model, see *Toward Modernity: The European Jewish Model*, edited by Todd Endelman (Brunswick, NJ, 1987).

4. For a sophisticated recent formulation, see the brilliant study by David Sorkin, *The Transformation of German Jewry* (New York, 1987).

5. Reinhard Rürup, "The Tortuous and Thorny Path to Legal Equality – 'Jew Laws' and Emancipatory Legislation in Germany from the Late Eighteenth Century" *Leo Baeck Institute Year Book*, XXXI (1986), pp. 3–34.

6. See, most recently, *A History of Scottish Economic Thought*, edited by Alexander Dow and Sheila Dow (London and New York, 2006), esp. pp. 219–25.

7. Mainusch, "Einleitung" to John Toland, *Gründe für die Einbürgerung der Juden in Grossbritanien und Irland*; Freudenthal, "the First Call of an Improvement of the Civil Rights of Jews in Germany (1753)."

8. Ilsegret Dambacher, *Christian Wilhelm von Dohm: Ein Beitrag zur Geschichte des preußischen aufgeklärten Beamtentums und seiner Reformbestrebungen am Ausgang des 18. Jahrhunderts* (Frankfurt-am-Main, 1974).

9. See Dombacher, *Christian Wilhelm von Dohm*, pp. 112–13. But compare Jonathan Hess, *Germans, Jews, and the Claims of Modernity* (New Haven, 2002), pp. 25–26.

Balancing his roles as government advisor entrusted with designing measures to enhance state revenue and scholar devoted to liberal reform, Dohm was hardly in a position to be consistent. See Franz Reuß, "Christian Wilhelm Dohm's Schift, "Über die bürgerliche Verbesserung der Juden" und deren Einwirkung auf die gebildeten Stände Deutschlands," in the reissued edition of Dohm's *Über die bürgerliche Verbesserung der Juden* (Hildesheim, 1973), pp. 8–16.

10. Ibid.

11. A detailed account of the background to the writing of Dohm's tract appears in Alexander Altmann, *Moses Mendelssohn: A Biographical Study* (London, 1998), pp. 449–61.

12. See, most recently, Ronald Schechter, *Obstinate Hebrews: Representations of Jews in France, 1715–1815* (Berkeley, CA, 2003), pp. 67–73, 82–109.

13. The *Verbesserung* was translated into French within a year of its initial publication as *De la réforme politique des Juifs*, translated by Jean Bernoulli (Dessau, 1782). Schechter discusses earlier precursors, such as Pierre-Louis Lacretelle, without once mentioning Dohm. Yet the essays of Thiéry, Grégoire, Zalkind Hourwitz, and especially Mirabeau resounded throughout with echoes of Dohm's book. See ibid., pp. 77–82. On the complex relations between Dohm's text, the writings on Jews of the Abbe Gregoire, and the Metz essay contest, see Alyssa Goldstein Sepinwall, *The Abbé Grégoire and the French Revolution* (Berkeley, CA, 2005), pp. 59–70.

14. Robert Lieberles, "The Historical Context of Dohm's Treatise on the Jews," in *Das Deutsche Judentum und der Liberalismus: Dokumentation eines internationalen Seminars der Friedrich-Naumann-Stiftung in Zusammenarbeit mit dem Leo Baeck Institute* (Sankt-Augustin, 1986), pp. 43–54.

15. Tucker, *Elements of Commerce*, p. 35.

16. Michael Toch, "Aspects of Stratification of Early Modern German Jewry: Population History and Village Jews," in Hsia and Lehmann, *In and Out the Ghetto*, pp. 77–124. On the early disappearance or, rather, *transformation* of the English peasantry, see Richard M. Smith, "The English Peasantry, 1250–1650," in *The Peasantries of Europe from the Fourteenth to the Eighteenth Centuries* (London, 1998), pp. 339–71.

17. Szajkowski, Zosa. *The Economic Status of the Jews in Alsace, Metz, and Lorriane 1648–1789* (New York, 1954); Steven M. Lowenstein, "The Rural Community and the Urbanization of German Jewry," in idem., *The Mechanics of Change: Essays in the Social History of German Jewry* (Atlanta, 1992), pp. 133–49. Of course, the Jewish rural peddler was increasingly a stock figure of English caricature by the mid-eighteenth century, but crucially Jews' role as moneylenders in rural England was far less pronounced. See Cecil Roth, "The Jew Peddler – An 18th Century Rural Character," in idem., *Essays and Portraits in Anglo-Jewish History* (Philadelphia, 1962), pp. 130–38.

18. The best detailed overview of this topic remains Selma Stern, *Der Preussische Staat und die Juden*, 2 vols. (Tübingen, 1962).

19. Stern, *Der Preussische Staat*, vol. 1, pp. 14–33. See also Mordechai Breuer, "The Early Modern Period," in Michael Meyer, ed., *German-Jewish History in Modern Times* (New York, 1996), pp. 144–155; Katz, *Out of the Ghetto*, pp. 12–18

20. Christian Wilhelm Dohm, *Ueber die bürgerliche Verbesserung der Juden* (Berlin and Stettin, 1783), p. 1. Unless otherwise indicated, I have used the 1783 edition of the text, which includes Dohm's responses to his critics. A partial English translation of

Dohm's book appeared as *Concerning the Amelioration of the Civil Status of the Jews*, translated by Helen Lederer (Cincinnati, 1957).

21. Mendelssohn attacked this notion of a limit to desirable population growth (or, rather, insisted that free labor markets would solve the problem of itself). Dohm insisted his point was only a theoretical and at present not a practical one. Although, as noted in the previous chapter, few contemporary economists dissented from populationism in theory, both Richard Cantillon and Adam Smith conceded an inevitable limit on the desirable numbers of men. See Guy Routh, *The Origin of Economic Ideas*, pp. 66, 98.

22. Dohm, *Verbesserung*, pp. 3–4.

23. In drawing this analogy between Dohm and the English theorists, it should be acknowledged that the tenor of German populationist doctrine at this time aimed as much at consumption as production. See Keith Tribe, *Governing Economy: The Reformation of German Economic Discourse, 1750–1840* (Cambridge, 1988), pp. 30–2, 80.

24. See Mordeché Wolf Rappaport, *Christian Wilhelm Dohm: Ein Beitrag zur Geschichte der Nationalökonomie* (Leipzig, 1907), pp. 62–72.

25. Dambacher, *Christian Wilhelm von Dohm*, pp. 124–27. Dambacher identifies Dohm's views on money with those of Büsching. But in fact the work to which she refers is not Büsching's but Johann Georg Büsch's *Abhandlung von dem Geldsumlauf in anhaltender Rucksicht auf die Staatswirtschaft und Handlung* (Hamburg, 1780), which was expressly an attack on bullionist theories of wealth.

26. Smith's nominalist view of money as well as his recognition of increased circulation as a stimulant is nicely expressed in the following: "It is not by augmenting the capital of the country, but by rendering a greater part of that capital active and productive than would otherwise be so, that the most judicious operations of banking can increase the industry of the country." Smith, *Wealth of Nations*, Bk. II, Ch. ii, p. 341. For Hume's views, see Hume, *Essays*, p. 286 and Rotwein's introduction to *Hume's Economic Writings*, pp. xv–xvi.

27. *Deutsches Museum* I (Berlin, 1777), p. 184. See also Dombacher, *Christian Wilhelm von Dohm*, p. 126.

28. See Chapter 3 of this volume. The velocity of money argument that was also employed by Dohm was advanced, *inter alia*, by Petty and Locke, the former remarking that "... a hundred pound passing a hundred hands for Wages, causes a 10000 l. worth of Commodities to be produced, which hands would have been idle and useless, had there not been this continual motive to their employment." See Routh, *The Origin of Economic Ideas*, pp. 43, 49.

29. According to Smith, merchants are "an order of men, whose interest is never exactly the same with that of the public, who have generally an interest to deceive and even to oppress the public, and who accordingly have, upon many occasions, both deceived and oppressed it." Smith, *Wealth of Nations*, Bk. I, Ch. xi, p. 278.

30. John Stoye, *Europe Unfolding, 1648–1688* (Glasgow, 1978), pp. 27–28, 31; for more recent and more conservative estimates, see Peter H. Wilson, *From Reich to Revolution: German History, 1558–1806* (New York, 2004), pp. 144–45.

31. As Carlo Cipolla points out, the Peasants' Wars in the first quarter and the precipitous decline of the Hanse in the third quarter of the sixteenth century had already taken a severe toll, principally in the North. See Cipolla, *Before the Industrial Revolution* (New York, 1993), pp. 234–35.

32. Wilson, *From Reich to Revolution*, pp. 147–49.
33. See the discussion in Mack Walker, *German Home Towns: Community, State, and General Estate*, 1648–1871 (Ithaca, NY, 1971), 145–84.
34. Cf. Tribe, *Governing Economy*, pp. 63–72.
35. This duality helps account for the cameralist, Johann Becher's, attack on Jews' roles in international and domestic commerce. Becher was concerned with protecting both local industry and its native producers. Here, Jews were seen as intruding upon an established sphere and undermining domestic production. See *Politische Discurs von den eigentlichen Ursachen des Auf- und Abnehmens der Städte, Länder und Republicken*, 2nd edition (Frankfurt, 1673).
36. From a 1672 Estate petition to the Prussian Great Elector, Frederick William, (unsuccessfully) requesting the local expulsion of Jews. Quoted in Stefi Jersch-Wenzel, "Jewish Economic Activity in Early Modern Times," in *In and Out of the Ghetto: Jewish-Gentile Relations in Late Medieval and Early Modern Germany*, edited by R. Po-Chia Hsia and Hartmut Lehmann (Cambridge, 1995), pp. 92–93. On the clash between Jewish commercial practices and the mentality of central European guilds, see also Leon Poliakov, *The History of Anti-Semitism*, vol. 3 (New York, 1985), pp. 8–11.
37. Richard Olsen, *The Emergence of the Social Sciences, 1642–1792* (New York, 1993), pp. 32–34.
38. Becher, *Politische Discurs*, p. 89; Wilhelm Freyherr von Schröder, *Fürstliche Schatz- und Rentenkammer* (1686). For the sake of brevity, this account telescopes successive stages of Cameralist literature. From about 1648 to about the middle of the eighteenth century, the Cameralists displayed a marked hesitation to interfere in the prerogatives of the guilds and other corporations. But, later, as Cameralism merged with the new science of *Polizeiwissenschaft* (political science), the state was no longer depicted as merely coexisting harmoniously alongside alternative bodies and institutions but rather as absorbing them into itself. Now, without directly waging war upon guilds, the state nevertheless arrogated to itself the authority to regulate their by-laws and to classify their members on a basis that was essentially foreign to their own conceptions. See Walker, *Home Towns*, pp. 166–70; Dohm himself recognized how resistant guilds would be to the admission of Jews; all the more reason, he believed, to afford Jews privileges equal to those of guild members and thereby gradually break down the guilds' monopolies: "Vielleicht würde dieß überhaupt das sicherste und gelindeste Mittel sein, die für unsre itzige Staaten unstreitig nicht mehr passende ausschliessende Rechte der Zünfte wendiger nachteilig für den Staat zu machen." Dohm, *Verbesserung*, p. 27.
39. It has been noted that the populationist doctrines of cameralism were rooted as much in consumption as production. This is what Schumpeter labels "Becher's Principle," "that one man's expenditure is another man's income," see his *History of Economic Analysis*, p. 283; Yet Dohm does not mention consumption at all in relation to population. Rather, he lists as the four benefits of an "unceasing" [*unaufhörlich*] rise in population: (1) security from external attack; (2) enhancement of domestic productive resources; (3) international exchange; and most important, (4) the stimulation of the industry of the citizenry. See *Verbesserung*, p. 3.
40. Johann Heinrich Gottlieb von Justi, *Die Grundfeste zu der Macht und Glückseligkeit der Staaten, oder ausführliche Vorstellung der gesampten Polizeiwissensschaft*, I (Königsburg, 1760), pp. 743–51. See also Schumpeter, *History of Economic Analysis*,

pp. 170–73; Walker, *Home Towns*, 162–70; for a contrasting view, Albion Small, *The Cameralists: the Pioneers of German Social Polity* (Chicago, 1909), pp. 340–78.

41. Dohm, *Verbesserung*, pp. 7–9, 17. Cf. Goudar's observations on France's Jewish policies in 1757: "... il n'est pas bein aisé de dire pourquoi notre Geouvernment s'est fermé lui-même la port à une branche de population à laquelle une infinité d'autres Etats de l'Europe l'ont ouverte." Goudar, however, favored Jews almost exclusively on populationist grounds and argued their commercial and financial exertions would only assist large states like France, endowed with abundant resources but commercially underdeveloped. As we shall see, Dohm went far beyond these limited and utilitarian rationales for Jewish toleration. See Goudar, *Les Intérêts de la France*, pp. 421, 242–26.

42. On this, including populationism in state policy, see Stern, *Der Preussische Staat*, vol. 1, pp. 33–43; on the specific motive of raising cash by importing Jews, pp. 37–38.

43. See Reuß, "Christian Wilhelm Dohm's Schift," p. 11.

44. Rappaport's claim that in the *Verbesserung* Dohm sought extravagantly to defend Jewish commercial capacities extends from his (untenable) thesis that the *Verbesserung* was inspired by and represents a continued expression Dohm's hostility to Physiocratic doctrine. See Rappaport, *Christian Wilhelm Dohm*, p. 102.

45. See Chapter 1.

46. I am not suggesting that he was familiar with specific apologetics, although there is no doubt that he had read works by Menasseh ben Israel and Lessing. More importantly, as both a historian and a Prussian civil servant Dohm was deeply familiar with the history of commercial privileges German and other governments had applied to Jews. For Dohm's sources on Jewish history, see the discussion later in this chapter.

47. Dohm, *Verbesserung*, pp. 32–33.

48. See discussion and citations later.

49. Dohm, *Verbesserung*, pp. 34–35.

50. One of Dohm's earliest publications was a translation of one of Bonnet's works.

51. Sutcliffe, *Judaism and Enlightenment* passim.

52. Isaac de Pinto, "An Apology for the Jewish Nation," in *The Jews in the Modern Worl: A Documentary History*, 2nd edition, edited by Paul Mendes-Flor and Jehudah Reinharz (New York, 1995), p. 306.

53. Isaac de Pinto, *Reflexoëns Politicas, Tocante à Constitutiçam da Naçam Judaica, Exposiçam do estado de suas Finanças, causeas dos atrasos, e desordens que se experimentam, e meyos de os prevenir* (Amsterdam, 1748). Indeed, shortly after the publication of de Pinto's book, the Sephardic communal government or Mahamad developed plans to send six hundred poor Jews in the Dutch colony of Surinam, though the scheme was never realized. See Robert Cohen, "Passage to the New World: The Sephardi Poor of Eighteenth-Century Amsterdam," in *Neveh Ya'akov: Jubilee Volume Presented to Dr. Jaap Meijer*, edited by L. Dasberg and J. N. Cohen (Assen, 1982), pp. 31–42; Tirtsah Levie Bernfeld, "Financing Poor Relief in the Spanish-Portuguese Jewish Community in Amsterdam in the Seventeenth and Eighteenth Centuries," in *Dutch Jewry: Its History and Secular Culture (1500–2000)*, edited by Jonathan Israel and Reiner Salverda (Leiden, 2002), pp. 63–102, esp. pp. 84–91.

54. Benjamin Braude, "The Myth of the Sephardi Economic Superman," in *Trading Cultures: The Worlds of Western Merchants: Essays On Authority, Objectivity, and Evidence*, edited by Jeremy Adelman and Stephen Aron (Turnhout, 2001), pp. 163–91.

55. Israel, *European Jewry in the Age of Mercantilism*, pp. 237–53; Idem., *Diasporas within a Diaspora*, esp. pp. 366–570; Penslar, *Shylock's Children*, pp. 19–20, 36; Bernfeld, "Financing Poor Relief"; Karina Sonnenberg-Stern, *Emancipation and Poverty: The Ashkenazi Jews of Amsterdam 1761–1850* (New York, 2000), pp. 26–33.

56. The following section is strongly influenced by Israel, *European Jewry in the Age of Mercantilism*, pp. 237–53.

57. On the effects of the loss of Dutch Brazil, see Israel, *Diasporas within a Diaspora*, pp. 355–84 and Peter Emmer, "The Jewish Moment and the Two Expansion Systems in the Atlantic, 1580–1650," in Bernardini and Fiering, *The Jews and their Expansion to the West*, pp. 512–14; on the fall of the Portuguese New Christian bankers in Spain, see ibid., p. 228 and Daniel M. Swetschinski, *Reluctant Cosmopolitans: The Portuguese Jews of Seventeenth-Century Amsterdam* (London, 2000), p. 120; on the consequences for Jews of the Treaty of Utrecht, see Israel, *Diasporas within a Diaspora*, pp. 535–66.

58. Ibid., pp. 396–404.

59. Ibid., pp. 390–92; idem. *European Jewry in the Age of Mercantilism*, pp. 238–39.

60. Swetschinski, *Reluctant Cosmopolitans*, pp. 155–58; Israel, *European Jewry in the Age of Mercantilism*, p. 247.

61. Population figures based on Jacob Lestschinsky, "Die Umsiedlung und Umschichtung des juedischen Volkes im Laufe des lezten Jahrhunderts," in *Weltwirtschaftliches Archiv*, vol. II, no. 30 (Jena, 1929), pp. 149–58; Arthur Ruppin, *Soziologie der Juden* (Berlin, 1930–1), vol. I, pp. 1–25.

62. Otto Ulbricht, "Criminality and Punishment of the Jews in the Early Modern Period," in Hsia and Lehmann, *In and Out of the Ghetto*, p. 65; Jonathan Israel, "Germany and Its Jews: A Changing Relationship (1300–1800)," in ibid., p. 303; Penslar, *Shylock's Children*, p. 36.

63. Bernfeld, "Financing Poor Relief," p. 71.

64. Michael Toch, "Aspects of Stratification of Early Modern German Jewry: Population History and Village Jews," in Hsia and Lehmann, *In and Out the Ghetto*, p. 82.

65. Jacob Katz, *Tradition and Crisis: Jewish Society at the End of the Middle Ages* (New York, 1993), pp. 76–87.

66. Bernfeld, "Financing Poor Relief," p. 84. So as to accord increasing numbers of Jews the rights of local residency, eighteenth-century Jewish communities in central Europe tended to place them on the list of official *Kehilla* employees. Community officials fell into the lowest category of protected Jews in Frederick II's Revised General Code of 1750. See Breuer, "The Early Modern Period," pp. 136, 149.

67. Israel, *European Jewry in the Age of Mercantilism*, pp. 238–41; Stanford J. Shaw, *The Jews of the Ottoman Empire and the Turkish Republic* (New York, 1991), pp. 119–20; Herbert I. Bloom, *The Economic Activities of the Jews of Amsterdam in the Seventeenth Century* (Williamsport, PA, 1937), pp. 210–18.

68. Ibid., pp. 240; Wolfgang Ribbe, "Wirschaftlicher und politischer Status der Juden in Brandenburg-Preußen im Zeitalter des Merkantilismus," in Marianne Awerbuch and Stefi Jersch-Wenzel, eds., *Bild und Selbstbild der Juden Berlins zwischen Aufklärung und Romantik* (Berlin, 1992), pp. 10–11.

69. Israel, *Jews in the Age of Mercantilism*, pp. 247–48.

70. Ibid., pp. 243–6; Ribbe, "Wirschaftlicher und politischer Status," pp. 13–4, notes that numerous fortunes were made by Berlin Jews during the Seven Years' War, even while most Prussian Jews suffered from Frederick II's economic policies.

71. Steven M. Lowenstein, "Die Berliner Juden 1770–1830: Pioniere jüdischer Modernität," in *Jüdische Geschichte in Berlin*, edited by Reinhard Rürup (Berlin, 1996), pp. 25–26.

72. Margaret Levi, *Of Rule and Revenue* (Berkeley, CA, 1988); see also *Global Debates about Taxation. How International Transfers of Ideas Shaped Our Fiscal Systems*, edited by Holger Nehring und Florio Schui (Basingstoke, UK and New York, 2007).

73. Even during the Seven Years' War of 1756–1763, when the number of Jewish minters in Prussia reached an all-time peak, Frederick II exerted pressure on the court Jews to disengage themselves from vertical business entanglements with common Jews. See Breuer, "The Early Modern Period," pp. 145–46.

74. Compare, for instance, the highly conservative estimates of the numbers of Amsterdam's Sephardi poor cited Herbert Bloom *The Economic Activities*, pp. 213–14, with those of Bernfeld, "Financing Poor Relief."

75. Breuer, "The Early Modern Period," pp. 150–51, notes that "... the rise of the Jewish middle class [in Prussia], which owed its beginnings in large part to court Jewry, progressed substantially under Frederick II"; see also Lois Dubin, *The Port Jews of Habsburg Tireste: Absolutist Politics and Enlightenment Culture* (Stanford, CA, 1999), pp. 28–32.

76. Bernard D. Weinryb, *The Jews of Poland: A Social and Economic History of the Jewish Community in Poland from 1100–1800* (Philadelphia, 1973), p. 141; Gershon David Hundert, "Comparative Perspectives on Economy and Society: The Jews of the Polish Commonwealth – A Comment," in Hsia and Lehmann, *In and Out the Ghetto*, pp. 103–107. However, by the last third of the eighteenth century, evidence was mounting of the unsustainable nature of Jewish entanglement in the Polish economy, especially in light of the overwhelming political crises the country faced. See, idem., *Jews in Poland-Lithuania in the Eighteenth Century* (Berkeley, CA, 2004), pp. 32–33.

77. In fact, Luzzatto declared in his *Discourse*, p. 109, that, excluding a handful of state-sanctioned Jewish banks for the poor, "hardly any Jews earn their living through usury." Part of Luzzatto's defense of Venetian Jewry was to claim that the establishment of the Monte de Pietà had effectively ended the practice of Jewish usury there. This, of course, was a serious exaggeration, even accepting Robert Bonfil's claim that the later Renaissance period entailed a "radical revolution in the socioeconomic structure of the Jewish population," rooted in the decline in the proportion of Jewish moneylending. What this seems to mean is a decline in the wealth and prestige of the formerly most powerful and dominant Jewish lenders and a concomitant rise of Jewish merchants. See his *Jewish Life in Renaissance Italy* (Berkeley, CA, 1994), p. 97, 192–93.

78. This would seem to hold as well for the early-eighteenth-century Jewish commercial apologetics cited by Penslar, *Shylock's Children*, pp. 65–67.

79. To the literature cited earlier describing high levels of poverty within all spheres of the Sephardic Diaspora should be added the descriptions of widespread destitution within the Ashkenazic world, dating back as early as the fifteenth century. See Toch, "Aspects of Stratification, pp. 77–124 and Yacov Guggenheim, "Meeting on the Road: Encounters between German Jews and Christians on the Margins of Society," in Hsia and Lehmann, *In and Out of the Ghetto*, pp. 125–36; Moses A. Shulvass, *From East to West: The Westward Migration of Jews from Eastern Europe during the Seventeenth and Eighteenth Centuries* (Detroit, 1971).

80. William Chester Jordan, *The French Monarchy and the Jews: From Philip Augustus to the Last Capetians* (Philadelphia, 1989); James William Parkes, *The Jew in the Medieval Community: A Study of his Political and Economic Situation* (New York, 1976).

81. Martin Luther, "On the Jews and their Lies," in *The Christian in Society IV*, edited by Franklin Sherman. Vol. 47 of *Luther's Works* (Philadelphia, 1971), p. 272. Luther and other reformers like Martin Bucer advocated Jews' exclusion from usury and habituation to manual labor under the influence of Jewish converts such as Anthonius Margaritha and Johannes Pfefferkorn, who believed that Jews' concentration in usury was a critical factor preventing their conversion. See R. Po-Chia Hsia, "The Usurious Jew: Economic Structure and Religious Representations in an Anti-Semitic Discourse," in Hsia and Lehmann, *In and Out of the Ghetto*, pp. 170–72. On guild demands, see Otto Stobbe, *Die Juden in Deutschland während des Mittelalters in politischer, socialer und rechtlicher Beziehung*, reprint (Amsterdam, 1968), pp. 103–10.

82. As expressed, for instance, by late seventeenth-century founder of German Pietism, Philip Jakob Spener. See Penslar, *Shylock's Children*, p. 24.

83. Quoted in Tamar Bermann, *Produktivierungsmythen und Antisemitismus: Eine soziologische Studie* (Vienna, 1973), p. 48.

84. Yosef Kaplan, "The Self-Definition of the Sephardic Jews of Western Europe and Their Relation to the Alien and the Stranger," in Benjamin R. Gampel, ed., *Crisis and Creativity in the Sephardic World, 1391–1648* (New York, 1997), pp. 138–39.

85. See note 37. These efforts were not entirely unrealistic. Dutch and French trading companies often professed to prefer the settling of Jewish farmers in the colonies they controlled to Jews continued merchandising. In some settings, such as French Guyana during its brief duration, Jewish agricultural colonies proved successful. See Mordechai Arbell, "Jewish Settlements in the French Colonies in the Caribbean (Martinique, Guadeloupe, Haiti, Cayenne) and the 'Black Code'," in Fiering and Bernardini, *Jews and Expansion to the West*, pp. 291–308. For a parallel phenomenon in the Dutch Guyana of the 1650s, see Robert Cohen, "The Edgerton Manuscript," *American Jewish Historical Quarterly*, LXII (1973), 333–47.

86. The change is usually interpreted as a secular critique of Jews and Judaism aimed ultimately at attacking the roots of traditional Christianity. See Jacob Katz, *From Prejudice to Destruction* (Cambridge, MA, 1980), pp. 23–50; Ettinger, "Jews and Judaism in the Eyes of the English Deists," pp. 182–207.

87. Toland, "Reasons," in Rudin, *Pamphlets*, p. 48.

88. The so-called Bergonzi Affair involved collaboration between Jewish and Christian criminals. See Ravid, *Economics and Toleration*, 10–18, 51–53; Moses Shulvass, "The Story of Sorrows that Occurred in Italy" (Hebrew), *HUCA* 22 (1949), pp. 1–21.

89. Rudolf Glanz, *Geschichte des niederen jüdischen Volkes in Deutschland: Ein Studie über historisches Gaunertum, Bettelwesen und Vagantentum* (New York, 1968), pp. 7–59.

90. Shulvass, *East to West*, pp. 13, 21, 67–68, 32, 84, 99.

91. See Glanz, *Geschichte des niederen jüdischen Volkes*, pp. 61–81 and passim; Ulbricht, "Criminality and Punishment."

92. Perry, *Public Opinion*, p. 7; Endelman, *Jews in Georgian England*, pp. pp. 31–2, 202–03, 230–42. To some extent, these frightful images reflected an inevitable association within a still largely traditional society between criminality and the kind of

unorthodox functions that Jews were specifically constrained to perform, such as peddling and pawn brokerage.

93. In fact, the roots of this kind of criminality in German-Jewry go back to the late Middle Ages, but it is only in the eighteenth century that the general public appears to have become aware of specifically Jewish criminal gangs. Breuer, "The Early Modern Period," pp. 247–50; Glanz, *Geschichte des niederen judischen*, pp. 12–23; Azriel Shohet, '*Im Hilufe Tekufot: Reshit ha-Haskalah be Yahadut Germaniyah* [Changing Times: The Beginnings of the Haskalah among German Jewry] (Hebrew), (Jerusalem, 1960), pp. 150–59.

94. Kaplan, "The Self-Definition of the Sephardic Jews," pp. 132–38; Glanz, *Geschichte des niederen judischen Volkes*, pp. 137–39.

95. Joshua Trachtenberg, *The Devil and the Jews: the Medieval Conception of the Jew and its Relation to Modern Antisemitism* (Philadelphia, 1983), pp. 57–158. Similar points are made by Penslar, *Shylock's Children*, p. 20 and Ulbricht "Criminality and Punishment," p. 54.

96. Gotthold Ephraim Lessing, *Nathan the Wise, Minna Von Barnhelm, and Other Plays and Writings*, edited by Peter Demetz (New York, 1998), pp. 141–42.

97. Ibid., p. 96.

98. Anke Te Heesen, *The World in a Box: The Story of an Eighteenth-Century Picture Encyclopedia* (Chicago, 2002), pp. 105–06.

99. On these influences, see Dambacher, *Christian Wilhelm von Dohm*, pp. 5, 63.

100. Smith, *The Wealth of Nations*, pp. 302–03. The serious effort to reform labor in the interests of its practitioners would not begin until after the French Revolution, through the endeavors of socialists such as Charles Fourier and Robert Owen. Although not a socialist, Dohm may be considered an early voice in this development.

101. See Chapter 2.

102. The special preoccupation of many German authors with the social, psychological and spiritual nature of work has been noted in previous studies, which have identified its first appearance at the very end of the eighteenth century and have attributed its origins, as with so many other phenomena of German history, in a securalization of the spirit of German Pietism. See, for instance, Joan Campbell, *The Joy of Work, German Work* (Princeton, NJ, 1989), pp. 7–15; Werner Conze, "Arbeit," in Otto Brunner, ed., *Geschichtliche Grundbegriffe. Historisches Lexikon zur Politisch-Sozialen Sprache in Deutschaland*, vol. I (Stuttgart, 1972), pp. 155–85. However, Dohm's sensitivity to the psychological categories of work appears to have derived from other sources: first, from his empiricism, drawn from his intensive readings of the work of John Locke and Charles Bonnet; and, second, from his cameralist background with its encyclopedic and totalistic attention to every aspect of life in society and with its aim of maximizing the *Gluckseligkeit* of the population. On the influence of Bonnet, see Dambacher, *Dohm*, p. 63.

103. Coleman, "Labour in the English Economy of the Seventeenth Century," pp. 280–81.

104. Dohm, *Verbesserung*, p. 97.

105. Ibid., pp. 107–09.

106. Ibid., pp. 112–13.

107. Ibid., pp. 108–09.

108. Ibid., p. 113.

109. Ibid., p. 114.

110. Ibid., pp. 114–15.
111. Ibid., pp. 115–17.
112. A partial list of the sources Dohm consulted includes the following: Johann Caspar Ulrich, *Sammlung judischer Geschichten: welche sich mit diesem Volk in dem XIII. und folgenden Jahrhunderten bis auf MDCCLX in der Schweitz von Zeit zu Zeit zugetragen* (Berlin, 1768); Johann Christof Wagenseil, *Benachrichtigung wegen einiger die gemeine Judischheit betreffenden wichtigen Sachen* (Leipzig, 1705); Johann Friedrich Fischer, *Commentatio de statu et jurisdictione Judaeorum, secundum leges Romanas, Germanicas, Alsaticas* (Argentorati, 1763); Gottfried Mascov, *Exercitatio ivridica de censv ivdaico, oder, von der Juden-Schatzung* (Iena, 1736); Johann David Kohler, *Kurzgefasste und grundliche Teutsche Reichs-Historie vom Anfang des Teutschen Reichs mit Konig Ludwigen dem Teutschen bis auf den Badenschen Frieden: mit allen accurat im Kupfer vorgestellten koniglichen und kaiserlichen Hand-Zeichen oder Monogrammatibus* (Frankfurt und Leipzig, 1767); Heinrich Meibom, Rerum Germanicarum (Helmaestadii, 1688); Georg Heinrich Ayrer, *Tractatio iuridica: De Jvre recipiendi ivdaeos cvm generatim tvm speciatim in terris Brvnsvico-Lvnebvrgicis qvam . . .* (Gottingae, 1741); Johann Friedrich Pfeffinger, *Vitriarius illustratus, seu, Institutiones juris publici Romano-Germanici (Gothae, 1712).*
113. Dohm, "Vorerinnerung," in *Verbessung*, p. 3.
114. Dohm cites Michaelis' *Mosaisches Recht*, I (Frankfurt am Mayn, 1775), paragraphs 38–44: "Der alte jüdische Staat war ganz auf den Ackerbau gegrundet, und das mosaische Gestz besonders dem Handel nicht günstig. Auch die Handwerke wurden wenig von freien Menschen, sondern fast von den Leibeignen getrieben."
115. Cf. Dohm, *Verbesserung*, pp. 35–36, in which he writes: "Alles, was man den Juden vorwirst, is durch die politische Verfassung, in der sie ißt leben, bewirkt, und jede andre Menschengattung, in dieselben Umstände vresetzt, würde sich sicher eben derselben vergehungen schuldig machen. Denn jene übereinstimmende Eigenheiten der Denkart, der Gesinnungen und Leidenschaften, die man bei den grössern Theil der einselnen Glieder einer Nation findet, und die man ihren bestimmten Charakter nennt, sind nicht unterscheidende und unabänderliche Eigenschäften einer ihnen eignen Modification der menschlichen Natur; sondern, wie man in unsern Zeiten deutlich anerkannt hat, theils des Himmelsstreichs, der Nahrungsmittel u. theils und vornehmlich aber der politischen Verfassung, in der sich eine Nation befindet."
116. Toland, "Reasons," in Rudin, *Pamphlets*, p. 48.
117. Dohm accepts the (specious) claim that all first-century Alexanrian Jews were granted equal citizenship with the Greeks. See *Verbesserung*, p. 43: "Der Kaiser Klaudius gab allen Juden die Rechte, welche bisher die alexandrinischen nur allein genossen hatten und befahl ausdrücklich, daß sie in allen, auch den griechischen Städten, völlig gleicher Freiheiten mit den übrigen Bürgern geniessen sollten."
118. "Die Geschichte bestätigt also hier das Urtheil der uneingenommenen Vernunft, das die Juden eben so gut, wie alle andre Menschen, nützliche Glieder der bürgerlichen Gesellschaft sein können." Dohm, *Verbesserung*, p. 42. On the modern scholarly debate over whether and how many Jews enjoyed citizenship rights in Alexandria, see John M. G. Barclay, *Jews in the Mediterranean Diaspora, From Alexander to Trajan (323 BCE–117 CE)* (Berkeley, CA, 1996), pp. 63–71.
119. Dohm, *Verbesserung*, p. 44–47. Cf. Jonathan Hess's recent discussion of Dohm's Jewish history in *Germans, Jews, and the Claims of Modernity*, pp. 25–49.

120. Dohm, *Verbesserung*, p. 50: "Endlich wurde auch den Gliedern derselbenn alle Fähigkeit bürgerliche Ehre zu erwerben, und um das gemeinschaftliche Vaterland sich derdeint zu machen, genommen."
121. Hess, *Germans, Jews, and the Claims of Modernity*, pp. 25–49.
122. Frank L. Borchardt, *German Antiquity in Renaissance Myth* (Baltimore, 1971).
123. *Germania* would also exert an important impact of nineteenth-century Romantic antisemitism. See George L. Mosse, *The Crisis of German Ideology: Intellectual Origins of the Third Reich* (New York, 1964), pp. 67–71.
124. Dohm, *Verbesserung*, p. 50.
125. Ibid., pp. 50–52.
126. Tucker, *Second Letter*, pp. 10–11.
127. Dohm, *Verbesserung*, pp. 55–57.
128. Dohm's essential argument was repeated by Otto Stobbe, *Die Juden*, p. 8, and later developed into a far-reaching and highly influential theory of the historical shifts in Jewish status in Europe by Wilhelm Roscher, "Die Stellung der Juden im Mittelalter, betrachtet vom Standpunkte der allgemeinen Handelspolitik," in *Zeitschrift für gesamte Staatswissenschaft*, XXXI (1875), pp. 503–26. There is no evidence that Roscher was directly influenced by Dohm, yet their arguments are similar not only with regard to the Jews but also with regard to other trading populations (what would later be labeled "middleman minorities"). Roscher's arguments also exerted an important impact on Zionist political economists, among others. On Roscher's influence, see Walter P. Zenner, *Minorities in the Middle: A Cross Cultural Analyis*. (Albany, NY, 1991), pp. 2–3. Guido Kisch, *Historia Judaica*, vol. vi (April 1944), pp. 1–12; Jonathan Frankel, *Prophecy and Politics: Socialism, Nationalism, and the Russian Jews, 1862–1917* (Cambridge, 1981), p. 575, n. 202.
129. Luzzatto, *Discourse*, pp. 89–92, 153–54; Wolf, *Menasseh ben Israel's Mission to Oliver Cromwell*, pp. 82–83; Toland, "Reasons," in Rudin, *Pamphlets*, p. 44.
130. Dohm, *Verbesserung*, p. 78.
131. The idea that Jews had fallen from a position of former cultural and technical superiority was also expressed by Simone Luzzatto, and itself reflected a long-standing tradition within medieval Jewish apologetics. See Ravid, *Economics*, p. 51, n. 50; Of course, lack of originality should not be confused with lack of significance. Dohm's intentions here were quite dissimilar to the tradition continued by Luzzatto.
132. Dohm, *Verbesserung*, pp. 56–65.
133. See Dambacher, *Dohm*, 88–114.
134. Dohm, *Verbesserung*, p. 12.
135. Ibid., p. 12–15.
136. Smith, *Wealth of Nations*, Bk. IV, Ch. II, p. 478.
137. Turgot cited in Emma Rothschild, *Economic Sentiments: Adam Smith, Condorcet, and the Enlightenment* (Cambridge, MA, 2001), p. 161.
138. Dohm may have adapted this phrase from the physiocratic, "the natural order of things." See David F. Lindenfeld, *The Practical Imagination: The German Sciences of State in the Nineteenth Century* (Chicago, 1997), p. 27. Smith used the expression "the natural course of things." Smith, *Wealth of Nations*, Bk. III, Ch. I, p. 404.
139. Ibid.; Smith, *Wealth of Nations*, Bk. II, Ch. iv, pp. 379–80. In his 1692 *Some Considerations of the Lowering of Interest and Raising the Value of Money*, Locke had first

advanced the argument that low legal interest rates encourage contempt for the law. See Routh, *The Origin of Economic Ideas*, pp. 47–48.

140. Dohm, *Verbesserung*. p. 12.

141. Although Dohm regarded tobacco and coffee as "evils," he refused to sanction prohibitions on their importation and consumption, (1) because such laws could not be effectively enforced and would therefore invite criminality, and (2) because individuals of all classes must ultimately enjoy the right to consume as they will. It is true, as Dambacher emphasizes, that Dohm was at the same time willing to countenance tariffs and tolls to discourage consumption of foreign luxury items and encourage domestic production. See *Dohm*, pp. 109–11. First, Dohm never justified such measures in terms he believed violated his general principle of non-intervention, but, rather, as practical tools judiciously applied to achieve limited ends. Second, seeking the economic advantage of the home country does not in itself constitute mercantilism, if that term is to retain any historical specificity. In this light, it should be remembered that for Adam Smith a major virtue of commercial freedom was that it tended inevitably to draw capital back into home industry. Thus, Smith concluded that, "upon equal, or nearly equal profits . . . every individual naturally inclines to employ his capital in the manner in which it is likely to afford the greatest support to domestic industry, and to give revenue and employment to the greatest number of people of his own country." See *Wealth of Nations*, p. 477.

142. Moses Mendelssohn, *Schriften zum Judentum*, II, Band 8, edited by Alexander Altmann (Stuttgart, 1971), pp. 3–25.

143. See, for instance, Mendelssohn's disapproval of David Hartley's theory of sense vibrations, in Altmann, *Moses Mendelssohn*, p. 317.

144. Here, too, however, Mendelssohn's intention was at least partly ironic, for he proceeded in the preface to discuss recent cases of blood libel accusations and other such "outmoded" slanders. See Mendelssohn, *Schriften*, pp. 7–10.

145. Ibid., p. 6.

146. See Mendelssohn's letter of September 22, 1783, to Herz Homberg, in Alfred Jospe, ed., *Jerusalem and other Jewish Writings* (New York, 1969), p. 148; idem., *Jerusalem, or on Religious Power and Judaism*, pp. 134–39.

147. The January decree, often taken as *the* Edict of Toleration, was issued for the Jews of Lower Austria; earlier decrees for Jews were issued in October and December of the preceding year Bohemia and Silesia respectively; subsequent decrees were issued by Joseph for Moravia (1782), Hungary (1783), and Galicia (1785, 1789). Josef Karniel, *The Policy towards the Religious Minorities in the Habsburg Monarchy in the Time of Joseph II*, vol. II (Hebrew, Ph.D. Dissertation, University of Tel-Aviv, 1980), pp. 531–62 and Charles H. O'Brien, "Ideas of Religious Toleration at the Time of Joseph II: A Study of the Enlightenment among Catholics in Austria," in *Transactions of the American Philosophical Society*, no. 59 (1969), pp. 157–78 place the Jewish edicts in the framework of Joseph's general toleration policies.

148. *The Jew in the Modern World: A Documentary History*, edited by Paul Mendes-Flohr and Jehuda Reinharz (New York, 1995), pp. 37–39.

149. Apparently, a similar suspicion of the missionary aims of the *Toleranzpatent* was held by Dohm and Michaelis, see Altmann, *Moses Mendelssohn*, p. 462.

150. Mendelssohn, *Jerusalem, or on Religious Power and Judaism*, p. 135.

151. Mendelssohn, *Schriften*, p. 13.
152. Mendelssohn, *Jerusalem, or on Religious Power and Judaism*, p. 139.
153. Mendelssohn, *Schriften*, p. 15. Cf. Mendes-Flohr and Reinharz, *The Jew in the Modern World*, p. 47.
154. Ibid.
155. Including Locke, Hume, and Adam Ferguson, among others. See Altmann, *Moses Mendelssohn*, pp. 30–31, 523.
156. David Hume, "Of Interest," in Eugene F. Millar, ed., *Essays Moral, Political, and Literary* (Indianapolis, 1985), p. 301.
157. See, generally, Perrot, *Une histoire intellectuelle de l'écononomie politique*, pp. 220–36.
158. Smith, *The Wealth of Nations*, p. 352.
159. For Smith, of course, it was the division of labor (absent in a society comprised entirely of farmers) which made the industrious laborers even in a society top-heavy with nonproductive persons more prosperous than an "African king" who was "the master of the lives and liberties of ten thousand naked savages." See Istvan Hunt and Michael Ignatieff, "Needs and Justice in the *Wealth of Nations*: An Introductory Essay," in *Wealth and Virtue: The Shaping of Political Economy in the Scottish Enlightenment*, edited by idem. (Cambridge, 1985), pp. 3–4. Still, in emphasizing the distinction Smith was being prescriptive – favoring the removal of protections and subsidies to the nonproductive – and not merely descriptive.
160. In the "Introduction and Plan of the Work," Smith makes it clear that the wealth of a nation in any given year is the ratio of the "annual produce" to the size of the population, on the one hand, and the ratio of productive to nonproductive labor within that population, on the other. Smith, *Wealth of Nations*, p. 1.
161. Mendelssohn, *Schriften*, p. 13.
162. The quotation derives from the first edition of Say's *Traité d'economie politique, ou Simple exposition de la manière don't se forment, se distribuent et se consomment les richesses* (Paris, 1803). For a translation of the passage, R. R. Palmer, *J.-B. Say, An Economist in Troubled Times* (Princeton, NJ, 1997), pp. 69–70.
163. Smith, *Wealth of Nations*, Bk. II, Ch. iv, p. 381–83.
164. Quoted in Routh, *The Origin of Economic Ideas*, p. 100.
165. The distinction between productive and nonproductive labor parallels that between "capital" and "revenue." Indeed, it is productive labor that produces, replaces, and augments capital. Thus economic growth depends on an economical proportion of productive to non-productive laborers. See Smith, *The Wealth of Nations*, Bk. II, Ch. iii, pp. 352–53.
166. See Altman, *Moses Mendelssohn*, pp. 468–69.
167. Justi, *Die Grundfeste zu der Macht und Glückseligkeit der Staaten*, pp. 744–52.
168. Schumpeter, *History of Economic Analysis*, p. 227.
169. Johann August Schlettwein, "Bitte an die Grossen wegen der Juden zu Verhütung traurigen Folgen in den Staaten," in *Ephemeriden der Menschheit oder Bibliothek der Sittenlehre, der Politik, und der Gesetzgebung*, 4 (Leipzig, October–December, 1776), pp. 41–46. See also Lieberles, "The Historical Context of Dohm's Treatise," p. 48.
170. Von diesen Grundsätzen ist man in den meisten Ländern noch sehr weit entfernt, und wenn man es von einer Seite zu einem Hauptnahrungsmittel des Juden macht,

sein Geld auszuleihen, so beweisen sich die Gesetze fast immer parthehisch für die Schuldner, und diese werden nur zu oft durch ihr Bedürfniss gezwungen, den jüdischen Gläubiger zur Uebertretung dieser Gesetze zu nothigen, und ihn unaufhörlichen Strafen auszusetzen. Dohm, *Verbesserung*, pp. 13–14.

171. On this point, see Rothschild, *Economic Sentiments*, p. 145. On Smith's consistent position, see Donald Winch, *Riches and Poverty: An Intellectual History of Political Economy in Britain, 1750–1834* (Cambridge, 1996), p. 88.

172. Dohm, *Über die bürgerliche Verbesserung der Juden*, 2nd edition (Berlin, 1783), p. 295.

173. These included the requirement that Jewish fathers permit one of their sons to train as artisans; the imposition of residential quotas or special taxes on Jewish merchants; the requirement that Jewish factory owners hire a quota of Jewish workers; and even if necessary to positively forbid Jews from peddling in rural and small town regions. See Ibid., pp. 120–21; Dambacher, *Dohm*, p. 193.

174. Dohm also worried about the failed past experience of settling Gypsy and other colonists. By contrast, he thought a Jewish *Handwerk* policy would be effective and relatively cheap. See ibid., pp. 87–90, 120.

175. For the application of the term, see Sorkin, *The Transformation of German Jewry*, pp. 21–40, especially pp. 29–30; Dohm's response to the criticism of the preacher, J. M. Schwager, which originally appeared in the *Mindenschen Intelligenzblatt*, and that was reprinted in the second (1783) edition of the *Verbesserung*, is in this light instructive. The latter had suggested that the Jews' moral improvement must serve as a precondition for their political incorporation. Dohm responded that "The one must bring about the other, just as [up to now] the *political degradation* has brought about the moral; this viewpoint must never be lost sight of, otherwise the true relation of things will be entirely reversed." Quoted in Dambacher, *Dohm*, p. 179.

176. Dohm, *Verbesserung*, p. 34.

177. The anonymous author in *Ephemeriden der Menschheit* (Leipzig, 1794), pp. 289–90, for instance, remarked that "Numerous authors seem to have recognized the chief object [of Dohm's work] as directed not so much at the oppressed Hebrews...as at humanity and the states." Quoted in Horst Möller, "Über die bürgerliche Verbesserung der Juden: Christian Wilhelm von Dohm und seine Gegner," in Awerbuch and Jersch-Wenzel, eds., *Bild und Selbstbild*, pp. 68–69.

178. Dohm, *Verbesserung.*, pp. 25–26, 87.

179. Dohm's admiration for Turgot's reforms of the 1750s was tempered only by his awareness that they had failed. He did not dispute the ends Turgot was trying to achieve – the elimination of the guilds and the reduction, leading to the elimination, of aristocratic feudal privileges – but he claimed to see that in retrospect such goals could only be achieved through gradualism. See Dohm, "Neueste politische Gerüchte," in *Der Teutsche Merkur* (Weimar, 1777), pp. 221–46.

180. Jacob Katz, "The Term 'Jewish Emancipation': Its Origin and Historical Impact," *Studies in Nineteenth-Century Jewish Intellectual History*, edited by Alexander Altmann (Cambridge, MA, 1964), pp. 1–25.

181. This was noted by Jacob Katz, *Out of the Ghetto: The Social Background of Jewish Emancipation, 1770–1879* (Syracuse, NY, 1998), p. 192.

182. See, for instance, Goudar, *Les Intérêts de la France*, pp. 8–9 ff.

5. A STATE WITHIN A STATE

1. Guy Chaussinand-Nogaret, *The French Nobility in the Eighteenth Century*, translated by William Doyle (Cambridge, 1985), p. 1.
2. Hannah Arendt, *Antisemitism: Part One of the Origins of Totalitarianism* (New York, 1968), pp. 20–21.
3. Hertzberg, *The French Enlightenment and the Jews*, pp. 9–10.
4. Penslar, *Shylock's Children*, pp. 29–32.
5. Deborah Hertz, *Jewish High Society in Old Regime Berlin* (New Haven, 1988), pp. 35–36. In this vein, one should also mention the statement of Leon Poliakov, both a historian of antisemitism and of Jewish commerce, who insisted on the importance of understanding "the psychological affinities between nobles and Jews" to grasp the solidity of their premodern alliance. Poliakov, *The History of Anti-Semitism*, vol. 3, p. 11.
6. As William H. Sewell notes, "[i]t was by all accounts the most influential pamphlet of the thousands published in the months leading up to the French Revolution." On this and on Sieyes's early years and religious attitudes, see Sewell's *A Rhetoric of Bourgeois Revolution: The Abbé Sieyes and 'What is the Third Estate?'* (Durham, NC, 1994), pp. 1, 8–10. For a facsinating recent discussion of the French Revolution focusing on Sieyes, see Michael Sonnenscher, *Before the Deluge: Public Debt, Inequality, and the Intellectual Origins of the French Revolution* (Princeton, NJ, 2007). Unfortunately, this book appeared to late for me to incorporate it into the analysis in this chapter.
7. Jacqueline Hecht, "Un problème de population active au XVIIIe siècle, en France: la quarelle de la nobesse commerçante," *Population*, no. 2 (April–May 1964), p. 268.
8. Hecht, "Un problème de population," p. 273.
9. Montesquieu, *The Spirit of the Laws*, Part I, Bk. 5, Ch. 8.
10. Abbé Gabriel François Coyer, *La Noblesse commerçante* (Paris, 1756).
11. Henri Lévy-Bruhl, "La Noblesse de France et le Commerce à la fin de l'ancien Régime," *Revue d'Histoire Moderne*, no. 8 (1933), p. 218.
12. Hecht, "Un problème de population," p. 277.
13. Jay M. Smith, *Nobility Reimagined: The Patriotic Nation in Eighteenth-Century France* (Ithaca, NY, 2005), p. 13. For a qualified restatement of the older view of noble taxation privilege through 1789, see Michael Kwaas, "A Kingdom of Taxpayers: State Formation, Privilege, and Political Culture in Eighteenth-Century France," *Journal of Modern History*, vol. 70, no. 2 (June 1998), pp. 295–338, esp. p. 313.
14. Emmanuel Sieyes, *Qu'est-ce que le Tiers état?*, edited by Roberto Zapperi (Genève, 1970) p. 121. I also have used and sometimes adapted the English translation by M. Blondel in Emmanuel Joseph Sieyès, *What Is the Third Estate*, edited by S. E. Feiner (New York, 1963). Hereafter cited as Blondel.
15. Ibid., p. 125. Blondel, p. 57.
16. Sieyes remarks in a footnote that he does not consider the clergy as an actual order, but a profession. At the same time, the nobility's monopolization of the high offices of the clergy (something Sieyes had firsthand experience with), indicates that it is a profession corrupted by the privileged order of the nobility. See ibid., p. 124, note 1.
17. Article 3 of the "Declaration of the Rights of Man and Citizen," in Van Kley, *The French Idea of Freedom: The Old Regime and the Declaration of Rights of 1789* (Stanford, 1994), p. 1.

18. Reinharz and Mendes-Flor, *The Jew in the Modern World*, pp. 305–06.
19. Dale Van Kley, "From the Lessons of French History to Truths for All Times and All People: The Historical Origins of an Anti-Historical Declaration," in idem., ed., *The French Idea of Freedom*, pp. 80–81.
20. Chaussinand-Nogaret, *The French Nobility*, pp. 3, 16–17.
21. Article 1. The Declaration was largely based on a draft by Sieyes. See Sieyes, *Préliminaire de la constitution françoise: Reconnaissance et exposition raisonée de droits de l'homme et du citoyen* (Paris, 1789); Dale Van Kley, "From the Lessons of French History," p. 76.
22. Sieyes, *Qu'est-ce que le Tiers état?*, p. 14.
23. Ibid., p. 32.
24. Jacob Katz, "A State within a State – the History of an anti-Semitic Slogan," in *Zur Assimilation und Emanzipatin der* Juden, edited by idem. (Darmstadt, 1982), pp. 124–53.
25. Sieyes viewed the monarchy as the captive of the nobility and not the other way around. See Van Kley, "From the Lessons of French History," pp. 72–113.
26. Sieyes, *Qu'est ce que le Tiers état?* p. 124.
27. "le corps d'un malheureux une maladie affreuse qui lui dévoreroit la chair vive." Ibid., 211. Blondel, p. 164.
28. Ibid., p. 218. Blondel, p. 165.
29. A view classically formulated by Henri, compte de Boulainvilliers in his 1732 *Essai sur la noblesse de France*.
30. The rest of the sentence indicates that the nobility are foreign to the nation because they do not derive their powers from the people. Sieyes uses the dual sense of the word *principe* as both "origin" (suggesting alien derivation) and "principle" suggesting powers derived illegitimately in terms of natural rights. In reality, Sieyes was not interested in racial or even necessarily cultural definitions of citizenship, although he often compared the nobility (unfavorably) to foreign nations who were traditional enemies of France, such as the British. Sieyes, *Qu'est ce que le Tiers état?*, p. 126.
31. Ibid., p. 196.
32. Ibid., p. 147.
33. Ibid., p. 196 (my emphasis). Blondel, p. 145.
34. Ibid., p. 150. This was an interpretation which had a significant amount of truth to it, and one that furthermore would have been widely recognized when Sieyes wrote. As Chaussinand-Nogaret explains, following the defeat of the old feudal nobility in the Fronde, and especially in the "guilded ghetto" established by Louis XIV, a "new" nobility arose (composed largely of formerly ennobled merchants) which owed direct allegiance to the king. Chaussinand-Nogaret designates this as "royal" as opposed to a "liege" nobility (though the latter continued to exist despite the loss of its former power). But where modern historical scholarship differs from Sieyes is in recognizing this "new" nobility less as a power unto itself than as a prop of absolutism. See Chaussinand-Nogaret, *The French Nobility*, pp. 7–8.
35. *Qu'est ce que le Tiers état?*, p. 132.
36. Ibid., p. 126.
37. Montesquieu, *The Spirit of the Laws*, edited and translated by Anne Cohler, Basia Miller, and Harold Stone (Cambridge, 1995), pp. 167–68. According to

Chaussinand-Nogaret, Montesquieu represented a synthesis of earlier defenses of the nobility as a check against tyranny. See Chaussinand-Nogaret, *The French Nobility*, p. 17.

38. "... for if *ability* derives from the exclusive employment and long application of intelligence, and if members of the Third Estate have been required for a hundred reasons to distinguish themselves through such a course, the *illumination* [*les lumières*] of public morality must [nevertheless] more readily manifest itself among men who are better situated to grasp the grand relations of society and among men whose original course of development are less commonly cut short." Sieyes, pp. 156–57. Blondel, pp. 94–95.

39. Quoted in *Qu'est ce que le Tiers état?*, p. 164. Blondel, pp. 94–95.

40. For this reason, Sieyes favored a system of representation rather than direct democracy. In accordance with his reading of modern political economy, he applied the division of labor to the political as well as the economic sphere. On this point, see Sewell, *Rhetoric*, pp. 68–69.

41. This phrase is Sewell's, *Rhetoric*, p. 163.

42. This phrase is Sieyes's, quoted in ibid., p. 164.

43. Quoted in Sewell, p. 164.

44. Smith, as noted, believed that only state-supplied public education could counteract the mind-numbing effects of the division of labor on working men. See Smith, *Wealth*, pp. 308–09, 340.

45. Sieyes, *Qu'est ce que le Tiers état?*, p. 139.

46. Ibid., p. 128 (his emphasis). Blondel, pp. 60–61.

47. Sieyes, *Qu'est ce que le Tiers état?*, p. 164.

48. As events soon proved, it would be delegates of the Third who in a sense wound up seceding.

49. Sieyes, *Qu'est ce que le Tiers état?*, p. 194. Blondel, p. 143.

50. J. M. Roberts, *French Revolution Documents*, vol. 1 (Oxford, 1966), pp. 151–53.

51. Patrice Higonnet, *Class, Ideology, and the Rights of Nobles during the French Revolution* (Oxford, 1981), pp. 57–78.

52. *Recueil des lois décrets, ordonnances, avis du conseil d' état, arêtes et règlements concernant les israélites dupuis la Révelution de 1789*, edited by Achille-Edmond Halphen (Paris, 1851), pp. 186–87. On the profession of toleration by Maury and other opponents of Jewish citizenship, see Schechter, *Obstinate Hebrews*, pp. 157–58. Schechter notes that thirteen of the twenty-six deputies who spoke in favor of the Jews were noble and speculates that this epitomized the theatrical display of symbolic and largely inconsequential noblesse oblige that Schechter believes characterized the emancipation episode as a whole. See pp. 150–65.

53. Zalkind Hourwitz, *Apologie des Juifs: en réponse à la question: Est-il deesmoyens de render les Juifs plus heureux et plus utiles en France?* (Paris, 1789), p. 73.

54. Quoted in Yerachmiel (Richard) Cohen, "Jewish Emancipation Rhetoric and the Image of the Future" (Hebrew), in *Ha-Mahapkhah ha-Tsarfatit ve-Rishumah: Kovets Ma'amarim* [The French Revolution and its Impact: Collected Essays] (Hebrew), edited by Yerachmiel (Richard) Cohen (Jerusalem, 1991), p. 155.

55. The point is not to claim that the nobility question *caused* the Jewish question, but simply to suggest a common structural dynamic insofar as both groups, *mutatis*

mutandis, were construed as part of the ancien régime and as sharing certain social and economic characteristics.

56. Quoted in Reinharz and Mendes-Flor, *The Jew in the Modern World*, p. 115.
57. Although some historians see their "assimilationist" aims as emblematic of the broader flaws of French and European citizenship concepts. See most recently the doctoral dissertation by Scott B. Glotzer, *Napoleon, the Jews, and the Construction of Modern Citizenship in Early Nineteenth Century France*. Rutgers University, New Brunswick, NJ, 1996.
58. Simon Schwarzfuchs, *Napoleon, the Jews and the Sanhedrin* (London, 1979).
59. This much, at least, is accepted by even the "revisionist" schools of Revolution historiography. See T. C. W. Blanning, *The French Revolution: Aristocrats versus Bourgeois?* (London, 1987).
60. Saul Ascher, *Eisenmenger der Zweite: Nebst einem vorangesetzten Sendscreiben an Herrn Prof. Fichte in Jena* (Berlin, 1794).
61. Paul Lawrence Rose, *Revolutionary Antisemitism in Germany* (Princeton, NJ, 1990), pp. 131. As Jonathan Hess points out, the great nineteenth-century Jewish historian Heinrich Graetz had labeled Fichte, "the father and apostle of national German hatred of the Jews, of a kind unknown before, or rather never before so clearly manifested." See Hess, *Germans, Jews and the Claim to Modernity*, p. 142.
62. Jacob Katz notes the context of the general attack on corporations but neglects to mention the nobility. Katz rightly sees Fichte's statements as antisemitic but fails to situate these comments within the overarching *Tendenz* of the book, which is an attack on the noble order. See Katz, "A State within a State," pp. 139–41.
63. *Emmanuel Sieyès. Politische Schriften*, edited by Konrad Engelbert Ölsner (n.p., 1796). On this effort see the references in Sonenscher, *Before the Deluge*, pp. 71–71, n. 139.
64. Wilhelm G. Jacobs, *Johann Gottlieb Fichte* (Reinbek bei Hamburg, 1984), p. 43.
65. James J. Sheehan, *German History: 1770–1886* (Oxford, 1994), pp. 210–18; Koppel S. Pinson, *Modern Germany: Its History and Civilization* (New York, 1966), pp. 25–30; Klaus Peter, *Die Politische Romantik in Deutschland* (Stuttgart, 1985), pp. 9–73.
66. "To every revolution belongs the renunciation of the previous contract and the joining together through a new one. Both are legally valid, consequently so too is every revolution in which both occur through legal means, that is, out of free will." Johann Gottlieb Fichte, "Beitrag zur Berichtigung der Urtheile des Publicums über die Französische Revolution," in J. H. Fichte, ed., *Johann Gottlieb Fichte's sämtliche Werke*, Pt. III, vol. 1 (Berlin, 1845), p. 148.
67. Ibid., p. 148.
68. Ibid., p. 149.
69. Ibid., p. 149.
70. Klaus Epstein, *The Genesis of German Conservatism* (Princeton, NJ, 1966), p. 571.
71. La Vopa, *Fichte: The Self and the Calling of Philosophy, 1762–1799* (Cambridge, 2001), p. 95.
72. Annelise Mayer, *England als politisches Vorbild un sein Einfluß auf die politische Entwicklung in Deutschland bis 1830* (Endingen, 1931), pp. 34–35.
73. Fichte, "Beitrag," p. 151.
74. Ibid., p. 152 (footnote).
75. Ibid., p. 149.
76. Ibid.

77. This is certainly along the lines of the title phrase "revolutionary antisemitism" of Paul Lawrence Rose's book.

78. Fichte, "Beitrag," p. 149. The accusation that the Jews serve the state by extracting illicit taxes goes back to Martin Luther, "On the Jews and Their Lies," pp. 272–73.

79. The specific episode Fichte may have had in mind was the Prussian government's dismissal of a state official, Johann Heinrich Schulz, for a published attack on Jewish "fanaticism." See La Vopa, *Fichte*, p. 147.

80. An allusion to Kant's "What Is Enlightenment," the famous first sentence of which reads, "Enlightenment is man's emergence from his self-imposed nonage [*Unmündigkeit*]. Characteristic is the contrast between Kant's diagnosis of a "self-imposed nonage" and Fichte's of a nonage at least equally imposed from outside. Immanuel Kant, *Perpetual Peace and other essays on Politics, History, and Morals.* Translated by Ted Humphrey (Indianapolis, 1983), pp. 41, 47 f. 2.

81. Fichte, "Beitrag," p. 151 f.

82. Ibid., pp. 150–51, 266–68; cf. Johann Gottlieb Fichte, *The Characteristics of the Present Age*, translated by William Smith (London, 1847), in which, as a reflection of his mature views (1806) on the ideal political order, Fichte insists on the "duty of both [Church and State] to keep themselves absolutely separate . . . ," p. 197.

83. Fichte, "Beitrag," p. 151 f.

84. Ibid., p. 150.

85. Ibid., p. 151 f.

86. Otto Stobbe, *Die Juden in Deutschland*, pp. 20–36, 128–31; Georg Caro, "Die Juden des Mittelalters in ihrer wirschaftlichen Betätigung," in *Monatschrift für Geschichte und Wissenschaft des Judentums*, vol. 45 (1912), pp. 600–01.

87. Hertz, *Jewish High Society in Old Regime Berlin*, pp. 28, 46.

88. Fichte, "Beitrag," p. 96. On the increasing rejection in intellectuals of Fichte's generation of the application of the Newtonian machine metaphor to society, see La Vopa, *Fichte*, p. 89. See also Roy Pascal, "'Bildung' and the Division of Labour," in *German Studies Presented to Walter Horace Bruford* (London, 1962), pp. 14–28.

89. Fichte, "Beitrag," pp. 235–36.

90. According to La Vopa, the example of Revolutionary France where the elimination of labor services and the subdivision of estates into smallholdings was projected to significantly increase agricultural productivity may have influenced Fichte. See *Fichte*, p. 122.

91. Fichte, "Beitrag," p. 187–88.

92. Ibid., p. 187 (Fichte's emphasis).

93. Ibid., p. 189 (emphasis added).

94. Ibid., p. 186.

95. Ibid., p. 189 (emphasis added).

96. Richard Beinacki, *The Fabrication of Labor: Germany and Britain, 1640–1914* (Berkeley, CA, 1995), pp. 264–65. J. F. Schiller's translation of *The Wealth of Nations* appeared in 1776 and 1778. The work received considerable attention, including extensive summaries, in the German periodical literature of the 1770s and 1780s. Subsequent translations quickly followed. See Wilhelm Treue, "Adam Smith in Deutschland: Zum Problem des 'Politischen Professors' zwischen 1776 und 1810," in Werner Conze, ed., *Deutschaland und Europa, Historische Studien zur Völker- und Staatenordnung des Abendlandes: Festschrift für Hans Rothfels* (Dusseldorf, 1993), pp. 101–02.

97. Klaus Hammacher and Hans Hirsch, *Die Wirtschaftspolitik des Philophen Friedrich Heinrich Jacobi* (Amsterdam, 1993), p. 69.

98. Hardenberg himself studied Smith under Pütter. See Treue, "Adam Smith," pp. 105, 107, 108.

99. Ibid., p. 108.

100. Johann Gottlieb Fichte, *Der geschlossne Handelsstaat: e. philos. Entwurf als Anh. zur Rechtslehre, u. Probe e. künftig zu liefernden Politik: mit e. bisher unbekannten Ms. Fichtes "Ueber StaatsWirthschaft,"* edited by Hans Hirsch (Hamburg, 1979), p. 7.

101. See La Vopa, *Fichte*, pp. 304-19; Susan Shell, "A Determined Stand: Freedom and Security in Fichte's Science of Right," *Polity* 25:1 (Fall 1992), pp. 95-121; R. R. Palmer, *The Age of Democratic Revolutions*, vol. II (Princeton, NJ, 1970), p. 451.

102. Johann Gottlieb Fichte, *Das System der Sittenlehre nach den Principien der Wissenschaftslehre* (Berlin, 1798).

103. Johann Gottlieb Fichte, *Grundlage des Naturrechts nach Principien der Wissenschaftslehre* (Berlin, 1797). On these points, see Wayne M. Martin, "Fichte's Transcendental Phenomenology of Agency Commentary on Fichte's Introduction to the *Sittenlehre*," in *Fichte: System der Sittenlehre*, edited by J. Merle and A. Schmidt (Berlin, 2007).

104. Cf. La Vopa, *Fichte*, p. 277.

105. Ibid., p. 189.

106. Cf. Reinhold Aris, *History of Political Thought in Germany from 1789 to 1815* (New York, 1965), pp. 130-35.

107. Cf. Zwi Batscha's "Einleitung" to Fichte's *Ausgewählte Politische Schriften*, edited by Zwi Batscha and Richard Saage (Frankfurt-am-Main, 1977), pp. 41-42.

108. Fichte had defended such liberty in his earlier "Einige Vorlesungen über die Bestimmung des Gelehrten," in *Sämtliche Werke*, vol. 1, pp. 317-18.

109. Fichte, *Der geschlossne Handelsstaat*, p. 23.

110. Ibid., p. 22.

111. Fichte, *Beitrag*, pp. 197-214.

112. Fichte, *Handelsstaat*, p. 65.

113. Ibid., pp. 66-67.

114. Ibid.

115. Ibid., p. 67.

116. Ibid.

117. Ibid.

118. Ibid., p. 72.

119. Ibid., p. 55.

120. Sieyes, *Qu'est ce que le Tiers état?*, pp. 113, 124.

6. THE ISRAELITES AND THE ARISTOCRACY

1. Novalis, *Fragmente und Studien; Die Christenheit oder Europa* (Stuttgart, 1984). The poem, or "fragment," was not published in its entirely until 1826, many year's after Hardenberg's death. For an English translation, see *The Early Political Writings of the German Romantics*, edited by Frederick C. Beiser (Cambridge, 1996), pp. 61-79.

2. Fania Oz-Salzburger, "The Jewish Roots of Western Freedom," *Azure* 13 (Summer 2002), 88-132.

3. Adam Müller, "Die Lehre vom Gegensatze," in *Kritische/Ästhetische Schriften*, vol. 2, edited by Walter Schroeder and Werner Siebert (Berlin, 1967), pp. 195–252.

4. German romantics are usually divided in three groups, the early or *Frühromantik*, from 1797 to 1802, the High or *Hochromantik*, with which Müller is identified (1803–1815), and the late or *Spätromantik* (1816–1830). See Beiser's introduction to *Early Political Writings*, p. xii.

5. Klaus Peter, *Die politische Romantik in Deutschland*, pp. 405–06.

6. Adam Müller, *Die Elemente der Staatskunst: oeffentliche Vorlesungen, vor Sr. Durchlaucht dem Prinzen Bernhard von Sachsen-Weimar und einer Versammlung von Staatsmännern und Diplomaten, im Winter von 1808 auf 1809, zu Dresden*. 3 volumes (Berlin, 1809).

7. Idem., *Versuche einer neuen Theorie des Geldes* (Jena, 1922).

8. The standard biography is Jakob Baxa, *Adam Müller, ein Lebensbid aus den Befreiungskriegen und aus der deutschen Restauration* (Jena, 1930).

9. Epstein, *Genesis*, pp. 181–82.

10. Peter, *Die politische Romantik*, pp. 14–15, 27.

11. On Müller's relation to von Marwitz and Metternich, see Benedict Koehler, *Ästhetik der Politik: Adam Müller und die politische Romantik* (Stuttgart, 1980), pp. 126–33, 190–99. Müller often has been regarded both by contemporaries and later commentators as something of an opportunist. His legacy in the history of German conservativism was not advanced by his conversion or his service to Austria. See Koehler, pp. 11–31.

12. See the dismissive remarks in the standard histories of economic thought: Schumpeter, *History of Economic Analysis*, pp. 421–24; Roll, *A History of Economic Thought*, pp. 218–27.

13. He derides these methods as mere "Plusmachen"; see Müller, *Versuche*, p. 42.

14. Müller, *Elemente*, vol. 1, pp. 91–92.

15. Ibid., p. 289.

16. Ibid., 237–40.

17. Rothschild, *Economic Sentiments*, p. 65.

18. See Friedrich Bulow's Introduction to Adam Müller, *Vom Gest der Gemeinschaft* (Leipzig, 1931), p. xxvii.

19. Fichte, *Beitrag*, p. 266.

20. Idem., "Einige Vorlesungen über die Bestimmung des Gelehrten," in *Sämtliche Werke*, vol. 1, pp. 318–19.

21. Müller, *Elemente*, vol. 1, p. 223.

22. "As the ends of such a partnership [i.e., a state] cannot be obtained in many generations, it becomes a partnership not only between those who are living, but between those who are dead, and those who are to be born." Edmund Burke, *Reflections on the Revolution in France* (Indianapolis, 1987), p. 85. On Burke's criticisms of Smith and contemporary political economy, see Rothschild, *Economic Sentiments*, pp. 53–54.

23. Müller, *Elemente*, vol. 1, p. 84.

24. William Robertson, *A View of the Progress of Society in Europe from the Subversion of the Roman Empire to the Beginning of the Sixteenth Century* (Chicago:, 1972 – originally published in 1769); Adam Ferguson, *History of the Progress and Termination of the Roman Empire* (London, 1783). Ferguson was widely read in Göttingen in the years when Müller was a student and Müller had almost certainly encountered his

work. I have not been able to determine whether Müller read Robertson directly or absorbed him through Burke. On the relationship of Robertson and Ferguson to Burke, see J. G. A. Pocock's introduction to Burke, *Reflections*, pp. xxxii–xxxiii. On Ferguson's reception in Germany, see Pascal, "'Bildung'," p. 15.

25. Müller, *Elemente*, vol. 3, p. 66.
26. Ibid., pp. 268–69.
27. Müller, *Versuche*, p. 6.
28. Müller, *Elemente*, Vol. 1, pp. 146–48.
29. Ibid., pp. 84, 146–48.
30. See Melamed, *The Philosopher King*, pp. 144–54. On the same theme in the writings of Hobbes, Spinoza, and many of the English deists, see, generally, Champion, *The Pillars of Priestcraft Shaken*.
31. For instance, Carlo Sigonio, Cornelius Bertram, and Petrus Cunaeus, all mentioned in Chapter 2. See Neuman, *The Literature of the Respublica Judaica*. For similar approaches in contemporary Germany, see Johannes Althusius, *Politica*, edited and translated by Frederick S. Carney (Indianapolis, 1995), pp. 146–47, and in seventeenth-century England, Christopher Hill, *Puritanism and Revolution: Studies in Interpretation of the English Revolution of the Seventeenth Century* (London, 1990), pp. 68–73.
32. Burchardt, *German Antiquity*, p. 12.
33. Laurence Dickey, *Hegel: Religion, Economics, and the Politics of Spirit, 1770–1807* (Cambridge, 1987), pp. 31–110.
34. Epstein, *Genesis*, pp. 572–74.
35. Müller, *Elemente*, vol. 3, pp. 16–18.
36. Cunaeus, *Of the Common-wealth of the Hebrews*, p. 87; Josephus, *Against Apion*, 1:12.
37. "...a living state, and a living freedom: that is the true Mosaic sense of all the institutions which he erected, so as to protect his people from intermixture with commerce and trade with foreign nations. This pride in sublime suffering is the first, most splendid and at the same time gentlest feeling of life. It is also the surest foundation of a true nobility." Müller, *Elemente*, vol. 3, pp. 23–24.
38. Ibid., p. 20.
39. Ibid., p. 21; One recalls here the notion of Adam Smith that "the merchant has no country." See Smith, *Wealth*, p. 444.
40. Müller, *Elemente*, vol. 3, p. 21.
41. I owe this formulation to Nicholas Riasanovski, *The Emergence of Romanticism* (New York, 1992).
42. Müller, *Versuche*, p. 298.
43. Müller, *Elemente*, vol. 1, p. 166.
44. Ibid., p. 268; Ernst Cassirer, *The Philosophy of the Enlightenment*, trans., Fritz C. A. Koelln and James Pettigrove (Princeton, NJ, 1979), pp. 31–32.
45. Müller, *Elemente*, vol. 1, p. 63.
46. Ibid., vol. 3, pp. 24–26.
47. Ibid., p. 93.
48. Burke, *Reflections on the Revolution in France*, pp. 95–96.
49. Dohm, *Verbesserung*, p. 50–52.
50. Müller, *Elemente*, vol. 3, pp. 89–91.
51. Ibid., pp. 95–97.

52. Ibid., p. 97.
53. Ibid., vol. 1, p. 264.
54. Ibid., vol. 3, p. 77.
55. Ibid., p. 99.
56. "Roman civitas [*Römisches Bürgerwesen*] and European *tiers-état* are two entirely different, mutually-opposing and mutually-exclusive essences." Ibid., p. 98.
57. Ibid., pp. 37–38.
58. Ibid., p. 37, note.
59. Ibid., pp. 96–97.
60. Ibid., pp. 37–38.
61. Ibid., p. 36.
62. Baxa, *Adam Müller*, pp. 360–63.
63. Hertz, *Jewish High Society*, pp. 271–78; Hannah Arendt, *Rahel Varnhagen: Lebensgeschichte einer deutschen Jüdin aus der Romantik* (Munich, 1959), pp. 118–20.
64. Alfred D. Low, *Jews in the Eyes of Germans, from the Enlightenment to Imperial Germany* (Philadelphia, 1979), pp. 197–203.
65. *Allegemeine Zeitung*, no. 69 (June 11, 1816), pp. 6–9; Low, *Jews in the Eyes*, p. 204. Müller later pursued this same line in a remarkable letter from 1823, written to the Duke of Anhalt-Köthen. Here he insisted that from a liberal standpoint Christians could not in justice deny equality to Jews. "The mere *interest* of Christians and the possible future risk they might engender cannot *in and for itself* supply grounds for denying Jews rights stemming from the concept of equality." But, of course, this was to underscore Müller's disdain for individual rights and equality. Adam Müller, *Lebenenzeugnisse*, vol. 2, edited by Jacob Baxa (Munich, 1966), p. 622.
66. Frederick was influenced only indirectly by Müller via the formulation of the medieval *Ständesstaat* provided by Karl Ludwig von Haller. See Klaus von See, *Freiheit und Gemeinschaft: Völkisch-nationales Denken in Deutschland zwischen Französischer Revolution und Erstem Weltkrieg* (Heidelberg, 2001), pp. 71–78. See also Chapter 8.
67. Horst Möller, *Fürstenstaat oder Bürgernation: Deutschand 1763–1815* (Berlin, 1989), pp. 595–632, especially pp. 616–17.
68. See Eric Dorn Brose, *German History, 1789–1871* (Providence, RI, 1997), pp. 93–114.
69. Theodore S. Hamerow, *Restoration, Revolution, Reaction: Economics and Politics in Germany, 1815–1871* (Princeton, NJ, 1958), pp. 47–60, 68–74; Joachim Whaley, "The German Lands before 1815," in *Nineteenth-Century Germany: Politics, Culture and Society 1780–1918*, edited by John Breuilly (New York, 2001), 33–34.
70. Hertz, *Jewish High Society*, p. 276; on Buchholz's anti-Jewish writings, see Peter R. Erspamer, *The Elusiveness of Tolerance* (Chapel Hill, NC, 1997), pp. 120–22; Hess, *Germans, Jews and the Claims of Modernity*, pp. 198–201.
71. Allen W. Woods comment, that " . . . whatever it may do to our moral sensibilities, antisemitism (or lack of it) is not, in this period, a reliable barometer of a person's general political position," may be useful in this light. See G. W. F. Hegel, *Elements of the Philosophy of Right*, translated by H. B. Nisbett (Cambridge, 1991), p. 386.
72. See Hertz, *Jewish High Society*, pp. 33–35, 251–78.
73. Friedrich Ludwig Jahn was perhaps the major exception. See Low, *Jews in the Eyes of the Germans*, pp. 164–65.
74. See Katz, "A State within a State," pp. 141–44; Erspamer, *The Elusiveness of Tolerance*, pp. 113–150; Hess, *Germans, Jews and the Claims of Modernity*, pp. 169–203, who notes

that Grattenauer's *Wider die Juden*, with six editions, "was one of the best-selling titles of its era" (p. 174).

75. M. de Bonald, "Sur les Juifs," in *Melanges Littéraires, Politiques et Philosophiques*, Vol. 2 (Paris, 1858). Bonald's emphasis.

76. Quoted in Poliakov, *History of Antisemitism*, vol. 3, p. 11.

77. He served in this position from 1805 to 1816, and from 1816 to 1843 he was Professor of Physics at Jena. Fries is also known to posterity as the nemesis of Hegel, famously ridiculed in *The Philosophy of Right*, pp. 15–16.

78. Charles E. McClelland, *State, Society, and University in Germany* (Cambridge, 1980), pp. 146–47.

79. Jacob Friedrich Fries, *Von Deutschem Bund und Deutscher Staatsverfassung* (Heidelberg, 1816), pp. 10–13.

80. Ibid., pp. 53–54.

81. Ibid., pp. 53–54.

82. Ibid., p. 65.

83. Jakob Friedrich Fries, *Ueber die Gefärdung des Wolhstandes und Charakters der Deutschen durch die Juden* (Heidelberg, 1816), pp. 3–4. Elsewhere (p. 12) Fries refers to Jews as "eine Mäkler- und Trödlerkaste."

84. Ibid., p. 15.

85. Jakob Friedrich Fries, *Politik oder philosophische Staatslehre*, edited by E. F. Apelt (Jena, 1848), p. 105.

86. Fries, *Ueber die Gefärdung*, p. 18 (my emphasis).

87. See Karl Marx, *The German Ideology*, Pt. I, section 24.

88. Fries, *Ueber die Gefärdung*, p. 18.

89. Ibid., p. 10.

90. Ibid., p. 22.

91. Ibid., p. 23.

92. Friedrich Rühs, *Die Rechte des Christenthums und des deutschen Volks: vertheidigt gegen die Ansprüche der Juden und ihrer Verfechter* (Berlin, 1816); Idem., *Über die Ansprüche der Juden an das deutsch Bürgerrecht; mit einem Anhange über die Geschichte der Juden in Spanien*, (Berlin, 1816). On the background, see Selma Stern-Täubler, "Die literarische Kampf um die Emanzipation in den Jahren 1816–1820 und seine ideologischen und soziologischen Voraussetzungen," in *Hebrew Union College Annual*, vol. xxiii, pt. ii (Cincinnati, 1950–1951), p. 181–82.

93. Erspamer, *The Elusiveness of Tolerance*, pp. 124–26.

94. Friedrich Rühs, *Entwurf einer Propädeutik des historischen Studiums* (Berlin, 1911). Idem., *Historische Entwickelung des Einflusses Frankreichs und der Franzosen auf Deutschland und die Deutschen* (Berlin, 1815).

95. Saul Ascher's pamphlet of that title was published slightly before Rühs's pamphlets appeared and do not refer to him, although it frequently invokes Müller as (incorrectly) an exemplar of "Germanomanie." See "Die Germanomanie: Skizze zu einem Zeitgemälde, in *4 Flugschriften: Eisenmenger der Zweite, Napoleon, Die Germanomanie, Die Wartburgfeier* (Berlin, 1991), pp. 193–232.

96. In his *Handbook of the History of the Middle Ages*, published in the same year as his antiemancipation tracts, Rühs noted the cruel treatment suffered by Jews during the Crusades. Although his characterizations of Jews are hardly more sympathetic in the *Handbook* than in his antiemancipation pamphlets, his tone is less violent. See Friedrich Rühs, *Handbuch der Geschichte des Mittelalters* (Berlin, 1816), pp. 142–44.

97. Friedrich Rühs, *Ueber die Ansprüche*, pp. 14–15.
98. Ibid., p. 15.
99. Ibid., pp. 15–17.
100. Ibid., pp. 18.
101. Ibid., pp. 18–22.
102. Rühs's attempt to show that in Antiquity and biblical times, Jews had not been "farmers in their own land," but, rather, already largely "usurers and traders," proved a total failure. His plundering of *Maccabees*, Josephus, Chrysostum, Tacitus, and the Bible, showed merely that there had existed wealthy Jews, and not a *Handelskaste* at this time. Ibid., p. 19.
103. Rühs made clear at the start of his pamphlet that he would set out to overturn Dohm's account. Ibid. p. 3.
104. Ibid., pp. 3–4.
105. In the introduction to *Ueber die Ansprüche*, Rühs explained that his pamphlet was an outgrowth of a book on the fall of Germany that he had planned to write. One part of that larger effort was his *Historische Entwickelung des Einflusses Frankreiches und der Franzosen auf Duetschland und die Deutschen* (Berlin, 1815).
106. Rühs, *Veber die Ansprüche*, p. 4.
107. Ibid., p. ix.
108. Ibid., pp. xiv–xv, p. 7.
109. Ibid., p. 164; Rühs, *Ueber die Ansprüche*, pp. 3–4.
110. Ibid., pp. 24–25.
111. Ibid., p. 5.
112. Solomon Maimon, *The Autobiography of Solomon Maimon*, trans. J. Clark Murray (London, 1954), p. 168.
113. Martin Luther, "On the Jews and their Lies," p. 140.
114. Ibid., pp. 272–73.
115. Ibid., p. 266.
116. Martin Luther, "That Jesus Christ was Born a Jew," in *The Christian in Society, IV* p. 201.
117. Luther, "On the Jews and their Lies," p. 271.
118. Rühs, *Ueber die Ansprüche*, pp. 24–25; cf. *Handbuch*, in which Rühs points to the demoralizing effects of Rabbinic contempt for the Jewish peasant, the "*Amharez*," sapping his spirit as well as his physical strength. The effect, according to Rühs, is not merely to debilitate Jews for manual labor but also to undermine the spirit of independence within the masses. Thus, they lack that "love of freedom" (*Freiheitsliebe*) which characterizes other nations. "A pure fanaticism substitutes for it, and it alone is now and then responsible for efforts at [popular] rebellion." Finally, Judaism treats women too effectively as chattel. *Handbuch der Geschichte des Mittelalter*, p. 151.
119. Rühs, *Veber die Ansprüche.*, pp. 29–30.
120. Ibid., p. 32.
121. Hundert, *Jews in Poland-Lithuania*, 211–40.
122. See the articles in *Jews in the Hungarian Economy, 1760–1945: Studies Dedicated to Moshe Carmilly-Weinberger on his Eightieth Birthday*, edited by Moshe Carmilly and Michael K. Silber (Jerusalem, 1992).
123. Schechter, *Obstinate Hebrews*, p. 178.
124. See the defenses of Jews along the lines of Dohm in Sigmund Zimmern, *Versuch einer Würdigung der Angriffe des herrn Professor Fries auf die Juden* (Heidelberg, 1816), esp.

pp. 3–19. Similarly, Johann Ludwig Ewald, who writes *contra* both Fries and Rühs, "Die Quellen dieser Fehler, liegen nicht in ihrer Religion, weder in dem Mosaismus, noch in dem Talmudismus; auch nicht in dem Aristokratismus ihrer Rabbiner; sondern in ihrer Beschränkung auf den Handel und in ihrem noch nicht gehörig organisirten Schulunterricht." *Ideen, über die nöthige Organisation der Israeliten in christlichen Staaten* (Karlesruhe and Baden, 1816), p. viii. For other responses, see Stern-Täubler, "Die literarische Kampf."

7. JEWS, COMMERCE, AND HISTORY

1. See Raphael Mahler, *Historiker un vegveiser* (Tel Aviv, 1967), pp. 66, 260–67; Bernard Dov Weinryb, "Prolegomena to an Economic History of the Jews in Germany in Modern Times," *Leo Baeck Institute Year Book* I (1956), pp. 279–306, esp. 286–92.
2. Penslar, *Shylock's Children*, pp. 158–60.
3. Sieyes, *Qu'est ce que le Tiers état*, pp. 156–57; see Chapter 5 of this volume.
4. See Moshe Pelli, *The Age of Haskalah: Studies in Hebrew Literature of the Enlightenment in Germany* (Leiden, 1979).
5. See, however, Maimon's criticisms of Mendelssohn, *Autobiography*, pp. 163–64.
6. See Alan Mintz, *Banished from Their Father's Table: Loss of Faith and Hebrew Autobiography* (Bloomington, IN, 1988).
7. Michael Meyer, *Response to Modernity: A History of the Reform Movement in Judaism* (New York, 1988), pp. 16–25.
8. Jacob Katz, *Out of the Ghetto*, pp. 124–41. For an excellent comprehensive overview of the Haskalah, see Shmuel Feiner, *The Jewish Enlightenment* (Philadelphia, 2002). See also the important collection, *New Perspectives on the Haskalah*, edited by Shmuel Feiner and David Jan Sorkin (Oxford, 2001).
9. Many of these themes are discussed in Mordecai Levin, *'Erkhe hevrah ve-kalkalah ba-'ideologyah shel tekufat ha-Haskalah* [Social and Economic Values: The Idea of Professional Modernization in the Ideology of the Haskalah Movement] (Hebrew) (Jerusalem, 1975), pp. 39–73.
10. Naphtali Herz Wessely, *Divre Shalom ve-Emet le-Kahal 'Edat Yisra'el ha-Garim be-'Arazot Memshelet ha-Kisar ha-Gadol ha-'Ohev 'et ha-'Adam u-Mesameah ha-Briyot* [Words of Peace and Truth to the Community of Israel that Dwells in the Lands of the Kingdom of the Great Emperor who Loves Humanity and Gladdens Mankind] (Hebrew), 2nd edition (Vienna, 1826), p. 8. The translation here is taken from Mendes-Flor and Reinharz, *The Jew in the Modern World*, p. 72.
11. Wessely, p. 8. Mendes-Flor, pp. 70–71.
12. Levin, *'Erkhe hevrah ve-kalkalah*, p. 54.
13. Wessely, *Words*, pp. 2–5.
14. Levin, *'Erkhe hevrah ve-kalkalah*, p. 54.
15. Friedländer, *Ueber die Verbesserung der Israeliten im Königreich Pohlen* (Berlin, 1819), pp. 11–13.
16. Friedländer, *Briefe über die Moral des Handels, geschrieben im Jahr 1785*, in *Jedidja, eine religiöse, moralische und pädagogische Zeitschrift*, Vol. 1 (1817), pp. 178–213. See also Penslar, *Shylock's Children*, pp. 76–77.
17. Wessely, *Masekhet Avot 'im Perush Yen Levanon* [Wine of Lebanon: a Commentary on Tractate 'Avot] '(Hebrew), (Warsaw, 1884), pp. 43–45.

18. Although note the use of Yiddish in the early Haskalah plays of Isaak Euchel and Aaron Halle-Wolfsohn, in which Jewish beggars and idlers often were lampooned. See Max Eric, editor, *Di komedyes fun der Berliner ufklerung* (Yiddish) (Kiev, 1933); Jacob Shatzky, *Arkhiv far der geshikhte fun yidishn teater un drame* (Yiddish) (Vilna, 1930), pp. 147–49.

19. Levin, '*Erkhe hevrah ve-kalkalah*, pp. 71–72.

20. Ibid., pp. 54–55.

21. See Harris Bor, "Enlightenment Values, Jewish Ethics: The Haskalah's Transformation of the Traditional Musar Genre," in Feiner and Sorkin, *New Perspectives*, pp. 48–63. On an earlier attempt by Moses Mendelssohn to adapt *musar* to the ethos of the *Haskalah*, see Jonathan Karp, "The Aesthetic Difference: Moses Mendelssohn's *Kohelet Musar* and the Origins of the Berlin Haskalah," *Renewing the Past, Reconfiguring Jewish Culture*, edited by Ross Brann and Adam Sutcliffe (Philadelphia, 2004), pp. 93–120.

22. Levin, '*Erkhe hevrah ve-kalkalah*, p. 45. On Franklin's influence, see Nancy Beth Sinkoff, *Out of the Shtetl: Making Jews Modern in the Polish Borderlands* (Providence, RI, 2003), pp. 135–41.

23. See Ismar Schorsch, *From Text to Context: The Turn to History in Modern Judaism* (Hanover, NH and London, 1994).

24. See the criticisms of the movement by Gershom Scholem, "Thoughts on the Science of Judaism" (Hebrew), in *Devarim be-Go: Pirke Morashah u-Tehiyah* [There Is Something in It: Chapters in Tradition and Rebirth] (Jerusalem, 1975), pp. 385–403.

25. McClelland, *State, Society, and University in Germany*, pp. 122–32.

26. See Chapter 6 of this volume.

27. See Salman Rubischoff "Erstlinge: Einleitung zu den drei Reden von Eduard Gans," in *Der jüdische Wille* (Berlin, 1919), pp. 30–35.

28. Shmuel Feiner, *Haskalah and History: The Emergence of a Modern Jewish Historical Consciousness*, translated by Chaya Naor and Sondra Silverston (Oxford, 2002), pp. 45–50.

29. Although here, as Feiner points out, it shared some of its celebratory tone with certain *Haskalah* authors. See ibid., 54–55, 86.

30. Schorsch, *Text*, p. 195.

31. This is essentially the emphasis of Leopold Zunz, "Etwas über die rabbinische Litteratur. Nebst Nachrichten über ein altes bis jeztzt ungedrucktes hebräisches Werk," in Idem., *Gesammelte Schriften*, Vol. 1 (Berlin, 1875), pp. 3–31. For an English translation, see Mendes-Flor and Reinharz, *The Jew in the Modern World*, pp. 221–30.

32. Reinhard Rürup, "The Tortuous and Thorny Path to Legal Equality – 'Jew Laws' and Emancipatory Legislation in Germany from the Late Eighteenth Century," *Leo Baeck Institute Year Book*, XXXI (1986), pp. 3–34, esp. 23–24.

33. Hans Liebeschütz, "Judentum und deutsche Umwelt in Zeitalter der Restauration," in *Deutsche Judentum in der Deutsche Umwelt: 1800–1850*, edited by idem. and Arnold Pauker (Tübingen, 1977), p. 17.

34. Friedländer, *Verbesserung der Israeliten*, pp. 7–10.

35. Rubischoff, "Erstlinge," pp. 109–10; Friedländer, *Verbesserung*, p. 15.

36. *Zeitschrift für die Wissenschaft des Judentums*, edited by Leopold Zunz (Berlin, 1822), pp. 395–97; Friedländer, *Verbesserung*, pp. xlv–xlvi; but cf. pp. 15–16.

37. Thus, for instance, Anhalt-Bernburg and Saxony-Hildburghausen in 1813, and Hesse-Kassel in 1816. See Rürup, "Tortuous Path," pp. 12, 23–24.

38. Stefi Jersch-Wenzel, "Legal Status and Emancipation," in *German Jewish History in Modern Times*, Vol. 2, edited by Michael Meyer (New York, 1997), pp. 29–30.

39. Hans Liebeschütz, "Judentum und deutsche Umwelt," p. 8.

40. The anti-Jewish literature is reviewed and refuted in the pamphlet of the civil servant, Wolfgang Heinrich Puchta, *Ueber Guterzertrümmerungen und Grundstückhandel, besonders in Beziehung auf die Frage: Ist es zweckmässiger, den jüdischen Güterhandel auch von Juden oder bloss von Christen treiben zu lasse?* (Erlangen, 1816), pp. 13–16, 36.

41. Low, *Jews in the Eyes of Germans*, p. 129–31.

42. Michael Brenner states that "... one can assume that in the period from 1815 to 1848 the proportion of Jewish students relative to the total Jewish population was twice the proportion of Christian students." See idem., "From Subject to Citezen," in Meyer, *German Jewish History*, p. 270; see, generally, Monika Richarz, *Der Eintritt der Juden in die akademischen Berufe. Jüdische Studenten und Akademiker in Dutschland 1787–1848* (Berlin, 1974); In this light, it also is curious to note that Johann Gottlieb Fichte, appointed Rector of the University of Berlin in 1812, had resigned his position one year later after receiving criticism for defending Jewish students from violent attacks and denunciations.

43. Sinai (Sigfried) Ucko, "Geistesgeschichtliche Grundlagen der Wissenschaft des Judentums," in *Wissenschaft des Judentums im deutschen Sprachbereich*, Vol. 1, edited by Kurt Wilhelm (Tübingen, 1967), pp. 316–18.

44. Richarz, *Der Eintritt*, p. 46.

45. Thus, both in the period before 1819 and after 1825, several of the movement's founders, such as Moses Moser, Joel Abraham List, Gans, and, later, Heinrich Heine, did not appear committed to a lifetime's labor in the field of Jewish history. Rather, for these individuals, at least, a primary interest in Judaism represented a passing phenomenon prompted by immediate circumstances. In the most famous cases of Gans and Heine, conversion provided the means of achieving *continuity* with the aspirations they had held prior to their involvement in *Wissenschaft*.

46. The degree of urbanization should not be overstated, as Steven M. Lowenstein warns. But even though most German Jews still lived in small communities in 1815, their percentage of the urban population was double that of their percentage of the population as a whole. See Lowenstein, "The Rural Community and the Urbanization of German Jews," in idem., *The Mechanics of Change*, pp. 135–36.

47. Although the phenomenon of displaced peasants and artisans was certainly underway by this time, it would not become a public issue until the late 1820s and 1830s. Hence, although members of these groups were indeed already subject to economic pressures for "retraining," they were not yet subject to ideological ones, as were the Jews. See Hamerow, *Restoration, Revolution, Reaction*, pp. 25–55; Klaus Epstein, *Genesis*, pp. 208–09.

48. Thus, the by-laws of the school established by the "Union" actually prohibited students from engaging in or from preparing for a life of traditional Jewish commerce. See Rubischoff, "Erstlinge," p. 115.

49. Ucko, "Geistesgeschichtliche Grundlagen," pp. 332–33.

50. Rubischoff, "Erstlinge," p. 119.

51. These are detailed in Ucko, "Geistesgeschichtliche Grundlagen," pp. 332–37.

52. Ibid., p. 340.

53. Rubischoff, "Erstlinge," pp. 119–20.

54. Dohm, *Verbesserung*, p. 87.

55. On the background to this pamphlet and the nature of the collaboration between Hellwitz and Zunz, see Jacob Toury, "Ein Dokument zur bürgerlichen Einordnung der Juden (Hamm/Westfalen, 1818)," in *Michael*, Vol. 7 (1967), pp. 77–91.

56. L. L. Hellwitz, *Die Organisation der Israeliten in Deutschland*, 3rd edition (Arnsberg, 1837), pp. 15–16.

57. Ibid., pp. 16–17.

58. *Zeitschrift für die Wissenschaft des Judentums* (Berlin, 1822), p. 396.

59. Paula Hyman, *Gender and Assimilation in Modern Jewish History: The Roles and Representation of Women* (Seattle and London, 1995), p. 29.

60. *Zeitschrift für die Wissenschaft*, p. 397.

61. Special laws restricting the numbers of Jewish youngsters inheriting their father's occupations were justified on this basis; see Hellwitz, *Organisation*, p. 18; Toury, "Ein Document," p. 89, n. 41 points out that in this Hellwitz and Zunz went further than the local legislation of Hamm, Westphalia.

62. Quoted in Schorsch, *Text*, p. 116.

63. The reason is that, in the eyes of Jost, Jewish internal solidarity, seen as properly the norm, was being destroyed by the wealthy selling out their brethren to powerful gentiles; see the remarks on Jost in the conclusion to this chapter. See also the somewhat similar remarks on Gans in "Aus dem Archiv des Vereins," in *Zeitschrift für die Wissenschaft*, pp. 533–37.

64. This is the whole tenor of Gans's "Third Address," in Rubischoff, "Erstlinge," pp. 195–99.

65. See the evaluation by Ignacy Schipper, quoted in Raphael Mahler, "Yizhak Schipper (1884–1943), in *Historiker un vegveizer* (Yiddish) (Tel-Aviv, 1967), p. 260; Salo W. Baron, *History and Jewish Historians* (Philadelphia, 1964), p. 255; Michael Meyer, *The Origins of the Modern Jew: Jewish Identity and European Culture in Germany, 1749–1824* (Detroit, 1967), pp. 173–77; Benjamin Braude, "Jewish Economic History – Review Essay," in *Association for Jewish Studies Newsletter* 19 (February, 1977), pp. 25–28; Schorsch, *Context*, pp. 119, 260–61.

66. Zunz, "Etwas," p. 15.

67. George Iggers, *The German Historical Conception of History: The National Tradition of Historical Thought from Herder to the Present* (Hanover, NH, 1983), p. 4; similarly, Karl Hardach, "Some Remarks on German Economic Historiography and its Understanding of the Industrial Revolution in Germany," *The Journal of European Economic Thought*, Vol. 1, No. 1 (Spring 1972), pp. 37–99.

68. J. H. Clapham, "Economic History," *Encyclopedia of the Social Sciences*, Vol. 12 (New York, 1934), p. 316.

69. Theodore M. Porter, *The Rise of Statistical Thinking, 1820–1900* (Princeton, NJ, 1986), pp. 25–26.

70. Charlotte Lorenz, "Statistik," in *Handwörterbuch der Sozialwissenschaften*, Vol. 10 (Stuttgart-Tübingen-Göttingen, 1959), p. 31.

71. Tribe, *Governing Economy*, pp. 66–95.

72. Dambacher, *Dohm*, pp. 32–40.

73. Friedrich Lenz, *Friedrich List: Der Mann und das Werk* (München-Berlin, 1936), pp. 26–31.

74. Friedrich List, for instance, held a definition of economically productive forces that broadly encompassed the institutions of state and civil society. See McClelland, *State, Society, and University in Germany*, p 17.

75. Wilhelm Roscher, *Grundriss zu Vorlessung über die Staatswirtschaft, nach geschichtlicher Methode* (Göttingen, 1843).

76. Leopold Zunz, "Grundlinien zu einer künftigen Statistik der Juden," in *Gesammelte Schriften*, pp. 134, 136–37.

77. Ibid. p. 136.

78. Ibid.

79. Ibid., p. 134.

80. Ibid., p. 136

81. Ibid.

82. Ibid., p. 138 (Zunz's emphasis).

83. Zunz, "Etwas," p. 15.

84. With the exception of Friedländer, in his *Briefe* and of Mendelssohn, as discussed in Chapter 4 of this volume.

85. Penslar also notes the indeterminate nature of Zunz's analysis. See *Shylocks' Children*, p. 159.

86. Eduard Gans, "Gesetzgebung über Juden in Rom, nach den Quellen des Römischen Rechts," in *Zeitschrift für Wissenschaft des Judentums*, Vol. 1 (Berlin, 1822), p. 25.

87. Eduard Gans, "Vorlesung über die Geschichte der Juden im Norden von Europa und in den slavischen Ländern," in ibid., p. 98.

88. Ibid.

89. Gans, "Gesetzgebung," pp. 40–41.

90. Gans, "Vorlesung," pp. 98–99.

91. Gans, "Gesetzgebung," p. 26.

92. Gans, "Vorlesungen," p. 99.

93. See Gans, "Third Address," in Rubishoff, "Erstlinge," p. 195.

94. Gans, "Gesetzgebung," pp. 28–29.

95. Gans, "Vorlesung," p. 99.

96. Gans pointed to the case of the Greeks as a parallel instance of a dispersion that had given rise to commercial functionality, "Vorlesung," p. 104.

97. On this relationship, see Michael H. Hoffheimer, *Eduard Gans and the Hegelian Philosophy of Law* (Dordrecht-Boston-London), pp. 12–22; Hans Gunther Reissner, *Eduard Gans: Ein Leben im Vormärz* (Tübingen, 1965), pp. 58–72.

98. Gans, "Gesetzgebung," pp. 39–40.

99. G. W. F. Hegel, *Elements of the Philosophy of Right*, edited by Allen W. Wood, translated by H. B. Nisbett (Cambridge, 1991), pp. 222–23.

100. Gans, "Second Address," in Rubashoff, "Erstlinge," p. 111. For an English translation, see Mendes-Flohr and Reinharz, *The Jew in the Modern World*, pp. 215–19.

101. Ibid., pp. 111–12 (my emphasis).

102. Ibid., p. 112.

103. Hegel, *Elements*, pp. 234–39.

104. As noted, Gans's *other* explanation for the Jews' occupational development was to see it as a necessary and inevitable consequence of dispersion. Gans pointed to the

case of the Greeks as a parallel instance of a Diaspora that had given rise to group commercial functionality.

105. Hegel, *Elements*, p. 237 (his emphasis).
106. Eduard Gans, *Naturrecht und Univrsalgeschichte*, edited by Manfred Reidel (Stuttgart, 1981), pp. 20–31, 84–85, 93.
107. Hegel, *Elements*, p. 223.
108. Ibid., p. 380.
109. Gans, *Naturrecht*, p. 93.
110. Ibid., p. 102.
111. Gans, in Rubischoff, p. 115.
112. Ibid.
113. Ibid.
114. Gans was successful in obtaining an academic position, but Heine was not. See Mendes-Flor and Reinharz, *The Jew in the Modern World*, pp. 258–59.
115. Gans published the first volume of his *Das Erbrecht des Mittelalters* in 1824, a year before his baptism.
116. See Ismar Schorsch, "Scholarship in the Service of Reform," *Leo Baeck Institute Yearbook*, xxxv (1990), pp. 78–79.
117. Isaak Markus Jost, *Geschichte der Israeliten seit der Zeit der Maccabaer bis auf unsre Tage*, Vol. VII (Berlin, 1827), pp. 426–28.
118. Schorsch, *Text*, p. 72.
119. Jost, *Geschichte*, Vol. III, pp. 127–45.
120. Ibid., Vol. VII, pp. 206–07.
121. Ibid., p. 212.
122. Ibid., p. 208.
123. Uriel Tal, "German-Jewish Social Thought in the Mid-Nineteenth Century," in *Revolution and Evolution: 1848 in German-Jewish History*, edited by Werner Mosse, Arnold Pauker, and Reinhard Rürup (Tübingen, 1981).
124. Abraham Geiger, *Urschrift und Uebersetzungen der Bibel in ihrer Abhängigkeit von der innern Entwickelung des Judenthums* (Breslau, 1857), pp. 100, 149–50. See also, Susannah Heschel, *Abraham Geiger and the Jewish Jesus* (Chicago, 1998), pp. 83–84, 101.
125. See, for instance, Graetz's remarks in volume 6 of his of *Geschichte der Juden von den ältesten Zeiten bis auf die Gegenwart* (Leipzig, 1859–1877), in which he discusses the transition between a Jewish community in which land ownership was not uncommon and one that, through the prohibitive influence of the feudal system, forced Jews to become overwhelmingly mercantile (pp. 127–29). In the same volume, he details the merchandising activities of French Jewry under the Capetian Kings (p. 186), decries the fiscal policies of Philip Augustus (p. 208), distinguishes between the concepts of chamber serfdom as applied in England and Germany, where it entailed a further dispossession of estates (pp. 220–23). Other volumes contain an additional wealth of examples. Although Graetz believed that the exclusive practice of usury had dulled the Jews moral sensibilities (saved only by their immersion in the Talmud), he nevertheless praised the Jews' contributions to a commercial civilization whose expansion he celebrated for breaking "though the narrow bonds of superstition and enlarging men's range of vision." See idem., *History of the Jews*, Vol. 4 (Philadelphia, 1894), p. 286.

126. George-Herbert Depping, *Les Juifs dans le Moyen Âge: essai historique sur leur état civil, commercial et littéraire* (Paris, 1834). I have consulted the German translation, *Die Juden im Mittelalter: ein von der Akademie der Inschriften und schönen Wissenschaften zu Paris durch Ehrenerwähnung ausgezeichneter historischer Versuch über ihre bürgerlichen, literärischen und handels–Verhältnisse* (Stuttgart, 1834); Otto Stobbe, *Die Juden in Deutschland wärend des Mittelalters in politischer, sozialer und rechtlicher Beziehung (Leipzig, 1865)*.

127. See Guido Kisch, "Otto Stobbe und die rechtsgeschichte der Juden," in *Jahrbuch der Gesellschaft für die Geschichte der Juden in der Tschechoslovakischen Republik*, IX (1938), pp. 1–41, especially p. 36.

128. Schorsch, *Text*, p. 192.

129. "Wollte man von diesem Zeitraume ein deutliches, entsprechendes Bild entwerfen, so könnte man ihn nur unter einem 'Doppelbilde' darstellen." Heinrich Graetz, *Geschichte der Juden*, Vol. IV (Leipzig, 1866), pp. 1–2. It is true that in his 1846 *Die Konstruction der jüdischen Geschichte* Graetz outlined his theory of Jewish history as comprised of a unity of political and religious spheres. He even showed how he believed that unity functioned in different periods, when the "polarities" of religion and politics were variously weighted. Nevertheless, this theory did not attempt to explain how Jews might have been politically or economically integrated into the social systems of the European medieval Diaspora. At most, Graetz claimed that scholarship, the Talmud, Law, and literature of the Jews provided a sort of government in exile. Thus, Jewish literature was the *"Grundeigenthum"* of the Jewish People in Exile. See Heinrich Graetz, *The Structure of Jewish History*, translated by Ismar Schorch (New York, 1975).

130. The development of a subfield of Jewish economic or commercial history within the tradition established by *Wissenschaft des Judentums* proceeded as follows. For the period of Jewish Antiquity, the starting point was the works of Levi Herzfeld, *Metrologische Untersuchungen zu einer Geschichte des ibräishen rep. altjüdischen Handels* (Leipzig, 1865) and idem., *Handelsgeschichte der Juden des Alterthums* (Braunschweig, 1894), esp. pp. iii–xlvi. For the Middle Ages, the starting place was Moritz Güdemann, *Geschichte des Erziehungswesens und der Cultur der Juden in Frankreich und Deutschland: von der Begründung der jüdischen Wissenschaft in diesen Ländern bis zur Vertreibung der Juden aus Frankreich (X.–XIV. Jahrhundert)* (Vienna, 1880), pp. 66–73, 168–211, 239–49; Julius Aronium, *Regesten zur Geschichte der Juden im fränkischen und deutschen Reiche* (Berlin, 1887); Israel Abrahams, *Jewish Life in the Middle Ages* (New York, 1896); Georg Caro, *Sozial- und Wirtschaftsgeschichte der Juden im Mittelalter und der Neuzeit* (Leipzig, 1908). A true synthetic theory of Jewish historical-economy was early developed along Marxist (and nationalist) lines by Ber Borochov, *Di klasen-interesen un di natsionale frage* (Vilna, 1906) and extended in a historical, scholarly fashion by Ignaz Schipper, *Anfänge des Kapitalismus bei den abendländischen Juden im früheren Mittelalter* (Vienna, 1906) and later by Raphael Mahler and Emmanuel Ringelblum in a series of articles beginning with "Religion and the Development of Society (Yiddish)," in *Di Fraye Yugent*, January 12 (Warsaw, 1925). See the bibliography in *Sefer Refa'el Mahler: Kovets Mehkarim be-Toldot Yisrael, Mugash lo bi-Melot lo Shiv'im ve-Hamesh Shanah* [Studies in Jewish History Presented to Professor Raphael Mahler on his Seventy Fifth Birthday] (Hebrew), edited by Shmuel Yeiven (Merhavyah, 1974), p. 221.

8. CAPITALISM AND THE JEWS

1. Gans, "Gesetzgebung," pp. 49–50.
2. See Rose, *German Question/Jewish Question*, pp. 113–14.
3. Gans, "Gesetzgebung," p. 50.
4. "Wie lange wird jene verderbliche Halbheit noch währen! Hat die Geschichte nicht hinreichend gelehrt, dass man nur zwischen zwei Wegen die Wahl habe: entweder von dem Princip der allein selig machenden Kirche auszugehen, und auf eine streng consequente (und wenigstens in so fern lobenswerthe) Weise die Juden vom Erdball zu vertilgen, und die bestehende Kluft mit ihren gegrabenen Leibern zu füllen, oder ind der Gesetzgebung zu vergessen, dass es Juden gäbe, und so die Kluft zu füllen mit ihren auferstandenen Geistern. Nur was in der Mitte liegt, ist vom Uebel." Ibid.
5. Liebeschütz, "Judentum und deutsche Umwelt," p. 16; Shulamit S. Magnus, *Jewish Emancipation in a German City: Cologne, 1798–1871* (Stanford, CA, 1997), pp. 102–17.
6. As Stefi Jersch-Wensel has commented, the institution of the plan would have meant a renunciation of the long-standing aim "of bringing about the Jews' 'civil improvement' through their education with the intent of integrating them into state and society..." Jersch-Wenzel, "Legal Status and Emancipation," p. 46.
7. Ibid.
8. Rürup, *"Tortuous Path,"* pp. 24–26.
9. Julius Carlebach, *Karl Marx and the Radical Crituque of Judaism* (Boston, 1978), pp. 134–35.
10. See Sheehan, *German History*, pp. 569–70. Marx himself refers to the immediate circumstances occasioning the essay, when he accuses Bauer of ignoring their implications. See Marx, "On the Jewish Question," in *The Marx-Engles Reader*, edited by Robert C. Tucker (New York, 1978), p. 28. See also David McLellan, *Marx before Marxism* (New York, 1970), pp. 158–59. The *Rheinische Zeitung*, the newspaper Marx edited in 1842–1843, adopted a vigorous stance against the king's policies. See Jerry Z. Muller, *The Mind and the Market: Capitalism in Modern European Thought* (New York, 2002), p. 171.
11. Carlebach, *Karl Marx*, pp. 63.
12. McLellan, *Marx before Marxism*, pp. 170–71, 204.
13. Douglas Moggach, *The Philosophy and Politics of Bruno Bauer* (Cambridge, 2003), p. 151.
14. Bruno Bauer, "Die Fahigkeit der heutigen Juden und Chrsiten frei zu werden," in *Eindundzwanzig Bogen aus der Schweiz*, edited by G. Herwegh (Zurich und Winterhur, 1843), pp. 56–71; idem., *Die Judenfrage* (Braunschweig, 1843); on Jewish reactions, see Nathan Rotenstreich, "For and Against Emancipation: The Bruno Bauer Controversy," in *The Leo Baeck Institute Yearbook*, iv (London, 1959), pp. 3–36; Marx himself mentions the reviews of Bauer by Hirsch and Geiger. See Marx, "Die heilige Familie," in Karl Marx and Friedrich Engels, *Werke*, vol. iv (Berlin, 1968), p. 141.
15. Julius Carlebach, "Judaism," in *A Dictionary of Marxist Thought*, edited by Tom Bottomore, Laurence Harris, V.G. Kiernan, and Ralph Miliband (Cambridge, MA, 1983), pp. 245–46.
16. Ibid., pp. 16–17. Robert Wistrich, *Socialism and the Jews: The Dilemmas of Assimilation in Germany and Austria-Hungary* (Rutherford, NJ, 1982), p. 97; Paul Massing, *Rehearsal for Destruction* (New York, 1949), p. 158.

17. Enzo Traverso, *The Marxists and the Jewish Question* (New Jersey, 1990), pp. 17–87; Jack Jacobs, *On Socialists and the Jewish Question after Marx* (New York, 1992), pp. 1–6.

18. Ibid., p. 9.

19. For the literature up through 1978, see the bibliography in Carlebach, *Karl Marx*.

20. See, for instance, Edmund Silberner, "Was Marx an Anti-Semite?," in *Essential Papers on Jews and the Left*, edited by Ezra Mendelsohn (New York, 1994), pp. 361–401.

21. See Sidney Hook, *From Hegel to Marx: Studies in the Intellectual Development of Karl Marx* (New York, 1994).

22. Silberner makes a similar point. See his "Was Marx," p. 379.

23. Karl Marx, "Zur Judenfrage," in *Deutsche-Französische Jahrbücher*, edited by Arnold Ruge (Paris, 1844), p. 209.

24. As Marx would later formulate it, "[t]he religious world is but a reflex of the real world." See Marx, *Capital*, vol. 1, in Tucker, *Reader*, p. 326.

25. Marx, "Zur Judenfrage," p. 209.

26. On the theme of a Judaizing (*Verjudung*) of society or the world in nineteenth-century German literature, see the essay by Steven E. Aschheim, "'The Jew Within': The Myth of 'Judaization' in Germany," in *The Jewish Response to German Culture: From the Enlightenment to the Second World War*, edited by Jehuda Reinharz and Walter Schatzberg (Hanover, NH, and London, 1985), pp. 211–41.

27. For example: "Society can no longer live under this bourgeoisie, in other words, its existence is no longer compatible with society." See Marx, "Manifesto of the Communist Party," in Tucker, *Reader*, p. 483.

28. Although in some Latin and medieval German usages "Judaism" had the secondary meaning of commerce, in the later Middle Ages and in nineteenth-century German that meaning had shifted to "moneylending" and "usury." Marx's use of *Schacher*, as opposed to *Handel* or *Verkehr*, suggested something more or less in between. See Maurice Walsch, *A Concise German Etymological Dictionary* (London, 1952), pp. 196–97.

29. McLellan, *Marx before Marxism*, p. 184.

30. Marx, "Zur Judenfrage," p. 211.

31. For Bauer, it was Christianity's Jewish descent that called into question its own heavenly origins. As Bauer writes, "[Judaism] is the incarnate doubt in the heavenly origin of Christianity, the religious adversary of the religion which announced itself as the perfect, the only true religion, and could not even overcome the small number of those in the midst of whom it was born." Bruno Bauer, *The Jewish Question*, translated by Helen Lederer (Cincinnati, OH, 1958), p. 123. Bauer, *Die Judenfrage*, p. 114. Yet this formulation did not explain why Judaism had persisted alongside of Christianity, which as noted was the question that interested Marx.

32. Marx, "Zur Judenfrage," p. 211.

33. See Ascher, "'The Jew Within,'" pp. 220–21.

34. Augustine writes: "[I]t is their own Scriptures that bear witness that it is not we who are the inventors of the prophecies touching Christ.... [T]hese enemies, who are scattered over the whole earth wherever the Church is expanding and who possess and preserve these books, are living witnesses, however reluctant to the truth of our position." Saint Augustine, *The City of God*, Books XVII–XXII, translated by Gerald G. Walsh and Daniel J. Honan (New York, 1954), p. 164. In contrast, for Protestant

NOTES TO PAGES 241–245

spokesmen such as Martin Luther, Jews indeed embody a doubt, though not over Christian origins. Rather, the doubt Jews embody is over the Catholic Church's claim to possess the correct doctrine and praxis for Christian life. For Luther, the restoration of pristine Christian doctrine would therefore be a precondition for Jewish conversion. Luther writes: "Our fools, the popes, bishops, sophists, and monks – the crude asses' heads – have hitherto so treated the Jews that anyone who wished to be a good Christian would almost have had to become a Jew. . . . When the Jews see then that Judasim has such strong support in Scripture, and that Christianity has become a mere babble without reliance on Scripture, how can they possibly compose themselves and become right good Christians?" Martin Luther, "That Jesus Christ was Born a Jew," p. 200.

35. See Alisdair MacIntyre, *Marxism and Christianity* (Notre Dame, IN, 1968), pp. 42–43.
36. Marx, "Zur Judenfrage," p. 209.
37. In addition to Eduard Gans's formulation cited in the previous chapter, see Ludwig Feuerbach, *Principles of the Philosphy of the Future*, translated by Manfred H. Vogel (Indianapolis, 1966), pp. 21–22.
38. As Carlebach notes, the emphasis of Hegel's own characterization of Judaism was its abstractness, its separation of Jews from their alien surroundings as well as from the joyful immersion in nature. See Carlebach, *Karl Marx*, pp. 80–81.
39. Marx, "Zur Judenfrage," p. 212.
40. Rose, *German Question/Jewish Question*, pp. 111–14.
41. Bauer, *The Jewish Question*, pp. 28–30.
42. Idid., p. 211.
43. Carlebach, *Karl Marx*, p. 123.
44. Shlomo Avineri, among others, posits that Hess's "Über das Geldwesen" was a direct influence Marx's "On the Jewish Question," a hypothesis challenged by Carlebach. The debate comes down to the question of whether or not Marx had seen Hess's essay (written in 1843 but only published two years later by Hess) in time. See Shlomo Avineri, *The Making of Modern Zionism* (New York, 1981), pp. 40–41; Carlebach, *Karl Marx*, pp. 110–24. The influence of "Über das Geldwesen" is assumed by Zwi Rosen, who nevertheless treats Marx as if his conception of "capitalism" was already complete by 1844. See his "Moses Hess' Einfluß auf die Entfremdungstheorie von Karl Marx," in *Juden im Vormärz und in der Revolution von 1848*, edited by Walter Grab and Julius H. Schoeps (Stuttgart, 1983), pp. 169–213.
45. Loyd D. Easton and Kurt H. Guddat, eds., *Writings of the young Marx on Philosophy and Society* (Garden City, NY, 1967), pp. 96–105.
46. Quoted in Jacob Katz, *From Prejudice to Destruction*, pp. 160–61.
47. Ibid., cf., Tucker, *Reader*, p. 50.
48. See the extensive comments in, and the numerous quotations culled from, patristic literature by Ludwig Feuerbach, *The Essence of Christianity*, translated by George Eliot (Buffalo, NY, 1989), pp. 308–20, esp. p. 309.
49. For example, Saint Augustine, "In Answer to the Jews," in *Treatises on Marriage and Other Subjects*, edited by Roy J. Deferrari and Sister Mary Ligouri (New York, 1955), pp. 405–06.
50. Matthew 6:25.
51. "Das Chistenthum hatte das reale Judenthum nur zum Schein überwunden. Es war zu vornehm, zu spirtitualistisch, um die Rohheit des praktischen Bedürfnisses anders

als durch die Erhebung in die blaue Luft zu beseitigen." Marx, "Zur Judenfrage," p. 213.

52. Cf. Tucker, *Reader*, p. 52.

53. This is a composite account, admittedly somewhat closer to Heine's position than to Börne's. But there is enough in Börne to suggest a parallel tendency. See Heinrich Heine, *Self-Portrait and Other Prose Writings*, edited by Frederick Ewen (Secaucus, NJ, 1948), pp. 424–32; Ludwig Börne, *Sämtliche Schriften*, Vol. 1 (Düsseldorf, 1964), pp. 499–505. Orlando Figes's article on Börne's radical critique of Judaism is a tour de force performance. But he does not succeed in establishing that Börne had a coherent theory of Judaism's relationship to money and commerce. "Ludwig Börne and the Formation of a Radical Critique of Judaism," in *LBIYB*, vol. xxix (1984), pp. 351–382.

54. This point provides much of the unifying tissue between the two sections of Marx's "Zur Judenfrage" – corresponding to the reviews of Bauer's two discussions of Jewish emancipation. It is Christianity's reabsorption of Judaism that for Marx corresponds to the establishment of modern social relations in the place of feudalism, which is the topic of the first part of Marx's essay.

55. Bauer, "Die Fahigkeit," p. 57.

56. On deist views of Judaism, see Shmuel Ettinger, "Jews and Judaism as Seen by English Deists of the Eighteenth Century" [in Hebrew], *Zion*, XXIX, n. 3–4, (1964), pp. 182–207. On the tensions between toleration of Jews and the purgation of Judaism, see the excellent treatment by Adam Sutcliffe, *Judaism and Enlightenment*. See also Frank Manuel, *The Broken Reed: Judaism through Christian Eyes* (Cambridge, MA, 1992), pp. 180, 189.

57. A good summation of these developments is presented in William Sewell, *Work and Revolution in France: The Language of Labor in the Old Regime to 1848* (Cambridge, 1980).

58. Dohm, *Verbesserung*, pp. 56–65.

59. On Dohm, see Chapter 4 of this volume.

60. Marx, "Zur Judenfrage," pp. 187–88. In support of this contention, Marx (citing Gustave de Baumont's *Marie ou l'esclavage aux États-Unis*, Alexander de Tocqueville's *Demcocracy in America*, and Thomas Hamilton's *Men and Manners in North America*) offered the example of the United States where *because* of the separation of Church and State, "ist Nordamerika vorzugsweise das Land der Religiosität."

61. This also was a dig against Bauer. Marx was saying, in effect, that the liberal "atheistic" state is the truly "Christian" state. Marx writes, "In fact the perfected Christian state is not the so-called *Christian* state which acknowledges Christianity as its basis, as the state religion, and thus adopts an exclusive attitude towards other religions; it is, rather the *atheistic* state, the democratic state, the state which relegates religion among the other elements of civil society." Tucker, *Reader*, p. 36.

62. Marx, "Zur Judenfrage," p. 204 (his emphases). Cf. Tucker, *Reader*, p. 44.

63. Ibid. (his emphases).

64. "Allein die Volendung des Idealismus des Staats war zugleich die Vollendung des Materialismus der bürgerlichen Gesellschaft.... Der Mensch wurde daher nicht von der Religion befreit, er erhielt die Religionfreiheit." Ibid., pp. 205–06.

65. Ibid., p. 211; Tucker, *Reader*, p. 51.

66. "The Jews have emancipated themselves insofar as the Christians have become Jews." Marx, "Zur Judenfrage," p. 210.

67. Tucker, *Raader*, p. 327; Marx, "Zur Judenfrage," p. 212.
68. Bauer, *Die Judenfrage*, p. 47.
69. Tucker, *Reader*, p. 50; Marx, "Zur Judenfrage," p. 211.
70. Tucker, *Reader*, p. 52; Marx, "Zur Judenfrage," p. 214.
71. The years 1842–1844 were ones in which Marx shifted from a criticism of Hegel's theory of the modern state (as historical and rational apotheosis) to a recognition of civil society as the "real" conditioning force in both social and political existence. This development helped focus Marx's attention of the contrast between feudal and modern social relations. The present period, Marx wrote to his colleague Arnold Ruge, was one in which reactionaries will be compelled to become even more entrenched in the past. See Hook, *From Hegel to Marx*, p. 157; McLellan, *Marx*, pp. 157–65.
72. Muller, *The Mind and the Market*, p. 177.
73. Marx, "Zur Judenfrage," p. 209.
74. This point is most fully developed in Marx, *The Economic and Philosophic Manuscripts of 1844*, edited and translated by Dirk J. Struik (New York, 1964), p. 113. "Indeed labor, *life-activity, productive life* itself, appears in the first place merely as a *means* of satisfying a need – the need to maintain physical existence. Yet the productive life is the life of the species. It is life-engendering life. The whole character of a species – its species character – is contained in the character of its life activity; and free, conscious activity is man's species character. Life itself appears only as a *means to life*. . . . Man makes his life activity itself the object of his will and of his consciousness. . . . It is just because of this that he is a species being . . ." The *Manuscripts* were composed in the two months following the publication of "On the Jewish Question," but were not themselves published until 1932.
75. Marx, "Zur Judenfrage," p. 214.
76. Ibid. p. 214 (Marx's emphasis).
77. Ibid.
78. Hook, *From Hegel to Marx*, pp. 243–51.
79. Feuerbach, *Christianity*, pp. 1–32.
80. "Marx on the History of his Opinions," in Tucker, *Reader*, p. 3.
81. Fichte, *Vorlesungen*, pp. 321–23; Karl Löwith, *From Hegel to Nietzsche: the Revolution in Nineteenth Century Thought*, translated by David E. Green (Garden City, NY, 1967).
82. "Der Wechsel ist der wirkliche Gott des Juden." Marx, "Zur Judenfrage," p. 212.
83. Ibid., p. 211.
84. Tucker, *Reader*, pp. 16–25.
85. Marx, "Zur Judenfrage," p. 213 (my emphasis).
86. See also Warren Breckman, *Marx, the Young Hegelians and the Origins of Radical Social Theory: Defining the Self* (Cambridge, 1999), pp. 292–95.
87. Ibid.
88. In fact, one might say that the duality appears in the very term "industrial capitalism" that Muller himself employs. Muller, *The Mind and the Market*, p. 189.
89. Marx, *Capital*, vol. 3, in Tucker, *Reader*, pp. 440–41.
90. Marx, *Capital*, vol. 1, in Tucker, *Reader*, pp. 84–155.
91. Marx, *Capital*, vol. 3, in Tucker, *Reader*, p. 440.
92. Marx, *Capital*, vol. 1, in Tucker, *Reader*, p. 333.
93. Marx, "Communist Manifesto," in Tucker, *Reader*, p. 486.

94. Friedrich Engels, *Socialism, Utopian and Scientific*, translated by Edward Bibbons Aveling (New York, 1935).

95. Ibid., p. 486.

96. Smith, *Wealth of Nations*, Bk. II, Ch. iv, pp. 381–87.

97. Hume, *Essays*, p. 355.

98. Charles Fourier, *Œuvres Complètes*, Vol. I (Paris, 1966), pp. 222–23.

99. Jonathan Beecher, *Charles Fourier: The Visionary and His World* (Berkeley, CA, 1986), p. 292; Frank Manuel, *Prophets of Paris*, p. 217.

100. Pierre-Joseph Proudhon, *System of Economical Contradictions: or, The Philosophy of Misery*, translated by Benjamin R. Tucker (Boston, 1888). I borrow the term from Seymour Melman, *Profits Without Production* (New York, 1983).

101. William Coleman, "Anti-Semitism in Anti-economics," *History of Political Economy*, 35:4 (2003), p. 768.

102. Edmund Silberner, *Sozialisten zur Judenfrage: Ein Beitrag zur Geschichte des Sozialismus vom Anfang des Jahrhunderts bis 1914* (Berlin, 1962).

103. As early as the 1830s and 1840s, the rise of the Rothschilds and other Jewish banking firms led to a perceptible shift; whereas formerly it was common to associate the Jewish "financial aristocracy" with the reactionary forces of Restoration absolutism, writers such as Börne and Heine increasingly, if ironically, trumpeted Jewish bankers as generals leading the social transformation of Europe. "Strangely enough," noted Heine, "it is once again the Jews who invented this new religion [of finance capitalism]." Ferguson, *The House of Rothschild: Money's Prophets, 1798–1848* (New York, 1998), pp. 210–25.

104. Alphonse Toussenel, *Les Juifs, rois de l'epoque: histoire de la féodalité financière* (Paris, 1845); Silberner, *Sozialisten zur Judenfrage*, pp. 29–34; Niall Ferguson explains the immediate backdrop to Toussenel's book in Baron James Rothschild's recent "securing of the rail concession to link Paris and Belgium." Ferguson also explores the broader background to the family's image as "kings of the age." *The House of Rothschild*, pp. 15–27, esp. 17.

105. Pamela Pilbeam, *French Socialists before Marx: Workers, Women and the Social Question* (Montreal, 2000), pp. 16–17, 112; Manuel, The *Prophets of Paris*, p. 177.

106. Henri de Saint-Simon, *The Political Thought of Saint-Simon*, edited by Ghita Ionescu (Oxford, 1976), pp. 138–39; Manuel, *The Prophets of Paris*, p. 177.

107. For example, the Fourierists, anarchist movements associated with Proudhon and Bakunin, the Kommunistenbund of Wilhelm Weitling, the Catholic socialism of Bishop Wilhelm Freiherr von Ketteler, and of course the socialism of Stoecker, Marr, Dühring, and Liebermann von Sonnenberg, in which antisemitism was one of the cardinal features. See Massing, *Rehearsal for Destruction*; Rose, *German Question/ Jewish Question*; Wistrich, *Socialism and the Jews*.

108. The other attraction, as Michael Graetz points out, was the Saint-Simonian affirmation of the Mosaic Constitution. See his *The Jews in Nineteenth-Century France: From the French Revolution to the Alliance Israélite Universelle*, translated by Jane Marie Todd (Stanford, CA, 1996), pp. 115–60.

109. Werner Sombart was among the first to recognize the 1850s as the critical juncture in Germany's economic transition. See Sombart, *Die deutsche Volkswirtschaft im neunzehnten Jahrhundert* (Berlin, 1903), pp. 66, 90. See also Karl W. Hardach, "Some Remarks on German Economic Historiography and its Understanding of the

Industrial Revolution in Germany," in *The Journal of European Economic History*, Vol. 1, No. 1 (Spring, 1972), pp. 37–99.

110. Albert S. Lindemann, *A History of European Socialism* (New Haven, 1983), p. 100.
111. See Maurice Glasman, *Unnecessary Suffering: Managing Market Utopia* (London, 1996), pp. 29–55.
112. See Jacobs, *On Socialists and the Jewish Question*.
113. See the remarks on the Sombart-Weber debate in Walter P. Zenner, *Minorities in the Middle: A Cross Cultural Analysis* (Albany, NY 1991), pp. 5–6.
114. Wilhelm Roscher, *Grundriss zu Vorlesungen über die Staatswirtschaft, nach geschichtlicher Methode* (Göttingen, 1843), pp. 76–77.
115. Ibid.; Roscher, "Die Stellung der Juden im Mittelalter."
116. Ber Borochov, *Di klasen-interesen un di natsionale frage* (Vilna, 1906).
117. Quoted in Raphael Mahler, "Yitzhak Schipper (1884–1943)" (Yiddish), in *Historiker un vegveizer* (Tel Aviv, 1967), p. 260.

AFTERWORD: INDUSTRIALIZATION AND BEYOND

1. Eric Hobsbawm, *The Age of Revolution* (New York, 1962), p. 46 and passim.
2. *The Industrial Revolution in National Context: Europe and the U.S.A.*, edited by Roy Porter and Mikuláš Teich (Cambridge, 1996); *The Industrial Revolution and Work in Nineteenth-Century Europe*, edited by Leonard R. Berlanstein (New York, 1992); Musgrave, *The Early Modern European Economy*, pp. 197–200.
3. Quoted in David Landes, *The Wealth and Poverty of Nations* (London, 2002), p. 192.
4. Idem, *Prometheus Unbound: Technological Change and Industrial Development in Western Europe from 1750 to the Present* (Cambridge, 1969).
5. This theme is explored throughout Weber's *Economy and Society*, edited by Guenther Roth and Claus Wittich, 2 vols. (Berkeley, 1978). See also the discussion in Muller, *The Mind of the Market*, 240–41 and 445, n. 44 and 45.
6. For a key example, see Max Weber's introduction to *The Protestant Ethic and the Spirit of Capitalism* (London and New York, 1992), pp. 20–22, in which he distinguishes speculative, financial capitalism, the "capitalism of promoters," which "has existed everywhere," on the one hand, and "a very different type of capitalism which has appeared nowhere else" but in the Occident, "the rational capitalist organization of (formally) free labor," on the other. One of the "typical representatives of financial and political capitalism [is] the Jews," p. 185, n. 6. See Muller, *The Mind of the Market*, pp. 238–39 for Weber's early and more positive discussions of the stock market and futures trading. In reality, the latter does not contradict the former, because Weber saw the market as a rational organization of speculation quite different from premodern forms of speculation.
7. Milton Friedman, "Comment on Capitalism and the Jews," in *Morality and the Market: Religious and Economic Perspectives*, edited by Walter Block, Geoffrey Brennen, Kenneth Elzinga (Vancouver, BC, 1985), pp. 419–429.
8. Werner Sombart, *The Quintessence of Capitalism: A Study of the History and Psychology of the Modern Businessman* (New York, 1967), a translation of *Der Bourgeois: Zur Geistesgeschichte des modernen Wirtschaftsmenschen* (Munich, 1913). See also John F. McGovern, "The Rise of New Economic Attitudes," pp. 219–220.

9. John Day, *Money and Finance in the Age of Merchant Capitalism* (Oxford, 1999), pp. 117–34.
10. Thorstein Veblen, "The Intellectual Preeminence of the Jews in Modern Europe," in *Essays on our Changing Order* (New York, 1963).
11. Raphael Mahler, *A History of Modern Jewry* (New York, 1971); Jacob Lestshinsky, *Yiddishe ekonomik* (Warsaw, 1931); Arthur Ruppin, *The Jews in the Modern World* (London, 1934); Calvin Goldscheider and Alan S. Zuckerman, *The Transformation of the Jews* (Chicago, 1984); Yuri Slezkine, *The Jewish Century* (Princeton, NJ, 2004).
12. See Arcadius Kahan, "Impact of Industrialization on the Jews in Tsarist Russia," in idem., *Essays in Jewish Social and Economic History,*" edited by Roger Weiss (Chicago, 1986), pp. 1–46. Kahan emphasizes discrimination as a key factor contributing to Jewish impoverishment in late nineteenth-century Russia, but he also acknowledges the dislocating effects of industrialization. See pp. 24–5, 43–6.
13. Daniel Soyer, "Class Conscious Workers as Immigrant Entrepreneurs: The Ambiguity of Class among Eastern European Jewish Immigrants to the United States at the Turn of the Century," *Labor History*, 42:1 (2001), pp. 45–59.
14. Nathan Reich, "The Economic Structure of Modern Jewry," in *The Jews: Their History, Culture, and Religion*, 3rd edition, vol. 3 (New York, 1960), p. 1250.
15. Walter P. Zenner, *Minorities in the Middle: A Cross-Cultural Analysis* (Albany, NY, 1991).
16. See the excellent discussion of social scientific analysis of Jewish conditions and prospects in Mitchell B. Hart, *Social Science and the Politics of Modern Jewish Identity* (Stanford, 2000).
17. I am of course compressing a richly complex body of economic thought – much of which is not new – into a too simplistic formula. But the point is that the industrialist is no longer seen, even by the historical sociologist, as the exclusive fulcrum of growth.
18. See generally Musgrave, *The Early Modern European Economy*.
19. Although it does not deal with the crucial matter of reconciling ethnic economic enclaves with political liberalism and cultural cohesiveness, Ivan Light and Steven J. Gold's *Ethnic Economies* (San Diego, 2000) offers a stimulating discussion of the viability of ethnic business in the United States and elsewhere.

Bibliography

PRIMARY SOURCES

Ascher, Saul. *Eisenmenger der Zweite: Nebst einem vorangesetzten Sendschreiben an Herrn Prof. Fichte in Jena.* Berlin: C. Hartmann, 1794.

———. *4 Flugschriften: Eisenmenger der Zweite, Napoleon, Die Germanomanie, Die Wartburgfeier.* Berlin: Aufbau-Verlag, 1991.

Addison, Joseph and Richard Steele. *The Spectator. A new ed., reproducing the original text, both as first issued and as corr., by its authors,* edited by Henry Morley. 3 vols. London: Routledge, 1891.

Althusius, Johannes. *Politica,* edited and translated by Frederick Smith Carney. Indianapolis: Liberty Fund, 1995.

Aristole. *The Politics,* translated by T. A. Sinclair. London: Penguin, 1981.

Bauer, Bruno. "Die Fahigkeit der heutigen Juden und Christen frei zu werden," in *Eindundzwanzig Bogen aus der Schweiz,* edited by George Herwegh. Zurich und Winterhur: Verlag des literarischen Comptoirs, 1843.

———. *Die Judenfrage.* Braunschweig: H. Otto, 1843.

———. *The Jewish Question,* translated by Helen Lederer. Cincinnati, Ohio: Hebrew Union College Institute of Religion, 1958.

Becher, Johann. *Politische Discurs von den eigentlichen Ursachen dess Auff- und Abnehmens der Städte, Länder und Republicken.* Frankfurt: Verlegung Johann David Zunners, 1673.

Beiser, Theodore C., editor. *The Early Political Writings of the German Romantics.* Cambridge: Cambridge University Press, 1996.

Bertram, Corneille Bonaventure. *De politia Judaica, tam civili quàm Ecclesiastica: iam inde à suis primordiis, hoc est, ab Orbe condito, repetita.* Geneva: Apvd Eustathium Vignon, 1574.

Boie, Heinrich Christian and Dohm, Christian Wilhelm von. *Deutsches Museum,* 1 (1777).

Bolingbroke, Henry St. John, Viscount. *Contributions to the Craftsman,* edited by Simon Varey. Oxford: Oxford University Press, 1982.

———. *Political Writings,* edited by David Armitage. Cambridge: Cambridge University Press, 1997.

Bonald, Louis-Gabriel-Ambroise, vicomte de. *Mélanges Littéraires, Politiques et Philosophiques,* 2 vols. Paris: Librairie D'Adrien Le Clere, 1858.

Börne, Ludwig. *Sämtliche Schriften,* 4 vols. Düsseldorf: Joseph Melzer Verlag, 1964.

Borochov, Ber. *Di klasen-interesen un di natsionale frage*. Vilna: Drukeray Vitve un Gebrider Rom, 1906.

Boulainvilliers, Henri, compte de. *Essai sur la noblesse de France*. Paris: n.p., 1732.

Botero, Giovanni. *The Reason of State*, translated by P. J. and D. P. Waley, and *The Greatness of Cities*, translated by Robert Peterson. New Haven: Yale University Press, 1956.

Büsch, Georg. *Abhandlung von dem Geldsumlauf in anhaltender Rucksicht auf die Staatswirtschaft und Handlung*. Hamburg: C.E. Bohn, 1780.

Cicero. *On Duties*, edited by M. T. Griffin. Cambridge: Cambridge University Press, 1991.

Cobbett, William, editor. *Parliamentary History of England from the Earliest Period to the Year 1803*, 36 vols. London: T.C. Hansard, 1806.

Britannicus, editor. *A Collection of the Best Pieces in Prose and Verse against the Naturalization of the Jews*. London: M. Cooper at the Globe, 1753.

Coyer, Abbé Gabriel François. *La Noblesse commerçante*. London and Paris: Chez Duchesne, 1756.

Cuneaus, Petrus. *De republica Hebraeorum*. Leiden: Apud Ludovicum Elzevirium, 1617.

Depping, George-Herbert. *Die Juden im Mittelalter: ein von der Akademie der Inschriften und schönen Wissenschaften zu Paris durch Ehrenerwähnung ausgezeichneter historischer Versuch über ihre bürgerlichen, literärischen und handels-Verhältnisse*. Stuttgart: E. Schweizerbart, 1834.

Dohm, Christian Wilhelm von. "Neueste politische Gerüchte," *Der Teutsche Merkur* (1777): 221–246.

———, editor. *Materialien für die Statistick und die neuere Staatengeschichte*, Christian Wilhelm von Dohm. 5 vols. Lemgo: Meyer, 1777–1785.

———. *Über die bürgerliche Verbesserung der Juden*. Berlin: Friedrich Nicholai, 1781.

———. *Über die bürgerliche Verbesserung der Juden*. Berlin and Stettin: Friedrich Nicholai, 1783.

Ewald, Johann Ludwig. *Ideen, über die nöthige Organisation der Israeliten in christlichen Staaten*. Karlesruhe: D. R. Marx, 1816.

Feuerbach, Ludwig. *The Essence of Christianity*, translated by George Eliot. Buffalo, NY: Prometheus Books, 1989.

———. *Principles of the Philosophy of the Future*, translated by Manfred H. Vogel. Indianapolis: Bobbs-Merrill, 1966.

Fichte, Johann Gottlieb. *Grundlage des Naturrechts nach Principien der Wissenschaftslehre*. Jena und Leipzig: Christian Ernst Gabler, 1797.

———. *Johann Gottlieb Fichte's sämtliche Werke*, 8 vols., edited by J. H. Fichte. Berlin: Veit und Comp, 1845.

———. *The Characteristics of the Present Age*, translated by William Smith. London: John Chapman, 1847.

———. *Ausgewählte politische Schriften*, edited by Zwi Batscha and Richard Saage. Frankfurt am Main: Suhrkamp, 1979.

———. *Der geschloßne Handelsstaat: e. philos. Entwurf als Anh. zur Rechtslehre, u. Probe e. künftig zu liefernden Politik: mit e. bisher unbekannten Ms. Fichtes "Ueber StaatsWirthschaft*, edited by Hans Hirsch. Hamburg: Meiner, 1979.

———. *The Vocation of Man*, translated by Peter Preuss. Indianapolis: Hackett, 1979.

Fourier, Charles. *Œvres Complètes*, 12 vols. Paris: Editions Anthropos, 1966–1968.

Friedländer, David. *Ueber die Verbesserung der Israeliten im Königreich Pohlen: Ein von der Regierung daselbst im Jahr 1816 abgefordertes Gutachten*. Berlin: Nicolaische Buchhandlung, 1819.

_____. *Briefe über die Moral des Handels, geschrieben im Jahr 1785*, in *Jedidja, eine religiöse, moralische und pädagogische Zeitschrift*, vol. 1. (1817).

Fries, Jakob Friedrich. *Politik oder philosophische Staatslehre*, ed., E. F. Apelt. Jena: Cröker, 1848.

_____. *Ueber die Gefährdung des Wolhstandes und Charakters der Deutschen durch die Juden. Eine aus den Heidelberger Jahrbüchern der Litteratur besonders abgedruckte Recension der Schrift des Professors Rühs... "Ueber die Ansprüche der Juden an das deutsche Bürgerrecht. Zweyter verbesserter Abdruck &c."* Heidelberg: Mohr und Winter, 1816.

_____. *Von Deutschem Bund und Deutscher Staatsverfassung: allgemeine staatsrechtliche Ansichten.* Heidelberg: Mohr und Winter, 1816.

Gans, Eduard. "Erstlinge: Drei Reden von Eduard Gans," in *Der jüdische Wille; Zeitschrift des Kartells Jüdischer Verbindungen* 1 (1919): 30–42, 108–121, 193–203.

_____. *Naturrecht und Universalgeschichte*, edited by Manfred Reidel. Stuttgart: Klett-Cotta, 1981.

Geiger, Abraham. *Urschrift und Uebersetzungen der Bibel in ihrer Abhängigkeit von der innern Entwickelung des Judenthums.* Breslau: J. Hainauer, 1857.

Goudar, Ange. *Les interets de la France mal entendus dans les branches de l'agriculture, de la population, des finances, du commerce, de la marine, et de l'industrie.* Amsterdam: Chez Jean Schreuder, & Pierre Mortier le jeune, 1757.

Graetz, Heinrich. *Geschichte der Juden von den ältesten Zeiten bis auf die Gegenwart aus den Quellen bearbeitet.* 11 vols. Leipzig: O. Leiner, 1853–1876.

_____. *The Structure of Jewish History and other Essays*, translated by Ismar Schorch. New York: Ktav, 1975.

Graetz, Michael, editor. *Mahapekhah ha-Tsarfatit ve-ha-Yehudim: Diyune ha-'asefah ha-Le'uimit, 1789–1791: mi-tokh ha-protokolim shel ha-Asefah ha-leumit veha-tazkirim she-hugshu 'al yede netsige ha-Yehudim* [The French Revolution and the Jews: Deliberations of the National Assembly: from the Protocols of the National Assembly and the Memoranda presented by the Jewish Representatives] (Hebrew) translated by Michael Graetz. Jerusalem: Mosad Bialik, 1989.

Grattenauer, Karl Wilhelm Friedrich. *Wider die Juden. Ein Wort der Warnung an alle unsere christliche Mitbürger.* 4th edition. Berlin: W. Schmidt, 1803.

Grégoire, Henri. *Essai sur la régénération physique, morale et politique des Juifs: ouvrage couronné par la Société royale des sciences et des arts de Metz le 23 Août 1788.* Paris: Éditions d'histoire sociale, 1968 [reprint 1789].

Grove, Joseph. *A reply to the famous Jew question: in which, from the public records and other undoubted authorities, is fully demonstrated... that the Jews born here before the late act were never intitled to purchase and hold lands to them and their heirs... In a letter to the gentleman of Lincoln's Inn.* London: J. Robinson; J. Woodyer; and J. Swan, 1754.

Halphen, Achille-Edmond, editor. *Recueil des lois décrets, ordonnances, avis du conseil d'état, arrêttés et règelments concernant les israélites dupuis la Révelution de 1789.* Paris: Bureaux des archives israélites, 1851.

Hanway, Jonas. *Letters admonitory and argumentative, from J. H-----y, merchant, to J. S-----r, merchant in reply to particular passages, and the general argument, of a pamphlet, entitled, Further considerations on the bill, &c.* London: Dodsley, et al., 1753.

_____. *A review of the proposed naturalization of the Jews being a dispassionate enquiry into the present state of the case: with some reflexions on general naturalization.* London: J. Waugh, 1753.

Harrington, James. *The Oceana of James Harrington and his other works, som wherof are now first publish'd from his own manuscripts: the whole collected, methodiz'd, and review'd, with an exact account of his life prefix'd*, edited by John Toland. London: The Booksellers of London and Westminster, 1700.

—————. *The Political Works of James Harrington*, edited by J. G. A. Pocock. Cambridge: Cambridge University Press, 1977.

Hartmann, Friedrich Traugott. *Untersuchung, ob die bürgerliche Freiheit den Juden zu gestatten sei.* Berlin: S. F. Hesse, 1783.

Hegel, GeorgeWilliam Friedrich. *Elements of the Philosophy of Right*, translated by H.B. Nisbett. Cambridge: Cambridge University Press, 1991.

—————. *Frühe Schriften*, edited by Eva Moldenhauer and Karl Markus Michel. Frankfurt am Main: Suhrkamp, 1994.

—————. *Grundlinien der Philosophie des Rechts*, edited by Eva Moldenhauer and Karl Markus Michel. Frankfurt am Main: Suhrkamp, 1996.

Heine, Heinrich. *Self-Portrait and Other Prose Writings*, edited by Frederick Ewen. Secaucus, N.J.: Citadell Press, 1948.

Hellwitz, L. L. *Die Organisation der Israeliten in Deutschland.* 3rd edition. Arnsberg, 1837.

Herzfeld, Levi. *Metrologische Untersuchungen zu einer Geschichte des ibräishen rep. altjüdischen Handels.* Leipzig: Leiner, 1865.

Hourwitz, Zalkind. *Apologie des Juifs: en réponse à la question: Est-il des moyens de rendre les Juifs plus heureux et plus utiles en France?* Paris: Éditions d'histoire sociale, 1968 [reprint 1789].

Hunt, Lynn, editor. *French Revolution and Human Rights: A Brief Documentary History*, Boston: St. Martins, 1996.

Hume, David. *Writings on Economics*, edited by Eugene Rotwein. Madison: University of Wisconsin Press, 1955.

—————. *An Enquiry Concerning the Principles of Morals*, edited by J. B. Schneewind. Indianapolis: Hackett, 1988.

—————. *Essays Moral, Political, and Literary*, edited by Eugene F. Millar. Indianapolis: Liberty Fund, 1985.

Israel, Levy. *Schreiben eines Juden an einen Philosophen nebst der Antwort.* Hamburg, n.p., 1759.

Jost, Isaak Markus. *Geschichte der Israeliten seit der Zeit der Maccabaer bis auf unsre Tage.* 10 vols. Berlin: Schlessinger, 1822–1847.

Justi, Johann von. *Die Grundfeste zu der Macht und Glückseligkeit der Staate, oder ausführliche Vorstellung der gesampten Polizeiwissensschaft.* Königsburg und Leipzig: Johann Heinrich Hartung, 1760.

Kant, Immanuel. *Perpetual Peace and other essays on Politics, History, and Morals*, translated by Ted Humphrey. Indianapolis: Hackett, 1983.

Kortum, E. T. von. *Über Judentum und Juden, hauptsächlich in Rücksicht ihres Einflusses auf bürgerlichen Wohlstand.* Nürnberg: n.p., 1795.

Lessing, Gotthold Ephraim. *Nathan the Wise, Minna Von Barnhelm, and Other Plays and Writings*, edited by Peter Demetz. New York: Continuum, 1998.

A Letter to the Right Honourable Sir Thomas Chitty, Knt. Lord Mayor of London shewing the true causes and reasons why so small a number of men has accepted of the great and extraordinary encouragements of the late Guild-hall subscription, and pointing out a certain and most effectual method whereby our government may, at all times, procure a sufficient number of men to fight our battles, both by sea and land, without any compulsive methods, or advance-money, and without distressing our manufactures, or at all hindering the cultivation of our lands. [au: "An English Merchant of London"] London: J. Scott, 1760.

Luther, Martin. *The Christian in Society IV*, edited by Franklin Sherman. Vol. 47 of *Luther's Works*, general editor Helmut T. Lehmann. Philadelphia: Fortress Press, 1971.

Luzzatto, Simone. *Discorso circa il stato de gl'Hebrei in particolar dimoranti nell' inclita città di Venetia, di Simone Luzzatto.* Venice: Appresso Gioanne Calleoni, 1638.

―――. *Socrate, overo dell'Humano Sapere exercitio soriogiocoso di Simone Luzzatto Hebreo Venetiano.* Venice: Tomasini, 1651.

―――. *Ma'amar 'al Yehunde Venitsiyah [Discourse on the Jews of Venice]* (Hebrew), translated by Dan Lattes. Jerusalem: Mosad Bialik, 1950.

Machiavelli, Niccolo. *Selected Political Writings*, edited by David Wootton. Indianapolis: Hackett, 1994.

Maimon, Solomon *The Autobiography of Solomon Maimon*, translated by J. Clark Murray. London: East and West Library, 1954.

Marx, Karl. "Zur Judenfrage," in *Deutsche-Französische Jahrbücher*, edited by Karl Marx and Arnold Ruges. Paris: Bureau der Jahrbücher, 1844.

―――. *The Economic and Philosophic Manuscripts of 1844*, edited by Dirk J. Struik, translated by Martin Milligan. New York: International Publishers, 1964.

―――and Friedrich Engles. *The Marx-Engles Reader*, edited by Robert C. Tucker. New York: Norton, 1978.

―――. *Gesamtausgabe (MEGA).* 36 vols. Berlin: Dietz, 1972.

Menasseh ben Israel. *Menasseh ben Israel 's Mission to Oliver Cromwell: being a reprint of the pamphlets published by Menasseh Ben Israel to promote the re-admission of the Jews to England, 1649–1656*, edited by Lucien Wolf. London: Jewish Historical Society of England, 1901.

Mendelssohn, Moses. *Jerusalem and other Jewish Writings*, edited by Alfred Jospe. New York: Schocken, 1969.

―――. *Jerusalem, or, On Religious Power and Judaism*, edited by Alexander Altmann, translated by Allan Arkush. Hanover-London: University Press of New England, 1983.

―――. *Schriften zum Judentum*, edited by Simon Rawidowicz. 4 vols. Stuttgart: F. Frommann, 1974.

Mendes-Flohr, Paul and Jehuda Reinharz, editors. *The Jew in the Modern World: A Documentary History*, New York: Oxford University Press, 1995.

Modena, Leone. *The Autobiography of a Seventeenth-Century Venetian Rabbi, Leon Modena's "Life of Judah,"* edited and translated by Mark R. Cohen. Princeton: Princeton University Press, 1988.

Montesquieu, Charles de Secondat, baron de. *The Spirit of the Laws*, edited and translated by Anne Cohler, Basia Miller and Harold Stone. Cambridge: Cambridge University Press, 1995.

Müller, Adam. *Die Elemente der Staatskunst.* Berlin: D. Sander, 1809.

―――. *Lebenszeugnisse*, edited by Jacob Baxa. 2 vols. Munich: F. Schöningh, 1966.

―――. *Kritische/Ästhetische Schriften*, edited by Walter Schroeder and Werner Siebert. 2 vols. Berlin: Luchterhand, 1967.

―――. *Versuche einer neuen Theorie des Geldes.* Jena: G. Fischer, 1922.

_____. *Vom Gest der Gemeinschaft*, edited by Friedrich Bulow. Leipzig: Friedrich Bülow, 1931.

Pamphlets Relating to Jews in England during the Seventeenth and Eighteenth Centuries, edited by Paul Radin. California State Library, occasional papers, reprint series no. 8. San Francisco: Works Progress Administration, 1939.

Philo-Patriae. *Considerations of the Bill to Permit Persons Professing the Jewish Religion to be Naturalized by Parliament, in Several Letters from a Merchant in Town to his Friend in the Country, wherein the Motives of all Parties interested therein are examined; The Principles of Christianity, with Regard to the Admission of Jews, are fully discussed; and their Utility in Trade clearly Proved*. London: R. Baldwin, 1753.

_____. *Further Considerations on the Bill to Permit Persons Professing the Jewish Religion to be Naturalized by Parliament*. London: R. Baldwin, 1753.

Proudhon, Pierre-Joseph. *System of Economical Contradictions: or, The Philosophy of Misery*, translated by Benjamin R. Tucker. Boston: Benjamin R. Tucker, 1888.

Prynne, William. *A Short Demurrer to the Jews Long discontinued barred Remitter into England*. London: E. Thomas, 1656.

Puchta, Wolfgang Heinrich. *Ueber Guterzertrümmerungen und Grundstückhandel, besonders in Beziehung auf die Frage: Ist es zweckmässiger, den jüdischen Güterhandel auch von Juden oder bloss von Christen treiben zu lasse?* Erlangen: J. J. Palm und E. Enke, 1816.

Roscher, Wilhelm. "Die Stellung der Juden im Mittelalter, betrachtet vom Standpunkte der allgemeinen Handelspolitik," *Zeitschrift für gesamte Staatswissenschaft*, XXXI (1875), pp. 503–26.

_____. *Grundriss zu Vorlessung über die Staatswirtschaft, nach geschichtlicher Methode*. Göttingen: Verlag der Dieterichschen Buchhandlung, 1843.

Rühs, Friedrich. *Entwurf einer Propädeutik des historischen Studiums*. Berlin: Realschul-buchhandlung, 1811.

_____. *Historische Entwickelung des Einflusses Frankreichs und der Franzosen auf Deutschland und die Deutschen*. Berlin: der Nicolaischen Buchhandlung, 1815.

_____. *Handbuch der Geschichte des Mittelalters*. Berlin: Realschulbuchhandlung, 1816.

_____. *Die Rechte des Christenthums und des deutschen Volk: vertheidigt gegen die Ansprüche der Juden und ihrer Verfechter*. Berlin: Realschulbuchhandlung, 1816.

_____. *Über die Ansprüche der Juden an das deutsch Bürgerrecht; mit einem Anhange über die Geschichte der Juden in Spanien*. Berlin: Realschulbuchhandlung, 1816.

Saint-Simon, Henri de. *The Political Thought of Saint-Simon*, edited by Ghita Ionescu. Oxford: Oxford University Press, 1976.

Say, Jean-Baptiste. *Traité d'economie politique, ou Simple exposition de la manière dont se forment, se distribuent et se consomment les richesse*. Paris: Chez Deterville, 1803.

Schlettwein, Johann August. "Bitte an die Grossen wegen der Juden zu Verhütung traurigen Folgen in den Staaten," *Ephemeriden der Menschheit oder Bibliothek der Sittenlehre, der Politik, und der Gesetzgebung*, 4 (October–December, 1776), pp. 41–46.

Serra, Antonio. *Breve trattato delle cause che possano far abbandonare li regni d'oro et d'argento dove non sono mintiere, con applicatione al Regno di Napoli*. Reggio: Editori meridionali riuniti, 1974.

Shakespeare, William. *The Merchant of Venice*, edited by Barbara A. Mowat and Paul Werstine. New York: Washington Square Press, 1992.

Sieyes, Emmanuel-Joseph. *Préliminaire de la constitution françoise: Reconnaissance et exposition raisonée de droits de l'homme et du citoyen.* Versailles: Ph.-D. Pierres, 1789.

_____. *Qu'est-ce que le Tiers état?*, ed. Roberto Zapperi. Genève: Droz, 1970.

_____. *Oeuvres des Sieyès*, ed. Marcel Dorigny. 3 vols. Paris: EDHIS, 1989.

Smith, Adam. *An Inquiry into the Nature and Causes of The Wealth of Nations*, edited by Edwin Cannan. Chicago: University of Chicago Press, 1976.

_____. *Wealth of Nations*, edited by Lawrence Dickey. Indianapolis: Hackett, 1993.

Spinoza, Benedict de. *A Theologico-Political Treatise; A Political Treatise*, translated by, R. H. M. Elwes. New York: Dover, 1951.

_____. *Theological-Political Treatise*, translated by Samuel Shirley. Indianapolis: Hackett, 1998.

Stobbe, Otto. *Die Juden in Deutschland während des Mittelalters in politischer, socialer und rechtlicher Beziehung.* Amsterdam: B. R. Grüner, 1968 [reprint 1866].

Tama, M. Diogene, editor. *Transactions of the Parisian Sanhedrin*, translated by F. D. Kirwan. Lanham, MD: University Press of America, 1985 [reprint 1807].

Toland, John. *Dissertationes Duae, Adeisidaemon et Origines Judicae.* The Hague: Rodopi, 1970 [reprint 1709].

_____. *Reasons for Naturalizing the Jews in Great Britain and Ireland.* London: J. Roberts, 1714.

_____. *Nazarenus or Jewish, Gentile, and Mahometan Christianity containing the history of the antient Gospel of Barnabas, and the modern Gospel of the Mahometans, attributed to the same apostle, this last Gospel being now first made known among Christians: also, the original plan of Christianity occasionally explain'd in the history of the Nazarens, whereby diverse controversies about this divine (but highly perverted) institution may be happily terminated: with the relation of an Irish manuscript of the four Gospels, as likewise a summary of the antient Irish Christianity, and the reality of the Keldees (an order of lay-religious) against the two last bishops of Worcester.* London: J. Brotherton, 1718.

_____. *State-Anatomy of Great Britain: containing a particular account of its several interests and parties, their bent and genius, and what each of them, with all the rest of Europe, may hope or fear from the reign and family of King George: being a memorial sent by an intimate friend to a foreign minister, lately nominated to come for the court of England....* London: John Philips, 1717.

_____. *Tetradymus: Containing I. Hodegus; or, The pillar of cloud and fire, that guided the Israelites in the wilderness, not miraculous: but, as faithfully related in Exodus, a thing equally practis'd by other nations, and in those places not onely useful but necessary. II. Clidophorus; or, Of the exoteric and esoteric philosophy, that is, of the external and internal doctrine of the antients: the one open and public, accommodated to popular prejudices and the establish'd religions; the other private and secret, wherin, to the few capable and discrete, was taught the real truth stript of all disguises. III. Hypatia; or, The history of a most beautiful, most virtuous, most learned, and every way accomplish'd lady; who was torn to pieces by the clergy of Alexandria, to gratify the pride, emulation, and cruelty of their Archbishop Cyril. IV. Mangoneutes: being a defense of Nazarenus, address'd to the Right Reverend John, lord bishop of London; against his lordship's chaplain Dr. Mangey, his dedicator Mr. Patterson, and... the Reverend Dr. Brett....* London: J. Brotherton and W. Meadows, 1720.

_____. *Pantheisticon. Sive Formula celebrandae sodalitatis Socraticae, in tres particulas divisa; quae pantheistarum, sive sodalium, continent I, Mores et axiomata: II, Numen et philosophiam: III, Libertatem, et non fallentem legem, neque fallendam. Praemittitur de antiquis et novis eruditorum sodalitatibus, ut et de universo infinito et aeterno, diatriba. Subjicitur de duplici pantheistarum philosophia sequendi, ac de viri optimi et ornatissimi idea, dissertatiuncula.* London: Cosmopoli, 1720.

_____. *A Collection of Several Pieces of Mr. John Toland now first published from his original manuscripts. . . . To the whole is prefixed a copious account of Mr. Toland's life and writings, by Mr. Des Maizeaux. (An appendix containing some pieces found among Mr. Toland's papers,* edited by Pierre Des Maizeaux, 2 vols. London: J. Whiston, 1726.

Tucker, Josiah. *Reflections on the Expediency of a Law for the Naturalization of Foreign Protestants in Two Parts.* London: T. Trye, 1751.

_____. *The Elements of Commerce, and Theory of Taxes.* London: n.p., 1755.

_____. *A Letter to a Friend concerning Naturalizations Shewing, I. What naturalization is not, II. What it is, III. What are the Motives for the Present Clamours against the Bill Passed last Sessions for Enabling Parliament to Naturalize such Jews, as they shall Approve of. . .* London: T. Trye, 1753.

_____. *A second letter to a friend concerning naturalizations wherein the reasons are given why the Jews were antiently considered as the immediate vassals and absolute property of the crown, but are now in a state of liberty and freedom like other subjects: to which are added, the opinions of the most eminent lawyers . . . relating to the same subject.* London: T. Trye, 1753.

_____. *The Elements of Commerce, and Theory of Taxes.* Bristol, n.p., 1768?.

Webb, Philip Carteret. *The question, whether a Jew born within the British Dominions was, before the making the late act of Parliament, a person capable by law to purchase and hold lands to him and his heirs, fairly stated and considered.* London, 1753, reprint New York: Garland, 1978.

Wessely, Naphtali Herz *Masekhet Avot 'im Perush Yen Levanon* [Wine of Lebanon: a Commentary on Tractate 'Avot]. Warsaw: Y. Goldman, 1884.

_____. *Divre Shalom ve-Emet le-Kahal 'Edat Yisra'el ha-Garim be-'Arazot Memshelet ha-Kisar ha-Gadol ha-'Ohev 'et ha-'Adam u-Mesameah ha-Briyot* [Words of Peace and Truth to the Community of Israel that Dwells in the Lands of the Kingdom of the Great Emperor who Loves Humanity and Gladdens Mankind]. Vienna: B. Shamir, 1826.

Zeitschrift für die Wissenschaft des Judentums, edited by Leopold Zunz. Berlin, 1822–1823.

Zimmern, Sigmund. *Versuch einer Würdigung der Angriffe des herrn Professor Fries auf die Juden.* Heidelberg: n.p., 1816.

Zunz, Leopold. *Gesammelte Schriften.* 3 vols. Berlin: L. Gerschel, 1875–1876.

SECONDARY SOURCES

Altmann, Alexander. *Moses Mendelssohn: A Biographical Study.* London: Littman Library of Jewish Civilization, 1998.

Andreau, Jean. *Banking and Business in the Roman World.* New York: Cambridge University Press, 1999.

Anthony, Peter. *The Ideology of Work.* London: Tavistock, 1978.

Appleby, Joyce. *Economic Thought and Ideology in Seventeenth Century England.* Princeton, N.J.: Princeton University Press, 1978.

Arbell, Mordechai. "Jewish Settlements in the French Colonies in the Caribbean (Martinique, Guadeloupe, Haiti, Cayenne) and the 'Black Code'," in Paolo Bernardini and Norman Fiering, *The Jews and their Expansion to the West, 1450–1800.* New York: Berghahn Books, 2001, pp. 291–308.

Arendt, Hannah. *Rahel Varnhagen: Lebensgeschichte einer deutschen Jüdin aus der Romantik.* Munich: R. Piper, 1959.

———. *Antisemitism: Part One of the Origins of Totalitarianism.* New York: Harcourt Brace Javonovich, 1968.

Aris, Reinhold. *History of Political Thought in Germany from 1789 to 1815.* New York: Russell and Russell 1965.

Aschheim, Steven E. "'The Jew Within': The Myth of 'Judaization' in Germany," in *The Jewish Response to German Culture: From the Enlightenment to the Second World War,* edited by Jehuda Reinharz and Walter Schatzberg. Hanover, NH and London: University Press of New England, 1985, pp. 211–41.

Assmann, Jan. *Moses the Egyptian: The Memory of Egypt in Western Monotheism.* Cambridge, MA: Harvard University Press, 1997.

Avineri, Shlomo. *The Making of Modern Zionism.* New York: Basic Books, 1981.

Baer, Fritz. *Die Juden in Christlichen Spanien,* 2 vols. Berlin: Akademie-Verlag, 1929–36.

———. *Galut,* translated by Robert Warshow. New York: Schocken, 1957.

Barbour, Reid. *John Selden: Measures of the Holy Commonwealth in Seventeenth-Century England.* Toronto: University of Toronto Press, 2003.

Baron, Hans. "Franciscan Poverty and Civic Wealth as Factors in the Rise of Humanistic Thought," *Speculum,* vol. XIII, no. 1 (January, 1938), pp. 1–37.

———. "Cicero and the Roman Civic Spirit in the Middle Ages and Early Renaissance," *Bulletin of the John Rylands Library,* vol. 22 (1938), pp. 72–97.

———. "A Sociological Interpretation of the Early Renaissance in Florence," *The South Atlantic Quarterly,* XXXVIII (Oct. 1939), pp. 434–36.

———. *The Crisis of the Early Italian Renaissance: Civic Humanism and Republican Liberty in an Age of Classicism and Tyranny.* Princeton, NJ: Princeton University Press, 1955.

Baron, Salo W. "Emphases in Jewish History," *Jewish Social Studies,* I (1939).

———. "The Modern Age," in Leo W. Schwarz, *Great Ages and Ideas of the Jewish People.* New York, 1956.

———. *History and Jewish Historians: Essays and Addresses.* Philadelphia: Jewish Publication Society of American, 1964.

———. and Arkadius Kahan, editors. *Economic History of the Jews.* New York: Schocken, 1975.

Barzilay, Isaac E. "John Toland's Borrowings from Simone Luzzatto," *Jewish Social Studies,* vol. xxxi, no. 2 (April, 1969), pp. 75–81.

Baxa, Jakob. *Adam Müller, ein Lebensbild aus den Befreiungskriegen und aus der deutschen Restauration.* Jena: G. Fischer, 1930.

Beecher, Jonathan. *Charles Fourier: The Visionary and His World.* Berkeley: University of California Press, 1986.

Beinacki, Richard. *The Fabrication of Labor: Germany and Britain, 1640–1914.* Berkeley: University of California Press, 1995.

Bermann, Tamar. *Produktivierungsmythen und Antisemitismus: Eine soziologische Studie.* Vienna: Europaverl, 1973.

Bernardini, Paolo and Norman Fiering, editors, *The Jews and their Expansion to the West, 1450–1800.* New York: Berghahn Books, 2001.

Bernfeld, Tirtsah Levie. "Financing Poor Relief in the Spanish-Portuguese Jewish Community in Amsterdam in the Seventeenth and Eighteenth Centuries," in *Dutch Jewry: Its History and Secular Culture (1500–2000)*, edited by Jonathan Israel and Reiner Salverda. Brill: Leiden, 2002.

Berti, Silvia. "At the Roots of Unbelief," *Journal of the History of Ideas*, vol. 56, n. 4 (October, 1995), pp. 555–75.

Black, Antony. *Guilds and Civil Society in European Political Thought from the Twelfth Century to the Present.* London and New York: Methuen, 1984.

Blanning, T. C. W. *The French Revolution: Aristocrats Versus Bourgeois?.* Atlantic Highlands, NJ: Humanities Press International, 1987.

Bloom, Herbert I. *The Economic Activities of the Jews of Amsterdam in the Seventeenth Century.* Williamsport, Pa: Bayard Press, 1937.

Bonfil, Robert. *Jewish Life in Renaissance Italy.* Berkeley: University of California Press, 1994.

Bor, Harris. "Enlightenment Values, Jewish Ethics: The Haskalah's Transformation of the Traditional Musar Genre," in Shmuel Feiner and David Sorkin (eds.), *New Perspectives on the Haskalah.* Oxford: Littman Library, 2001, pp. 49–63.

Boraleva, Lea Campos. "Classical Foundational Myths of European Republicanism: The Jewish Commonwealth," in *Republicanism, a Shared European Heritage*, vol. 1, edited by Martin Van Gelderen and Quentin Skinner. Cambridge: Cambridge University Press, 2002, pp. 247–262.

Bouwsma, William J. *Venice and the Defense of Republican Liberty: Renaissance Values in the Age of Counter-Reformation.* Berkeley: University of California Press, 1968.

Braude, Benjamin. "Jewish Economic History – Review Essay." *Association for Jewish Studies Newsletter* 19 (February, 1977), pp. 25–28.

Breckman, Warren. *Marx, the Young Hegelians and the Origins of Radical Social Theory: Defining the Self.* Cambridge: Cambridge University Press, 1999.

Breuer, Mordechai. "The Early Modern Period," in Michael Meyer, ed., *German-Jewish History in Modern Times.* New York: Columbia University Press, 1996.

Brewer, John *The Sinews of Power, War, Money and the English State, 1688–1783.* Cambridge, Ma.: Harvard University Press, 1988.

Brose, Eric Dorn. *German History, 1789–1871.* Providence, R. I.: Berghahn, 1997.

Burchardt, Frank. *German Antiquity in Renaissance Myth.* Baltimore: Johns Hopkins University Press, 1971.

Burgess, Glenn. *The Politics of the Ancient Constitution: An Introduction to English Political Thought, 1603–1642.* University Park, PA: Pennsylvania State University Press, 1992.

Bush, Jonathan A. "'You're Gonna Miss Me When I'm Gone': Early Modern Common Law Discourse and the Case of the Jews," *Wisconsin Law Review*, (September/October, 1993), pp. 1225–1285.

Campbell, Joan. *The Joy of Work, German Work.* Princeton: Princeton University Press, 1989.

Carabelli, Giancarlo. *Tolandiana: materiali bibliographici per lo studio dell'opera e della fortuna di John Toland.* Florence: La Nuova Italia, 1975.

Carlebach, Julius. *Karl Marx and the Radical Crituque of Judaism.* Boston: Routledge and Kegan Paul, 1978.

Carmilly, Moshe and Michael K. Silber (eds.). *Jews in the Hungarian Economy, 1760–1945: Studies Dedicated to Moshe Carmilly-Weinberger on his Eightieth Birthday.* Jerusalem: Magnes Press, 1992.

Caro, Georg. "Die Juden des Mittelalters in ihrer wirschaftlichen Betätigung," in *Monatschrift für Geschichte und Wissenschaft des Judentums* vol. 45 (1912), pp. 600–633.

Cassirer, Ernst. *The Philosophy of the Enlightenment,* translated by Fritz C. A. Koelln and James Pettigrove. Princeton: Princeton University Press, 1979.

Champion, J. A. I. *The Pillars of Prienstcraft Shaken.* Cambridge: Cambridge University Press, 1992.

―――. "Toleration and Citizenship in Enlightenment England: John Toland and the Naturalization of the Jews, 1714–1753," in *Toleration in Enlightenment Europe,* edited by Ole Peter Grell and Roy Porter. Cambridge: Cambridge University Press, 2000.

―――. *John Toland and the Crisis of Christian Culture, 1696–1722.* Manchester: Manchester University Press, 2003.

Chaussinand-Nogaret, Guy. *The French Nobility in the Eighteenth Century,* translated by William Doyle. Cambridge: Cambridge University Press, 1985.

Chibnall, Marjorie. *The Debate on the Norman Conquest.* Manchester and New York: Manchester University Press, 1999.

Cipolla, Carlo. *Before the Industrial Revolution.* New York: Norton, 1993.

Cohen, Edward E. *Athenian Economy and Society: a Banking Perspective.* Princeton, N.J.: Princeton University Press, 1992.

Cohen, Robert. "Passage to the New World: The Sephardi Poor of Eighteenth-Century Amsterdam," in L. Dasberg and J. N. Cohen editors, *Neveh Ya'akov: Jubilee Volume Presented to Dr. Jaap Meijer.* Assen: Van Gorcum, 1982.

―――. "The Edgerton Manuscript," *American Jewish Historical Quarterly,* LXII (1973), 333–47.

Cohen, Yerachmiel (Richard). "Jewish Emancipation Rhetoric and the Image of the Future" in Yerachmiel Cohen, editor, *ha-Mahapekhah ha-Tsarfatit ve-Rishumah: Kovets Ma'amarim* [The French Revolution and its Legacy] (Hebrew). Jerusalem: Zalman Shazar le-Toldot Yisrael, 1991, pp. 141–158.

Coleman, D. C. "Labour in the English Economy of the Seventeenth Century," *Economic History Review,* series 2, 8: 3 (1955), pp. 280–95.

Coleman, William. "Anti-Semitism in Anti-Economics," *History of Political Economy,* 35:4 (2003), pp. 781–99.

Conze, Werner. "Arbeit," in Otto Brunner, Werner Conze and Reinhard Kosseleck, editors, *Geschichtliche Grundbegriffe. Historisches Lexikon zur Politisch-Sozialen Sprache in Deutschaland,* vol. I. Stuttgart: E. Klett, 1972, pp. 155–185.

Bernard Dov Cooperman, Trade and Settlement: The Establishment of the Jewish Communities of Leghorn and Pisa. Ph.D. Dissertation. Harvard University. Cambridge, Ma. 1976.

Dambacher, Ilsegret. *Christian Wilhelm von Dohm: Ein Beitrag zur Geschichte des preußischen aufgeklärten Beamtentums und seiner Reformbestrebungen am Ausgang des 18. Jahrhunderts.* Bern: H. Lang, 1974.

Daniel, Stephen H. *John Toland, His Methods, Manners, and Mind.* Kingston: McGill-Queen's University Press 1984.

Davis, Natalie Zeman. "Sixteenth-Century French Arithmetics on the Business Life," *Journal of the History of Ideas*, vol. 21, no. 1. Jan.–March 1960, pp. 24–25.

De Vries, Jan. *The Economy of Europe in an Age of Crisis*. Cambridge: Cambridge University Press, 1988.

Dickey, Laurence. *Hegel: Religion, Economics, and the Politics of Spirit, 1770–1807*. Cambridge: Cambridge University Press, 1987.

Dickinson, H. T. "The Poor Palatines and the Parties," *English Historical Review*, vol. lxxxii (1967), pp. 464–85.

Dickson, P. G. M. *The Financial Revolution in England: a Study in the Development of Public Credit, 1688–1756*. St. Martin's Press: New York, 1967.

Dow, Alexander and Sheila Dow. *A History of Scottish Economic Thought*. London and New York: Routledge, 2006.

Downie, J. A. *Robert Harley and the Press: Propaganda and Public Opinion in the Age of Swift and Defoe*. Cambridge: Cambridge University Press, 1979.

Draper, John W. "Usury in 'The Merchant of Venice'," *Modern Philology*, vol. 33, no. 1. August, 1935, pp. 37–47.

Dubin, Lois. *The Port Jews of Habsburg Trieste: Absolutist Politics and Enlightenment Culture*. Stanford: Stanford University Press, 1999.

Emmer, Peter. "The Jewish Moment and the Two Expansion Systems in the Atlantic, 1580–1650," in Paolo Bernardini and Norman Fiering, *The Jews and their Expansion to the West, 1450–1800*. New York: Berghahn Books, 2001.

Epstein, Klaus. *The Genesis of German Conservatism*. Princeton: Princeton University Press, 1966.

Erspamer, Peter R. *The Elusiveness of Tolerance*. Chapel Hill: University of North Carolina Press, 1997.

Ettinger, Shmuel. "The Beginnings of the Change in the Attitude of European Society towards the Jews," *Scripta Hierosolymitana*, VII (1961), pp. 193–219.

––––––. "Jews and Judaism in the Eyes of the English Deists of the Eighteenth Century" (Hebrew), *Zion*, xxix (1964), pp. 182–207.

Endelman, Todd. *The Jews of Georgian England*. Oxford: Oxford University Press, 1978.

––––––, editor. *Toward Modernity: The European Jewish Model*, Brunswick, N.J.: Transaction Press, 1987.

Evans, Robert Reese. *Pantheisticon: The Career of John Toland*. New York: P. Lang, 1991.

Feiner, Shmuel. *Haskalah ve-Historiyah: Toldotehah shel Hakarat-'Avar Yahadut*. [Haskalah and History: The Development of Jewish Historical Consciousness] (Hebrew). Jerusalem: Merkaz Zalman Shazar le-toldot Yisrael, 1995.

––––––. *New Perspectives on the Haskalah*, edited by Shmuel Feiner and David Jan Sorkin. Oxford: Littman Library, 2001.

––––––. *Haskalah and History: The Emergence of a Modern Jewish Historical Consciousness*, translated by Chaya Naor and Sondra Silverston. Oxford: The Litman Library of Jewish Civilization, 2002.

Felsenstein, Frank. *Anti-Semitic Stereotypes: A Paradigm of Otherness in English Popular Culture, 1660–1830*. Baltimore: Johns Hopkins University Press, 1995.

Ferguson, Niall. *The House of Rothschild*. 2 vols. New York: Viking, 1998.

Figes, Orlando. "Ludwig Börne and the Formation of a Radical Critique of Judaism," in *LBIYB*, vol. xxix (1984), pp. 351–382.

Finley, M. I. *The Ancient Economy*. Berkeley: University of California Press, 1985.

Freudenthal, Gad. "Aaron Salomon Gumpertz, Gotthold Ephraim Lessing, and the First Call of an Improvement of the Civil Rights of Jews in Germany (1753)," *AJS Review*, 29:2 (2005), pp. 299–353.

Furet, F. and M. Ozouf, editors, *A Critical Dictionary of the French Revolution*. Cambridge, Ma.: Harvard University Press., 1989.

Gager, John. *The Origins of Anti-Semitism*. New York: Oxford University Press, 1985.

Gerber, Jane S. *The Jews of Spain: A History of the Sephardic Experience*. The Free Press: New York, 1994.

Giuntini, Chiara. *Panteismo e ideologia republicana: John Toland (1670–1722)*. Bologna, Il mulino, 1979.

Glanz, Rudolf. *Geschichte des niederen judischen Volkes in Deutschland; eine Studie uber historisches Gaunertum, Bettelwesen und Vagantentum*. New York: n.p., 1968.

Glasman, Maurice. *Unnecessary Suffering: Managing Market Utopia*. London: Verso Press, 1996.

Glassman, Bernard. *Protean Prejudice: Antisemitism in England's Age of Reason*. Atlanta: Scholars Press, 1998.

Glotzer, Scott B. *Napoleon, the Jews, and the Construction of Modern Citizenship in Early Nineteenth Century France*. Ph.D. dissertation: Rutgers University. New Brunswick, N.J., 1996.

Goldsmith, M. M. "Liberty, Virtue, and the Rule of Law, 1689–1770," in *Republicanism, Liberty, and Commercial Society, 1649–1776*, edited by David Wootton. Stanford: Stanford University Press, 1994, pp. 197–232.

Goubert, Pierre. *Initiation à l'histoire de la France: suivi d'une chronologie, de cartes, de tableaux généalogiques et d'une bibliographie*. Paris: Tallandier, 1984.

Graetz, Michael. *The Jews in Nineteenth-Century France: From the French Revolution to the Alliance Israélite Universelle*, translated by Jane Marie Todd. Stanford: Stanford University Press, 1996.

Grassby, Richard. *The Business Community of Seventeenth-Century England*. Cambridge: Cambridge University Press, 1995.

Gross, John J. *Shylock: A Legend and its Legacy*. New York: Simon and Schuster, 1992.

Hamerow, Theodore S. *Restoration, Revolution, Reaction: Economics and Politics in Germany, 1815–1871*. Princeton: Princeton University Press, 1958.

Hammacher, Klaus and Hans Hirsch. *Die Wirtschaftspolitik des Philophen Friedrich Heinrich Jacobi*. Amsterdam: Editions Rodopi, 1993.

Hardach, Karl. "Some Remarks on German Economic Historiography and its Understanding of the Industrial Revolution in Germany," *The Journal of European Economic Thought*, vol. 1, no. 1 (Spring, 1972).

Hankins, James. "The 'Baron Thesis' after Forty Years, and Some Recent Studies of Leonardo Bruni," *Journal of the History of Ideas* 56, no. 2 (1995), pp. 309–338.

———, editor. *Renaissance Civic Humanism: Reappraisals and Reflections*. Cambridge University Press, 2000.

Hayton, David. "The 'Country' Interest and the Party System, 1689–1720," in Clyve Jones, editor, *Party and Management in Parliament, 1660–1784*. New York: St. Martin's Press, 1984, pp. 37–85.

Hazard, Paul. *The European Mind*, translated by James Lewis May. Harmondsworth: Penguin, 1973.

Hecht, Jacqueline. "Un problème de population active au XVIIIe siècle, en France: la quarelle de la nobesse commerçante" *Population*, no. 2 (April–May 1964), pp. 267–90.

Heesen, Anke Te. *The World in a Box: The Story of an Eighteenth-Century Picture Encyclopedia*. Chicago: University of Chicago Press, 2002.

Hertz, Deborah. *Jewish High Society in Old Regime Berlin*. New Haven: Yale University Press, 1988.

Herzberg, Arthur. *The French Enlightenment and the Jews: The Origins of Modern Anti-semitism*. New York: Columbia University Press, 1968.

Hess, Jonathan. *Germans, Jews, and the Claims of Modernity*. New Haven: Yale University Press, 2002.

Higonnet, Patrice. *Class, Ideology, and the Rights of Nobles during the French Revolution*. Oxford: Clarendon, 1981.

Hill, Christopher. *Society and Puritanism in Pre-Revolutionary England*. New York: Schocken, 1964.

Hirsch, Helmut. *Marx und Moses, Karl Marx zur 'Judenfrage' und zu Juden*. Frankfort au Main; Lang, 1980.

Hirschmann, Albert O. *The Passions and the Interests: Political Arguments for Capitalism before its Triumph*. Princeton, N.J.: Princeton University Press, 1977.

Honohan, Iseult. *Civic Republicanism*. London and New York: Routledge, 2002.

Hont, Istvan. "Free Trade and the Economic Limits to National Politics: Neo-Machiavellian Political Economy Revisited," John Dunn, editor, *The Economic Limits to Modern Politics*. Cambridge: Cambridge University Press, 1990.

_____. "The 'Rich Country–Poor Country' Debate in Scottish Classical Political Economy," in Istvan Hont and Michael Ignatieff, editors, *Wealth and Virtue: The Shaping of Political Economy in the Scottish Enlightenment*. Cambridge: Cambridge University Press, 1985, pp. 285–301.

_____ and Michael Ignatieff, "Needs and Justice in the *Wealth of Nations*: An Introductory Essay," in Istvan Hont and Michael Ignatieff, editors, *Wealth and Virtue: The Shaping of Political Economy in the Scottish Enlightenment*. Cambridge: Cambridge University Press, 1985.

Hopkins Keith, "Taxes and Trade in the Roman Empire (200 B.C.–A.D. 400)," *The Journal of Roman Studies* LXX (1980), pp. 105–25.

Höffding, Harald. *A History of Modern Philosophy*, 2 vols. New York: Dover, 1955.

Holmes, Geoffrey. *British Politics in the Age of Queen Anne*. New York: St. Martins Press, 1967.

_____ and Daniel Szechi, *The Age of Oligarchy: Pre-Industrial Britain, 1722–1784*. London: Longman, 1993.

Hook, Sidney. *From Hegel to Marx: Studies in the Intellectual Development of Karl Marx*. New York: Columbia University Press, 1994.

Houston, Alan. "Republicanism, the Politics of Necessity, and the Rule of Law," in Alan Houston and Steve Pincus, editors, *A Nation Transformed: England after the Restoration*. Cambridge: Cambridge University Press, 2001.

Hsia, R. Po-Chia. "The Usurious Jew: Economic Structure and Religious Representations in an Anti-Semitic Discourse," in R. Po-Chia Hsia and Hartmut Lehmann, editors, *In and Out of the Ghetto: Jewish-Gentile Relations in Late Medieval and Early Modern Germany*. Cambridge: Cambridge University Press, 1995.

Hundert, Gerson David. *Jews in Poland-Lithuania in the Eighteenth Century*. Berkeley: University of California Press, 2004.

Hutchison, Terence. *Before Adam Smith: The Emergence of Political Economy, 1662–1776*. Oxford: Oxford University Press, 1988.

Hyman, Paula. *Gender and Assimilation in Modern Jewish History: The Roles and Representation of Women*. Seattle and London: University of Washington Press, 1995.

Iggers, George. *The German Historical conception of History: The National Tradition of Historical Thought from Herder to the Present*. Middletown, Ct.: Wesleyan University Press, 1983.

Israel, Jonathan. *European Jewry in the Age of Mercantilism*. Oxford: Oxford University Press, 1991.

————. "Germany and Its Jews: A Changing Relationship (1300–1800)," in R. Po-Chia Hsia and Hartmut Lehmann editors, *In and Out of the Ghetto: Jewish-Gentile Relations in Late Medieval and Early Modern Germany*. Cambridge: Cambridge University Press, 1995.

————. *Diasporas within a Diaspora: Jews, Crypto-Jews and the World Maritime Empires (1540–1740)*. Leiden: Brill, 2002.

Jacob, Margaret C., *Living the Enlightenment: Freemasonry and Politics in Eighteenth-Century Europe*. New York: Oxford University Press, 1991.

————. "John Toland and the Newtonian Ideology," *Journal of Warburg and Courtauld Institute*, XXXII (1969).

Jacobs, Jack. *On Socialists and the Jewish Question after Marx*. New York: New York University Press, 1992.

Jacobs, Wilhelm G. *Johann Gottlieb Fichte: mit Selbstzeugnissen und Bilddokumenten*. Reinbek bei Hamburg: Rowohlt, 1984.

Jersch-Wenzel, Stefi. "Jewish Economic Activity in Early Modern Times," in R. Po-Chia Hsia and Hartmut Lehmann, editors, *In and Out of the Ghetto: Jewish-Gentile Relations in Late Medieval and Early Modern Germany*. Cambridge: Cambridge University Press, 1995.

Jones, J. R. *Country and Court England, 1658–1714*. Cambridge, MA: Harvard University Press, 1979.

Jones, Philip. *The Italian City-State: From Commune to Signoria*. Oxford: Oxford University Press, 1997.

Jordan, William Chester. *The French Monarchy and the Jews*. Philadelphia: University of Pennsylvania Press, 1989.

Jurdjevic, Mark. "Virtue, Commerce, and the Enduring Florentine Republican Moment: Reintegrating Italy into the Atlantic Republican Debate." *Journal of the History of Ideas*, v. 62 n. 4. Oct 2001, pp. 721–43.

Kaplan, Yosef. "The Self-Definition of the Sephardic Jews of Western Europe and Their Relation to the Alien and the Stranger," in Benjamin R. Gampel, editor, *Crisis and Creativity in the Sephardic World, 1391–1648*. New York: Columbia University Press, 1997.

Karniel, Josef. *The Policy towards the Religious Minorities in the Habsburg Monarchy in the Time of Joseph II*, vol. II (Hebrew), Ph.D. Dissertation, University of Tel-Aviv. Tel-Aviv, 1980.

Karp, Jonathan. "The Aesthetic Difference: Moses Mendelssohn's *Kohelet Musar* and the Origins of the Berlin Haskalah," in Ross Brann and Adam Sutcliffe, editors, *Renewing the Past, Reconfiguring Jewish Culture.* Philadelphia: University of Pennsylvania Press, 2004, pp. 93–120.

Katz, David S. *Jews in the History of England, 1485–1850.* New York: Oxford University Press, 1994.

———. *Philo-Semitism and the Readmission of the Jews to England, 1603–1655* Oxford: Oxford University Press, 1982.

Katz, Jacob. "The Term 'Jewish Emancipation': Its Origin and Historical Impact," in Alexander Altmann, editor, *Studies in Nineteenth-Century Jewish Intellectual History.* Cambridge, MA: Harvard University Press, 1964.

———. "A State within a State – the History of an anti-Semitic Slogan," *The Israel Academy of Sciences and Humanities,* IV (1971) pp. 32–58.

———. *Out of the Ghetto: The Social Background of Emancipation, 1770–1870.* New York: Schocken, 1978.

———. *From Prejudice to Destruction.* Cambridge, MA: Harvard University Press, 1980.

———. *Halakhah ve-Kabbalah* (Hebrew). Jerusalem: Hebrew University Press, 1984.

———. *Tradition and Crisis: Jewish Society at the End of the Middle Ages.* New York: New York University Press, 1993.

Kenyon, J. P. *Revolution Principles: The Politics of Party, 1689–1720.* Cambridge: Cambridge University Press, 1977.

Keynes, J. M. *General Theory of Employment, Interest and Money.* New York: Harcourt, Brace, 1936.

Kirschenbaum, S. "Jewish and Christian Theories of Usury in the Middle Ages," *Jewish Quarterly Review,* 75, no. 3 (1985), pp. 270–289.

Kisch, Guido. "Otto Stobbe und die Rechtsgeschichte der Juden," in *Jahrbuch der Gesellschaft für die Geschichte der Juden in der Tschechoslovakischen Republik,* IX (1938).

———. *The Jews in Medieval Germany: A Study of their Legal and Social Status.* Chicago, University of Chicago Press, 1949.

Kley, Dale Van, editor, *The French Idea of Freedom: The Old Regime and the Declaration of Rights of 1789.* Stanford: Stanford University Press, 1994.

Koehler, Benedict. *Ästhetik der Politik: Adam Müller und die politische Romantik.* Stuttgart: Klett-Cotta, 1980.

Kolbrener, William. "'Commonwealth Fictions' and 'Inspiration Fraud': Milton and the *Eikon Basilike* after 1689," *Milton Studies,* 37 (1999), pp. 166–97.

Kramnick, Isaac. *Bolingbroke and his Circle: The Politics of Nostalgia in the Age of Walpole.* Ithaca-London: Cornell University Press, 1992.

———. *Republicanism and Bourgeois Radicalism: Political Ideology in Late Eighteenth-Century England and America.* Ithaca: Cornell University Press, 1990.

Kwass, Michael. "A Kingdom of Taxpayers: State Formation, Privilege, and Political Culture in Eighteenth-Century France," *Journal of Modern History,* vol. 70, n. 2 (June 1998), pp. 295–339.

Lamont, W. M. *Marginal Prynne.* London: Routledge and Paul, 1963.

Lane, Frederick C. *Venice: A Maritime Republic.* Baltimore and London: Johns Hopkins University Press, 1973.

Langford, Paul. *A Polite and Commercial People: England 1727–1783.* Oxford: Oxford University Press, 1989.

Langmuir, Gavin. "'Judei nostri' and the Beginning of Capetian Legislation." *Traditio* 16 (1960), p. 203–40.

_____. "The Jews and the Archives of Angevin England: Reflections on Medieval Anti-Semitism," *Traditio* 19 (1963), pp. 183–244.

La Vopa, Anthony J. *Fichte: The Self and the Calling of Philosophy, 1762–1799*. Cambridge: Cambridge University Press, 2001.

Lefebvre, George. *The French Revolution*, 2 vols. New York: Columbia University Press, 1962.

Le Goff, Jacques. *Time, Work, and Culture in the Middle Ages*, translated by Arthur Goldhammer. Chicago: Chicago University Press, 1980.

Lenz, Friedrich. *Friedrich List: der Mann und das Werk*. München-Berlin: R. Oldenbourg, 1936.

Lerner, Ralph. "Commerce and Character: The Anglo-American as New-Model Men." *The William and Mary Quarterly*, 36 (January 1979), pp. 3–26.

Lestschinsky, Jacob. "Die Umsiedlung und Umschichtung des juedischen Volkes im Laufe des lezten Jahrhunderts," in *Weltwirtschaftliches Archiv*, vol. II, no. 30 (Jena, 1929), pp. 149–158.

Levin, Mordecai. *Erkhe hevrah ve-kalkalah b-'ideologyah shel tekufat ha-Haskalah* [Social and Economic Values: The Idea of Professional Modernization in the Ideology of the Haskalah Movement] (Hebrew). Jerusalem: Mosad Byalik, 1975.

Lévy-Bruhl, Henri. "La Noblesse de France et le Commerce a la fin de l'ancien Régime," *Revue d'Histoire Moderne*, no. 8 (1933), pp. 209–35.

Lieberles, Robert. "The Historical Context of Dohm's Treatise on the Jews," in *Das Deutsche Judentum und der Liberalismus: Dokumentation eines internationalen Seminars der Friedrich- Naumann-Stiftung in Zusammenarbeit mit dem Leo Baeck Institute*. Sankt-Augustin: Comdok-Verlagsabteilung, 1986, pp. 43–54

Liebeschütz, Hans "Judentum und deutsche Umwelt in Zeitalter der Restauration," in Idem. and Arnold Pauker, editors., *Deutsche Judentum in der Deutsche Umwelt: 1800–1850*. Tübingen, 1977.

_____. *Das Judentum im deutschen Geschichtsbild vom Hegel bis Max Weber*. Tübingen: J. C. B. Mohr, 1967.

Liljegren, S. B. *Harrington and the Jews*. Lund: C. W. K. Gleerup, 1932.

Lindemann, Albert S. *A History of European Socialism*. New Haven: Yale University Press, 1983.

Lindenfeld, David F. *The Practical Imagination: The German Sciences of State in the Nineteenth Century*. Chicago: University of Chicago Press, 1997.

Little, Lester K. *Religious Poverty and the Profit Economy in Medieval Europe*. Ithaca: Cornell University Press, 1978.

Lo Cascio, Elio and Dominic Rathbone, editors. *Production and Public Powers in Classical Antiquity*. Cambridge: Cambridge Philological Society, 2000.

Lopez, Robert. "Hard Times and Investment in Culture," in *Social and Economic Foundations of the Italian Renaissance*, edited by Anthony Molho. New York: Wiley, 1969.

Low, Alfred D. *Jews in the Eyes of Germans, from the Enlightenment to Imperial Germany*. Philadelphia: Institute for the Study of Human Issues, 1979.

Lowenstein, Steven M. "The Rural Community and the Urbanization of German Jewry," in idem, editor, *The Mechanics of Change: Essays in the Social History of German Jewry*. Atlanta: Scholars Press, 1992, pp. 133–149.

————. "Die Berliner Juden 1770–1830: Pioniere jüdischer Modernität," in Reinhard Rürup, editor, *Jüdische Geschichte in Berlin*. Berlin: Edition Hentrich, 1996.

Löwith, Karl. *From Hegel to Nietzsche: the Revolution in Nineteenth Century Thought*, translated by David E. Green. Garden City, NY: Anchor, 1967.

Luzzatto, Gino. "Sulla condizione economica degli Ebrei veneziani nel secolo XVIII," in *Sritti in onore di Riccardo Bachi*. Città di Castello, Perugia: Unione Arti Grafiche, 1950, pp. 161–72.

Martines, Lauro. *Power and Imagination: City-States in Renaissance Italy*. New York: Alfred A. Knopf, 1979.

McClelland, Charles E. *State, Society, and University in Germany*. Cambridge: Cambridge University Press, 1980.

McGovern, John F., "The Rise of New Economic Attitudes – Economic Humanism, Economic Nationalism – during the later Middle Ages and Renaissance, A.D. 1200–1550, *Traditio*, XXVI (1970), pp. 218–253.

————. "The Rise of New Economic Attitudes in Canon and Civil Law," *The Jurist*, 32 (1972), pp. 39–50.

McGrath, Alister E. *The Intellectual Origins of the European Reformation*. Malden, MA: Blackwell, 2004.

McKendrick, Neil, John Brewer and J. H. Plumb, editors, *Birth of a Consumer Society: The Commercialization of eighteenth-century England*. Bloomington: Indiana University Press, 1982.

McLaughlin, T. P. "The Teaching of the Canonists on Usury," *Medieval Studies*, 1 (1939), pp. 81–147.

McLellan, David. *Marx before Marxism*. New York: Harper Row, 1970.

McNally, David. *Against the Market: Political Eonomy, Market Scialism and the Marxist Critique*. London: Verso, 1993.

————. *Political Economy and the Rise of Capitalism: A Reinterpretation*. Berkeley: University of California Press, 1988.

MacCulloch, Diarmaid. *The Reformation*. New York: Viking, 2003.

Magnus, Shulamit S. *Jewish Emancipation in a German City: Cologne, 1798–1871*. Stanford: Stanford University Press, 1997.

Mahler, Raphael. *A History of Modern Jewry, 1780–1815*. New York: Schocken, 1971.

————. "Yizhak Schipper (1884–1943)," in *Historiker un vegveizer: essayen*, edited by Raphael Mahler. Tel-Aviv: Yisroel-Bukh, 1967.

Mainusch, Herbert. "Einleitung" to John Toland, *Gründe für die Einbürgerung der Juden in Grossbritannien und Irland*, edited and translated by Herbert Mainusch. Stuttgart: W. Kohlhammer Verlag, 1965.

Malino, Frances. *A Jew in the French Revolution: The Life of Zalkind Hourwitz*. Oxford and Cambridge, MA: Blackwell, 1996.

Manuel, Frank. *The Broken Staff: Judaism through Christian Eyes*. Cambridge, MA: Harvard University Press, 1992.

Matar, Nabil. "The Idea of the Restoration of the Jews in English Protestant Thought, from the Reformation to 1660," *Durham University Journal*, 78 (1985), pp. 23–36.

————. "The Controversy over the Restoration of the Jews in English Protestant Thought, 1701–1753," *Durham University Journal*, 80 (1988), pp. 241–56.

Mayer, Annelise. *England als politisches Vorbild und sein Einfluß auf die politische Entwicklung in Deutschland bis 1830*. Endingen: Wild, 1931.

Méchoulan, Henry. "Menasseh and the World of the Non-Jew," in Yosef Kaplan, Henry Méchoulan, and Richard H. Popkin, editors, *Menasseh ben Israel and His World*. New York, Copenhagen, Cologne: E.J. Brill, 1989.

Melamed, Abraham. "Ahotan ha-ketanah shel ha-hokhmot: ha-mahashavah ha-medinit shel ha-hogim ha-Yehudiyim ba-Renesans ha-Italki" [Wisdom's Little Sister: The Political Thought of Jewish Thinkers in the Italian Renaissance] (Hebrew). Ph.D. dissertation. Tel Aviv University, 1976.

———. "Medieval and Renaissance Jewish Political Philosophy," in Daniel H. Frank and Oliver Leaman, editors, *History of Jewish Philosophy*. London: Routledge, 1997, pp. 415–419.

———. *The Philosopher King in Medieval and Renaissance Jewish Thought*. Albany: SUNY Press, 2003.

Merquior, J. G. *Liberalism Old and New*. Boston: Twayne, 1991.

Mendle, Michael. Review of Andrew Lacey, *The Cult of King Charles the Martyr*. Studies in Modern British Religious History Series. (Woodbridge and Suffolk: Boydell Press, 2003) on H-Albion (http://www.h-net.org/reviews/showrev.cgi?path= 255891083547450).

Meyer, Michael, editor, *German Jewish History in Modern Times*, 2 vols. New York: Columbia University Press, 1997.

———. *The Origins of the Modern Jew: Jewish Identity and European Culture in Germany, 1749–1824*. Detroit: Wayne State University Press, 1967.

———. *Response to Modernity: A History of the Reform Movement in Judaism*. New York: Oxford University Press, 1988.

Moggach, Douglas. *The Philosophy and Politics of Bruno Bauer*. Cambridge: Cambridge University Press, 2003.

Möller, Horst. *Fürstenstaat oder Bürgernation: Deutschand 1763–1815*. Berlin: Siedler, 1989.

———. "Über die bürgerliche Verbesserung der Juden: Christian Wilhelm von Dohm und seine Gegner," in Marianne Awerbuch and Stefi Jersch-Wenzel, editors, *Bild und Selbstbild der Juden Berlins zwischen Aufklärung und Romantik*. Berlin: Colloquium Verlag, 1992. pp. 68–9.

Mossé, Claude. *The Ancient World at Work*. New York: Norton, 1969.

Mosse, George L. *The Crisis of German Ideology: Intellectual Origins of the Third Reich*. New York: Grosset and Dunlop, 1964.

Muller, Jerry Z. *The Mind and the Market: Capitalism in Modern European Thought*. New York: Knopf, 2002.

Murphy, Antoin E. "John Law and the Scottish Enlightenment" in *A History of Scottish Economic Thought*, edited by Alexander Dow and Sheila Dow. London and New York: Routledge, 2006.

Musgrave, Peter. *The Early Modern European Economy*. New York: St. Martins, 1999.

Nederman, Carrie. "Nature, Sin, and the Origins of Society: The Ciceronian Tradition in Medieval Political Thought," *Journal of the History of Ideas*, vol. 49, no. 1 (Jan.–Mar., 1988), pp. 3–26.

Nelson, Benjamin N. *The Idea of Usury: From Tribal Brotherhood to Universal Otherhood*. Princeton, N. J.: Princeton University Press, 1949.

Netanyahu, B. *Don Isaac Abravanel*. Philadelphia: Jewish Publication Society of America, 1982.

Neuman, Kalman. "Sifrut *Respublica Judaica*: Tiore' ha-Medinah ha-'Ivrit ha-kedumah bi-ketivah ha-Antiquariyah shel ha-ma'ot ha-tet-zayin ve-ha-yod-zayin." [The Literature of the *Respublica Judaica*: Descriptions of the Ancient Israelite Polity in the Antiquarian Writing of the Sixteenth and Seventeenth Centuries] (Hebrew). Ph.D. dissertation. Hebrew University of Jerusalem, 2002.

————. "Political Hebraism and the Early Modern 'Respublica Hebraeorum': On Defining the Field." *Hebraic Political Studies*, 1 : 1 (Fall, 2005), pp. 57–70.

Nicholas, David. *The Later Medieval City, 1300–1500*. London and New York: Longman, 1997.

Noonan, John T. *The Scholastic Analysis of Usury*. Cambridge, Ma.: Harvard University Press, 1957.

O'Brien, Charles H. *Ideas of Religious Toleration at the Time of Joseph II: A Study of the Enlightenment among Catholics in Austria*. Philadelphia: American Philosophical Society, 1969.

Olson, Richard. *The Emergence of the Social Sciences, 1642–1792*. New York: Twayne, 1993.

Oz-Salzburger, Fania. "The Jewish Roots of Western Freedom," *Azure* 13 (summer, 2002), pp. 88–132.

————. "The Political Theory of the Scottish Enlightenment," in Alexander Broadie editor, *The Cambridge Companion to the Scottish Enlightenment*, Cambridge: Cambridge University Press, 2003.

Don Patinkin, "Mercantilism and the Readmission of the Jews to England," *Jewish Social Studies*, 8 (1946), pp. 161–78.

Parkes, James. *The Jew in the Medieval Community*. London: Soncino Press, 1938.

Palmer, Gesine and Claus-Michael Palmer, *Ein Freispruch für Paulus: John Tolands Theorie des Judenchristentums*. Berlin: Institut Kirche und Judentum, 1996.

Palmer, Michael. *Adeisidaemon, Vernunft zwischen Atheismus und Aberglauben: Materialismus und Commonwealth bei John Toland*. Ph.D. dissertation. University of Berlin. Berlin. 2002.

Palmer, R. R. *The Age of Democratic Revolutions*, 2 vols. Princeton: Princeton University Press, 1970.

————. *J.-B. Say, An Economist in Troubled Times*. Princeton: Princeton University Press, 1997.

Pascal, Roy. "'Bildung' and the Division of Labour," in Walter H. Bruford, editor, *German Studies Presented to Walter Horace Bruford*. London: George G. Harrap, 1962, pp. 14–28.

Penslar, Derek. *Shylock's Children: Economics and Jewish Identity in Modern Europe*. Berkeley: University of California Press. 2001.

Peter, Klaus. *Die Politische Romantik in Deutschland*. Stuttgart: Suhrkamp, 1985.

Pelli, Moshe. *The Age of Haskalah: Studies in Hebrew Literature of the Enlightenment in Germany*. Leiden: Brill, 1979

Perrot, Jean Claude. *Une Histoire Intellectuelle de 'l'économie politique, xviie-xviiie*. Paris: École des Hautes Études en Sciences Sociales, 1992.

Perry, Thomas W. *Public Opinion, Propaganda, and politics in Eighteenth-Century England; a Study of the Jew Bill of 1753*. Cambridge MA: Harvard University Press, 1962.

Pilbeam, Pamela. *French Socialists before Marx: Workers, Women and the Social Question*. Montreal: Queens University Press, 2000.

Pincus, Steve. "Neither Machiavellian Moment nor Possessive Individualism: Commercial Society and the Defenders of the English Commonwealth," *American Historical Review*, 103: 3 (June, 1998), pp. 705–736.

Pinson, Koppel S. *Modern Germany: Its History and Civilization*. New York: Macmillan, 1966.

Plumb, J. H. *Sir Robert Walpole: The Making of a Statesmen*. Cambridge, MA: Houghton Mifflin, 1956.

Pocock, J. G. A. *The Ancient Constitution and the Feudal Law: A Study of English Historical Thought in the Seventeenth Century*. New York: Norton, 1967.

————. *The Machiavellian Moment*. Princeton: Princeton University Press, 1975.

————. *Virtue, Commerce, and History*. Cambridge: Cambridge University Press, 1985.

————. "Gog and Magog, The Republican Thesis and the Ideologia Americana," *Journal of the History of Ideas*, vol. 48, n. 2. (April–June, 1987), pp. 325–346.

————. "Introduction" to Edmund Burke, *Reflections on the Revolution in France*, edited by J. G. A. Pocock. Indianapolis: Hackett, 1987.

Polanyi, Karl. *The Great Transformation: The Political and Economic Origins of Our Time*. Boston: Beacon, 1957.

————. *The Livelihood of Man*, edited by H. W. Pearson. New York and London: Academic Press, 1977.

Poliakov, Leon. *The History of Anti-Semitism*, 3 vols. New York: Vanguard Press, 1985.

Popkin, Richard H. "The Rise and Fall of the Jewish Indian Theory," in Yosef Kaplan, Henry Méchoulan, and Richard H. Popkin, editors, *Menasseh ben Israel and His World*. Leiden: E. J. Brill, 1989.

Porter, Theodore M. *The Rise of Statistical Thinking, 1820–1900*. Princeton: Princeton University Press, 1986.

Pullan, Brian. *The Jews of Europe and the Inquisition of Venice, 1550–1670*. Oxford: Basil Blackwell, 1983.

Rappaport, Mordché Wolf. *Christian Wilhelm Dohm: Ein Beitrag zur Geschichte der Nationalökonomie*. Leipzig: Robert Noske, 1907.

Rashid, Salim. "Josiah Tucker, Anglican Anti-Semitism, and the Jew Bill of 1753, *Historical Magazine of the Protestant Episcopal Church* (June, 1982), pp. 191–201.

————. "Christianity and the Growth of Liberal Economics," *Journal of Religious History* (1982), pp. 221–32.

————. *The Myth of Adam Smith*. Cheltenham, UK: E. Elger, 1998.

Ravid, Benjamin C. I. *Economics and Toleration in Seventeenth-Century Venice: The Background and Context of the 'Discorso' of Simone Luzzatto*. Jerusalem: American Academy of Jewish Research, 1978.

————. "How Profitable the Nation of the Jews Are': *The Humble Addresses* of Menasseh ben Israel and the *Discorso* of Simone Luzzatto," in Jehudah Reinhartz and Daniel Swetschinsky, editors, *Mystics, Philosophers, and Politicians: Eassays in Jewish Intellectual History in Honor of Alexander Altmann*. Durham, NC: Duke University Press, 1982.

————. "A Tale of three Cities and the Raison d'Etat: Ancona, Venice, Livorno, and the Competition for Jewish Merchants in the Sixteenth Century," in *Mediterranean Historical Review*, 6: 2 (December, 1991), pp. 138–162

Rahe, Paul A. "Antiquity Surpassed: The Repudiation of Classical Republicanism," in David Wootton, editor, *Republicanism, Liberty, and Commercial Society, 1649–1776.* Stanford: Stanford University Press, 1994, pp. 232–269.

Reissner, Hans Gunther. *Eduard Gans: Ein Leben im Vormärz.* Tübingen: Mohr, 1965.

Reynolds, Robert L. *Europe Emerges: Transition toward an Industrial World-Wide Society, 600–1750.* Madison: University of Wisconsin Press, 1961.

Reich, Nathan. "The Economic Structure of Modern Jewry," in Louis Finkelstein, ed., *The Jews: Their History, Culture, and Religion,* vol. IV. Philadelphia: Jewish Publication Society of America, 1949.

Reuß, Franz. "Christian Wilhelm Dohm's Schift, 'Über die bürgerliche Verbesserung der Juden' und deren Einwirkung auf die gebildeten Stände Deutschlands," in Christian Wilhelm von Dohm's *Über die bürgerliche Verbesserung der Juden: Teile in 1 Bd.* Hildesheim: Goerg Olms, 1973.

Riasanovsky, Nicholas. *The Emergence of Romanticism.* New York: Oxford University Press, 1992.

Ribbe, Wolfgang. "Wirschaftlicher und politischer Status der Juden in Brandenburg-Preußen im Zeitalter des Merkantilismus," in Marianne Awerbuch and Stefi Jersch-Wenzel, editors, *Bild und Selbstbild der Juden Berlins zwischen Aufklärung und Romantik.* Berlin: Colloquium Verlag, 1992.

Richarz, Monika. *Der Eintritt der Juden in die akademischen Berufe. Jüdische Studenten und Akademiker in Dutschland 1787–1848.* Tübingen: Mohr, 1974.

Roll, Eric. *A History of Econonomic Thought.* 5th edition. London: Faber and Faber, 1992.

Rose, Paul Lawrence. *Revolutionary Antisemitism in Germany.* Princeton: Princeton University Press, 1990.

Rosen, Zwi. "Moses Hess' Einfluß auf die Entfremduntstheorie von Karl Marx," in Walter Grab and Julius H. Schoeps, editors, *Juden im Vormaärz und in der Revolution von 1848,* Stuttgart, 1983.

Rotenstreich, Nathan. "For and against Emancipation: The Bruno Bauer Controversy," in *The Leo Baeck Institute Yearbook,* iv (1959), pp. 3–36.

Roth, Cecil, editor. *Anglo-Jewish Letters.* London: Soncino Press, 1938.

———. "The Jew Peddler – An 18th Century Rural Character," in Cecil Roth, *Essays and Portraits in Anglo-Jewish History.* Philadelphia: Jewish Publication Society of America, 1962, pp. 133–149.

———. *A History of the Jews in England,* 3rd edition. Oxford: Clarendon Press, 1978.

Rothschild, Emma. *Economic Sentiments: Adam Smith, Condorcet, and the Enlightenment.* Cambridge, Ma.: Harvard University Press, 2001.

de Roover, Raymond. *La Pensée Économique des Scolastiques: Doctrines et Méthodes.* Montréal and Paris: Institute d'études médiévales, 1971.

Routh, Guy. *The Origin of Economic Ideas.* Dobbs Ferry, N. Y.: Sheridan House, 1989.

Ruderman, David. "Champion of Jewish Economic Interests," in Jeremy Cohen, ed., *Essential Papers on Judaism and Christianity in Conflict.* New York: New York University Press, 1991.

———. *Jewish Thought and Scientific Discovery in Early Modern Europe.* New Haven: Yale University Press, 1995.

———. *Jewish Enlightenment in an English Key.* Princeton, NJ: Princeton University Press, 2000

Ruppin, Arthur. *Soziologie der Juden,* 2 vols. Berlin: Jüdischer Verlag, 1930–1.

Saltman, Avrom. *The Jewish Question in 1655: Studies in Prynne's Demurrer*. Ramat-Gan: Bar Ilan University Press, 1995.

Samuel, Edgar R. "'Sir Thomas Shirley's Project for the Jews' – the Earliest Known Proposal for the Resettlement," in *Transactions of the Jewish Historical Society of England*, vol. xxiv. Spring, 1975.

Schechter, Ronald. *Obstinate Hebrews: Representations of Jews in France, 1715–1815*. Berkeley: University of California Press, 2003.

Scholem, Gershom. "Mitokh hirhure hokhmat yisro'el" (Hebrew), in *Devarim be-Go: Pirke Morashah u-Tehiyah* [Chapters in Tradition and Rebirth]. Jerusalem: 'Am 'oved, 1975.

Schorsch, Ismar. *From Text to Context: The Turn to History in Modern Judaism*. Hanover, NH: University Press of New England, 1994.

Schumpeter, Joseph. *History of Economic Analysis*, edited by Elizabeth Boody Schumpeter. New York: Oxford University Press, 1954.

Schwarzfuchs, Simon. *Napoleon, the Jews and the Sanhedrin*. London: Routledge and Keegan Paul, 1979.

Schwarzschild, Steven S. "Do Noachites have to Believe in Revelation," *The Jewish Quarterly Review*, 52 (1961–1962), pp. 296–306 and 53 (1962–1963), pp. 30–65.

Sepinwall, Alyssa Goldstein. *The Abbé Grégoire and the French Revolution*. Berkeley: University of California Press, 2005.

Septimus, Bernard. "Biblical Religion and Political Rationality in Simone Luzzatto, Maimonides and Spinoza," in Isadore Twersky and Bernard Septimus editors, *Jewish Thought in the Seventeenth Century*. Cambridge: Cambridge University Press, 1987.

Sewell, William H. *A Rhetoric of Bourgeois Revolution: The Abbé Sieyes and 'What is the Third Estate?*. Durham, NC: Duke University Press, 1994.

———. *Work and Revolution in France: The Language of Labor from the Old Regime to 1848*. Cambridge, 1989.

Shapiro, James. *Shakespeare and the Jews*. New York: Columbia University Press, 1996.

Shatzmiller. Joseph. *Shylock Reconsidered: Jews, Moneylending, and Medieval Society*. Berkeley: University of California Press, 1990.

Shatzky, Jacob. *Arkhiv far der geshikhte fun yidishn teater un drame*. Vilna: Yidisher visnshaftlekher institut, 1930.

Shaw, Stanford J. *The Jews of the Ottoman Empire and the Turkish Republic*. New York: New York University Press, 1991.

Sheehan, James J. *German History: 1770–1866*. Oxford: Clarendon Press, 1994.

Shell, Susan. "A Determined Stand: Freedom and Security in Fichte's Science of Right," *Polity* 25:1 (Fall 1992), pp. 95–121.

Shelton, George. *Dean Tucker and Eighteenth-Century Economic and Political Thought*. London: Macmillan, 1981.

Shohet, Azriel,'*Im Hilufe Tekufot: Reshit ha-Haskalah be Yahadut Germaniyah* [Changing Times: The Beginnings of the Haskalah among German Jewry](Hebrew). Jerusalem: Mosad Byalik, 1960.

Shulvass, Moses A. "The Story of Sorrows that Occurred in Italy" (Hebrew), *HUCA* 22 (1949), pp. 1–21

———. *From East to West: The Westward Migration of Jews from Eastern Europe During the Seventeenth and Eighteenth Centuries*. Detroit: Wayne State University Press, 1971.

Silberner, Edmund. *Sozialisten zur Judenfrage: Ein Beitrag zur Geschichte des Sozialismus vom anfang des Jahrhunderts bis 1914*. Berlin: Colloquium Verlag, 1962.

_____. "Was Marx an Anti-Semite?," in Ezra Mendelsohn, editor, *Essential Papers on Jews and the Left*. New York: New York University Press, 1994.

Silver, Morris. *Economic Structures of the Ancient Near East*. Totowa, NJ: Barnes & Noble Books, 1986.

_____. *Economic Structures of Antiquity*. Westport, CT: Greenwood Press, 1995.

Simms, J. G. "John Toland (1670–1722), a Donegal Heretic," in David Hayton, Gerard O'Brien, and J. G. Simms, editors, *War and Politics in Ireland 1649–1730*. London: Hambledon Press, 1986.

_____. *The Williamite Confiscation in Ireland, 1690–1703*. London: Faber and Faber, 1956.

Sinkoff, Nancy Beth. *Out of the Shtetl: Making Jews Modern in the Polish Borderlands*. Providence: Brown Judaic Studies, 2003.

Skinner, Quentin. *The Foundations of Modern Political Thought*. 2 vols. Cambridge: Cambridge University Press, 1978.

Small, Albion. *The Cameralists: The Pioneers of German Social Polity*. Chicago: University of Chicago Press, 1909.

Smith, Jay M. *Nobility Reimagined: The Patriotic Nation in Eighteenth-Century France*. Ithaca, N.Y.: Cornell University Press, 2005.

Smith, Richard M. "The English Peasantry, 1250–1650," in Tom Scott, editor, *The Peasantries of Europe from the Fourteenth to the Eighteenth Centuries*. London: Longman, 1998, pp. 339–71.

Smyth, Jim. *The Making of the United Kingdom, 1660–1800*. New York: Longman, 2001.

Sombart, Werner. *Die deutsche Volkswirtschaft im neunzehnten Jahrhundert*. Berlin: G. Bondi, 1903.

Sommerville, J. P. *Politics and Ideology in England, 1603–1640*. London and NY: Longman, 1986.

Sonnenberg-Stern, Karina. *Emancipation and Poverty: The Ashkenazi Jews of Amsterdam 1761–1850*. St. Martin's Press: New York, 2000.

Sorkin, David. *The Transformation of German Jewry 1780–1840*. New York: Oxford University Press, 1990.

Spufford, Peter. *Money and its Use in Medieval Europe*. Cambridge: Cambridge University Press, 1988.

Stearns, Peter S. *European Society in Upheaval; Social History since 1750*. New York: Macmillan, 1967.

Stein, Siegfried. "Interest Taken by Jews from Gentiles." *Journal of Semitic Studies*, 1: 2 (April, 1956), pp. 141–164.

Stern, Menahem. *Greek and Latin Authors on Jews and Judaism*. 2 vols. Jerusalem: Israel Academy of Sciences and Humanities, 1974.

Stern, Selma. *Der Preussische Staat und die Juden*, 2 vols. Tübingen: J. C. B. Mohr, 1962.

Stern-Täubler, Selma. "Die Literarische Kampf um die Emanzipation in den Jahren 1816–1820 und seine ideologischen und soziologischen Voraussetzungen," in *Hebrew Union College Annual*, xxiii: pt. ii. (1950–1), pp. 171–96.

Stone, Lawrence. *The Causes of the English Revolution 1529–1642*. New York: Harper & Row, 1972.

Stoye, John. *Europe Unfolding, 1648–1688*. Glasgow: Fontana, 1978.

Stow, Kenneth. "The Jewish Community of the Middle Ages was Not a Corporation," in Isaiah Gafni and Gabriel Motzkin, editors, *Kehunah u-Melukhah: Yahase Dat u-Medinah be-Yisra'el uva-'Amim* [Priesthood and Monarchy: Church-State Relations in Israel and Among the Nations] (Hebrew) Jerusalem: Zalman Shazar Center, 1987, pp. 141–48.

Sumberg, Theodore A. "Antonio Serra: A Neglected Herald of the Acquisitive System," *American Journal of Economics and Sociology*, 50: 3. (July, 1991), pp. 365–373.

Sutcliffe, Adam. *Judaism and Enlightenment.* Cambridge: Cambridge University Press, 2003.

Swetschinski, Daniel M. *Reluctant Cosmopolitans: The Portuguese Jews of Seventeenth-Century Amsterdam.* London: Littman, 2000.

Szajkowski, Zosa, *Jews and the French Revolutions of 1789, 1830 and 1848.* New York: Ktav, 1970.

Tal, Uriel. "German-Jewish Social Thought in the Mid-Nineteenth Century," in Werner Mosse, Arnold Pauker, and Reinhard Rürup, editors, *Revolution and Evolution: 1848 in German-Jewish History.* Tübingen: Mohr, 1981.

Tawney, R. H. *Religion and the Rise of Capitalism: A Historical Study.* Gloucester, MA: P. Smith, 1962.

Toch, Michael "Aspects of Stratification of Early Modern German Jewry: Population History and Village Jews," in R. Po-Chia Hsia and Hartmut Lehmann, editors, *In and Out of the Ghetto: Jewish-Gentile Relations in Late Medieval and Early Modern Germany.* Cambridge: Cambridge University Press, 1995, pp. 77–124.

Toury, Jacob. "Ein Dokument zur bürgerlichen Einordnung der Juden (Hamm/ Westfalen, 1818)," in *Michael*, 7 (1967), pp. 77–91.

Trachtenberg, Joshua. *The Devil and the Jews: the Medieval Conception of the Jew and its Relation to Modern Antisemitism.* Philadelphia: Jewish Publication Society of America, 1983.

Traverso, Enzo. *The Marxists and the Jewish Question.* Atlantic Highlands, N.J.: Humanties Press, 1990.

Treue, Wilhelm. "Adam Smith in Deutschland: Zum Problem des 'Politischen Professors' zwischen 1776 und 1810," in Werner Conze, editor, *Deutschland und Europa, Historische Studien zur Völker- und Staatenordnung des Abendlandes: Festschrift für Hans Rothfels.* Goldbach: Kiep, 1993, pp. 101–166.

Tribe, Keith. *Governing Economcy: The Reformation of German Economic Discourse, 1750–1840.* Cambridge: Cambridge University Press, 1988.

————. *Strategies of Economic Order: German Economic Discourse, 1750–1950.* Cambridge: Cambridge University Press, 1995.

Ulbricht, Otto. "Criminality and Punishment of the Jews in the Early Modern Period," in R. Po-Chia Hsia and Hartmut Lehmann, editors, *In and Out of the Ghetto* Cambridge: Cambridge University Press, 1995.

Ucko, Sinai (Sigfried). "Geistesgeschichtliche Grundlagen der Wissenschaft des Judentums," in Kurt Wilhelm, editor, *Wissenschaft des Judentums im deutschen Sprachbereich*, vol. I. Tübingen: Mahr, 1967.

Van Cleve, John Walter. *The Merchant in German Literature of the Enlightenment.* Chapel Hill: University of North Carolina Press, 1986.

Veltri, Guiseppe. "Alcune considerazioni sugli Ebrei e Venezia nel pensiero politico di Simone Luzzatto," in Cesare Ioly Zorattini, editor, *Percorsi di storia ebraica. Atti del*

XVIII convegno internazionale dell'AISG, Cividale del Friuli-Gorizia, 7/9 settembre 2004. Udine: Forum, 2005, pp. 247–266.

Vennant, J. P. *Mythe et Penseè chez les Grecs: études de psychologie historique.* Paris: F. Maspero, 1965.

Von See, Klaus. *Freiheit und Gemeinschaft: Völkisch-nationales Denken in Deutschland zwischen Französischer Revolution und Erstem Weltkrieg.* Heidelberg: Universitätsverlag, 2001.

Walker, Mack. *German Home Towns: Community, State, and General Estate, 1648–1871.* Ithaca: Cornell University Press, 1971.

Waszek, Norbert. "Eduard Gans on Poverty: Between Hegel and Saint-Simon," in *The Own of Minerva,* 18:2 (Spring, 1987), pp. 167–178.

Weinryb, Bernard D. *The Jews of Poland: A Social and Economic History of the Jewish Community in Poland from 1100–1800.* Philadelphia: Jewish Publication Society of America, 1973.

Wiles, Richard C. "Mercantilism and the Idea of Progress," *Eighteenth-Century Studies,* vol. 18, no. 1 (Autumn, 1974), pp. 56–74.

Williamson, Arthur H. "'A Pil for Pork-Eaters': Ethnic Identity, Apocalyptic Promises, and the Strange Creation of the Judeo-Scots," in Raymond B. Waddington and A. H. Williamson, editors, *The Expulsion of the Jews: 1492 and After,* New York: Garland, 1994, pp. 237–58.

Wilson, Peter H. *From Reich to Revolution: German History, 1558–1806.* New York: Palgrave, 2004.

Winch, Donald. *Riches and Poverty: An Intellectual History of Political Economy in Britain, 1750–1834.* Cambridge: Cambridge University Press, 1996.

Wischnitzer, Mark. *A History of Jewish Crafts and Guilds.* New York: J. David, 1965.

Wistrich, Robert. *Socialism and the Jews: The Dilemmas of Assimilation in Germany and Austria-Hungary.* Rutherford, NJ: Fairleigh Dickenson University Press, 1982.

Wood, Andy. *Riot, Rebellion and Popular Politics in Early Modern England.* New York: Palgrave, 2002.

Wood, Ellen Meiksins. *Peasant-Citizen and Slave.* London: Verso, 1988.

Wood, Neal. "Machiavelli's Concept of *Virtù* Reconsidered," *Political Studies* (June 1967), pp. 159–72.

Wootton, David. "The Republic Tradition: From Common Wealth to Common Sense," 1–41 in David Wootton editor, *Republicanism, Liberty, and Commercial Society, 1649–1776.* Stanford: Stanford University Press, 1994.

Worden, Blair. "Marchamont Nedham and English Republicanism," in David Wootton, editor, *Republicanism, Liberty, and Commercial Society, 1649–1776.* Stanford: Stanford University Press, 1994.

———. "Whig History abnd Puritan Politics: The *Memoirs* of Edmund Ludlow Revisited," in *Historical Research,* 75: 188 (May 2002), pp. 209–37.

Zenner, Walter P. *Minorities in the Middle: A Cross Cultural Analyis.* Albany: State University of New York Press, 1991.

Ziskind, Jonathan R. "Cornelius Bertram and Carlo Sigonio: Christian Hebraism's First Political Scientists. *Journal of Ecumenical Studies* (Summer-Fall 2000), pp. 321–332.

Zook, Melinda S. *Radical Whigs and Conspiratorial Politics in Late Stuart England.* Pennsylvania State University Press, University Park, 1999.

Zuckert, Michael. *Natural Rights and the New Republicanism.* Princeton: Princeton University Press, 1994.

Index

Württemberg, 178, 210
Work *see* Labor

Young, Arthur (1741–1820), 162
Yunge Historiker, 263

Zeitschrift für die Wissenschaft des Judentums, 213, 216

Zionism, 7, 201, 262–3, 264, 267, 307n.128
Zoroaster, 156
Zunz, Leopold (1794–1886), 202, 210, 231, 234, 325n.55, n.61
  "Something Regarding Rabbinic Literature" (1818), 222–23
  "Organization of the Israelites" (1819), 215–8, 222

203   Haskala